QUICK REFERENCE TABLE OF CONTENTS

PERSONAL FINANCE

PERSONAL FINANCE

Jack R. Kapoor
College of DuPage

Les R. Dlabay
Lake Forest College

Robert J. Hughes
Richland College

1988

IRWIN

Homewood, Illinois 60430

© RICHARD D. IRWIN, INC., 1988

All rights reserved. No part of this publication may be
reproduced, stored in a retrieval system, or transmitted,
in any form or by any means, electronic, mechanical,
photocopying, recording, or otherwise, without the prior
written permission of the publisher.

This book was set in Caledonia by York Graphic Services.
The editors were Gary L. Nelson, Ann M. Granacki, Dale Boroviak, Merrily D. Mazza.
The production manager was Irene H. Sotiroff.
The designer was Tim Kaage.
The drawings were done by Tom Mallon.
R. R. Donnelly & Sons Company was the printer and binder.

ISBN 0-256-05665-X

Library of Congress Catalog Card No. 87–81573

Printed in the United States of America

1 2 3 4 5 6 7 8 9 0 DO 5 4 3 2 1 0 9 8

To my wife, Theresa Kapoor, and to my children,
Karen Tucker, Kathryn and Dave Kapoor.

To my wife, Linda Dlabay, and to my children,
Carissa and Kyle.

To my wife, Peggy Hughes.

Preface

Spending, saving, borrowing, and investing decisions are the foundation of personal financial planning. These basic decisions are influenced by various economic and social factors, including:

- Changing economic conditions, such as changes in inflation rates, interest rates, and employment opportunities.
- Technological advances that stimulate new financial services and increase the access to information needed for financial planning decisions.
- Changes in tax laws and other legislative actions that require individuals to know about the dynamic financial marketplace.

These and other factors that affect personal financial planning are continually addressed in this textbook because it is important to study the role of personal financial planning in a changing environment.

ORGANIZATION OF THE TEXT

This textbook follows a logical sequence of personal finance topics. The topics covered by the six text parts are as follows:

Part One, "Planning Your Personal Finances," introduces personal financial planning and discusses career planning and the basics of financial record-keeping and budgeting.

Part Two, "Managing Your Personal Finances," discusses such financial services as savings and checking accounts. The use of credit and the planning and paying of your taxes are also covered in this part.

Part Three, "Making Your Buying Decisions," presents the background you need to purchase housing, transportation, and other products and services.

Part Four, "Protecting Your Resources," discusses insurance coverage for your life, health, and property.

Part Five, "Investing Your Money," considers the various ways in which you can make your money work for you.

Part Six, "Controlling Your Financial Future," addresses the subject of long-term financial security as it relates to retirement and estate planning.

This sequencing will make it easier for you to develop and implement the overall financial plan that will best serve your personal economic needs.

A Personal Finance course provides the framework for additional study in the area of finance. Advanced and specialized finance courses will expand your knowledge of this area. These courses include Financial Management, Investments, Insurance, Taxes, Real Estate, and Estate and Retirement Planning. Taking such courses will give you the background you need to pursue career opportunities in financial planning.

TEXT FEATURES

This textbook has a number of components that will stimulate and enhance the learning process. The supplementary information sources, chapter format, end-of-part cases, and appendixes will be valuable to both students and teachers.

Sources of Personal Finance Information

To supplement your study of Personal Finance, a list of personal finance periodicals and sources of information is presented on the front and back inside covers of the book. This feature will help you update the knowledge you need to make rational economic choices.

Chapter Format

Each chapter is organized so that learning will occur in a logical and thought-provoking manner. The major components of each chapter are:

- A chapter overview and a list of the chapter learning objectives.
- An interview with a personal finance expert.
- An opening scenario that introduces the chapter through a real-world situation; questions about the opening scenario are included among the discussion questions that appear at the end of each chapter.
- A listing of each chapter objective in the margin at the beginning of the section in which the topic pertaining to that objective is covered.
- Boxed features on *real-world applications* that expand the chapter content. These features appear under the following headings: "In the Real World," "In the News," "Today's Lifestyles," "Technology for Today," "Personal Financial Planning and You," and "Careers in Personal Finance."
- The chapter summary, a point-by-point synopsis of the chapter content based on the chapter objectives.
- The chapter glossary, which defines the key terms in the chapter.
- Review questions that help you assess your understanding of the chapter content.
- Discussion questions and activities that help you expand your knowledge of the chapter content.
- An additional readings list consisting of books and articles that will expand your understanding of the chapter material.
- The cases, real-world situations to which you apply your financial planning skills.

These chapter components create a total learning package that can be adapted to any educational setting.

End-of-Part Cases

At the end of Chapters 3, 7, 10, 14, 18, and 20 are comprehensive cases. Each of these embraces a number of financial planning concepts and allows students to practice their decision-making skills by coping with realistic situations.

Appendixes

This textbook also has four appendixes that supplement the main content: "Choosing a Financial Planner," "Buying a Personal Computer and Financial Planning Software," "The Time Value of Money," and "Consumer Agencies and Organizations." These appendixes provide practical guidelines on the topics they cover.

SUPPLEMENTARY MATERIALS

The instructional package for our book consists of the following materials:

- *The Student Resource Manual.* This study guide is designed to review and apply the concepts developed in each chapter. It contains a chapter overview, a pretest, self-guided study questions, a posttest, problems, projects, and field research and financial planning activities. The *Student Resource Manual* also includes recent articles on personal financial planning topics from *The Wall Street Journal;* each reading is accompanied by study questions.
- *Course Planning Guide.* This publication provides a basic framework for the use of *Personal Finance.* The first section provides suggestions for planning and implementing various instructional strategies. The second component of the *Course Planning Guide* lists periodicals, publications, audio-visual materials, software, and community resources available to supplement the instructional process. This publication also includes a guide to reading and using *The Wall Street Journal.*
- *Instructor's Manual.* This supplement provides the basic material needed for teaching the course, including a chapter overview, a list of learning objectives with content summaries, and answers to end-of-chapter questions and cases. The *Instructor's Manual* also includes ready-to-duplicate chapter outlines, chapter quizzes, and personal finance research sheets for use by students in doing their own financial planning and comparison of financial services.
- *Lecture Notes.* The lecture guide presents instructional suggestions for each chapter including points to highlight, references to transparencies, in-class exercises, examples from current readings, suggested discussion questions, and references to supplementary resources.
- *Transparencies.* Transparency masters for 100 text and other visuals are offered for class presentations. Also, 30 major concepts from *Personal Finance* are presented on color acetates.
- *Test Bank.* An extensive evaluation program is available with *Personal Finance* involving over 1200 true–false, multiple choice, and essay questions keyed to specific textbook pages with an indication of difficulty level. These test items are available in a printed manual as well as in COMPUTEST II format which allows the use of a personal computer to

create tests based on chapter, type of question, and difficulty level. The COMPUTEST II system also allows instructors to add their own test items. The printed manual of tests also includes end-of-part tests and a final examination consisting of selected items from the test bank.

- *Personal Finance Software.* This comprehensive software package includes financial planning routines for each chapter of the text. These programs may be used to do problems included in the *Student Resource Manual* or the *Software Manual,* or the software can be of value in your own personal financial planning situation. The *Software Manual* includes operating instructions, an overview of all routines, sample problems, and other applications.

ACKNOWL-EDGMENTS

We would like to express our appreciation to the colleagues who gave us comments and suggestions that contributed to the development of this book:

Bill Bailey
Casper College

Robert Ek
Seminole Community College

Robert Flammang
Louisiana State

Jeanette Klosterman
Hutchinson Community College

Jerry Leadham
Clackamus Community College

Robert Kegel
Cypriss College

William Marrs
Vincennes University

Jeanne Peters
University of Nevada

David Pingree
University of Utah

Rosemary Walker
Michigan State University

In addition, we are indebted to the professionals who provided their expertise on various personal financial planning topics for use in the opening interview in each chapter, and for the supplemental audio tape programs.

Wally Knighton
Naomi T. Ewing
Richard and Kathryn Holland
John Searer
Joseph D'Agostino
C. E. "Gene" Jernigan
Joyce Bryant
Joanne Carmody
Joanne L. Kron
Elaine Strubbe
Jack Rasmussen
Holley A. Fryman
Tracey Murphy
Edward T. Clark

Gene Curelo
Joseph Bonnice
Rod Iwema
Thomas Drews
M. Jerome Houghton
Anthony J. Mooney
Robert W. Petrie
Gene R. Huxhold
Dan Bergman
Howard Shank
William E. Boylan
Bruce Hubbel
Michael Sirota
Pat Dziekzic

We are grateful to many colleagues below for their comments and ideas which were invaluable in preparing the manuscript.

Donald M. Albanito
Bradley University

Charles L. Alford
Forman University

Larry C. Allen
Oklahoma Baptist University

James O. Armstrong II
John Tyler Community College

Donald W. Avery
Springfield Technical Com. College

Emerson R. Bailey III
Casper College

V. Ward Bennett
Manatee Community College

Richard R. Bennington
High Point College

Homer G. Benton
Pacific Christian College

Catherine L. Bertelson
Central Washington University

Charles Blanchard
Northwood Institute

Archille O. Bourque
University of Kansas

Harvey Bronstein
Oakland Community College

Gordon L. Brookhart
Purdue University

Thomas M. Brooks
Southern Illinois University

Bill Brunsen
Northern Arizona University

John Buss
Lemoyne-Owen College

Harold L. Caddell
Cal Baptist College

John E. Carr III
Longwood College

Clyde J. Cooley
Weber State College

Robert H. Cox
Edison State Community College

Sheran L. Cramer
University of Nebraska, Omaha

Jennifer Craven
Coleman College

Ellen Daniel
University of Southwestern Louisiana

Helen M. Davis
Jefferson Community College

A. Terrance Dickens
California State University, Fullerton

Elizabeth Dolan
University of New Hampshire

Emilie Duggan
Grossmont College

Robert Ek
Seminole Community College

Richard Ellis
Barber-Srotia College

Barry Farber
University of Maine at Augusta

John F. Ficks
College of DuPage

Robert A. Flammang
Louisiana State University

George B. Flanigan
University of No. Carolina, Greensboro

Barbara G. Foley
Castleton State College

Steven M. Foulks
Northern Michigan University

Donald L. Frampton
St. Cloud Technical Institute

Gary M. Frandson
Southwest State University

Erlinda F. Ganiron
Los Angeles City College

A. Sam Ghanty
*University of Wisconsin,
    Green Bay*

L. Milton Glisson
North Carolina A&T State University

Rae Jean B. Goodman
U.S. Naval Academy

Wendy Gray
Skagit Valley College

Geoffrey D. Greer
Findlay College

Henry J. Gruthues
St. Louis University

Carl M. Guelzo
Catonsville Community College

Virginia A. Haldeman
University of Nevada, Reno

Marcy Hall
College of the Sequoias

Marvin H. Halldorson
University of Northern Colorado

A. R. Hamlin
So. Utah State College

Dave Hancock
Tarkio College

Zen C. Hanger
Muskegon Business College

Paul W. Hart
Northeastern Oklahoma A&M College

David Hawk
Univeristy of Akron

C. Beth Haynes
Coastal Carolinia College

Roger Hill
University of North Carolina, Wilmington

Lou Hoekstra
Grand Rapids Jr. College

Ester L. Hogans
Sierra College

S. Thomas Holbrook
Tennessee State University

Arlene Holyoak
Oregon State University

Edward L. Houghton
Southern Oregon State College

Nancy P. Houston
Slippery Rock University

Thomas R. Humphrey
Palomar College

Travis Hyde
Central State University of Oklahoma

Thomas L. Jackson
Cerritos College

Jeannette R. Jesinger
University of Nevada, Las Vegas

Clint Johnson
University of Central Arkansas

Jack Johnson
Cosumnes River College

Thomas A. Johnson
Harper College

Ray G. Jones, Jr.
Appalachian State University

Jerry Jones
Spokane Community College

Vernon R. Kalvestrand
Simpson College

Delbort M. Kangas
University of Wisconsin, Superior

Alan Kardoff
Northern Illinois University

Bob Kegel
Cypress College

Ray Kerlagon
Webster University

M. Barbara Killen
University of Minnesota

Wayne Kirklin
Heidelberg College

Fred J. Kittrell
Middle Tenn. State University

Jeanette Klosterman
Hutchinson Community College

John R. Knight
Austin-Peay State University

Duane A. Krenz
Mesagi Community College

Robert H. Landry
Massasoit Community College

Bernard J. Landwehr
West Liberty State College

Keith F. Lawson
West Liberty State College

Jerry Leadham
Clackamas Community College

Charles A. Malouf
Pasadena City College

Joseph Marchese
Monroe Community College

William C. Marrs
Vincennes University

Jim Martens
San Jacinto College

Emiddio Massa
National University

Robert Masters
Fort Hays State University

Ike Mathur
Southern Illinois University, Carbondale

Pamela Matthews
Missouri Western State College

Joan L. Maupin
Murray State University

Charles W. Miller
Marymount University

David B. Milton
Bentley College

Lon L. Mishler
Northeast Wisconsin Technical Institute

Chalmers A. Monteith
Kent State University

Peter J. Moutsatson
Montcalm Community College

Clifford Mpare
Wingate College

Theresa D. McConnell
Manchester Community College

Sally J. Nelson
University of Dubuque

R. V. Nuttall
University of South Carolina

John M. Olson
University of Wisconsin, Parkside

Beverly M. Osier
Hamilton Business College

Alvarene G. Peace
Southern Arkansas University

Albert R. Pender
Northern Illinois University

Jeanne M. Peters
University of Nevada, Reno

William S. Phillips
Memphis State University

David R. Pingree, Jr.
University of Utah

Steven W. Puch
J. Sargeant Reynolds Community College

Ira W. Pyron
Troy State University

Marlene M. Reed
Samford University

Morris D. Reed
East Central University

Marcia Rhodes
Chamberlayne Jr. College

J. H. Richardson
S F Austin State

S. Ritter
Chamenade University

William V. Rollins
Ventura College

Eileen Porkoski Rosenberg
Elms College

Hossein Sarjehpeyma
Langston University

Michael Schellenger
Appalachian State University

Daniel L. Schneid
Central Michigan University

Elmer B. Shellenberger
Southern Nazarene University

Katie Simmons
Gainesville Jr. College

Brian W. Simpson
Mohegan Community College

Patricia Smytne
The Wichita State University

Horacio Soberon-Ferrer
University of Maryland

Carl Stern
Randolph-Macon Woman's College

Carma Sutherland
Ricks College

Skip Swerdlow
University of Nevada, Las Vegas

Raymond D. Teague
Jackson State University

William K. Templeton
Ohio Northern University

Francis C. Thomas
Stockton State College

Judith A. Tibbetts
Alpena Community College

James P. Trebby
Marquette University

Malcolm S. Torgerson
Western Illinois University

W. Bob Turner
Golden Gate University

MaryAnn VanSlyke
North Central Technical Institute

Ashvin P. Vibhakar
University of Arkansas, Little Rock

Rosemary Walker
Michigan State University

James E. Walsh
Tidewater Community College

Mark A. Walsvick
Santa Rosa Junior College

Daniel M. Watson
Sullivan Jr. College of Business

Richard Widdows
Purdue University

John F. Wiederspan
Lincoln School of Commerce

Bill Wilcox
Northwestern Business College

Walter J. Woeheide
University of Michigan, Flint

Glen R. Wood
Broome Community College

Elizabeth Yelland
North Hennepin Community College

Alex R. Yguado
L. A. Mission College

Leonard V. Zumpano
University of Alabama

Many talented editorial and staff professionals at Richard D. Irwin have contributed to the development of this book. We are especially grateful to Ann Granacki, Developmental Supervisor, whose assistance, guidance, and support made this project possible. We also express our appreciation to the individuals at Irwin with whom we had frequent contact, including Gary Nelson, Paula Meyers, Gail Mack, Dale Boroviak, Nancy Lanum, and Dora Jeffers. In addition, Jack Kapoor expresses his appreciation to his wife,

Theresa, and daughter, Kathy, for their typing, proofreading, and research assistance. Finally, we thank our wives and families for their patience, understanding, and encouragement during the past two years.

Jack R. Kapoor

Les Dlabay

Bob Hughes

A NOTE TO STUDENTS

Since most fundamentals of successful personal financial management remain constant, we are sure you will find this book a valuable reference for many years.

Contents

PART TWO
Managing Your Personal Finances 101

PART SIX
Controlling Your Financial Future   611

PERSONAL FINANCE

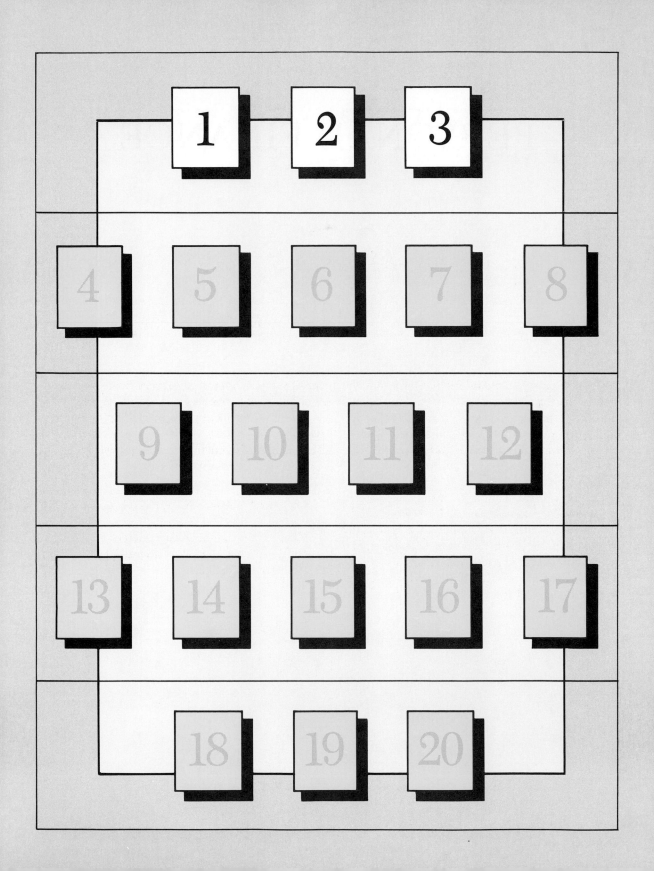

PART ONE

Planning Your Personal Finances

The first part of *Personal Finance* provides the foundation for studying and applying personal financial planning techniques. First, we examine the benefits, elements, and implementation of personal and family financial planning. Also examined are the many personal, social, and economic influences on financial planning. Then we discuss how careful career planning can lead you to financial independence and personal fulfillment. Also discussed is the need for continuing education as the work environment evolves due to technological and social changes. Finally, we focus on financial recordkeeping and budgeting. The guidelines given will help you develop a money plan to meet your special needs and goals. Practical suggestions are offered to improve your handling of financial records. Budgeting will not change the basic realities of income and expenses, but this plan for spending can help you get the most out of your income. This part consists of:

1

Personal Financial Planning in Our Society

We all want to handle our finances successfully so that we can get the most value possible from each dollar we spend. Our many goals may include such things as a new car, a nice apartment, extended travel and vacations, education, and the assurance of self-sufficiency during our working and retirement years. However, we need to identify and set priorities for these goals. This process is commonly referred to as personal money management, the financial side of living, or personal financial planning.

After studying this chapter, you will be able to:

- Discuss the meaning of personal financial planning.

- Identify the benefits of personal financial planning.

- List the steps involved in personal financial planning.

- Explain the various factors that affect financial planning.

- Discuss the operation of the American economic system.

- Identify the effects of changing economic conditions on personal financial planning.

- Describe the components of a personal financial plan.

- List the resources that are available to supplement and expand your knowledge of personal finance.

- Implement a personal financial plan.

Interview with **Wally Knighton,**
Account Executive Dean Witter Reynolds

Wallace L. Knighton is an account executive for Dean Witter Reynolds and is responsible for assisting clients with decisions on selecting stocks, bonds, and other investments. He is licensed by the New York Stock Exchange, the Chicago Board of Trade, and the State of Illinois Insurance Department. Mr. Knighton also teaches adult education courses on personal financial planning and investments.

Personal financial planning is a strategy that can help you get from where you are to where you want to be. Financial planning begins with an inventory of your personal resources to pinpoint your strengths and weaknesses. Then you can more accurately define your specific short- and long-term financial goals. Once you have defined your goals, you can devise a plan of action to make sure that those goals are achieved.

When asked about the importance of financial planning, Knighton stated, "I can't stress how important it is to start a financial plan, especially in today's economic environment." Always start by asking these three questions: (1) Financially, where am I today, (2) where am I going, and (3) where do I eventually want to be? The financial plans you make today will determine the standard of living you'll have tomorrow. Financial planning should be a part of your everyday life.

A number of basic steps should be taken for effective financial planning. Identify your available income. Establish goals according to your needs. Establish a family budget, and review it often. Once you have prepared a budget, make careful spending decisions to stretch your dollars. Finally, review and modify your financial plan at least once a year.

Knighton suggests that as you develop your financial plan, you get more information or advice from a financial counselor or someone else trained to assist you on financial matters. For example, your attorney can verify that the methods you adopt for transferring your wealth comply with the law and are appropriate to your personal financial goals. Your investment adviser can show you how to use your wealth so that you get the best rate of return on your investments. Your insurance representatives can review your financial goals, determine your financial needs, and coordinate your insurance and annuity program. Finally, your financial counselor can help you coordinate the efforts of your other key advisers to ensure that you accomplish your financial goals.

Poor personal financial management is the most important cause of bankruptcy and the greatest cause of anxiety in American households. Consider the case of Erika Earnhart of Lexington Park, Maryland, who won $1 million in the Maryland lottery. Erika says she is in debt, lives in a trailer park, and is unable to work because of a knee injury.

"I thought I'd be on easy street the rest of my life," said Erika. "Now I live from April to April. I admit I've had some fun, but it's not every-thing it's cracked up to be."

Each April Erika receives her annual $50,000 check, a prize guaranteed for 20 years. Erika spent the first $50,000 on a four-bedroom house, gifts of money to her parents and sister, a Volkswagen, and some travel. She did not pay taxes on this money, so when her second check came, she had to pay $18,000 in taxes on the first year's winnings plus advance taxes for the second year. Consequently, the second annual windfall immediately plunged from $50,000 to about $20,000.

Now—after two divorces, a still unresolved child custody case, two knee operations without any health insurance to defray costs, and moves to Michigan, Colorado, California, and back to Maryland—Erika is broke. She sold her house and lives in a nearly new, extra-wide trailer. She visits her bank frequently. The bank vice president does not even ask Erika the purpose of her visit. He knows that Erika is borrowing against her next lottery check, and he just needs to know what amount she wants

AN INTRODUCTION TO PERSONAL FINANCIAL PLANNING

- Meaning of Personal Financial Planning

Personal financial planning is the art and science of putting your money to work for you and living within your means. It is the process by which you take control of your financial situation. It begins by recognizing that every person or family has a unique financial position and that any course of financial action must therefore also be unique—that is, carefully planned to meet specific needs and goals.

One person may need to accumulate cash to pay for tuition, room and board, and books for next semester. You, on the other hand, may already have sufficient money reserves. You may be more concerned about reducing the amount of your taxes while you are building a nest egg for retirement. Obviously, what's right for another person may not be right for you. But what *is* your best course of action? When you consider that the average income earner will make over a million dollars in his or her lifetime and that many will make much more, you can see that your financial decisions are important.

While you may take care of your day-to-day financial matters competently, you should also consider the interrelationship of your savings, spending, borrowing, insuring, investing, and tax planning. Most people can live within the limits of their income, but only a limited number can adequately plan for the future. The U.S. Department of Health and Human Services has estimated that only 5 out of every 100 people who are employed upon reach-to withdraw. "When I got this year's check, I already owed the bank $10,000," she said.

There are still several checks to come, but Erika said that if she had known what would happen after she won the million dollars, "I'd have torn up the ticket or put it in someone else's name." Still she continues to play the Maryland lottery periodically in the hope of winning again, "to pay off my debts."

Erika's financial woes demonstrate that using money effectively is one of the biggest problems in the lifetime of any individual or family. But personal financial planning and money management are skills that can be learned, developed, and enjoyed.

The job of managing your money is lifelong. Some people do it well and live smoothly and pleasantly, free from monetary cares and worries. They enjoy the pleasures and satisfactions of a full life. Others ineptly stumble from one financial mess to the next. They never seem to solve their personal financial problems. Some families can live comfortably and save money on an annual income of $25,000. Others, with annual incomes of more than $100,000, can't make ends meet. Most of us work hard for our money. We should make an additional effort to see that it is managed and used wisely.

*Adapted from "'I'm Broke,' Says Winner of Lottery," *Chicago Tribune*, October 11, 1984, sec. 1A, p. 32.

ing age 65 will continue to have a financially successful income. These five people had a financial plan and coordinated their personal economic resources.

As you study the topics in this book, you will be developing the tools you need for a successful financial existence. Your total efforts for personal financial planning can be described as

- A tax and investment discipline and a learning process.
- A procedure, much like an annual physical or dental checkup, that pulls the myriad financial pieces together and renders an opinion on family health in financial and tax terms.
- A process that allows all family assets and liabilities to be screened to see whether major mistakes are apparent, with possible dire consequences at hand or downstream. What is examined includes taxes, savings, investments, insurance protection, estate transfer, monthly and annual budgets, family liquidity, and whether all of these diverse and complex elements, current and future, are integrated to work cohesively and in unison.[1]

[1]Carl E. Andersen, *Andersen on Financial Planning* (Homewood, Ill.: Dow Jones-Irwin, 1986), p. 6.

The various elements and factors that make up financial planning are presented in Figure 1–1.

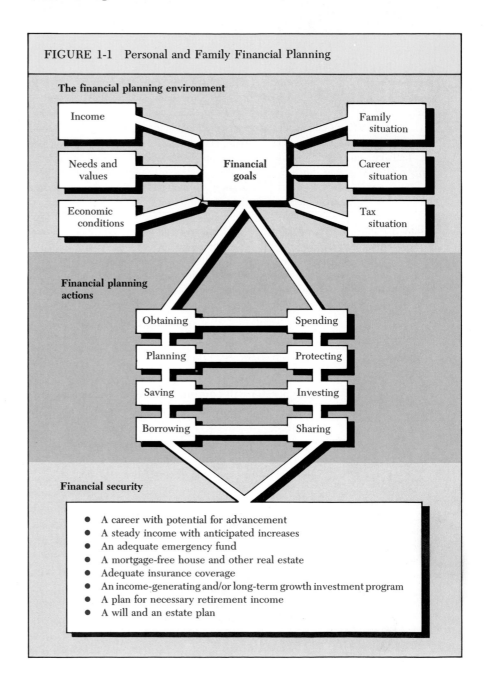

FIGURE 1-1   Personal and Family Financial Planning

The financial planning environment

Income

Needs and values

Economic conditions

Financial goals

Family situation

Career situation

Tax situation

Financial planning actions

Obtaining

Planning

Saving

Borrowing

Spending

Protecting

Investing

Sharing

Financial security

- A career with potential for advancement
- A steady income with anticipated increases
- An adequate emergency fund
- A mortgage-free house and other real estate
- Adequate insurance coverage
- An income-generating and/or long-term growth investment program
- A plan for necessary retirement income
- A will and an estate plan

Financial planning requires an understanding of the benefits of achieving your various personal economic goals and of having a logical process for your financial planning efforts.

Why Study Personal Financial Planning?

Throughout life, each individual and family has needs that can be satisfied by the intelligent use of available financial resources. Financial planning is the process of deciding how to obtain, protect, and use these resources.

Financial planning is both individual and family centered, as well as future oriented. Of primary importance in financial planning is the idea that both your needs and your resources will change as you progress from one stage of life to another. The **adult life cycle** is the stages that an individual goes through based on age, financial needs, and family situation. Figure 1–2 highlights the need for a realistic financial plan for people in all phases of the adult life cycle and at all income levels.

- Benefits of Personal Financial Planning

A comprehensive financial plan can enhance your quality of life by reducing uncertainty about your future needs and resources. Such a blueprint for financial success helps foster a sense of well-being and satisfaction that accompanies the achievement of a desired standard of living. The specific advantages of personal and family financial planning include:

- Increased effectiveness in obtaining, using, and protecting resources throughout the adult life cycle.
- Reduced economic uncertainty about whether a desired product or service can be afforded.
- Increased control of financial affairs to prevent excessive debt, bankruptcy, and dependence on others for economic security.
- Improved family relationships resulting from well-planned and -communicated financial decisions.
- An instilled sense of freedom from financial worries that is obtained by looking to the future, anticipating expenses, and achieving economic goals.

The Financial Planning Process

- Steps Involved in Personal Financial Planning

The steps used in financial planning are:

1. Analyze your current personal and financial situation.
2. Develop financial goals.
3. Create a financial plan of action.
4. Implement the financial plan.
5. Evaluate and revise your actions.

This process for financial planning does not establish a standard. It does not recommend a set formula for spending money. It does not address one set of values and prescribe a means for attaining set goals. It does not provide

FIGURE 1-2 Major Financial Tasks in the Adult Life Cycle

18 to 24
- Train for career
- Establish household and attain financial independence
- Develop a savings and investment plan
- Purchase insurance
- Create effective financial record-keeping and planning system
- Make will

25 to 34
- Provide for expanding housing needs and living costs
- Expand career goals
- Manage increased need for credit
- Purchase additional insurance coverages

35 to 44
- Upgrade career training
- Maximize protection for major income earners
- Establish and work toward retirement goals
- Provide greater income for expanding needs

45 to 54
- Maximize investments
- Evaluate and update retirement plans
- Analyze and adjust estate plan as needed
- Evaluate future financial needs of parents or other dependents

55 to 64
- Consolidate financial assets
- Plan for part-time or volunteer work during retirement
- Investigate housing location and expense for retirement

65 and over
- Adjust living conditions and spending based on health and income
- Obtain assistance with managing financial affairs
- Finalize estate plan

Source: Adapted from *Personal and Family Financial Planning* (Washington, D.C.: American Council of Life Insurance, 1983), sec. 1, pp. 20d–21d.

principles that apply only to a traditional concept of family. It does not present a set of facts that are applicable across time. However, this process for financial planning does apply to persons of any age, any income level, any lifestyle, and any family size.

Analyze Your Current Situation. Analyzing your values and goals involves identifying how you feel about money and why you feel that way. Are your feelings based on factual knowledge? On your family's model? On peer practices? Are your priorities based on social pressures, family needs, or desires for luxury items? How will current economic conditions affect your goals and priorities? The purpose of this analysis is not to establish basic needs but to differentiate needs from wants for a family or an individual.

In this first step of the financial planning process, you must also determine your current financial position with regard to available income, savings, living expenses, and money owed. There should be a match between goals and the earning power or potential earning power of family members. How do you address the reality of unlimited wants and limited income? How does your lifestyle fit with the expectations of persons in your career field? What job-related expenses must have priority in your financial plan? How will you achieve balance between earning and spending?

Finally, this step of the financial planning process requires an understanding of changing income patterns and income demands as the family life cycle changes. When you have children and as they grow older, unique financial needs evolve. Your decisions about marriage, children, education, and career are a few of the milestones of life that will influence your financial existence.

Develop Financial Goals. An old saying is that if you don't know where you're going, you might end up somewhere else and not even know it. While others can suggest financial goals, you must decide which ones to pursue. Your goals can range from spending all of your current income to developing an extensive savings and investment program for future financial security. The topics, discussion, and examples in this book are likely to suggest some goals that you may try to accomplish.

Establishing financial goals should involve all of the people affected by the financial planning process. In a family situation, each member should participate in the listing, evaluating, discussing, and ranking of potential financial objectives. This goal evaluation effort should consider available resources along with individual and group values. **Values** are the ideas and principles that are considered correct, desirable, or important. These values will greatly influence the creation and achievement of goals. Decisions about spending now versus saving for the future, or about continuing school versus getting a job, may be the result of personal or family help values. Such decisions also demonstrate the economic concept of **opportunity cost.** If you use money or other resources in a particular way, you cannot at the same time use them for anything else. Time spent for recreation cannot be used for schoolwork; money allocated for the rent cannot be spent for other items.

(Further discussion of personal and financial goals may be found in Chapter 3.)

Create a Financial Plan of Action. The first step of the financial planning process is to identify where you are now. The second step is to determine where you would like to be. The third step is to develop a plan of action for achieving your goals. Since there is more than one way to attain your goals, you will need to choose a specific path to follow. For example, increases in savings may be achieved by reducing spending or by increasing income through extra time on the job. A person concerned with year-end tax payments may increase the amount withheld for taxes from each paycheck, file quarterly tax payments, or shelter current income in a tax-deferred pension program.

Creating an action plan will require you to investigate the possible alternatives. Besides assessing how each possibility will affect your personal and financial situation, also obtain information regarding costs, benefits, and ease of implementation. While several methods may be used to achieve the same end, each path may not have the same desirability based on values, needs, and other factors. You may choose to increase your savings through participating in a payroll deduction plan instead of taking a trip to the bank to make a deposit.

In the News
Financial Advisers Help Younger Clients

Individuals and couples in their 20s and 30s are calling their financial advisers before going out to dinner, making a major purchase, or taking money out of savings. To prevent wasteful and unnecessary buying and thus to assist young clients in reaching financial goals and avoiding money problems, some financial advisers closely monitor the spending habits of such clients. These financial advisers are acting more like parents than consultants. But many clients appreciate the effort since it has enabled them to save for new cars, vacations, and down payments on homes.

The financial advisers do not stop their clients from spending; they just try to encourage moderate purchasing habits and increased savings. To encourage setting aside money for the future, some financial advisers send clients a monthly bill for an amount to be invested for the clients or urge clients to place a graph of their savings progress on the refrigerator door. Some advisers help clients open savings accounts but provide very little information on how to make a withdrawal. The clients are then required to talk to the adviser before making any major purchase.

Source: Alexandra Peers, "Advisers Help Younger Clients Curb Spending," *The Wall Street Journal,* September 26, 1986, p. 21.

Implement the Financial Plan. This stage of financial planning may require assistance from others. You may contact an insurance agent for property insurance. Or you may contact an investment broker to purchase stocks, bonds, or mutual funds. The individuals and organizations available to help you achieve financial goals are discussed later in this chapter.

All of your efforts should be geared to avoiding the many financial mistakes that are made by individuals and families (see Table 1–1). Specific strategies for the different components of a financial plan are the basis of this book. Techniques to achieve goals related to savings, spending, borrowing, and investing are covered in the chapters that follow.

TABLE 1-1   15 Money Blunders

Among the most common financial planning mistakes are the following:

1. Not setting financial goals.
2. Making an unrealistic budget.
3. Maintaining poorly organized financial records.
4. Not establishing a credit history in both spouses' names.
5. Using credit unwisely.
6. Not having enough insurance for your home and valuables.
7. Not having an emergency savings fund.
8. Buying insurance without taking discounts.
9. Failing to shop for the best interest rates.
10. Not insuring lives and earning power.
11. Not putting money to work for you.
12. Paying too much in taxes.
13. Making major financial decisions without professional help.
14. Making spur-of-the-moment investments based on tips.
15. Not having a will.

Source: *15 Money Blunders and How to Avoid Them* (Hartford, Conn.: Aetna Life and Casualty Company, n.d.).

Evaluate and Revise Your Actions. Changes in your income, your values, and even your family situation will require changes in your goals and actions. When uncontrollable events such as loss of a job or a family member affect your finances, the financial planning process provides a vehicle for dealing with them by delaying or altering priorities. As immediate or short-term goals are achieved, goals next in priority come into focus. Some changes in your life situation or your values can result in changes in your long-term goals.

Financial planning is a dynamic process. It doesn't end when you take a particular action. You need to regularly reassess your financial decisions. While a complete reevaluation of your finances should be made once a year, various personal, economic, and tax factors may require more frequent evaluation. These and other factors that influence personal financial planning are the subject of the next section.

THE FINANCIAL PLANNING ENVIRONMENT

Your personal financial planning efforts are affected both by personal factors and by social and economic influences. Your needs, wants, values, and goals will be the foundation of your financial decisions. These factors will combine with your family situation, income, and life-cycle stage to determine your economic choices. The economy will also affect your financial planning since basic economic principles and changing economic conditions create the dynamic environment in which your financial decisions are made.

Personal Factors

● Factors That Affect Financial Planning

As previously discussed, your values—that is, ideas and principles of importance to you and your family—will guide your financial planning. For example, if you value advanced training and education, one of your financial goals might be to save money for college expenses.

Your financial planning is also affected by the basic needs and wants of daily living. Spending and saving decisions will determine the resources available for future financial security. Some people spend their entire income on current consumption items, such as food, clothing, furniture, recreation, and education. Other people save and invest some portion of their income or purchase insurance to achieve a degree of financial security. These spending habits reflect individual and family values and goals.

Your income level also affects your financial planning. Many people believe that personal economic goals can be achieved only by individuals whose income allows the purchase of expensive items or extended vacations. However, everyone can achieve such goals. A financial plan is not based on the amount of income available but rather on how resources are used. Moreover, financial planning can help you identify methods for increasing income through additional education or new careers.

Finally, your life-cycle stage strongly influences your financial planning. Age, marital status, and the ages of children dictate certain decisions. An unmarried individual will have financial priorities that are different from those of a single parent with school-age children. The financial activities related to different family situations are reported in Table 1–2.

The American Economic System

● Operation of the American Economic System

An **economic system** is the mechanism that brings labor, resources, and skills together to produce and distribute the goods and services that people want and need. While every country has an economic system, each of these systems is unique. An economic system is used to answer three basic economic questions: what to produce, how to produce, and for whom to produce? In the United States, basic economic decisions are influenced by the principles of supply, demand, prices, government involvement, and competition.

Basic Economic Questions. Economics is the study of how wealth is created and distributed. Wealth is anything that has value, including food,

TABLE 1-2 Family Situation and Financial Activities

Group	Household Income	Percent Who Own Home	Amount of Liabilities	Savings Rate (1984)	Financial Profile
Singles (one in household; average age: 35)	$34,000	57%	$27,000	8%	Least active group for investing; group reporting most disorganized financial records
Young couples (two in household, both working; average age: 39)	50,000	79	42,000	8	Least conservative investment strategy; seek advice from financial advisers and publications
Traditionals (married, one income, two children; average age: 39)	47,000	88	46,000	6	Most likely group to use budget; quite conservative investments, such as U.S. savings bonds
Moderns (married, two incomes, two children; average age: 39)	50,000	89	45,000	5	High expenses for transportation due to two workers and transporting children; least likely group to own stock; concerned about their high level of debt
Empty Nesters (two in household, one working; average age: 56)	49,000	90	32,000	8	High level of satisfaction with finances; high level of accumulated wealth; spend the most per person on food
Retirees (two in household, at least one retired; average age: over 65)	36,000	95	7,000	7	Most satisfied with finances; high level of investments, low level of debt; low amounts spent for clothing, transportation and housing

Source: "Where Does All the Money Go?" *Consumer Reports*, September 1986, pp. 581–92. Copyright 1987 by Consumers Union of United States, Inc., Mount Vernon, NY 10553. Excerpted by permission from *Consumer Reports*, September 1986.

clothing, automobiles, savings accounts, education, real estate, and vacations. In the process of creating and distributing wealth, three basic economic questions must be answered:

1. *What to Produce?* This question is answered continually by consumers as they spend their dollars for goods and services. When consumers buy every Camcorder that RCA can produce, they are casting dollar votes for the

production of more Camcorders. Changes in consumer preferences influence decisions by producers to offer certain items. As more investors purchased mutual funds, new and different funds were offered by investment companies.

2. *How to Produce?* In years past, greater physical labors were required to harvest food and produce clothing. As technology improved, new manufacturing methods were employed. These mass production methods lowered costs and increased the availability of everything from food to electronic entertainment devices. In the financial services marketplace, information on bank accounts is being produced increasingly by computers rather than people.

3. *For Whom to Produce?* Productive efforts along with ownership of capital, land, and other resources determine what income a person will have to purchase goods and services. Income in the form of wages, rents, profits, and interest is the basis of spending and financial success. The income you receive from your work, savings, investments, or ownership of a business is the basis of the wealth you will possess.

Supply, Demand, and Prices. While money is used to buy goods and services, the price of a specific item is determined by a balance of supply and demand. A high demand to borrow available money will force interest rates up. This price of money reflects the supply of money and the demand for it.

Generally, the price of any good or service will increase if its supply decreases or if the demand for it increases, or both. Shortages of wheat and corn due to poor weather will cause food prices to increase. In the same way, the price of an item will usually decrease if the supply increases or the demand decreases, or both. An increased number of businesses that provide eyeglasses and contact lenses has caused reduced prices for these products.

Our Mixed Economy. In a **market economy,** the forces of supply and demand operate freely. The actions of buyers and sellers answer the three basic economic questions and determine prices. One of the best examples of supply and demand is the actions of stock exchange traders representing buyers and sellers of investments. The ups and downs of stock prices demonstrate the forces of supply and demand.

The complexity of our society has created a situation in which market forces do not always operate freely. As a result, government is involved in various economic activities that create a mixed, rather than a market, economy. A **mixed economy** combines a market economy with selected efforts by government. The main economic functions of government are to protect the rights of individuals, ensure the fair distribution of goods and services, promote a fair and safe business environment, maintain stable economic conditions, and support individuals who are in need due to special circumstances or lack of employment. The performance of these functions is intended to create equity in the economy and to reduce the chances that any individual or organization will take advantage of others. For example, the Securities and Exchange Commission closely regulates information from corporations that could affect the price of the stock they issue. Corporate officers and employees are not allowed to benefit from inside information that could enable them to buy stock for less than it will cost once the public is aware of the information. Buying such stock before the information has been announced and then selling it when buying by others pushes the price up can result in illegal profits.

Competition. While the economic role of government is greater than it was in the past, rivalry among businesses is still fundamental to economic growth. Competition among suppliers of goods and services gives the American economy its vitality. The most successful suppliers will be those that provide the best goods and services at the best prices. Few people realize that this country once had ten times as many automobile manufacturers as the ones that exist today. The surviving companies were those that were able to compete successfully. In recent years, competition among personal computer companies and among financial services companies has intensified. Once again, competitive forces have been stimulating changes in our constantly evolving economy.

Changing Economic Conditions

- Effect of Changing Economic Conditions on Financial Planning

Economic expansion and contraction are influenced by many factors, including new technology, increased savings, government policies, crop failures, wars, and public confidence in the economy. In good economic times, individuals, businesses, and governments are confident about the future and spend more money, which stimulates the economy. Such changes in economic conditions affect personal financial decision making. Our spending and savings patterns are influenced by inflation, employment, interest rates, and taxes.

Inflation. Inflation is a rise in the general level of prices. In times of inflation, the buying power of the dollar decreases. If prices increase 5 percent in a year, items that cost a total of $100 last year would now cost $105. It takes more money to buy the same amount of goods and services. Consequently, a given dollar has less buying power.

Inflation is most harmful to people who live on fixed incomes. Some retired persons continue to receive the same amount of income each year, but due to inflation they buy ever fewer goods and services.

Lenders of money can also be affected by inflation. Unless an adequate interest rate is charged, dollars paid back by borrowers in times of inflation have less value than the amount that was originally borrowed. If you are paying 10 percent interest on a loan and the inflation rate is 12 percent, the dollars received in payment by the lender have lost buying power. For this reason, a strong relationship exists between inflation and interest rates. Interest rates usually rise in periods of increased inflation.

The rate of inflation varies. During the late 1950s and early 1960s, the annual inflation rate was in the 1–3 percent range. During the late 1970s and

Pepper . . . and Salt

"—and when I grow up, please give me
lots of buying power."

From *The Wall Street Journal,* with permission of Cartoon Features Syndicate.

early 1980s, it was 10–12 percent. At a 12 percent inflation rate, prices would double in about six years. More recently, the annual price increase of most goods and services as measured by the Consumer Price Index has been in the 3–5 percent range. The Consumer Price Index (CPI), published monthly by the Bureau of Labor Statistics, is based on a selected group of goods and services. Although different indexes are computed for various cities, the Consumer Price Index is probably not a reliable measure of your personal living costs. You do not buy goods and services in the proportion that is used in calculating the index. Remember, however, that the Consumer Price Index will give you an indication of changes in prices and in the value of the dollar that will assist you in financial planning.

Employment. Your financial situation and your personal economic choices will also be influenced by the availability of work and the wages you receive. Although hundreds of thousands of new jobs are created each year, the demand for these positions exceeds the supply, which causes unemployment. The natural growth and development of the economy have caused major shifts in employment. In recent years, jobs were plentiful in the South and West as businesses expanded into these areas and high-tech companies and service organizations offered more employment opportunities than did manufacturing businesses.

The total demand for goods and services also influences employment levels. Consumer purchasing of an item increases employment in the industry that produces it. Reduced spending causes unemployment. The financial hardships of unemployment are a major concern of business, labor organizations, and government. Retraining programs, income assistance, and job services help individuals adjust to changing employment conditions. (Further discussion of the factors affecting employment is given in Chapter 2.)

Interest Rates. While prices balance the supply of and demand for goods and services, interest rates serve the same purpose for money. The price of money in the form of interest rates is a vital factor in personal economic and financial planning. As a saver and investor, you add to the supply of money and you want to receive a good return in exchange for the use of your funds. In contrast, when you borrow money for a car, a house, or some other purchase, you will be required to pay an interest rate for using someone else's money. Much like inflation, interest rates vary based on the available supply of and demand for money. These rates influence many personal financial decisions.

Interest rate changes reflect economic ups and downs. The interest rates charged for mortgages on homes ranged from 5 percent in the 1960s to 15 percent in the early 1980s.

Taxes. Just as we depend on wages or other income to pay our living expenses, the government depends on tax revenues to pay its bills. As the demand for government services increases, tax collections must also increase. While Americans experienced reductions in federal income rates in the early 1980s, other types of federal taxes along with state and local taxes increased to fund public services. Your tax payments are a fundamental component of your financial plan. Although taxes are a requirement, careful financial decisions can minimize this expenditure.

PERSONAL FINANCIAL PLANNING AND YOU

This book is designed to provide a framework for the study and planning of personal financial decisions. Table 1–3 presents an overview of the areas covered along with some of the concerns associated with each area. The information that you obtain from this book can be supplemented by people, current publications, and other resources that are available to guide your financial planning.

- Components of a Personal Financial Plan

Components of Personal Financial Planning

To achieve a successful financial existence, eight major components of personal financial planning must be coordinated. Your financial planning efforts will involve decisions related to obtaining, planning, saving, borrowing, spending, protecting, investing, and sharing personal economic resources.

Obtaining. Your available resources will be mainly income from your employment or profits from a personally owned business. Your ability to

TABLE 1-3   Components of Personal Financial Planning

Component/Text Chapter	Major Financial Planning Questions
Obtaining/ Chapter 2	Is your income appropriate to your level of education and training? Have you made plans for achieving an improved career situation? What plans are you making to increase your income now and in the future?
Planning/ Chapters 3, 7	Have you set specific financial goals and developed a plan for achieving these goals? Do you have a realistic budget for your current financial situation? Is your tax situation appropriate to your level and type of income?
Saving/ Chapter 4	Do you have an adequate emergency fund? Are your savings earning the best interest rates? Should some of your savings be transferred to higher-risk, higher-return investments?
Borrowing/ Chapters 5, 6	Is you level of borrowing appropriate to your income? Are the interest rates on your loans the lowest available? Are you attempting to reduce your level of debt?
Spending/ Chapters 8–10	Do you plan purchases with the best price, quality, and service in mind? Is your housing situation appropriate to your financial situation? Are your transportation expenses minimized through careful planning?
Protecting/ Chapters 11–14	Do you have adequate insurance protection for your home and possessions? Are you covered for life and health risks? Have there been any changes in your life situation that would require an increase or a decrease in your insurance coverage?
Investing/ Chapters 15–19	Is your investment program appropriate to your income and tax situation? Have you assessed the risk of your various investments? Do you continually reassess your investment portfolio?
Sharing/ Chapter 20	Is your will current? Does your plan for distributing your estate minimize taxes? Have you prepared for the orderly transfer of your property to dependents or others?

increase income will usually result from increased education or training, career advancement, or higher profits from your business. Obtaining financial resources is the foundation of your financial plan since these resources will be the basis for all of your other financial actions. To reach your goals, you must save and invest part of the income you earn. Your savings and investments will provide an additional income source.

Planning. Budgeting the spending, saving, and investing of your income is the basis of successful financial planning. Allocating part of your current resources to cover necessary living expenses while setting aside another part for future financial security is the key to such planning. Efforts made to anticipate expenses and other financial decisions can help reduce taxes. The ability to pay your fair share of taxes—no more, no less—is vital to the growth of your financial resources.

Saving. Long-term financial security starts with a regular savings plan for emergencies, unexpected bills, replacement of needed home items, and the purchase of special goods and services, such as a boat, a vacation home, or a college education. Once the basic savings component has been established, additional money saved may be used for investments that offer greater potential returns.

A certain amount of savings must be readily available to meet individual or family needs. **Liquidity** is the ability to convert financial resources into usa-

---

Careers in Personal Finance
Financial Planning Careers

As you learn to handle your personal finances, you may wish to use your money management skills in a financial planning career. To embark on such a career, you will be required to have a basic knowledge of insurance, taxes, investments, and estate planning. Also important will be your study of such business subjects as accounting, economics, and marketing and your development of public speaking and writing skills.

Employment in financial planning usually starts with experience as a stockbroker, insurance agent, bank officer, or accountant. As your practical background increases, you can get involved as a personal and family financial planner through your employer or you can start your own service.

The expanding field of financial services is creating a demand for individuals who desire to help others analyze and plan their finances. For further information on a career in financial planning, contact the International Association for Financial Planning, Two Concourse Parkway, Suite 800, Atlanta, GA 30328, or the College for Financial Planning, 9725 East Hampton Avenue, Denver, CO 80231.

Source: *Financial Planning as a Career* (Atlanta, Ga.: International Association for Financial Planning, 1985).

ble cash with ease. Liquidity needs vary with the age, health, and personal requirements of family members. Such savings plans as money market accounts, money market funds, and SuperNOW accounts allow you to get better than average returns while still having a high degree of liquidity.

Borrowing. Maintaining control over credit buying habits will help you achieve your financial goals. Using credit so that you will not have to make excessive credit payments is crucial to successful financial planning. The overuse and misuse of credit are major causes of personal economic difficulties. **Bankruptcy** is a situation in which a person is not able to pay debts on time. This results in legal proceedings to arrange payments to creditors. The thousands of people who have declared bankruptcy each year could have avoided this trauma through better borrowing and spending decisions.

Spending. Your living expenses and your other financial obligations should be detailed in a spending plan. Decisions on necessities and other items are a vital aspect of financial planning. Quite often, people buy what they need and want without considering the effect of their shopping. A few individuals shop compulsively and are thus led to financial ruin. An organization called Spender Menders was formed to assist people who have difficulty in controlling their purchasing.[2] Restricting your spending is necessary if you are to accumulate resources for future financial security.

Protecting. Another financial necessity is adequate insurance coverage for yourself, your family, and your property. Insurance is an overlooked aspect of many financial plans. The number of people who suffer disabling injuries or diseases at age 50 is greater than the number who die at that age, so individuals may need disability insurance more than they need life insurance. Yet surveys reveal that most people have adequate life insurance, while few have disability coverage. As health care costs continue to rise, you should consider this aspect of insurance.

In contrast, some individuals have excessive or overlapping insurance coverages. Insuring property for more than it is worth wastes money. So does having a husband and wife both pay for similar family health insurance.

Investing. Many types of investment vehicles are available. Those who desire assurance of long-term capital safety should select investments with minimal risk, such as government securities, corporate bonds, or stocks of well-established companies.

Investment diversification can be achieved by selecting a variety of assets, such as stocks, real estate, and rare coins. It can also be achieved through the purchase of a mutual fund. Obtaining investment advice can be easy; more difficult is obtaining investment advice that is appropriate to your individual needs and goals.

---

[2]"Compulsive Buying—It's No Joke," *Consumers Digest*, September 1986, pp. 55–57.

Sharing. Timing your decision to transfer money or property to others is crucial to your financial plan. Maximizing benefits for family members while minimizing taxes is a primary goal of estate planning. The investigation of property transfer methods can help you in choosing a course of action that will fund the current and future living costs, educational expenses, and retirement needs of family members.

Financial Planning Assistance

● Resources Available to Supplement and Expand Your Knowledge of Personal Finance

This book offers the foundation you need for successful financial planning. Due to changing social and economic conditions, however, you will need to continually supplement and update your knowledge. Various resources are available to provide personal financial planning assistance. These resources include financial specialists, printed materials, financial institutions, courses and seminars, and computer software.

Financial Specialists. Specialists from different fields can provide specific kinds of financial assistance and advice. These specialists are as follows:

- *Accountants* specialize in tax matters and financial documents.
- *Bankers* assist you with financial services and trusts.
- *Credit counselors* suggest ways to reduce spending and eliminate credit problems.
- *Certified financial planners* coordinate your finances into a single plan.
- *Insurance agents* sell types of insurance coverage that will protect your wealth and property.
- *Investment brokers* provide information on stocks, bonds, and other investments and handle transactions for their purchase and sale.

"Your guess is as good as mine. That'll be $350."

From *The Wall Street Journal,* with permission of Cartoon Features Syndicate.

- *Lawyers* help you with wills, estate planning, tax problems, and other legal matters.
- *Real estate agents* assist you in handling the details of buying and selling a home or other real estate.
- *Tax preparers* specialize in the completion of income tax returns and other tax forms.

In recent years, many of these specialists have expanded their services to include various aspects of financial planning. However, you may wish to obtain complete financial assistance from one source. If so, Appendix A, "Choosing a Financial Planner," has additional information that will be useful to you.

Printed Materials. As presented inside the back cover, a variety of personal finance periodicals are available to expand and update your knowledge

Technology for Today
Financial Data at Your Fingertips

The demand for financial planning and personal business information is being met by various technologies. Regular public television programs such as *Wall Street Week* and the *Nightly Business Report* have been joined by cable and network shows such as *Business Day* on CNN and *Business World* on ABC.

For those who are unable to wait for a television report to get the latest stock prices, electronic information systems are available. Such organizations as Quotron, Telerate, Automatic Data Processing, and Reuters provide instant access to stock, bond, and other financial data

through your computer terminal. With investment prices changing every minute of every business day, brokers and investors require much information to make the decisions that will give them the largest profits. Not being plugged into the appropriate data base can mean a financial loss.

Home computers can be used to access data bases that provide business and investment news as well as general news and sports, entertainment, and travel information. CompuServe, The Source, and Dow Jones News/Retrieval allow all of us to use electronic data bases in the comfort of our home or office. The Dow Jones

system provides more than 30 types of information, including articles in *The Wall Street Journal* and *Barron's*, stock prices, research reports of companies, government industry reports, movie reviews, sports scores, and weather reports.

Source: Donald R. Woodwell, *Using and Applying the Dow Jones Information Services* (Homewood, Ill.: Dow Jones-Irwin, 1986); "On-Line Services Can Put World at Your Fingertips," *Chicago Tribune*, April 6, 1986, sec. 19, pp. 11–12; "Hooking into Electronic Data Bases," *U.S. News & World Report*, February 10, 1986, p. 59; and "Financial Facts at Your Finger Tips," *U.S. News & World Report*, September 15, 1986, pp. 53–54.

in this area. These periodicals, as well as an extensive number of books on various personal finance topics, can be found in your library.

In addition to these sources, there are a vast number of specialized publications. Financial planning newsletters key in on such specific topics as mutual funds, commodity investments, low-priced stocks, real estate investments, tax planning, and investments in gold and coins. You can find a newsletter on any financial area that is of interest to you.

As with any purchase, you should determine whether the amount you pay for a newsletter will give you a commensurate benefit. The unregulated financial newsletter industry has many participants that promise much more than they deliver. Investment advisers publish recommendations and charge clients high fees for this service. Not all investment services offer more information than you can obtain from other, less expensive resources. Obtain a sample copy of any high-priced newsletter before you subscribe to it.

Financial Institutions. Some financial advisers, such as insurance agents and investment brokers, are affiliated with companies that sell financial services and assistance. Through national marketing efforts or local promotions, banks, savings and loan associations, credit unions, insurance companies, investment brokers, and real estate offices offer suggestions on budgeting, saving, investing, and other aspects of financial planning. These organizations also offer booklets, financial planning worksheets, and other materials.

Courses and Seminars. Colleges and universities offer courses in investment, real estate, insurance, tax, and estate planning that will enhance your knowledge of financial planning. Civic clubs and community business organizations schedule free or inexpensive programs featuring speakers and workshops on career planning, budgeting, life insurance, tax form preparation, and investment in stocks. Financial institutions and financial services trade associations present seminars for preferred and prospective customers and members.

Computer Software. Personal computers and financial planning software have become more affordable. Experts do not recommend buying a personal computer for financial planning unless doing so will help you improve your decision-making skills. A personal computer will not change your saving, spending, and borrowing habits; this must be done by you. But a personal computer can provide you with fast and current analyses of your financial situation and progress.

Many financial planning software programs are on the market; these range in price from $30 to $200. Two of the most popular programs are *Andrew Tobias' Managing Your Money* and *Sylvia Porter's Personal Finance: Your Personal Financial Planner.* Each of the programs helps you analyze your current situation and project your future financial position. Specialized computer programs are also available for conducting investment analyses, preparing taxes, and determining the costs of financing and owning a home. For further information, see Appendix B, "Buying a Personal Computer and Financial Planning Software."

FIGURE 1-3   Financial Planning in Action: Two Examples

	Carl Nolan	Ken and Ellen Snyder
Step 1. Analyze current personal and financial situation.	• Single, age 25 • Annual income $24,000 • Desires advanced career training • Financial needs of elderly parents • Buy a house	• Married, Ken age 31, Ellen age 29 • Two children, ages four and two • Annual family income $38,000 • Income in the event of family member disability or death • Education for children • Comfortable retirement
Step 2. Develop financial goals.	• Savings for school tuition • Savings or investment program for parent's financial needs • Investment program for future housing	• Adequate disability and life insurance • Savings and investment program for education fund • Investment and pension plan for retirement
Step 3. Create a plan of action.	• Increase savings deposits • Investigate investment alternatives and life insurance options	• Discuss insurance needs with insurance agent • Increase savings and investment amounts • Investigate additional contributions to pension plans
Step 4. Implement the financial plan.	• Make regular savings deposits • Purchase life insurance with parents as beneficiaries • Make monthly payments to investment program	• Purchase additional disability and life insurance to supplement current and employer-provided coverage • Purchase long term government bonds for children's education • Start stock and bond investments for retirement fund
Step 5. Evaluate and review actions taken.	• Assess increased amount and reduced use of credit cards • Assess life insurance coverage in relation to parents' needs • Evaluate performance of investments; consider different investment vehicles and putting a portion of savings fund into investment program	• Evaluate insurance coverage in relation to changing needs • Assess performance of education fund investment • Evaluate stock and bond performance in relation to retirement needs • Investigate additional types of investments based on changing needs and tax situation

PERSONAL FINANCIAL PLANNING IN ACTION

• Implementation of Personal Financial Planning

A **financial plan** is a formalized report that summarizes your current financial situation, analyzes your financial needs, and recommends a direction for your financial activities. You can create this document on your own, or you can seek assistance from others such as with computerized financial plans (see Appendix A). Regardless of the financial planning actions you take, specific implementation techniques are needed.

The financial planning process, discussed previously, can be implemented in many ways. Figure 1–3 offers an overview of two situations—that of Carl Nolan and that of Ken and Ellen Snyder. In these situations, the individuals involved concentrated on assessing current concerns, developing financial planning strategies, and evaluating the effectiveness of their financial plan.

Current Concerns

Financial forecasting is the process of predicting your future financial situation. Such predictions are only educated guesses based on current information and anticipated needs. For example, Carl Nolan sees a possible need to take care of his parents in the future. This possibility influences his financial goals and actions. Ken and Ellen Snyder want to provide for the family's basic financial needs in the event of the disability or death of either spouse. This concern is reflected in their financial plan.

One method for assessing the future financial needs of an individual or a family is to list the following items for each anticipated financial concern:

- Estimate how much money would be needed to deal with the financial concern.
- Determine when the estimated funds would be needed.
- Indicate how long the funds will be needed.
- Determine a priority for each need.
- Indicate how much investment risk can be taken with regard to the financial concern.

Funds for education will be needed by the Snyder children in about 14 years, and each child will need enough money to pay for four years of college. This is a high-priority financial item that should involve low-risk investments. In contrast, a higher risk may be taken when investing for a retirement that is more than 30 years away.

Your current financial concerns and your future financial needs are based on your financial resources (see Figure 1–4). The components of these resources require frequent evaluation. For example, changing personal situations may allow you to take advantage of employment benefits offered by your company. Increases in life insurance may be possible through a group policy, or your employer may offer a special investment program to assist you in setting aside funds for children's educational expenses or for retirement. Existing and potential financial resources are the foundation of your efforts to achieve your goals.

Financial Strategies

The 1986 tax law changes affected the financial direction of many individuals. Lower tax rates created less of a need for tax shelters and increased the emphasis on income producing investments.[3] The exact techniques you use will be influenced by the factors presented earlier in this chapter, but some commonly recommended courses of action include the following:

- Develop a large savings reserve for unexpected financial needs.
- Invest in corporate bonds to receive a steady income from earned interest.

[3]Earl C. Gottschalk, Jr., and Robert L. Rose, "Changing Times for Financial Planners," *The Wall Street Journal*, October 24, 1986, p. 21.

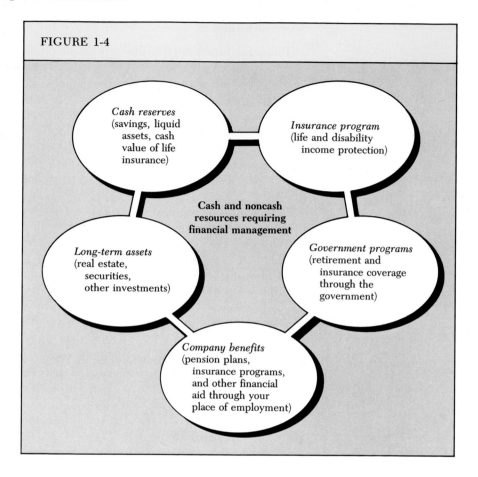

FIGURE 1-4

- Purchase antiques and other collectibles that can appreciate in value.
- Buy real estate that can be rented for income.
- Invest in U.S. government securities for a steady income and ultimate safety.
- Contribute money to programs that offer tax advantages.
- Minimize the use of credit cards and other borrowing.
- Make regular deposits into a savings account.
- Invest in gold jewelry, coins, bars, or certificates.
- Diversify your financial situation by owning a variety of investments.[4]

These are only a few of the many strategies that can be used to achieve financial security. These and other personal financial strategies will be developed in later chapters.

[4]"10 Ways to Financial Security," *Sylvia Porter's Personal Finance*, December 1984, pp. 37ff.

SUMMARY

- Personal financial planning is the art and science of putting your money to work for you and living within your means. It is the process by which you take control of your financial situation.
- The major benefits of personal financial planning are increased effectiveness in financial decision making, reduced economic uncertainty, increased control of financial affairs, improved family relationships, and freedom from financial worries.
- Personal financial planning involves the following steps: (1) analyze your needs, wants, values, and current financial position; (2) develop financial goals; (3) create a financial plan of action; (4) implement the financial plan; and (5) evaluate and revise your actions.
- Personal financial planning is influenced by values, needs and wants, income, life-cycle stage, economic principles, and changing economic conditions.

- The American economic system answers basic economic questions through supply, demand, prices, and competition, with an interaction among consumers, producers, and government.
- Changes in consumer prices, the availability of a job, interest rates, and taxes affect personal financial decisions.
- Personal financial planning involves decisions about obtaining, planning, saving, borrowing, spending, protecting, investing, and sharing personal economic resources.
- Assistance with personal financial decisions is available from financial specialists, printed materials, financial institutions, courses and seminars, and computer software.
- Personal financial planning in action requires decisions about current concerns, future needs, and financial strategies to create and implement a financial plan.

GLOSSARY

Adult life cycle. The stages that an individual goes through based on age, financial needs, and family situation.

Bankruptcy. A situation that exists when an individual is not able to pay debts on time.

Economic system. The mechanism that brings labor, resources, and skills together to produce and distribute goods and services in a country.

Economics. The study of how wealth is created and distributed.

Financial forecasting. The process of predicting your future financial situation.

Financial plan. A formalized report that summarizes your current financial situation, analyzes your financial needs, and recommends a direction for your financial activities.

Inflation. A rise in the general level of prices.

Liquidity. The ability to convert financial resources into usable cash with ease.

Market economy. An economic system that is based on the forces of supply and demand.

Mixed economy. An economic system that combines a market economy with selected efforts by government.

Opportunity cost. An economic concept that states that if resources are used for a particular purpose, they cannot be used for another purpose.

Personal financial planning.   The art and science of putting your money to work for you and living within your means.

Values.   Ideas and principles that are considered correct, desirable, or important.

REVIEW QUESTIONS

1. What is personal financial planning? What benefits does it have for individuals and families?

2. What steps are involved in personal financial planning?

3. What influences the financial goals set by an individual or a family?

4. Why is it necessary to evaluate the actions you take after making personal financial decisions?

5. How can age, family situation, and children affect a person's financial planning?

6. What are the basic questions that every economic system must answer?

7. What effects do the forces of supply and demand have in our economy?

8. How does inflation affect personal financial decisions?

9. What are the main components of financial planning?

10. What resources are available to help you make financial decisions?

11. What is the purpose of financial forecasting?

12. What are some common strategies that are used to achieve financial security?

DISCUSSION QUESTIONS AND ACTIVITIES

1. What financial planning mistakes did Erika Earnhart make?

2. What actions would you suggest that Erika take to improve her financial position?

3. Survey friends, relatives, or other people to determine the major financial problems they face?

4. Describe how an individual's goals and financial strategies are affected by the stage of the adult life cycle.

5. Use the steps in the financial planning process to develop a direction for your personal economic situation. Are these steps adaptable to different age, income, and family situations?

6. What goals and values do you and members of your family have that influence personal financial decisions?

7. Are supply and demand still viable forces in our economy?

8. Interview three individuals about the effect of changing consumer prices and interest rates on their financial position and decisions.

9. What do you believe to be the three most important financial decisions that a person makes in a lifetime?

10. Prepare a list of financial specialists, library materials, and other resources in your community that can assist people with personal financial decisions.

ADDITIONAL READINGS

Andersen, Carl E. *Andersen on Financial Planning.* Homewood, Ill.: Dow Jones-Irwin, 1986.

Daugherty, Greg. "Great Moments in Personal Finance," *Sylvia Porter's Personal Finance,* April 1987, p. 95.

Duncan, Greg J. "On the Slippery Slope." *American Demographics,* May, 1987, pp. 30–35.

"Financial Planning: A Special Report." *The Wall Street Journal,* December 1, 1986, Section 4, pp. 1–44.

"Is Your Advisor as Sharp as You Think?" *Changing Times,* February 1987, pp. 37–38, 40, 42.

"Planning Your Future, Byte by Byte." *U.S. News and World Report,* January 19, 1987, p. 54.

Richards, Robert William. *The Dow Jones-Irwin Dictionary of Financial Planning.* Homewood, Ill.: Dow Jones-Irwin, 1986.

Shafran, Alice Priest. "The Two-Hour, Do-It-Yourself Financial Plan." *Sylvia Porter's Personal Finance,* November 1986, pp. 31–56.

CASE 1–1 Beth Plans for Graduate School—and Beyond

Beth Mahoney, 23, completed college two years ago with a degree in physical therapy. The major cost of her education was covered by a scholarship. Beth finished second in two events in the national collegiate swimming championships. Through wise planning by her parents, Beth has $22,000, which was set aside for her education. This fund, which was started when she was eight, consists of savings certificates and stocks that increased in value over the years.

Beth works for a hospital in Manhattan, Kansas, and earns $19,000 a year. In about three years, she would like to go to graduate school to get a master's degree. Then she would like to buy a house and perhaps get married. Beth wants to live on her salary and invest the $22,000 for her education and future needs.

Questions

1. How did Beth benefit from financial planning by her parents?

2. What decisions does Beth need to make regarding her future?

3. How could various personal and economic factors influence Beth's financial planning?

4. Develop a financial plan for Beth.

CASE 1–2 The Penningtons' Plan for Parenthood

Paul and Carla Pennington are in their mid-20s and have no children, but they are considering starting a family in the near future. They both have jobs with very stable companies and good opportunities to advance within their respective organizations. Their combined income is $43,000.

Each month, the Penningtons spend about

$1,800 of their $2,600 after-tax income for rent, utilities, credit payments, and insurance. They owe money on an automobile loan and on a student loan that helped pay Paul's college expenses. The other $800 goes for food, clothing, savings, and miscellaneous expenses. Currently, the Penningtons have $2,500 in a savings account.

Questions

1. How could the Penningtons benefit from financial planning?

2. Which goals are likely to be priorities in the Penningtons' plan?

3. What financial planning resources might be helpful to the Penningtons?

4. What financial strategies would you suggest for the Penningtons?

2

Planning
Your Career

A job means that you work regular hours, receive a paycheck, and may experience only limited satisfaction from your employment. In contrast, a career is a commitment to training and growth in a particular field. While both a job and a career contribute to your financial existence, a career provides you with the opportunity to obtain high levels of economic and personal fulfillment. Therefore, the selection of your career is an integral part of your financial plan.

After studying this chapter, you will be able to:

- Explain the relationship between education and income.

- List the steps involved in career planning.

- Discuss the factors that influence career choice.

- Describe the factors that determine the future availability of jobs.

- Name sources and uses of career information.

- Use the process of preparing a résumé and cover letter.

- Explain the job interview process.

- Describe the factors that should be considered when accepting a job offer.

- Recognize the need for continued career growth.

Interview with **Naomi T. Ewing**, Director, Career Planning and Placement, Lake Forest College

Naomi T. Ewing is the Director of Career Planning and Placement at Lake Forest College, Lake Forest, Illinois. She works as a liaison between graduating students and employers. Ms. Ewing also plans and implements workshops for students on such topics as résumé preparation and interviewing skills.

Several career planning experts have estimated that 80 percent of job openings are never advertised. For that reason, the development of a network of career contacts is necessary. Talk to anybody and everybody you know and meet. If five people introduce you to five others, your network is developing. It may be the friend of a friend who leads you to a job. Your contacts are also helpful for informational interviewing. Ask to visit their business or organization, not for a job interview, but to learn more about the career field.

A well-rounded background should include quantitative courses, such as mathematics, statistics, computers, economics, or accounting, and courses to develop your verbal skills.

To put it another way, your course work should include *numbers* and *words*. Grades are important, but they are not the most important factor in a person's employability. Leadership skills are important to most employers. They will look for people who organized activities and were respected by peers in sports, campus activities, or work situations.

Students need to obtain some type of experiential education. This doesn't necessarily mean a part-time job during school or in the summer; it could mean an internship, involvement in a cooperative education program, or volunteer work. The experience doesn't have to be in your planned career field. The important thing is your demonstration of an ability to discipline yourself and to show dependability in an organizational setting.

The classes you have taken, the skills you possess, the areas in which you excel, and the things you enjoy in your spare time can help you assess a career direction. Do you see yourself in a business suit at a

desk, or moving about, or working outdoors? What type of setting do you see for yourself? You don't have to describe the specific work, but think about the type of working environment.

It takes an average of six months to get a job from the time you first send out résumés and cover letters. Don't expect to send out a résumé and be offered a job in a couple of weeks. The process is slow, and it takes determination on your part. Remember, résumés are read from top to bottom, not left to right. Make sure you keep your résumé short; have a layout that allows the reader to quickly pick out desired information; and use such action verbs as *organized*, *developed*, *researched*, and *created* to describe your experience. In the interview, take control of questions that can be turned to your advantage. If a question relates to a weakness in your background, respond to it quickly, but then turn it to your favor by presenting one of your strong points.

When Betsey Collins received her B.A. degree from a small college in Wisconsin, she started to look for a job. She sent out many letters and made numerous telephone calls to companies in the towns and cities near her school. Betsey really liked that area of the country and wanted to live and work there. Despite her efforts, few businesses were interested in her. After months of disappointment, she expanded her job search to companies in nearby states. Even with this additional effort, Betsey still could not obtain employment.

Frank Manchester had a degree in computer science. While he was in school, his efforts and achievements were outstanding. However, Frank had limited his endeavors to classwork. As he applied for jobs, he discovered that most employers were looking for individuals who had had some practical experience in cocurricular activities. Because of his weakness in this area, Frank had to accept a job with less responsibility than he believed he could handle.

CAREER CHOICE AND YOUR FUTURE

The selection of your lifework is one of the most important financial decisions you will make. You may want a **job**, an employment position that is obtained mainly to earn money. Many people work in one or more jobs during their lives without considering their interests or their opportunities for advancement. Or you may want a **career**, which is a commitment to a profession that requires continued training and offers a clear path for occupational growth. A career decision is strongly related to your level of education and your lifestyle.

The Effect of Education on Income

- Relationship between Education and Income

The level of your formal training combined with various career-flexible skills will be the foundation of your financial and personal success. Figure 2–1 reports the influence of education on earnings.

As you make career and training decisions, try to develop the following traits of successful individuals:

- A desire to excel in your course work.
- The discipline to work hard and organize your time in order to complete assignments.
- A broad educational background before and after you specialize in a particular field.
- Extensive reading interests.

Marla Kenner began her job search by sending hundreds of letters to companies. She sent the same letter to all of these companies despite the fact that they were involved in different industries. Marla's letter did not specify what type of employment she was seeking, but since she sent so many letters, she believed that her chances of getting a job were good. Marla received only a few encouraging responses.

In attempting to obtain employment, these applicants used the approach that they believed was most effective. But limiting the job search to one geographic area, not having appropriate skills and experience, and sending out letters without researching a job situation are common problems of career planning. Also, none of the applicants had formed a clear and carefully planned career search program. Preparing for and obtaining employment is a systematic process. You should begin your career planning activities by deciding how your work will affect your life.

- Well-developed thinking skills.
- The patience and commitment to do well in college, to complete a course of graduate work, and to develop a lifelong plan of study.[1]

The increased demand for education in our society is quite evident. While a high school education was considered adequate some years ago, today a bachelor's degree is required in most career areas. The popularity of master's degrees, especially in business, points to the growing desire for career and financial success. The number of MBAs (masters of business administration) awarded grew from 5,787 in 1962 to over 60,000 in the mid-1980s.[2]

Your formal education is not the only measure of your ability. While technical skills are important, you also need broader, flexible skills to excel in your career. Among these are the "occupational survival skills" presented in Table 2–1. The demand for employees with flexible skills is indicated by the increase in salaries and the number of interviews being reported by liberal arts graduates.[3]

[1]George Gallup, Jr., and Alec M. Gallup, *The Great American Success Story* (Homewood, Ill.: Dow Jones-Irwin, 1986), p. 52.

[2]Michael Stanton, "MBA's: Where They Work and Where They're Needed," *Occupational Outlook Quarterly*, Winter 1985, pp. 3–4.

[3]Harriet C. Johnson, "Jobs Will Be Tight for Grads in '86," *USA Today*, June 18, 1986, pp. B1–2.

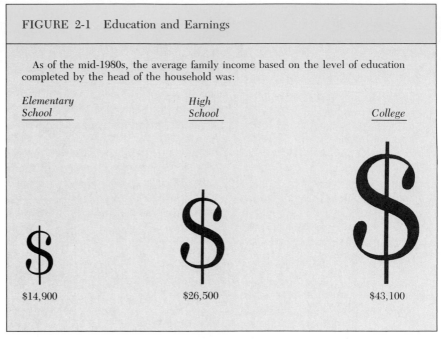

FIGURE 2-1   Education and Earnings

As of the mid-1980s, the average family income based on the level of education completed by the head of the household was:

Elementary School   High School   College

$14,900 $26,500 $43,100

Source: U.S. Department of Commerce, Bureau of the Census.

Choosing a Career Is Choosing a Lifestyle

Because your lifestyle is directly or indirectly influenced by your work, when you choose a career, you also choose a way of life. Your income level, business associates, and available time will affect your buying habits and your daily activities. Your work duties may coincide with your personal activities. However, if you do not find your job activities interesting, you will probably pursue other activities during nonworking hours. Either way, your employment situation reflects your needs, wants, goals, beliefs, and values.

SELECTING A CAREER

Your choice of a career should be approached seriously because this decision has serious personal and financial implications. Various steps may be taken in selecting a career. You should begin this process by avoiding certain common mistakes and by examining personal and other factors that can affect your choice of a career.

The Career Planning Process

- Steps Involved in Career Planning

For a systematic approach to career selection, follow the steps presented in Figure 2–2. Each of these steps in career planning will be discussed in

TABLE 2-1   Occupational Survival Skills

The following skills will help every person achieve a satisfying and successful career.

Working in an organization	A knowledge of the reasons for organizations and of the common characteristics that they possess.
Understanding self and others	Insight into the causes of human behavior and an ability to interpret your own behavior and that of others.
Motivation for work	An understanding of the motivations for work and the ability to build positive work motivations.
Interpersonal relations	The ability to develop concepts and skills when working with others.
Effective communication	An understanding of communication processes and techniques and an ability to use them effectively.
Creativity on the job	An awareness of your creative potential and of how creativity can be used in work situations.
Authority and responsibility	An understanding of the concepts of authority, power, influence, and responsibility in formal organizations.
Problem solving	An ability to apply problem-solving skills in work situations.
Coping with conflict	An awareness of the sources and types of conflicts and of techniques for coping with conflicts.
Coping with change	An awareness of the process of organizational change and of methods for implementing such change.
Leadership	An ability to recognize the need for leadership in work groups and an understanding of the leadership role.
Adapting and planning for the future	An ability to develop perspectives regarding future work roles as well as methods for adapting to anticipated changes.

Source: *Occupational Survival Skills* (Springfield: Illinois State Board of Education, 1978).

FIGURE 2-2   The Career Planning Process

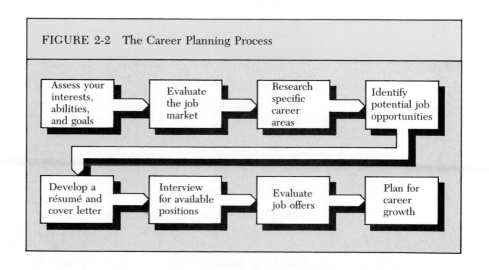

this chapter. But remember that these steps only provide a framework for selecting a career and obtaining employment. This exact approach may not be appropriate for everyone. For example, if you have a technical degree or experience in a specific field, you may find it best to use the services of an executive recruiting organization. Such organizations specialize in finding candidates for top-level positions in major companies. Or you may learn about an available job while attending a meeting of a community organization or a campus club. In career selection, you must be ready to adapt your efforts to many factors.

Common Job Search Mistakes

It is difficult to find the right job, but many people make this process even more difficult by violating certain common sense aspects of career planning. First, there is no single right way to select a career. The steps mentioned in Figure 2–2 should be a guide, not an exact formula for obtaining employment.

Second, make others aware of your interest in selecting a career and obtaining employment. People are your most valuable resource. Friends, relatives, teachers, counselors, community leaders, and local businesspeople can assist you in a variety of ways. Asking for training suggestions, obtaining experience through part-time jobs, and discussing career opportunities are ways in which you can use others to enhance your job-hunting efforts.

Third, be flexible about the type of work you will accept. While you may train for and desire a specific job, be willing to consider other positions. Experience in related or diverse fields will improve your potential for future success. An ability to understand and work at different jobs will make you a more valued member of an organization. In addition to taking courses in your main area of interest, be sure to take liberal arts and general education classes that will expand your awareness and knowledge and thus increase your future career flexibility.

Finally, jobs go to those who persevere. Be persistent in obtaining the education and training you need for the career you desire. Also, it may take many letters, telephone conversations, and interviews before you find a position. Attaining financial success and personal satisfaction requires time, effort, and determination. The attitudes you develop must include a willingness to make a consistent and concentrated effort in your career pursuits.

Assessing Your Career Desires and Potential

● Factors that Influence Career Choice

A variety of methods exist to identify your abilities, interests, and personal qualities. The most common methods are guidance tests that can help you identify a satisfying career direction.

What Do You Do Best? Aptitudes are natural abilities that people possess. Working well with numbers, problem-solving skills, and physical dexterity are examples of aptitudes. Since certain employment situations require certain competencies, aptitude tests can identify the tasks at which you excel.

What Do You Enjoy? Interest inventories determine the activities that give you the most satisfaction. These instruments measure the qualities that are related to various types of work. Individuals with strong social tendencies may be best suited for careers that involve dealing with people, while work in research areas may be desirable for individuals with investigative interests. Commonly used interest inventories are the Kuder General Interest Survey and the Strong-Campbell Interest Inventory.

Aptitude tests, interest inventories, and other types of career planning tests are available at vocational centers and school counseling offices. Using books from a library or bookstore, you can take many of these tests at home.

In the News
The Entrepreneurial Spirit

More and more individuals are working for themselves rather than for someone else. Each year, more than half a million people start a business. These entrepreneurs are involved in everything from restaurants and gift shops to child care services and computer software.

Would running your own business be an appropriate career for you? That depends on the qualities you possess. Are you a highly motivated, confident individual? Do you have the ability to manage the many different phases of a business? Are you an individual who enjoys challenges and is willing to take risks? Despite the efforts and desires of small-business owners, about 40 percent of the new companies created each year fail within five years.

If you decide that entrepreneurship is for you, there are three main areas of knowledge that can improve your chances for success. First, get to know all aspects of the production, sales, and service of the item you are planning to sell. Second, carefully define your potential customers, select a location, and identify competitors. Finally, consider your financing sources. Most new business owners use a combination of personal funds and loans to get started.

As you start and operate a business, get professional help from experts. A lawyer can assist you in organizing and obtaining the necessary business permits in dealing with the legal matters that you encounter during the operation of your company. A local banker can provide financial advice or a loan to expand your business. An accountant will help you handle tax matters and the fi-nancial records of the business. Finally, an insurance agent will suggest necessary coverages to protect you from financial disaster.

Small-business management is a career option that is open to anyone willing to take the risks involved. The number of self-employed women grew by 75 percent between 1975 and 1985, while the number of self-employed men grew by only about 12 percent. By the year 2000, women are expected to own half of the small businesses in the United States.

Sources: *Starting a Business* (Springfield: Illinois State Bar Association); "Starting Your Own Business," *Sylvia Porter's Personal Finance*, October 1984, pp. 40–45; "Starting Your Own Small Business," *Consumer Views*, Citicorp, September 1986; and "Women Entrepreneurs Thrive," *The New York Times*, August 18, 1986, pp. 25, 27.

For a fee, some testing services will mail you the results of a completed test after you send it in to them.[4]

Does a Dream Job Exist? Test results will not tell you which job to pursue. They will only give you an indication of factors to consider because of your abilities and interests. Another important dimension of career selection is your personality. Are you the type of person who performs best in structured or high-pressure situations? Or do you prefer an unstructured or creative work environment? To find a satisfying career, you need to assess these and many other factors.

It has been said that the best job is the one you look forward to on Monday morning. You want a situation in which the rewards, location, and satisfactions are balanced. Some people adapt to any work situation, while others constantly think that the next job will be the best. A vital ingredient in this process is flexibility, since change will be an integral part of your working life.

Factors Affecting the Job Market

● Factors that Determine the Future Availability of Jobs

The career opportunities that are available to you are influenced by economic, industrial, technological, social, and geographic factors.

The Economy. In certain industries, high interest rates, increases in prices, or reduced demand for goods and services can restrict the need for workers. Unemployment rates vary as a result of these and other economic conditions. While it is impossible to eliminate the effect of the economy on career opportunities, changes in the economy affect some businesses more than others. For example, high interest rates reduce employment in housing-related industries since people are less likely to buy homes when interest rates are high.

Industry Trends. In manufacturing, reduced employment has been caused by two factors. First, increased competition from Japanese, German, and other foreign companies has reduced the demand for such American-made products as automobiles and electronic goods. Second, automated production methods have reduced the need for such employees as assembly line workers.

While career opportunities dwindle in one sector of the economy, other sectors grow and thrive. Such fields as health care, financial services, marketing and retailing, computer services, and office administration are expected to experience the greatest growth. Table 2–2 is a list of some specific employment positions that will be in demand in the 1990s.

Technology. Recently, the use of computerized banking, automated gas stations, and office video displays has increased. Other developments, many

[4]"Take a Test to Find Your Niche," *Changing Times,* July 1986, pp. 57–60.

TABLE 2-2   Hot Job Prospects for the 1990s

Occupations with the Highest Projected Growth Rates	Occupations with the Largest Projected Increases in Number of Jobs
Paralegal personnel	Cashiers
Computer programmers	Registered nurses, nursing aides
Computer systems analysts	Janitors, cleaners, and maintenance workers
Medical assistants	Truckdrivers
Data processing equipment repairers	Restaurant and food service workers
Electrical and electronic engineers	Wholesale and retail salespeople
Electrical and electronic technicians	Accountants and auditors
Computer operators	Secretaries; general office clerks
Travel agents	Teachers (preschool, elementary)
Physical therapists	Computer programmers and analysts
Physician assistants	Electrical and electronic engineers and technicians
Securities and financial services salespeople	Automotive mechanics
Mechanical engineering technicians	Lawyers
Lawyers	Cosmetologists
Correction officers and jailers	Computer operators
Accountants and auditors	Physicians and surgeons
Mechanical engineers	Teacher aides/educational assistants
Registered nurses	Licensed practical nurses
Employment interviewers for private and public employment services	Carpenters and electricians
	Receptionists and information clerks
	Mechanical engineers
	Bookkeeping, accounting, and auditing clerks
	Supervisors of blue-collar workers

Source: *Occupational Outlook Quarterly,* Spring 1986, p. 34.

still in the planning stages, are also expected to change the nature of work. However, designers, producers, installers, operators, and repairers of these new technologies will be needed. In addition, people in other jobs will have to learn how to use the new devices. Technology is also influencing the entertainment and leisure industries. As people have more spare time and higher incomes, the sales of recreational goods and services will grow.

Social Influences. The demands and activities of consumers directly affect jobs. In recent years, smaller families and an increased number of working mothers have resulted in more opportunities in food service industries and child-care businesses. Growing consumer concerns about personal health and fitness are evident in the number of products and services that have been made available to meet these needs.

Geographic Movement. Changes in the location of jobs can affect your career choice. During certain periods in our history, various geographic areas were targeted for population expansion. According to estimates from the National Planning Association, the Los Angeles, Boston, San Jose, Phoenix, Washington, D.C., Houston, Chicago, Dallas, and Atlanta metropolitan areas will have the largest employment increases between now and the year 2000.[5]

USING CAREER INFORMATION

Planning a career and finding work require information. Many occupational data sources are available to assist you in selecting, researching, and identifying career opportunities.

Finding Relevant Career Data

● Sources and Uses of Career Information

Like any other financial decision, the selection of a career should be made after you study pertinent data. Information about career opportunities, training requirements, financial benefits, and future prospects can make your job search more efficient. The vast array of available career-related information is shown in Figure 2–3.

Library Materials. Your school or community library has a wealth of career information ranging from job search guides to in-depth materials on specific careers. Also available are federal government publications that report employment levels, salaries, and career forecasts.

The most comprehensive source of career information is the *Occupational Outlook Handbook*, which is prepared by the Bureau of Labor Statistics, a division of the U.S. Department of Labor. Updated every two years, this extensive volume gives information related to all aspects of career planning and job searching. Besides presenting the fundamental aspects of a job search, the *Occupational Outlook Handbook* provides detailed information on jobs in various career clusters. This publication offers information on approximately 200 occupations. Other helpful government resources related to careers are the *Dictionary of Occupational Titles* and the *Occupational Outlook Quarterly*. These publications supplement the information contained in the *Occupational Outlook Handbook*.

Mass Media Career Information. Another source of career information is daily news articles and news broadcasts. Most newspapers have a column that contains job search tips and career trend data. Newspapers, television, and radio news reports offer helpful information on the economic, social, and business aspects of career planning. Changes in interest rates, consumer preferences, and foreign imports are good indications of the demand for jobs in certain occupational categories.

Magazines are also helpful sources of career information. Timely information is provided by specialized publications such as *Business Week's Guide to Careers* and by regular features in various periodicals, such as "Job Strategies," which appears each month in *Glamour*.

[5]"Where the Jobs Will Be in the Year 2000," *USA Today*, June 4, 1986, p. B5.

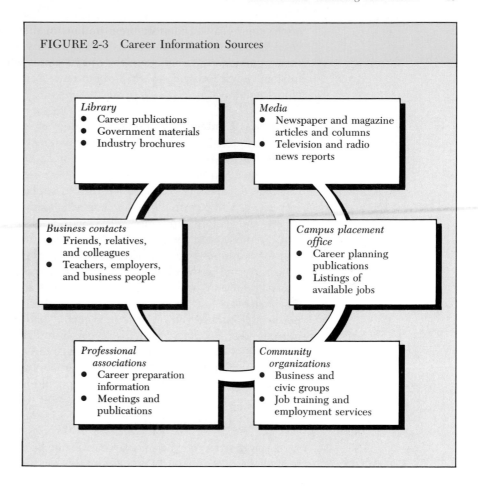

FIGURE 2-3   Career Information Sources

Campus Placement Office. Your school probably has a career planning and placement service to assist you. This office makes available booklets and other materials on various career planning topics. It will also guide you in creating a résumé and preparing for an interview.

Community Organizations. Every community has a variety of business and civic groups that you can use in your career search. Public meetings featuring industry leaders and business owners provide opportunities to become acquainted with local businesspeople. Members of the Chamber of Commerce, Jay-Cees, Rotary Club, and other organizations can give you information about current and future jobs in a geographic area.

Professional Associations. Professionals in every career area have organizations that assist them and promote their interests. Examples of such organizations are the American Marketing Association, the Independent Insurance Agents of America, the American Society of Women Accountants, and the National Association of Real Estate Brokers. The *Encyclopedia of Associ-*

ations can help you identify organizations in the career areas that interest you. Most of these organizations will provide you with information about career opportunities and about the qualifications you need to enter the professions they represent. Many of them have local chapters and conduct regional meetings.

Business Contacts. The people you meet at school and at work can be a valuable source of career assistance. Professional contacts will be most helpful in advising you about career preparation and job opportunities. The people you meet through community and professional organizations and friends, relatives, and people you have met through school, work, church, or other activities are all potential business contacts. Campus activities such as clubs, sports, and lecture programs will provide you with valuable contacts. You will also meet people who can help you with your career choice if you volunteer for community service activities related to voter registration, recycling centers, or aid to the elderly. Every person you talk to is a potential career contact who may provide information or assistance.

Contacts are only sources of information. While the people you meet may not be able to hire you, if jobs are available, they can refer you to the right person. Also, a contact can help you get an **informational interview,** that is, a meeting designed to gather information about a career or an organization. Informational interviews are valuable sources of career planning information because they allow you to interact with people in their actual work setting.

Identifying Job Opportunities

As you narrow your career search to a specific type of work, you will begin to apply for available positions. Before this can be done, you need to identify job openings for people with your interests and abilities. Information about career opportunities is available from many of the sources discussed in the previous section. Advertisements in newspapers and professional periodicals are also valuable sources of available positions. Newspapers such as *The Wall Street Journal*, the *New York Times*, the *Chicago Tribune*, and the *Los Angeles Times* have job listings covering a wide geographic area. Local and regional newspapers should also be checked. For opportunities in a specific career field, refer to specialized publications such as *Advertising Age*, *Marketing News*, the *Journal of Accountancy*, and the *American Banker*.

The various career contacts you develop through community organizations, professional associations, and campus activities will help you identify potential jobs. Your campus placement office probably maintains a list of various openings. Also, many businesses send representatives to campuses to recruit potential employees.

If you want to work in a specific career or for a particular company, conduct research about your interests. Determine what background is needed for your desired occupation. Also, obtain detailed information about companies for which you would like to work. After learning about your targeted job, present your qualifications to these companies in the form of a letter or a telephone call. Using this method, you can create job opportunities that didn't exist previously.

One final aid in obtaining job leads is an employment agency. This for-profit organization matches job hunters with prospective employers. Often the hiring company pays the fee charged by an employment agency, but be careful of situations where you pay a fee and have no guarantee of getting a job. Government-supported employment services are also available. Contact your state employment service or your state department of labor for further information.

PRESENTING YOURSELF TO PROSPECTIVE EMPLOYERS

Every business presents its product or service to potential customers in an appealing manner. You must do the same thing in marketing yourself to prospective employers. Your efforts along these lines require listing your background, developing a personal informational sheet, and creating a letter to obtain an interview.

Doing an Inventory of Your Background

- Process of Preparing a Résumé and Cover Letter

A résumé is a summary of your education, training, experience, and other job qualifications. This personal information sheet is a vital component of most career searches. It gives references and includes information about your personal situation, career objective, education, experience, related information, and references.

Personal Data. You need to give the prospective employer your name, address, and telephone number. It may be appropriate to give both a school and home address and telephone number. Your birth date, sex, height, and weight are usually not included in a résumé unless these items are related to specific qualifications for the job. Otherwise, these items are not submitted to avoid job discrimination.

Career Objective. You may want to include a career objective in your résumé. The problem with doing this is that if the career objective is too vague, it will be meaningless to the prospective employer; and if it is too specific, you may not be considered for another position within the organization. If you decide to use a career objective in your résumé, be sure that it communicates not only your interest in a particular type of job but also your willingness to consider other positions. The career objective should be revised, if necessary, when you apply for different jobs. Some career advisers suggest that your career objective is best communicated in the letter that you send with your résumé. Detailed discussion of cover letters is presented later in this chapter.

Education. Your school experiences are an important component of your résumé. This component should include dates, schools attended, fields of study, and degrees earned. The listing of specific courses completed may be included if these relate directly to the prospective job. You should list the courses you have taken in accounting, computer science, or marketing when you apply for jobs in these areas. When your grade point average is exceptionally high, include it in the résumé to demonstrate your ability to excel.

Experience. Previous jobs, school activities, and community service can provide experiences that will be valuable in work situations. Prepare a list of the organizations, the dates of your involvement, and your responsibilities. As an officer of a campus organization, you have developed skills in managing, organizing, and coordinating people and activities. Other valuable career skills include:

- Public speaking experience from class, campus, and community presentations.
- Supervising and delegating experience from community service, class projects, and service on club committees.
- Financial planning and budgeting experience gained from organizing fund-raising projects, managing personal finances, and handling monies for campus organizations.
- Goal-setting and planning experience from personal time management, part-time employment, and work on campus committees.
- Research skills gained from class projects, community involvement, and campus activities.

All of your experiences enhance your ability to perform effectively on the job. But first you need to gain these experiences. Be willing to become involved in activities, organizations, and committees. Part-time, summer, and work-study employment programs are excellent opportunities to expand your career-related skills. Maintain a resource file with information on your various experiences; this will allow you to quickly prepare or update your résumé.

Related Information. A résumé may also list any honors or awards that you have received. This will communicate your ability to produce quality work. A list of other interests and activities may be appropriate if these relate to your career field. However, a long list of this kind might give the impression that work is not your top priority.

References. Finally, develop a list of people who can verify your skills and competences. These individuals may be teachers, previous employers, supervisors, or business colleagues. Do not include these references in your résumé, but have this information available when it is requested by a prospective employer. Be sure to obtain permission from the individuals you plan to use as references.

Preparing Your Résumé

After you have accumulated the data necessary to create a résumé, you need to make several decisions regarding the presentation of your background.

Résumé Formats. There are three main types of résumés: chronological, functional, and targeted. The first two types may be used in a variety of situations; the third is designed for a specific job.

The **chronological résumé** (see Figure 2–4) presents your education, work experience, and other information in a reverse time sequence (the most recent item first). This type of résumé is most appropriate for individuals

---

Today's Lifestyles
Careers that Move when You Do

A lmost 75 percent of all families are two-income households. If one working spouse relocates for career advancement, the other working spouse may have difficulty in finding employment at the new location. In such situations, flexibility of career direction becomes increasingly important. When her family moved, Joan Senner, an assistant vice president for human resources with a bank, was unable to obtain similar employment. However, her experience in personnel allowed her to get a job with an employment office that eventually led to a better position than she had had with the bank.

People in entry-level positions, legal professionals, medical and health care workers, and sales personnel usually have the least trouble in getting a job in a new geographic area. But even individuals with specialized skills can find employment if they are willing to keep an open mind about work opportunities. One example is a former high school teacher, who, when his family moved, obtained a variety of positions, including insurance agent, park district supervisor, business training specialist, and seminar director for an employment agency.

Flexibility of employment is especially important when a particular geographic area has few jobs available for certain careers. When medical employees are not in demand in a region, but information processing positions offer excellent wages, flexibility may be crucial to your financial existence. This flexibility may include using your skills and experience to serve a company in an innovative position. Former teachers and counselors, for example, possess an ability to train and guide employees in a way that can improve the overall work environment of an organization. Workers needing to learn new skills and employees involved in difficult situations can be helped by individuals who previously worked as teachers and counselors. A willingness and an ability to adapt your talents are vital for continuous employment.

Source: Mary Ellen Schoonmaker, "Careers that Move when You Do," *Working Mother*, December 1985, pp. 28, 30–31.

FIGURE 2-4   A Chronological Résumé

CHAD BOSTWICK

SCHOOL ADDRESS   HOME ADDRESS
234B University Drive   765 Cannon Lane
Jasper, MO 54321   Benton, KS 67783
(316) 555-7659   (407) 555-1239

CAREER   An entry-level position in medical or health care
OBJECTIVE   administration.

EDUCATION   Bachelor of Science in Business Administration and Health
                Care Marketing, University of South Arkansas, June 1988.

                Associate of Arts, Medical Technician Assistant, Arrow Valley
                Community College, Arlington, Kansas, June 1986.

EXPERIENCE   Patient account clerk, University Hospital, Jasper, Missouri,
                November 1987–present. Researched overdue accounts,
                created collection method for faster accounts receivable
                turnover, assisted in training billing clerks.

                Sales data clerk, Jones Medical Supply Company, Benton
                Kansas, January–August 1986. Maintained inventory records,
                processed customer orders.

CAMPUS   Newsletter editor, University of South Arkansas chapter of
ACTIVITIES   Financial Management Association, January–June 1988.

                Tutor for business statistics and computer lab, 1987–1988.

HONORS   College of Business Community Service Award, University
                of South Arkansas, June 1988.

                Arrow Valley Health Care Society Scholarship, June 1986.

REFERENCES   Furnished upon request.

---

with a continuous school and work record leading to a specific career area. Many people find that a résumé of this kind is the best vehicle for presenting their career qualifications.

The **functional résumé** (see Figure 2–5) is suggested for individuals with diverse skills and time gaps in their background. This type of résumé emphasizes a person's abilities and skills in such categories as communication, supervision, research, human relations, and planning. Each section of the résumé stresses experiences and qualifications rather than dates, places, and job titles. This type of résumé is especially valuable for someone who is changing careers or whose most recent experiences are not directly related to the available position.

You may want to develop a résumé for a specific job—that is, a **targeted résumé.** Such a résumé highlights the capabilities and experiences that are appropriate to the available position. Its format may be similar to that of the chronological or functional résumés, except that it will include a very specific career objective to communicate your intentions. The targeted résumé takes extra time to prepare, but this effort may give you the opportunity to interview for a particularly desirable position.

Résumé Details. There is no specific formula for the preparation of an effective résumé. However, a résumé must be presented in a professional manner. Modern typewriters and personal computers make the layout process easier. Quick-print businesses will duplicate résumés. Many of the businesses specialize in the preparation and reproduction of personal data sheets.

Limit your résumé to one page if possible; send a two-page résumé only if you have enough material to fill three pages. Then use the most valid information to prepare an impressive two-page data sheet. For best results, seek help in preparing and evaluating your résumé. Counselors, the campus placement office, and friends can suggest improvements and find errors.

FIGURE 2-5 A Functional Résumé

NANCY FRANK
670 Dove Circle
Reston, ME 01267
(203) 555-6710

CAREER OBJECTIVE

Human resources department position with training responsibilities.

EDUCATION

Master of Arts, Columbia College, Hamilton, New Jersey, 1985.
Bachelor of Science, Oral Communications, Martin University, Cooper, New Hampshire, 1980.

SUPERVISORY EXPERIENCE

Coordinated conference committees for National Communication Association.
Developed and implemented training program for Ashton Graphics, Harper, Maine.

COMMUNICATION EXPERIENCE

Created training manuals for Benton Printing Company, Reston, Maine.
Wrote press releases for local government agencies, Reston, Maine.

RESEARCH EXPERIENCE

Investigated training problems of large industrial organizations in northeastern United States.

REFERENCES

Furnished upon request.

Résumé Gimmicks. Thousands of résumés are received from job seekers each day. As a result of this intense competition, some prospective employees have used creative résumés to draw attention to their abilities. Personnel directors have reported receiving résumés in the form of comic strips, wanted posters, advertisements, and menus; résumés attached to balloons, pizzas, and plants; and résumés on videotapes and computer discs. While some of these unusual résumés have been effective, many employers see them as inappropriate gimmicks. The creative approach does work, however, when the job is in a field requiring original thinking, such as advertising, journalism, photography, or public relations.[6]

Developing an Effective Cover Letter

Your résumé presents your qualifications, which must be targeted to a specific organization and job. **A cover letter** is designed to express your interest in a job and obtain an interview. This communication accompanies your résumé and highlights the aspects of your background that are related to the available position. A cover letter will usually consist of an introductory paragraph, one or two development paragraphs, and a concluding paragraph.

The introductory paragraph should get the reader's attention. Indicate your reason for writing by referring to the job or type of employment in which you are interested. Communicate what you have to offer the company based on your experience and qualifications. This first paragraph must motivate the reader to continue reading.

The development section should highlight the aspects of your background that specifically qualify you for the job. Refer the employer to the enclosed résumé for more details. At this point, you should also elaborate on experiences that will contribute to the organization.

The concluding paragraph should request action from the employer. Ask for the opportunity to meet the employer to discuss your qualifications and potential in more detail. Include information that will make contacting you convenient, such as telephone numbers and the times when you are available. Close your letter by summarizing how you can benefit the organization.

A separate cover letter should be typed for each of the positions for which you apply. A form cover letter will usually guarantee rejection. Be sure to address your correspondence to the appropriate person in the organization. It may take some research to find out who that person is, but your chances of obtaining a positive response are enhanced when your cover letter and résumé are sent to a specific person rather than to "Dear Sir or Madam."

A résumé and cover letter are your ticket to the interview. You may possess outstanding qualifications and career potential, but you need an interview to communicate this information. The time, effort, and care you expend in presenting yourself on paper will help you achieve your career goal.

[6]Laura R. Walbert, "A Foot in the Door," *Forbes*, November 18, 1985, pp. 240, 244.

THE JOB
INTERVIEW

● Job Interview Process

A major step in your job search is getting the opportunity to present your abilities and potential in person. The interview stage of job hunting is limited to candidates who possess the specific qualifications that the employer wants. Being invited for an interview puts you closer to receiving a job offer. Several activities are required before you actually meet with a company representative. Upon completing the interview, you should acknowledge and assess it.

Preparing for the Interview

Prepare for your interview by obtaining additional information about your prospective employer. The best sources are the company's annual report and other publications that are available to the public. The library has business periodicals and reference volumes with company profiles and current industry news. Attempt to talk with at least one person who is currently employed by the company.

During your research, try to obtain information about the company's past development and current situation. Facts about its operations, competitors, recent successes, planned expansion, and personnel policies will be helpful when you discuss your potential contributions to the company.

Another essential preinterview activity is the development of questions that you would like to ask the interviewer. These questions have two purposes. First, they show that you prepared for the interview. Second, the answers you receive will help you decide whether you would like to work for the company. Some questions to ask in an interview are:

What training opportunities are available to employees who desire to advance?

What do your employees like best about working here?

What plans does the company have for new products or expanded markets?

What actions of competitors are likely to affect the company in the near future?

Also prepare questions on your specific interests and on the particular organization with which you are interviewing. Request information about company policies and employee benefits.

Successful interviewing requires practice. By using a tape recorder or working with friends, you can develop the confidence needed for effective interviewing. Work to improve your ability to organize ideas, to speak clearly and calmly, and to communicate enthusiasm. Many campus organizations and career placement offices offer opportunities for practice by conducting mock interviews. Take advantage of these situations to polish your interviewing skills.

As you get ready for the interview, proper dress and grooming will be a consideration. Current employees are the best source of information on how

From *The Wall Street Journal*, with permission of Cartoon Features Syndicate.

to dress. In general, dress more conservatively than the employees. A business suit is usually appropriate for both men and women. Avoid trendy and casual styles, and don't wear too much jewelry.

The Interview Process

The meeting between the candidate and the employer is usually the key to getting the job. This process, which may include several interviews along with various follow-up activities, requires strong interpersonal and communication skills.

A Screening Interview. Many companies use a preliminary personal encounter to identify the best candidates. A **screening interview** is an initial meeting, usually brief, that reduces the pool of job candidates to a workable number. In this situation, interviewees are processed on the basis of overall impression and a few general questions. Screening interviews are frequently conducted on college campuses by corporate recruiters. Success in such an interview qualifies you for closer scrutiny by the employer.

An In-Depth Interview. Once you have been judged to be a serious candidate for a job, your next interview can last from one hour to several days. This **in-depth interview**, which is reserved for the finalists in the job search, may involve a series of activities, including responses to questions, meetings with several people on the staff, and a seminar presentation.

When an in-depth interview is conducted, the first few minutes of the interview usually occur in an informal setting. This process is designed to help the interviewee relax and to establish rapport. Next a brief discussion of

TABLE 2-3   Common Interview Questions

Education and Training Questions

What experience and training prepare you for this job?
Why are you interested in working for this company?
In addition to going to school, what activities have you been involved in to expand your interests and increase your knowledge?
What did you like best about school? What did you like least?

Work and Other Experience Questions

In what types of situations have you done your best work?
Describe the supervisors who motivated you best.
Which of your past accomplishments are you proud of?
Have you ever been involved in a situation in which you had to coordinate the activities of several people?
Describe some people whom you have had difficulty in working with.
Describe a situation in which your determination helped you achieve a specific goal.
What situations frustrate you?
Other than past jobs, what experiences have you had that helped prepare you for this job?
What do you believe are the best methods for motivating employees?

Personal Qualities Questions

What are your major strengths? Your major weaknesses? What have you done to overcome your weaknesses?
What do you plan to be doing 5 or 10 years from now?
Which individuals in your life have had the greatest influence on you?
What traits make a person successful?
How well do you communicate your ideas orally and in writing?
How would your teachers and your past employers describe you?
What do you do in your leisure time?
How persuasive are you in presenting ideas to others?

the available job position may occur. Then the main part of the interview takes place. It involves questions to assess your abilities, potential, and personality. Table 2–3 lists some commonly used interview questions. In the last portion of the interview, you are given an opportunity to ask questions.

Follow-Up Activities. Most interviewers will conclude the in-depth interview by telling you when you can expect to hear from the company. While waiting, there are two things you should do. First, send a follow-up letter to the company expressing your appreciation for the opportunity to interview. If you don't get the job, this thank-you letter can make a positive impression for future consideration.

Second, do a self-evaluation of your interview performance. Write down those areas that could be improved. Try to remember the questions you were asked that were different from what you expected. These can be used for future interview preparation.

ACCEPTING A JOB

When you are offered a position, you should examine several factors. Salary is a major consideration, but job duties, the work environment, company policies, and supplementary financial benefits are also vital to your final decision.

Is This the Job for You?

● Factors that Should Be Considered when Accepting a Job Offer

Before accepting a position, you may want to do further research about the job and the company. Request information about your specific duties and job expectations. If someone currently has a similar position, ask to talk to that person. If you are replacing a person who is no longer with the company, obtain information about the circumstances of that person's departure.

Another area that you should investigate is the work environment. In the mid-1980s, the term *corporate culture* emerged. This label refers to such matters as management style, work intensity, dress codes, and social interactions within an organization. For example, some companies have rigid lines of communication, while others have an open-door atmosphere. Are the values, goals, and lifestyles of current employees similar to yours? If not, you

---

In the Real World

The Best Companies to Work for in America

T he best-selling book *The 100 Best Companies to Work for in America* reported that pay, benefits, job security, and chances for advancement, but most likely a combination of these, were the factors that made an employment opportunity desirable. To identify such factors, the authors first compiled a list of several hundred organizations that were recommended by the media, teachers, employees, and others. Then they conducted in-depth interviews with workers rang-

ing from top executives to custodial personnel.

This research revealed great diversity of benefits among the companies for which people enjoyed working. Among the favorite amenities reported were a 25-cent French gourmet lunch and multimillion-dollar employee health centers. In most cases, strong allegiance to an organization was the result of one or more of the following:

Workers made to feel part of a team or family.

Open communication encouraged.

Promotion from within.

Strong pride in the quality of the goods and services produced.

Profit sharing and other generous benefits.

An informal environment, with all employees on a first-name basis.

A pleasant, physically attractive workplace.

Employees encouraged to be active in community service.

Assistance in placing employees in other jobs or with other companies

may find yourself in an uncomfortable situation that doesn't allow you to perform according to your capabilities.

You should also look into company policies and procedures. For example, how does the company handle salary increases, evaluations of employees, and promotions? Talking with current workers can give you a good indication of the answers to such questions.

What Are the Benefits of the Job?

While salary will be an important factor in your job choice, you should also consider perquisites (also called perks), that is, privileges and financial benefits other than salary. Traditionally, perquisites have included paid time off for holidays, vacations, and sick leaves; medical, dental, disability, and life insurance; profit sharing programs; retirement plans; educational tuition reimbursement; employee discounts; lunch facilities; and facilities for recreational activities. More recently, organizations have expanded the nonsalary benefits of employees to include child care services, either conducted on the premises of the organization or reimbursed by the organization; programs

when layoffs were necessary.

An emphasis on physical fitness and health care.

Training programs and generous tuition reimbursement plans.

Working mothers were concerned about how their needs were provided for at their place of employment. A follow-up study assessed how the needs of women with children were accommodated at the workplace. While most companies accommodated the needs of working mothers, some provided them with better advancement opportunities and benefits that included parental leaves of absence, child care facilities, and flexible working schedules.

The organizations that served the employment and personal needs of working mothers ranged from large, national companies, such as Campbell Soup, General Motors, IBM, and Procter & Gamble, to such small, local companies as South Shore Bank in Chicago and Stride Rite, the leading manufacturer of children's shoes. All of these companies demonstrated an economic and social concern for the special situation of female employees with children.

Sources: Robert Levering, Milton Moskowitz, and Michael Katz, *The 100 Best Companies to Work for in America* (Reading, Mass.: Addison-Wesley Publishing, 1984); and Milton Moskowitz and Carol Townsend, "The 30 Best Companies for Working Mothers," *Working Mother*, August 1986, pp. 25–28, 109–12.

that provide employees with legal assistance; counseling for health, emotional, and financial needs; and exercise and fitness programs. Such perquisites benefit not only the employee but also the organization, which because of them has happier, healthier workers who miss fewer workdays and have a higher level of productivity.

Cafeteria-style employee benefits are programs that allow workers to base their benefits on a credit system and personal needs. This flexible basis for job benefits has become quite common. A married employee with children may opt for increased life and health insurance, while a single parent may use benefit credits for child care services. Since the financial value of employee benefits can be significant both now and in the future, these benefits should be an important criterion for accepting a job.

FUTURE CAREER SATISFACTION AND PROFESSIONAL GROWTH

A job is for today, but a career can be forever. Will you always enjoy the work you do today? Will you be successful in the career you select? These questions cannot be answered right away. But there are a number of skills and attitudes that can lead to a fulfilling working life. Figure 2–6 presents some of these ingredients of career success. Other factors can also contribute to job satisfaction. Whether you've just started to work or have been employed many years, a number of activities are available to enhance your career.

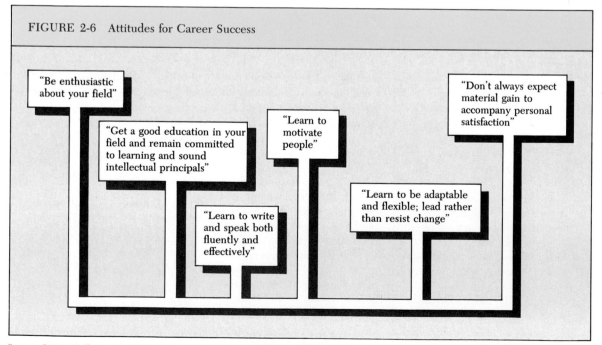

FIGURE 2-6   Attitudes for Career Success

"Be enthusiastic about your field"

"Don't always expect material gain to accompany personal satisfaction"

"Get a good education in your field and remain committed to learning and sound intellectual principals"

"Learn to motivate people"

"Learn to write and speak both fluently and effectively"

"Learn to be adaptable and flexible; lead rather than resist change"

Source: George Gallup, Jr., and Alec M. Gallup, *The Great American Success Story* (Homewood, Ill.: Dow Jones-Irwin, 1986), pp. 167–75.

From *The Wall Street Journal*, with permission of Cartoon Features Syndicate.

On-the-Job Initiatives

- Need for Continued Career Growth

Every day of your working life, you can perform duties that will contribute to your career success. Communicating and working well with others will enhance your chances for financial advancement and promotion. Flexibility and an openness to new ideas will help you expand your abilities, knowledge, and career potential.

Develop more efficient work habits. The use of lists, goal setting, note cards, and other time management techniques will help you in this effort. Combine increased productivity with quality. Every activity with which you are associated should reflect your best performance. This extra effort will be recognized and rewarded.

Finally, learn to anticipate problems and areas for action. A willingness to assist others combined with the creation of ideas that can help the entire organization will contribute to your enjoyment of your work and your career growth.

Continuing Education

On-the-job demands and your desire for advancement affect your need for increased training and knowledge. First, society requires a continual updating of information and skills. Today, there are computerized work situations that did not exist a couple of years ago. Many of the job skills that you will need in the future have yet to be created. Second, you desire success, and, as noted earlier in this chapter, education is one of the primary determinants of career and financial advancement.

Various methods are available for updating and expanding your knowledge after you have completed a training program or college degree. Formal methods that serve these purposes range from company development activities to seminars offered by professional organizations in your career field. They also include graduate and advanced college courses. Many companies encourage and pay for such continuing education.

Informal methods for updating and expanding your knowledge include reading and discussion with colleagues. Newspapers, popular magazines, business periodicals, and professional journals offer a wealth of information on business, economic, and social trends that will influence your job. Informal meetings with fellow workers and associates from other companies are also a valuable source of current information.

CONSIDERING A CAREER CHANGE

At some time in their lives, most workers will change jobs. This may be done to obtain a better position or a different position within the same career field or to move into a new career. Changing your job may be more difficult than selecting your first job. Unless their present situation is causing mental stress or physical illness, most people are unwilling to exchange the security of an existing position for the uncertainty of an unfamiliar position.

The following are frequently indications that it is time to move on:

- Weak motivation toward your current work.
- Physical or emotional distress caused by your job.
- Consistently poor performance evaluations.
- A lack of social interactions with your fellow workers.
- Limited opportunity for salary or position advancement.
- A poor relationship with your superior.[7]

Whether you view a job as a stepping-stone to a higher level or you believe that your present position is also your future, you should continually reevaluate your career situation. Regularly assess your personal values, your career goals, and the satisfactions that you receive from your work. At the same time, look at your company and its industry to determine whether your personal situation will remain compatible with their situation. These efforts will help you achieve a satisfying working life.

[7]Rita Stollman, "When to Switch Jobs," *Business Week's Guide to Careers*, March 1986, pp. 62–63.

SUMMARY

- Your level of education can significantly influence the amount of your future earnings. Technical training and flexible skills are vital for economic success and personal satisfaction.
- The career planning process involves the following steps: (1) assess your interests, abilities, and goals; (2) evaluate the job market; (3) research specific career areas; (4) identify potential job opportunities; (5) develop a résumé and cover letter; (6) interview for available positions; (7) evaluate job offers; and (8) plan for career growth.
- An evaluation of your abilities, interests, and personality can help indicate the type of work that you would find most satisfying.
- The availability of jobs is influenced by economic, industrial, technological, social, and geographic factors.
- A vast amount of career planning information is available from libraries, government agencies, mass media sources, campus placement offices, community organizations, and businesses. The best sources of information regarding available jobs are personal business contacts, newspaper and magazine advertise-

ments, businesses, and private and public employment agencies.
- A résumé is a summary of your background that includes personal data, information about your education, experiences, and references and may include a career objective. A résumé mailed to a prospective employer is accompanied by a cover letter indicating your interest in a position and requesting an opportunity to interview.
- Prior to an interview, you should obtain additional information about your prospective employer, prepare questions to ask, and practice your interviewing skills. Effective interviewing requires strong personal qualities along with an ability to communicate your enthusiasm and your work potential.
- Before you accept a job, you should investigate the environment and the policies of the organization. You should also assess the salary offered as well as other employee benefits.
- Your career advancement and financial success will be the result of various personal and educational efforts that you make to foster your professional growth.

GLOSSARY

Cafeteria-style employee benefits. Programs that allow workers to choose supplemental job benefits from a variety of benefits.

Career. A commitment to a profession that requires continued training and offers a clear path for occupational growth.

Chronological résumé. A data sheet that presents a person's background in a reverse time sequence.

Cover letter. A communication that accompanies a

person's résumé and expresses interest in a particular job.

Functional résumé. A data sheet that presents a person's background by emphasizing various skills and abilities.

Job. An employment position that a person obtains mainly to earn money, without regard to his or her interests or opportunities for advancement.

In-depth interview. A series of question sessions and

other activities that are designed to select one of several candidates for a job.

Informational interview.   A visit to a company or with an individual for the purpose of gathering career information.

Perquisites.   Financial benefits and privileges other than salary received by employees; also called perks.

Résumé.   A summary of a person's education, training, experience, and other job qualifications.

Screening interview.   An initial meeting with job candidates to reduce the number of applicants to a workable number.

Targeted résumé.   A personal data sheet that is developed for use in applying for a specific job.

REVIEW QUESTIONS

1. How is a job different from a career?

2. What is the common relationship between education and income? What personal factors can enhance an individual's economic and career success?

3. What job search mistakes are frequently made?

4. How do aptitude tests and interest inventories assist a person in selecting a career?

5. What factors influence the availability of jobs in our society?

6. What are the main sources of career information?

7. How can career contacts help you with your career planning?

8. When would each of the three types of résumés be appropriate?

9. What are the main sections of a cover letter?

10. How does an in-depth interview differ from a screening interview?

11. What factors should a person consider when deciding whether to accept a job offer?

12. What efforts can a person make to grow and advance in a career?

DISCUSSION QUESTIONS AND ACTIVITIES

1. How could Betsey Collins improve her efforts to find a job?

2. What practical experience could Frank Manchester have obtained during his time in college?

3. How could Marla Kenner revise her cover letter to improve her chances of obtaining employment?

4. Should all individuals go to college? Name other alternatives for advanced training.

5. What courses should be required of all students? How will these courses help you on the job?

6. Arrange to take an aptitude test or an interest inventory through your school's career planning office. Talk about your results with a school counselor.

7. Use the *Occupational Outlook Handbook* to research one or more careers that interest

you. What answers do you need in addition to those provided in this reference book?

8. Make arrangements to have an informational interview at a local company or with a person you know. Prepare a list of questions to ask during your visit.

9. Is whom you know more important than what you know when it comes to getting a job?

10. List all of the experiences you have had that could be mentioned in a résumé. Be sure to consider work, school, club, church, and community activities.

11. Should employees be required to take tests every few years to determine the quality of their skills?

ADDITIONAL READINGS

Business Week's Guide to Careers. 1221 Avenue of the Americas, New York, NY 10020.

The Employment Kit: A Practical Guide to Achieving Success in the Job Market. American Marketing Association, 250 South Wacker Drive, Chicago, IL 60606-5819.

National Business Employment Weekly. Dow Jones & Company, Inc., 420 Lexington Avenue, New York, NY 10170.

Occupational Outlook Handbook. U.S. Government Printing Office, Washington, DC 20402.

Occupational Outlook Quarterly. U.S. Government Printing Office, Washington, DC 20402.

CASE 2–1 An Unsuccessful Job Hunt

Frances Melton has tried to get a sales job for three months. She has applied for a position with companies that sell everything from automobiles and electronic products to medical supplies and restaurant equipment. Frances has always worked in an office. She completed two years of college and took several business courses. She sees sales as a chance to meet interesting people and earn a higher salary.

During interviews, Frances displays a very pleasant and outgoing personality. The company representatives like talking with her, but they have not offered her a job due to her limited knowledge and her limited sales experience.

Questions

1. As a career counselor, what suggestions would you offer Frances?

2. What experiences might Frances have that could be adapted to a sales career?

3. How could a specific career objective be valuable to Frances?

4. What types of career information materials could Frances use to improve her chances of obtaining a sales job?

CASE 2–2 Job Prospects of a Longtime Employee

For the past 22 years, Tom Bartwell has been employed by Galloway Department Stores. He was promoted from salesclerk to department manager and then to store manager. Currently, as the regional manager for the Mountain Division, Tom is responsible for 14 stores in six states.

Galloway was recently sold to BXT Industries, a diversified, multinational company involved in oil exploration, athletic equipment, European resorts, and computer components. Tom is fearful that the takeover will result in a reorganization that would eliminate his job.

Questions

1. What research efforts might Tom take to investigate his future with BTX Industries?

2. What types of career alternatives does Tom have?

3. What should Tom do at this point in his career?

3

Financial Recordkeeping and Budgeting

When people watch a baseball or football game, they usually know the score. With financial planning, the score is also important. Various financial records provide information on your wins and losses in the money game. Maintaining financial documents and planning your spending are the foundation of many financial decisions. While the time and effort you use for personal financial recordkeeping may seem extensive, the organization and information that result are valuable.

After studying this chapter, you will be able to:

- Explain the purpose of financial records.

- List the types of financial documents.

- Use the process of preparing a personal balance sheet.

- Describe the components of a personal income statement.

- Identify the steps used to develop and implement a budget.

- Explain techniques for successful budgeting and effective money management.

- Discuss different types of budgeting systems.

- Describe the role of the time value of money in budgeting and financial planning.

Interview with **Kathryn Holland,**
Certified Public Accountant, Oppenheimer & Co.

Kathryn Holland started her securities career with Merrill Lynch before joining Oppenheimer & Co. She writes a newspaper column and produces a radio program on financial planning.

Sound financial recordkeeping is the basis for making sound financial decisions. Good recordkeeping can save you money, time, and trouble. It ensures that important documents will be available when you need them, without the cost and waiting time required to obtain duplicates.

Current records can be kept in a file cabinet, an accordion file, or even a cardboard box. Stationery stores often have inexpensive cardboard filing cabinets that can also be used for this purpose. Each month, you should file such items as bills to be paid; and recent bank statements; receipts for recent premium, utilities, mortgage, and credit card payments. Other documents that you should keep on hand are insurance policies, warranties, mortgage statements, employment and health records, and a list of what's in your safe-deposit box.

You need a safe-deposit box for irreplaceable records such as automobile titles, birth certificates, bonds, stock certificates, marriage certificates, bills of sale, contracts, military records, deeds, and wills.

Keep receipts for household utility bills only until you are sure that the payment has been recorded. However, receipts for mortgage payments and taxes, along with other tax-deductible items, should be kept for three years from the date you file your taxes.

You should sort your canceled checks by category as you reconcile each month's bank statement. Then store the checks in files according to tax categories, such as medical bills, donations, and home improvement.

Holland suggests that you create a budget. Your budget should be one that fits your individual circumstances. Don't be concerned about what the typical budget or average expenses are. Some families may be spending 25 percent of their incomes for housing and 10–12 percent for clothing. However, your budget depends on your or your family's goals and priorities. The budget you use depends largely on your individual situation. The budget of a young working couple with a rental apartment and no children will differ from that of a young couple with children and a mortgaged home.

Don't expect that a budget will work miracles or change the basic realities of income and expenses. Budgeting will give you a clear picture of your actual income and your planned expenses. It will tell you how much is left over for savings and investments. An individual or family will have financial difficulties if expenses exceed income. Facing the problem immediately gives you a better opportunity to cut down or perhaps eliminate some expenses. The budget process can assist you in reaching your ultimate objective, to have financial security in the future.

Opening Scenario
The Importance of Financial Records and Budgeting

Bob Jameson completed high school two years ago. Afterward, he continued to live with his parents while attending college across town. He had a part-time job as a sales and inventory clerk at a department store. With his income, he was able to pay his school expenses and save $1,000. Since his parents paid for housing and food, Bob was able to make car payments, buy clothes, and spend money on entertainment activities.

During the past two years, Bob never kept track of his spending habits. His financial recordkeeping consisted of depositing half of his income in a checking account and half in a savings account. Whenever he needed to pay a bill or make a purchase, Bob would write a check. If he didn't have enough money in checking, he would transfer funds from savings to checking. When Bob decided to get his own apartment, he didn't have a realistic picture of his finances and living expenses.

During the first few months

PERSONAL
FINANCIAL
RECORDS

- Purposes of Personal Financial Records

Organized money management requires a system of financial records. Budgets, receipts, bank statements, and tax forms are some of the financial documents that make up a person's financial existence. Your efforts to develop organized financial records will provide a basis for:

- Handling daily business affairs, including the payment of bills on time.
- Planning and measuring your financial progress.
- Completing required tax reports.
- Making effective investment decisions.
- Determining available resources for current and future buying.

As shown in Figure 3–1, most financial records are kept in one of two places—a home file or a safe-deposit box. A home file should be used to keep records for current needs and documents with limited value. Your home file may be a series of folders that hold various papers, or it may be a cabinet that has several drawers to store documents. It is most important that your home file be simply organized to allow quick access to required documents and information.

Important financial records and valuable articles should be kept in a location that provides better security than a home file. A safe-deposit box is a private storage area at a financial institution that offers maximum security for valuables. Access to the contents of a safe-deposit box requires two keys. One key is issued to you; the other is kept by the financial institution where

in his apartment, Bob was able to work full-time and could pay his bills on time. When school started in September, however, his income decreased since he worked fewer hours. Also, Bob had to use most of his savings to pay for tuition and books. These school costs were higher than those he had paid the previous year.

As time passed, Bob had other expenses, such as automobile repairs, insurance for his car and other property, and medical bills. The cost of food, electricity, and telephone was higher than Bob had anticipated. Bob's financial independence was not as pleasant as he had hoped it would be.

Budgeting and an under- standing of living expenses are skills that many people learn only after difficult experiences. An ability to plan and document spending is the starting point of successful money management and effective financial planning.

the safe-deposit box is located. Items commonly kept in a safe-deposit box include stock certificates, contracts, insurance policies, and rare coins and stamps.

● Types of Financial Documents

The number of financial records and documents may seem overwhelming, but they can easily be organized into 10 basic categories. These categories correspond to the major topics covered in this textbook. You may not need to use all of the following records and documents at present. However, as your financial situation changes, you will use them.

1. *Money Management Records.* The foundation of your financial records is documents listing your possessions, debts, and spending patterns. A budget is a specific plan for spending your income. This device helps an individual or family control spending while working toward various financial goals. The creation of a budget and other personal financial statements is discussed later in this chapter.

2. *Personal and Employment Records.* From the day you are born, legal and financial documents are a part of your life. Your birth certificate and later a social security card and, perhaps, a marriage license are among the items that you should keep in your financial records file. Once you are employed, employee benefit information, pension data, and other work records will be added to your recordkeeping system.

3. *Financial Services Records.* Most people use one or more services offered by financial institutions. The documents associated with savings

FIGURE 3-1   Where to Keep Your Financial Records

Records	Home File	Safe-Deposit Box
Money management records	Current budget Recent personal financial statements (balance sheet, income statement) List of financial goals List of safe-deposit box contents	(None appropriate)
Personal and employment records	Current résumé Employee benefit information	Birth, marriage, and death certificates Citizenship papers Adoption, custody papers Military papers
Financial services records	Checkbook, unused checks Bank statements, canceled checks Savings passbooks Location information and number of safe-deposit box	Savings certificates List of checking and savings account numbers and financial institutions
Credit records	Unused credit cards Payment books Receipts, monthly statements List of credit account numbers and telephone numbers of issuers	Credit contracts List of credit card, charge account numbers and telephone numbers of issuers
Tax records	Paycheck stubs, W-2 forms, 1099 forms Receipts for tax-deductible items Records of taxable income Old income tax returns and documentation	(None appropriate)
Consumer purchase records	Warranties Receipts for major purchases Owner's manuals for major appliances	Serial numbers of expensive items Photographs of valuable belongings

and checking accounts are canceled checks, bank statements, savings passbooks, certificates of deposit, and interest earnings reports.

4. *Credit Records.* Buying on credit is an accepted part of our business environment. Therefore, a credit user needs to keep records of the various loans and charge accounts being used. The legal agreements between a borrower and a lender, along with payment books monthly statements, unused credit cards, and other credit-related information, need to be stored carefully.

5. *Tax Records.* Your annual tax return will be easier to prepare if you keep organized records and documents. Information about income and information about deductible expenses are the main components of this as-

FIGURE 3-1 *(concluded)*

Records	Home File	Safe-Deposit Box
Housing and automobile records	Lease (if renting) Property tax records Home repair, home improvement receipts Automobile service and repair records Automobile registration Automobile owner's manual	Mortgage papers, title deed Automobile title
Insurance records	Original insurance policies List of insurance premium amounts and due dates Medical information (health history, prescription drug information)	List of insurance policy numbers and company names
Investment records	Records of stock, bond, and mutual fund purchases and sales List of investment certificate numbers Broker statements Dividend records Company annual reports	Stock and bond certificates Rare coins, stamps, gems, and other collectibles
Estate planning and retirement records	Copy of will (original of will should be filed with your lawyer) Pension plan information IRA statements Social security information	Copy of will

pect of your financial recordkeeping system. Tax forms, earnings statements, government publications, and articles about changes in tax laws will minimize the burden associated with preparing a tax return.

6. *Consumer Purchase Records.* Whenever you make a purchase, several documents may be involved. A receipt provides evidence of payment for the item. Some products have a *warranty,* which is a written statement from the manufacturer giving the conditions under which an item can be returned, replaced, or repaired. Expensive items such as appliances and recreational equipment may come with a serial number document and service information booklets. This information should become part of your financial record file.

7. *Housing and Automobile Records.* Housing and transportation are usually the two items on which we incur the largest costs. Various documents associated with these items need to be kept on file or stored in a safe-deposit box.

Pepper . . . and Salt

"I've completely broken with my parents,
Sylvia. Now they have to send my allowance
by mail."

From *The Wall Street Journal*, with permission of Cartoon Features Syndicate.

If you rent, the lease is your main document; if you buy a home, you will be concerned with various mortgage papers and other real estate documents. Such automobile records as the title, registration report, and service information are also an important part of your financial file.

8.   *Insurance Records.* The protection of your belongings and of your financial well-being is another aspect of your economic existence. An insurance policy is the contractual agreement between you and an insurance company that specifies the type, amounts, and costs of coverage for your life, health, home, and automobile.

9.   *Investment Records.* Once you provide for current living expenses and you have adequate insurance coverage, you will probably want to increase your wealth through an investment program. The documents associated with this phase of financial planning include investment research reports, stock and bond certificates, and statements from brokers summarizing transactions.

10.   *Estate Planning and Retirement Records.* Your long-term financial plan will include information and documents about your and your family's

future economic status. One of the fundamental aspects of this area of personal finance is a will. This legal document states how a person wants his or her wealth to be distributed after death. Other information related to long-range finances includes social security data, individual retirement account (IRA) statements, and pension plan information.

As you accumulate an increased number of documents and records, you will want to dispose of some. How long should information be kept? The answer to this question differs for various kinds of items. Such records as birth certificates, wills, and social security data should be kept permanently. Property and investment records should be kept as long as you own the items that they cover. Federal tax laws influence the length of time that tax-related information should be kept. Copies of tax returns and supporting data should be saved for six years. Normally, an audit will go back only three years, but under certain circumstances the Internal Revenue Service may request information six years back.

In the Real World
Survival Tips

To survive in the real world, remember the following tips:

Insurance premiums are not like stock premiums. You pay them. They don't pay you.

People aren't kidding when they say, "Wash whites separately."

The rate of interest is what kills you, not the down payment.

Cars need not only gasoline but also oil, antifreeze, brake and transmission fluid, and about one third of your annual wage for other automobile-related expenses.

Grocery coupons are not socially unacceptable.

Greasy burgers will eventually damage your health; eat good meals.

Buy good stuff. It lasts longer.

Push-ups are just as effective on the living room floor as they are at a $50 a month, $320 a year, Eros Total Body Fitness Center.

If you don't like your job, quit. Otherwise, shut up.

There is no such thing as a self-cleaning oven.

Shower curtains are replaceable.

You are going to need silverware.

No one sells a car because it runs too well.

Never chew red peppers during a job interview.

Get a credit card. Sales clerks are suspicious of cash.

Avoid credit cards. The heck with salesclerks.

Plastic garbage bags are not a luxury item. Look in the bottom of the wastebasket for proof.

Anything-of-the-month clubs are the mail-order equivalent of chronic lower back pain.

You need to hurry up and learn patience.

Source: Wes Smith, "Hey Grads, Your Real Final Exam Awaits," *Chicago Tribune*, June 1, 1986, sec. 3, pp. 1, 4.

PERSONAL
FINANCIAL
STATEMENTS:
MEASURING
FINANCIAL
PROGRESS

Most of the financial documents that we have discussed come from financial institutions, insurance companies, investment brokers, retail stores, government agencies, or employers. Two financial documents that you create yourself, the personal balance sheet and the personal income statement, are called personal financial records. These documents provide information about your current financial position and present a summary of your current income and expenses. The main purposes of personal financial statements are to

- Report your current financial position in relation to the value of the items you own and the amounts you owe.
- Measure your progress toward your financial goals.
- Maintain information on your financial activities.
- Provide data that you can use in preparing tax forms or applying for credit.

Your Personal Balance Sheet

- Process of Preparing a Personal Balance Sheet

The financial position of an individual or a family is a common starting point for financial planning. A balance sheet, also known as a statement of net worth, specifies what you own and what you owe. A personal balance sheet is prepared to determine your current financial position using the following process:

If your possessions are worth $4,500 but you owe $800 to others, your net worth is $3,700.

Listing Items of Value. Personal spending money and money in bank accounts combined with other items that have a value are the basis of your current financial position. Assets are cash and other property that has a monetary value. The balance sheet for Cheryl and Steve Belford (Figure 3–2) lists their assets under these three categories:

1. Liquid assets are cash and items of value that can easily be converted into cash. Monies in checking and savings accounts are liquid and available to the Belfords for current spending. Also, the cash value of their life insurance may be obtained quickly if needed. While assets other than liquid assets can also be converted into cash, the process is not quite as easy.
2. Household assets and possessions are the major portion of assets for most families. Included in this category are a home, an automobile, and other personal belongings. While these items have value, it would be

FIGURE 3-2

CHERYL AND STEVE BELFORD
Personal Balance Sheet as of October 31, 1988

Assets

Liquid assets:

Checking account balance	$ 450	
Savings/money market accounts	2,235	
Cash value of life insurance	1,685	
Total liquid assets		$ 4,370

Household assets and possessions:

Current market value of home	86,500	
Market value of automobile	4,300	
Furniture	5,900	
Clothing	3,400	
Stereo and video equipment	2,600	
Home computer	1,400	
Jewelry	2,200	
Total household assets		106,300

Investment assets:

Individual retirement accounts	6,780	
Mutual funds	1,890	
Total investment assets		8,670
Total assets		$119,340

Liabilities

Current liabilities:

Medical bills	$ 150	
Charge account and credit card balances	2,340	
Balance due on auto loan	450	
Total current liabilities		$ 2,940

Long-term liabilities:

Mortgage	52,800	
Home improvement loan	1,760	
Total long-term liabilities		54,560
Total liabilities		$ 57,500
Net worth (assets minus liabilities)		$ 61,840

difficult to quickly convert them into cash. Your possessions will usually be listed on the balance sheet at their original cost. However, these values may be revised as time passes. A five-year-old television would be worth less than it was worth when new. Jewelry would probably increase in value over time.

3. Finally, investment assets consist of money set aside for long-term financial needs. The Belfords' investments will be used for such things as

financing their children's education, purchasing a vacation home, and planning for retirement. Like household assets, investment assets fluctuate in value. Each time a balance sheet is prepared, the amount listed should reflect the current value.

Determining Amounts Owed. Looking at the Belfords' total assets, you might conclude that they have a strong financial position. But we need to consider any debts they have. **Liabilities** are amounts owed to others. Like assets, liabilities can be divided into two categories:

1. **Current liabilities** are debts that must be paid within a short period of time, usually less than a year. These liabilities include such things as medical bills, tax payments, and amounts due for loans and charge accounts.
2. **Long-term liabilities** are debts that are not required to be paid in full until some time in the more or less distant future. One of the most common long-term liabilities is a mortgage. A mortgage is an amount borrowed to buy a house that will be repaid over a period of 15 to 30 years. In a similar way, a home improvement loan may be repaid to the lender over the next 5 or 10 years.

The debts listed in the liability section of a balance sheet do not include the interest charged for using someone else's money. However, each debt payment usually includes a portion for interest. Further discussion of the cost of borrowing is presented in Chapters 5 and 6.

Computing Your Net Worth. Your **net worth** is the difference between your total assets and your total liabilities. Net worth is the amount that a person would get if all of his or her assets were sold for the listed amounts and all of his or her debts were paid in full. Also, total assets equal total liabilities plus net worth. The balance sheet of a business is usually expressed as:

$$\text{Assets} = \text{Liabilities} + \text{Net worth}$$

As shown in Figure 3–2, the Belfords have a net worth of $61,840. Since very few, if any, people will liquidate all of their assets, the amount of net worth has a more practical purpose. Your net worth is a measurement of your current financial position.

Insolvency is the financial position in which your total liabilities are greater than the value of your assets. When a person is in this position, it may be difficult to make scheduled payments on time. A continued position of insolvency may require a person to declare bankruptcy, which is discussed in Chapter 6.

Your net worth can be increased in various ways. Among the most common ways are:

FIGURE 3-3   Developing a Personal Balance Sheet

Step 1. Prepare a total of all items of value (assets). Include amounts in bank accounts, investments, and the current market value of possessions. The market value of an item is the amount that you would get for the item if you sold it. The market value usually has to be estimated.

Assets

Checking account balance	$ 250
Savings account	980
Automobile	2,800
Furniture	2,100
Clothing and other possessions	2,450
Total assets	$8,580

Step 2. List and total the amounts owed to others (liabilities). This list will include current debts, charge account/credit card balances, and amounts due on loans and mortgages.

Liabilities

Cash loan balance	$ 280
Gasoline credit card balance	78
Department store charge account	180
Automobile loan balance	830
Total liabilities	$1,368

Step 3. Subtract total liabilities from total assets to determine net worth. This amount is an expression of the current financial position of an individual or a family.

Net Worth

Total assets	$8,580
Less: Total liabilities	$1,368
Net worth	$7,212

- Increased earnings from wages, salary, or investments.
- Reduced spending for current living expenses.
- Increased values of investments such as stocks, rare coins, or real estate.
- Reduced amounts owed to others.
- Increased values of personal belongings and other possessions.

Remember, your net worth is *not* money available for use, but it is an indication of your financial position on a given date. The steps for creating a personal balance sheet are summarized in Figure 3–3.

Your Personal Income Statement

- Components of a Personal Income Statement

Each day, financial events can affect your net worth. As you receive a paycheck, make payments for living expenses, or purchase items on credit, your total assets and liabilities will change. Since it would not be practical to prepare a new balance sheet each day, another statement—the income statement—is helpful in personal financial planning. An **income statement** is a summary of your income and expenses for a given period of time, such as a month or a year. This document provides data on your spending patterns that will be helpful later in the chapter when we prepare a budget. The process for preparing an income statement is:

Total cash received during the time period	minus	Payments made during the time period	equals	An increase (or decrease) in net worth

Sources of Income. The preparation of an income statement starts by identifying the cash received during the time period involved. Income is the inflows of cash to an individual or a family. For most people, the main source of income is money received from a job. Common income sources include:

- Wages, salaries, and commissions.
- Self-employment income.
- Savings and investment income (interest, dividends, rent).
- Payments from government for social security, public assistance, and unemployment benefits.
- Amounts received from pension and retirement programs.
- Alimony and child support payments.

In Figure 3–4, notice that Susan Morgan's monthly salary of $2,350 is her main source of income. But she does not have use of the entire amount. Take-home pay is a person's earnings after deductions for taxes and other items. Susan's deductions for federal, state, and social security taxes are $470. Her take-home pay is $1,880. This amount plus earnings from savings and investments is the income she has available for use during the current month.

Recording Expenses. Living expenses, which are cash payments for various items, make up the second component of an income statement. Susan Morgan divides her living expenses into three major categories: fixed expenses, emergency fund and savings, and variable expenses. While every individual and family has different living expenses, the main categories used by Susan can be adapted to most situations.

1. Fixed expenses are payments that do not vary from month to month. Examples of fixed expenses are rent or mortgage payments, payments on installment purchases or loans, fees for cable television service, and a monthly train ticket for commuting to work. Other items, such as food or gasoline, would only be fixed if you limit the amount you spend on those items.

For Susan, another type of fixed expenses is the amount that she sets aside each month for payments due only once or twice a year. For example, Susan pays $240 for life insurance every March. Each month, she puts $20 in a special savings account so that the money will be available when her insurance payment falls due.

FIGURE 3-4

SUSAN MORGAN
Personal Income Statement for the Month Ended September 30, 1988

Income

Salary (gross)		$2,350	
Less deductions:			
Federal income tax..................	$235		
State income tax	45		
Social security	190		
Total deductions		$ 470	$1,880
Interest earned on savings			34
Earnings from investments			62
Total income			$1,976

Expenses

Fixed expenses:			
Rent	$ 690		
Loan payment	86		
Cable television....................	43		
Monthly train ticket	147		
Life insurance	20		
Apartment insurance	23		
Total fixed expenses		$1,009	
Emergency fund and other savings:			
Emergency fund savings	25		
Financial goals savings	30		
Long-term financial security	25		
Total savings		80	
Variable expenses:			
Food at home	212		
Food away from home	168		
Clothing	76		
Telephone.........................	52		
Electricity.........................	48		
Personal care (dry cleaning,			
laundry, cosmetics)................	47		
Medical expenses	55		
Recreation/entertainment............	78		
Gifts	38		
Donations.........................	45		
Total variable expenses		819	
Total expenses			$1,908
Additional savings/increased net worth			$ 68

2. An emergency fund and other savings is the second main category of the expense section of the income statement. A very common mistake in financial planning is to save only the amount that you have left at the end of the month. Very often, nothing is left for savings. Since savings is a vital component of a financial plan, advisers suggest that you consider your payments to savings as a fixed expense. Susan has three items in this part of her income statement. Each month she sets aside money for her emergency fund. This account is used to meet unexpected expenses or to pay bills if Susan did not receive her salary. Susan also has two other parts to her savings plan. One part is for various financial goals, such as a new car, a

---

FIGURE 3-5   Developing a Personal Income Statement

Step 1. For a period of time, such as a month, total your income from various sources—wages, salary, interest, payments from government, and other sources.

Income

Salary for month (take-home pay)	$2,380
Earnings on savings	56
Total	$2,436

Step 2. For each month, develop categories for keeping track of expenses, such as fixed expenses, savings, and variable expenses.

Expenses

Fixed expenses:	
Mortgage payment	$ 780
Loan payment	84
Credit card payments	165
Amount set aside for automobile, home, and life insurance	87
Emergency fund and savings	85
Variable expenses:	
Food	236
Clothing	134
Gasoline	178
Auto repair	86
Gifts/donations	95
Electricity	72
Telephone	68
Medical costs	125
Recreation	79
Education/books	73
Total expenses	$2,347

Step 3. Subtract your total expenses from your income. A positive number represents an additional amount available for savings or investment. A negative number means that you have spent more than was available. This money must be borrowed or the amount in savings is decreased.

Surplus for additional savings	$ 89

vacation, or going back to school; the other part is for long-term financial security—her retirement.

3. Variable expenses are flexible living costs that change from month to month. Common examples of variable expenses are food, clothing, utilities such as telephone and electricity, recreation, medical expenses, gifts, and donations. Keeping accurate records of expense payments is very helpful in budgeting and for increasing your net worth.

Changes in Net Worth. The completion of the income statement involves subtracting your total expenses and payments from your monthly income. The process for developing a personal income statement is summarized in Figure 3–5.

Since Susan's expenses for September were less than her income, an additional amount can go into savings. This amount, plus other payments to savings and investment accounts, will increase her net worth. In other months, Susan may have more payments than income, which will mean a temporary decrease in her net worth. When Susan has more expenditures than income, she may take this additional expense amount from her savings or she may decide to borrow or buy on credit.

Changes in your net worth are a result of the current month's income and expenses. This relationship between your personal income statement and your personal balance sheet is as follows:

Income Statement   *Balance Sheet*

If income for the month is greater
   than expenses and payments - — — — — — — — → Net worth increases

If expenses and payments for the
   month are greater than income — — — — — — — — → Net worth decreases

---

Evaluating Your Financial Statements

Assessing your financial progress through your personal balance sheet and income statement can help you achieve your goals. You are experiencing financial improvement if each time you prepare a balance sheet, your net worth increases. Your financial status will improve as you are able to set aside more money each month for savings and investments.

The relationship between various balance sheet items can also give you an indication of changes in your financial position. In general, a lower debt ratio—liabilities divided by net worth—indicates a more favorable financial position. For example, if you have $50,000 in debts and a net worth of $25,000, your debt ratio is 2 ($50,000/$25,000); but if you have $25,000 in debts and a net worth of $50,000, your debt ratio is 0.5 ($25,000/$50,000).

Another balance sheet evaluation technique is the current ratio, determined by dividing liquid assets by current liabilities. This relationship is an indication of how well you will be able to pay your upcoming debts. If you have $4,000 in liquid assets and $2,000 in current liabilities, your current ratio is 2 ($4,000/$2,000). This means that you have $2 in liquid assets for every dollar in current liabilities.

The debt ratio, the current ratio, and other financial statement analysis methods can assist you in planning your spending and reaching your financial goals.

THE BUDGETING PROCESS

Improvements in your financial position are the direct result of an effective budget. Yet a study conducted by *Money* magazine reported that only 23 percent of those surveyed had a planned budget and that another 48 percent only had "somewhat of a budget."[1]

A budget is the foundation of successful financial planning. The common financial problems of overusing credit, not having a savings and investment program, and failing to ensure future financial security can all be minimized through budgeting. The main purposes of a budget are to help you:

- Live within your income.
- Spend your money wisely.
- Reach your financial goals.
- Prepare for financial emergencies.
- Develop wise financial management habits.

The process of creating and implementing a budget involves three major phases:

- Steps Used to Develop and Implement a Budget

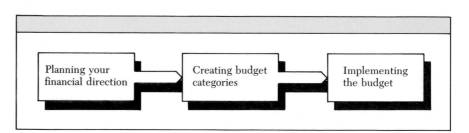

Planning Your Financial Direction

Making some decisions about your life is the starting point of budgeting. You must make a variety of choices about your daily living patterns and your plans for the future.

Your Lifestyle. Each day, you make many decisions that add up to a statement about you. Your lifestyle is how you spend your time and money.

[1]*Americans and Their Money/2: The Second National Survey from MONEY Magazine* (1984), p. 67.

The clothes you wear, the food you eat, and your interests contribute to your lifestyle. Some people spend time and money on automobiles or stereo equipment; other people travel, engage in home gardening, or are involved in church or community activities. Each of these actions reflects a lifestyle that is greatly affected by the following factors:

- *Career.* Your job situation will influence the amount of income, the way you spend your leisure time, and even your choice of the people with whom you wish to associate.
- *Family.* The size of your household and the ages of the people in it will also affect your lifestyle. The spending priorities of a couple without children will be different from those of a couple with several youngsters.
- *Values.* The ideas and beliefs that you regard as important will strongly influence your interests, activities, and purchasing habits.

These factors combine to create planned spending patterns that are reflected in your financial goals.

Financial Goals. Future plans are another important dimension of your financial direction. Financial goals are plans for future activities that require you to plan your spending, saving, and investing. Figure 3–6 gives examples of common financial goals based on family situation and time.

Using your personal financial statements along with a budget can play an important role in achieving financial goals. Your income statement tells you where you have been over a certain time period, such as the past month. Your balance sheet tells you your current financial position—where you are now. And your budget expresses where you would like to be in the future. A budget is a major tool for achieving financial goals by planning spending and saving.

FIGURE 3-6   Common Financial Goals

Family Situation	Short-Term Goals (less than two years)	Intermediate Goals (2–5 years)	Long-Term Goals (over 5 years)
Single person	Complete college Pay off auto loan	Take vacation Pay off education loan Return to school for graduate degree	Buy vacation home Ensure retirement income
Married couple (no children)	Take annual vacation Buy new car	Remodel home Build stock portfolio	Buy retirement home Ensure retirement income
Married couple (young children)	Increase life insurance Increase savings	Increase investments Buy new car	Accumulate college fund Move to larger home

Savings Methods. Regular savings is vital to future financial security. Common savings goals are

- To set aside money for irregular and unexpected expenses.
- To pay for the replacement of expensive items such as appliances or to have money for the down payment on a new car or house.
- To buy special items such as home video equipment or recreational equipment or to pay for a vacation.
- To provide for long-term expenses such as the education of children or retirement.
- To earn income from the interest on savings for use in paying living expenses.

Since most people find saving difficult, financial advisers suggest several methods to assist you. Each payday, write a check and deposit it in a special savings account at a distant financial institution. This savings deposit can be a percentage of income, such as 5 or 10 percent or a specific dollar amount.

Another method to help force you to save is payroll deduction, which is available at many places of employment. Under this system, an amount is automatically deducted from your salary and deposited in a savings account or used to purchase U.S. savings bonds.

Finally, saving coins or reducing spending on certain items can also help you achieve your savings goals. Each day, put your change in a container. In a short time, you will have enough money to make a substantial deposit in a savings account. You can also add to your savings by taking a sandwich in-

Courtesy of Honeywell, Inc.

stead of buying your lunch or by not buying snacks or magazines. How you save, however, is less important than saving regularly by making periodic deposits into a savings plan that will help you achieve your financial goals.

Creating Budget Categories

After you have decided on an overall plan for your lifestyle, financial goals, and savings, the next phase of budgeting is to assign income into spending categories. How much you budget for various items will depend on your current needs and on your plans for the future. The following sources are available to assist you in planning your spending:

- Personal income statement.
- Sample budgets from government reports (Figure 3–7).
- Personal financial planning magazines such as *Changing Times* and *Money.*
- Estimates of your future income and expenses and of future cost changes due to inflation.

Today's Lifestyles
Budgeting for the New Baby

Thirty years ago, expenses during the first year of a child's life were approximately $800 for food, clothing, and other necessities. Today, the figure is estimated to be four or five times that amount. Luxuries can increase the amount to about $10,000.

The most certain aspect of child-rearing costs is that there will be many unexpected items. To transport the child, parents will probably spend money for car seats and portable cribs and high chairs. These items are, of course, in addition to a regular high chair, crib, and stroller.

Many child-related products are now on the market that didn't exist thirty years ago. Disposable diapers, safety latches for cabinets, electronic monitoring systems for the baby's room, and pumps for expressing breast milk have added to the financial costs of having a baby.

Designer strollers, cribs, and clothing can also add to those costs. A basic stroller costs $30 or $40, but a luxury model goes for several hundred dollars. Famous label shirts, shorts, and other clothing can result in an outlay of $500 during the child's first year.

These expenses do not include medical and hospital bills, which can range from $2,000 to $6,000 for prenatal care, delivery, and related costs. While the first year of life is expensive, later you can anticipate such costs as braces, piano lessons, and a college education!

Source: Roger Lowenstein, "Expecting a Baby Soon? Expect to Spend a Pile of Money during the First Year," *The Wall Street Journal,* April 16, 1986, p. 29.

A combination of this information should be used to develop your budget.

The format previously used to prepare an income statement can be the basis for your budget. The major categories of this spending plan are estimates for income, fixed expenses, emergency fund and savings, and variable expenses.

Income. Estimate the amount of available money for a given period of time. A common budgeting period is a month, since many payments, such as rent or mortgage, utilities, and charge accounts, are made during that time frame. In determining available income, only include monies that you are sure you'll receive. Bonuses, gifts, or unexpected income should not be considered until the money has actually been received.

If you get paid once a month, planning your budget is easy since you will work with a single amount. But if you get paid weekly or twice a month, you will need to plan how much of each paycheck will go for various expenses. If you get paid every two weeks, plan your spending based on the two paychecks that you will receive each month. Then, during the two months each

---

FIGURE 3-7   Budget Expenditures by Income Level

	$15,000–$19,999	$20,000–$29,999	$30,000–$39,999	Over $40,000
Food (both at home and away from home)	20%	18	16%	15%
Housing (rent or mortgage payment and taxes)	17	16	16	17
Utilities	9	8	7	6
Furnishings and household purchases	5	5	6	7
Clothing	5	5	5	6
Transportation (automobile operation and insurance, public transportation)	20	21	21	19
Personal and health care, miscellaneous expenses	7	6	6	5
Entertainment	5	6	6	6
Reading and education	2	2	2	2
Personal insurance and pension payments	7	10	12	13
Contributions and donations	3	3	3	4

Source: *Consumer Expenditure Survey: Interview Survey, 1982–83* (Washington, D.C.: Department of Labor, Bureau of Labor Statistics).

year that have three paydays, you can put additional amounts in savings, pay off some debts, or make a special purchase.

Fixed Expenses. Definite financial obligations are the basis for the expense portion of your budget. As you can see in Figure 3–8, the Frazier family has fixed expenses for housing, taxes, and payment for the use of

---

FIGURE 3-8   A Monthly Budget for the Frazier Family

	Budgeted amounts (dollar)	(percent)	Actual amounts	Variance
Income				
Salary	2874	100	2874	—
Expenses				
Fixed expenses				
Mortgage payment	518	18	518	—
Property taxes	115	4	115	—
Auto loan payment	144	5	144	—
Life insurance	29	1	29	—
Total fixed expenses	806	28	806	—
Emergency fund and savings:				
Emergency fund savings	115	4	115	—
Savings for auto insurance	29	1	29	—
Savings for vacation	57	2	57	—
Savings for investments	57	2	57	—
Total savings	258	9	258	—
Variable expenses				
Food	402	14	417	−15
Utilities (telephone, heat, electric, water)	172	6	164	+8
Clothing	116	4	93	+23
Transportation (automobile operation, repairs, public transportation)	460	16	471	−11
Personal and health care	172	6	163	+9
Entertainment	172	6	201	−29
Reading, education	86	3	78	+8
Gifts, donations	144	5	150	−6
Personal allowances, miscellaneous expenses	86	3	90	−4
Total variable expenses	1810	63	1827	−17
Total expenses	2874	100	2891	−17

credit. The family also has a monthly payment of $29 for life insurance. The total of the Fraziers' budgeted fixed expenses is $806, or 28 percent of their income.

Emergency Fund and Savings. In an attempt to set aside money for unexpected expenses as well as future financial plans, the Fraziers have budgeted several amounts for saving and investing. Financial advisers suggest that an emergency fund representing three to six months of income be established for unexpected financial situations.

The Fraziers also set aside an amount each month for their automobile insurance payment, which is due every six months. Each of the amounts set aside in a savings or other bank account will grow in value over the months and years. The **time value of money** refers to increases in an amount of money as a result of interest earned. The methods used to compute the time value of money are discussed later in this chapter.

Variable Expenses. A major portion of the planned spending by the Fraziers—63 percent of their budgeted income—is for various living costs.

Pepper . . . and Salt

"Now suppose you give us the answer *without* inflation."

From *The Wall Street Journal,* with permission of Cartoon Features Syndicate.

The Fraziers base their estimates on needs and desires for the items listed. These expenses are also influenced by changes in the cost of living. The Consumer Price Index is a measure of the general price level of consumer items in the United States. This government statistic gives consumers an indication of changes in the buying power of a dollar. As consumer prices increase due to inflation, people must spend more to buy the same amount.

Changes in the cost of living will vary depending on what you buy and where you live. Changes in food prices from June 1985 to June 1986 varied

Personal Financial Planning
Computing Your Own Cost-of-Living Index

E ach month, the Bureau of Labor Statistics (BLS) publishes the Consumer Price Index (CPI). The CPI measures the cost of living based on changes in a selected market basket of goods and services. In addition to the U.S. average CPI, the BLS develops monthly reports for selected large cities.* While the CPI provides an indication of the cost of living, few people use the exact products that are used to compute the monthly index. You can prepare your own consumer price index by monitoring the price of commonly used items over a period of time. For example:

	Base		Time Period 1		Time Period 2	
Item	Price	Index	Price	Index	Price	Index
Gallon of milk	$1.49	100	$1.63	109	$1.78	119
Gallon of gas	1.09	100	0.93	85	1.06	97
Apartment rent	$450	100	$480	107	$510	113

To compute a personal cost-of-living index, use the following format:

$1.49 x = $1.63 (100)

Base price   New index number   New price   Base index

$$1.49x = 163$$

$$x = \frac{163}{1.49}$$

New index number = 109

*For a copy of the latest consumer price index, contact the U.S. Department of Labor, Bureau of Labor Statistics, 600 E Street, NW, Washington, DC 20212.

Now prepare your personal consumer price index using the price of items you commonly use.

by city. Chicago shoppers experienced an 11 percent increase, while food prices in Phoenix fell 8.1 percent. At the same time, a similar market basket of 35 food items ranged in price from $59.64 in Honolulu to $39.97 in San Diego.[2]

Implementing the Budget

After your spending plan has been set, you will need to keep records about your actual income and expenses similar to those you keep in preparing an income statement. In Figure 3–8, you will notice that the Fraziers estimated specific amounts for income and expenses. These are presented under "Budgeted Amounts." The family's spending was not always the same as planned. A **budget variance** is the difference between the amount budgeted and the actual amount received or spent. The total variance for the Fraziers was a $17 **deficit**, since actual spending exceeded planned spending by this amount. The Fraziers would have had a **surplus** if their actual spending had been less than they had planned to spend.

Spending more than planned for an item may be justified by reducing spending for another item or by putting less into savings. However, it may be necessary to revise the budget and reevaluate your financial goals and spending patterns.

SUCCESSFUL BUDGETING TECHNIQUES

- Techniques for Successful Budgeting and Effective Money Management

Having a budget will not eliminate your financial worries. A budget will work only if you follow it and if nothing in your life changes. Changes in income, expenses, and goals will require changes in your budget. Money experts state that a successful budget has the qualities of being:

- *Well planned.* A good budget takes time and effort. Planning a budget should involve everyone affected by it. Children can learn important money management lessons by helping develop and use the family budget.
- *Realistic.* If you have a moderate income, don't expect to immediately save enough money for an expensive car or a European vacation. A budget is not designed to prevent you from enjoying life but to help you achieve what you most want out of life.
- *Flexible.* Unexpected expenses and changes in your cost of living will require a budget that can easily be revised. Also, special situations, such as two-income families or the arrival of a baby, may require an increase in certain types of expenses.
- *Clearly communicated.* Unless you and the others affected by a budget are aware of the spending plan, the budget will not be valuable. It should be written and available to all family members. While many variations of written budgets are possible, such budget formats as a notebook or a computerized system are also available.

[2]"Grocery Bag Harder to Fill in 'Paradise,'" *USA Today*, July 31, 1986, p. 5A.

TYPES OF BUDGETING SYSTEMS

- Different Types of Budgeting Systems

Your checkbook is a simple, yet effective method of financial recordkeeping. If you deposit all of your paychecks and other income into a checking account and then pay all of your bills by check, your checkbook will give you a fairly complete record of your expenses. But a checkbook does not serve the purpose of planning for spending. A budget requires that you outline how you will spend your available income. Various types of budgeting systems exist, from informal procedures to computerized spending plans.

A mental budget is one that exists only in a person's mind. This simple system may be quite appropriate for an individual with limited resources and minimal financial responsibilities. The major drawback of a mental budget is the danger of forgetting what amounts you plan to spend on various items.

A physical budget involves the use of envelopes, folders, or containers to hold the money or slips of paper that represent the amounts allocated for your spending categories. This system allows a person to actually see where the money goes. Envelopes would contain the amount of cash or a note listing the amount to be used for "Food," "Rent," "Clothing," "Auto Payment," "Entertainment," and other expenses.

Financial advisers and experienced money managers recommend that you use a written budget. The exact system used and the amount of detail involved will depend on the time, effort, and information that you put into the budgeting process. A written budget can be kept on notebook paper or in a specialized budgeting book available in office supply stores or bookstores. A common budget format is a spreadsheet that has several sets of monthly columns for comparing budgeted and actual amounts for various expense items.

As the use of personal computers increases, so too does the use of computerized budgeting systems. In addition to creating a spreadsheet budget presentation, a home computer is capable of doing other financial recordkeeping duties such as writing checks and projecting the future value of savings accounts. Software packages ranging in cost from $15 or $25 to several hundred dollars can assist with budgeting and with the preparation of personal financial statements. Information about the use of a personal computer for financial recordkeeping and planning is available through computer stores, books, and articles in such computer magazines as *Personal Computing* and *Family Computing*. Also refer to Appendix B, "Buying a Personal Computer and Financial Planning Software." It takes time and effort to learn the system and enter data, but a computerized budgeting and recordkeeping procedure yields fast and accurate data vital to successful financial planning.

TIME VALUE OF MONEY

- Role of the Time Value of Money in Budgeting and Financial Planning

The money you set aside in a savings account will grow in value as a result of interest earned. Interest is calculated based on three items:

- The amount of savings.
- The annual interest rate.
- The length of time the money is on deposit.

These three amounts are multiplied to obtain the amount of interest. The interest formula is as follows:

| Interest | equals | Amount in savings | times | The annual interest rate | times | Time period |

For example, $500 on deposit for six months at 6 percent would earn $15 ($500 × 0.06 × 6/12, or ½ year).

The increased value of your money from interest earned can be viewed in two ways. You can calculate the total amount that will be available in the future, or you can determine the current value of an amount desired in the future.

Future Value

Deposited money earns interest that will increase over time. **Future value,** also referred to as compounding, is the amount to which current savings will increase based on a certain interest rate and a certain time

TABLE 3-1   Future Value of $1

	Percent				
Year	5%	6%	7%	8%	9%
1	1.050	1.060	1.070	1.080	1.090
2	1.103	1.124	1.145	1.166	1.188
3	1.158	1.191	1.225	1.260	1.295
4	1.216	1.262	1.311	1.360	1.412
5	1.276	1.338	1.403	1.469	1.539
6	1.340	1.419	1.501	1.587	1.677
7	1.407	1.504	1.606	1.714	1.828
8	1.477	1.594	1.718	1.851	1.993
9	1.551	1.689	1.838	1.999	2.172
10	1.629	1.791	1.967	2.159	2.367
11	1.710	1.898	2.105	2.332	2.580
12	1.796	2.012	2.252	2.518	2.813
13	1.886	2.133	2.410	2.720	3.066
14	1.980	2.261	2.579	2.937	3.342
15	2.079	2.397	2.759	3.172	3.642
16	2.183	2.540	2.952	3.426	3.970
17	2.292	2.693	3.159	3.700	4.328
18	2.407	2.854	3.380	3.996	4.717
19	2.527	3.026	3.617	4.316	5.142
20	2.653	3.207	3.870	4.661	5.604

period. For example, $100 deposited in a 6 percent account for one year will grow to $106. This amount is computed as follows:

$$\text{Future value} = \$100 + (\$100 \times 0.06 \times 1 \text{ year}) = \$106$$

|
Original
amount in
savings

|
Amount of
interest
earned

The same process could be continued for a second, third, and fourth year, but the computations are time consuming. To simplify the process, future value tables are available (see Table 3–1). To use a future value table, multiply the amount of savings by the factor for the desired interest rate and time period. For example, $650 at 8 percent for 12 years would have a future value of $1,636.70 ($650 × 2.518). The future value of an amount will always be greater than the original amount. As seen in Table 3–1, the future value factors are all larger than one.

To determine the future value of equal yearly savings deposits, use Table 3–2. For this table to be used, the deposits must earn a constant interest

TABLE 3-2   Future Value of a Series of Deposits

			Percent		
Year	5%	6%	7%	8%	9%
1	1.000	1.000	1.000	1.000	1.000
2	2.050	2.060	2.070	2.080	2.090
3	3.153	3.184	3.215	3.246	3.278
4	4.310	4.375	4.440	4.506	4.573
5	5.526	5.637	5.751	5.867	5.985
6	6.802	6.975	7.153	7.336	7.523
7	8.142	8.394	8.654	8.923	9.200
8	9.549	9.897	10.260	10.637	11.028
9	11.027	11.491	11.978	12.488	13.021
10	12.578	13.181	13.816	14.487	15.193
11	14.207	14.972	15.784	16.645	17.560
12	15.917	16.870	17.888	18.977	20.141
13	17.713	18.882	20.141	21.495	22.953
14	19.599	21.015	22.550	24.215	26.019
15	21.579	23.276	25.129	27.152	29.361
16	23.657	25.673	27.888	30.324	33.003
17	25.840	20.213	30.840	33.750	36.974
18	28.132	30.906	33.999	37.450	41.301
19	30.539	33.760	37.379	41.446	46.018
20	33.066	36.786	40.995	45.762	51.160

rate. A person who deposits $50 a year at 7 percent for six years, starting at the end of the first year, would have $357.65 at the end of that time ($50 × 7.153).

Present Value

Another aspect of the time value of money involves determining the current value of a desired amount for the future. **Present value** is the current value for a future sum based on a certain interest rate and a certain time period. Present value computations allow you to determine how much to deposit now to obtain a desired total in the future. Present value tables (Table 3–3) can be used in making the computations. If you want $1,000 three years from now and you earn 5 percent on your savings, you need to deposit $864 ($1,000 × 0.864). The present value of the amount you want in the future will always be less than the future value since all of the factors on Table 3–3 are less than one and since interest earned will increase the present value amount to the desired future amount.

Present value computations can also be used to determine how much you need to deposit so that you can take a certain amount out of the account for a desired number of years. If you want to take $400 out of savings each year for

---

TABLE 3-3   Present Value of $1

Year	5%	6%	7%	8%	9%
			Percent		
1	0.952	0.943	0.935	0.926	0.917
2	0.907	0.890	0.873	0.857	0.842
3	0.864	0.840	0.816	0.794	0.772
4	0.823	0.792	0.763	0.735	0.708
5	0.784	0.747	0.713	0.681	0.650
6	0.746	0.705	0.666	0.630	0.596
7	0.711	0.665	0.623	0.583	0.547
8	0.677	0.627	0.582	0.540	0.502
9	0.645	0.592	0.544	0.500	0.460
10	0.614	0.558	0.508	0.463	0.422
11	0.585	0.527	0.475	0.429	0.388
12	0.557	0.497	0.444	0.397	0.356
13	0.530	0.469	0.415	0.368	0.326
14	0.505	0.442	0.388	0.340	0.299
15	0.481	0.417	0.362	0.315	0.275
16	0.458	0.394	0.339	0.292	0.252
17	0.436	0.371	0.317	0.270	0.231
18	0.416	0.350	0.296	0.250	0.212
19	0.396	0.331	0.277	0.232	0.194
20	0.377	0.312	0.258	0.215	0.178

TABLE 3-4   Present Value of a Series of Deposits

Period	Percent				
	5%	6%	7%	8%	9%
1	0.952	0.943	0.935	0.926	0.917
2	1.859	1.833	1.808	1.783	1.759
3	2.723	2.673	2.624	2.577	2.531
4	3.546	3.465	3.387	3.312	3.240
5	4.329	4.212	4.100	3.993	3.890
6	5.076	4.917	4.767	4.623	4.486
7	5.786	5.582	5.389	5.206	5.033
8	6.463	6.210	5.971	5.747	5.535
9	7.108	6.802	6.515	6.247	5.995
10	7.722	7.360	7.024	6.710	6.418
11	8.306	7.887	7.499	7.139	6.805
12	8.863	8.384	7.943	7.536	7.161
13	9.394	8.853	8.358	7.904	7.487
14	9.899	9.295	8.745	8.244	7.786
15	10.380	9.712	9.108	8.559	8.061
16	10.838	10.106	9.447	8.851	8.313
17	11.274	10.477	9.763	9.122	8.544
18	11.690	10.828	10.059	9.372	8.756
19	12.085	11.158	10.336	9.604	8.950
20	12.462	11.470	10.594	9.818	9.129

nine years and your money is earning 8 percent, you can see from Table 3–4 that you would need to make a current deposit of $2,498.80 ($400 × 6.247).

The formulas for calculating future and present values as well as tables covering a wider range of interest rates and time periods are presented in Appendix C.

SUMMARY

- An organized system of financial records and documents is the foundation of effective financial planning.
- Financial records will be stored either in a home file or in a safe-deposit box. These records include budgets, personal financial statements, employment documents, banking account information, credit contracts, tax forms, warranties, receipts, insurance policies, investment reports, and retirement materials.

- A personal balance sheet is prepared by deducting the total amount owed to others from the value of your assets to determine your net worth.
- An income statement reports the income and expense payments for a period of time to determine changes in the net worth of an individual or a family. Fixed expenses are financial obligations that cannot be avoided. An emergency fund allows for unexpected ex-

penses and unplanned living costs. Variable expenses can be adapted to the amount of income that is currently available.
- The budgeting process involves planning your financial direction, creating budget categories, and implementing the budget.

- Successful budgets are well planned, realistic, flexible, and clearly communicated.
- The budgeting system may be mental, physical, written, or computerized.
- Future value and present value computations enable a person to calculate the increased value of savings as a result of interest earned.

GLOSSARY

Assets.   Cash and other property that has a monetary value.

Balance sheet.   A financial statement that reports what an individual or a family owns and owes; also called a statement of net worth.

Budget.   A plan for spending.

Budget variance.   The difference between the amount budgeted and the actual amount received or spent.

Current liabilities.   Debts that are due within a short period of time, usually a year.

Deficit.   The amount by which actual spending exceeds planned spending.

Future value.   The amount to which current savings will increase based on a certain interest rate and a certain time period; also referred to as compounding.

Income.   Inflows of cash to an individual or a family.

Income statement.   A summary of income and expenses for a given time period.

Insolvency.   The financial position in which your total liabilities are greater than the value of your assets.

Liabilities.   Amounts owed to others.

Liquid assets.   Cash and items of value that can easily be converted into cash.

Long-term liabilities.   Debts that are not required to be paid in full until some time in the more or less distant future.

Net worth.   The difference between a person's or family's total assets and total liabilities.

Present value.   The current value for a future sum based on a certain interest rate and time period.

Safe-deposit box.   A private storage area at a financial institution that offers maximum security for valuables.

Surplus.   The amount by which actual spending falls short of planned spending.

Take-home pay.   A person's earnings after deductions for taxes and other items.

Time value of money.   Increases in an amount of money as a result for interest earned.

REVIEW QUESTIONS

1. What are the benefits of an organized system of financial records?

2. Where should you store the various financial records discussed in this chapter?

3. How does the preparation of personal financial statements help a person in financial planning?

4. What are the main components of a personal balance sheet?

5. How do current liabilities differ from long-term liabilities?

6. What does a person's net worth represent?

7. What are the main sections of an income statement?

8. How does the difference between a person's income and expenses affect his or her net worth?

9. What are the main purposes of a budget?

10. What formats can be used for a budget?

11. What information is needed to compute interest?

12. How can future value and present value computations be used to plan your savings?

DISCUSSION QUESTIONS AND ACTIVITIES

1. What actions could Bob Jameson have taken to prepare for his financial independence from his parents?

2. What records would help Bob in planning his finances?

3. What other problems could occur for Bob as a result of not having an organized system of financial records?

4. Prepare a list of your personal financial records. Develop a system for organizing and storing these records.

5. Contact a local financial institution to determine the cost of a safe-deposit box.

6. Based on the procedures presented in the chapter, prepare your current balance sheet and your income statement for the past month.

7. Compute a cost-of-living index for items you regularly purchase.

8. Ask two or three friends or relatives about their budgeting system. Obtain information on how and why they maintain their spending records.

9. What items are people likely to spend less on when expenses exceed income?

10. Many people do not believe that they need a written budget. How would you convince them to change their mind?

11. Visit a computer store to see a demonstration of money management software that assists with personal budgeting and financial recordkeeping.

ADDITIONAL READINGS

Consumer Budget Planner. American Financial Services Association, 1101 14th Street, NW, Washington, DC 20005.

Lawrence, Judy. *Common Cents: The Complete Money Management Workbook*. Homewood, Ill.: Dow Jones-Irwin, 1986.

"The Spending Habits of American Consumers." *American Demographics*, March 1986, pp. 22–25, 51–54.

"Where Does All the Money Go?" *Consumer Reports*, September 1986, pp. 581–92.

Your Financial Plan. Money Management Institute, Household Financial Services, 2700 Sanders Road, Prospect Heights, IL 60070.

CASE 3–1 A Recordkeeper's Personal Budgeting Difficulties

Alice Fredericks is employed as a word processing supervisor for an investment company. She lives in a small house about 20 minutes from work, and she drives a two-year-old car. She is making payments on both the house and the car. Alice has a steady income and can afford to buy many other items. She recently redecorated several rooms in her house, and for the past five years she has taken a yearly vacation.

Even though Alice handles business records and documents at work, she is frequently late in making payments to her creditors. Also, the insurance coverage for her home and car is not ade-quate to cover their value. After working for al-most 10 years, Alice has only $800 in her savings and investment accounts.

Questions

1. Which financial documents does Alice need?
2. How could Alice become more organized in handling her personal finances?
3. How would the preparation of a personal balance sheet and a personal income statement assist Alice in her financial planning?

CASE 3–2 Income High, Liabilities High

Debi and Fred Conklin have been married six years. They have a combined income of $50,000. With total assets of $110,500, they have only $500 in savings. Their liabilities total $80,600.

Each time the Conklins have a sum of money, they spend it for such things as vacations, furniture, or home entertainment equipment. Currently, their annual expenses include $11,325 listed as "unaccounted for." This amount is in addition to the amounts they spend for food, housing, utilities, transportation, loan payments, insurance, donations, gifts, and taxes. The Conklins live in a town house but would like to buy a detached house.

Questions

1. What is the net worth of the Conklins? What is your opinion of their current financial position?
2. How could the Conklins improve their financial position?
3. What changes would you suggest in the Conklins' budgeting techniques?
4. How could the Conklins be more effective in their financial planning?

Comprehensive Case for Part One
Planning Is Everything

Martha Wallace recently started her first full-time job at Browning Associates, a real estate development company that builds, rents, and manages shopping malls. While attending college, Martha worked part-time as a receptionist, a department store clerk, and an assistant manager of a restaurant. Martha has a degree in business with special interests in finance and marketing.

Browning offers its employees a very generous package of financial benefits. In addition to salary, paid vacations, holidays, and basic health insurance, Martha can select from a variety of other benefits. These benefits include contributions to a retirement program, extra vacation days, additional health insurance, life insurance, and the services of a financial planner.

The pension plan, if Martha selects that as part of her benefits, consists of a $600 annual contribution by the company toward her savings for use after retirement. This amount is in addition to her regular pension fund and social security deductions.

As an assistant account manager with Browning, Martha contacts current clients to identify their changing needs. However, the company offers employees a number of opportunities for career advancement and training. These opportunities include employee seminars, management training programs, and tuition reimbursement for additional college courses. Martha plans to use one or more of these opportunities to advance her career.

As a single person, Martha has a strong interest in improving her skills and advancing her career. She doesn't think a formal budget is necessary, since she lives alone. Her resources are good because of the money she has saved and the salary from her new job. Martha can now afford many of the things she dreamed about while growing up. As the second youngest of seven children, she was frequently required to use her older sisters' clothing and toys. But now, as Martha puts it, "those days are gone. I can afford to enjoy the things that I worked hard for during college."

Questions

1. What values does Martha possess that will influence her financial goals?

2. What might be some financial goals that Martha will want to achieve within the next few years? In the distant future?

3. What factors should Martha consider when building a savings and investment program? How can having a budget contribute to her savings goals?

4. What factors should Martha consider when determining whether she will take advantage of the company's training opportunities?

5. Which of the supplementary employee benefits should Martha consider selecting? How might this decision change if her family situation changes?

6. If Martha selects the additional pension plan, how much money will be in her retirement account after 40 years if the $600 annual contribution earns 10 percent compounded annually?

7. What other financial decisions should Martha start thinking about at this point in her life?

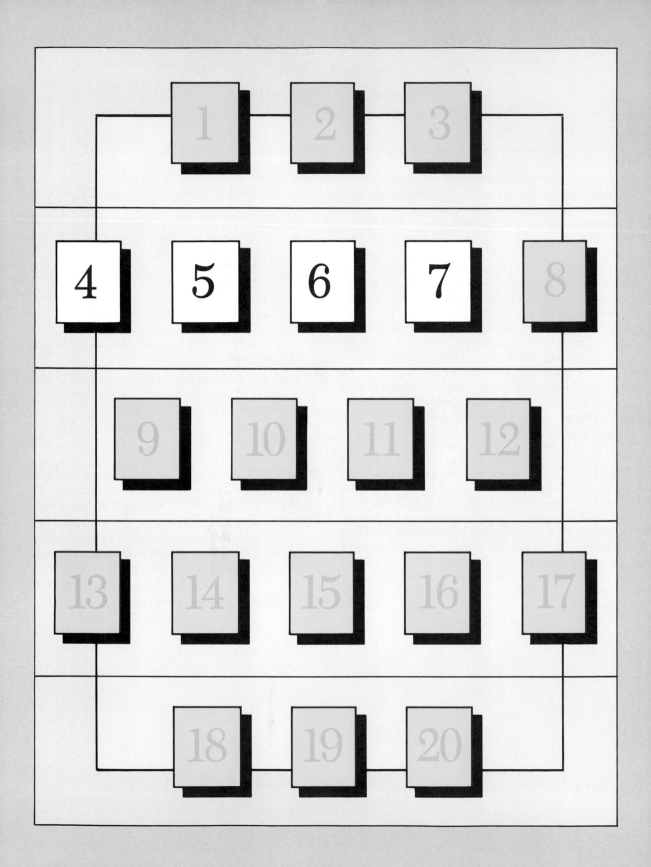

PART TWO

Managing Your Personal Finances

The second part of *Personal Finance* is concerned with financial services and tax decisions. Legislative actions have increased the number and availability of banking services. As a result, greater effort is needed to compare the costs and benefits of savings plans, checking accounts, and other financial services. The discussion of consumer credit provides complete information on the sources, costs, and types of credit plans. Since almost everyone uses credit, knowledge of this area is usually a vital component of successful financial planning. The problems associated with buying on credit are considered along with actions that can be taken to avoid and solve these problems. Finally, the recently enacted changes in our tax laws are discussed. Understanding, planning, and paying your government obligations will contribute to an effective financial existence. This part consists of:

4

Financial Services and Banking Basics

Someone who says "I'm going to the bank" may be referring to a savings and loan association, a credit union, or even an automatic teller machine in a shopping mall. In recent years, the types and availability of financial services have expanded. A bank is no longer the only source of checking accounts. Mortgages are now available from financial institutions other than savings and loan associations. Many new options have been created for saving, spending, borrowing, and investing your money.

After studying this chapter, you will be able to:

- Explain the factors that influence the availability of financial services.

- Describe the business operations of financial institutions.

- List the types of financial institutions commonly used by consumers.

- Identify the services offered by financial supermarkets.

- Discuss the factors to consider when selecting a financial institution.

- Explain the factors to consider when choosing a savings plan.

- Describe the types of savings instruments that are available to consumers.

- List the types of checking accounts.

- Explain the activities involved in using a checking account.

Interview with **John Searer,** Vice President, Gary-Wheaton Bank, and **Joseph D'Agostino,** President, DuPage Bank and Trust Company

John A. Searer is the Assistant Vice President for Consumer Services at the Gary-Wheaton Bank, Wheaton, Illinois. Mr. Searer is also a certified financial planner. Joseph V. D'Agostino is the president of the DuPage Bank and Trust Company, Glen Ellyn, Illinois. Mr. D'Agostino has over 35 years of experience in the banking industry.

The traditional view of a commercial bank is changing as we are offering many types of savings and investment services in addition to loans, checking accounts, and safe-deposit boxes. Instead of just passbook savings accounts and certificates of deposit, also available to savers are money market accounts, NOW accounts, and SuperNOW accounts. Investment departments offer bank customers the opportunity to place their money in government securities and high-quality corporate securities. The services of a bank's investment department are very much like those of most stock brokerage companies.

Probably the most important change in financial institutions has been the movement toward money management. As bankers, we try to point out four aspects for being a good money manager. First, we want to teach people to become good money managers through effective use of a checking account and other payment services. Second, everyone needs a savings and investment program, which can be in the form of a savings account, certificates of deposit, or a money market account. Third, everyone needs a retirement account to plan for long-range financial security. And finally, everyone needs a line of credit or a loan account to meet possible borrowing needs.

Banks have been facing increased competition from other financial institutions, such as savings and loan associations, credit unions, investment brokers, insurance companies, and even retailers such as Sears. This increased competition means increased availability of services for consumers. But

with more choices, consumers need to spend more time comparing services, costs, and savings rates to get the best deal. While many accounts offer higher interest rates than were offered in the past, higher minimum balances are also required.

Probably the most exciting area of change in banking is electronic funds transfer (EFT). The 24-hour teller machines give customers a convenient way of getting cash at any time. Another EFT service is direct deposit of payroll and government "checks." Under this system, no check is actually created; instead, computerized data transfer money from an employer's or government's account to the customer's account. These transactions take far less time than having the customer bring checks in for deposit. The reduced costs of EFT will probably result in savings that are passed on to the customer in the form of lower fees and charges.

Marlene and Bill Sullivan have separate checking accounts. They each pay part of the household and living expenses. Marlene pays the mortgage and telephone bill, while Bill pays for food and utilities and makes the insurance and car payment. This arrangement allows them the freedom to spend whatever extra money they have each month without needing to explain their actions. Marlene and Bill believe that their separate accounts have minimized family disagreements about money. Since they both spend most of their money each month, they have low balances in their checking accounts, resulting in a monthly charge totaling $15.

In the same financial institution where Marlene has her checking account, the Sullivans have $600 in a passbook savings account that earns 5.5 percent interest. If the savings account balance exceeded $1,000, they would earn 6 percent. If the balance stayed above $1,000, they would not have to pay the monthly service charge on Marlene's checking account. This financial institution has a

THE CHANGING ENVIRONMENT OF FINANCIAL SERVICES

- Factors that Influence the Availability of Financial Services

In the past, people often had their savings, checking, and loan accounts at the bank closest to their home or their place of work. Also, there was a limited choice of financial institutions and services. For example, commercial banks were the only organizations that offered checking accounts and most homeowners obtained a mortgage through a savings and loan association. Recently, changing laws, changing economic conditions, and computerized information systems have created a financial services marketplace very different from "the good old days."

Legislative Actions

In the early 1980s, two congressional actions significantly changed the role of banks and other financial institutions. The Depository Institutions Deregulation and Monetary Control Act of 1980 made it possible for nonbank financial institutions to offer checking accounts and other services previously limited to banks. It also eliminated restrictions on the amount that an institution could pay savers. In 1982, the Garn-St. Germain Depository Institutions Act went further in the deregulation of financial institutions by allowing banks and other organizations to merge. This legislation opened the financial services marketplace to a variety of institutions competing for your banking business. The many advertisements in newspapers and magazines offering savings, checking, and investing opportunities are evidence of the changes

program that moves money from checking to savings. The program would allow the Sullivans to increase their savings and work toward a secure financial future.

Bill has his checking account at a bank offering an electronic money system that allows a customer to obtain cash at many locations, 24 hours a day. Bill believes that this feature is valuable when cash is needed to cover business expenses and personal spending. For an additional monthly fee, the bank would also provide Bill with a credit card, a safe-deposit box, and a single monthly statement summarizing all transactions.

While most people plan their spending for living expenses, few plan their use of financial services. Therefore, many people are charged high fees for checking accounts and earn low interest on their savings. Despite a wide choice of financial institutions and services, you can learn to compare their costs and benefits. Your awareness of financial services and your ability to evaluate them are vital skills for a healthy personal economic future.

due to deregulation. Specifically, deregulation of financial institutions has resulted in new competitors, new services, changing costs and benefits, and name changes for financial institutions.

New Competitors. Many types of businesses, such as insurance companies, investment brokers, and credit card companies, have become involved in financial services that were previously limited to banks. At the same time, banks have expanded their competitive efforts by opening offices that specialize in such financial services as investments, insurance, or real estate. Increased competition has included the opening of many limited-service offices, sometimes called *nonbank banks*. These limited-service offices specialize in a particular banking activity such as savings or personal loans to avoid certain regulations that still affect full-service banks. Nonbank banks have been started by companies involved in other types of business, such as Sears, General Motors, and Dreyfus.[1]

New Services. Interest on checking accounts, variable rate loans, and savings plans with earnings based on market interest rates are the results of the changing financial services environment. The availability of these new

[1]Norman Brown, "Manage Your Money like a Pro," *Consumers Digest*, September 1986, p. 22.

From *The Wall Street Journal*, with permission of Cartoon Features Syndicate.

banking services has allowed consumers to avoid paying high interest rates on certain types of loans while also receiving competitive returns on their savings. But the new services have also created a more complex marketplace in which consumers have many more alternatives from which to choose.

Changing Benefits and Rates. Early in 1986, the limit on interest rates for savings accounts was eliminated. Financial institutions can now pay savers interest based on changing market interest rates. As savers received higher earnings on deposited money, the cost of checking accounts increased because of higher service charges and increased minimum balances. Many low-income consumers who needed basic banking services such as checking could no longer afford this luxury.

Name Changes. Many savings and loan associations are taking advantage of the banking revolution by revising their names to better reflect the services they offer. Since 1984, over 100 of these organizations have added the word *bank* to their company names. In 1983, the Charleston Federal Savings and Loan in West Virginia became the Magnet Bank, FSB (federal savings bank). This name change is effective in communicating a sense of trust among customers.[2]

Economic Conditions

Changing interest rates, changing consumer prices, and other economic factors are major influences on the availability and use of financial services. In the late 1970s and early 1980s, high interest rates strongly affected the savings and investment choices of consumers. Savers wanted to earn interest rates that exceeded cost-of-living increases. At the same time, lenders had to charge rates that covered their money costs. This situation resulted in savings plans in which earnings were based on current market interest rates and in loans whose interest rates varied over the life of the borrowing period.

As you read this textbook, interest rates and inflation rates are likely to change. For successful financial planning, you need to be aware of the current trends and future prospects for interest rates. You can learn about these trends and prospects by reading articles in *The Wall Street Journal*, the business section of daily newspapers, and various business periodicals such as *Business Week* and *Forbes*.

Technology

In the past, banking transactions had to be conducted during set business hours. Computerized information systems now make 24-hour banking possible. Cash is now available from terminals in food stores, and you can make payments through a home banking system.

Electronic funds transfer (EFT) is a system of making payments and recording receipts through the use of computerized data rather than cash and checks. This process involves the use of an **EFT card**, or debit card, which is a plastic access card needed to make computerized banking transactions. The EFT card is called a *debit* card, as opposed to a *credit* card, because when you use it, you are spending existing funds rather than borrowing additional money. Using an EFT card is similar to writing a check, with the amount of payment automatically deducted from your account. This automatic transfer of funds eliminates the *float*, the time delay between the writing of a check and the deduction of the amount from your account.

The main component of the EFT system is the **automatic teller machine (ATM)**, which is a computer terminal at a financial institution or some other location. This terminal allows customers to conduct banking transactions such as transferring amounts among savings, checking, and loan accounts. Some financial institutions have made the banking terminal very convenient by offering ATMobiles that travel to the customers at their place of employment or some other location.

[2]"When Is a Bank Not a Bank?" *Changing Times*, June 1986, p. 7.

The point-of-sale (POS) terminal is a computer device at a store that allows customers to transfer funds from their account to the store's account to pay for purchases. The process is like writing a check, but the money is transferred between accounts in seconds rather than in days. Figure 4–1 shows the process used in various EFT transactions, including banking and making electronic payments at home.

The development of the *smart card* could expand the capabilities of existing electronic banking systems. This device has a miniature microcomputer chip for activating and storing data on financial transactions. The smart card

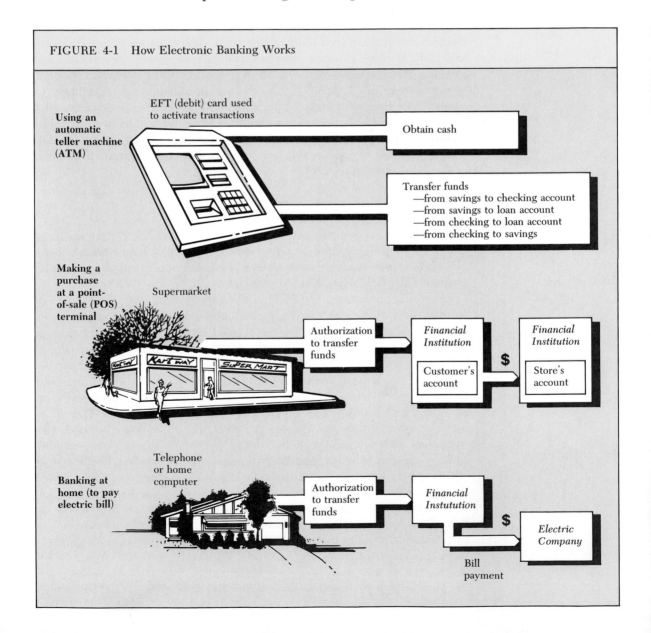

FIGURE 4-1   How Electronic Banking Works

Using an automatic teller machine (ATM)

EFT (debit) card used to activate transactions

Obtain cash

Transfer funds
—from savings to checking account
—from savings to loan account
—from checking to loan account
—from checking to savings

Making a purchase at a point-of-sale (POS) terminal

Supermarket

Authorization to transfer funds

Financial Institution

Customer's account

$

Financial Institution

Store's account

Banking at home (to pay electric bill)

Telephone or home computer

Authorization to transfer funds

Financial Instutution

$

Electric Company

Bill payment

can retain extensive personal and financial information and could replace your need for identification cards, cash credit cards, and a checkbook. The storage of your fingerprints on the computer chip would reduce the unauthorized use of your card.

The technology of banking will continue to evolve as the effort to offer new services intensifies among financial institutions.

OPERATIONS OF FINANCIAL INSTITUTIONS

Financial institutions accept, store, and use money for the benefit of customers and owners. These main activities of financial institutions may be expressed as follows:

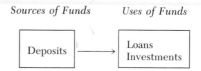

Sources of Funds   Uses of Funds

Deposits ⟶ Loans Investments

- Business Operations of Financial Institutions

The main sources of funds are deposits made by individuals, businesses, governments, and other financial institutions, including foreign companies and banks. **Demand deposits** are money held in checking accounts. These funds are very liquid and can quickly flow out of the financial institution. **Time deposits** represent savings accounts and certificates. This money will be on deposit longer than funds in checking accounts.

The money in financial institutions must be put to work so that they can pay interest to savers and earn profit for stockholders. The main interest-earning activities of financial institutions are making loans and investments. Money is lent to businesses and individuals for commercial needs, real estate purchases, consumer buying, and agricultural pursuits. It is also used to purchase investments, mainly government securities. Earnings from loans and investments allow banks and other financial institutions to pay interest on savings, to expand their activities and services, and to grow.

TYPES OF FINANCIAL INSTITUTIONS

Despite significant changes in the banking environment, many of the financial institutions with which you are familiar still serve your needs. Most of these institutions have expanded their services to remain competitive. Commercial banks, thrift institutions, credit unions, and investment companies are quite evident. But these institutions have been joined by others in the banking marketplace.

Commercial Banks

- Common Types of Financial Institutions Used by Consumers

Traditionally, the **commercial bank** has offered the widest range of financial services to individuals, businesses, and government agencies. In addition to checking, savings, and lending services, commercial banks offer most of the services listed in Figure 4–2. Commercial banks are organized as corporations, with individual investors contributing the capital they need to

---

FIGURE 4-2   An Overview of Financial Services

Savings	Regular (passbook) savings accounts
	Certificates of deposit
	Money market accounts
	U.S. savings bonds
	Individual retirement accounts (IRA)
Payment services	Checking accounts
	NOW accounts
	SuperNOW accounts
	Electronic funds transfer
	Payments by telephone
	Cashier's checks, money orders
	Traveler's checks
Borrowing	Cash loans for automobiles, education, home improvement, and other purposes
	All-purpose credit cards
	Mortgages
	Overdraft protection
Other services	Insurance (automobile, home, life, and health)
	Investments (stocks, bonds, mutual funds, government securities)
	Financial management (trust service, tax preparation, investment advice, retirement accounts)
	Safe-deposit boxes
	Foreign currency exchange
	Credit and budget counseling
	Estate planning

---

operate. National banks are chartered by the federal government; state banks, by state governments. State-chartered banks have fewer restrictions placed on them by their regulators.

Thrift Institutions

While the commercial bank serves mainly businesses and customers with large amounts of money, the **savings and loan association** specializes in savings accounts and loans for mortgages. In recent years, savings and loan associations have expanded their offerings to include interest-bearing checking accounts, specialized savings plans, loans to businesses, and other investment and financial planning services. Like banks, savings and loan associations have either federal or state charters.

Another financial institution that concentrates on serving individuals is the **mutual savings bank,** which is owned by depositors and, like the savings and loan association, specializes in savings and mortgages. Mutual savings banks are located mainly in the northeastern United States. Unlike the profits of other types of financial institutions, the profits of a mutual savings bank go to the depositors rather than to stockholders.

Credit Unions

Another user-owned financial institution is the **credit union,** a nonprofit, cooperative organization. Traditionally, credit union members had to have a common bond such as a work, church, or community affiliation. As the common bond restriction was loosened, the membership of credit unions increased. Today, over 50 million people belong to credit unions.

Credit unions offer low-cost loans and high earnings rates on savings. Many credit unions paid 7 percent on savings accounts when other financial institutions were paying between 5 and 6 percent. Most observers believe that credit unions provide more personal service than other financial institutions. Many credit unions have expanded their services to include checking accounts, credit cards, mortgages, retirement accounts, investment services, and even electronic payment systems.

Investment Companies

In recent years, various investment companies, also referred to as *mutual funds,* have become involved in banking-type activities. A common service of these organizations is the **money market fund,** a combination savings-investment plan in which the investment company uses your money to purchase a variety of financial instruments. Your earnings are based on the interest received by the investment company. The money market fund usually pays higher interest rates than regular savings accounts, but it is not insured. Investors in money market funds are usually allowed to write a limited number of checks on their accounts. The expanded services of investment companies are only one example of the wider range of financial activities now being engaged in by types of businesses other than the traditional financial institutions.

Financial Supermarkets

- Services Offered by Financial Supermarkets

Such financial services as savings, checking, and borrowing have traditionally been offered only by banks and related financial institutions. When you wanted to buy insurance, make a stock investment, or purchase a home, you had to deal with a separate business to meet each of these financial needs. Today, the **financial supermarket**—a large business operation—offers a complete range of financial services. Such organizations allow you to save, make payments, take out loans, apply for a credit card, buy investment securities, insure your property, and purchase real estate through one office. While many people are familiar with the financial supermarkets, some concern has been expressed that a few of the large ones will dominate the financial industry if the smaller financial institutions are unable to compete with them.

Which Firms Are the Financial Supermarkets? All types of large financial services organizations as well as other businesses are expanding their activities to offer banking and related financial services. The term *financial supermarket* is used to describe a variety of companies, including:

- Banks such as BankAmerica and Citicorp, which have become involved in investments, real estate, and insurance.
- Consumer credit companies such as American Express, which has expanded its services into real estate and investment planning, or Household Financial Services, which has acquired control of a bank and an insurance company.
- Retail businesses such as Sears, J. C. Penney, and K mart, which offer various financial services in selected stores. The Sears financial network consists of Allstate Insurance; Dean Witter, an investment brokerage company; Coldwell Banker, which sells real estate; Sears Savings Bank; and Discover, an all-purpose credit card.
- Insurance companies such as Prudential and John Hancock, which have made a concentrated effort to compete in the financial planning and investment securities markets.
- Investment companies such as Merrill Lynch, Dreyfus, and E. F. Hutton, which offer services to meet the many financial needs of customers.

Should You Use a Financial Supermarket? The biggest advantage of financial supermarkets seems to be the convenience of one-stop shopping. Through a financial supermarket, you can take care of all your financial

Courtesy of K mart.

needs, and even buy clothes or automotive products, at a single location. The price of this convenience may be higher costs and less personal service. The large financial businesses are able to compete in a manner that may reduce the number of organizations offering financial services, resulting in fewer choices for consumers in the long run. As for personal service, you must decide what you are willing to give up in order to have convenience.

SELECTING A FINANCIAL INSTITUTION

As you use financial services, you must decide what you want from the organization that will serve your needs. Because the financial marketplace is constantly changing, you must assess the various services and other factors before selecting the organization that will handle your financial matters.

- Factors to Consider when Selecting a Financial Institution

An Overview of Financial Services

The basic concerns of every financial services customer are simple. Where can I get the best return on my savings? How can I minimize the cost of checking? Will I be able to borrow money when I need it? While the number and types of financial services seem to increase every day, these services may be grouped into the basic categories of savings, payment services, borrowing, other financial services, and all-purpose accounts.

Savings. The safe storage of funds for future use is a basic need of every individual. The selection of a savings plan requires consideration of the growth of your money, liquidity, safety, and convenience. These factors are discussed later in this chapter.

Payment Services. The ability to transfer money to others is a necessity for conducting business. Checking accounts and other types of payments will be covered in the final section of this chapter.

Borrowing. Most people use credit sometime during their lives. Credit alternatives range from short-term accounts such as credit cards and cash loans, to long-term borrowing in the form of a home mortgage. The types and costs of credit are discussed in Chapters 5 and 6.

Other Financial Services. Insurance protection, investing for the future, real estate purchases, tax assistance, and financial planning are additional services that may be needed for a successful economic existence. Many financial plans entail the need to have someone else manage your funds. A **trust** is a legal agreement that provides for the management and control of assets by one party for the benefit of another. This type of arrangement is most commonly created through a commercial bank or a lawyer. A trust may be desirable when parents want to set aside certain funds for their children's education. The investments and money in the trust would be managed by a bank, with the necessary amounts going to the children for their educational expenses.

All-Purpose Accounts. To simplify the maze of financial services and to attract customers, many financial institutions offer all-in-one accounts. A **central management account (CMA)**, or central asset account, provides a complete financial services program for a single fee. CMAs were first offered by investment brokers as a method of combining various security investments into a single account. Now banks and other financial institutions offer this service. The all-purpose account will usually include the following:

- A minimum balance of $5,000 or more.
- A checking account.
- One or more all-purpose credit cards.
- A line of credit to obtain quick cash loans.
- Access to various types of investments, such as stocks, bonds, mutual funds, commodities, and government securities.
- Use of an electronic funds transfer system.
- A *sweep* feature in which cash that is not currently invested or needed in the checking account earns a money market interest rate.
- A single monthly statement that summarizes all aspects of the account.

In mid-1986, the Chemical Bank of New York announced its ChemPlus account, which combined checking, saving, and credit card services. This

---

In the Real World
Special Banking Privileges

T ired of waiting in line at the bank? Just keep a balance of $25,000 in your checking account, and you are likely to receive special attention.

To attract the current and future business of affluent customers, financial institutions such as BankAmerica and Chase Manhattan offer special sitting rooms with elegant decor for their preferred customers. Coffee is served in fine china, and depositors have immediate access to top-level staff members. This type of service is reserved for individuals with income over $100,000 and a net worth approaching $1 million.

More important to these financial institutions than the current deposits of such clients are the borrowing, investment, and trust services that clients of this kind may use in the future. The potential earnings for the financial institution are quite sizable. Therefore, preferred customers are assigned a personal banker with a direct telephone line.

Can the less affluent reduce the time spent in bank lines? Citibank and other financial institutions are offering you a special teller with a minimum deposit of only $2,000!

Sources: "Banking for the Privileged," *Bottom Line/Personal*, December 30, 1984, pp. 7–8; and Jeff and Marie Blyskal, "How Good Is Your Bank?" *New York*, March 7, 1983, pp. 40–41.

all-purpose account is similar to those offered by other large banks such as Citibank and Chase Manhattan. Beside paying top earnings on the savings portion of the account, Chemical plans to offer users the opportunity to obtain discounts on other financial services.[3]

Factors that Affect Choice

If everyone wanted personal financial service, we would have credit unions only. If everyone wanted one-stop shopping, financial supermarkets would dominate the industry. But since consumers have different needs and concerns, you will probably consider a variety of factors when you are selecting a financial institution.

The services offered by the institution are likely to be a primary concern. Table 4–1 suggests some of the best services that may be available. Personal service is also important to many customers. You may want a strong working relationship with the institution's staff.

TABLE 4-1   The 10 Best Financial Services

In sorting through the many financial services available to consumers, the following are seen as the most beneficial:

1. *Fee waivers.* The cost of checking accounts, cashier's checks, and other payment services may be avoided if you do business at certain financial institutions
2. *Free checks.* To attract customers, some institutions do not charge for the printing of checks.
3. *Immediate credit.* Since most financial institutions have a waiting period for deposited checks, see whether you can write checks immediately against your deposits.
4. *Check protection.* This involves an advance of funds to cover checks written in excess of the account balance.
5. *Overdraft privileges.* Preferred customers are notified that their checking account is overdrawn; this enables them to avoid an overdraft fee.
6. *Loan services.* Preferred customers can qualify for lower than usual borrowing rates and may not be charged for the preparation of loan documents.
7. *Financial advice.* Being a regular customer at certain financial institutions can result in suggestions about investments, tax matters, and potential clients for your business.
8. *Avoiding lines.* Such methods as messenger services, computer banking terminals, and banking by mail can save time.
9. *Avoiding red tape.* Preferred clients of financial institutions can usually receive quick assistance with statement errors, lost credit cards, and other financial difficulties.
10. *Banking at home.* Computerized linkups that allow you to handle all types of financial transactions from your home or office are likely to become common.

Source: "The Ten Best Services," *Sylvia Porter's Personal Finance,* October 1985, pp. 91–93.

---

[3]Sarah Stiansen, "Chemical Pushes Integrated Account," *Adweek,* May 12, 1986, p. 1.

Convenience is another consideration. It is provided by convenient business hours, conveniently located branch offices and automatic teller machines, and banking by mail service. Convenience and service have a cost; be sure to compare the fees and other charges at several financial institutions.

Finally, safety factors and the interest rates of the business should be assessed. Obtain information on the earnings you will receive on your savings and checking accounts and on the amount you will pay for borrowed funds. Most financial institutions have deposit insurance to protect customers against losses, but not all of these institutions are insured by federal government programs. Investigate the type of protection that your money will have.

Your selection of a financial institution should be based on a combination of your needs and conditions in the financial services marketplace. The decision you reach should be based on valid information. Never assume that one financial institution will provide a better interest rate or service than another. You need to compare the earnings on savings and the costs of loans at banks, savings and loan associations, and credit unions with those of other financial institutions.

USING SAVINGS SERVICES

Savings is one of your basic financial needs. To best meet this need, you should evaluate and understand the savings choices that are available.

Evaluating Savings Alternatives

- Factors to Consider when Choosing a Savings Plan

Your selection of a savings plan will be influenced by the rate of return, the interest method, liquidity, safety, and restrictions and costs.

Rate of Return. Your earnings on savings are likely to be an important consideration. Earnings can be measured by the **rate of return,** or yield, which is the percentage of increase in the value of your savings due to earned interest. For example, a $100 savings account that earned $5 after a year would have a rate of return, or yield, of 5 percent. This rate of return was determined by dividing the interest earned ($5) by the amount in the savings account ($100).

Since interest is usually paid more often than once a year, the actual yield on your savings will be greater than the stated interest rate. **Compounding** refers to interest that is earned on previously earned interest. Each time that interest is added to your savings, the next interest is computed on the basis of the new amount in the account. The more frequent the compounding, the higher your rate of return, or effective yield, will be. For example, $100 in a savings account that earns 6 percent compounded annually will increase $6 after a year. But the same $100 in a 6 percent account compounded daily will earn $6.19 for the year. With various numbers of compounding periods per year, 6 percent has different effective yields:

6 percent compounded annually has an effective yield of 6.00 percent.

6 percent compounded quarterly has an effective yield of 6.14 percent.

6 percent compounded monthly has an effective yield of 6.17 percent.

6 percent compounded weekly has an effective yield of 6.18 percent.

6 percent compounded daily has an effective yield of 6.19 percent.

Although these differences may not seem like much, with large amounts in savings for long periods of time, the higher yields will result in many more dollars earned.

The rate of return you earn on your savings should be compared with the inflation rate. When the inflation rate was over 10 percent, people whose money in savings accounts was earning 5 or 6 percent were experiencing a loss in the buying power of that money. In general, as inflation increases, the interest rates offered to savers also increase; this gives you an opportunity to select a savings option that will minimize the erosion of your dollars on deposit.

Interest Method. The balance used for interest computation will affect the earnings on your savings. Financial institutions use different methods to determine the amount that will be used to compute earnings. These methods include:

- *Day of deposit to day of withdrawal (DD/DW).* Your money earns interest every day that it is on deposit. In general, DD/DW is the most advantageous method for savers.
- *Last in, first out (LIFO).* This method assumes that withdrawals are deducted from the most recent deposits. These deposits would not earn interest if withdrawals were made on them.
- *First in, first out (FIFO).* This method deducts withdrawals from either the beginning balance of the period or the earliest deposit. In either case, an amount on deposit early in the interest period would earn nothing if it were withdrawn before the end of the compounding period.
- *Low balance.* Interest is based on the lowest balance in the account during the interest period. This method is the least desirable for savers since it results in the fewest dollars earned.

In addition to these four interest computation methods, there are combination methods that can further complicate your savings decision. Studies have been conducted on the interest obtained from the same amounts in savings accounts at different institutions. As a result of different interest computation techniques, three-month earnings ranged from $79.13 to $29.25 in one such study.

Liquidity. Liquidity allows you to withdraw your money on short notice. Some savings plans have penalties for early withdrawal. With certain types of savings certificates and accounts, early withdrawal may be penalized by a loss of interest or a lower earnings rate.

From *The Wall Street Journal*, with permission of Cartoon Features Syndicate.

Safety. Most savings plans at banks, savings and loan associations, and credit unions are insured by agencies affiliated with the federal government. This protection prevents a loss of money due to the failure of the insured institution. Coverage for banks is provided by the Federal Deposit Insurance Corporation (FDIC); for savings and loan associations, by the Federal Savings and Loan Insurance Corporation (FSLIC); and for credit unions, by the National Credit Union Administration (NCUA).

In recent years, more financial institutions have failed than at any other time since the 1930s. However, savers with deposits in federally insured institutions have not lost any money. Depositors of failed organizations have either been paid the amount in their account or have had the account taken over by a financially stable institution.

Since not all financial institutions have federal deposit insurance, investigate this matter when you are selecting a savings plan. Additional information on the regulation and consumer protection aspects of financial institutions is included in Appendix D.

Restrictions and Costs. Other limitations can affect your choice of a savings program. For example, there may be a delay between the time interest is earned and the time it is added to your account. This means that it will not be available for your immediate use. Also, some institutions charge a transaction fee for each deposit or withdrawal. These fees can become expensive when several transactions are made each month.

Some institutions have promotions offering a *free* gift when a certain savings amount is deposited. For this gift, you will probably have to leave your money on deposit for a certain time period; or you may receive less interest, since some of the institution's earnings may be used to cover the cost of the free gifts. Economists tell us that "there is no such thing as a free lunch"; the same holds true for toasters and television sets.

Types of Savings Plans

● Types of Savings Instruments Available to Consumers

Deregulation of savings rates and other changes in financial services have created a wide choice of savings alternatives (see Table 4–2). The number of savings plans may seem overwhelming, but they can be grouped into regular

TABLE 4-2 Savings Alternatives

Type of Account	Benefits	Restrictions
Regular savings accounts/ passbook accounts/share accounts (credit unions)	Low minimum balance Ease of withdrawal Insured	Low rate of return
Certificates of deposit	Good rate of return Insured	Penalty for early withdrawal Minimum deposit
NOW accounts/ share drafts (credit unions)	Checking privileges Interest earned Insured	Service charge for going below minimum balance Cost for printing checks; other fees may apply
SuperNOW accounts	Checking privileges Good rate of return Insured	High minimum balance Low return if below a certain balance
Money market accounts	Good rate of return (based on current interest rates) Allows some check writing Insured	High minimum balance No interest or service charge if below a certain balance
Money market funds	Good rate of return (based on current interest rates) Some check writing	Minimum balance Not insured
Individual retirement accounts (IRAs)	Taxes deferred on earnings May be insured (depends on type of savings plan used— see above)	Tax penalty if withdrawn before certain age
U.S. savings bonds	Fairly good rate of return (varies with current interest rates) Low minimum deposit Government guaranteed Exempt from state and local income taxes	Long maturity; penalty for withdrawal before five years

savings accounts, club accounts, certificates of deposit, interest-earning checking accounts, money market accounts, and savings bonds.

Regular Savings Accounts. Traditionally referred to as passbook accounts, since savers had a small book showing deposits and withdrawals, regular savings accounts usually involve a low or no minimum balance and allow savers to withdraw money as it is needed. The rate earned on regular savings accounts is usually low. Early in 1986, after interest rates on savings were deregulated, many institutions established an agreement for regular passbook savings in which earnings would vary based on the balance in the account.[4] A typical situation could be as follows:

Balance of . . .	Would Earn . . .
Less than $500	No interest
$500–$9,999	5¾%
$10,000–$24,999	6¼%
$25,000–$49,999	6½%
More than $50,000	6¾%

Banks, savings and loan associations, and most other financial institutions offer passbook savings plans. **A share account** is a regular savings account at a credit union.

Club Accounts. Club accounts are savings plans designed for a certain goal or a certain time of the year. Examples are vacation or Christmas club accounts in which a person makes a weekly deposit and then withdraws a large sum after a set time period, usually a year. Interest on club accounts may be very low; savers are therefore encouraged to compare them with other savings alternatives.

Certificates of Deposit. Higher earnings result from leaving money on deposit longer. **A certificate of deposit** is a savings plan that requires you to leave a certain amount on deposit for a set time period in order to earn a certain interest rate. Although these time deposits are an attractive savings alternative, a penalty for early withdrawal usually applies. This penalty will reduce the amount earned on savings.

Interest-Earning Checking Accounts. A variety of checking accounts can be used as savings vehicles. These interest-earning accounts will be discussed in the next section of this chapter.

Money Market Accounts. To meet consumer demands for higher savings rates, federal legislation created an account with a floating interest rate. A **money market account** is a savings plan that has a minimum balance and earnings based on market interest rates. Earnings on money market accounts will vary based on interest rates such as those shown in Figure 4–3.

[4]"Why Bank Passbooks Are Still Bad Deals," *Money*, May 1986, p. 14.

6.17%   **9.5%**

FIGURE 4-3   Which Interest Rate Are You Talking About?   **13.1%**

10.43%   **11%**

When people say interest rates have increased or decreased, they could be referring to one or more of the following:

	1965*	1970	1975	1980	1985	1986
Prime rate—an indication of the rate charged large corporations by banks	4.53%	7.91%	7.85%	15.26%	9.93%	8.33%
Discount rate—the rate financial institutions are charged to borrow funds from Federal Reserve banks	4.03	5.95	6.25	11.77	7.69	6.33
T-bill rate—the yield on short-term (13 weeks) U.S. government debt obligations	3.95	6.39	5.78	11.43	7.48	5.98
Treasury bond rate—the yield on long-term (20 years) U.S. government debt obligations	4.27	6.86	8.19	11.39	10.97	7.85
Mortgage rate—the amount being paid by individuals to borrow for the purchase of a new home	5.81	8.45	9.00	12.66	11.58	9.82
Corporate bond rate—the cost of borrowing for large U.S. corporations	4.49	8.04	8.83	11.94	11.37	9.02
Certificate of deposit rate—the rate for six-month time deposits at savings institutions	4.43	7.65	6.89	12.99	8.25	6.51

*These rates represent an annual average for the various categories for the year indicated.

Sources: Board of Governors of the Federal Reserve System and the United States League of Savings Institutions.

Money market accounts allow savers to write a limited number of checks to make large payments or to transfer money to other accounts.

The main difference between the money market *account* and the previously discussed money market *fund* is the financial institution. While money market accounts are offered by banks and savings and loan associations, money market funds are products of investment and insurance companies. Although money market funds are not covered by federal deposit insurance, they are quite safe since their investments usually consist of government securities and the securities of reputable companies.

U.S. Savings Bonds. In the past, buying savings bonds was a patriotic act rather than a wise savings choice. But as interest rates rose, U.S. savings bonds became less attractive. In order to compete with other savings plans, the Treasury Department now uses a floating interest rate on savings bonds. Earnings rise and fall based on changes in the level of interest rates. One drawback of U.S. savings bonds is that savers earn less if the bonds are redeemed within five years of purchase. U.S. savings bonds have tax advantages: the interest they earn is exempt from state and local taxes, and you do not have to pay the federal income tax on it until the bonds mature or are redeemed.

CHOOSING AND USING A CHECKING ACCOUNT

Each day, millions of checks are used to transfer payments among individuals and businesses. With more than 90 percent of business transactions conducted by check, a checking account is a necessity for most people. Selecting and using a checking account should be based on the types available and consideration of certain factors.

Different Types of Checking Accounts

- Types of Checking Accounts

As with other financial services, the types and availability of checking accounts have increased. Several institutions offer regular, special, and interest-bearing checking accounts.

Regular Checking Accounts. A regular checking account does not earn interest and usually has a monthly service charge. At many institutions, you may avoid the service charge by maintaining a minimum balance in the account or by keeping a certain amount in savings at the same financial institution. In recent years, minimum balances on regular checking accounts have increased, causing higher cost for consumers as larger amounts of money are in an account not earning interest.

Special Checking Accounts. An activity account is designed for people who write few checks. Customers are charged on a per check basis instead of being required to maintain a minimum balance or to pay a set monthly fee.

For a single monthly fee, a package account provides checking as well as other financial services such as a safe-deposit box, traveler's checks, low-rate loans, and travel insurance. Financial experts observe that package accounts benefit only those individuals—a small group—who make constant use of the services included in the program.

Interest-Bearing Checking Accounts. Major changes in checking accounts occurred when financial institutions were allowed to pay interest on them. The **NOW account** (NOW is an abbreviation for negotiable orders of withdrawal) is a checking account that earns interest. Like regular checking accounts, NOW accounts usually require a minimum balance. If your account balance falls below this amount, you may not earn interest and often you are assessed a service charge.

The **share draft account** is an interest-bearing checking account at a credit union. Credit union members write credits, called share drafts, against their account balance. Share draft accounts usually have fewer restrictions than other types of interest-bearing checking accounts.

The **superNOW account** benefits customers who keep large amounts in their checking account. This interest-bearing checking account earns interest higher than that earned by regular savings accounts. Money in a Super-NOW account earns the same rate as money in a NOW account except for amounts above a certain balance. For those amounts, the customer is paid a rate based on market interest rates.

Selecting the Best Checking Account

Variations and combinations of checking accounts should be evaluated on the basis of restrictions, costs, interest, and special services.

Restrictions. Beside minimum balances, most financial institutions require a holding period for deposited checks. That is, they require a period of time for checks to clear before you are allowed to use the funds they represent. Several state legislatures have enacted laws to limit this holding period; similar legislation has been considered by Congress.

Costs. Nearly all financial institutions require a minimum balance or service charges for checking accounts. When using an interest-bearing checking account, you will need to compare your earnings with any service charge or fee. Also consider the cost of lost or reduced interest due to the minimum balance.

Checking account fees have increased in recent years. Since the early 1980s, such items as check printing, overdraft fees, and stop-payment orders have doubled or tripled in cost at some institutions.

Interest. As discussed earlier in this chapter, the interest rate, the frequency of compounding, and the interest computation method will affect the earnings on your checking account.

Special Services. Financial institutions may offer checking account customers such extra services as 24-hour teller machines and home banking services.

Financial institutions are attempting to reduce the paper and postage costs associated with checking accounts. One solution is not to return canceled checks to customers. Microfilm is then used by the financial institution to store checks, and customers are provided with statements summarizing the checks written. If a customer requests a copy of a canceled check, the institution reproduces the copy from its microfilm file for a fee.

Overdraft protection is an automatic loan made to checking account customers to cover checks written in excess of the available balance. This service is convenient but costly. Most overdraft plans make loans based on $50 or $100 increments. An overdraft of just a dollar might trigger a $50 loan and the corresponding finance charges.

Your Checking Account in Action

• Activities Involved in Using a Checking Account

After you select a checking account by considering the questions in Table 4–3, several procedures are involved in using your account. These procedures include opening the account, making deposits, writing checks, reconciling the account, and using other forms of payment.

Opening a Checking Account. Deciding on the owner of the account is your starting point for opening a checking account. An individual account allows only one person to write checks on the account. A joint account has two or more owners, with any authorized person allowed to write checks.

Technology for Today
Banking at Home

Each year, more and more individuals are handling their financial transactions at home. When you do this, instead of writing checks, licking envelopes, and purchasing postage stamps, you process your payments electronically by pressing one or two buttons. You can also have a regular payment, such as your mortgage payment or a loan payment, automatically processed each month, or you can have various bills paid while you are on vacation. In the future, banking-at-home arrangements will allow customers to obtain current balance information, apply for loans, and request special assistance from the financial institution.

The convenience of home banking does have costs. Since your payments are transferred instantly, there is no float— that is, no time elapses between your authorization of a payment and the deduction of that amount from your account. Therefore, as soon as you authorize a payment, you will cease to earn interest on the funds whose payment you have authorized. Also, there is usually a monthly fee for home banking service plus charges for the use of computer time. These costs assume that you already have the equipment needed to access the system.

The services available from your financial institution will continue to expand as home banking gains in popularity. Budgeting assistance, tax advice, and investment information will be available to certain customers. Ultimately, everyone may have a bank branch office in his or her living room.

TABLE 4-3   Choosing the Best Checking Account

The following items should be considered when you are selecting a checking account:

1. What are the location and hours of the financial institution? Is a 24-hour banking machine available at various locations?
2. What minimum balance is required to avoid a service charge and/or earn interest on the account? What is the monthly service charge for falling below the minimum balance?
3. Are fees charged for each check or deposit?
4. Does the account earn interest? At what rate? What method is used to compute interest?
5. Do certain groups (students, senior citizens, employees of certain companies) qualify for free or reduced-rate checking accounts?
6. What other services are available to checking account customers—overdraft protection, traveler's checks, money orders, and so on?
7. What fees are charged for the printing of checks, stop-payment orders, overdrafts, and certified checks?
8. How long does the financial institution require deposited checks to be held before you can draw funds against them?
9. Will canceled checks be returned? If not, what fee is charged for obtaining a copy of a canceled check?
10. Does the financial institution offer an electronic transfer and payment system by telephone?

With both an individual account and a joint account, a signature card is required. This document is a record of the official signatures of the persons who are authorized to write checks on an account.

Making Deposits. A deposit ticket is the form used for adding money to your checking account (see Figure 4–4). On this document, you list the amount of the cash and the checks you are depositing. Each check you deposit requires an endorsement, which consists of your signature on the back of the check to authorize the transfer of the funds into your account. Three common endorsements are:

- A *blank endorsement* is your signature. This endorsement form should be used only when you are actually depositing or cashing a check, since once the back of the check has been signed, the check can be cashed by anyone.
- A *restrictive endorsement* consists of the words *for deposit only* followed by your signature. This endorsement is especially useful when you are depositing checks by mail.
- A *special endorsement* allows you to transfer a check to another person or organization. In this endorsement form, the words *pay to the order of* are followed by the name of the person to whom you want to give the check and then by your signature.

FIGURE 4-4

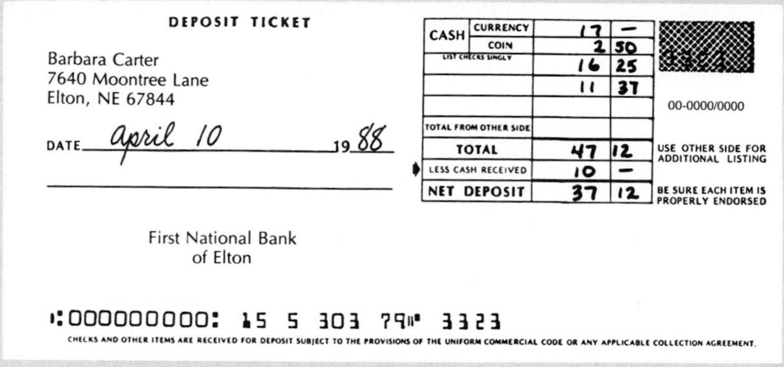

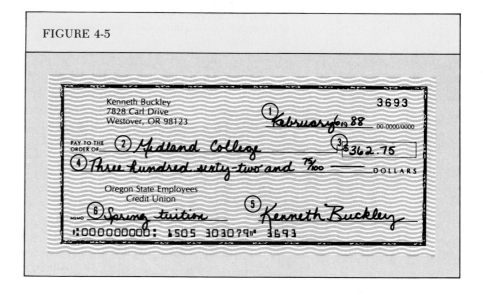

DEPOSIT TICKET

Barbara Carter
7640 Moontree Lane
Elton, NE 67844

DATE April 10 19 88

First National Bank
of Elton

CASH	CURRENCY	17	—
	COIN	2	50
LIST CHECKS SINGLY		16	25
		11	37
TOTAL FROM OTHER SIDE			
TOTAL		47	12
LESS CASH RECEIVED		10	—
NET DEPOSIT		37	12

00-0000/0000

USE OTHER SIDE FOR ADDITIONAL LISTING

BE SURE EACH ITEM IS PROPERLY ENDORSED

⑆000000000⑆ 15 5 303 79⑈ 3323

CHECKS AND OTHER ITEMS ARE RECEIVED FOR DEPOSIT SUBJECT TO THE PROVISIONS OF THE UNIFORM COMMERCIAL CODE OR ANY APPLICABLE COLLECTION AGREEMENT.

FIGURE 4-5

Kenneth Buckley
7828 Carl Drive
Westover, OR 98123

3693

(1) February 6 19 88

00-0000/0000

PAY TO THE ORDER OF (2) Midland College (3) $362.75

(4) Three hundred sixty-two and 75/100 DOLLARS

Oregon State Employees
Credit Union

MEMO (6) Spring tuition (5) Kenneth Buckley

⑆000000000⑆ 1505 303079⑈ 3693

Writing a Check. Before writing a check, record the information in your check register and deduct the amount of the check from your balance. Otherwise, you will think that you have more money available than you really do.

The procedure for proper check writing, displayed in Figure 4–5, consists of the following steps:

1. Record the current date.
2. Write the name of the person or organization that is receiving the payment.

3. Record the amount of the check in figures.
4. Write the amount of the check in words; checks for less than a dollar should be written as, say, "only 79 cents," with the word *dollars* on the check crossed out.
5. Sign the check the same way you signed the signature card when you opened your account.
6. Make a note of the reason for payment, if desired.

Maintaining a Checking Account. Each month, you will receive a *bank statement*, which is a summary of transactions for a checking account. This document reports deposits made, checks paid, interest earned, and fees for such things as service charges and the printing of checks. The balance reported on the bank statement will probably be different from the balance in your checkbook. The reasons for the difference are checks that you have written but that have not yet cleared, deposits that you have made since the bank statement was prepared, interest added to your account, and deductions for fees and charges.

To determine your true balance, a *bank reconciliation* should be prepared. This report accounts for differences between the bank statement and your checkbook balance. The steps that you take in this process are as follows:

1. Compare the checks that you have written over the past month with those reported as paid on your bank statement. Use the canceled checks from the financial institution, or compare your check register with the check numbers reported on the bank statement. *Subtract* from the *bank statement balance* the total of the checks written but not cleared.
2. Determine whether any recent deposits are not on the bank statement. If so, *add* the amount of the deposits to the *bank statement balance.*
3. *Subtract* any fees or charges on the bank statement from your *checkbook balance.*
4. *Add* any interest earned to your *checkbook balance.*

At this point, the revised balances for both your checkbook and the bank statement should be the same. If the two do not balance, attempt to find the error by checking your addition and making sure that every check and deposit was recorded correctly in your checkbook and on the bank statement.

Other Payment Forms. While personal checks are the most common payment form, other methods are available. A certified check is a personal check with guaranteed payment. The amount of the check is deducted from your balance when the check is certified by the financial institution.

A cashier's check is the check of a financial institution. A customer may purchase one by paying the amount of the check plus a fee. A money order may be purchased in a similar manner from financial institutions, post offices, and stores. Certified checks, cashier's checks, and money orders allow you to make a remittance that the recipient knows is valid.

Finally, traveler's checks allow you to make payments when away from home. This payment form requires the user to sign each check twice. First, the traveler's checks are signed when they are purchased. Then, to identify the authorized person, the checks are signed again as they are cashed.

Savings and checking services were discussed in this chapter. Other major financial services, consumer credit, insurance, investments, and retirement planning are discussed in following chapters.

SUMMARY

- Recent changes in financial services have been influenced by deregulation, economic conditions, and technology.
- Financial institutions accept deposits in the form of demand deposits (checking accounts) and time deposits (savings accounts). These funds are used to make loans and investments to earn money for the savers and owners of the institutions.
- Commercial banks, savings and loan associations, and credit unions have traditionally been the main suppliers of financial services. Credit card companies, insurance companies, and investment brokers have expanded their offerings of financial services.
- Financial supermarkets offer a wide variety of financial services, including savings, checking, borrowing, investing, insurance, and real estate purchases.
- Financial institutions are selected on the basis

of services offered, personal service, convenience, interest rates, costs of services, and safety.
- When comparing savings plans, you should consider the rate of return, the interest computation method, liquidity, safety, restrictions, and costs.
- The types of savings plans used by consumers are regular savings accounts, club accounts, certificates of deposit, interest-bearing checking accounts, money market accounts, and U.S. savings bonds.
- The main types of checking accounts are regular checking accounts, special checking accounts, and interest-bearing checking accounts.
- Using a checking account involves opening the account, making deposits, writing checks, reconciling the account, and, when necessary, using payment forms other than checks.

GLOSSARY

Automatic teller machine.   A computer terminal that is used to conduct financial transactions.

Central management account (CMA).   An all-in-one bank account that includes savings, checking, borrowing, investing, and other financial services for a single fee; also called a central asset account.

Certificate of deposit.   A savings plan requiring that a certain amount be on deposit for a set time period to receive a specific rate of interest.

Commercial bank.   A financial institution that offers a wide range of services to individuals, businesses, and government agencies.

Compounding.   Interest that is earned on previously earned interest.

Credit union.   A nonprofit, cooperative financial institution that is organized for the benefit of its members.

Demand deposit.   Money in checking accounts.

EFT card.   A plastic access card used in computerized banking transactions; also called a debit card.

Electronic funds transfer (EFT).   A system of making payments and recording receipts with computer data rather than cash or checks.

Financial supermarket.   A large business that offers a complete range of financial services.

Money market account.   A savings account offered by banks, savings and loan associations, and credit unions that requires a minimum balance and has earnings based on the current level of interest rates.

Money market fund.   A savings-investment plan offered by investment companies, with earnings based on investments in various financial instruments.

Mutual savings bank.   A financial institution that is owned by depositors and specializes in savings and mortgage loans.

NOW account.   An interest-bearing checking account; NOW is an abbreviation for negotiable orders of withdrawal.

Overdraft protection.   An automatic loan to checking account customers to cover the amount of checks written over the available balance in the checking account.

Rate of return.   The percentage increase in the value of your savings as a result of interest earned; also called yield.

Savings and loan association.   A financial institution that traditionally specialized in savings and mortgage loans.

Share account.   A regular savings account at a credit union.

Share draft account.   An interest-bearing checking account at a credit union.

Super NOW account.   An interest-bearing checking account that earns interest at a rate higher than that earned by a regular savings account; requires a high minimum balance.

Time deposits.   Money in savings accounts.

Trust.   A legal agreement that provides for the management and control of assets by one party for the benefit of another.

REVIEW QUESTIONS

1. How has deregulation affected financial institutions and the services they offer?

2. In what ways do economic conditions affect financial services?

3. How have electronic banking systems made financial services more convenient?

4. What are the advantages of a credit union over other financial institutions?

5. What are the advantages and possible disadvantages of financial supermarkets?

6. What factors should be considered when selecting a financial institution?

7. What factors can be used to compare different types of savings plans?

8. How does frequency of compounding affect the earnings on savings?

9. What are the main types of savings plans that are available to consumers?

10. How does a money market *account* differ from a money market *fund?*

11. What are the main types of checking accounts that are available to consumers?

12. What is the purpose of a bank reconciliation?

DISCUSSION QUESTIONS AND ACTIVITIES

1. Which financial services are most important to Marlene and Bill Sullivan? Are they currently making the wisest use of financial services?

2. What actions would you suggest that the Sullivans take to improve their use of financial services?

3. Has the deregulation of financial services helped or hurt consumers? Explain.

4. Collect information on current interest rates and consumer prices from *The Wall Street Journal* and other sources of business news. How will savers and lenders be affected by his information?

5. Compare the services and costs of a local bank, savings and loan association, and credit union.

6. Should retail stores sell insurance, real estate, investments, and other financial services as part of their product line? Explain.

7. Conduct an informal survey of friends and relatives. Obtain information on why they use a certain financial institution.

8. Collect advertisements to compare the interest rates paid on various types of savings plans at different financial institutions.

9. Contact four financial institutions to obtain information on the type of interest method they use to compute earnings on savings.

10. Is a checking account a necessity in our society? Should the government require banks and other financial institutions to provide low-cost checking accounts to people whose income falls below a certain amount?

ADDITIONAL READINGS

Alice in Debitland: Consumer Protection and Electronic Banking. Washington, D.C.: Board of Governors of the Federal Reserve System.

Avery, Robert B.; Gregory Elliehausen; and Thomas A. Gustafson. "How People Use Financial Services." *American Demographics*, September 1985, pp. 34–37, 46–48.

Financial Services Fact Book. Washington, D.C.: American Bankers Association.

Hoffman, Naphtali, and Stephen Brobeck. *The Bank Book.* New York: Harcourt Brace Jovanovich, 1986.

"You and the Banks." *Consumer Reports*, September 1985, pp. 508–16.

CASE 4–1 The Credit Union versus the Investment Company

Joan Ellis is a member of the credit union at her place of work. This financial institution offers regular savings accounts, share draft checking, and a variety of loans. It does not offer electronic banking, mortgages, or investment advice.

Joan's husband, Hal, is a manager at a department store in a local shopping center. Recently, an investment company opened a store in the mall. It offers free checking, low-cost loans, investment assistance, insurance, and real estate service. Hal believes that Joan and he should do business with this nationally known company.

Questions

1. What are the benefits of doing business with the credit union instead of the investment company?

2. What factors should Joan and Hal consider when they compare financial institutions?

3. What recommendations would you make to Joan and Hal about their use of financial services?

CASE 4–2 Marv's Savings Goals

Marv Hammerling, age 24, has a well-paying job and rents an apartment a few miles from work. Over the past two years, he has been able to save $650, which he keeps in a regular savings account. Marv would like to buy a house in about five years. In about a year or two, he will need to buy a new car.

Marv expects a salary increase within the next two months. He plans to use the additional money to buy new furniture for his apartment and to repair the air-conditioning system in his car.

Questions

1. What are Marv's short-term and long-term savings goals?

2. What could Marv do to make his savings grow faster?

3. What options for saving does Marv have other than a regular savings account?

4. What do you recommend that Marv do when evaluating various savings plans and attempting to reach his savings goals?

5

Using Consumer Credit

The use of credit is an important element in personal and family financial planning. When credit is used, needs satisfied in the present are paid for in the future. While the use of credit is often necessary and even advantageous, responsibilities and disadvantages are associated with its use. After studying this chapter, you will be able to:

- Define consumer credit and list its advantages and disadvantages.

- Differentiate between closed-end credit and open-end credit.

- State what information creditors look for when you apply for credit and what information they can or cannot use.

- Measure your credit capacity.

- List the procedures you can use to build and maintain your credit rating.

- State the steps you can take to avoid and correct credit mistakes.

- Discuss the laws that protect you if you complain about consumer credit.

Interview with C. E. Jernigan,
Associate Sales Vice President, Equifax Services, Inc.

C. E. Jernigan, currently Associate Sales Vice President of Equifax Services, Inc., joined the company in 1970. Before assuming his present assignment in Chicago, Mr. Jernigan served Equifax Services in such locations as Tulsa, New Orleans, San Francisco, and Jackson, Mississippi. He is a member of the International Credit Association, the American Surety of Industrial Security, the Illinois Mortgage Bankers Association, the Minnesota Mortgage Bankers Association, and the Michigan Mortgage Bankers Association.

If you have ever applied for a charge account, a personal loan, insurance, or a job, someone is probably keeping a file on you. This file may contain information on how you pay your bills or on whether you've been sued or arrested or have filed for bankruptcy.

The companies that gather and sell such information are called consumer reporting agencies, or CRAs. The most common type of CRA is the credit bureau. The information sold by CRAs to creditors, employers, insurers, and other businesses is called a consumer report. This report states where you work and live and contains information about your bill-paying habits.

In 1970, Congress passed the Fair Credit Reporting Act to give consumers specific rights in dealing with CRAs. The act protects you by requiring credit bureaus to furnish correct and complete information that businesses can use in evaluating your applications for credit, insurance, or a job. The Federal Trade Commission enforces the act.

If your application was denied because of information supplied by a CRA, the company to which you applied must give you that agency's name and address. Otherwise, you can find the CRA that has your file by calling the agencies listed in the yellow pages under "credit" or "credit rating and reporting." According to Mr. Jernigan, more than one CRA may have a file about you; therefore, you should call each of the agencies listed until you locate all of the agencies maintaining your file.

You have the right to know what the agency's report says about you, but you must request this information from the agency. The information is free if your application was denied because of it and if you request it within 30 days of receiving the denial notice.

To maintain a good credit rating, pay your bills on time. If you can't make a payment on or before the due date, contact your creditor immediately.

Mr. Jernigan suggests that to get your first credit card from a bank, you begin by opening a retail charge account, since such accounts are easy to obtain. Then use your charge card to make small purchases that you would have otherwise used cash to buy and pay your bills promptly.

Anita Peoples, a 27-year-old nurse and single mother in Shaker Heights, Ohio, fell on hard times in the fall of 1985. Surgery and a family death forced her to skip three mortgage payments, and her four-bedroom home nearly became an object of foreclosure proceedings.

The parents of a mason in San Fernando, California, moved into a house he owned and promised to make the mortgage payments. However, they didn't tell him that they had missed five payments totaling more than $3,000, nor did they give him the bank's notices threatening foreclosure. "We never did get any calls from the bank," recalled the mason's wife. She learned about the unpaid debt from a Mortgage Guaranty Insurance Corporation's loan counselor, who arrived while she was visiting her in-laws. At the counselor's urging, the younger couple used their vacation money to repay $2,000 immediately. They planned to pay the rest of the money soon.

The normal wait for an appointment at a Washington counseling center that helped people with debt problems had been a week to 10 days. Early in 1986, the swamped office required clients to arrange visits five weeks in advance. At the beginning of 1986, surveys showed that consumer confidence was falling, while personal bankruptcies and delinquency rates on loan payments

WHAT IS CONSUMER CREDIT?

- Meaning of Consumer Credit

Credit is an arrangement to receive cash, goods, or services now and pay for them in the future. **Consumer credit** refers to the use of credit for personal needs by individuals and families as contrasted to credit used for business or agricultural purposes.

Although Polonius cautioned, "Neither a borrower nor a lender be," using and providing credit have become a way of life for many individuals in today's economy. In January, you pay a bill for electricity that you used in December. A statement arrives in the mail for medical services that you received last month. You write a check for $40—a minimum payment on a $300 department store bill. With a bank loan, you purchase a new car. All of these are examples of using credit, that is, paying later for goods and services obtained now.

Consumer credit is based on trust in the consumer's ability and willingness to pay bills when due. It works because people, by and large, are honest and responsible. But how does consumer credit affect our economy, and how is it affected by our economy?

The Importance of Consumer Credit in Our Economy

Consumer credit dates back to colonial times. While it was originally a privilege of the affluent, it came to be used extensively by farmers. No direct

and credit cards were rising. "Monthly payments have reached a pain threshold," said Michael J. Drury, a senior economist in New York. According to Susan M. Sterne, a chief economist in Vermont, "Consumers are just stretched out beyond their limits." Meanwhile, such companies as Sears Roebuck & Co., J. C. Penney Company and Household International, Inc. reported that delinquency rates were rising.

In addition, economists noted that an increasing number of consumers had lost control of their budgets. In 1985, personal bankruptcies in the United States were up 6 percent. "What's going to happen when more and more credit is extended and things go bad again?" asked Ralph Spurgin, general credit manager at J. C. Penney. "The credit problem is going to be worse than ever."

Julie Lee, a Temple Hill, Maryland, teacher, destroyed her credit cards after accumulating $4,000 in bills in two years. Like others, Julie had used the cards to pay her bills. Eventually, she noticed that she was doubling her normal spending on clothing, sporting goods, and a vacation to England. As a result, she was "just buying the necessities and paying the bills."

*Adapted from *The Wall Street Journal*, February 18, 1986, p. 29.

finance charge was imposed; instead, the cost of credit was added to the price of goods. With the advent of the automobile in the early 1900s, installment credit—in which the debt is repaid in equal installments over a specified period of time—exploded on the American scene.

All economists now recognize consumer credit as a major force in the American economy. Any forecast or evaluation of the economy includes consumer spending trends and consumer credit as a sustaining force. To paraphrase an old political expression, as the consumer goes, so goes the U.S. economy.

In the post–World War II period, the use of consumer credit and the ability to borrow expanded rapidly. People are now buying items on credit and increasing personal debt to an extent never before known. The prices of such products as VCRs, stereo color TV sets, personal computers, washing machines, automobiles, motorboats, and recreational vehicles do not permit the average person to buy them with available cash. But some people want the satisfaction of owning these products even though they do not have the ready cash. For them, the use of credit is the answer. As a result, the volume of consumer debt (outstanding consumer credit) has assumed vast proportions. In 1985, for example, consumer credit compared with disposable income (income after all taxes), was at a record 18.9 percent, and the savings rate (savings as a percentage of disposable income) was 1.9 percent—the lowest in 35 years. Figure 5–1 shows that as the savings rate falls, consumer debt rises. Much of that debt, however, has been taken on by the high-income households that are probably best able to service it. Rich or poor, people must now set aside 3½ percent of their after-tax incomes just to pay interest on consumer debt, compared with less than 2½ percent, on average, during the 1970s.

According to a Federal Reserve System study, nearly three fourths of the households in the highest and the next highest income bracket use installment debt. By contrast, less than one third of the households in the lowest income bracket are in debt; they account for less than 5 percent of total consumer credit outstanding. As shown in Table 5–1, in 1985 consumer credit (median) ranged from $677 for families making less than $5,000 per year to $5,529 for families with annual incomes of $50,000 and more.

The movement of the baby boom generation into the age groups that tend to use credit most heavily has added to the growth of consumer credit. The 25–44 age group currently represents about 30 percent of the population but holds nearly 60 percent of the debt outstanding. The people in this age group have always been disproportionate users of credit, since at these ages consumption is highest as families are formed and homes are purchased and furnished. Thus, while the intensive use of debt by this group is nothing new, the fact that it is growing rapidly adds to overall debt use.[1]

Uses and Misuses of Credit

Using credit to purchase goods and services may allow consumers to be more efficient or more productive or to lead more satisfying lives. There are many valid reasons for using credit. A medical emergency may cause a per-

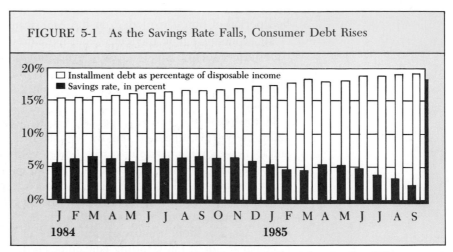

FIGURE 5-1   As the Savings Rate Falls, Consumer Debt Rises

Source: *The Wall Street Journal*, October 22, 1985, p. 33; based on information from U.S. government sources and Dean Witter Reynolds, Inc.

[1]Manufacturers Hanover, *Economic Report*, October 1985, p. 2. Copyright 1985.

TABLE 5-1   Consumer Credit

At the beginning of 1985, the median amount of consumer debt for the average U.S. family was $2,382.

Income (000)	Percent of U.S Families*	Percent with Debt	Median Amount of Debt
Less than $5.0	9%	33%	$ 677
$ 5.0–$ 7.4	8	40	573
$ 7.5–$ 9.9	7	48	1,006
$10.0–$14.9	14	54	1,451
$15.0–$19.9	13	66	1,639
$20.0–$24.9	11	72	2,336
$25.0–$29.9	9	72	2,929
$30.0–$39.9	13	77	3,594
$40.0–$49.9	7	80	4,365
$50.0 and more	10	75	5,529

*Includes single-person households.

Source: *The Wall Street Journal*, February 7, 1985, p. 37; based on information from Federal Reserve System.

son to be strapped for funds. A homemaker returning to the work force may need a car. Or it may be possible to buy an item now for less money than it will cost later. But it is probably not reasonable to finance an African safari on credit when a week at the beach is all your budget allows.

Using credit increases the amount of money that a consumer can spend to purchase goods and services now, but it decreases the amount of money that will be available to spend in the future. However, many people expect their incomes to increase, and they therefore expect to be able to make payments on past credit purchases and still make new purchases.

Here are some questions that you should ask before you decide how and when to buy a car: Do I have the cash I need to make this purchase? Do I want to use my savings for this purchase? Does the purchase fit my budget? Could I use the credit I need for this purchase in some better way? Could I postpone the purchase? What are the costs of postponing the purchase? (Alternative transportation costs; a possible increase in the price of the car.) What are the dollar costs and psychological costs of using credit? (Interest; other finance charges; being in debt and responsible for a monthly payment.)

If you decide to use credit, the benefits of making the purchase now (increased efficiency or productivity, a more satisfying life, etc.) should outweigh the costs (financial and psychological) of using credit. Thus, effectively used, credit can help us have more and enjoy more. Misused, credit can result in default, bankruptcy, and loss of reputation.

Advantages of Credit

● Advantages of Using Credit

Consumer credit enables us to have and enjoy goods and services now—a car, a home, education, help in emergencies—and to pay for them through payment plans based on future income.

Charge cards permit the purchase of goods even when funds are low. Customers with previously approved credit may receive other extras, such as advance notice of sales and the right to order by phone or to buy on approval. In addition, many shoppers believe that it is easier to return merchandise that has been purchased on account. Charge cards also provide shopping convenience and the efficiency of paying for several purchases with one monthly payment.

With credit, you are better equipped to cope with financial emergencies. If an aching tooth requires extensive dental surgery or a windstorm causes property damage, you'll be able to take immediate action without dipping into savings or borrowing money from friends and relatives.

Credit is more than a substitute for cash. Many of the services it provides are taken for granted. Every time you turn on the water tap, flick the light switch, or telephone a friend, you are using credit.

It is also safer to use credit. Charge accounts and credit cards let you shop and travel without carrying a large amount of cash. Credit cards are also used for identification when cashing checks, and the use of credit provides a record of expenses.

Frequently, you can use credit as a leverage to receive a cash discount on a purchase. Furthermore, the use of credit is a form of forced saving and it can be a hedge against inflation as a loan is paid off with inflated, cheaper dollars.

Lastly, credit indicates stability. The fact that lenders consider you a good risk usually means that you are a responsible individual. But if you do not pay your debts back on a timely basis, credit has many disadvantages.

Disadvantages of Credit

● Disadvantages of Using Credit

When considering the use of credit, remember that credit costs money and that it may cause overspending, result in loss of merchandise or income, and tie up your future income.

Perhaps the greatest disadvantage of using credit is the temptation to overspend, especially during periods of inflation. It seems easy to buy today and pay tomorrow using cheaper dollars. But continued overspending leads to serious trouble. Remember the problems faced by Anita Peoples and Julie Lee, mentioned at the beginning of the chapter? Remember, too, that if payments are not made on time, you may have to give up your home or the merchandise.

Whether or not credit involves security (something of value to back the loan), failure to pay a loan may result in the loss of income, valuable property, and your good reputation. Further difficulties could be court action, garnishment of salary, and bankruptcy. Misuse of credit can create serious long-term financial problems, damage to family relationships, and a slowing of progress toward goals. Therefore, credit should be approached with caution and must not be used more extensively than your budget permits.

Although credit permits more immediate satisfaction of needs and desires, it does not increase total purchasing power. Credit purchases must be paid for out of future income; therefore, credit ties up the use of future income. Furthermore, if your income does not increase to cover rising costs, your ability to repay credit commitments will be diminished. Before buying goods and services on credit, consider whether they will have lasting value, whether they will increase your personal satisfaction during present and future income periods, and whether your current income will continue or increase.[2]

Finally, credit costs money. It is a service for which you must pay. Paying for purchases over a period of time is more costly than paying for them cash. You must decide whether making a credit purchase is worth the extra cost— or whether it is advisable to wait until you can save the necessary money and pay cash. The cost of credit may cancel a bargain.[3]

In summary, the use of credit provides immediate access to goods and services, flexibility in money management, safety and convenience, a cushion in emergencies, a means of increasing resources, a character recommendation if the debt is paid back on a timely basis, and forced saving. But remember, the use of credit is a two-sided coin. An intelligent decision as to its use demands careful evaluation of the debt factor, future income, the added cost, and the consequences of overspending.

There are many forms of credit. As a consumer and a borrower, you should select the kind of credit that most appropriately meets your economic and personal needs in given situations. The accompanying box lists a few helpful tips about the use of credit.

Kinds of Credit

● Two Types of Consumer Credit

There are two types of consumer credit—closed-end credit and open-end credit. With closed-end credit, or installment credit, you pay back onetime loans in a specified period of time and the payments are of equal amounts. With open-end credit, or revolving credit, loans are made on a continuous basis and you are billed periodically to make at least partial payment. Figure 5–2 shows examples of closed-end and open-end credit.

---

[2]*Managing Your Credit*, rev. ed. (Prospect Heights, Ill.: Money Management Institute, Household Financial Services, 1985), p. 6.
[3]Ibid.

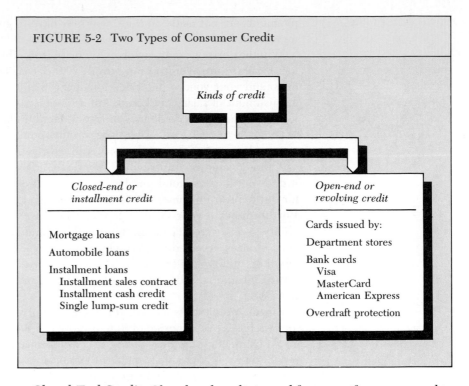

FIGURE 5-2 Two Types of Consumer Credit

Kinds of credit

Closed-end or
installment credit

Mortgage loans

Automobile loans

Installment loans
   Installment sales contract
   Installment cash credit
   Single lump-sum credit

Open-end or
revolving credit

Cards issued by:

Department stores

Bank cards
   Visa
   MasterCard
   American Express

Overdraft protection

Closed-End Credit. Closed-end credit is used for a specific purpose and is for a specified amount. Mortgage loans, automobile loans, and installment loans for purchasing furniture or appliances are examples of closed-end credit. An agreement, or contract, lists the repayment terms—the number of payments, the payment amount, and how much the credit will cost. Closed-end payment plans usually involve a written agreement for each credit purchase. A down payment or trade-in may be required, with the balance to be repaid in equal weekly or monthly payments over a period of time. Generally, the seller holds title to the merchandise until the payments have been completed.

The three most common types of closed-end credit are installment sales credit, installment cash credit, and single lump-sum credit. *Installment sales credit* is a loan that allows the consumer to receive merchandise, usually high-priced items such as refrigerators or furniture. The consumer makes a down payment and usually signs a contract to repay the balance, plus interest and service charges, in equal installments over a specified period.

Installment cash credit is a direct loan of money for personal purposes, home improvements, or vacation expenses. No down payment is made, and payments are made in specified amounts over a set period.

Single lump-sum credit is a loan that must be repaid in total on a specified day. Lump-sum credit is generally used to purchase a single item.

Open-End Credit. Using a credit card issued by a department store, using a bank credit card (VISA, MasterCard) to make purchases at different stores, charging a meal at a restaurant, and using overdraft protection are examples of open-end credit. As you will see in the next section, you do not apply for open-end credit to make a single purchase, as is done with closed-end credit. Rather, you can use open-end credit to make any purchases you wish if you do not exceed your **line of credit,** the maximum amount of credit you can use. You may have to pay **interest,** a periodic charge for the use of credit, or other finance charges. Some creditors allow you 30 days to pay a bill in full before you incur any interest charges. This type of credit is often called *convenience credit.*

All of us have probably had an appointment with a doctor or a dentist that we did not pay for until later. Professionals and small businesses often do not demand immediate payment. *Incidental credit* is a credit arrangement that has no extra costs and no specific repayment plan.

Personal Financial Planning and You
Helpful Tips about Credit

A lways budget your credit spending carefully.

Shop around for the lowest credit rates. The rates sometimes vary tremendously.

Use credit only when it is to your advantage.

Buy items on credit that will last at least until the last payment is due. You will receive more satisfaction that way.

Pay your bills on time to ensure that you can continue to use credit.

Understand the credit contract before signing it.

Notify the creditor if, for any reason, you cannot make scheduled payments.

Keep an eye on your card when you give it to salespeople. Make certain they use it for your transaction only, and then be sure the card you receive back is yours.

Tear up the carbons after you sign credit card receipts. This will make it more difficult for anyone to steal your account number in order to use it for fraudulent purposes.

Do not give your credit card numbers over the phone to anyone unless *you* initiate the call. Ask callers to put their request to you in writing.

Keep your receipts after you make any charges. Compare them with your monthly statement. Carefully read your monthly bill.

If you find any incorrect charges on your monthly credit card statements, notify your credit card issuer in writing.

Keep a list of your credit card numbers and the issuers' phone numbers in a safe place for quick reference in case of loss or theft.

Report your lost or stolen cards at once. Most card issuers have toll-free telephone numbers for this purpose.

Federal law limits your liability for unauthorized charges to $50 per credit card. But you don't have to pay for *any* charges made after you have notified card companies of your loss. After calling, follow up with a telegram or registered letter.

Open-end, or revolving, credit is a form of credit that many retailers use. Customers can purchase goods or services up to a fixed dollar limit at any time. Usually, they have the option of paying the bill in full within 30 days without interest charges or of making stated monthly installments based on the account balance plus interest.

Revolving check credit is a service extended by many banks. It is a prearranged loan for a specific amount that the consumer can use by writing a special check. Repayment is made in installments over a set period. The finance charges are based on the amount of credit used during the month and on the outstanding balance.

Credit Cards. About 22,000 financial institutions participate in the credit card business, and the vast majority of them are affiliated with VISA International or the Interbank Card Association, which issues MasterCard. A bank credit card differs from other credit cards in that it is issued by a bank or

---

In the Real World
Choosing a Credit Card?

1. Department stores and gasoline companies are good places to obtain your first credit card. Pay your bills in full and on time, and you will begin to establish a good credit history.
2. Bank cards are offered through banks and savings and loan associations. Fees and finance charges vary considerably (from 12.5 percent to 21.6 percent), so shop around. The average finance charge on bank cards for 1985 was 18.5 percent.
3. If you usually pay your bill in full, try to deal with a financial institution with an interest-free grace period, which is the time after a purchase is made and before a finance charge is imposed, typically 25 to 30 days.
4. If you're used to paying monthly installments, look for a card with a low monthly finance charge. Be sure you understand how that finance charge is calculated. For a list of banks offering low finance charges send $1, check or money order, to BankCard Holders of America, 333 Pennsylvania Avenue, SE, Washington, DC, 20003. Request "Low Interest Rate List." A "No Annual Fee List," a list of banks offering cards with no annual fee, is available for $1.95.
5. Consider the option of obtaining a card from an out-of-state financial institution if it offers better terms than those offered locally.
6. Be aware of some credit cards that offer "no fee" or low interest, but start charging interest from the day an item is purchased.
7. Be aware of some credit cards that do not charge annual fees but instead charge a "transaction fee" each time the card is used.
8. If you're only paying the minimum amount on your

other financial institution. According to *Bank Credit Card Observer*, the number of Americans age 18 and older who hold bank credit cards is as follows:

At least one bank credit card	82 million
Two or more	39 million
Three or more	14 million
Four or more	7.5 million[4]

The unique feature of bank credit cards is that they extend a line of credit to the cardholder, much like a bank's consumer loan department. They provide prompt and convenient access to short-term credit for the cardholder, who instructs the bank to pay the merchant immediately and reimburses the bank later.

[4]*The Wall Street Journal*, November 14, 1986, p. 23.

monthly payments, you need to plan your budget more carefully. The longer it takes for you to pay off a bill, the more interest you pay. You could end up paying more in finance charges than the item is worth.

9. With a grace period of 25 days, you are actually getting a free loan when you pay bills in full each month.

10. In order to avoid delays that may result in finance charges, follow the card issuer's instructions as to where, how, and when to make bill payments.

11. If you have a bad credit history and problems in getting a credit card, look for a savings institution that will give you a card if you open a savings account with it. Your line of credit will be determined by the amount you have on deposit.

12. Travel and entertainment cards often charge higher annual fees than most credit cards. Payment usually must be made in full within 30 days of receiving your bill or, typically, no further purchases will be approved on the account.

13. Often, credit cards on your account for a spouse or child (over 18) are available with a minimum additional fee, or no fee at all.

14. Be aware that "debit" cards are not credit cards but simply a substitute for a check or cash. The amount of the sale is immediately subtracted from your checking account.

Source: American Institute of Certified Public Accountants and U.S. Office of Consumer Affairs.

Under most bank credit card systems, you enjoy the use of free credit from the time of purchase until the due date shown on the monthly statement. The bank will allow you to extend payment beyond the due date but will charge you interest for doing so.

APPLYING FOR CREDIT

- How to Apply for Credit

Mary and John Jones, whose joint income is more than enough for payments on their dream house, are turned down for a mortgage loan. The lender says that Mary might become pregnant and leave her job.

It is illegal for creditors to ask or assume anything about a woman's childbearing plans. It's even illegal to discourage the Joneses from applying for a loan because Mary is of childbearing age. And Mary's income must be acknowledged fully by a lender.

When you are ready to apply for credit, you should know what creditors think is important in deciding whether you are creditworthy. You should also know what they cannot legally consider in their decisions.

The **Equal Credit Opportunity Act (ECOA)** starts all credit applicants off on the same footing. It states that race, color, age, sex, marital status, and certain other factors may not be used to discriminate against you in any part of a credit dealing.

What Creditors Look For[5]

When a lender extends credit to its customers, it recognizes that some customers will be unable or unwilling to pay for their purchases. Therefore, lenders must establish policies for determining who will receive credit. Most lenders build their credit policies around the five C's of credit: character, capacity, capital, collateral, and conditions.

Character. By **character**, we mean the borrower's attitude toward his or her credit obligations. Lenders often see this attitude as the most important factor in predicting whether a borrower will make regular payments and ultimately repay a loan.

In judging a borrower's character, consider these typical questions: Is the borrower prompt in paying bills? Have other lenders had to dun the borrower with overdue notices before receiving payments? Have lenders been forced to take the borrower to court to obtain payment? Has the borrower ever filed for bankruptcy? If so, did the borrower make an attempt to repay debts voluntarily?

Capacity. By **capacity**, we mean the borrower's financial ability to meet credit obligations, that is, to make regular loan payments as scheduled in the credit agreement. The lender checks your salary and outstanding financial obligations before credit is approved. For example, the lender wants to

---

[5]Adapted from Robert J. Hughes and Jack R. Kapoor, *Business* (Boston: Houghton Mifflin, 1985), pp. 409–10. Copyright 1985, Houghton Mifflin Company.

know your occupation, how long you have worked, and how much you earn. The lender also wants to know your expenses: how many dependents you have and whether you pay or receive alimony or child support.

Capital. As used here, the term **capital** refers to the borrower's assets or net worth. The greater the borrower's capital, the greater the borrower's ability to repay a loan of a specific size. Information on net worth can be obtained by requiring that a borrower complete a credit application. The borrower must also authorize employers and financial institutions to release information to confirm the claims made in the application.

Collateral. For large amounts of credit, and especially for large loans, the lender may require some type of collateral. **Collateral** is a valuable asset pledged to assure loan payments and is subject to seizure upon default. That is, if the borrower fails to live up to the terms of the credit agreement, the collateral can be sold to satisfy the debt.

Conditions. The term **conditions** refers to the general economic conditions that can affect a borrower's ability to repay a loan or other credit obligations. The basic question of conditions focuses on the security of both the applicant's job and the firm for which he or she works.

Creditors use different combinations of the above facts to reach their decisions. Some creditors set unusually high standards, and others simply do not make certain kinds of loans. Creditors also use different kinds of rating systems. Some rely strictly on their own instinct and experience. Others use a

From *The Wall Street Journal*, with permission of Cartoon Features Syndicate.

FIGURE 5-3 Sample Credit Application

CREDIT APPLICATION IMPORTANT: Read these Directions before completing this Application. [Closed end, secured credit]

Check Appropriate Box

☐ If you are applying for individual credit in your own name and are relying on your own income or assets and not the income or assets of another person as the basis for repayment of the credit requested, complete Sections A, C, D, and E, omitting B and the second part of C.

☐ If this is an application for joint credit with another person, complete all Sections, providing information in B about the joint applicant.

☐ If you are applying for individual credit, but are relying on income from alimony, child support, or separate maintenance or on the income or assets of another person as the basis for repayment of the credit requested, complete all Sections to the extent possible, providing information in B about the person on whose alimony, support, or maintenance payments or income or assets you are relying.

Amount Requested   Payment Date Desired   Proceeds of Credit

$................................   To be Used For..

SECTION A—INFORMATION REGARDING APPLICANT

Full Name (Last, First, Middle): .... Birthdate: / /

Present Street Address: .... Years there: ....

City: .... State: .... Zip: .... Telephone: ....

Social Security No.: .... Driver's License No.: ....

Previous Street Address: .... Years there: ....

City: .... State: .... Zip: ....

Present Employer .... Years there: .... Telephone: ....

Position or title: .... Name of supervisor: ....

Employer's Address: ....

Previous Employer: .... Years there: ....

Previous Employer's Address: ....

Present net salary or commission: $................ per .... No. Dependents: .... Ages: ....

Alimony, child support, or separate maintenance income need not be revealed if you do not wish to have it considered as a basis for repaying this obligation.

Alimony, child support, separate maintenance received under: court order ☐ written agreement ☐ oral understanding ☐

Other income: $................ per .... Source(s) of other income: ....

Is any income listed in this Section likely to be reduced before the credit requested is paid off?
☐ Yes (Explain in detail on a separate sheet.) No ☐

Have you ever received credit from us? .... When? .... Office: ....

Checking Account No. .... Institution and Branch: ....

Savings Account No. .... Institution and Branch: ....

Name of nearest relative
not living with you: .... Telephone: ....

Relationship: .... Address: ....

SECTION B—INFORMATION REGARDING JOINT APPLICANT OR OTHER PARTY (Use separate sheets if necessary.)

Full Name (Last, First, Middle): .... Birthdate: / /

Relationship to Applicant (if any): ....

Present Street Address: .... Years there: ....

City: .... State: .... Zip .... Telephone: ....

Social Security No.: .... Driver's License No.: ....

Present Employer: .... Years there: .... Telephone: ....

Position or title: .... Name of supervisor: ....

Employer's Address: ....

Previous Employer: .... Years there: ....

Previous Employer's Address: ....

Present net salary or commission: $................ per .... No. Dependents: .... Ages: ....

Alimony, child support, or separate maintenance income need not be revealed if you do not wish to have it considered as a basis for repaying this obligation.

Alimony, child support, separate maintenance received under: court order ☐ written agreement ☐ oral understanding ☐

Other income: $................ per .... Source(s) of other income: ....

Is any income listed in this Section likely to be reduced before the credit requested is paid off?
☐ Yes (Explain in detail on a separate sheet.) No ☐

Checking Account No.: .... Institution and Branch: ....

Savings Account No.: .... Institution and Branch: ....

Name of nearest relative not living with Joint
Applicant or Other Party: ....

Relationship: .... Address: ....

SECTION C—MARITAL STATUS

Applicant: ☐ Married   ☐ Separated   ☐ Unmarried (including single, divorced, and widowed)
Other Party: ☐ Married   ☐ Separated   ☐ Unmarried (including single, divorced, and widowed)

Source: Board of Governors of the Federal Reserve System.

credit-scoring or statistical system to predict whether you are a good credit risk. They assign a certain number of points to each characteristic that has proven to be a reliable sign that a borrower will repay. Then they rate you on this scale. A typical credit application is shown in Figure 5–3, and Figure 5–4 shows how your credit application might be scored.

Age. Many older persons have complained about being denied credit because they were over a certain age. Or when older persons retired, their credit may have been suddenly cut off or reduced.

The law is very specific about how a person's age may be used in credit decisions. A creditor may ask your age, but if you're old enough to sign a binding contract (usually 18 or 21 years old, depending on state law), a creditor may not turn you down or decrease your credit because of your age, may not ignore your retirement income in rating your application, may not close your credit account or require you to reapply for it because you reach a certain age or retire, and may not deny you credit or close your account because credit life insurance or other credit-related insurance is not available to persons of your age.

Because age has economic consequences, the law permits a creditor to consider certain information related to age—such as how long it will be until you retire or how long your income will continue. On a risky venture, an older applicant might not qualify for a large loan with a 5 percent down

---

FIGURE 5-4   How Is a Consumer's Application Scored?

To illustrate how credit scoring works, consider the following example, which uses only three factors to determine whether someone is creditworthy. (Most systems have 6 to 15 factors).

Monthly income	Points Awarded
Less than $400	0
$400–$650	3
$651–$800	7
$801–$1,200	12
$1,200 +	15
Age	
21–28	11
28–35	5
36–48	2
48–61	12
61 +	15
Telephone in home	
Yes	12
No	0

Source: *Scoring for Credit: Facts for Consumers from the Federal Trade Commission* (Washington, D.C.: Federal Trade Commission, August 1986).

payment. That same person might qualify for a smaller loan with a bigger down payment, secured by good collateral. Remember that while declining income may be a handicap if you are older, you can usually offer a solid credit history. The creditor has to look at all the facts of your particular situation and to apply the usual standards of creditworthiness to it.

Public Assistance. You may not be denied credit because you receive social security or public assistance. But, as is the case with age, certain information related to this source of income could have a bearing on your creditworthiness. So a creditor may consider such things as the age of your dependents (you may lose benefits when they reach a certain age) and whether you will continue to meet the residency requirements for receiving benefits. Factors of this kind help the creditor determine whether your public assistance income will continue.

Housing Loans. The ECOA covers your application for a mortgage or a home improvement loan. It bans discrimination because of such characteristics as your race, color, or sex or because of the race or national origin of the people in the neighborhood where you live or want to buy your home. Creditors may not use any appraisal of the value of your property that considers the race of the people in your neighborhood.

Discrimination against Women

When she was divorced, Louise Martin changed her name. Although she had had several successful credit accounts in her married name, her applications for credit in her maiden name were repeatedly denied. Creditors said: "We can't find a record of your credit history under the name you gave on your application form."

Bess Fenton, a young single woman, recently moved to the West Coast to start a new job. She applied for her first credit card with a national oil company, but since she had no record with the local credit bureau, her application was denied. Her question is: "If it takes credit to get credit, how do I begin?"

You may have faced similar problems when you applied for credit. Each year, many women are denied credit because they cannot show their own credit history. A good credit history is the way most companies predict your future success in using credit. Your payments on credit cards, charge accounts, installment loans, and other credit accounts are how you get a track record, and that record gives creditors evidence that you are a good risk.

Fill an Empty File. If creditors have failed to supply information to your credit file, or if you have never had credit in your own name, a no-file report can cause your credit application to be rejected. For example, when a woman is widowed or divorced or wants credit in her own name, a credit bureau may report that no file exists. She may have a great credit history, but in her husband's name. Old accounts held in her maiden name may not have been transferred to a file listed under her married name. For all practical purposes, her credit history has been lost.

For your own protection, you should learn how to prevent credit history evaporation. There are steps you can take to fill an empty file with your past credit history or to build a file with new information.

If you were recently married or divorced and changed your name, ask your creditors to change your name on your accounts. (Figure 5–5 is a form that can be used for this purpose.) Once these accounts are in your new name, your complete credit history should be reported to the credit bureau correctly.

FIGURE 5-5   Credit Histories for Married People

If you are married, but want to establish a credit history in your own name, simply write your creditors and request it. Creditors have an obligation to provide the history in both names when accounts are shared. As a sample of what you should say, you can use the following format.

Acme Department Store
Credit Division
1798 Third Street
Cincinnati, OH 70239

Dear Madam or Sir:
   Under the Equal Credit Opportunity Act, I request that you report all credit information on this account in both names.

_____
                    Account Number

Account Names (print or type):

_____
First   Middle   Last

_____
First   Middle   Last

_____
Street Number, Apartment

_____
City, State, Zip

                                        _____
                                        Signature of Either Spouse

Source: Federal Trade Commission.

Ask Questions if Your Application Is Denied. The ECOA gives you the right to know the specific reasons for denial if you receive a notice that your application was denied. If the denial was based on a credit report, you are entitled to know the specific information in the credit report that led to the denial. After you receive this information from the creditor, you should visit or telephone the local credit bureau to find out what information it reported. The bureau cannot charge for disclosure if you ask to see your file within 30 days of being notified of a denial based on a credit report. You may ask the

---

FIGURE 5-6 Statement of Credit Denial

ABC BANK

STATEMENT OF CREDIT DENIAL,
TERMINATION, OR CHANGE

DATE January 2, 19xx

Applicant's Name: Lynn E. Jones

Applicant's Address: 123 Main Street
Anytown, US 91233

Description of Account, Transaction or Requested Credit:
Automobile Loan

Description of Adverse Action Taken:
Loan Denied.

PRINCIPAL REASON(S) FOR ADVERSE
ACTION CONCERNING CREDIT

_____ Credit application incomplete
_____ Insufficient credit references
_____ Unable to verify credit references
_____ Temporary or irregular employment
_____ Unable to verify employment
_____ Length of employment
_____ Insufficient income
_____ Excessive obligations
_____ Unable to verify income
_____ Inadequate collateral
_____ Too short a period of residence

_____ Temporary residence
_____ Unable to verify residence
_____ No credit file
_____ Insufficient credit file
__X__ Delinquent credit obligations
_____ Garnishment, attachment, foreclosure, repossession, or suit
_____ Bankruptcy
_____ We do not grant credit to any applicant on the terms and conditions you request.
_____ Other, specify: _____

DISCLOSURE OF USE OF INFORMATION
OBTAINED FROM AN OUTSIDE SOURCE

_____ Disclosure inapplicable
__X__ Information obtained in a report from a consumer reporting agency
Name: Anytown Credit Bureau

Street address: 456 First Street
Anytown, US 91234
Telephone number: (123) 456-789

Information obtained from an outside source other than a consumer reporting agency. Under the Fair Credit Reporting Act, you have the right to make a written request, within 60 days of receipt of this notice, for disclosure of the nature of the adverse information.

Creditor's name: ABC Bank
Creditor's address: 789 Second Street
Anytown, US 91234

Creditor's
telephone number: (123) 789-4560

The Federal Equal Credit Opportunity Act prohibits creditors from discriminating against credit applicants on the basis of race, color, religion, national origin, sex, marital status, age (provided that the applicant has the capacity to enter into a binding contract); because all or part of the applicant's income derives from any public assistance program; or because the applicant has in good faith exercised any right under the Consumer Credit Protection Act. The Federal agency that administers compliance with this law concerning this creditor is the Federal Reserve Bank of Anytown, 400 Third Street, Anytown, US 91234.

Source: Board of Governors of the Federal Reserve System.

bureau to investigate any inaccurate or incomplete information and correct its records. The accompanying box summarizes the credit rights of women, and Figure 5–6 shows a sample statement of credit denial.

MEASURING YOUR CREDIT CAPACITY

● How Much Credit Can You Afford?

The only way to determine how much credit you can assume is to first learn how to make an accurate and sensible personal or family budget. Budgets, as you learned in Chapter 3, are simple, carefully considered outlines of plans to distribute dollars of earnings. With budgets, you first provide for basic necessities, such as rent, mortgage, food, and clothing. Then you provide for such items as furniture, home furnishings, and other heavy, more durable goods.

Can You Afford a Loan?

Before you take a loan, ask yourself whether you can meet all of your essential expenses and still afford the monthly loan payments. You can make this calculation in two ways. One is to add up all of your basic monthly expenses and then to subtract this total from your take-home pay. If the difference will not cover the monthly payment and still leave funds for other expenses, you cannot afford the loan.

Personal Financial Planning and You
Credit Rights of Women

A creditor *cannot:*

1. Refuse you individual credit in your own name.
2. Require a spouse to cosign a loan. Any creditworthy person can be your cosigner if one is required.
3. Ask about your birth control practices or family plans or assume that your income will be interrupted to have children.
4. Consider whether you have a telephone listing in your own name.

A creditor *must:*

5. Evaluate you on the same basis as applicants who are male or who have a different marital status.
6. Consider income from part-time employment.
7. Consider reliable alimony, child support, or separate maintenance payments.
8. Consider the payment history of all joint accounts that accurately reflects your credit history.

9. Report the payment history on an account if you use the account jointly with your spouse.
10. Disregard information on accounts if you can prove that it does not reflect your ability or willingness to repay.

Source: Reprinted, courtesy of Office of Public Information, Federal Reserve Bank of Minneapolis, Minneapolis, MN 55480.

difference will not cover the monthly payment and still leave funds for other expenses, you cannot afford the loan.

An even more reliable method is to ask yourself what you plan to give up in order to make the monthly loan payment. If you currently save a portion of your income greater than the monthly payment, then you can use these savings to pay off the loan. But if you do not, you will have to forgo spending on entertainment, new appliances, or perhaps even necessities. Are you prepared to make this trade-off?

Although it is difficult to precisely measure your credit capacity, there are certain rules of thumb that you can follow.

General Rules of Credit Capacity

Experts suggest that you spend no more than 20 percent of your net (after-tax) income on credit purchases. Thus, a person making $15,000 per year after taxes should spend no more than $3,000 on credit purchases.

The 20 percent estimate is the maximum; however, the 15 percent shown in Figure 5–7 is much safer. The 20 percent estimate is based on the average family, with average expenses; it does not take any major emergencies into account. If you are just beginning to use credit, you should not consider yourself safe if you are spending 20 percent of your net income on credit purchases.

Spend no more on credit purchases than you can afford to pay off in 12 months. (This rule applies to short-term debts, but it does not include car loans or college education expenses.) If, for instance, you have two loans that total $2,000 on which you are paying $100 per month, you would have to increase the payments to $167 per month in order to pay off the loan within 12 months.

Only you, based on the money you earn, your current obligations, and your financial plans for the future, can determine the exact amount of credit you need. You must be your own credit manager.

BUILDING AND MAINTAINING YOUR CREDIT RATING

- Establishing and Maintaining Your Credit

If you apply for a charge account, credit card, car loan, personal loan, or mortgage, your credit experience—or lack of it—will be a major factor considered by the creditor. Your credit experience may even affect your ability to get a job or buy life insurance. A good credit rating is a valuable asset that should be nurtured and protected. If you want a good rating, you must use credit with discretion; limit your borrowing to your capacity to repay, and live up to the terms of your contracts. The quality of your credit rating is entirely up to you.

In reviewing your creditworthiness, a creditor seeks information from credit bureaus located in your area.

FIGURE 5-7   Recommended Budget for a Typical Family

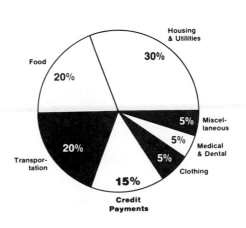

Housing & Utilities **30%**

Food **20%**

5% Miscellaneous

5% Medical & Dental

5% Clothing

15% Credit Payments

Transportation **20%**

WHERE DOES YOUR MONEY GO?*

While each household has a different situation, and everyone's budget is unique, this pie chart depicts a recommended budget for a typical family. The figures represent percentages of the household's total income. Remember, these are averages. They should be used for general guidelines only. Your expenses may vary from this to reflect your own priorities and situation.

Source: "Advice for Consumers Who Use Credit" (Consumer Credit Counseling Service of Maryland, Inc., n.d.).

Credit Bureaus

Across the United States, there are several thousand credit bureaus that collect credit information about consumers. Many of these credit bureaus are connected by teletype to centralized computer files that contain data about millions of individuals. From these files, a credit bureau can produce for a subscribing creditor, almost instantaneously, a report about your past and present credit activity.

Who Provides Data to Credit Bureaus?

Credit bureaus obtain their data from banks, finance companies, merchants, credit card companies, and other creditors. These sources regularly send reports to credit bureaus containing information about the kinds of credit they extend to customers, the amount and terms of that credit, and customers' paying habits. Credit bureaus also collect some information from other sources, such as court records.

What's in Your Credit Files?

As shown in a sample credit report (Figure 5–8), the credit bureau file contains your name, your address, your social security number, and your birth date. It may also include the following information:

Your employer, position, and income.

Your former address.

Your former employer.

Your spouse's name, social security number, employer, and income.

Whether you own your home, rent, or board.

Your credit file may also contain detailed credit information. Each time you buy from a reporting store on credit or take out a loan at a bank, a finance company, or some other reporting creditor, a credit bureau is informed of your account number and of the date, amount, terms, and type of credit. As you make payments, your file is updated to show the outstanding balance, the number and the amounts of payments past due, and the frequency of 30-, 60-, or 90-day latenesses. Your record may indicate the largest amount of credit you have had and the maximum limit permitted by the creditor. Each inquiry about you may be recorded. If you have been refused credit, that may also be entered into your file. If this has happened frequently a creditor may be wary; he will at least want to consider the reasons for the refusals. Any suits, judgments, or tax liens against you may appear as well. However, a federal law protects your rights if the information in your credit file is erroneous.

Fair Credit Reporting

You can see that fair and accurate credit reporting is vital to both creditors and consumers. Therefore, Congress enacted the **Fair Credit Reporting Act** of 1971, which regulates the use of credit reports, requires the deletion of obsolete information, and gives the consumer access to his or her file and the right to have erroneous data corrected. Furthermore, only authorized persons are allowed to obtain your credit report.

FIGURE 5-8 Sample Credit Report

EQUIFAX SERVICES/RETAILERS COMMERCIAL AGENCY
CREDIT REPORT (INDIVIDUAL)

Report Made By Equifax Services ☒ Retailers ☐

Acct. No.	00000	File No. & Requestor's Name 1821 Faye	Macon, GA OFFICE

Date	7/15/83	
NAME (& Spouse)	BRYAN, JOHN A. (MARY)	**REPORT FROM** _(If not city in heading)_ _(State whether former addr., etc.)_
Address	Macon, GA, 248 Poplar St., N.E.	
Emp-Occ.	Johnson Realty Co., Salesman	**Transaction:** Books
Bus. Add.	Macon, GA, 301 Main St., S.W.	**Amount $** 200
		Mo. Notes $ 10

1. Time known by each source? — 1. 3, 3, 1, 2yrs
2. Are name and address correct as given above? — 2. yes
3. About what is age? (If around 21 verify if possible.) — 3. 33
4. Is applicant married, single, divorced or widowed? No. dependents? — 4. married No. dependents 2
5. Name of employer? (Give name of firm.) — 5. Johnson Realty Co.
6. What is nature of business? (State the kind of trade or industry?) — 6. Real Estate
7. Position held—how long with present employer? (If less than 1 year, explain.) — 7. Salesman How long? 1½ yrs
8. Work full time steadily? (If not, how many days per week?) — 8. yes
9. Are prospects for continued employment regarded as good? — 9. yes
10. What would you estimate NET WORTH? — 10. $8,500
11. List principal assets (Real estate, cash, stocks, bonds, etc.). — 11. Car, equity in home, personals
12. Does applicant own home, rent or board? — 12. buying
13. What is ANNUAL EARNED INCOME from work or business? — 13. $18,000 Exact ☐ Estimated ☒
14. ADDED ANNUAL income from investments, rentals, pensions, disability, etc.? — 14. $none Source:
15. If spouse employed, give name of employer. — 15. A&B Insurance Co.
    a. Position held—approximate ANNUAL INCOME. — a. Clerk (part- Income $5,000
    b. Approximate number of years employed. — b. 2 time)
16. Any foreclosures, garnishments, suits, judgments or bankruptcies known to sources? (If yes, explain below.) — 16. no
17. Any factors that may affect doing business with applicant on a credit basis? — 17. no
18. **CREDIT RECORD:** Set out CREDIT RECORD in tabular form below.
19. **BUSINESS-FINANCES:** Comment on present and any past business connections developed, irregular employment or lack of stability. Cover subject's financial position, giving breakdown on worth.
20. **RESIDENCE:** Show how long subject has lived at this address and former addresses, if developed.

Comment when information developed on credit responsibility or financial difficulties may affect earnings or paying ability.

Trade Line	How Long Selling	Date Last Sale	Highest Credit	Terms of Sale	Amount Owing	Amount Past Due	Paying Record
Sundial Finance Company	2 yrs	10/82	1200	24 x $35	885	–	prompt
Al's Dept. Store	9/79	10/80	100	30 days	–	–	30 days
GA State Bank		7/79	3850	48x $80.20	962.40	–	as agreed
FROM FILE DATED 8/14/81							
Al's Dept. Store	9/79	–	264	10 mos.	none	none	as agreed
GA State Bank	11/77	–	1321	24 x $65	none	none	as agreed

BUSINESS FINANCES: John A. Bryan is employed as shown. He sells on a commission basis and has been successful in this work. His employer expects his earnings to increase. Prior to this employment, he was an insurance salesman for A&B Insurance Co. for two years, where he was well regarded. His wife is employed by this company. Their worth is composed of equity in home, auto (78 Chev.), household goods, personal effects and cash.

RESIDENCE: Prior to buying their present home 6 months ago, they rented an apartment at 29 Maple Lane, N.W., Macon for 1 year. They have one child age 2.

Equifax Services Inc.
Equifax Services Ltd.
Form 63LE—2-78 U.S.A.

Source: Courtesy of Equifax Services, Inc.

Who May Obtain a Credit Report?

Your credit report may be issued only to properly identified persons for approved purposes. It may be furnished in response to a court order or in accordance with your own written request. It may also be provided to someone who will use it in connection with a credit transaction, an employment application, the underwriting of insurance, or some other legitimate business need or in the determination of eligibility for a license or other benefit granted by a governmental agency. Your friends and neighbors may not obtain credit information about you. If they request such information, they may be subject to fine and imprisonment.

Time Limits on Adverse Data

Most of the information in your credit file may be reported for only seven years. If you have declared personal bankruptcy, however, that fact may be reported for 10 years. After 7 years or 10 years, the information in your credit file can't be disclosed by a credit reporting agency unless you are being investigated for a credit application of $50,000 or more, for an application to purchase life insurance of $50,000 or more, or for employment at an annual salary of $20,000 or more. In those situations, the time limits on releasing the information in your credit file do not apply. Nor do those time limits apply if a creditor chooses to use prior adverse information to deny a credit application.

Incorrect Information in Your Credit File

Credit bureaus are required to follow reasonable procedures to ensure that subscribing creditors report information accurately. However, mistakes may occur. Your file may contain erroneous data or records of someone with a similar name. When you notify the credit bureau that you dispute the accuracy of information, it must reinvestigate and modify or remove inaccurate data. You should give the credit bureau any pertinent data you have concerning an error. If reinvestigation does not resolve the dispute to your satisfaction, you may place a statement of 100 words or less in your file, explaining why you think the record is inaccurate. You may also want to place a statement in your file to explain a period of delinquency caused by some unexpected hardship, such as serious illness, a catastrophe, or unemployment, that cut off or drastically reduced your income. The credit bureau must include your statement about disputed data—or a coded version of that statement—with any report it issues about you. At your request, the credit bureau must also send a correction to any recipient of a report in the preceding six months if the report was for a credit check or in the preceding two years if the report was for employment purposes.

What Are the Legal Remedies?

Any consumer reporting agency or user of reported information that willfully or through negligence fails to comply with the provisions of the Fair

Credit Reporting Act may be sued by the consumer. If the agency or the user is found guilty, the consumer may be awarded actual damages, court costs, and attorney's fees, and in the case of willful noncompliance, punitive damages as allowed by the court. The action must be brought within two years of the occurrence or within two years after the discovery of material and willful misrepresentation of information. An unauthorized person who obtains a credit report under false pretenses may be fined up to $5,000 or imprisoned for one year, or both. The same penalties apply to anyone who willfully provides credit information to someone not authorized to receive it.

Figure 5–9 outlines the steps you can take if you are denied credit.

AVOIDING AND CORRECTING CREDIT MISTAKES

- How to Avoid and Correct Credit Mistakes

Has the department store's computer ever billed you for merchandise that you returned to the store or never received? Or has a credit card company ever charged you for the same item twice or failed to properly credit a payment on your account?

The best way to maintain your credit standing is to repay your debts on time. But there may still be complications. To protect your credit and to save your time, your money, and your future credit rating, you should learn how to correct the mistakes and misunderstandings that may tangle your credit accounts. If there is a snag, first try to deal directly with the creditor. The credit laws can help you settle your complaints.

The Fair Credit Billing Act (FCBA), passed in 1975, sets the procedure for promptly correcting billing mistakes, for refusing to make credit card payments on defective goods, and for promptly crediting your payments.

The act defines a billing error as any charge for something you did not buy or for something bought by a person not authorized to use your account. Also included among billing errors is any charge that is not properly identified on your bill, that is for an amount different from the actual purchase price, or that was entered on a date different from the purchase date. A billing error may also be a charge for something that you did not accept on delivery or that was not delivered according to agreement.

Finally, billing errors include errors in arithmetic; failure to reflect a payment or other credit to your account; failure to mail the statement to your current address, provided you notified the creditor of an address change at least 20 days before the end of the billing period; and questionable items or items on which you need additional information.

In Case of Error

If you think your bill is wrong or you want more information about it, follow these steps. First, notify the creditor *in writing* within 60 days after the bill was mailed. Be sure to write to the address that the creditor lists for billing inquiries, to give the creditor your name and account number, and to say that you believe the bill contains an error and what you believe the error to be. State the suspected amount of the error or the item you want explained.

FIGURE 5-9 What If You're Denied Credit?

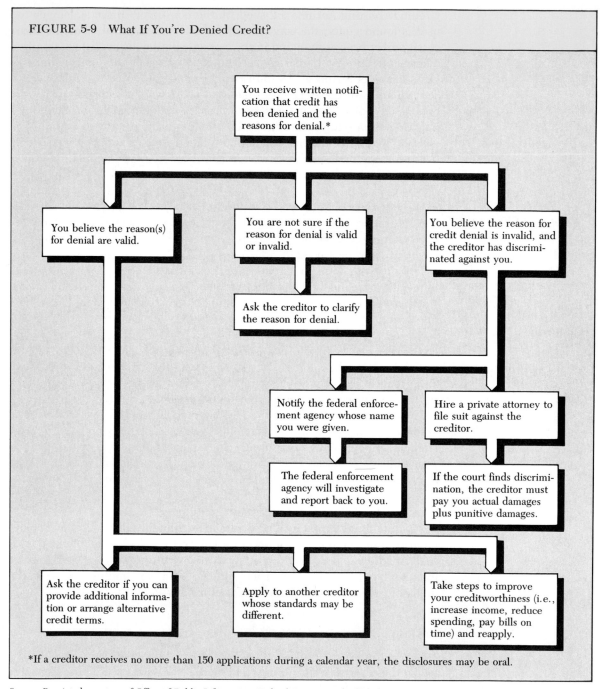

You receive written notification that credit has been denied and the reasons for denial.*

You believe the reason(s) for denial are valid.

You are not sure if the reason for denial is valid or invalid.

You believe the reason for credit denial is invalid, and the creditor has discriminated against you.

Ask the creditor to clarify the reason for denial.

Notify the federal enforcement agency whose name you were given.

Hire a private attorney to file suit against the creditor.

The federal enforcement agency will investigate and report back to you.

If the court finds discrimination, the creditor must pay you actual damages plus punitive damages.

Ask the creditor if you can provide additional information or arrange alternative credit terms.

Apply to another creditor whose standards may be different.

Take steps to improve your creditworthiness (i.e., increase income, reduce spending, pay bills on time) and reapply.

*If a creditor receives no more than 150 applications during a calendar year, the disclosures may be oral.

Source: Reprinted, courtesy of Office of Public Information, Federal Reserve Bank of Minneapolis, Minneapolis, MN 55480.

Then pay all the parts of the bill that are not in dispute.

While waiting for an answer, you do not have to pay the disputed amount or any minimum payments or finance charges that apply to it.

The creditor must acknowledge your letter within 30 days, unless your bill can be corrected sooner. Within two billing periods, but in no case longer than 90 days, either your account must be corrected or you must be told why the creditor believes the bill is correct. If the creditor made a mistake, you do not pay any finance charges on the disputed amount. Your account must be corrected, and you must be sent an explanation of any amount you still owe.

If no error is found, the creditor must promptly send you an explanation of the reasons for that determination and a statement of what you owe, which may include any finance charges that have accumulated and any minimum payments that you missed while you were questioning the bill. You then have the time usually given on your type of account to pay any balance. If you are still not satisfied, you should notify the creditor within the time allowed to pay your bill.

Maintaining Your Credit Rating

A creditor may not threaten your credit rating while you are resolving a billing dispute. Once you have written about a possible error, a creditor is prohibited from giving out information that would damage your credit reputation to other creditors or credit bureaus. And until your complaint has been answered, the creditor may not take any action to collect the disputed amount.

Pepper . . . and Salt

"We're sorry about the mistake, sir—our administrative computer is chewing out our billing computer right now."

From *The Wall Street Journal,* with permission of Cartoon Features Syndicate.

After the creditor has explained the bill, you may be reported as delinquent on the amount in dispute and the creditor may take action to collect if you do not pay in the time allowed. Even so, you can still disagree in writing. Then the creditor must report that you have challenged your bill and give you the name and address of each recipient of information about your account. When the matter has been settled, the creditor must report the outcome to each recipient of information. Remember that you may also place your version of the story in your credit record.

Defective Goods or Services

Your new sofa arrives with only three legs. You try to return it; no luck. You ask the merchant to repair or replace it; still no luck. The Fair Credit Billing Act provides that you may withhold payment on any damaged or shoddy goods or poor services that you have purchased with a credit card, as long as you have made a real attempt to solve the problem with the merchant. This right may be limited if the card was a bank credit card or a travel and entertainment credit card or any other credit card not issued by the store where you made your purchase. In such cases, the sale must have been for more than $50 and it must have taken place in your home state or within 100 miles of your home address.

COSIGNING A LOAN

● Should You Cosign a Loan?

What would you do if a friend or relative asked you to cosign a loan? Before you give your answer, make sure you understand what cosigning involves. Under a recent Federal Trade Commission rule,[6] creditors are required to give you a notice to help explain your obligations. The cosigner's notice says:

> You are being asked to guarantee this debt. Think carefully before you do. If the borrower doesn't pay the debt, you will have to. Be sure you can afford to pay if you have to, and that you want to accept this responsibility.
>
> You may have to pay up to the full amount of the debt if the borrower does not pay. You may also have to pay late fees or collection costs, which increase this amount.
>
> The creditor can collect this debt from you without first trying to collect from the borrower. The creditor can use the same collection methods against you that can be used against the borrower, such as suing you, garnishing your wages, etc. If this debt is ever in default, that fact may become a part of *your* credit record.

Cosigners Often Pay

Some studies of certain types of lenders show that as many as three out of four cosigners are asked to repay the loan. That statistic should not surprise you. When you are asked to cosign, you are being asked to take a risk that a professional lender will not take. The lender would not require a cosigner if the borrower met the lender's criteria for making a loan.

[6]*Facts for Consumers* (Washington, D.C.: Federal Trade Commission, Bureau of Consumer Protection, January 1986), p. 1.

In most states, if you do cosign and your friend or relative misses a payment, the lender can collect from you immediately without pursuing the borrower first. And the amount you owe may be increased—if the lender decides to sue to collect. A lender that wins the case may be able to take your wages and property.

If You Do Cosign

Despite the risks, there may be times when you decide to cosign. Perhaps your son or daughter needs a first loan, or a close friend needs help. Here are a few things to consider before you cosign:

1. Be sure you can afford to pay the loan. If you are asked to pay and cannot, you could be sued or your credit rating could be damaged.
2. Before you cosign a loan, consider that even if you are not asked to repay the debt, your liability for this loan may keep you from getting other credit that you may want.
3. Before you pledge property, such as your automobile or furniture, to secure the loan, make sure you understand the consequences. If the borrower defaults, you could lose these possessions.
4. Check your state law. Some states have laws giving you additional rights as a cosigner.

COMPLAINING ABOUT CONSUMER CREDIT

- Effective Complaining about Credit

First try to solve your problem directly with the creditor. Only if that fails should you bring more formal complaint procedures. Here's the way to file a complaint with the federal agencies responsible for administering consumer credit protection laws.

Complaints about Banks

If you have a complaint about a bank in connection with any of the federal credit laws or if you think that any part of your business with a bank has been handled in an unfair or deceptive way, you may get advice and help from the Federal Reserve System. You don't need to have an account at the bank to file a complaint.

You should submit your complaint, in writing whenever possible, to the Director of the Division of Consumer and Community Affairs, Board of Governors of the Federal Reserve System, Washington, DC 20551, or to the Federal Reserve bank for your district, as listed in Figure 5–10. Be sure to give the name and address of the bank involved and to describe the bank practice to which you object. (See Figure 5–11 for the complaint form.)

The Federal Reserve bank or the Board of Governors will try to respond in full within 15 days. If that is not possible, the reply will set a reasonable date for furnishing you with complete information.

The Board of Governors has supervisory responsibility only for state-chartered banks that are members of the Federal Reserve System. It will

---

FIGURE 5-10   Addresses of the Board of Governors and the Federal
Reserve Banks

Board of Governors
of the Federal
Reserve System
20th and Constitution Avenue, NW
Washington, DC 20551
(202) 452-3000

Atlanta, Georgia
104 Marietta Street, NW
ZIP 30303
(404) 586-8500

Boston, Massachusetts
600 Atlantic Avenue
ZIP 02106
(617) 973-3000

Chicago, Illinois
230 South LaSalle Street
P.O. Box 834
ZIP 60690
(312) 322-5322

Cleveland, Ohio
1455 East Sixth Street
P.O. Box 6387
ZIP 44101
(216) 579-2000

Dallas, Texas
400 South Akard Street
Station K
ZIP 75222
(214) 651-6111

Kansas City, Missouri
925 Grand Avenue
ZIP 64198
(816) 881-2000

Minneapolis, Minnesota
250 Marquette Avenue
ZIP 55480
(612) 340-2345

New York, New York
33 Liberty Street
Federal Reserve P.O. Station
ZIP 10045
(212) 791-5000

Philadelphia, Pennsylvania
100 North Sixth Street
P.O. Box 66
ZIP 19105
(215) 574-6000

Richmond, Virginia
701 East Byrd Street
P.O. Box 27622
ZIP 23219
(804) 643-1250

St. Louis, Missouri
411 Locust Street
P.O. Box 442
ZIP 63166
(314) 444-8444

San Francisco, California
400 Sansome Street
P.O. Box 7702
ZIP 94120
(415) 544-2000

---

refer complaints about other institutions to the appropriate federal bank
regulatory agency and then let you know to which agency your complaint has
been referred. The practice you wish to complain about does not have to be
subject to federal regulation.

Protection under Consumer Credit Laws

You may also take legal action against a creditor. If you decide to file a
lawsuit, here are important consumer credit laws you should know.

Truth in Lending and Consumer Leasing Acts. If any creditor fails to
disclose information required under the Truth in Lending Act or the Consumer Leasing Act, or gives inaccurate information, or does not comply with

the rules about credit cards or the right to cancel them, you may sue for actual damages, that is, any money loss you suffer.

Class action suits are also permitted. A class action suit is one filed on behalf of a group of people with similar claims.

Equal Credit Opportunity Act. If you think you can prove that a creditor has discriminated against you for any reason prohibited by the ECOA, you may sue for actual damages plus punitive damages (that is, damages for the fact that the law has been violated) of up to $10,000.

Fair Credit Billing Act. A creditor who fails to comply with rules applying to the correction of billing errors automatically forfeits the amount owed on

---

FIGURE 5-11   Complaint Form to Report Violations of Federal Credit Laws

COMPLAINT FORM   **Federal Reserve System**

Name _____   Name of Bank _____

Address _____   Address _____
         Street   City   State   Zip
   City   State   Zip

Daytime telephone _____   Account number (if applicable) _____
         (include area code)

The complaint involves the following service: Checking Account ☐   Savings Account ☐   Loan ☐

   Other: Please specify _____

I have attempted to resolve this complaint directly with the bank: No ☐   Yes ☐

   If "No", an attempt should be made to contact the bank and resolve the complaint.

   If "Yes", name of person or department contacted is _____
                                                Date

MY COMPLAINT IS AS FOLLOWS (Briefly describe the events in the order in which they happened, including specific dates and the bank's actions to which you object. Enclose copies of any pertinent information or correspondence that may be helpful. Do not send us your only copy of any document):

_____

_____

_____

_____

_____

_____

_____

_____

_____

_____

This information is solicited under the Federal Trade Commission Improvement Act. Providing the information is voluntary; complete information is necessary to expedite investigation of your complaint. Routine use of the information may include disclosing it to bank(s) or others involved or to other governmental agencies as deemed appropriate.

Date _____   Signatures _____

                                               _____

Source: Board of Governors of the Federal Reserve System.

TABLE 5-2   Summary of Federal Consumer Credit Laws

Act (date effective)	Major Provisions
Truth in Lending (July 1, 1969)	Provides specific cost disclosure requirements for the annual percentage rate and the finance charge as a dollar amount. Requires disclosure of other loan terms and conditions. Regulates the advertising of credit terms. Provides the right to cancel a contract when certain real estate is used as security.
(January 25, 1971)	Prohibits credit card issuers from sending unrequested cards. Limits a cardholder's liability for unauthorized use of a card to $50.
(October 1, 1982)	Requires that disclosures for closed-end credit (installment credit) be written in plain English and appear apart from all other information. Allows credit customer to request an itemization of the amount financed, if the creditor does not automatically provide it.
Fair Credit Reporting Act (April 24, 1971)	Requires disclosure to consumers of the name and address of any consumer reporting agency that supplied reports used to deny credit, insurance or employment. Gives a consumer the right to know what is in his file to have incorrect information reinvestigated and removed, and to include his version of a disputed item in the file. Requires credit reporting agencies to send the consumer's version of a disputed item to certain businesses or creditors. Sets forth identification requirements for consumers wishing to inspect their files. Requires that consumers be notified when an investigative report is being made. Limits the time that certain information can be kept in a credit file.
Fair Credit Billing Act (October 28, 1975)	Establishes procedures for consumers and creditors to follow when billing errors occur on periodic statements for revolving credit accounts. Requires creditors to send a statement setting forth these procedures to consumers periodically. Allows consumers to withhold payment for faulty or defective goods or services (within certain limitations) when purchased with a credit card. Requires creditor to promptly credit customers' accounts and to return overpayments if requested.
Equal Credit Opportunity Act (October 28, 1975)	Prohibits credit discrimination based on sex and marital status. Prohibits creditors from requiring women to reapply for credit upon a change in marital status. Requires creditors to inform applicants of acceptance or rejection of their credit application within 30 days of receiving a completed application. Requires creditors to provide a written statement of the reasons for adverse action.
(March 23, 1977)	Prohibits credit discrimination based on race, national origin, religion, age, or the receipt of public assistance.
(June 1, 1977)	Requires creditors to report information on an account to credit bureaus in the names of both husband and wife if both use the account and both are liable for it.
Fair Debt Collection Practices Act (March 20, 1978)	Prohibits abusive, deceptive, and unfair practices by debt collectors. Establishes procedures for debt collectors contacting a credit user. Restricts debt collector contacts with a third party. Specifies that payment for several debts be applied as the consumer wishes and that no monies be applied to a debt in dispute.

Source: *Managing Your Credit*, rev. ed. (Prospect Heights, Ill.: Money Management Institute, Household Financial Services, 1985), pp. 36–37. © Household Financial Services, Prospect Heights, Illinois.

the item in question and any finance charges on it, up to a combined total of $50, even if the bill was correct. You may also sue for actual damages plus twice the amount of any finance charges.

Fair Credit Reporting Act. You may sue any credit reporting agency or creditor for violating the rules about access to your credit records and the correction of errors in your credit file. Again, you are entitled to actual damages plus such punitive damages as the court may allow if the violation is proven to have been intentional.

Table 5–2 summarizes the major federal consumer credit laws. The Federal Reserve System has set up a separate office in Washington—the Division of Consumer and Community Affairs—to handle consumer complaints. This division also writes regulations to carry out the consumer credit laws, enforces these laws for state-chartered banks that are members of the Federal Reserve System, and helps banks comply with these laws.

The Federal Reserve System is advised by the Consumer Advisory Council, a panel of experts in consumer credit, representing both business and consumer interests across the country. The council meets four times a year, and its meetings are open to the public.

SUMMARY

- Consumer credit is the use of credit by individuals and families for personal needs. Among the advantages of using credit are purchasing goods when they are needed and paying for them gradually, meeting financial emergencies, achieving convenience in shopping, establishing a credit rating, making forced savings, and employing credit as leverage. But credit costs money, encourages impulse buying and overspending, and ties up future income, and its misuse can create serious long-term financial difficulties.

- Closed-end and open-end credit are two types of consumer credit. With closed-end (or installment) credit, the borrower pays back a onetime loan in a specified period of time and with a specified number of payments. With open-end (or revolving) credit, the borrower is permitted to take loans on a continuous

basis and is billed for partial payments periodically.

- Creditors determine creditworthiness on the basis of the five C's: character, capacity, capital, collateral, and conditions.

- Two general rules of thumb for measuring credit capacity are: spend no more than 20 percent of your net income on credit purchase (15 percent is much safer), and spend no more than you can afford to pay off in 12 months.

- You are responsible for building and maintaining your credit rating. The credit bureaus collect credit information and reveal it to creditors.

- The Fair Credit Reporting Act gives you the right to know what your credit file contains, and the credit bureau must provide someone to help you interpret the data. Erroneous information must be corrected to your satisfaction; if not, you may enter your version in 100 words or less.

- If you have a complaint against a creditor, try to solve the problem directly with the creditor. If all else fails, you are protected under the federal consumer protection laws.

GLOSSARY

Capacity.   The borrower's financial ability to meet credit obligations.

Capital.   The borrower's assets or net worth.

Character.   The borrower's attitude toward his or her credit obligations.

Closed-end credit.   Onetime loans that the borrower pays back in a specified period of time and in payments of equal amounts; also called installment credit.

Conditions.   The general economic conditions that can affect a borrower's ability to repay a loan.

Collateral.   A valuable asset that is pledged to assure loan payments.

Consumer credit.   The use of credit for personal needs.

Credit.   An arrangement to receive cash, goods, or services now and pay for them later.

Credit bureau.   A reporting agency that assembles credit and other information on consumers.

Equal Credit Opportunity Act (ECOA).   Bans discrimination against women and forbids other forms of discrimination.

Fair Credit Billing Act (FCBA).   Sets procedures for consumers and creditors to follow when billing errors occur on periodic statements for revolving credit accounts.

Fair Credit Reporting Act.   Requires disclosure to consumers of any consumer reporting agency that supplied reports used to deny credit, insurance, or employment.

Interest.   The dollar cost of borrowing money.

Line of credit.   The dollar amount, which may or may not be borrowed, that a lender is making available to a borrower.

Open-end credit.   A line of credit extended by many retailers that may be used repeatedly up to a certain specified limit; also called revolving credit.

Revolving check credit.   A prearranged loan from a bank for a specified amount.

REVIEW QUESTIONS

1. What is consumer credit, and what is its importance in our economy?
2. What factors are important in making a decision to borrow or not to borrow, and what options are available to consumers?
3. List and discuss advantages and disadvantages of using credit.
4. Describe and distinguish between open-end and closed-end credit. Give examples of each type, and explain when one type is better than the other.
5. What are the five C's of credit? How do creditors evaluate the five C's in granting or denying credit?
6. Describe existing federal credit laws that affect consumer credit availability and consumer credit problems.

7. What information can the creditor not use in evaluating your application for credit?

8. List steps that women can take to build a favorable credit history and credit rating. How do these steps differ for men?

9. How can you measure your credit capacity? What are general guidelines in determining your credit capacity?

10. What are credit bureaus? Who needs them? What functions do they perform?

11. What information is in your credit files, and what sources provide this information to credit bureaus?

DISCUSSION QUESTIONS AND ACTIVITIES

1. How could the situations presented in the opening scenario have been avoided?

2. Discuss and compile a list of places that can be called to report dishonest credit practices, to get advice and help with credit problems, and to check out a creditor's reputation before signing a contract.

3. Interview credit representatives such as bankers, managers of credit departments in retail stores, managers of finance companies, credit union officers, managers of credit bureaus, and savings and loan officers. Ask what procedures they follow in granting or refusing a loan.

4. Discuss the following statements: (a) Credit should be used only for emergencies and absolute necessities. (b) Bankruptcy is the best solution for overindebtedness. (c) Credit tempts people to overspend.

5. How can the wise use of credit help individuals and families raise their standard of living? How can it help the economy?

6. Why does the amount of credit that individuals and families can safely assume vary significantly?

7. What are some of the potential spending needs for which people between the ages of 18 and 35 might use credit?

8. Discuss this issue: "In the long run, spending cannot exceed income—consumers must ultimately pay for all of their purchases."

ADDITIONAL READINGS

Consumer Credit. Silver Spring, Md.: National Foundation for Consumer Credit, n.d.

Consumer Handbook to Credit Protection Laws. Washington, D.C.: Board of Governors of the Federal Reserve System, June 1980.

Credit Handbook for Women. New York: American Express Company, 1982.

Getting a Hold on Credit. Silver Spring, Md.: National Foundation for Consumer Credit, n.d.

Managing Your Credit. Prospect Heights, Ill.: Money Management Institute, Household Financial Services, 1985.

Managing Your Credit. San Francisco: Bank of America, 1983.

Measuring and Using Our Credit Capacity. Silver Spring, Md.: National Foundation for Consumer Credit, n.d.

Solving Credit Problems. Washington, D.C.: Federal Trade Commission, May 1985.

Story of Consumer Credit. New York: Federal Reserve Bank of New York.

Using Retail Credit. Chicago: Sears Roebuck & Co., Consumer Information Services.

"Why There's Such a Rush to Deal Out Credit Cards." *U.S. News & World Report*, November 11, 1985, pp. 84–85.

Your Credit Options. Washington, D.C.: Consumer Federation of America, n.d.

CASE 5-1 Applying for Credit and Getting It*

Betty Carson applied for credit at Friendly Finance Company. She was denied credit and received a form letter stating that information had been obtained from a consumer reporting agency. The letter included the name, address, and phone number of Anytown Credit Bureau.

Betty called Anytown Credit Bureau to find out what information it had given the finance company. She was told that it generally did not give out such information on the phone but that she could come to the office to learn the contents of her credit file. Betty said that she would be able to come at 1 p.m. on Monday.

When Betty arrived at the credit bureau, she was asked to show her driver's license and one other piece of identification. A trained interviewer talked with her and revealed that the inquiry from Friendly Finance Company was the only inquiry about her that the credit bureau had received during the past six months. The only other information in her file was that an account held five years earlier with AAA Department store had been paid. Betty was surprised at the lack of credit information in her file, but she explained that until recently she had lived in a different state. The interviewer asked whether she could provide the names of her creditors there. The credit bureau would then check with those firms and add any new credit information. Betty did so and then applied for credit again at Friendly Finance Company. This time, she was granted credit.

Questions

1. Why do you think Ms. Carson was denied credit?

2. Was it legal for the Friendly Finance Company to deny her credit request?

3. How could Ms. Carson have avoided being denied credit the first time?

*Source: *Your Credit Rights* (Minneapolis: Federal Reserve Bank of Minneapolis, 1982), p. 65. ©1982 by Federal Reserve Bank of Minneapolis. Reprinted, courtesy of Office of Public Information, Federal Reserve Bank of Minneapolis, Minneapolis, MN 55480.

CASE 5-2 Measuring Hank's Credit Capacity

Hank Hansen is 24 years old, single, and employed as a computer operator at a local manufacturing company. He recently purchased a two-bedroom condominium, and he plans to marry his high school sweetheart when she graduates from college in two years.

Hank's net monthly income is $2,000. He spends the following amounts each month for essential items:

Mortgage loan	$ 600
Utilities	130
Food	260
Transportation	130
Clothing	40
Medical expenses	40
Total	$1,200

Hank wants to buy a $10,000 car, and he has a down payment of $2,000. He figures that automobile insurance will be about $900 a year but that if he buys this new, fuel-efficient car, he will save about $30 a month on transportation.

Questions

1. How much can Hank spend on credit payments each month?

2. What percentage of his net monthly income can Hank spend safely on credit (not including housing) payments?

3. Will Hank get a loan from a bank if he applies for it?

6

Sources of Consumer Credit

All of us can get into credit difficulties if we do not understand how and when to use credit. Credit problems are rarely identical. Consumers are motivated by the desire for a higher standard of living, persuasive advertising, ignorance of the real cost of credit, lack of realistic planning, impatience, and a desire to keep up with the Joneses! When, as a result, credit problems begin to arise, they lack the skills to deal with those problems and to find alternative solutions. After studying this chapter, you will be able to:

- Identify major sources of consumer credit.

- Shop for credit by comparing the finance charge and the annual percentage rate.

- Determine the cost of credit by calculating interest with various interest formulas.

- List the steps you can take to deal with your debts.

- Describe various private and governmental sources that assist consumers with debt problems.

- Distinguish between the Chapter 7 and Chapter 13 bankruptcy laws.

Interview with **Joyce Bryant,**
Vice President and Director, Money Management Institute,
Household Financial Services Household International

Joyce Bryant is Vice President, Consumer Affairs, of Household Financial Services, an arm of Household International. Her consumer education department, which has been a public service activity for over 50 years, provides financial guidance to individuals and families in the United States and Canada. Ms. Bryant frequently speaks on financial issues and serves as a national media spokesperson on credit issues for Household Financial Services.

With a number of credit sources available, it is important to shop for credit and evaluate its costs and terms—choosing the credit source that is best for you. Now that laws require creditors to state finance charges in terms of dollar amount and annual percentage rate, it might appear that the only thing necessary to make a decision is to determine which credit source offers the lowest price by comparing these two figures. However, other factors should also be considered.

In evaluating the plan and source that best meet your needs and requirements, Ms. Bryant suggests that you consider several factors. First, consider the maturity of the contract. Will you be able to fit the size and number of payments into your spending plan without straining? Second, consider the total cost—that is, both the price of the credit and the price of the goods and services purchased. Third, consider the security pledged—what you would lose if you defaulted on your payments. Finally, consider the other conditions for credit—services or terms that may outweigh differences in credit charges.

Ms. Bryant suggests that money problems occur when expenses and obligations become greater than income or ability to meet payments. These problems may be the result of inexperience in handling finances, mismanagement, marital problems or divorce, unexpected emergencies, interrupted income, or any number of situations that cause a difference in the ability of the credit user to pay. Whatever the problem, it is important to know what to do about it and to act promptly.

Last summer, John Grey's old car finally had to be junked. John needed another one, so he checked local newspaper ads for used cars. He finally saw two ads that interested him. Both were for the same kind of car, and the prices were identical. Lucky's Used Car Lot advertised credit terms and required a $200 down payment. But Wheels and Deals Used Cars advertised "No Money Down." That sounded good to John, so he visited Wheels and Deals.

At Wheels and Deals, John looked at the car, liked it, and asked about financing terms. The salesperson told John that he could pay $80.61 a month for 24 months and gave him a contract that was already filled in.

The contract was confusing to John, but he did notice that a $200 down payment was included in the figures. He asked the salesperson about this, since "no money down" was the phrase that had attracted him to Wheels and Deals.

The salesperson told John that the credit department could only finance $1,495. However, he told John that he could borrow $200 for the down payment from a loan company down the street and said that the loan company payments would be less than $20 a month for only 12 months. John thought about this but decided that he probably wouldn't need a loan. He had already saved about $200 that he could use for the down payment.

John looked at the car contract again, saw a charge for credit life insurance, and asked about it. The salesperson quickly told him that the insurance was a good thing to have.

Finally, John noticed the words *annual percentage rate* and asked what they meant. The salesperson told him that this term was required by the Truth in Lending Act but really didn't mean a thing. He said that the only important figure was the amount John would owe on the car—$1,934.63. That was a lot of money, and John decided to think things over before signing the contract.

John started home and then remembered that Lucky's Used Car Lot had advertised a car like the one he had just

SOURCES OF CONSUMER CREDIT

- Major Sources of Consumer Credit

We all have short- or long-term needs for money or credit. Whether your furnace quit in the middle of January or short-term disability has limited your monthly income, unexpected incidents can create a need for several hundred or several thousand dollars.

Financial institutions, the sources of credit, come in all shapes and sizes. They play an important role in our economy, and they offer a broad range of financial services.

Just look in your yellow pages under "credit," "financing," and "loans." You will find that a variety of financial institutions in your area offer cash and credit. In this section, you will learn about the major sources of consumer credit—commercial banks, savings and loan associations, credit unions, finance companies, life insurance companies, pawnshops, loan sharks, and family and friends.

seen. The Lucky's ad had had a lot of terms—one was *annual percentage rate*. John decided to go to Lucky's and compare its credit terms with those offered by Wheels and Deals.

The salesperson at Lucky's showed John the car and asked whether he had seen the Lucky's ad. John said that he had but confessed that he hadn't understood all the terms. The salesperson then got a blank contract, sat down with John, and explained the credit terms, pointing out that some of them could be used to great advantage by a shopper. John examined the various alternatives.

John was about to buy the car when the salesperson suggested another option: John could pay for the car in 18 months at $98.33 a month. The salesperson filled out a contract to show John the very real difference between his choices. John immediately noticed that the APR was much lower on the 18-month plan. He also saw that he could save nearly $100 on the finance charge by making the higher monthly payments for fewer months.

John considered his choice of payment plans and finally decided on 24 months. Although the second option would have saved him money, he felt that it was more important to be sure he could meet his monthly payments than it was to reduce his finance charge. If he couldn't afford the higher payments, he might lose his car.

After making his decision, John read his contract carefully, asked questions about things he didn't understand, and then signed. The salesperson gave him a copy of his contract and the keys to his new car. Breathing a sigh of relief, John drove away—a happy car owner.

*John W. Tibbetts and Dorothy Westby-Gibson, *Personal and Family Financial Planning for Multicultural Adults: A Staff Development Program for Adult Basic Education Teachers and Trainers* (Washington, D.C.: American Council of Life Insurance, 1982), pp. 4/62d, 63d.

Commercial Banks

Banks make loans to borrowers who need them and who have the capacity to repay them. Loans are the sale of the use of money by those that have it (such as banks) to those that want it (borrowers) and are willing to pay a price (interest) for it.[1] Banks make several types of loans including consumer loans, housing loans, and credit card loans.

Consumer Loans. Consumer loans represent about 20 percent of all bank loans. Banks did not enter this field until the 1930s, but they greatly expanded their consumer loan operations after World War II. Today, banks

[1]*Financial Services Fact Book* (Washington, D.C.: American Bankers Association, 1984), pp. 6–7.

lead all other types of lenders in consumer loans. Most of these loans are for installment purchases, repaid with interest on a monthly basis; the bulk of such loans are for cars, boats, furniture, and other expensive durable goods.

Housing Loans. More than 20 percent of the residential mortgages in this country originate in banks. Only savings and loan associations and mortgage pools or trusts write more housing loans than banks. But the contributions of banks to the housing market extends far beyond the writing of mortgages. At the beginning of 1984, close to 35 percent of all home construction loans ($18.9 billion) and about 50 percent of all home improvement loans ($7.8 billion) were held by banks. In addition, about 50 percent of all loans for the purchase of mobile homes ($9.7 billion) were made by banks.[2] Most of the contractors that build homes borrow money from banks in order to buy supplies and equipment.

Credit Card Loans. As you learned in Chapter 5, the functions of a bank credit card include consumer credit, access to automated banking systems, and check guarantee. Bank cards are accepted by millions of retail outlets. The average bank card purchase is about $49, and the average outstanding bank card balance is about $1,600. Although most often used as a convenient source of credit for purchases of goods and services, bank cards are also used to obtain a cash advance within a prearranged credit limit.

As shown in Figure 6–1, about half of bank loans are real estate loans, loans to individuals, and other loans and leases.

[2]Ibid.

Pepper . . . and Salt

"It's nothing personal, Sir. We just aren't granting loans to any Scorpios this month."

From *The Wall Street Journal,* with permission of Cartoon Features Syndicate.

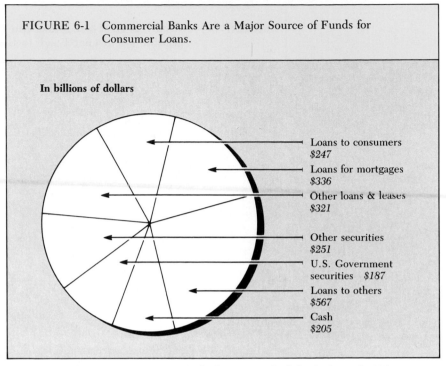

FIGURE 6-1   Commercial Banks Are a Major Source of Funds for Consumer Loans.

In billions of dollars

Loans to consumers
$247

Loans for mortgages
$336

Other loans & leases
$321

Other securities
$251

U.S. Government
securities   *$187*

Loans to others
$567

Cash
$205

Source: *Financial Institutions in Transition* (Federal Reserve Bank of Cleveland, March 1985), p. 3.

Savings and Loan Associations (S&Ls)

Before the deregulation of financial institutions, S&Ls specialized in long-term mortgage loans on houses and other real estate. Today, S&Ls offer personal installment loans, home improvement loans, second mortgages, education loans, and loans secured by savings accounts.

S&Ls lend to all creditworthy people, even though collateral may be required. The loan rates of S&Ls vary depending on the amount borrowed, the payment period, and the collateral. The interest charges of S&Ls are lower than those of some other types of lenders because S&Ls lend depositors' money, which is a relatively inexpensive source of funds.

In addition, S&Ls offer financial counseling services and handle credit transactions confidentially. As shown in Figure 6–2, S&Ls are a major source of loans for mortgages.

Credit Unions (CUs)[3]

As discussed in Chapter 4, credit unions are nonprofit cooperatives organized to serve people who have some type of common bond. Nearly 53 million Americans belong to credit unions, and the number is growing stead-

[3]Condensed from *The Wall Street Journal*, August 30, 1985, p. 11.

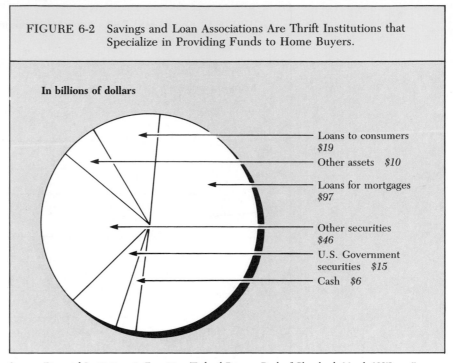

FIGURE 6-2 Savings and Loan Associations Are Thrift Institutions that Specialize in Providing Funds to Home Buyers.

In billions of dollars

Loans to consumers $19

Other assets $10

Loans for mortgages $97

Other securities $46

U.S. Government securities $15

Cash $6

Source: *Financial Institutions in Transition* (Federal Reserve Bank of Cleveland, March 1985), p. 5.

ily. The nonprofit status and lower costs of credit unions usually allow them to provide better terms on loans and savings than commercial institutions. The costs of credit unions are lower because sponsoring firms, such as Hewlett-Packard Company, provide staff and office space and because some firms agree to deduct loan payments and savings installments from members' paychecks and apply them to credit union accounts.

Credit unions often offer good value in personal loans and savings accounts. CUs often require less stringent qualifications and provide faster service on loans than do banks or S&Ls. In many cases, their loans are cheaper and their savings rates more attractive. And while consumer lending is still their primary business, some of the larger CUs have recently been offering such products as credit cards, individual retirement accounts, discount brokerage services, automated teller machine networks, and computer-authorized loans.

Of course, you must join a CU and pay membership fees to use its services. Some CUs require members to be enrolled three to six months before they can take out loans, but others allow borrowing the first day. Figure 6–3 shows that almost two thirds of CU assets are committed to consumer loans and mortgages.

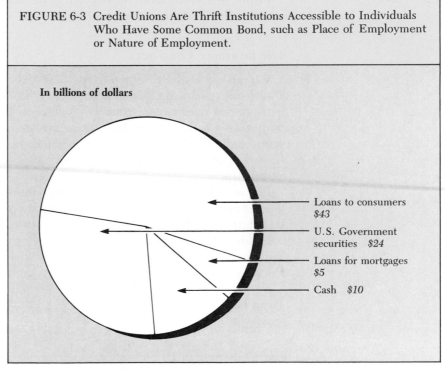

FIGURE 6-3 Credit Unions Are Thrift Institutions Accessible to Individuals Who Have Some Common Bond, such as Place of Employment or Nature of Employment.

In billions of dollars

Loans to consumers $43

U.S. Government securities $24

Loans for mortgages $5

Cash $10

Source: *Financial Institutions in Transition* (Federal Reserve Bank of Cleveland, March 1985), p. 21.

Finance Companies

The **consumer finance company (CFC)** specializes in personal installment loans and second mortgages. Consumers without an established credit history can often borrow from CFCs without collateral. CFCs are often willing to lend money to consumers who are having difficulty in obtaining credit somewhere else, but because the risk is higher, so is the interest rate.

The interest rate of CFCs varies according to the size of the loan balance and the repayment schedule. CFCs process loan applications quickly, usually on the same day that the application is made, and design repayment schedules to fit the borrower's income.

The **sales finance company (SFC)** lets you pay for big-ticket items, such as an automobile, major appliances, furniture, and stereo equipment, over a longer period of time. You don't deal with SFCs directly, but you are generally informed by the dealer that your installment note is sold to a sales finance company. You make your monthly payments to the sales finance company, not to the dealer from which you purchased the product.

Finance companies have been viewed historically as a lender of last resort to consumers because of the relatively high cost of their credit. But their image has been changing since General Motors Acceptance Corporation and others began offering attractive loans to both consumers and businesses.

Figure 6–4 shows that over one half of the assets of finance companies is committed to installment and mortgage loans.

Life Insurance Companies

You can usually borrow up to 80 percent of the accumulated cash value of a whole life (or straight life) insurance policy. The older policies were written with interest rates ranging from 4 to 8 percent. Loans against these policies do not have to be repaid, but the balance remaining upon your death is subtracted from the amount your beneficiaries receive. Repayment of at least the interest portion is important, as compounding interest works against you.

Life insurance companies charge lower interest rates than some other lenders because they take no risks and pay no collection costs and because their loans are secured by the cash value of the policy.

Figure 6–5 shows that in 1985 life insurance companies held $55 billion in loans to consumers and $152 billion in mortgage loans. However, most of the mortgage loans of life insurance companies are for commercial real estate.

Pawnshops

Pawnshops require some property of value as security for a loan, and will

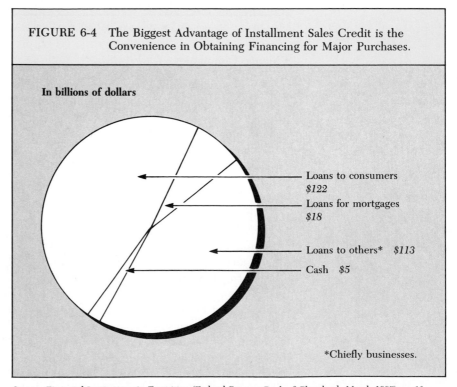

FIGURE 6-4   The Biggest Advantage of Installment Sales Credit is the Convenience in Obtaining Financing for Major Purchases.

In billions of dollars

Loans to consumers *$122*
Loans for mortgages *$18*
Loans to others*   *$113*
Cash   *$5*

*Chiefly businesses.

Source: *Financial Institutions in Transition* (Federal Reserve Bank of Cleveland, March 1985), p. 13.

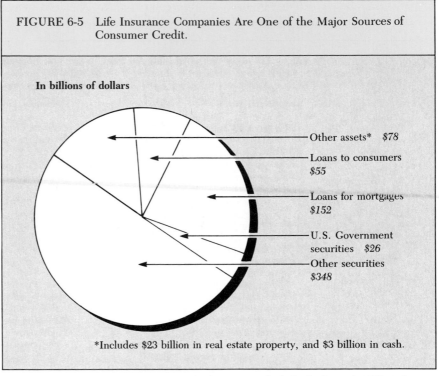

FIGURE 6-5   Life Insurance Companies Are One of the Major Sources of Consumer Credit.

In billions of dollars

Other assets* $78

Loans to consumers $55

Loans for mortgages $152

U.S. Government securities $26

Other securities $348

*Includes $23 billion in real estate property, and $3 billion in cash.

Source: *Financial Institutions in Transition* (Federal Reserve Bank of Cleveland, March 1985), p. 9.

sell that property if the loan is not paid back on time. Pawnshops almost never lend amounts comparable to the full value of the property pawned. Furthermore, pawnshops charge high interest rates.

Loan Sharks

Loan sharks are usurious lenders that charge unlawful interest rates and have no state license to engage in the lending business. Often, loan sharks use a brokerage system: a middleman arranges a loan and receives a large commission from a loan shark.

Loan sharks charge excessive rates for refinancing, repossession, late payments, and credit life insurance, and they allow only a very short time for repayment. They use collection methods that involve violence or other criminal conduct. In addition, they may obtain mortgages on property owned by the borrower and they may date the loan prior to the time that it is made.

Family and Friends

Family and friends can sometimes be your best source of credit. However, all such transactions should be treated in a businesslike manner; otherwise, misunderstandings may develop that can ruin family ties and friendships.

Table 6–1 summarizes the major sources of consumer credit—commercial

TABLE 6-1   Summary of Sources of Consumer Credit

The following table outlines the major sources of consumer loans. It attempts to generalize the information and to give an average picture of each source in regard to the type of credit available, lending policies, and customer services. Due to the dramatic fluctuations in interest rates during the 80s, it is no longer possible to provide a

Credit Source	Commercial Banks	Consumer Finance Companies
Type of Loan	Single-payment loans Personal installment loans Passbook loans Check-credit plans Credit card loans Second mortgages	Personal installment loans Second mortgages
Lending policies	Seek customers with established credit history Often require collateral or security Prefer to deal in large loans, such as auto, home improvement, and home modernization, with the exception of credit card and check-credit plans Determine repayment schedules according to the purpose of the loan Vary credit rates according to the type of credit, time period, customer's credit history, and the security offered May require several days to process a new credit application	Often lend to consumers without established credit history Often make unsecured loans Often vary rates according to the size of the loan balance Offer a variety of repayment schedules Make a higher percentage of small loans than other lenders Maximum loan size limited by law Process applications quickly, frequently on the same day as the application is made
Cost	Lower than some lenders because they: Take fewer credit risks Lend depositors' money, which is a relatively inexpensive source of funds Deal primarily in large loans, which yield a larger dollar income without an increase in administrative costs	Higher than some lenders because they: Take greater risks Must borrow and pay interest on money to lend Deal frequently in small loans, which are costly to make and yield a small amount of income
Services	Offer several different types of consumer credit plans May offer financial counseling Handle credit transactions confidentially	Provide credit promptly Make loans to pay off accumulated debts willingly Design repayment schedules to fit the borrower's income Usually offer financial counseling Handle credit transactions confidentially

common range of annual percentage rates for each source of credit. Check with your local lender for current interest rates.

Study and compare the differences to determine which source can best meet your needs and requirements.

Credit Unions	*Life Insurance Companies*	*Savings and Loan Associations*

Personal installment loans
Share draft–credit plans
Credit card loans
Second mortgages
	Single-payment or partial
	   payment loans
		Personal installment loans
		   (generally permitted by state-
		   chartered savings associations)
		Home improvement loans
		Education loans
		Savings account loans
		Second mortgages

Lend to members only
Make unsecured loans
May require collateral or cosigner
   for loans over a specified amount
May require payroll deductions to
   pay off loan
May submit large loan applications
   to a committee of members for
   approval
Offer a variety of repayment
   schedules
	Lend on cash value of life
	   insurance policy
	No date or penalty on repayment
	Deduct amount owed from the
	   value of policy benefit if death
	   or other maturity occurs before
	   repayment
		Will lend to all creditworthy
		   individuals
		Often require collateral
		Loan rates vary, depending on
		   size of loan, length of payment,
		   and security involved

Lower than some lenders because
   they:
   Take fewer credit risks
   Lend money deposited by
      members, which is less
      expensive than borrowed
      money
   Often receive free office space
      and supplies from the
      sponsoring organization
   Are managed by members whose
      services, in most cases, are
      donated
   Enjoy federal income tax
      exemptions
	Lower than some lenders because
	   they:
	   Take no risk
	   Pay no collection costs
	   Secure loans by cash value of
	      policy
		Lower than some lenders because
		   they:
		   Lend depositors' money, which
		      is a relatively inexpensive
		      source of funds
		   Secure most loans by savings
		      accounts or real estate

Design repayment schedules to fit
   the borrower's income
Generally provide credit life
   insurance without extra charge
May offer financial counseling
Handle credit transactions
   confidentially
	Permit repayment at any time
	Handle credit transactions
	   confidentially
		Often offer financial counseling
		Specialize in mortgages and other
		   housing-related loans
		Handle credit transactions
		   confidentially

Source: *Managing Your Credit,* rev. ed. (Prospect Heights, Ill.: Money Management Institute, Household Financial Services, 1985), pp. 18–19. ©
Household Financial Services, Prospect Heights, Illinois.

banks, consumer finance companies, credit unions, life insurance companies, and savings and loan associations.

Borrowing and credit are more complex than ever. As more and more types of financial institutions offer financial services, your choices of what to borrow and from whom to borrow grow wider. Shopping for credit is just as important as shopping for an automobile, furniture, or major appliances.

COST OF CREDIT

- Determining the Cost of Credit

The **Consumer Credit Protection Act** of 1968, which launched **Truth in Lending**, was a landmark piece of legislation. For the first time, creditors were required to state the cost of borrowing in a common language so that you, the customer, could figure out exactly what the charges would be, compare costs, and shop for credit.

If you are thinking of borrowing money or opening a credit account, your first step should be to figure out how much it will cost you and whether you can afford it. Then you should shop for the best terms. As you learned in the opening scenario, two key concepts that you should keep in mind are the finance charge and the annual percentage rate.

The Finance Charge and the Annual Percentage Rate (APR)

Credit costs vary. By remembering the finance charge and the APR, you can compare credit prices from different sources. Under the Truth in Lending law, the creditor must inform you, in writing and before you sign any agreement, of the finance charge and the APR.

Pepper . . . and Salt

"May I have $125,000 Dad?—I have a
chance to buy into a clinic."

From *The Wall Street Journal*, with permission of Cartoon Features Syndicate.

The **finance charge** is the total dollar amount you pay to use credit. It includes interest costs and sometimes other costs, such as service charges, credit-related insurance premiums, or appraisal fees.

For example, borrowing $100 for a year might cost you $10 in interest. If there were also a service charge of $1, the finance charge would be $11. The **annual percentage rate (APR)** is the percentage cost (or relative cost) of credit on a yearly basis. The APR is your key to comparing costs, regardless of the amount of credit or how much time you have to repay it.

Suppose you borrow $100 for one year and pay a finance charge of $10. If you can keep the entire $100 for the whole year and then pay it all back at once, you are paying an APR of 10 percent. But if you repay the $100 and the finance charge (a total of $110) in 12 equal monthly payments, you don't get to use the $100 for the whole year. In fact, you get to use less and less of that $100 each month. In this case, the $10 charge for credit amounts to an APR of 18 percent.

All creditors—banks, stores, car dealers, credit card companies, finance companies—must state the cost of their credit in terms of the finance charge and the APR. The law says that these two pieces of information must be shown to you before you sign a credit contract. The law does not set interest rates or other credit charges, but it does require their disclosure so that you can compare credit costs.

A comparison. Even when you understand the terms a creditor is offering, it's easy to underestimate the difference in dollars that different terms can make. Suppose you're buying a $7,500 car. You put $1,500 down, and you need to borrow $6,000. Compare the three credit arrangements below.

	APR	Length of Loan	Monthly Payment	Total Finance Charge	Total Cost
Creditor A	14%	3 years	$205.07	$1,382.52	**$7,382.52**
Creditor B	14	4 years	**163.96**	1,870.08	7,870.08
Creditor C	**15**	4 years	166.98	2,015.04	8,015.04

How do these choices compare? The answer depends partly on what you need. The lowest-cost loan is available from Creditor A. If you were looking for lower monthly payments, you could repay the loan over a longer period of time. However, you would have to pay more in total costs. A loan from Creditor B—also at a 14 percent APR, but for four years—will add about $488 to your finance charge.

If that four-year loan were available only from Creditor C, the APR of 15 percent would add another $145 to your finance charges. Other terms—such as the size of the down payment—will also make a difference. Be sure to look at all the terms before you make your choice.

Cost of Open-End Credit. As discussed earlier, open-end credit includes credit cards, department store charge plates, and check overdraft accounts that allow you to write checks for more than your actual balance. Open-end credit can be used again and again, until you reach a prearranged borrowing limit. The Truth in Lending law requires that open-end creditors let you know how the finance charge and the APR will affect your costs.

First, they must tell you how they calculate the finance charge. Creditors use various systems to calculate the balance on which they assess finance charges. Some creditors add finance charges after subtracting payments made during the billing period, this is called the **adjusted balance method.** Other creditors give you no credit for payments made during the billing period; this is called the **previous balance method.** Under a third method, the **average daily balance method,** creditors add your balances for each day in the billing period and then divide by the number of days in the period.

Here is a sample of the three billing systems:

	Adjusted Balance	Previous Balance	Average Daily Balance
Monthly interest rate	1½%	1½%	1½%
Previous balance	$400	$400	$400
Payments	$300	$300	$300 (payment on 15th day)
Interest charge	**$1.50** ($100 × 1.5%)	**$6.00** ($400 × 1.5%)	**$3.75** (average balance of $250 × 1.5%)

As the example shows, the finance charge varies for the same pattern of purchases and payments.

Second, creditors must tell you when finance charges on your credit account begin, so that you know how much time you have to pay your bills before a finance charge is added. Some creditors, for example, give you 30 days to pay your balance in full before imposing a finance charge.

The Truth in Lending law does not set the rates or tell the creditor how to make interest calculations. It only requires that the creditor tell you the method that will be used. You should ask for an explanation of any terms you don't understand.

Leasing Costs and Terms

Leasing gives you temporary use of property in return for periodic payments. It has become a popular alternative to buying—under certain circumstances. For instance, you might consider leasing furniture for an apartment you will use for only a year. The **Truth in Leasing** law requires leasing companies to give you the facts about the costs and terms of their contracts, to help you decide whether leasing is a good idea.

The law applies to personal property leased to you for more than four months for personal, family, or household use. It covers, for example, long-term rentals of cars, furniture, and appliances, but not daily car rentals or leases for apartments.

Before you agree to a lease, the leasing company must give you a written statement of the costs, including the amount of any security deposit, the amount of your monthly payments, and the amount you must pay for licenses, registration, taxes, and maintenance.

The leasing company must also give you a written statement about the terms, including any insurance you need, any guarantees, any standards for wear and tear, information on who is responsible for servicing the property, and whether or not you have an option to buy the property.

Open-End Leases and Balloon Payments

Your costs will depend on whether you choose an open-end or a closed-end lease. Open-end leases usually offer lower monthly payments than closed-end leases, but with an open-end lease you may owe a large extra payment, often called a balloon payment, based on the value of the property when you return it.

Suppose you lease a car under a three-year open-end lease. The leasing company estimates that the car will be worth $4,000 after three years of normal use. If the car is worth only $3,500 when you bring it back, you may owe a balloon payment of $500.

The leasing company must tell you whether you might owe a balloon payment and how it will be calculated. You should also know that you have the right to an independent appraisal of the property's worth at the end of the lease; you must pay the appraiser's fee, however. Also, the law usually limits a balloon payment to no more than three times the average monthly payment. If your monthly payment is $100, your balloon payment can't be more than $300, unless, for example, the property has received more than average wear and tear (as might happen if you drove a car for more than the average mileage).

Closed-end leases usually have a higher monthly payment than open-end leases, but there is no balloon payment at the end of the lease.

Advertising Leasing and Credit Terms. Both the Truth in Lending law and the Truth in Leasing law require accurate advertising of terms. These laws say that if a business mentions one important feature of a credit sale or lease, such as the down payment, it must also state the APR and other important terms, such as the terms of repayment. Thus, an ad that states "only $2 down" must also state that you will have to pay $10 a week for the next two years. An ad must also specify whether a leasing arrangement is involved.

Understanding how to calculate the cost of money can be very useful to you. In the next section, you will learn how to calculate interest rates to become a better-educated and more informed consumer.

Interest Calculations

The two most common methods of calculating interest are compound and simple interest formulas; perhaps the most basic method is simple interest calculation.

Simple Interest. **Simple interest** is the dollar cost of borrowing money. This cost is based on three elements: the amount borrowed, which is called the *principal;* the *rate of interest;* and the amount of *time* for which the principal is borrowed.

The following formula may be used to find simple interest:

$$\text{interest} = \text{principal} \times \text{rate of interest} \times \text{time, or}$$
$$I = P \times R \times T$$

Interest Rate, R. As the term implies, an interest rate is a ratio or fraction of two numbers. For example, an interest rate of 12 percent means 12 divided by 100. Interest rates can also be written in decimal form. For example, 12 percent becomes 0.12. If it is to be used correctly in any formula, the interest rate must be stated as a fraction or a decimal. For example, multiplying $5,000 by 13½ percent does not make sense, but multiplying $5,000 by 13.5 ÷ 100, or 0.135, does.

Amount of Time, T. The amount of time for which simple interest is calculated is usually stated in years. If the time is less than a year, it may be expressed as a fraction of days per year, that is, as days/year. The term *year* in the denominator may take one of three values: a 360-day year, normally used by bankers; a standard 365-day calendar year; or a 366-day leap year. The amount of time may also be written in months per 12-month period. For example, three months is ³/₁₂ of ¼ of a year.

Simple Interest Example. Suppose you borrow $1,000 at 12 percent simple annual interest and repay it in one lump sum at the end of one year. To find the interest on the loan, use the simple interest formula:

$$I = \$1,000 \times 0.12 \times 1 = \$120$$

Now suppose that the loan is for two years and that you are required to repay the loan (principal *and* interest) at the *end* of two years. What will be the interest charge?

Over the first year, you have the full use of the $1,000 principal and you therefore incur an interest of $120, or $1,000 × 0.12 × 1. This first year's interest expense, however, is payable at the *end* of the second year.

Over the second and last year of the loan, you again have the full use of the original amount borrowed ($1,000) and you incur another $120 in interest. In other words, you have to pay interest only on the amount borrowed and not on any accumulated interest charges. This is the essence of simple interest.

To calculate the total amount of a simple interest loan that is due at the end of two years, the following formula may be used:

$$
\begin{aligned}
\text{Total loan repayment} &= \text{Principal} + \text{Interest charges} \\
\text{(or future amount due)} &\qquad\text{on the principal only} \\
&= P + I \\
&= P + (P \times R \times T) \\
&= \$1{,}000 + (\$1{,}000 \times 0.12 \times 2) \\
&= \$1{,}000 + \$240 \\
&= \$1{,}240
\end{aligned}
$$

Compound Interest. Unlike simple interest, **compound interest** is the amount paid on the original principal *plus* the accumulated interest. With interest compounding, the more the periods for which interest is calculated, the more rapidly he amount of interest and interest on principal builds.

Compounding annually means that there is only *one* period annually when interest is calculated. On a *one-year* loan, interest charges are identical whether figured on a simple basis or on an annual compound basis. However, a new interest formula, based on the simple interest formula, must be used if there is annual compounding for more than a year or compounding with more than one compound period per year.

Multiple-Year Annual Compounding. Suppose you take a two-year loan of $1,000 at 12 percent per year, compounded annually. While not due until the loan's maturity, interest charges accrue on the principal and interest at the end of each year or annual compound period. In this example, the nature of annual compounding requires you to pay interest at the end of the *second* year on the *first* year's accumulated interest on principal. In addition, you are obligated to pay 12 percent interest on the principal for each of the two annual compound periods.

What is the amount (principal and compound interest) you must pay at the end of two years? The total amount of interest consists of the following:

a.	Interest on $1,000 for the first year	$120.00
b.	Interest on $1,000 for the second year	120.00
c.	Interest on the first year's interest of $120 for the second year	14.40
	Total	$254.40

Adding the total amount of interest to the original sum borrowed gives the amount of the loan that you must repay at the *end* of two years:

$$ I + P = \$254.40 + \$1{,}000 = \$1{,}254.40 $$

Compare this result of compounding annually for two years with simple interest. On a two-year, $1,000 loan at 12 percent simple interest, the amount of interest is $240: $I = PRT = \$1{,}000 \times 0.12 \times 2$. This is $14.40 less than the result found with annual compounding. The difference, of course, is attributable to paying interest on interest—which is what compounding is all about.

Compound Formula. A compact formula that describes compound interest calculations is:

$$F = P(1 + R)^T$$

where

F = Total future repayment value of a loan (principal plus total accumulated or compound interest)
P = Principal
R = Rate of interest per year, or annual percentage rate
T = Time in years

Now use the compound interest formula to solve the following example problem.

Compound Interest Example. What is the total amount of interest that must be paid on a $3,000 loan for six years at 10 percent per year, compounded annually?

First, find the lump-sum amount that must be repaid (F) at the end of six years:

$$F = \$3,000(1 + 0.10)^6 = \$3,000(1.10)^6$$

The factor $(1.10)^6$ can be obtained easily using pencil and paper, a calculator, or a compound interest table. Using pencil and paper, $(1.10)^6$ is obtained as follows: $(1.10) \times (1.10) \times (1.10) \times (1.10) \times (1.10) \times (1.10)$, or 1.771561. Now place this result into the compound interest formula:

$$F = \$3,000 \times 1.771561 = \$5,314.68$$

Subtracting the principal (P) from the total amount due (F) equals the total amount of accumulated compound interest on the loan:

$$I = F - P$$
$$= \$5,314.68 - \$3,000 = \$2,314.68$$

Multiple Compound Periods per Year. So far, we have been discussing annual compounding—with each year consisting of one compound period. For multiple-period compounding, each year is divided into a corresponding number of equal periods. For example, compounding semiannually means that there are 2 compound periods per year, compounding quarterly means that there are 4 compound periods per year, and compounding daily means that there are 360 compound periods per year.

An Example. What is the total amount that must be repaid on a $2,500, three-year loan at 18 percent per year, compounded monthly?

Pepper . . . and Salt

"The whole is equal to the sum of
its parts—until you add the
finance charges."

From *The Wall Street Journal*, with permission of Cartoon Features Syndicate.

The total amount of compound interest on this loan is $1,772.85, or $4,272.85 − $2,500.

$$F = \$2,500(1 + 0.18/12)^{3 \text{ years} \times 12 \text{ compound periods/year}}$$
$$= \$2,500(1 + 0.015)^{36}$$
$$= \$2,500(1.70914)$$
$$= \$4,272.85$$

As you can see, the solution to this problem is complicated. A calculator or a compound interest table can help make interest calculations more manageable. See Appendix C for compound interest tables.

When you borrow from a bank or another lender, you usually arrange to repay the loan with interest by a specific date in a number of installments. But after several payments, you may decide to repay the entire loan at one earlier date than the one originally scheduled. How is interest calculated if you repay the loan early?

When the Repayment Is Early: The Rule of 78's

Creditors use tables based on a mathematical formula called **the rule of 78's**, or sometimes "the sum of the digits," to determine how much interest you have paid at any point in a loan. This formula dictates that you pay more interest at the beginning of a loan when you have the use of more of the money and that you pay less and less interest as the debt is reduced. Because all of the payments are the same in size, the part going to pay back the amount borrowed increases as the part representing interest decreases.

The laws of several states authorize the use of the rule of 78's as a means of calculating finance charge rebates when you pay off a loan early. The Truth in Lending law requires that your creditor disclose whether or not you are entitled to a rebate of the finance charge if the loan is paid off early.

Read the accompanying box to learn how to use the rule of 78's.

Credit Insurance

Credit insurance ensures the repayment of your debt in the event of death, disability, or loss of property. The lender is named the beneficiary and directly receives any payments made on submitted claims.

In the Real World
The Rule of 78's

How to Use the Rule of 78's

The first step is to add up all the digits for the number of payments scheduled to be made. For a 12-installment loan, add the numbers 1 through 12:

$$1 + 2 + 3 + 4 + 5 + 6 + 7 + 8 + 9 + 10 + 11 + 12 = 78$$

The answer—"the sum of the digits"—explains how the rule was named. One might say that the total interest is divided into 78 parts for payment over the term of the loan.

In the first month, before making any payments, the borrower has the use of the whole amount borrowed and therefore pays 12/78 of the total interest in the first payment; in the second month, he still has the use of 11 parts of the loan

and pays 11/78 of the interest; in the third, 10/78; and so on down to the final installment, 1/78.

To add all the numbers in a series of payments is rather tedious. One can arrive at the answer quickly by using this formula:

$$\frac{N}{2} \times (N + 1)$$

N is the number of payments. In a 12-month loan, it looks like this:

$$\frac{12}{2} \times (12 + 1) = 6 \times 13 = 78$$

A Loan for Ann and Dan

Let us suppose that Ann and Dan Adams borrow $3,000 from the Second Street Na-

tional Bank to redecorate their home. Interest comes to $225, and the total of $3,225 is to be paid in 15 equal installments of $215.

Using the rule of 78's, we can determine how much of each installment represents interest. We add all the numbers from 1 through 15:

$$\frac{15}{2} \times (15 + 1) = 7.5 \times 16 = 120$$

The first payment will include 15 parts of the total interest, or 15/120; the second, 14/120; and so on.

Notice in the following table that the interest decreases with each payment and the repayment of the amount borrowed increases with each payment.

There are three types of credit insurance: credit life, credit accident and health, and credit property. The most commonly purchased type of credit insurance is credit life insurance, which provides for the repayment of the loan if the borrower dies. At the beginning of 1985, there were nearly 66 million credit life policies with in-force coverage of $190 billion.[4]

Credit accident and health insurance, also called credit disability insurance, repays your debt in the event of a loss of income due to illness or injury. Credit property insurance provides coverage for personal property purchased with a loan. It may also insure collateral property, such as a car or furniture.

[4]*Economic Review*, Federal Reserve Bank of San Francisco, Summer 1986, p. 5.

Payment No.	Interest	Reduction of Debt	Total Payment
1	$ 28.13	$ 186.87	$ 215.00
2	26.25	188.75	215.00
3	24.37	190.63	215.00
4	22.50	192.50	215.00
5	20.63	194.37	215.00
6	18.75	196.25	215.00
7	16.87	198.13	215.00
8	15.00	200.00	215.00
9	13.13	201.87	215.00
10	11.25	203.75	215.00
11	9.37	205.63	215.00
12	7.50	207.50	215.00
13	5.63	209.37	215.00
14	3.75	211.25	215.00
15	1.87	213.13	215.00
	$225.00	$3,000.00	$3,225.00

How Much Is the Rebate?

Now let's assume that Ann and Dan want to pay off the loan with the fifth payment. We know that the total interest is divided into 120 parts. To find out how many parts will be rebated, we add up the numbers for the remaining 10 installments, which will be pre-paid:

$$\frac{10}{2} \times (10 + 1) = 5 \times 11 = 55$$

Now we know that 55/120 of the interest will be deducted as a rebate; it amounts to $103.12.

$$\frac{55}{120} \times \$255 = \frac{\$12,375}{120}$$
$$= \$103.12$$

We see that Ann and Dan do not save two thirds of the interest (which would be $150) by paying off the loan in one third of the time. But the earlier they repay the loan, the higher the portion of interest they do save.

Source: *The Rule of 78's*, (Philadelphia: Federal Reserve Bank of Philadelphia, May 1984).

Survey findings show that consumers generally do not feel pressured into buying credit insurance and that they view it quite favorably. These findings indicate that past abuses in the marketing and sale of credit insurance may have been overstated or may have declined in recent years.[5]

The cost of credit has increased with the passage of the Tax Reform Act of 1986. This act will change your borrowing habits. See the accompanying box for information on the gradual phaseout of consumer interest deductions under the act.

DEALING WITH YOUR DEBTS

- Handling Your Debts

A sudden illness or the loss of your job may make it impossible for you to pay your bills on time. If you find that you cannot make your payments, contact your creditors at once and try to work out a modified payment plan with them. If you have paid your bills promptly in the past, they may be willing to work with you. Do not wait until your account is turned over to a debt collector. At that point, the creditor has given up on you.

Automobile loans present special problems. Most automobile financing agreements permit your creditor to repossess your car anytime you are in default on your payments. No advance notice is required. If your car is repossessed, you may have to pay the full balance due on the loan, as well as

[5]Ibid.

Personal Financial Planning and You
The Tax Reform Act of 1986

The Tax Reform Law of 1986 calls a halt to interest deductions on your auto, credit card, education, and other consumer loans. However, you will not lose these deductions all at once; they will be phased out over five years. For 1987 taxes, you can still deduct 65 percent of your consumer interest expense; for 1988 taxes, 40 percent; for 1989 taxes, 20 per-cent; and for 1990 taxes, 10 percent. The new rules apply to existing loans as well as loans you take out after January 1, 1987. If you have investments, you can continue to deduct interest on loans to finance them. However, your interest deductions will be limited to the amount of your net investment income.

Remember that deductions for consumer loan interest, like all deductions, will be worth less than they are at present. This is because the tax rates will be lower once the new tax law goes into effect. For many people, such deductions will provide savings of no more than 15 cents on the dollar. For the rest, the savings will generally be no more than 28 cents on the dollar.

towing and storage costs, to get it back. If you cannot do this, the creditor may sell the car. Try to solve the problem with your creditor when you realize that you will not be able to meet your payments. It may be better to sell the car yourself and pay off your debt than to incur the added costs of repossession.

If you are having trouble paying your bills, you may be tempted to turn to a company that claims to offer assistance in solving debt problems. Such companies may offer debt consolidation loans, debt counseling, or debt reorganization plans that are guaranteed to stop creditors' collection efforts. Before signing with such a company, investigate it. Be sure you understand what services the company provides and what they will cost you. Do not rely on oral promises that do not appear in your contract. Also, check with the Better Business Bureau and your state or local consumer protection office. They may be able to tell you whether other consumers have registered complaints about the company.

Consumers who turn to such companies for help sometimes encounter additional problems. For example, debt consolidation or other short-term loans may have hidden costs and may require your home as collateral. An unscrupulous company may misrepresent the terms of such loan agreements; if so, you could end up losing your home.

Businesses offering debt counseling or debt reorganization may charge substantial fees or a percentage of your debts but fail to follow through on the services they sell. Some may do little more than refer indebted consumers to a bankruptcy lawyer, who charges an additional fee. Businesses advertising voluntary debt reorganization plans or Chapter 13 relief may fail to explain that a Chapter 13 debt adjustment is actually a form of bankruptcy. To qualify for it, you must have a source of regular income and a plan for repaying your creditors that meets the approval of the bankruptcy court. Businesses that sell bankruptcy-related services may not tell you all that is involved in a bankruptcy or that other, less dramatic alternatives may exist. They may also lack the expertise to assist you through a complex and lengthy legal process. Debt problems can be distressing, but be careful when selecting a solution. Some "solutions" may only add to your problems.

A constant worry for a debtor who is behind in payments is the fear of debt collection agencies. However, as you will see in the next section, a federal agency protects certain legal rights that you possess in your dealings with such agencies.

Debt Collection Practices

The Federal Trade Commission enforces the **Fair Debt Collection Practices Act (FDCPA),** which prohibits certain practices by agencies that collect debts for creditors. The act does not apply to creditors that collect debts themselves. While the act does not erase the legitimate debts that consumers owe, it does regulate the ways in which debt collection agencies do business.

Debt collection agencies may contact consumers in person or by mail, phone, or telegram. They may not contact consumers at inconvenient or unusual times or places, such as late at night or, if employers object, at work. If a consumer has an attorney, debt collection agencies may not contact anyone but the attorney. They may contact other third parties only to learn where the consumer is located. In most cases, they are not allowed to tell anyone other than the consumer or the attorney that the consumer owes money.

Within five days of the initial contact, debt collection agencies must send consumers a written notice, telling them the amount they owe, the creditors to which they owe the money, and what to do if they do not believe they owe the money. If consumers request written verification of the debt within 30 days, these agencies must stop their collection activities until they have supplied this information.

Consumers can stop debt collection agencies from contacting them by writing them and requesting no further contact. Once a debt collection agency receives such a letter, it may not contact the consumer again except to say that there will be no further contact or to provide notification of some specific legal action that is actually being taken. It may continue collection through other means, such as filing lawsuits, but it may not continue to contact the consumer directly.

Debt collectors are not permitted to harass consumers. For example, they may not threaten to harm individuals, property, or reputation; use obscene or profane language; make false statements; send any communication that looks like an official document that a federal, state, or local government agency might send; seize or threaten to seize consumers' wages or property unless they intend to do so and it is a legal action; give false information to anyone about consumers; or falsely claim that consumers have committed a crime or will be arrested. In addition, debt collectors may not collect any amount greater than the debt unless the contract creating the debt or state law permits; deposit a postdated check before the check's date; make consumers accept collect calls or pay for telegrams by concealing the purpose of the communications; or put anything on an envelope besides the agency's name and address—they cannot even use the name of the agency if it reveals that the letter concerns debt collection.

In addition to the FTC rules and the FTC-enforced laws, many states have their own laws dealing with credit practices and debt collection. Consumers should check with their state attorney general's office or their state or local consumer protection offices to determine their rights under state law.

The FTC relies on consumer complaints to decide which debt collection agencies to investigate and to identify trends that indicate problem areas. While the FTC cannot intervene in individual disputes, information from consumers about their experiences is vital to the FTC's enforcement program. Consumers can send complaints about debt collection agencies to the FTC's Office of the Secretary, Sixth Street and Pennsylvania Avenue, NW, Washington, DC 20580.

Figure 6–6 summarizes the steps you may take if a debt collector calls.

FIGURE 6-6   What If a Debt Collector Calls?

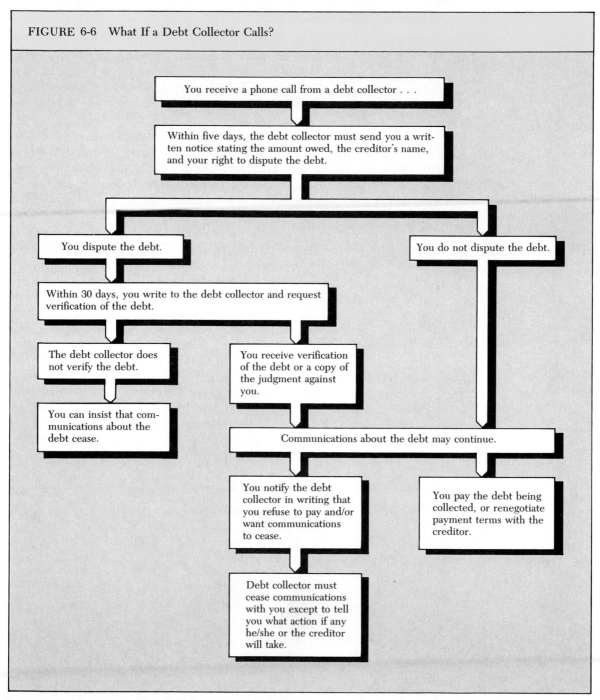

Source: Reprinted, courtesy of Office of Public Information, Federal Reserve Bank of Minneapolis, Minneapolis, MN 55480.

Consumer Credit Counseling

Bill Kenney is a vigorous, healthy man in his early 30s. He has a steady job with an annual income of $25,000 a year. Bill, his wife, and their two children enjoy a comfortable life; a new car is parked in the driveway of their home, a home furnished with such modern conveniences as a new microwave oven, a new freezer, an electric washer and dryer, a videocassette recorder, and a large-screen color television set.

However, Bill Kenney is in debt. He is drowning in a sea of bills; most of his income is tied up in repaying debts. Foreclosure proceedings on his home have been instituted, while several stores have court orders to repossess practically every major appliance in it. His current car payment is overdue, and three charge accounts at local stores are several months delinquent.

This case is neither exaggerated nor isolated. Unfortunately, a large number of people are in the same floundering state. The problem of these people is immaturity. Mature consumers have certain information; they demonstrate self-discipline, control of impulses, and sound judgment; they accept responsibility for money management; and they are able to postpone and govern expenditures when overextension of credit appears likely. As shown in Figure 6–7, overextension of credit is the second most common reason why consumers are unable to pay their bills on time.

Immature consumers, on the other hand, have been described as gullible, impulsive, and unsophisticated in their buying behavior. One authority claims that "they would save pennies on canned goods and waste dollars in high-markup neighborhood shops on expensive appliances." Another believes that they have a limited "frustration tolerance" and seek immediate gratification for goods by the use of easy credit. In less technical language, Bill Kenney's plight can be described in these words: "Easy credit, frivolous

---

FIGURE 6-7   Why Consumers Don't Pay

Reason for Default		Primary or Contributing Cause of Default (percent of cases)
Loss of income		48
Unemployment	24	
Illness	16	
Other	8	
Overextension		25
Defective goods or services or other perceived consumer fraud		20
Fraudulent use of credit	4	
Other		3

Source: Reprinted, courtesy of Office of Public Information, Federal Reserve Bank of Minneapolis, Minneapolis, MN 55480.

buying, low down payments, instant need for everything by young people, the need for status, exploitation by advertising specialists, and deceitful business practices."

Referring to overindebtedness as the nation's number one family financial problem, a nationally noted columnist on consumer affairs lists the following as frequent reasons for indebtedness:[6]

1. *Emotional problems,* such as the need for instant gratification, as in the case of a man who can't resist buying some costly sports equipment, or of a woman who lets herself be talked into an expensive purchase by a door-to-door salesperson.
2. *The use of money to punish,* as in the case of a husband who buys a new car without consulting his wife, who in turn makes an expensive purchase to get even.
3. *The expectation of instant comfort* among young couples who assume that they can have immediately, by use of the installment plan, the possessions that their parents acquired after years of work.
4. *Keeping up with the Joneses,* which is more apparent than ever, not only among families with more money but among limited-income families too.
5. *Expensive indulgence of children,* often because of both parents' emotional needs, but also sometimes because the two parents are in competition with each other or lack adequate communication with each other (they buy independently).
6. *Misunderstanding or lack of communication among family members.* For example, a salesperson selling an expensive freezer visited a Memphis family. Although the freezer was beyond the means of this already overindebted family, and too large for its needs anyway, the husband thought that his wife wanted it. Not until later, in an interview with a counselor, did the wife relate her concern when she signed the contract; she had wanted her husband to say no.
7. *The amount of the finance charges,* which can push a family over the edge of ability to pay, especially when it borrows from one company to pay another and these charges pyramid.

Figure 6–8 lists the 10 danger signals of potential debt problems.

The Serious Effects of Debt

If the causes of indebtedness vary, so too do a mixture of other personal and family problems that frequently occur with the overextension of credit.

Loss of a job because of garnishment proceedings may occur in a family that has a disproportionate amount of its income tied up in debts. Another possibility is that such a family may be forced to neglect vital areas. In the frantic effort to rob Peter to pay Paul, family skimping may seriously affect diet, the educational needs of children and the protection of the family's

[6]*Debt Counseling,* AFL–CIO Publication #140, rev. ed. March 1981.

FIGURE 6-8   The 10 Danger Signals of Potential Debt Problems

1. Paying only the minimum balance each month on credit card bills
2. Increasing the total balance due each month on credit accounts
3. Missing payments, paying late, or paying some bills this month and others next month
4. Intentionally using the overdraft or automatic loan features on checking accounts, or taking frequent cash advances on credit cards
5. Using savings to pay normal bills such as groceries or utilities
6. Receiving second or third notices from creditors
7. Not talking to your spouse about money, or . . . talking only about money
8. Depending on overtime, moonlighting, or bonuses to meet normal expenses
9. Using up your savings
10. Borrowing money to pay old debts

If your household is experiencing more than three of these warning signals, it's time to examine your budget for ways to reduce expenses.

Source: *Advice for Consumers who use Credit* (Consumer Credit Counseling Service of Maryland, Inc., n.d.).

---

health. Excessive indebtedness may also result in heavy drinking, a neglect of children, marital difficulties, and drug abuse. But help is available to those debtors who seek it.

What Is a Consumer Credit Counseling Service?

- Private and Governmental Sources of Help

A **Consumer Credit Counseling Service (CCCS)** is a local, nonprofit organization affiliated with the National Foundation for Consumer Credit. It provides debt counseling services for families and individuals with serious financial problems. It is not a charity, or a lending institution, a governmental or legal institution. It is supported by contributions from banks, consumer finance companies, credit unions, merchants, and other community-minded firms and individuals.

What a CCCS does. Credit counselors are aware that most people who are in debt over their heads are basically honest people who want to clear up their indebtedness. Too often, the problems of such people arise from a lack of planning or a miscalculation of what they earn. Therefore, the CCCS is just as concerned with preventing the problems as with solving them. As a result, its activities are divided into two parts:

1. Aiding families with serious debt problems by helping such families manage their money better and by setting up a realistic budget and plan for expenditures.
2. Helping prevent debt problems by teaching the necessity of family budget planning, providing education to people of all ages regarding the pitfalls of unwise credit buying, suggesting techniques for family bud-

geting, and encouraging credit institutions to provide full information about the costs and terms of credit and to withhold credit from those who cannot afford to repay it.

How a CCCS Works. Anyone overburdened by credit obligations can phone, write, or visit a CCCS office. There are over 200 CCCS offices all over the nation. The CCCS requires that an application for credit counseling be completed and then an appointment is arranged for a personal interview with the applicant.

CCCS counseling is usually free. However, when the CCCS administers a debt repayment plan, it sometimes charges a nominal fee to help defray administrative costs.

But what if the debtor is suffering from an extreme case of financial woes? Is there any relief? The answer is yes—bankruptcy proceedings.

The U.S. Bankruptcy Act of 1978: The Last Resort

● Chapters 7 and 13
  Bankruptcies

If your situation is hopeless, you have two choices in declaring personal bankruptcy: Chapter 7 and Chapter 11 bankruptcy.

Chapter 7 Bankruptcy. Chapter 7 bankruptcy requires a debtor to draw up a petition listing his or her assets and liabilities. The debtor submits the petition to a U.S. district court and pays a filing fee. A person filing for relief under the bankruptcy code is called a debtor; the term *bankrupt* is not used.

"The purpose of bankruptcy under Chapter 7 is to grant to the honest debtor who is overwhelmed by his debts a chance to make a fresh start in life and remain a useful member of society by relieving him of the oppressive burden of his debts."[7] The debtor must turn over to the bankruptcy court all of the property that he or she owns that is not exempted by law. The property is converted into cash, which is used to pay administrative costs and creditors. Usually, so little money is realized, however, that the creditors receive only a small fraction or none of the money owed to them.

The federal bankruptcy exemption law permits the debtor to keep up to $7,500 equity in a home; up to $1,200 equity in one motor vehicle; up to $200 equity per item in household goods, for a maximum of $4,000; and up to $500 in jewelry. In addition, the debtor may retain implements, professional books, or tools of the trade not to exceed $750 in value. If husband and wife file jointly, the dollar amounts double. Other protected assets include veterans' benefits, social security payments, unemployment compensation, pension funds, and alimony.

Chapter 13 Bankruptcy. Chapter 13 bankruptcy is a plan for a debtor with a regular income to extinguish his or her debts from future earnings or other property over a period of three years either by payment in full or by

---

[7]*Some General Information concerning Chapter 7 of the Bankruptcy Code* (Washington, D.C.: n.d.) Division of Bankruptcy, Administrative Office of the United States Courts.

payment of some percentage of total indebtedness under a plan approved by the bankruptcy court. Under special circumstances, the period may be extended to five years. During the repayment period, creditors may not harass the debtor or seek to collect their debts. They must receive payments only under the plan. This protection relieves the debtor from indirect and direct pressures from creditors and enables the debtor to support his or her family while repaying the creditors.

Need for an Attorney. To obtain the benefit of a debtor's plan under Chapter 13, the debtor will ordinarily need an attorney to:

1. Advise the debtor whether Chapter 13 or some alternative form of relief is the best solution to his or her financial problems.
2. Prepare the necessary legal papers incident to filing a petition for approval of the debtor's plan.
3. Obtain or assist the debtor in obtaining acceptances from the secured creditors dealt with in the plan.
4. Represent the debtor during the course of the proceedings.

If the debtor does not know a local attorney who handles Chapter 13 cases under the bankruptcy code, the local bar association or legal aid society may be able to give him or her the names of such attorneys. Frequently, attorneys who handle Chapter 13 cases will not require the fee to be paid in advance but will agree to be paid under the plan.

What Are the Costs? The monetary costs to the debtor under Chapter 13 include the following:

1. *Court Costs.* A $60 filing fee must be paid to the clerk of the court at the time the debtor's petition is filed. The filing fee may be paid in up to four installments if authorization is granted by the court.

2. *Attorney's Fees.* These fees are usually the largest single item of cost. Often the attorney does not require them to be paid in advance at the time of filing but agrees to be paid in installments after receipt of a down payment.

3. *Trustee's Fees and Costs.* The trustee's fees are established by the bankruptcy judge in most districts and by a U.S. trustee in certain other districts.

Although it is possible to reduce these costs by purchasing the legal forms in a local stationery store and completing them yourself, an attorney is strongly recommended.

There are also psychological costs. For example, obtaining credit in the future may be very difficult since bankruptcy reports are retained in credit bureaus for 10 years. Therefore, the extreme step of declaring personal bankruptcy should be taken only when no other options for solving financial problems exist.

SUMMARY

- The major sources of consumer credit are commercial banks, savings and loans, credit unions, finance companies, life insurance companies, pawnshops, loan sharks, and family and friends. Each of these sources has unique advantages and disadvantages.

- Compare the finance charge and the annual percentage rate as you shop for credit. Under the Consumer Credit Protection Act, which launched Truth in Lending, creditors are required to state the cost of borrowing so that you can compare credit costs and shop for credit.

- The various methods used to calculate interest are basically variations of the simple interest calculation method. The rule of 78's yields the percentage of the total interest amount that is returned to the borrower if the loan is prepaid.

- If you can't meet your obligations, contact your creditors immediately. Before signing up with a debt consolidation company, investigate it thoroughly. Better yet, contact your local Consumer Credit Counseling Service.

- The Fair Debt Collection Practices Act prohibits certain practices by debt collection agencies.

- A debtor's last resort is to declare bankruptcy, permitted by the U.S. Bankruptcy Act of 1978. Consider the financial and psychological costs of bankruptcy before taking this extreme step.

GLOSSARY

Adjusted balance method. The assessment of finance charges after payments made during the billing period have been subtracted.

Annual percentage rate (APR). The percentage cost (or relative cost) of credit on a yearly basis. The APR yields a true rate of interest for comparisons with other sources of credit.

Average daily balance method. A method of computing finance charges that uses a weighted average of the account balance throughout the current billing period.

Chapter 7 bankruptcy. Grants the honest debtor a chance to make a fresh start in life by relieving him or her of the oppressive burden of debts.

Chapter 13 bankruptcy. A voluntary plan that a debtor with regular income develops and proposes to a bankruptcy court.

Compound interest. Interest calculated on the original principal plus all interest accrued to that point in time.

Consumer Credit Counseling Service (CCCS). A local, nonprofit organization that provides debt counseling services for families and individuals with serious financial problems.

Consumer Credit Protection Act. Federal legislation, enacted in 1968, intended to provide each consumer with meaningful and uniform information concerning the cost of credit.

Consumer finance company (CFC). A financial institution that specializes in personal installment loans and second mortgages.

Credit insurance. Any type of insurance that provides coverage on a borrower in the event that the borrower is unable to pay.

Fair Debt Collection Practices Act (FDCPA). A federal law, enacted in 1978, that regulates debt collection activities.

Finance charge. The total dollar amount paid to use credit.

Previous balance method. A method of computing finance charges that gives no credit for payments made during the billing period.

Rule of 78's. A method of apportioning interest throughout the life of the loan so that an appropriate principal balance can be found for any time.

Sales finance company (SFC). A company specializing in the financing of big-ticket items by purchasing consumer installment notes.

Simple interest. Interest computed on the principal only and without compounding.

Truth in Leasing. A federal law that requires leasing companies to give the facts about the costs and terms of their contracts.

Truth in Lending. A federal law that requires that the cost for the APR and the finance charge be disclosed as a dollar amount.

REVIEW QUESTIONS

1. List the major sources of consumer credit. What are advantages and disadvantages of each?

2. What are the differences between the finance charge and the annual percentage rate? Which is the more reliable method of determining the real cost of credit, and why?

3. What are the three most commonly used methods that creditors use to calculate the finance charge for open-end credit?

4. Define open-end and closed-end leases. Which type usually offers lower monthly payments, and why?

5. Define interest. What federal law governs the disclosure of interest rates? What are the major provisions of this law?

6. What is the rule of 78's? When is it applied, and why? Whom does it favor, the lender or the borrower?

7. What are the major provisions of the Fair Debt Collections Practices Act? Which federal agency enforces this act?

8. List seven elements that often lead to overindebtedness.

9. What are 10 danger signals of potential debt problems?

10. Define a Consumer Credit Counseling Service. What does it do, and how does it help a debt-ridden consumer?

11. What are the major provisions of the U.S. Bankruptcy Act of 1978? What are the costs, financial and emotional, of filing a personal bankruptcy?

DISCUSSION QUESTIONS AND ACTIVITIES

1. Did John Grey make the right decision when buying his car on credit? Explain.

2. Discuss the dangers of dealing with usurious lenders, and examine the differences between reputable and disreputable lenders. Discuss appropriate action to take when encountering dishonest credit policies.

3. Discuss how the size and length of payments affect the dollar cost of credit. What are advantages of a large down payment? What are possible disadvantages?

4. Compare the dollar cost and APR of several department stores in your area. Discuss store policies that might be more important than the cost of credit, such as guarantee and service policies.

5. Return to the example of Ann and Dan discussed in "In the Real World: The Rule of 78's." Assume that Ann and Dan pay off their loan with the 11th payment. How much interest will they save? Remember that the interest over 15 months is divided into 120 parts and that you need to know how many payments will be prepaid. Fill in the blanks:

$$\frac{N}{2} \times (N + 1) = \frac{\_\_}{2} \times (\_\_\_\_ + 1) = \_\_\_\_ \times \_\_\_\_ = \_\_\_\_ .$$ Now multiply the rebate fraction by the total amount of interest on the loan: $\_\_\_\_ \times \_\_\_\_ = \$\_\_\_\_$ rebate.

6. Obtain several sample credit contracts and discuss the meaning of the terms they use.

7. Identify agencies in your area that are available to assist persons with credit problems.

ADDITIONAL READINGS

ABCs of Figuring Interest. Chicago: Federal Reserve Bank of Chicago, 1984.

Borrowing Basics for Women. New York: Citibank, 1980.

Credit Wise: A Guide to Consumer Credit. Toronto: Canadian Bankers Association, 1983.

Hughes, Kathleen A. "Credit Clinics May Make It Sound Too Easy to Clean Up a Bad Record." *The Wall Street Journal*, June 16, 1986, p. 33.

Langley, Monica. "Proposed Federal Rules May Limit Interest Charges on Credit Cards." *The Wall Street Journal*, September 27, 1985, p. 25.

Managing Your Credit. Prospect Heights, Ill.: Money Management Institute, Household Financial Services, 1985.

The Rule of 78's. Philadelphia: Federal Reserve Bank of Philadelphia, May 1984.

Some General Information concerning Chapter 7 of the Bankruptcy Code, Liquidation. Washington, D.C.: Office of the U.S. Courts, n.d.

Truth in Lending: What It Means for Consumer Credit. Philadelphia: Federal Reserve Bank of Philadelphia, n.d.

What to Do when Debts Pile Up. Consumer Information Report 27. San Francisco: Bank of America, 1982.

CASE 6–1 Karen's Predicament*

At 8 P.M., Karen Johnson received a phone call from a person who identified himself as a debt collector for ABC Collections, Inc. "I've had a difficult time locating you, Ms. Johnson," he says. "I'm calling you about the money you owe Fineline Furniture Company. You must pay, or we will be forced to take strong action against you."

Karen objects, stating that she has never purchased anything from Fineline Furniture. The caller responds, "That's what they all say."

*Taken from *Your Credit Rights* (Minneapolis: Federal Reserve Bank of Minneapolis, 1982), p. 91. Reprinted, courtesy of Office of Public Information, Federal Reserve Bank of Minneapolis, Minneapolis, MN 55480. Copyright 1982 by Federal Reserve Bank of Minneapolis.

Questions

1. What is the debt collector required by law to do at this point?

2. What action must Ms. Johnson take to protect her rights under the Fair Debt Collection Practices Act?

3. What can Ms. Johnson do if ABC Collections, Inc. continues to call her about the debt before it is verified?

CASE 6–2 John's Automobile Loan*

John Kilpatrick has been out of work for several months. His savings have been depleted, and he can no longer make payments on his loan. Since his account was turned over to a debt collection agency, it hasn't been uncommon for John to receive calls from the agency two or three times a day. John must answer his phone since he is expecting a call about a job he applied for recently. John does owe the money, but he is unable to pay right now and he wishes that the phone calls would stop.

Questions

1. Can John do anything about the annoying phone calls from the collection agency?

2. If a consumer requests that communications cease, a debt collector can take no further action to try to obtain payment. True or false? Explain.

*Taken from *Your Credit Rights* (Minneapolis: Federal Reserve Bank of Minneapolis, 1982), p. 91. Reprinted, courtesy of Office of Public Information, Federal Reserve Bank of Minneapolis, Minneapolis, MN 55480. Copyright 1982 by Federal Reserve Bank of Minneapolis.

7

Planning Your Tax Strategy

Taxes are a quiet, everyday financial fact. You pay certain taxes every time you get a paycheck or make a purchase. But many people are only concerned with taxes around April of each year. With about one third of each dollar earned going for taxes, an effective tax strategy is a vital component of successful financial planning. If you know and understand the tax rules and regulations, you may be able to reduce your tax liability. Your purchases, investments, and other financial decisions can affect the amount of tax you pay.

After studying this chapter, you will be able to:

- Recognize the importance of taxes in personal financial planning.

- Identify the different types of taxes in our society.

- List the components needed to compute taxable income.

- Discuss various federal income tax deductions.

- Describe methods for paying federal income tax.

- Explain who must file a federal income tax return.

- Identify tax assistance sources.

- Describe the process involved in a tax audit.

- Identify the major provisions of the Tax Reform Act of 1986.

Interview with **Joanne Carmody,**
Revenue Agent, Internal Revenue Service

Joanne Carmody graduated from Loras College, Dubuque, Iowa, with a major in business and accounting. Since 1980, she has been a Revenue Agent for the Internal Revenue Service, Department of the Treasury.

It takes a considerable amount of money to keep this country running smoothly. The amount of revenue raised through taxes determines the amount of services that the government can provide its citizens.

Ms. Carmody states that in recent years Americans have become increasingly concerned about the safety of the environment. One substantial expense for the government (paid for with tax dollars) is that of imposing regulations on manufacturers to ensure a safe and healthy environment. In addition, government agencies enforce numerous regulations controlling the use of billboards and signs; the reclamation of land after strip mines have

been closed; the dumping of industrial waste into streams, rivers, and lakes; and noise pollution at airports. Government agencies also regulate the services, prices, and profits of the utility companies to protect citizens from excessive rates.

Since the 1930s, the federal government has been providing financial aid for the disabled and unemployed, health services for the elderly, financial aid to families with dependent children, and social services for the poor.

Taxes are imposed to pay for these and other government services. The main source of revenue for the federal government is the income tax; for state governments, income and consumption taxes; and for local governments, property and wealth taxes.

According to Ms. Carmody, the principle of income tax laws is that people should pay according to their ability to pay. Those with high taxable in-

comes pay a larger percentage of their income in taxes.

In this country, the tax system is voluntary. That is, you are responsible for determining the amount of your tax liability. Federal income tax is collected on a pay-as-you-go basis. Most employers are required to withhold tax from your paycheck and to deposit it with the government. If you have not paid enough tax during the year, you must pay an additional tax. If you have paid too much tax, you will receive a refund.

Employers are also required to withhold money to pay your social security tax. This amount is based on your total earnings.

Ms. Carmody states that over the years many Americans have become intimidated by the Internal Revenue Service. They have picked up "facts" that are fictions. In order to dispel these misconceptions, they must learn to distinguish the facts from the fallacies.

Hugh and Margaret Lennon succeeded in beating the Internal Revenue Service in a lawsuit twice. But the Bronx, New York couple, who saved about $8,000 in the process, weren't high on the experience. After months of haggling with IRS officials and digging up five-year-old receipts, Hugh stated, "I don't know if I would do it again."

When it comes to suing the IRS, even winning can be a bummer. Many cases last years, and the chances of getting a clean victory are lousy. But experts say that the odds can be improved in two ways: First, exhaust all administrative appeals. Second, if you sue, do so over facts and not the law. And it may not be necessary to hire a lawyer when a lot of money is not involved. (Even the tax attorneys make that last suggestion.)

About 90 percent of all the cases filed in Tax Court are settled out of court; in July 1986, 70,000 cases were pending. Last fiscal year, only 54 taxpayers were winners in Tax Court trials, compared with 813 such victories for the IRS.

Taxpayers come out best, lawyers say, when they're arguing over substantiating deductions instead of challenging tax laws. "It seems that the Tax Court is more lenient on cases involving factual issues," says David Silverman, a New York accountant.

The Lennons, for example, in two cases sued the IRS for disallowing a total of $8,100 in charitable and miscellaneous deductions on their 1980 and 1981 returns. With the help of a letter from their church pastor, the couple convinced the IRS that their deductions were valid and settled out of court.

TAXES AND FINANCIAL PLANNING

Unlike other aspects of financial planning, taxes are affected not only by our personal choices but by a strong external influence—the government. Taxes are vital to society because they provide the funds needed for desired public services. A constant debate exists as to the fairness of taxes. Different types of taxes differ in their effects on an individual's financial situation.

Taxes in Our Society

- The Importance of Taxes in Personal Financial Planning

For about two thirds of our nation's history, the federal government did not have the specific constitutional power to directly tax the incomes of individuals. An income tax was imposed briefly during the Civil War. But when the income tax was used again in the 1890s, the U.S. Supreme Court ruled it unconstitutional. In 1913, the states ratified the 16th Amendment to the U.S. Constitution, granting Congress the power to tax personal income. Figure 7–1 highlights some of the major developments in the history of federal taxes.

Taxes have several purposes. Their principal purpose is to finance government activities. As citizens, we look to the government to provide services

The agency accepted all of the deductions in the 1980 return and all but $500 in the 1981 return.

But James and Carol Bowe of Dobbs Ferry, New York, got clobbered when they sued to challenge a law. In 1980, the couple took $1,500 off their taxes for an individual retirement account. At the time, the law prohibited such deductions because the Bowes were enrolled in a company retirement plan that year. "We really felt we had a pretty strong case since we hadn't gotten any benefits," said James Bowe, a senior vice president of a New York commodities company.

The Tax Court ordered the couple to pay $1,500, plus an additional $1,500 in interest and penalties. Moreover, the interest kept mounting while the Bowes were deciding whether to appeal the case in a higher court.

You don't need to hire an attorney to go to Tax Court. About 55 percent of the taxpayers who file suit don't have lawyers. Many tax lawyers say they're not needed in most cases about substantiation when large amounts aren't involved. Some lawyers say they won't take small cases.

"You can fight your own tickets in traffic court. There's no need to drag attorneys in on this," says Ira Kevelson, a New York lawyer and accountant.

*Condensed from "Your Money Matters," *The Wall Street Journal*, July 14, 1986, p. 17.

such as police and fire fighting services, road maintenance, parks and libraries, and inspection of food, drugs, and other products. Figure 7–2 shows how the federal government uses its funds.

Does a Fair Tax Exist?

Many people believe that the only fair tax is one that someone else pays. However, most people realize that taxes are a financial planning fact and that they must pay their fair share. Three criteria used in assessing the fairness of taxes are the benefits received criterion, the ability to pay criterion, and the payment burden criterion.

Benefits Received. This criterion of tax fairness states that people should pay taxes in proportion to the benefits they receive from the government. An application of this criterion is the use of gasoline taxes and driver's license fees for road construction and repairs.

Equitable as the benefits received criterion may seem, it is very difficult to implement. The value placed on a particular government service is not

FIGURE 7-1   Income Tax in the United States

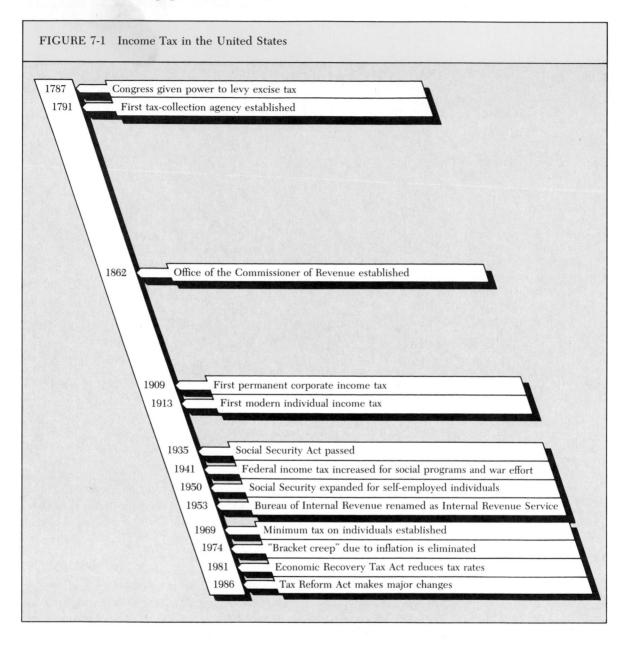

1787	Congress given power to levy excise tax
1791	First tax-collection agency established
1862	Office of the Commissioner of Revenue established
1909	First permanent corporate income tax
1913	First modern individual income tax
1935	Social Security Act passed
1941	Federal income tax increased for social programs and war effort
1950	Social Security expanded for self-employed individuals
1953	Bureau of Internal Revenue renamed as Internal Revenue Service
1969	Minimum tax on individuals established
1974	"Bracket creep" due to inflation is eliminated
1981	Economic Recovery Tax Act reduces tax rates
1986	Tax Reform Act makes major changes

easily measured. Some individuals may believe that recreational facilities are more important to the community than increased protection of property and citizens' rights; other individuals may hold the opposite view. It is not possible to establish a total tax system based on the value of services received.

Ability to Pay. A commonly accepted criterion of tax fairness is that individuals with different amounts of wealth or income should pay different

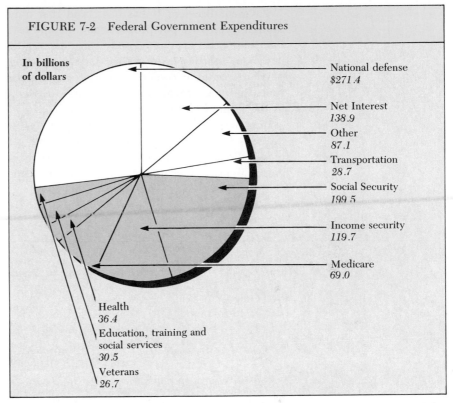

FIGURE 7-2   Federal Government Expenditures

In billions of dollars

National defense
$271.4

Net Interest
138.9

Other
87.1

Transportation
28.7

Social Security
199.5

Income security
119.7

Medicare
69.0

Health
36.4

Education, training and
social services
30.5

Veterans
26.7

Source: *Your Federal Income Tax*, IRS Publication 17, rev. ed. (Washington, D.C.: Department of the Treasury, Internal Revenue Service, November 1986), p. 201.

amounts of taxes. Supporters of the ability to pay criterion usually argue that high tax bills hurt the rich less than the poor. This argument is the basis for the **progressive tax,** in which tax rates increase as the level of taxable income increases. Until the 1986 tax reform, the federal income tax was a progressive tax.

Recent tax changes have made the federal income tax more like a **proportional tax,** or a flat tax, with a constant tax rate applied to all levels of the tax base. The new federal tax plan is not completely proportional since it involves two tax brackets for different income levels. Many state and local income taxes are examples of proportional taxes.

Some proportional taxes may seem fair, but they penalize people in low-income groups. For example, when all individuals are charged sales tax on food, low-income people, who use a larger portion of their income for necessities, will pay a greater percentage of their total income for sales tax than people with higher incomes. A **regressive tax** of this kind involves rates that decrease as the tax base increases and tends to place a heavier burden on the poor. For this reason, many states have chosen not to tax the sale of food and medications.

Payment Burden. It has been said that only individuals pay taxes. Although businesses pay property and income taxes, some observers contend that these taxes are passed on to consumers in the form of higher prices. We pay many *indirect* taxes of this kind. In addition to those just mentioned, a portion of building owners' real estate taxes is paid by tenants as part of their rent. Indirect taxes are taxes that can be passed on to someone else, usually in the form of higher prices.

In contrast, *direct* taxes cannot be passed on to someone else. Property taxes paid by homeowners and income taxes paid by individuals are examples of direct taxes. Your awareness of all types of taxes is vital for successful personal financial planning and long-term economic security.

In the Real World
Taxes in Other Countries

Most of the types of taxes used in the United States are also used in other countries. However, other types are imposed as well. In Canada, for example, a sales tax is assessed at the wholesale level. This tax is passed on to consumers in the form of higher costs.

Many Western countries have a *value-added tax*. This tax is assessed on the increased value of goods at each stage of their production and distribution. In France, most goods are taxed at about 18 percent, though luxury items are taxed at 33 percent and food at only 7 percent. Many developing nations in Asia and Africa depend on taxes based on their exports. In Sweden, a wealth tax is imposed annually, with a maximum rate of 2.5 percent.

The income tax rates in other countries differ from those in the United States. In Sweden, local governments use a flat 20 or 25 percent rate on all incomes. Australia uses only three income brackets; the lowest bracket is 32 percent. Most countries with income taxes use a progressive rate structure. In the United Kingdom, the lowest rate is 35 percent. This rate climbs slowly until it reaches the highest brackets—83 percent on salaries and 93 percent on investment income.

Other countries permit tax deductions and allowances that are not used in the United States. In Canada, taxpayers can deduct up to $1,000 each year by investing in the Registered Home Ownership plan. If the money is withdrawn to buy a house, it is not taxed. In the United Kingdom, businesses can deduct the full value of equipment purchases and other capital expenditures by taking 100 percent depreciation in the first year.

Tax administration methods also vary by country. In Australia, taxpayers file a return but do not calculate their own taxes. The Australian government uses the information on the return to assess the tax. France has no system for the withholding of taxes by employers. Instead, citizens must make their own payments three times a year.

Source: *Understanding Taxes, 1987*, IRS Publication 21, rev. ed. (Washington, D.C.: Internal Revenue Service, Department of the Treasury, October 1986), p. 27.

Types of Taxes

• The Different Types of Taxes in Our Society

Our financial existence is influenced by a variety of taxes. For example, the main sources of federal government revenue are income and social insurance taxes such as social security (see Figure 7–3). Most people pay taxes in four major categories: taxes on purchases, taxes on property, taxes on wealth, and taxes on income.

Taxes on Purchases. You are probably used to paying sales tax on many of your purchases. This state and local tax is added to the purchase price of a product. As mentioned, many states exempt food and drugs from sales tax to reduce the economic burden of this tax on the poor. In recent years, all but five states have had a general sales tax.[1]

An **excise tax** is imposed on specific goods and services, such as gasoline, cigarettes, alcoholic beverages, tires, air travel, and telephone service.

Taxes on Property. The real estate property tax is a major source of revenue for state and local governments. This tax is based on the value of land and buildings. A major concern of homeowners is the increasing amount of real estate property taxes. Retired individuals with a limited pension income

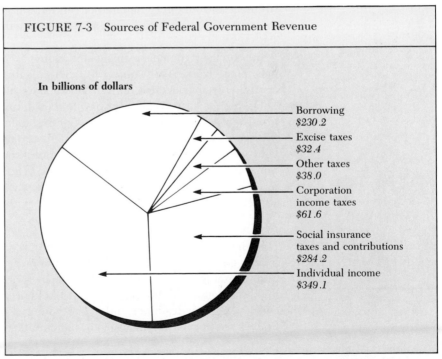

FIGURE 7-3   Sources of Federal Government Revenue

In billions of dollars

Borrowing
$230.2

Excise taxes
$32.4

Other taxes
$38.0

Corporation income taxes
$61.6

Social insurance taxes and contributions
$284.2

Individual income
$349.1

Source: *Your Federal Income Tax*, IRS Publication 17, rev. ed. (Washington, D.C.: Department of the Treasury, Internal Revenue Service, November 1986), p. 201.

[1]*The Dow Jones-Irwin Business and Investment Almanac, 1987* (Homewood, Ill.: Dow Jones-Irwin, 1987), p. 508.

may encounter financial difficulties if local property taxes increase at a fast rate.

Personal property taxes are also imposed in some areas. State and local governments may assess taxes on the value of automobiles, boats, furniture, and farm equipment.

Taxes on Wealth. An estate tax is imposed on the value of an individual's property at the time of his or her death. This tax is based on the fair market value of the deceased individual's investments, property, and bank accounts less allowable deductions and other taxes.

Money and property passed on to heirs is also subject to a tax. An inheritance tax is levied on the value of property received from a deceased individual. This tax is paid for the right to acquire the inherited property.

Individuals are allowed to receive gifts valued at $10,000 or less in a given year. Gift amounts greater than $10,000 are subject to a federal gift tax. Some states impose a gift tax on amounts that one person, before his or her death, transfers to another person since the action may be designed to avoid future estate and inheritance taxes.

Taxes on Earnings. The two main taxes on your wages and salary are social security and income taxes. Social security taxes are used to finance the retirement and disability benefits of the federal government's social security program. Various features of social security are discussed in Chapters 13 and 19.

Income tax is the major financial planning aspect of taxes for most individuals. Some workers are subject to federal, state, and local income tax. Currently, only seven states do not have a state income tax.

During the year, income tax payments will be withheld by your employer from your paycheck or you may be required to make estimated tax payments if you own your own business. Both types of payments are only estimates of your income and social security tax burden. You may need to pay an additional amount, or you may get a tax refund. The next sections will assist you in preparing your federal income tax return and in planning your future tax strategies.

INCOME TAX FUNDAMENTALS

Each year, millions of Americans are required to pay their fair share to the federal government in the form of income taxes. The process involves computing taxable income, determining the amount of taxes owed, and comparing this amount with the payments withheld or made during the year. Being aware of the tax deadlines and of the potential penalties for tax code violations is another basic aspect of the income tax process.

Computing Taxable Income

● The Components
   Needed to Compute
   Taxable Income

Taxable income is the net amount of income, after allowable deductions, on which income tax is computed. Figure 7–4 presents the components of taxable income and the process used to compute it.

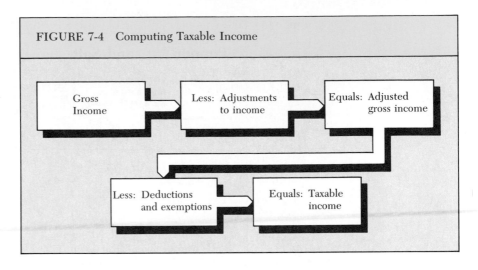

FIGURE 7-4   Computing Taxable Income

Types of Income. Most, but not all, income is subject to taxation. Your gross, or total, income can consist of several components. **Earned income** is money received by an individual for personal effort. Earned income is usually in the form of wages, salary, commission, fees, tips, or bonuses. **Investment,** or **portfolio income** is money received in the form of dividends or interest. While **passive income** is the result of business activities in which you do not actively participate such as a limited partnership.

Other types of income subject to federal income tax include alimony, awards, lottery winnings, and prizes. Cameron Clark, 14, won $30,533 in prizes on the television game show "Wheel of Fortune." In addition to paying California sales tax of $1,154, Cameron had to sell the car stereo, Ping-Pong table, camping gear, water ski equipment, bass guitar, and art drawing table and chair to pay the federal income tax. He did get to keep the Toyota Tercel, Honda Scooter, Gucci watches and Australian vacation.[2]

Total income is also affected by exclusions. An **exclusion** is an amount not included in gross income. For example, the foreign income exclusion allows U.S. citizens working and living in another country to exclude a certain portion ($70,000) of their income from federal income taxes.

Adjustments to Income. Adjusted gross income (AGI) is gross income after certain reductions have been made. These reductions include contributions to an individual retirement account (IRA) or a Keogh retirement plan, penalties for early withdrawal of savings, and alimony payments. Adjusted gross income is used as the basis for computing various income tax deductions, such as medical expenses.

Certain adjustments to income such as tax-deferred retirement plans are a type of **tax shelter.** Tax shelters are investments that provide immediate tax benefits and a reasonable expectation of a future financial return. In recent

[2]Jean Davidson, "Fortune's Smile Has Game Whiz Indebted," *Chicago Tribune*, December 12, 1986, sec. 2, p. 3.

Pepper . . . and Salt

"It's still considered income, Mr. Harris, whether you had it spent before you saw it or not."

From *The Wall Street Journal*, with permission of Cartoon Features Syndicate.

years, tax court rulings and changes in the tax code have disallowed various types of tax shelters that were considered abusive.

● Various Federal Income Tax Deductions

Deductions. A deduction is an amount subtracted from adjusted gross income to arrive at taxable income. Every taxpayer receives a **standard deduction**—a set amount on which no taxes are paid. As of 1987, single people received a standard deduction of $2,560 (married couples, $3,760).

TABLE 7-1 Tax Deductions	
Employees	Union dues
	Small tools and supplies
	Uniforms
	Job-hunting expenses
	Job-related moving expenses
Investors	Interest expense for borrowed funds to invest
	Capital losses
Homeowners	Mortgage interest
	Real estate property taxes
	Casualty losses
Parents	An exemption for dependent children
	Child care costs that allow you to work
Business owners	Necessary and ordinary operating expenses
	Travel expenses related to your trade or business
	Wages paid your children

Note: Many of these tax deductions have restrictions and usually require that you itemize your deductions.

Many individuals qualify for more than the standard deduction. **Itemized deductions** are expenses that a taxpayer is allowed to deduct from adjusted gross income. Your itemized deductions can include medical expenses, real estate property taxes, home mortgage interest, charitable contributions, casualty losses, and certain work-related expenses. The standard deduction is subtracted from the total itemized deductions and the remaining amount is used to reduce your taxable income. Table 7–1 lists some of the tax deductions that are available to various individuals.

You are required to maintain records to document your tax deductions. Financial advisers recommend that a home filing system be used to store receipts and other forms of expense documentation. Canceled checks will serve as proof of payment for such deductions as charitable contributions, medical expenses, and business-related expenses. Travel expenses must be maintained in a daily log with records of mileage, tolls, parking fees, and away-from-home costs.

Exemptions. An **exemption** is a deduction from adjusted gross income for yourself, your spouse, and qualified dependents. A dependent must not earn

---

Personal Financial Planning and You
Is It Taxable Income? Is It Deductible?

Certain financial benefits received by individuals are not subject to federal income tax. For each of the following items, indicate whether or not it would be included in taxable income when you compute your federal income tax.

		Yes	No
1.	Lottery winnings	—	—
2.	Child support received	—	—
3.	Worker's compensation benefits	—	—
4.	Life insurance death benefits	—	—
5.	Municipal bond interest earnings	—	—
6.	Bartering income	—	—

For each of the following items, indicate whether or not it would be deductible when you compute your federal income tax.

7.	Life insurance premiums	—	—
8.	The cost of commuting to work	—	—
9.	Fees for traffic violations	—	—
10.	Mileage for driving to volunteer work	—	—
11.	An attorney's fee for preparing a will	—	—
12.	Income tax preparation fee	—	—

Answers: 1, 6, 10, 12—yes; 2, 3, 4, 5, 7, 8, 9, 11—no.

Note: These taxable income items and deductions are based on the 1986 tax year, and may change due to changes in the tax code.

Pepper . . . and Salt

"Honestly, Edgar . . I don't think it will kill
you to enjoy something that isn't tax
deductible."

From *The Wall Street Journal*, with permission of Cartoon Features Syndicate.

more than a set amount unless he or she is under age 19; you must provide
more than one half of the dependent's support; and the dependent must
reside in your home or be a specified relative, and be a citizen. Deductions
for exemptions result in your taxable income, which is the amount you will
use to determine the amount of taxes you owe.

Determining Taxes Owed

Taxable income is the basis for the amount of your income taxes. The use
of tax rates and the benefits of tax credits are the two main phases in the final
step of computing your federal income taxes.

Tax Rates. Once you have determined your taxable income, you will use
the appropriate tax schedule in the tax instruction booklet. Taxpayers who
benefit from the special treatment given to some kinds of income and receive
special deductions may be subject to an additional tax. The *alternative minimum tax* is designed to make sure that those who receive tax breaks also pay
their fair share.

Tax Credits. The amount of taxes owed may be reduced as a result of
special considerations. A **tax credit** is an amount subtracted directly from the
amount of taxes owed. One example of a tax credit is the credit given for
child and dependent care expenses. This amount lowers the taxes owed by
an individual. A tax credit differs from a deduction in that a tax credit has a

full dollar effect in lowering taxes, whereas a deduction reduces the taxable income on which the tax liability is computed.

Payment Methods

● Payment Methods for Federal Income Tax

Your payment of taxes due the federal government will be made in one of two ways: through payroll withholding or through quarterly tax payments.

Withholding. The pay-as-you-go system, which was started in 1943, requires an employer to deduct an amount for federal income tax from your pay and send it to the government. The withheld amount is based on the number of exemptions claimed on the W-4 form. For example, a married individual with children would have less withheld than a single person with the same salary since the married person will owe less in taxes at year-end.

After the end of the year, you will receive a W-2 form (Figure 7-5) which reports your annual earnings and the amounts that have been deducted for federal income tax, social security, and, if applicable, state income tax. A copy of the W-2 form is filed with your tax return to document your earnings and the amount you have paid in taxes. The difference between the amount withheld and the tax owed is either the additional amount you must pay or the refund you will receive.

Estimated Payments. Taxpayers who have income from investments or their own business are required to make payments every three months if there has not been any income tax withheld. These quarterly payments are based on the individual's estimate of the taxes that will be due at year-end. Underpayment or failure to make the required quarterly payments can result in the payment of penalties and interest.

FIGURE 7-5   W-2 Form

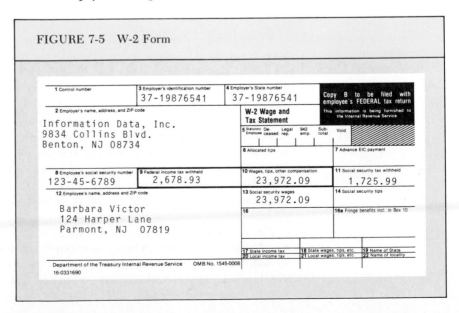

Deadlines and Penalties

Most people are required to file their federal income tax return each April 15. If you are not able to file on time, Form 4868 can be used to obtain an automatic four-month extension. This extension is for the 1040 form and other documents, but it does not delay your payment liability. You must submit any amount owed with Form 4868 by April 15.

Individuals who make quarterly deposits for estimated taxes must submit their payments by April 15, June 15, and September 15 of the current tax year, with the final payment due by January 15 of the following year.

The Internal Revenue Service (IRS) can impose penalties and interest for violations of the tax code. Failure to file a tax return can result in a 25 percent penalty in addition to the taxes owed.

Underpayment of quarterly estimated taxes requires that you pay interest on the amount that should have been submitted. Underpayment due to negligence or fraud can result in penalties of 50 to 75 percent. The good news is that if you claim a refund several months or years late, the IRS will pay you interest.

FILING YOUR FEDERAL INCOME TAX RETURN

The annual submission of your income tax form requires several decisions. First, you must determine whether you need to file a return and, if so, what filing status to claim. Second, you must determine which form to use. Finally, you must determine what types of information and assistance you desire. After filing your tax return, you may be identified for a tax audit. If this happens, there are several policies and procedures of which you need to be aware.

Who Must File?

- Who Must File a Federal Income Tax Return

Every citizen or resident of the United States and every resident of Puerto Rico is required to file a federal income tax return if his or her income is above a certain amount. This amount will vary based on marital status, filing status, and age. For example, a married couple (both under age 65) had to file a tax return on April 15, 1988 (for tax year 1987), if their gross income was at least $7,560. This amount will change each year based on changes in the standard deduction and in the amount allowed for personal exemptions. If your gross income is less than the amount required to file but taxes were withheld from your earnings, you will need to file a tax return to obtain a refund.

The main categories of filing status for your federal income tax are:

- *Single*—for never-married, divorced, or legally separated individuals.
- *Married filing joint return*—combines the income of both a husband and a wife.
- *Married filing separate return*—under certain conditions, a married couple can benefit from this filing status.

- *Head of household*—for married individuals with a dependent child who live apart from the spouse.
- *Qualifying widow or widower*—for individuals whose spouse recently died.

As mentioned, your filing status is determined by several factors. In some situations, you may have a choice. In such cases, compute your taxes under both alternatives to determine which is most advantageous.

Tax Form Selection

Taxpayers have a choice of three forms when filing their income tax. In 1985, 17 percent used Form 1040EZ, 19 percent used Form 1040A, and 64 percent used the regular Form 1040. Your decision on this matter will depend on your type of income, the amount of your income, the number of your deductions, and the complexity of your tax situation.

Form 1040EZ. You may use Form 1040EZ if you are single and claim only your own exemption; if your income consisted only of wages, salaries, and tips and not more than $400 of interest; if your taxable income is less than $50,000; and if you do not itemize deductions or claim any adjustments to income or any tax credits.

Form 1040EZ allows individuals with less complicated situations to file with a minimum of effort. For example, Matthew Collins, a college freshman, had a part-time job at a health center. Since he was single, earned less than the amount needed to file, and had $43 in interest income, Matthew was able to use Form 1040EZ to obtain a refund of income tax withheld during the past year.

Form 1040A. This form would be used by individuals who have less than $50,000 in taxable income from wages, salaries, tips, unemployment compensation, interest, or dividends. With Form 1040A, you can also take deductions for individual retirement account (IRA) contributions and a tax credit for child and dependent care expenses.

If you qualify for either Form 1040EZ or Form 1040A, you may wish to use one of them to simplify your tax return filing. But you are not required to use either form if the use of the regular Form 1040 lets you pay less tax.

Form 1040. Form 1040 is an expanded version of Form 1040A that includes sections for all types of income. You are required to use this form if your income is over $50,000 or if you can be claimed as a dependent on your parents' return *and* you had interest, or dividends, over a set limit.

Form 1040 makes it possible to itemize your deductions. You can list various allowable expenses (medical costs, home mortgage interest, real estate property taxes) that will reduce your taxable income and the amount you owe to the government. You should learn about all the possible adjustments to income, deductions, and tax credits for which you may qualify.

Information Sources and Tax Preparation Assistance

● Tax Assistance Sources

As with other aspects of personal financial planning, a variety of materials and sources are available to assist you with your taxes. The Internal Revenue Service offers a wide range of services to taxpayers. Libraries and bookstores have annually updated books and publications. Finally, professional tax preparers make their services available to individuals who desire this type of assistance.

IRS Services. If you wish to do your own tax return or just to expand your knowledge of tax regulations, the Internal Revenue Service has four methods of assistance.

1. *Publications.* The IRS has hundreds of free booklets and pamphlets. These publications can be obtained at a local IRS office, by mail request, or by a telephone call to the office listed in your tax packet or your local telephone directory. Especially helpful is *Your Federal Income Tax* (IRS Publication 17).

2. *Recorded Messages.* The IRS Tele-Tax system allows you access to 150 telephone tax tips covering everything from filing requirements to reporting gambling income. Your push-button phone gives you 24-hour-a-day availability to this recorded information. Again, telephone numbers can be found in your tax packet or your telephone directory.

3. *Toll-Free Hot Line.* You can obtain information on specific problems through a series of IRS-staffed phone lines. The appropriate telephone number can be obtained in the same manner as above. You are not asked to give your name when you use this service, so your questions are anonymous.

4. *Walk-In Service.* You can visit your local or district IRS office to obtain assistance with your taxes. More than 500 of these facilities are available to taxpayers.[3]

Other Publications. Each year, several tax guides are published and offered for sale. These publications include *J. K. Lasser's Your Income Tax*, the *H&R Block Income Tax Workbook*, and *Sylvia Porter's Income Tax Book*. You can purchase these books at bookstores, drugstores, or supermarkets or use them at your library.

Tax Preparers. Over 40 million U.S. taxpayers pay someone to do their taxes. The fee for this service can range from $40 at a tax preparation service for a simple return, to more than $700 at a certified public accountant for a complicated tax return.

Many people like doing their own taxes. This experience can help you improve your understanding of your actual financial situation. The IRS claims that anyone with an eighth grade education can fill out a 1040 form. The average person takes a little more than two hours to complete Form

---

[3]"IRS Information," *Changing Times Financial Services Directory*, issue 2, 1987, p. 110; and "Write Yourself Off as a Tax Expert," *USA Weekend*, February 13–15, 1987, p. 15.

1040, compared with 57 minutes for Form 1040A and 22 minutes for the one-page 1040EZ. But doing your own taxes can be complicated, particularly if you have sources of income other than salary. The sources available for professional tax assistance include:

- Tax services ranging from local, one-person operations to national firms such as H&R Block, which has over 4,500 offices open from January to April each year.
- Enrolled agents—government-approved tax experts who prepare returns and provide tax advice. You may contact the National Association of Enrolled Agents at 1-800-424-4339 for information on enrolled agents in your area.
- The many accountants who offer tax assistance along with their other business services. A certified public accountant (CPA) with special training in taxes can be valuable in your tax planning and in the preparation of your annual return.
- Attorneys, who do not usually complete tax returns and whose services can be best used when you are involved in a tax-related transaction or when you have a difference of opinion with the IRS.[4]

Even if you hire a professional tax preparer, you are responsible for supplying accurate and complete information. If you owe more tax because your return contains errors or because you have made entries that are not allowed, it is your responsibility to pay that additional tax plus any interest and penalties.

What if Your Return Is Audited?

- The Process Involved in a Tax Audit

The IRS reviews all returns to make sure that they have been properly completed. Computers check all of the arithmetic. If you have made an error, your tax is automatically refigured and you will receive a bill or a refund. If you have made an entry that is not allowed, you will be notified by mail. A tax audit is a detailed examination of your tax return by the IRS. In most audits, the IRS requests more information to support the entries on your tax return. You must keep accurate records to support your return. Keep receipts, canceled checks, and other evidence to prove amounts that you claim as valid. Avoiding common filing mistakes (see Table 7–2) helps minimize your chances of an IRS audit.

Who Gets Audited? In 1985, 1.31 percent (1.3 million) of all tax filers were audited.[5] While the IRS does not reveal its basis for selecting the returns that it audits, several indicators are evident. Individuals who claim large or unusual deductions increase their chances of an audit. Tax advisers suggest including a brief explanation or a copy of receipts for deductions that may be

---

[4]"Tax Preparers and Planners," *Changing Times Financial Services Directory*, issue 2, 1987, p. 104; and "When You Should Hire an Expert," *USA Today*, February 9, 1987, p. 4E.

[5]"Steps You Can Take to Keep Auditors Away," *USA Today*, February 9, 1987, p. 5E.

TABLE 7-2   Avoiding Common Filing Errors

Keep all tax-related information together for easy access.

Follow instructions carefully. Many people deduct total medical expenses rather than the amount that exceeds the set percentage of adjusted gross income. And people often forget to deduct the standard deduction from total itemized deductions before recording on the 1040 form.

Use the proper tax schedule.

Check your arithmetic several times.

Sign your return (both spouses must sign a joint return), or the IRS won't process it.

Attach necessary documentation such as your W-2 forms and required supporting schedules.

Put your social security number, the tax year, and a daytime telephone number on your check—and be sure to sign the check.

Keep a photocopy of your return.

Put the proper postage on your mailing envelope.

Finally, check everything again—and file on time!!

Taking care when you file your income tax can result in "many happy returns."

---

questioned. Individuals whose incomes are high, who have had large losses due to tax shelters or partnerships, or who have had their income or deductions questioned in the past may also be targeted for an audit.

Types of Audits. The simplest and most common type of audit is the *correspondence audit*. This mail inquiry requires you to clarify or document minor questions about your tax return. You usually have 30 days to provide the requested information, and your response may be by mail.[6]

The *office audit* requires you to visit an IRS office to clarify some aspect of your return. This type of audit usually takes an hour or two. The field audit is more complex. It involves having an IRS agent visit you at your home, at your place of business, or at the office of your accountant so that you will have quick access to all pertinent documents and records. A *field audit* may also be done to verify whether an individual has an office in the home as claimed.

Finally, the *research audit* is a line-by-line investigation of a tax return. Individuals audited in this way are selected at random so that the IRS can obtain information for use in developing future audit procedures. In a research audit, a person is asked to furnish proof for every item on the return, including proof of marriage.[7]

Your Audit Rights. When you are audited, you should be prepared to answer the IRS agent's questions clearly and completely. You may be accom-

---

[6] "Tax Audits: Improving Your Odds," *Consumer Reports*, March 1986, p. 156.
[7] Ibid.

panied by your tax preparer, accountant, or lawyer, who may assist you in answering questions.

If you disagree with the results of the audit, you may request a conference at the Regional Appeals Office. Although most differences of opinion are settled at this stage, some taxpayers take their cases further. An individual

---

In the News
A Wall Street Journal *Reporter Gets Audited by IRS— and Lives to Tell All about It*

On October 21, 1984, James B. Stewart, staff reporter for *The Wall Street Journal*, received a letter from the IRS. He was being audited for his 1983 tax return. Here is his account of the ordeal—in his own words:

When I first phoned my auditor, he gave me an option: He would come either to my home or office for our session. How thoughtful and convenient, I thought. How awful, I later learned. If you are invited into an IRS office, it probably means you are in for a fairly perfunctory review, possibly of only one or two suspicious areas in the return. The house call is reserved for full-scale scrutiny into every corner of your financial life.

When the auditor arrived, I offered him coffee. He refused as though it were a bribe. We got down to business with deductions. I was armed with receipts, charge slips, used airline tickets, etc. He chose two sample months and examined the expenses carefully. My appointment calendar, which he asked to see, proved invaluable. He checked to see that entries in the calendar matched receipts. Not all of them tallied, but he multiplied the two-month total of those that did by six. Since I was in the ballpark for total deductions, I was absolved.

Then the auditor asked for income statements, and the true purpose of this exercise became clear: I was suspected of having failed to report income. Not reporting income, my auditor casually mentioned, is a crime.

It had never occurred to me that I would have to produce a record of every deposit in every account—checking, money market, brokerage, savings. In fact, I could not do it, since I hadn't saved many of those records. Despite my pleas of innocence, the audit was adjourned until I could retrieve the data, along with an identification of the source of every deposit in every account.

Tracing the deposits took days of detective work, and it was three months before my audit resumed. I had no explanation for two substantial deposits, but the auditor said I'd have to provide an explanation before the audit was over. While rummaging through a drawer, I solved the mystery. One deposit was the proceeds of a tax-free certificate that had matured. The other was a friend's out-of-state check I had deposited in my account; I had then written him a local check. That favor I won't repeat.

I had one, final, heart-stopping moment when, at the end of a full day of scrutiny, the auditor called me in to say in solemn tones that it looked as if I was guilty of not reporting income. Fortunately, I recognized a simple arithmetic error. The auditor apologized profusely and I was subsequently cleared. My official letter of absolution came two weeks ago.

Source: James B. Stewart, "Your Money Matters," *The Wall Street Journal*, July 18, 1985, sec. 2, p. 23.

From *The Wall Street Journal*, with permission of Cartoon Features Syndicate.

may go to the U.S. tax court, or the U.S. claims court, or the U.S. district court. Some tax disputes have gone as far as the U.S. Supreme Court.

CHANGING TAX STRATEGIES

Revisions in the tax laws, like changes in prices and interest rates, are economic facts of life. Each year, the IRS modifies its forms and procedures. Also, Congress frequently passes legislation that changes the tax code. But none of these actions have had the major impact that we can expect as a result of the Tax Reform Act of 1986. This overhaul of our tax system (see Table 7–3) will require all of us to reassess our tax strategies for both the short term and the long run.

The Tax Reform Act of 1986

● Major Provisions of the Tax Reform Act of 1986

The Tax Reform Act of 1986 (TRA) will have a major impact on personal financial planning. TRA attempts to create an equitable distribution of taxes and to eliminate personal and corporate loopholes that allowed some to pay less than their fair share of taxes. It is estimated that 80 percent of American taxpayers will pay less federal taxes under the new system. However, the greater taxes assessed on businesses could result in increased prices for goods and services. Indirectly, therefore, the anticipated increase in spendable income might be eroded.

TRA will affect how much we pay in taxes. It will also influence how we spend, save, invest, and plan for retirement.

Reduced Tax Rates. In 1986, there were 14 tax rates, ranging from 11 to 50 percent. Starting in 1988, TRA replaces this rate structure with a two-rate system:

	Married Couples	*Single Taxpayers*
15 percent on taxable income of	up to $29,750	up to $17,850
28 percent on taxable income of	over $29,750	over $17,850

For the transition year of 1987, a five-rate system is used.

TRA also includes a 5 percent additional tax for individuals in higher income categories. The 33 percent tax rate applies to married taxpayers on taxable income between $71,900 and $149,250 and to single taxpayers on taxable income between $43,150 and $89,560. Taxable income above the upper limit amounts is taxed at the 28 percent rate. The additional tax is designed to eliminate the benefits of the personal exemption and the 15 percent tax bracket for taxpayers with high incomes.

Estimates suggest that the average taxpayer's bill will drop 6 percent as of 1988, when the new tax system is in place. What happens to your specific tax burden will, of course, depend on the size of your household and the amounts and types of deductions you were taking under the old law. Some observers believe that as a result of the lower tax rates, personal financial decisions will be based solely on the economic value of transactions rather than on tax considerations.

TABLE 7-3   Major Provisions of the 1986 Tax Reform Act

Reduction in the number of tax rates from 14 to 2 (15 and 28 percent).

Personal exemption amount increased; extra personal exemptions for the blind and the elderly (over 65) eliminated. Standard deduction increased (zero income bracket).

Mortgage interest deductible only on principal and second residences.

Deductibility of consumer interest phased out; no longer a tax deduction as of 1989.

Charitable contributions deductible only for those who itemize their deductions.

State sales tax no longer deductible.

Long-term and short-term capital gains taxed as ordinary income.

Individual retirement account (IRA) contributions phased out for upper-middle-income and high-income workers with pension plans.

401(k) tax-deferred savings plans limited to $7,000 a year.

Medical deductions required to exceed 7.5 percent of adjusted gross income.

Miscellaneous deductions required to exceed 2 percent of adjusted gross income.

Two-earner deduction and income averaging eliminated.

Losses from passive income offsetting other income phased out; prohibited as of 1991.

Increased Exemptions and Standard Deduction. Under TRA, the personal exemption will increase from $1,080 in 1986 to $2,000 in 1989. Starting in 1990, the amount will be revised annually based on inflation. Extra personal exemptions for the blind and elderly are eliminated, but these individuals will receive a higher standard deduction. In 1988, the standard deductions will increase from $2,480 to $3,000 for single taxpayers and from $3,670 to $5,000 for joint filers.

These increased exemptions and standard deductions will eliminate or reduce the taxes paid by many low-income Americans. In 1989, a family of four will not have to pay federal income tax on its first $13,000 of taxable income.

Changes in Exclusions. Many traditional exclusions have been repealed or modified. For example, dividends and unemployment benefits are now fully taxable. Under the old system, a taxpayer could exclude the first $100 ($200 for married couples filing a joint return) in dividends from taxable income and unemployment benefits were not taxable in certain situations.

Revised Investment Tax Rules. A capital gain is a profit realized from the sale of a capital asset, such as stocks, bonds, or real estate. Previously, 60 percent of long-term capital gains (gains on assets held for more than six months) was excluded from income tax. Under TRA, all capital gains will be included in taxable income and taxed in the same way as other ordinary income, such as wages and salaries. Capital losses may be deducted to offset capital gains and up to $3,000 of ordinary income.

Starting in 1991, taxpayers will no longer be allowed to write off losses from passive investments, such as limited partnerships, against earned income. The new tax rules also apply to businesses in which the investor does not materially participate. Real estate investments are considered passive even if the investor is actively involved.

Passive losses can be deducted only against income from passive investments. Special treatment is given to individuals who own and actively manage rental property. These investors can write off up to $25,000 in losses against other income. This tax benefit is phased out for individuals whose adjusted gross income is between $100,000 and $150,000. Individuals whose adjusted gross income is over $150,000 do not qualify for the benefit.

Eliminated or Reduced Deductions. As of 1987, most taxpayers will find it difficult to qualify for the medical expense deduction. Your medical bills have to exceed 7.5 percent of your adjusted gross income (AGI) before you can deduct a dollar. If your AGI is $20,000, for example, you must have $1,500 in unreimbursed medical expenses before you can claim a medical deduction. If your medical bills amount to $1,600, you qualify for a $100 deduction. Under the old law, medical expenses exceeding 5 percent of adjusted gross income were tax deductible.

You can continue to deduct the mortgage interest on your primary and second (or vacation) home. While TRA has eliminated many tax shelters and other tax preferences, it leaves homeowners' tax advantages intact. However, the interest deduction is limited to loan amounts of up to the purchase price plus improvements, except that home mortgage interest on debt in excess of the purchase price plus improvements, up to the fair market value of the residence, is deductible if the debt is incurred to meet educational or medical expenses.

Under the old law, interest paid on consumer loans was tax deductible. If you itemized, you could deduct interest paid on personal loans, lines of credit, bank loans, installment credit, auto loans, charge accounts, and credit cards. TRA eliminates these interest deductions. The interest deduction will be phased out as follows:

Year	Amount of Interest Allowed as Tax Deductible:
1987	65 percent
1988	40 percent
1989	20 percent
1990	10 percent
1991 and after	none

You can continue to deduct interest on loans made to finance investments. However, such interest deductions will be limited to the amount of your net investment income.

The new tax rules still leave homeowners plenty of borrowing power for consumer purchases. You can deduct interest on loans secured by your primary or secondary home up to the actual dollar amount that you have invested in it. For example, suppose that 10 years ago you bought a house for $85,000. If your mortgage is now $60,000 and you have made $15,000 in improvements, you can deduct the interest on a home equity loan of up to $40,000 ($85,000 + $15,000 − $60,000). TRA will allow you to use that line of credit to buy a car or to consolidate credit card or other debts on which interest is no longer tax deductible.

As of 1987, only taxpayers who itemize their deductions can write off their charitable contributions. Previously, nonitemizers were allowed to deduct a portion of their donations from taxable income.

Union dues, fees for tax return preparation, and other miscellaneous expenses related to earning income were fully deductible under the old law if you itemized. Under the new law, however, these expenses and other miscellaneous items are allowed only if their total amount exceeds 2 percent of adjusted gross income. Unreimbursed employee business expenses, which were previously an adjustment to income, are now taken as an itemized deduction. Work-related moving expenses, which previously could be deducted by anyone who filed, have now become an itemized deduction.

Affected Retirement Plans. An individual retirement account (IRA), discussed in more detail in Chapter 19, remains a valuable long-term investment, allowing you to put money aside for your retirement and to earn income on that money. Under the new tax law, however, an IRA deduction is available only to individuals who do not participate in employer-sponsored retirement plans or to joint filing taxpayers whose adjusted gross income is not greater than $40,000 and to single taxpayers whose adjusted gross income is not greater than $25,000. IRA contributions are partially deductible for participants in employer-sponsored retirement plans if, when filing jointly, they have an adjusted gross income of between $40,000 and $50,000 or if, when filing individually, they have an adjusted gross income between $25,000 and $35,000. No IRA deduction is allowed for joint and individual filers with adjusted gross incomes of above $50,000 and $35,000, respectively.

Even though an IRA contribution may not be deductible, all working Americans may continue to make annual IRA contributions of up to $2,000. All IRA accounts will earn interest on a tax-deferred basis; in other words, you will not have to pay taxes on the earnings of an IRA until you withdraw your money from it.

Retirement plans for self-employed individuals, referred to as Keogh plans, are not affected by TRA. These plans are discussed in detail in Chapter 19.

Tax Planning in Your Future

Most people want to pay their fair share of taxes—no more, no less. Your efforts to pay no more than your fair share can benefit from the practical suggestions offered in Table 7–4. **Tax avoidance,** the use of legitimate methods to reduce one's taxes, is an important part of good financial planning. **Tax evasion,** in contrast, is the use of illegal actions to reduce one's taxes.

TABLE 7-4   Financial Planning and Tax Reform

Pay off your consumer debt since the interest is no longer deductible.

Consider tax-exempt investments, such as municipal bonds, bond funds, and tax-exempt money market funds.

Examine single-premium whole life insurance policies, single-premium deferred annuities, and Series EE U.S. savings bonds, all of which delay taxes on accumulated earnings.

Consider high-yield investments, such as high-dividend stocks and high-yield bond funds. Lower tax brackets can make such investments more advantageous.

Take advantage of company 401(k) and 403(b) savings plans to help you set aside money for retirement.

Amounts paid into individual retirement accounts will still be deductible for many taxpayers. The earnings on IRAs are still deferred for everyone.

Be cautious of partnerships designed as tax shelters. Passive income can no longer offset your earned income.

Changes in personal and economic factors as well as changes in tax laws will challenge you to minimize your tax liability within the rules adopted by Congress. As you plan your tax strategies, bear in mind that your decisions not only affect your individual financial situation but also have far-reaching social implications. If government is to provide the services that we have come to expect from it, tax revenues are necessary.

SUMMARY

- Citizens pay taxes to provide public services. These required payments to government reduce the funds available for spending, saving, and investing. An individual's financial plan must consider the impact that taxes have on his or her economic situation.
- Sales tax, excise tax, property tax, estate tax, inheritance tax, gift tax, social security tax, and income tax are the taxes most commonly paid in our society.
- Taxable income is determined by subtracting adjustments to income, deductions, and exemptions from gross income.
- Common federal income tax deductions include medical expenses, real estate property taxes, home mortgage interest, charitable contributions, casualty losses, and certain work-related expenses.

- Individuals pay federal income tax through withholding from paychecks or quarterly estimated payments.
- Every citizen or resident of the United States whose income is above a certain level is required to file a federal income tax return.
- The main sources of tax assistance are IRS services and publications, other books and publications, and professional tax preparers.
- A tax audit involves a detailed examination of your tax return. Such an audit may be made by mail, at an IRS office, or at your home, your place of business, or the office of your accountant.
- The Tax Reform Act of 1986 reduced tax rates for federal income tax, and also reduced or eliminated certain deductions, exclusions, and tax preferences.

GLOSSARY

Adjusted gross income (AGI). Gross income reduced by certain adjustments, such as contributions to an individual retirement account (IRA) and alimony payments.

Capital gain. A profit realized from the sale of a capital asset, such as stocks, bonds, or real estate.

Earned income. Money received by an individual for personal effort, such as wages, salary, commission, fees, tips, or bonuses.

Estate tax. A tax imposed on the value of an individual's property at the time of his or her death.

Excise tax. A tax imposed on specific goods and services, such as gasoline, cigarettes, alcoholic beverages, tires, and air travel.

Exclusion. An amount not included in gross income.

Exemption. A deduction from adjusted gross income for yourself, your spouse, and qualified dependents.

Inheritance tax. A tax levied on the value of property received from a deceased individual.

Investment income. Money received in the form of dividends or interest; also called portfolio income.

Itemized deductions. Expenses that a taxpayer is allowed to deduct from adjusted gross income, such as medical expenses, real estate property taxes, home mortgage interest, charitable contributions, casualty losses, and certain work-related expenses.

Passive income. Money received as a result of business activities in which you do not actively participate.

Progressive tax. A tax in which tax rates increase as the level of taxable income increases.

Proportional tax. A tax in which a constant tax rate is applied to all levels of the tax base; also called a flat tax.

Regressive tax. A tax that tends to place a heavier burden on the poor because its rates decrease as the tax base increases.

Standard deduction. A set amount on which no taxes are paid.

Tax audit. A detailed examination of your tax return by the Internal Revenue Service.

Tax avoidance. The use of legitimate methods of reducing one's taxes.

Tax credit. An amount subtracted directly from the amount of taxes owed.

Tax evasion. The use of illegal actions to reduce one's taxes.

Tax shelter. An investment that provides immediate tax benefits and a reasonable expectation of a future financial return.

Taxable income. The net amount of income, after allowable deductions, on which income tax is computed.

REVIEW QUESTIONS

1. How can the fairness of a tax be evaluated?
2. What are some examples of taxes that individuals pay indirectly?
3. How does an excise tax differ from a general sales tax?
4. What taxes are imposed on an individual's wealth?
5. How is taxable income computed?
6. How does passive income differ from earned income?
7. What expenses can be included in the itemized deductions on an income tax return?
8. How does a tax credit affect the amount owed in federal income tax?
9. Who is required to make estimated tax payments to the government?
10. What are the main categories of filing status on a federal income tax return?
11. What factors will affect a taxpayer's choice of a 1040 form?
12. What services does the IRS provide to assist taxpayers in preparing their returns?
13. What does a tax audit involve?
14. How did the Tax Reform Act of 1986 affect tax rates?
15. Which tax benefits were eliminated or reduced by the 1986 Tax Reform Act?

DISCUSSION QUESTIONS AND ACTIVITIES

1. Had you been Hugh and Margaret Lennon, would you have sued the IRS? Explain.
2. Do you believe that the legal action taken by James and Carol Bowe was justified? Explain.

3. What types of taxes do you regard as fairest for all individuals?

4. Ask several people to name the various taxes they pay, both directly and indirectly.

5. What types of income do you believe should be excluded from taxable income?

6. Investigate various tax shelters that are available to taxpayers.

7. Some people make sure that more is withheld from their pay than is necessary so they will get a tax refund. Do you agree with this action?

8. Obtain copies of the current income tax forms and instruction booklet. Which 1040 form would you use?

9. Contact several local tax preparation services and obtain information on their charge for preparing a simple federal income tax return. What do you believe accounts for the differences in fees?

10. Talk to someone who has been asked for a clarification of his or her tax return. What information did the IRS question? How was the situation resolved?

11. Will the Tax Reform Act of 1986 reduce the total tax burden on low-income people? What provisions of the act support this idea?

12. What effect can changes in the taxing of capital gains have on economic growth in our country?

ADDITIONAL READINGS

"Choosing a Tax Preparer." *Money,* December 1986, p. 204.

Master Tax Guide. Commerce Clearing House, Inc., 4025 West Peterson, Chicago, IL 60646.

Strassels, Paul N. *The 1986 Tax Reform Act: Making It Work for You.* Homewood, Ill.: Dow Jones-Irwin, 1987.

Tax Hotline. 330 West 42 Street, New York, NY 10036.

Your Federal Income Tax. IRS Publication 17. Internal Revenue Service, Washington, DC 20224.

"Your Taxes: Up or Down?" *Consumer Reports,* March 1987, pp. 164–71.

CASE 7–1 Students Find New Federal Law Taxing*

Students, beware! Buried in the Tax Reform Act of 1986 is a provision that makes free room and board not so free anymore. Under the new tax law, any scholarship or grant used to cover tuition and such course-related expenses as fees, books, and supplies remains tax free, provided you're working toward a degree. But any portion of the scholarship or grant that goes for noneducation costs, such as room and board, will no longer be tax free. Therefore, a student on a full scholarship must list as income for tax purposes an amount equal to the cost of room and board. Students who are not in a program leading to a degree must declare all scholarships and grants, no matter what their purpose.

"This is going to be a devastating surprise to a lot of students," said Ted Bracken at the Consortium on Financing Higher Education in Washington, D.C. "What's most unfortunate is that it's generally those students who are most needy that get their room and board paid for."

The new rule, which took effect in 1987, applies to scholarships and fellowships granted after August 16, 1986. "I have a lot of sympathy for the

*USA Today, November 6, 1986, p. 13B.

next generation," said Dennis Clougherty, 24, who was working on a doctoral dissertation in theoretical physics at the Massachusetts Institute of Technology. Clougherty received a tax-free stipend of $760 a month but did not have to pay taxes on that amount because his fellowship had been renewed for 12 months before August 16, 1986.

Had the bill been fully in effect, however, he would have had to pay $618 tax on the $9,618 annual total. "Every penny counts when you're trying to get by in an expensive city like Boston,"

Clougherty said. "I'm going to work hard to finish up the dissertation before the fellowship is up for renewal next summer."

Questions

1. Do you think that full-time college students should be exempt from income taxes? Why or why not?

2. Is it fair to tax the scholarships and grants of students if the students are not in a program leading to a degree? Explain.

CASE 7–2 The Case of a Disappearing Summer Job

Michael Sims and his friends Cathy and Eric had just graduated from high school. All three of them had been counting on having summer jobs as summer interns at the community access television station. But when they reported for work, Mr. Walken, the station's producer, told them that because of cutbacks in state and federal funds the summer intern program had been canceled.

Michael's mother, an accountant for the state legislature, explained that because of recent tax cuts there wasn't enough government money to pay for the summer jobs program. Michael was still upset, and decided to write a newspaper article about what had happened to him and his friends.

Through research, Michael found many examples of limited tax resources, and he began to understand that often there were conflicting goals. He interviewed a state senator and a small-business owner and learned that special tax reductions were meant to encourage individuals to start businesses. Such reductions might mean higher taxes for others. Legislators also wanted to keep unpopular tax increases to a minimum, but

some programs might be cut, for example, the summer job program. A group of students told Michael that university housing was affordable because it was tax exempt but that the resulting loss in property taxes meant less revenue for public goods and services. At a day-care center, Michael learned that such operations were often considered charitable organizations and supported by tax-deductible contributions. Their tax-exempt status meant less revenue for government services.

Michael's research was thorough, and after long hours of work he finished his article. The article was published, and as a result of its publication he landed a summer job.

Questions

1. Why did Michael and his friends lose their summer jobs?

2. What is meant by the term *conflicting goals?* Give several examples of conflicting goals.

3. How do special interest groups affect tax rates and the allocation of tax revenues?

Comprehensive Case for Part Two
An Interest in Interest

Ken Emerson recently spent a lot of time reading advertisements for financial services. Among them were the following:

"Reduce Your Taxes with a Tax-Deferred Savings Account"

"Our Electronic Banking System Gives You a Personal Banker 24 Hours a Day"

"Auto Loans at 6.9% (some restrictions apply)"

"Fast, Easy Loans for Any Purpose (amount based on the value of your home)"

"Free Checking and No Charge for a Safe-Deposit Box with Convenience Savings ($5,000 minimum balance required)"

After seeing these and many other ads, Ken commented, "I thought gathering information was supposed to make financial planning easier, but I'm just more confused!"

"What's the big deal?" was the reaction of Devon, Ken's friend. "Just put some money in a savings account each month, and get a checking account at the bank near work." This was the way Devon handled her financial activities.

"But it seems that some savings accounts pay more interest than others and that not all checking accounts charge the same fees," was Ken's concern. "In fact, some checking accounts can earn you money instead of costing you."

"The amount of the fees and extra interest isn't really worth the time and effort," said Devon. "Besides, my bank has several 24-hour banking machines that make it all worth it."

"Well, you obviously have your ideas on this matter and I have mine," said Ken. "Personally, I think a little bit of effort can result in some wise financial choices."

"Come on, let's get something to eat," suggested Devon. "And I'll buy," she said.

"Now that's the best financial deal of the day," said Ken.

When dinner was over, Devon paid for the meal with a bank credit card. Ken asked, "I thought you can get cash at any time from the electronic banking machines?"

"Well," sighed Devon, "you have to have money in the account to withdraw cash!"

"Maybe the way a person selects financial services will affect money management habits and financial planning," commented Ken as he picked up a newspaper containing ads of different financial institutions.

"OK," said Devon, "maybe I can make better choices when I use financial services."

Questions

1. How would you describe Ken's and Devon's attitudes toward selecting and using financial services? Is one point of view necessarily better than the other? Explain your answer.

2. How can a person's use of financial services influence his or her financial planning success?

3. How helpful were the financial services ads that Ken read? What information could be used in planning the use of financial services?

4. How important should the amount of interest earned on savings be as a consideration in selecting a savings account or a financial institution?

5. What considerations should influence a person's selection of the place and type of his or her checking account?

6. Using one institution for all of your financial services is convenient. Describe a situation in which it would be better to do business with more than one financial institution.

7. How does your selection of financial services influence the process of preparing your tax return and paying your taxes?

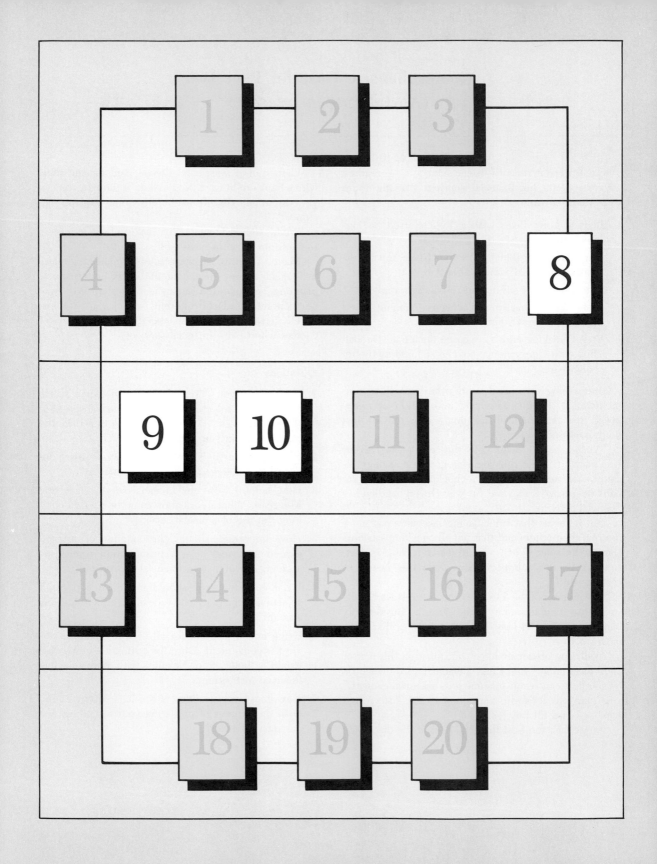

PART THREE

Making Your
Buying Decisions

The third part of *Personal Finance* considers the spending aspect of financial planning. First, we discuss the process of buying and the many influences that affect purchasing decisions. The buying process is presented in a form that can be adapted to most shopping situations. Effective buying strategies are described, as are actions that can be taken to resolve consumer complaints. Next, we take up housing and transportation, the two largest purchases of most individuals and families. The selection of a place to live is considered from the perspective of your needs, your financial resources, and your lifestyle. Your choice among buying, renting, or building is emphasized. The home buying process—which involves determining needs, selecting a location, and financing the purchase—is examined. In a similar manner, transportation alternatives are evaluated on the basis of needs, costs, and lifestyle. Finally, we present practical suggestions for buying a used car, selecting and financing a new car, and maintaining the vehicle. This part consists of:

Chapter 8   Daily Buying Decisions and Legal Protection
Chapter 9   Choosing a Place to Live
Chapter 10   Buying Transportation

8

Daily Buying Decisions and Legal Protection

We are all consumers. Regardless of age, income, or place of residence, each day we all use a variety of goods and services. To get the most for the many dollars we spend, we want to make wise buying decisions. Certain purchasing skills make this possible. These skills are based on information, experience, and common sense. This chapter will begin to provide you with the necessary information; you will develop the necessary experience and common sense as a result of your personal efforts.

After studying this chapter, you will be able to:

- Discuss the factors that influence your buying decisions.
- Explain the steps involved in the buying process.
- Use various sources of consumer information.
- Identify strategies for effective purchasing.
- State the causes of consumer problems.
- Describe basic consumer rights and responsibilities.
- Explain how to resolve consumer complaints.
- Discuss the assistance that is provided for consumers by government agencies.
- Identify the legal actions that are available to consumers.

Interview with **Joanne L. Kron,** Asst. Legal Counsel, Governor's Office of Interagency Cooperation, State of Illinois, and **Elaine Strubbe,** Director, Consumer Div., Better Business Bureau of Metro Chicago

Joanne L. Kron serves as an Assistant Legal Counsel to the governor of Illinois. Her responsibilities range from commenting on proposed legislation to advising clients on financial matters. Elaine Strubbe has served as the Director of the Consumer Division of the Better Business Bureau of Metropolitan Chicago. In that position, Ms. Strubbe organized numerous consumer information seminars and forums.

Caveat emptor is a Latin expression meaning "Let the buyer beware." This idea can be traced to Cicero, who said more than 2,000 years ago, "All things should be made bare so that the buyer may not be in any way ignorant of anything a seller knows."

The complexity of today's marketplace has required government at all levels to monitor potentially dangerous consumer products and to prose-cute illegal business practices. In the final analysis, however, it is the knowledge of consumers and the decisions of responsible businesspeople that determine the success and failure of goods and services in our economy.

When a problem occurs with a purchase, you need to let the seller know about the situation. Not only is this the fastest way to get your complaint resolved, but it also gives the seller a chance to keep you as a satisfied customer and gain new customers by learning from mistakes. Most companies welcome this opportunity as it may help them avoid future complaints.

Better Business Bureaus are nonprofit corporations financed by membership dues and subscriptions paid by responsible business and professional firms in the communities they serve. Without charge, the Better Business Bureau provides in-formation about companies, associations, and charities and refers to appropriate organizations inquiries in areas that it does not handle. It helps resolve disputes through mediation and, as a final step, arbitration. It fosters ethical advertising and selling practices through advertising reviews, shopping investigations, media information programs, and the development of standards.

However, Ms. Strubbe states, the Better Business Bureau does not endorse any company, product, or individual. It does not offer legal advice. It does not provide help in voiding contracts unless these involve fraud or misrepresentation. It does not make collections or provide credit information. Finally, the Better Business Bureau does not pass judgment on prices charged, the quality of services or workmanship, the efficiency of devices, or the durability of merchandise.

Each month, Fred and Lynn Bonner had difficulty in making ends meet. They had three children, and their housing, food, and other living expenses were constantly increasing. One day at work, a friend told Fred about a food-buying plan that would help the Bonners save money. For a monthly payment of $165, all the food they needed would be delivered and they would also qualify for a new refrigerator. Since the Bonners viewed this program as a way to save money and since they also needed a new refrigerator, they signed up for the plan.

After making two payments, the Bonners received a notice from the company with which they had signed up that delivery of their refrigerator had been delayed due to production problems. Meanwhile, they had received less food than they needed, so they had still had to spend money for groceries.

Two months later, the refrigerator still hadn't arrived and the Bonners were paying more for food than they had paid before they joined the plan. Two weeks later, the Bonners

THE CONSUMER BUYING PROCESS

- Factors that Influence Your Buying Decisions

Each day, American consumers spend an average of

- $700 million on entertainment.
- $300 million on clothes.
- $300 million at restaurants; $64 million in bars.
- $40 million on automobile repairs and replacement parts.
- $25 million to transport children to and from school.
- $6 million on plumbing repairs.
- $200,000 on roller skates.[1]

Such buying habits are affected by a wide variety of factors that can be grouped into three major categories: economic, personal, and social (see Figure 8–1).

Economic buying influences include such factors as inflation, taxes, interest rates, and government regulations. They also include product characteristics, such as quality, brand, safety, and convenience.

Personal buying influences include such factors as age, sex, income, family situation, and place of residence. Thus, when people get married at an older age and the birthrate drops, there is a decline in the demand for such products as children's clothing and toys.

Social buying influences include such factors as lifestyle, interests, hobbies, advertising, and the people with whom you associate. Your lifestyle is revealed in how you spend your time and money. It makes a statement to

[1]Tom Parker, *In One Day* (Boston: Houghton Mifflin, 1984), pp. 12, 16, 17, 31.

240

stopped receiving food from the company. "Well, I guess we won't have to make any more payments," commented Fred, "since we aren't receiving any of the services we were paying for." He attempted to notify the company of his intention to stop making payments, but its phone was disconnected and its office was empty. He sighed, saying,

"Now our food expenses can return to the amount they were before we got involved in this deal."

But the Bonners' problems weren't over. A few months later, a collection agency notified them that they still owed $495 for several months of service. The contract they had signed obligated them to pay for a minimum of eight months.

Such consumer problems occur all the time. People get involved in expensive situations that they could have avoided if they had known all the facts when they were making their purchasing choices.

others about the type of person you are, and it is the basis for most of your buying decisions.

While many factors affect your purchasing habits, your actual shopping decisions are based on a specific decision-making process. Figure 8–2 presents an overview of the steps that should be taken to ensure effective purchasing. This consumer buying process will be most valuable with large purchases, such as appliances, sports equipment, home improvements, or vacations. When you buy such items, you should take the time and effort needed to get the most for your money. However, you probably make many routine purchases of low-cost items—food, clothing, and the like—without thinking about them, and often this may be exactly what you should do. Following all the steps in the consumer buying process for such items may not be the best use of your time. But taking time to evaluate all of your purchases can improve the satisfaction you receive from each dollar you spend.

PREBUYING ACTIVITIES

Before every purchase, you will probably perform three steps: identify the problem, gather information, and evaluate alternatives. These steps will help you make informed buying decisions.

Problem Identification

- Steps Involved in the Buying Process

Identifying the problem in a purchasing situation may be difficult. Often you have made a predetermined choice. However, objective decision mak-

FIGURE 8-1 Influences on Consumer Buying

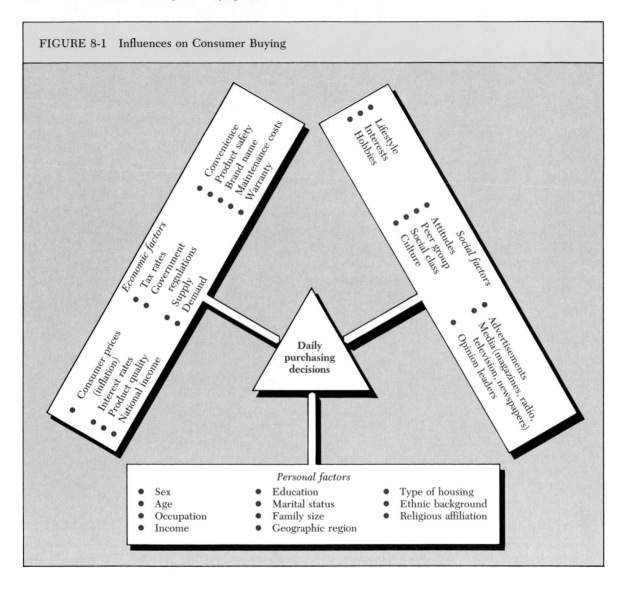

ing with regard to purchases must start without a planned course of action. Some people always buy the same brand when another brand at a lower price may serve their needs as well or when another brand at the same price may provide better quality.

A narrow view of the problem is another weakness in problem identification. For example, you may think that the problem is the need to get a car when the real problem is the need for transportation. Or you may confuse causes and symptoms with the problem itself. While many causes and symptoms enter into a purchasing problem, the actual basis on which action needs to be taken must be the main focus of this phase of the buying process. A

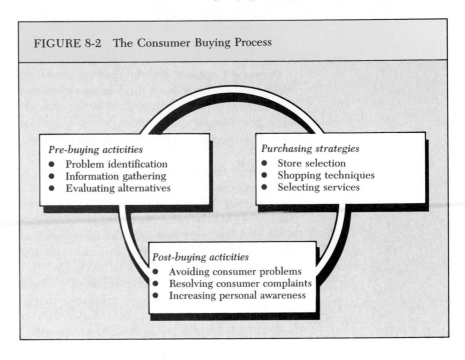

FIGURE 8-2   The Consumer Buying Process

Pre-buying activities
- Problem identification
- Information gathering
- Evaluating alternatives

Purchasing strategies
- Store selection
- Shopping techniques
- Selecting services

Post-buying activities
- Avoiding consumer problems
- Resolving consumer complaints
- Increasing personal awareness

clear, unbiased identification of the purchasing problem is vital to successful purchasing.

Information Gathering

Information is power. The better informed you are, the more likely you are to make the purchasing choice that best serves your interest. Knowing the least expensive place to buy an item or being aware of the ingredients of a food product can enhance your financial and physical well-being.

Some people spend very little, if any, time gathering and evaluating information relevant to their purchases. They buy on impulse; they have a gut feeling about their choices. While they may at times be satisfied with their decisions, there are probably other times when they are not.

At the other extreme are people who spend more time and effort than necessary on obtaining consumer information. While information is necessary for wise purchasing, too much information can create confusion and frustration.

The best course of action lies somewhere between the two extremes. Many of your simple, routine purchases may not require any information other than experience, but your large, expensive buying should involve some information gathering.

- Various Sources of Consumer Information

The main sources of information available to consumers are personal contacts, business organizations, media stories and reports, independent testing organizations, and government agencies. The information received from each of these sources should be evaluated for reliability, completeness, relevance, and objectivity.

Personal Contacts. Besides gaining knowledge from every purchase you make, you can learn from the buying experiences of the people with whom you associate. The information that they can give you on product performance, brand quality, and prices provides a valuable foundation for the information gathering phase of the buying process.

Business Organizations. Advertising is the most common type of consumer information. Each day, you are exposed to several hundred ads that appear along the road, in publications, at stores, and on television and radio. Table 8–1 lists the common techniques used in advertising to influence consumers. Advertising that provides information about product price, quality, and availability can be helpful. But many ads appeal to emotions and provide little assistance when purchases are made.

Other information sources provided by business organizations are the product label and the package. Like advertising, a product label can contain helpful information, such as information on content, weight, and price, as well as features that are designed only to stimulate sales. Many companies use the word *natural* on their food labels to imply a higher quality. Since

---

TABLE 8-1   Common Advertising Techniques

Product quality ads	Demonstrate a product Present scientific evidence Emphasize quality, brand, price, or other characteristic
Comparative ads	Direct presentation of competitive brands
Endorsement ad (or testimonials)	May involve one of the following: (a) Plain folks, average consumers expressing their support of the product or service (b) Corporate representative or character—a company executive or an animated person or animal (c) Famous person or company spokesperson—someone with high visibility, usually an entertainment or sports personality
Humorous ads	Use comedy to draw attention to a product or to stimulate sales
Lifestyle ads	Present the product or service in a common situation to which potential customers can relate—people at work, at home, or in recreational settings
Emotional ads	Obtain the attention and response of consumers by appealing to their feelings and desires—fear, guilt, sex, love, pleasure, convenience, safety, economy, beauty, popularity, power, security, and status.

FIGURE 8-3 Consumer Information from Product Labels

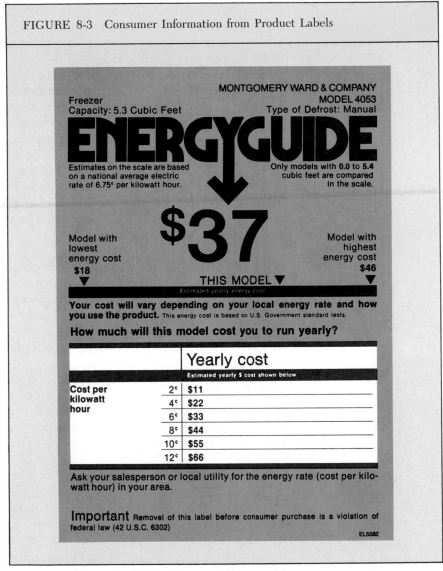

Product labeling for appliances includes information on operating costs. The data provided here can assist you in selecting the most energy-efficient model.

government regulations do not provide a specific definition for this word, this label may be misleading.

Almost every product and service we use is promoted by a trade association. The Electronics Industries Association represents companies that manufacture and distribute audio and video equipment, telephones, and home computers. Other trade association include the Brown Bag Institute, the American Bankers Association, the National Restaurant Association, the Radio Advertising Bureau, the Fresh Garlic Association, and the National

Frozen Pizza Institute. The main goal of such groups is to increase the use and sales of products or services. In addition, however, most of them offer information about the selection, safety, and use of those products or services.

Media Information. Among the most valuable, easily available, and least expensive consumer information sources are data from television, radio, newspapers, and magazines. Besides offering advertisements, these communication systems provide purchasing advice and general consumer information. Television and radio news stories and special reports can help you make wise buying choices. Most magazines and newspapers present regular columns and special articles on such topics as wise spending, budgeting, and insurance. Special topic magazines can also be helpful when you are buying such products as automobiles, boats, cameras, stereos, video recorders, or sports equipment.

Independent Testing Organizations. For over 50 years, Consumers Union has been providing information about the quality of products and services. Each month, *Consumer Reports* magazine presents test results on items ranging from automobiles, vacuum cleaners, and personal computers to hand soap, orange juice, and hot dogs. As we have evolved into a more service-oriented economy, Consumers Union has increased its coverage of such subjects as apartment renting, health care, insurance, investments, legal services, tax preparers, and banking.

Underwriters Laboratories (UL) is a business-sponsored organization that tests products for electrical and fire safety. Items that pass its tests can display the UL symbol. This emblem provides consumers with an assurance that the product has met rigorous safety standards.

Government Agencies. Local, state, and federal government agencies provide publications and other information services for consumers. The use of tax dollars to fund these efforts helps individuals make wiser, more informed purchasing choices. Booklets on most aspects of consumer purchases are available from the Office of Consumer Affairs, the Federal Trade Commission, the Food and Drug Administration, the Consumer Product Safety Commission, and other federal agencies. State and city consumer protection offices have materials relating to housing, insurance, and buying on credit. Beyond providing printed information, government agencies work to inform consumer through toll-free telephone numbers and displays at shopping centers, county fairs, and libraries. Appendix D details government sources on various consumer purchasing topics.

Evaluation of Alternatives

In every purchasing situation, several acceptable alternatives are usually present. These alternatives are based on various questions that you might ask yourself. Is it possible to delay the purchase or to do without the item?

Will you pay for the item with cash, or will you buy it on credit? Which brands should you consider? How do the price, quality, and service compare at different stores? Is it possible to rent the item instead of buying it? Considering such alternatives will result in the most effective purchasing decisions.

Each alternative needs to be evaluated on the basis of such factors as personal values and goals, available time and money, the costs of each alternative, the benefits of each alternative, and your specific needs with regard to product size, quality, quantity, and features. Figure 8–4 is an example of a consumer buying matrix that may be used to evaluate alternatives. In this figure, a person is considering the purchase of one of three brands of clock radios based on price, quality, style, and features. Each radio is rated for each attribute, and this number is multiplied by the weight assigned to that

---

FIGURE 8-4   Consumer Buying Matrix

Item _AM-FM CLOCK RADIO_

Information Sources/Comments _CONSUMER MAGAZINE / BRAND C HAS VERY SMALL SPEAKER_
FRIEND / BRAND B PERFORMS WELL

Attribute	Weight	Alternatives Brand _A_ Price _$37.95_ Rating (1-10)	Weighted score	Brand _B_ Price _$32.50_ Rating (1-10)	Weighted score	Brand _C_ Price _$26.00_ Rating (1-10)	Weighted score
PRICE	.3	6	1.8	8	2.4	10	3
QUALITY	.4	9	3.6	7	2.8	5	2
STYLE	.1	8	.8	8	.8	7	.7
FEATURES	.2	9	1.8	6	1.2	4	.8
■ Totals	1.0		8.0		7.2		6.5

attribute. This process results in an objective assessment of several purchase alternatives.

This type of buying matrix can be used for different products or services at different stores. You should consider various attributes such as location, price, and services provided. The result computed with the buying matrix may not be the clock radio you select. Factors related to the place of purchase and shopping procedures should also be considered.

PURCHASING STRATEGIES

- Strategies for Effective Purchasing

As a consumer, you must choose among different types of retail establishments and different methods of distribution. The choices you make will have a strong influence on the satisfaction you receive from purchasing products. Efforts to use various product comparison methods will also improve your shopping effectiveness. Finally, you should give special attention to the purchase of services since such purchases lack the physical qualities needed for easy comparison.

Store Selection

Your decision to shop at a particular store is probably influenced by the variety of its merchandise and the quality of its brands. Also important are the store's policies with regard to such matters as check cashing, exchanges, and frequency of sales. Most stores offer customers various services, including free parking and delivery, telephone and mail orders, and product advice. Finally, your selection of a store is affected by store hours, location, reputation, and the accessibility of shopping alternatives. The choices as to stores fall into three groups: traditional stores, contemporary retailers, and nonstore shopping.

Traditional Stores. Department stores have a wide variety of products grouped into specific departments such as appliances, clothing, garden supplies, and housewares. Each product type is available in various styles and types at such stores as Sears Roebuck and J. C. Penney.

Specialty stores concentrate on a limited product line—for example, shoes, clothing, flowers, or gifts. Such stores usually provide extensive personal service.

Discount stores, such as K mart and Zayre, offer a variety of products at prices lower than those charged by other stores. However, these stores do not provide many of the services that are obtainable at department and specialty stores.

In the mid 1930s, supermarkets were developed as alternatives to small, full-service grocery stores. Today, most supermarkets, while providing a wide variety of food-related products, also offer such items as housewares, tools, cosmetics, and clothing. In order to remain competitive in attracting customers, supermarkets have added departments that sell bulk food items, deli meats and cheeses, salad bars, fresh-baked foods, and gourmet items, such as exotic fruits, game, and imported foods and drinks.

Courtesy of Great Atlantic & Pacific Tea Company.

Contemporary Retailers. New types of stores have been developed to offer consumers additional choices of places to shop. Convenience stores are small-scale supermarkets that carry a limited product line consisting of groceries and other basic necessities. These stores are frequently located close to areas where people live and work; they are open long hours, and they provide fast service. At convenience stores, the prices for many products are higher than those at other types of stores.

Pepper . . . and Salt

"The food additives don't bother me half as much as the price additives."

From *The Wall Street Journal*, with permission of Cartoon Features Syndicate.

The catalog showroom is a store that uses catalogs to sell a wide variety of famous name brands at discount prices; many of these items are displayed in the showroom. Large warehouses are often attached to the showroom to facilitate filling orders. Service Merchandise is a company that does extensive business through its catalog showrooms.

Factory outlets are stores that carry certain products at discount prices. Originally, these retail establishments were located next to the factory and sold excessive inventory and slightly defective merchandise. As their popularity increased, manufacturers opened such outlets in various locations. Groups of these stores have created factory outlet shopping centers and malls.

The hypermarket, a store created in the early 1980s, combines the supermarket and the discount store to offer customers self-service and competitive prices. These superstores are at least twice the size of supermarkets and carry more products. The hypermarket is the ultimate in one-stop shopping for food, clothing, personal care products, automotive needs, lawn and garden items, tools, home appliances, and furniture. It also provides such services as dry cleaning, shoe repair, and video rental.

Nonstore Shopping. Because of social, economic, and technological influences, a variety of alternatives to store shopping have evolved. One method is the **cooperative,** a nonprofit organization created so that its member-owners can save money on certain products or services. As discussed in Chapter 4, a credit union is an example of a financial services cooperative. Food cooperatives, usually based in a community group or church, buy grocery items in large quantities. The money saved by these bulk purchases is passed on to the co-op's members in the form of lower food prices than they would pay at a supermarket. Although most food co-ops have a limited scope, some have thousands of members and have expanded their service to provide low-cost groceries to nonmembers. Cooperatives have also been organized to provide less expensive child care, recreational equipment, health care, cable television, and burial services.[2]

Another nonstore shopping option is buying clubs, organizations that allow members to purchase brand name products at prices lower than those charged by retail stores. Since most buying clubs charge exorbitant initiation fees, you usually have to buy hundreds of dollars of merchandise to break even. For example, if you paid $500 to join a buying club and saved 25 percent on the items you purchased, you would have to spend $2,000 to cover the cost of membership.

Shopping without leaving home, or direct selling, is popular. Direct selling refers to various distribution techniques that offer products for sale to customers in their homes. Direct selling includes door-to-door sales; mail-order sales; catalog sales; home parties to sell household products, cosmetics, and women's lingerie; telephone solicitation; and selling through televi-

[2]Andrea Rock, "Co-ops Can Feed, Finance, Doctor, and Bury You," *Money,* May 1985, pp. 197–204.

sion, in which use of a toll-free number enables you to place your order for an item "not available in stores."

Various electronic retailing devices are making direct selling more sophisticated. Some retailers offer shopping-at-home services through cable television or personal computer systems. These services enable consumers to view, order, and pay for purchases without leaving the video screen.

The influence of electronic retailing is also becoming widespread in stores. Electronic coupon dispensers provide customers with instant savings offers. In New York City, a clothing boutique uses a giant projection screen both to entertain customers and to allow them to call up videodiscs of available merchandise.[3] Fashion product companies use computer images to show potential customers how they will look in certain cosmetics and clothing.

[3]"This Store May Be Another Coke Classic," *Changing Times*, June 1986, p. 8.

Today's Lifestyles
Differences between Male and Female Food-Buying Habits

With the increase in the number of single-person households and in the number of working wives and mothers, there has been an increase in the number of male food shoppers. Men spend 40 percent of all the dollars spent on food products. However, a number of differences exist between male and female food shoppers.

While both men and women report that supermarkets are the type of store they use most frequently, women are more likely than men to shop at a small neighborhood grocery store, a fruit and vegetable market, a butcher shop, or a convenience store.

Both sexes regard convenience as a primary reason for selecting a particular store. But men rate low prices and the variety of products as more important than females do. Women prefer a good selection of meats and fresh produce in the stores they patronize.

Married men who shop for food with their wives spend more money and time in food stores than do married men who shop alone. In general, men and women have basically the same items on their shopping lists, but men are more likely to include beer, canned vegetables, and chips and pretzels and women are more likely to include crackers, salad dressings, butter/margarine, and cheese.

While such information-seeking behaviors as checking prices, looking at freshness dates, looking for special sales, and comparing prices and brands are used fairly regularly by both men and women, women tend to use the available information to a greater extent.

Source: *The Male Food Shopper: How Men Are Changing Food Shopping in America*, New York: The Campbell Soup Company and *People Weekly*, 1985).

Courtesy of Great Atlantic & Pacific Tea Company.

Shopping Techniques

Comparison shopping is the process of considering alternative stores, brands, and prices. In contrast, **impulse buying** is unplanned purchasing. While some impulse buying may be acceptable, too much can cause financial problems. A recent survey showed that 9 out of 10 consumers occasionally buy on impulse. Common emotions associated with impulse buying include excitement, conflicting feelings, an intense desire to buy, a dreaming sensation, and resistance.[4] Several tools available to consumers can minimize the emotional and financial costs of unplanned buying.

Comparing Brands. Since food and other products come in different brands, customers have a choice. Brand name products are highly advertised items that are available in many stores. You are probably familiar with such brands as Green Giant, Nabisco, Del Monte, Kellogg's, Kraft, Levi's, Sony, Kodak, and Tylenol. Brand name products are usually more expensive than nonbrand products but offer a consistency of quality for which many people are willing to pay.

Store brand products, sold by one chain of stores, are low-cost alternatives to famous name products. These products have labels that identify them with a specific chain such as Safeway, Kroger, A&P, Osco, Walgreen's, and K mart. Since store brand products may be manufactured by the same companies that produce their brand name counterparts, they give consumers an opportunity to save money.

[4]"Why Impulse-Consumers Can't Resist a Product That Screams 'Buy Me,'" *Chicago Tribune*, May 26, 1986, sec. 4, p. 6.

For many products, a third brand alternative is the plain package, nonbrand **generic** item. Introduced in the late 1970s, the generic alternatives for certain products provide customers with a low-cost choice. While, for some items, the generic equivalent may have a lower quality than the national and store brands, other items, such as aspirin, bleach, granulated sugar, and salt, are equal in quality to the national and store brands.

Label Information. Federal law requires that a label on all food products contain information on the common name of the product, the name and address of the manufacturer or distributor, the net weight of the product, and a list of the ingredients in decreasing order of weight. Nutritional labeling, which is not required for all food products, provides information about the serving size, the number of calories per serving, and the quantities of protein, carbohydrate, fat, sodium, potassium, vitamins, and other ingredients.

Open dating —information that tells consumers about the freshness or shelf life of a perishable product—is also found on labels. Open dating was originally used for bakery and dairy products, but it is now also used for many other kinds of foods. Such phrases as "Use before May 1989" or "Not to be sold after October 8" are found on most grocery items.

Pricing. Unit pricing uses a standard unit of measurement to compare the prices of packages of different sizes. An 8-ounce package of breakfast cereal selling for $1.52 would have a unit price of 19 cents per ounce, while an 11-ounce package with a price of $1.98 would have a unit price of 18 cents per ounce. The package that has the lowest unit price may not be the best buy for you since it may contain more food than you will use before the food spoils. Some stores are using computerized visual displays that inform customers of current selling prices and unit costs.[5]

Two common techniques that offer customers reduced prices are the use of coupons and rebates. Each year, millions of coupons are distributed on packages and through newspapers, magazines, and the mail. These coupons are especially valuable if you already intend to buy the product. **A rebate** is a partial refund of the price of a product. This technique was originally used to promote sales of automobiles, but it is now used in selling clothing, home appliances, food products, and alcoholic beverages.

Warranties. Most products come with some guarantee of quality. **A warranty** is a written guarantee from the manufacturer or distributor of a product that specifies the conditions under which the product can be returned, replaced, or repaired. Retailers of a product that costs more than $15 and has a warranty are required by federal law to make this document available to customers before they buy the product. Frequently, this disclosure is printed in a catalog or on the product carton.

An express warranty, usually in written form, is created by the seller or

---

[5]"Supermarkets Shelf Prices You Can Trust," *Changing Times*, December 1985, p. 8.

manufacturer and has two forms—the full warranty and the limited warranty. Full warranties state that a defective product can be fixed or replaced in a reasonable amount of time. Limited warranties cover only certain aspects of a product, such as parts, or require the buyer to incur part of the costs for shipping or repairs.

An implied warranty is the result of a product's intended use or of other suggested understandings that are not in writing. For example, the implied warranty of title indicates that the seller has the right to sell the product. The

In the Real World
Problems of Low-Income Consumers

I n 1963, a book entitled *The Poor Pay More* presented an analysis of the purchasing behaviors of low-income consumers. It revealed that the purchasing problems of these consumers were more intense than the purchasing problems of moderate-income consumers. Low-income consumers bought more on credit than other groups. As a result, they paid a higher cost for items that they probably couldn't afford in the first place. Also, their low income usually meant that they had to pay a higher rate of interest to borrow than others.

The problems of low-income consumers are the direct result of being poor. Usually, such consumers have achieved only a limited level of education and lack mobility for shopping purposes. Both of these factors reduce their ability to compare and select brands, prices, and stores. Uninformed individuals are not able to use various shopping aids, and the cost of an automobile or public transportation can make travel to the best stores prohibitive. Without the resources to comparison shop, the poor pay more through high prices and inferior products.

Since the original research on this topic was conducted, various consumer protection laws have been enacted and several new consumer agencies have been created. But evidence indicates that this has done little to correct the difficult situation of the poor. A continued lack of awareness makes certain sectors of society a prime target for deceptive advertisements and fraudulent sales practices. Despite the right to be informed, low-income consumers are still persuaded to buy low-quality products using *easy credit* plans. Or such consumers may pay several dollars to cash a check at a bank or a currency exchange instead of using the services of a community credit union.

Since consumer protection legislation has not eliminated the purchasing problems of low-income consumers, what else can be done? Many believe that community education and information programs are the answer. Only by going to the source of the difficulty will any changes occur. Low-income consumers must be taught to budget, to read and use consumer information, and to compare buying alternatives. Low-income consumers must learn skills that are automatic for many so that they will be better able to cope with the economic and social pressures faced by all consumers.

implied warranty of merchantability guarantees that the product is fit for the ordinary uses for which it is intended: a toaster must toast bread, and a stereo must play records or tapes. Since implied warranties vary from state to state, contact your state consumer protection office for additional information on them.

A **service contract** is an agreement between a business and a consumer to cover the repair costs of a product. Even though service contracts are frequently called extended warranties, they are not warranties. For a fee, they insure the buyer of a product against losses due to the cost of certain repairs. Owners of automobiles, home appliances, and other equipment buy these contracts to protect themselves against large repair expenses. In general, service contracts are very profitable for businesses since many more people buy them than need repair service. So buying a service contract may not be the best use of your money.

Table 8–2 provides a summary of techniques that can assist you in your buying decisions.

The Selection of Services

In this chapter, most of the emphasis has been on buying products. Each day, however, our society is increasing the amount it spends on services. Some experts estimate that by the year 2000 over 80 percent of our purchases will be for services. Buying services presents special problems that you do not have when you buy products. First, services are intangible, so it is difficult to assess their quality. Second, services must be performed before

---

TABLE 8-2   Wise Buying Techniques: A Summary

Compare brands of similar products to determine which is best for your intended use.

Compare stores and other sources of buying with regard to prices, services offered, product quality, and return privileges.

Read and evaluate label information.

Use coupons for products that you buy regularly or are trying out.

Use unit pricing to compare packages of different sizes.

Use open dating to determine the freshness and shelf life of perishable products.

Use various consumer information sources to assist you with your buying decisions.

Consider the nutritional value and the health aspects of the foods you buy.

Evaluate and compare the warranties of different brands.

Read product testing reports to determine which items are the safest and have the highest quality.

Plan your purchases to take advantage of sales and special offers.

Consider the time and effort it takes to evaluate alternatives and go to different stores.

their actual quality can be judged. This limits comparison shopping. Finally, variations among sources of services can be great. For example, two home improvement firms charging the same price may provide very different end results.

Your primary decision in selecting a service concerns the type of business you choose. National firms usually provide fast service at a low cost. In contrast, local businesses may be more concerned with quality and customer satisfaction. Certain types of services, such as automobile repair shops and beauty parlors, require certification in some states. Investigate this aspect of the companies you plan to patronize.

When obtaining price information for expensive services, get written estimates of the costs, the work to be performed, the time it will take, and the terms of payment. Such estimates will help assure that you get what you are paying for. Also get information about the guarantee the company offers for customer satisfaction.

For services, the main indicator of quality is the reputation of the business. The experiences of previous customers can help you in choosing service organizations, and the knowledge of previous customers can help you assess the price and quality of particular services.

POSTBUYING ACTIVITIES

You may believe that once a purchasing decision has been made, the buying process is over. However, decision making on purchases is an ongoing effort that requires reevaluation of your situation after the purchase has been made. Also, many purchases can give you experiences that will be helpful for the future.

Many of your postbuying activities will be dictated by the problems you meet. Increased buying satisfaction will result from efforts to avoid consumer problems and utilization of the avenues available to solve them if they arise.

Avoiding Consumer Problems

Every business transaction is a potential problem. Consumer protection experts suggest that to prevent being taken by deceptive business practices, you should:

1. Do business with reputable companies that have a proven record of satisfying customers.
2. Avoid signing contracts and other documents that you do not understand.
3. Be cautious about offerings that seem too good to be true—they probably are!
4. Compare the cost of buying on credit with the cost of paying cash; also compare the interest rates offered by the seller with those offered by a bank or a credit union.

TABLE 8-3   What People Are Complaining About

The most common consumer complaints relate to the following products and services:

Ordered product sales (mail-order purchases; magazine subscriptions; television, radio, newspaper, magazine, and telephone ads answered).

Home remodeling, home improvement companies.

Automobile repair shops.

Automobile dealers.

Home furnishings stores.

Financial companies (banks, credit card companies, savings and loan associations, investment brokers).

Direct selling companies.

Department stores.

Insurance companies.

Dry cleaning, laundry companies.

Source: *1986 Inquiries and Complaints Report: A Summary of 1985 Data* (Council of Better Business Bureaus).

5. Not be in a hurry to get a good deal; successful con artists depend on your impulse buying.

● **Causes of Consumer Problems**

Most customer difficulties are the result of defective products, low quality, short product lives, unexpected costs, and poor repairs. These problems are most commonly associated with the products and services listed in Table 8–3. A variety of protections have been created to assist consumers in avoiding deceptive advertising, unclear contracts, and other fraudulent business practices.

Consumer Protection Efforts. Every generation has unique consumer problems. At one time in our history, people were endangered by contaminated meat, poorly labeled foods, and adulterated drugs. More recently, food additives, radiation from color televisions, and automobile safety have been of concern.

In the 1960s, a broad range of consumer protection laws were enacted by Congress to supplement some of the earlier legislation (see Table 8–4). Most of the states also passed laws and created various consumer protection offices within their governmental structures. In general, a vast mechanism was formed to help consumers cope with potential marketplace difficulties. An attitude of consumerism has become embedded among individuals, businesses, and public officials. The consumer movement resulted in:

● Increased awareness among consumers regarding sources of product information and actions that they could take when dissatisfied.

TABLE 8-4   Consumer Protection Laws

Food, drugs, and cosmetics	Pure Food and Drug Act (1906) Meat Inspection Act (1906) Federal Food, Drug, and Cosmetic Act (1938) Delaney Amendment to Food, Drug, and Cosmetic Act (1958) Color Additives Amendment (1960) Drug Safety, Labeling, and Effectiveness Amendment (1962) Wholesale Meat Act (1967)
Labeling and product safety	Wool Products Labeling Act (1939) Fur Products Labeling Act (1951) Flammable Fabrics Act (1953) Textile Fiber Products Identification Act (1958) Federal Hazardous Substances Labeling Act (1960) Fair Packaging and Labeling Act (1966) Child Protection and Toy Safety Act (1969) Poison Prevention Packaging Act (1970) Consumer Product Safety Act (1972) Energy Policy and Conservation Act (1976)
Auto safety and environment	Automobile Information Disclosure Act (1958) Clean Air Act (1963) National Traffic and Motor Vehicle Safety Act (1966) Air Quality Act (1967) National Environmental Policy Act (1969) Water Quality Improvement Act (1970) Pesticide Control Act (1972) Noise Control Act (1972) Safe Drinking Water Act (1974) Toxic Substances Control Act (1976) Clean Water Act (1977)

- Acceptance by business that the health, safety, and well-being of individuals is vital to consumer satisfaction and to company profits.
- Laws and government offices to assist consumers.
- Initiatives by community organizations to inform consumers, protest marketplace injustices, and lobby legislative and regulatory bodies.
- A recognition of basic consumer rights and responsibilities.

● Basic Consumer
Rights and
Responsibilities

Consumer Rights and Responsibilities. In March 1962, President Kennedy delivered his Consumer Bill of Rights address to Congress. At that time, he identified four fundamental consumer rights: the right to be informed, the right to choose, the right to safety, and the right to be heard.

As with any democratic right, each of these rights is accompanied by certain responsibilities. For example, the right to be informed requires that you seek out, evaluate, and use available resources about products and services. And the right to safety demands that you read warning labels and use products properly. The consumer rights identified by President Kennedy are the foundation for various channels that have been established to resolve marketplace dilemmas.

Resolving Consumer Complaints

● Process for Resolving Consumer Complaints

You will probably never be completely satisfied with every purchase you make. Most consumers have problems related to poor quality, inadequate service, defective products, or incorrect pricing. The process for resolving differences between buyers and sellers includes the following steps:

1. Returning to the place of purchase.
2. Contacting the company's main office.
3. Obtaining assistance from a consumer agency.
4. Taking legal action.

Returning to the Place of Purchase. Most consumer complaints are resolved at the original sales location. Since most business firms are concerned with their reputation for honesty and fairness, retailers will usually honor legitimate complaints. As you talk with the salesperson, customer service

Pepper . . . and Salt

"Well what do you know? The little toy car supposed to be in this cereal has been recalled by the factory."

From *The Wall Street Journal*, with permission of Cartoon Features Syndicate.

person, or store manager, you should avoid yelling, threatening a lawsuit, or asking for unreasonable action. In general, a calm, rational, but persistent approach is recommended.[6]

Contacting the Company's Main Office. Most consumer advisers suggest that you express your dissatisfaction at the corporate level if your problem is not resolved at the local store. A letter like the one shown in Figure 8–5 provides the communication necessary.

Several publications have the addresses of companies that you may wish to contact. One of these publications is the *Consumer's Resource Handbook*, published by the U.S. Office of Consumer Affairs. Reference volumes at your local or school library also has that contain addresses and other information about major companies include Standard & Poor's *Register of Corporations, Directors, and Executives* and Dun & Bradstreet's *Million Dollar Directory*.

To handle complaints and requests for information, many companies have established toll-free telephone hot lines. Some companies print the toll-free hot line number on product packages. You can obtain a company's hot line number by using a directory of toll-free numbers in the library or by calling 1-800-555-1212, which is the toll-free information number.

Obtaining Assistance from a Consumer Agency. If you do not receive satisfaction from the company, several consumer, business, and government organizations are ready to serve you. During the 1960s and 1970s, various public interest and community action organizations were founded. These included national organizations specializing in such issues as automobile safety, nuclear energy, and nutrition and local organizations that were established to handle complaints, conduct surveys, and provide legal assistance.

The Better Business Bureaus are a network of offices throughout the country that resolve complaints against local merchants. These offices are funded by companies concerned about customer satisfaction. The Better Business Bureau in your area can be of most value to you before you make a purchase. Its files will tell you about the experiences of others who dealt with a firm with which you are planning to do business.

The Better Business Bureau and other organizations provide third-party assistance, or **mediation,** for settling grievances. In mediation, an impartial person tries to resolve a difference between a customer and a business through discussion and negotiation.

Arbitration is the settlement of a difference by a third party—the arbitrator—whose decision is legally binding. After both sides agree to abide by the arbitrator's decision, each side presents its case to the arbitrator. Arbitrators are selected from a pool of volunteers. The major automobile manufacturers and many industry organizations have arbitration programs.

---

[6]Michael Weiss, "How to Complain—and Get Results," *Chicago Sun-Times,* February 23, 1986, p. 25.

FIGURE 8-5   Sample Complaint Letter

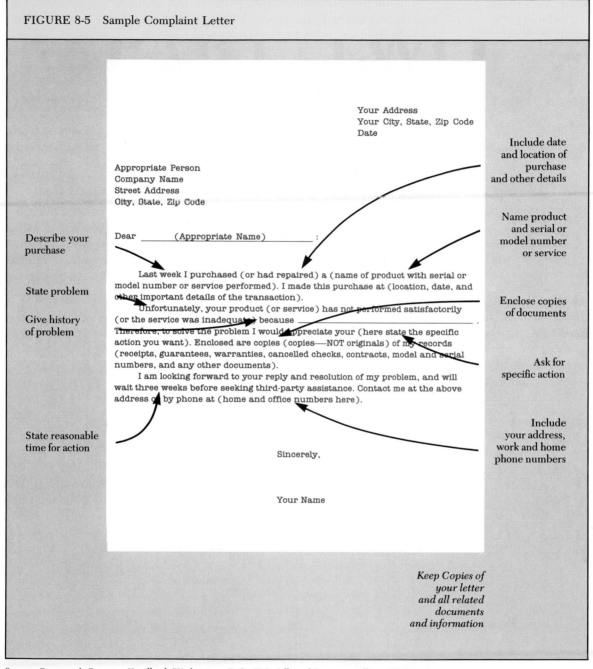

Source: *Consumer's Resource Handbook* (Washington, D.C.: U.S. Office of Consumer Affairs, 1986), p. 3.

● Assistance Provided
by Government
Agencies

A vast network of government agencies is also available to consumers. The type of problem will dictate which of these agencies should be approached for help. Problems with local restaurants or food stores may be handled by a city or county health department. Every state has a variety of agencies to handle problems involving deceptive advertising, fraudulent business practices, banking, insurance companies, and utility rates.

At the national level, the Federal Trade Commission (FTC) is concerned with the advertising and sales practices of businesses. It conducts investigations and takes legal action on such activities as fallacious labeling on the energy efficiency of products, fraudulent used car sales, deceptive credit contracts, and violations of product warranty laws.

The Food and Drug Administration (FDA) and the U.S. Department of Agriculture (USDA) are both involved in consumer protection related to food products. The USDA is mainly concerned with the inspection and grading of meat and other foods. The FDA is responsible for cosmetics, medicines, and medical devices, such as hearing aids and pacemakers.

Other federal agencies are also available to help resolve customer difficulties and provide information (see Appendix D). When you are uncertain about which agency to use, contact the U.S. Office of Consumer Affairs in Washington. This office can help channel your concern to the most appropriate consumer protection agency.

● Legal Actions
Available to
Consumers

Taking Legal Action. After you have tried to resolve your difficulty by means of communication, you may have to take more drastic action. Various legal mechanisms are available. Every state has a system of courts to settle minor legal differences. In a **small claims court,** a person may file a claim for legal matters involving amounts under a set limit. The maximum amount varies from state to state; most states have a limit of $500 to $1,500.

Before resorting to the small claims court, you should become familiar with its location, procedures, and fees. During the court hearing, you are allowed to present your case. Your evidence should include contracts, receipts, photographs, and other items that prove your position. You may also use witnesses to testify on your behalf.

Although obtaining a favorable judgment in a small claims court may be easy, the collection process is frequently difficult. Since the defendant may not appear, you may have to pay a sheriff to serve a court order or you may have to use a collection agency to get your money.

Occasionally, a number of people have the same problem—for example, people who claim to have been injured by a defective product, customers who believe they have been overcharged by a utility company, or travelers who feel that they have been cheated by a charter tour company. Such people may qualify for a **class action suit.** A class action suit is a legal action taken by a few individuals on behalf of many who have suffered the same alleged injustice. The group involved is called a class.

Once a situation qualifies as a class action suit, all of the affected persons must be notified of the suit. At this point, an individual may decide not to participate in the class action suit or may decide to file an individual lawsuit.

If the court ruling is favorable to the class, the funds awarded may be divided among all of the individuals involved, used to reduce rates in the future, or assigned to public funds for government use.

When the small claims court or a class action suit is not effective or appro-

---

Personal Financial Planning and You
Is It Legal?

Which of the following situations or actions are legal, and which are not?

	Yes	*No*
1. A store advertised a bottle of shampoo as "the $1.79 size, on sale for 99¢." If the store never sold the item for $1.79 but the manufacturer's recommended price was $1.79, was this a legitimate price comparison?	_____	_____
2. You purchase a stereo system for $650. Two days later, the same store offers the same item for $425. Is this legal?	_____	_____
3. You receive a sample of flower seeds in the mail. You decide to plant them to see how well they will grow in your yard. A couple of days later, you receive a bill for the seeds. Do you have to pay for the seeds?	_____	_____
4. A store has a "going out of business sale—everything must go" sign in its window. After six months, the sign is still there. Is this a deceptive business practice?	_____	_____
5. A 16-year-old is injured while playing ball at a local park and is taken to the hospital for medical care. The parents refuse to pay the hospital since they didn't request the service. Can the parents be held legally responsible for the expenses?	_____	_____
6. You purchase a shirt for a friend. The gift doesn't fit, but when you return to the store, you are offered an exchange, since the store policy is not to give cash refunds. Is this legal?	_____	_____
7. A manufacturer refuses to repair a motorcycle that is still under warranty. The manufacturer can prove that the motorcycle was used improperly. If this is true, must the manufacturer honor the warranty?	_____	_____
8. If an employee of a store incorrectly marks the price of an item, is the store obligated to sell the item at the incorrect price?	_____	_____

Circumstances, interpretations of the law, and store policies, as well as state and local laws, can affect the above situations. The generally accepted answers would be: 1, 3, 7, and 8—no; 2, 4, 5, and 6—yes.

priate, you may decide to use the services of an attorney. The most common sources of available lawyers are referrals from people you know, the local branch of the American Bar Association, and telephone directory listings. Since lawyers are now advertising in newspapers, on television, and in other media, consumers have more information on available legal services. However, you must be aware that impressive advertising does not mean competent legal counsel.

Deciding when to use a lawyer is difficult. In general, straightforward legal situations, such as appearing in small claims court, renting an apartment, or defending yourself on a minor traffic violation, usually do not require legal counsel. But for more complicated matters, such as writing a will, settling a real estate purchase, or suing for injury damages caused by a product, it is probably best to employ the services of a lawyer.

When selecting a lawyer, several questions should be considered. Is the lawyer experienced in your type of case? How will you be charged—on a flat fee basis, at an hourly rate, or on a contingency basis? Is there a fee for the initial consultation? How and when will you be required to make payment for services?

The cost of legal services is frequently a problem, especially for low-income consumers. A **legal aid society** is one of a network of publicly supported community law offices that provide legal assistance to consumers who cannot afford their own attorney. These community agencies provide legal assistance at a minimal cost or without charge.

Because of increased competition among lawyers, other efforts to cut the cost of legal assistance are available. Prepaid legal services are programs that provide unlimited or reduced-fee legal assistance for a set fee. Some prepaid legal programs provide certain basic services, such as telephone consultation and preparation of a simple will, for an annual fee ranging from $50 to $150 or more. More complicated legal assistance would require an additional fee, usually at a reduced rate. Other legal plans do not involve an advance fee but allow members of the program to obtain services at discount rates. There are also comprehensive plans in which a high prepaid fee covers the legal needs of most families. In general, prepaid legal plans are designed as preventive law by attempting to avoid complicated legal problems while they are manageable as minor troubles.[7]

Legal clinics, also called storefront lawyers, have grown in popularity. These clinics provide legal service in retail stores at competitive prices. They have made legal service readily available to consumers at a reasonable cost. Some major retailing companies, such as Montgomery Ward and Zayre, have attorneys in their stores to provide an additional dimension to their product line.

Personal Consumer Protection

While a vast array of laws, agencies, and legal tools is available to protect your rights, none of these will be valuable to you unless you know about

[7]"Pay Ahead and Save on Lawyers' Fees," *Changing Times*, May 1985, pp. 55–58.

them. To achieve a successful financial existence, you must be aware of and use the various information sources available to consumers and you must make effective purchasing decisions.

Overall, the consumer buying process is a logical system for making satisfying purchasing decisions. This process will help you make choices that fulfill your needs, values, and goals. It will also help you acquire decision-making skills that you can apply to situations in your life other than making purchases.

SUMMARY

- The main influences on your buying decisions are economic, personal, and social factors. Your lifestyle is the primary motivation for your buying decisions.
- The consumer buying process consists of (1) prebuying activities involving problem identification, information gathering, and the evaluation of alternatives; (2) purchasing strategies, such as store selection, shopping techniques, and the selection of services; and (3) postbuying activities, which include avoiding consumer problems and resolving complaints.
- The main sources of consumer buying information are personal experience and contacts, business organizations, the media, independent testing organizations, and government agencies.
- When selecting a place to shop, you should consider the merchandise available, the policies of the store, the services offered, and the location, size, and reputation of the store.
- The most common consumer problems are

the result of defective products, low quality, short product lives, unexpected costs, poor repair service, deceptive advertising, unclear contracts, and fraudulent business practices.
- The four fundamental consumer rights are the right to be informed, the right to choose, the right to safety, and the right to be heard.
- When attempting to resolve a consumer complaint, the following steps should be followed: return to the place of purchase, contact the company's main office, obtain assistance from a consumer agency, and, finally, consider taking legal action.
- A variety of private, business-sponsored, and government agencies provide consumers with information and assist them with marketplace difficulties.
- Resorting to the small claims court, filing class action suits, and hiring a lawyer are legal means for handling consumer problems that cannot be resolved through communication with the business involved or through the help of a consumer protection agency.

GLOSSARY

Arbitration.   The settlement of a difference by a third party whose decision is legally binding.

Class action suit.   A legal action taken by a few individuals on behalf of many who suffered the same alleged injustice.

Cooperative.   A nonprofit organization created so that

member-owners can save money on certain products or services.

Generic item.   A plain package, nonbrand version of a product, offered at a lower price than that of the brand version or versions.

Impulse buying.   Unplanned purchasing.

Legal aid society.   One of a network of community law offices that provide legal assistance to consumers who cannot afford their own attorney.

Mediation.   The attempt by a third party to resolve a difference between two parties through discussion and negotiation.

Open dating.   Information on freshness or shelf life found on the package of a perishable product.

Rebate.   A partial refund of the price of a product.

Service contract.   An agreement between a business and a consumer to cover the repair costs of a product.

Small claims court.   A court that settles legal differences involving amounts under a set limit and employs a process in which the litigants do not use a lawyer.

Unit pricing.   The use of a standard unit of measurement to compare the prices of packages of different sizes.

Warranty.   A written guarantee from the manufacturer or distributor of a product that specifies the conditions under which an item can be returned, replaced, or repaired.

REVIEW QUESTIONS

1. What factors influence your daily purchasing habits?

2. What activities are involved in the prebuying phase of the consumer buying process?

3. What are the main information sources that are available to help consumers in their buying decisions?

4. What factors can consumers consider when they are evaluating purchasing choices?

5. What attracts a person to shop at a particular store?

6. How do brand name products, store brand products, and generic products differ?

7. How do open dating and unit pricing assist consumers in making purchases?

8. How does a service contract differ from a warranty?

9. Why is buying services more difficult than buying products?

10. What are the common causes of consumer problems and complaints?

11. What actions should be taken to resolve a consumer problem?

12. How does arbitration differ from mediation?

13. What legal actions are available to consumers?

14. When is the use of a lawyer recommended as a means of dealing with consumer problems?

DISCUSSION QUESTIONS AND ACTIVITIES

1. What actions should the Bonners have taken before joining the food-buying plan?

2. How can the Bonners avoid paying the additional $495?

3. How does advertising affect the purchasing habits of consumers?

4. Use a recent issue of *Consumer Reports* to evaluate different brands of a product. Talk to several people about their experiences with the product.

5. Do people benefit more by always shopping at the same store and not expending time and effort to take advantage of lower prices and special sales at other stores?

6. Investigate the presence of buying clubs and cooperatives in your community.

7. Compare the prices of products merchan-dised by direct selling with the prices of products merchandised in traditional stores.

8. What factors influence a person's selection of a brand?

9. How well do warranties serve customers? Base your answer on library articles and on the experiences of people you know.

10. Prepare a survey of the legal services available to students and others in your community. Compare the fees charged and the services provided by individual lawyers, legal clinics, and other agencies.

ADDITIONAL READINGS

Buying Guide Issue, Consumer Reports. Consumers Union, 256 Washington Street, Mount Vernon, NY 10553.

Consumer's Resource Handbook. U.S. Office of Consumer Affairs, Washington, DC 20201.

"Service Contracts: Hype or Help?" *Changing Times,* August 1986, pp. 69–73.

Williams, Kay. "Attention, K Mart Shoppers: Stay Home!" *Money,* August 1986, pp. 76–78, 80–81.

Your Equipment Dollar; Your Shopping Dollar. Money Management Institute, Household Financial Services, 2700 Sanders Road, Prospect Heights, IL 60070.

CASE 8–1 Which Computer for Rose?

Rose Whitlow is planning to purchase a home computer. Friends have suggested a variety of brands and models. Also, Rose has heard about certain features that she would like to have on her computer. She plans to use her home computer to prepare school reports, to assist her in home money management, and to practice playing chess.

Rose likes the personal computer she uses at her part-time job, but the cost of that computer is more than she can afford. A friend has an inexpensive model that can handle most of the information processing that Rose wants to do now. But this model may not be able to handle the information processing that she hopes to do in the future.

Questions

1. How should Rose define the problem with regard to her planned purchase of a home computer?

2. What information sources are available to Rose?

3. What factors should Rose consider in evaluating her alternatives in buying a home computer?

CASE 8–2 Damages for a Faulty Air Conditioner

Jim Concord bought a new window air conditioner three weeks ago. A few days ago, the unit overheated and started a small fire in his apartment. Jim's rug and drapes were damaged, and Jim suffered some minor burns that required medical treatment.

The day after the fire, Jim returned to the store where he bought the air conditioner. He asked that the purchase price of the air conditioner be refunded, and he wanted the store to pay for his property damage and medical costs. The store's customer service manager was willing to give Jim the refund for the air conditioner but said that he was not authorized to make any additional payments.

Questions

1. What actions might Jim have taken to avoid buying a potentially defective air conditioner?

2. What additional courses of action can Jim take to resolve his complaint?

3. What types of legal action may be appropriate in this situation?

9

Choosing a Place to Live

Whether you rent an apartment, own a house, or live in a mobile home, the cost of your place of residence is a major budget item. Due to the economic significance of a housing decision, careful consideration of housing alternatives is vital. The type and location of the residence, renting versus buying, and financing are only a few of the factors that you should consider before you incur this major expense. The choice of housing is a major aspect of your personal finances.

After studying this chapter, you will be able to:

- Discuss the factors that should be considered in selecting a place to live.

- List the advantages and disadvantages of renting.

- Name the types of housing units that people can buy.

- Explain the positive and negative aspects of home ownership.

- Implement the process involved in buying a house.

- Describe the negotiating of a purchase price.

- Discuss the actions necessary to qualify for a mortgage.

- Explain the types of mortgages that are available to finance the purchase of a home.

- Name the costs associated with finalizing a real estate transaction.

- Identify the decisions involved in selling a home.

Interview with **Jack Rasmussen,** Manager, Merrill Lynch Realty, Glen Ellyn, Illinois

Jack Rasmussen is the Manager of the Merrill Lynch Realty office in Glen Ellyn, Illinois. He has had over 20 years of real estate experience as a sales manager, a broker, and a developer.

The choice between renting and buying your dwelling is influenced by such factors as financial condition and responsibility, family size, and general lifestyle.

Mr. Rasmussen points out that most of the people who eventually become homeowners pass through a pattern of residential changes. A young couple may rent an apartment until they have children. Then they may rent a small house to accommodate their growing family. Later they may purchase and acquire equity in their first house. Then they may sell that house as increased income and the need for more space dictate the purchase of a larger and a better-equipped house. When their children are grown, the couple may seek the convenience of a smaller residence, perhaps an apartment, that has fewer responsibilities and a minimum of maintenance care.

In our mobile society, few people remain in the same location throughout life. Those who rent may move to different apartments or houses for convenience, more space and comfort, or lower rental fees. A person's occupation may require a series of moves to new areas. Many people take advantage of opportunities to trade up progressively to better homes in more prestigious neighborhoods or at more convenient locations.

If you buy your dwelling, home ownership can contribute to your financial well-being. Monthly mortgage payments can be less expensive than rent when the tax-deductible costs of interest and real estate taxes are considered. As an investment, a home may weather changes in the economy better than other purchases. Furthermore, owning a home gives you greater independence and a sense of pride. Mr. Rasmussen also points out that equity in a home will improve your credit rating and give you an advantage if you decide to buy a larger, more expensive house.

On the other hand, if you rent, you retain mobility and you avoid the process of disposing of a house should you have to move. You also avoid expensive maintenance costs or unexpected loss if property values drop. You can leave upkeep problems and repairs to the landlord. Furthermore, you may be able to have the best of both buying and renting if you rent a house or a condominium with an option to buy. In this case, your rental contract must state that a portion of your rent is credited to the purchase price.

When Steven and Cherie Starkman first saw the house, they didn't like it. This could have been caused by the dark, rainy day. They viewed the house more favorably on their second visit, which they had expected to be a waste of time. Despite cracked ceilings, the need for a paint job, and a kitchen built in the 1950s, the Starkmans saw a potential for creating a place that they could call their own.*

Barbara Zeller purchased her condominium four years ago. She got a mortgage rate of 12.5 percent, which was very good then. Recently, when interest rates had dropped, Barbara was considering refinancing her mortgage at a lower rate.

Carl and Lois Alcott had been married for five years and were still living in an apartment. Several of the Alcotts' friends had purchased homes recently, but Carl and Lois were not sure that they wanted to follow this example. Although they liked their friends' homes and had viewed photographs of homes currently on the market, they also liked the freedom from responsibility that they had as renters.

Buying a home that needs improvement, refinancing a mortgage when interest rates decline, and deciding to rent instead of buying a home are just a few of the housing strategies used by individuals and families. The logical investigation of housing options and costs is an integral part of your overall financial decision making.

*William R. Greer, "First House: Rate Drop Makes It Affordable," *New York Times*, May 22, 1986, pp. 17–18.

EVALUATING HOUSING ALTERNATIVES

If you walk down any residential street, you are likely to see different types of housing. What makes people select a certain type of housing? As you assess various housing choices, you will identify the factors that will influence your choice. Your needs, lifestyle, and financial resources will determine whether you decide to rent, buy, or have a home built. In assessing these alternatives, you must make use of reliable housing information.

Your Lifestyle and Your Choice of Housing

- Factors to Consider when Selecting a Place to Live

While the concept of lifestyle—how a person spends his or her time and money—may seem intangible, it materializes in your consumer purchases. Every buying decision is a statement about your lifestyle. Thus, your lifestyle, along with your values, needs, desires, and attitudes, is reflected in your choice of a place to live. For example, a belonger may want a kitchen that is large enough for family-oriented, home-cooked meals. In contrast, a career-oriented achiever may want a lavish bathroom or a home spa in which he or she can escape from the pressures of work. Among the lifestyle factors that influence housing choices are status, fashion, individualism, and ecolog-

TABLE 9-1   Housing Alternatives

	Advantages	Disadvantages

Renting:
Apartment
	Easy to move
	Few responsibilities for
	  maintenance
	Minimal financial commitment
		No tax benefits
		Limitations regarding remodeling
		May have restrictions regarding
		  pets, other activities

Renting: House	More room than apartment Minimal financial commitment	Higher utility expenses Limitations regarding remodeling
Owning: New house	No previous owner Pride of ownership Tax benefits	Financial commitment Higher living expenses than renting Limited mobility
Owning: Previously owned house	Pride of ownership Established neighborhood Tax benefits	Financial commitment Possibility of repairs or replacements Limited mobility

Owning:
Condominium
	Tax benefits
	Less maintenance responsibilities
	  than house
	Usually good accessibility to
	  recreation and business
	  districts
		Less privacy than house
		Financial commitment
		Uncertain demand affecting
		  property value
		Potential disagreements with
		  condominium association
		  regarding rules

Owning:
Cooperative
	Ownership in form of nonprofit
	  organization
	Stable property values
		Frequently difficult to sell
		Potential disagreements among
		  members
		Other members may have to
		  cover costs of unrented units

Owing:
Manufactured home (mobile home)
	Less expensive than other
	  ownership options
	Flexibility in selection of home
	  features and appliances
		May be difficult to sell in future
		Financing may be difficult to
		  obtain
		Construction quality may be
		  poor.

ical concerns.[1] As you select housing, you will probably consider the alternatives in Table 9–1 as ways of meeting your needs and expressing your lifestyle.

How Much Home Can You Afford?

While personal preferences and tastes are the foundation of your housing decision, financial factors may modify your final choice. Traditional financial guidelines suggest that "you should spend no more than 25 or 30 percent of your take-home pay on housing" or that "your home should cost about 2½

[1]Lew Sichelman, "How Lifestyles Affect Choices in Housing," *Chicago Tribune*, May 24, 1986, sec. 3, pp. 1–2.

times your annual income." Because of changes in our economy and society, however, financial advisers now suggest that these guidelines are no longer completely valid. Some sort of financial guideline is necessary to determine the amount you should spend on housing. A budget and the other financial records discussed in Chapter 3 can assist you in evaluating your income, living costs, and other financial obligations to determine an appropriate amount for your housing payment. Later in this chapter, further consideration will be given to the amount you can afford to spend when buying a house.

Renting versus Buying Your Housing

Choosing between renting and owning your place of residence is an essential decision in the selection of housing. You will probably be able to resolve this dilemma by evaluating various lifestyle and financial factors. Mobility is a primary motivator of renters, while buyers usually want permanence.

Economic conditions can also influence your choice between renting and buying. Between 1973 and 1982, when housing prices increased by nearly 150 percent, buying a house made sound financial sense. In just a few years, a person was able to make a profit from the sale of a home. Since then, lower inflation rates have had a stabilizing effect on housing prices.

You can compare the financial aspects of renting and buying by using the following process:

1. Determine the annual total expenses of the purchased home.
2. Determine the portion of the total expenses that would be deductible from your federal income tax, such as mortgage interest and property taxes.
3. Multiply the deductible expenses by your marginal tax rate.
4. Subtract the amount in Step 3 from the total in Step 1.
5. Compare the result with the amount you pay in rent each year.

If the amount of your rent is less than the after-tax cost of owning a home, renting would be your best financial option. Remember, however, that this analysis does not consider the increased value of the home, rent increases, or home maintenance costs.[2]

The choice between renting and buying is usually not clear. In general, renting is less costly in the short run, but home ownership also has certain financial advantages. These aspects of renting and buying will be discussed later in this chapter.

Building Your Own Home

Some people want a home built according to their specifications. Building your own home allows you to create a customized residence while experi-

---

[2]Andrew Leckey, "Rent or Buy: How to Decide," *Chicago Tribune*, February 7, 1986, sec. 3, p. 1.

encing a certain challenge and satisfaction. Before you begin such a project, be sure you possess the knowledge, the money, and the perseverance that are needed to complete it.

When choosing a contractor to coordinate the project, be sure to consider the following:

Does the contractor have the experience needed to handle the type of building project you require?

Does the contractor have a good working relationship with the architect, materials suppliers, electricians, plumbers, carpenters, and other personnel needed to complete the project?

What assurance do you have about the quality of the materials used and about the quality of the finished home?

What arrangements have to be made for payments during the construction process?

What delays in the construction process will be considered legitimate?

Your written contract should include a time schedule, cost estimates, a description of the work, and a payment schedule.

As much as 25 percent of the cost of a new house can be saved by supervising its construction. Home building suppliers and owners of homes under

In the Real World
1-bdrm NY apt, no vu: $850–1,800

Finding satsfactory housing can be difficult, especially in high-demand areas such as New York City. A story is told about a woman who rushed to rent an apartment after she heard that the tenant had committed suicide, only to find that the policeman investigating the case had already signed the lease.

One buyer complained about the condition of a penthouse cooperative. Its skylights were broken, it had no kitchen, the bathroom was run-down, and plaster was falling from the ceiling. The real estate agent commented, "What do you want for $400,000?"

While New York City, where rents and housing prices some- times increase 35 percent a year, may not be typical, many areas are experiencing a situation in which the very rich have elegant housing, while the poor face a shortage of adequate living conditions.

Source: Philip Lentz, "1-bdrm NY apt, no vu: $850–1,800," *Chicago Tribune*, February 23, 1986, sec. 1, p. 17.

construction can suggest quality tradespeople.[3] Inexpensive blueprints are available from the U.S. Department of Housing and Urban Development; these building plans can save you thousands of dollars in architect's fees.

Housing Information Sources

As with other consumer purchases, a vast amount of information is available on housing. Start your data search with basic resources such as this book and books that are available in most libraries. Consult the weekly real estate section in your newspaper. That section carries useful articles about renting, buying, financing, remodeling, and other housing topics. Other helpful information sources are friends, and local real estate agents, and government agencies (see Appendix D). Your current and future housing decisions should be based on sound, up-to-date information.

RENTING YOUR RESIDENCE

If you are not one of the few people who can afford to buy a home when they first finish school or when they first get married, you may decide to rent. As a tenant, you pay for the right to live in a residence owned by someone else. When choosing a rental unit, you should consider the available types of rented housing and the advantages, disadvantages, and costs of renting.

Selecting a Rental Unit

An apartment is the most common type of rented housing. Apartments range from modern high rises and luxury suburban complexes with extensive recreational facilities to simple one- and two-bedroom units in quiet, family-oriented neighborhoods.

People who need more room should consider renting a house. The increased space will cost you more money, and you will probably have more responsibility for maintaining the property. People who need less space may rent a room in a house, over a garage, or in a basement.

The main sources of information on available rental units are newspaper ads, real estate and rental offices, and people you know. When comparing rental units, consider the factors presented in Figure 9–1.

Advantages of Renting

- Advantages and Disadvantages of Renting

The main advantages of renting are mobility, fewer responsibilities, and lower initial costs.

Mobility. Renting gives you mobility when a change of location becomes necessary or desirable. A new job, a rent increase, the need for a larger

---

[3]Allen Evans, "Building for the Future," *Sylvia Porter's Personal Finance,* September 1986, pp. 40, 42–43.

FIGURE 9-1 Selecting an Apartment

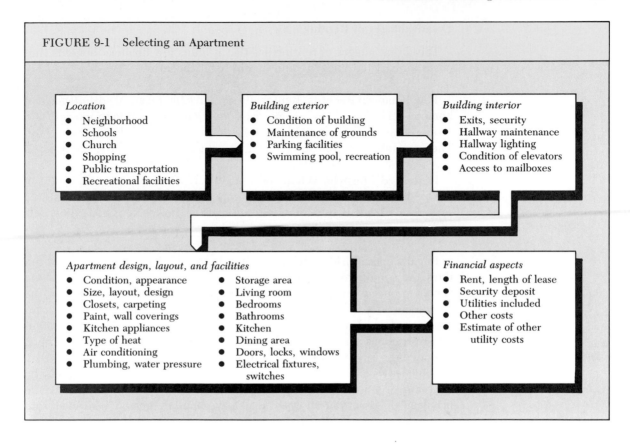

apartment, or the desire to live in a different community can make relocation necessary. It is easier to move when you are renting than when you own a home. After you have completed school and started your career, renting will make it easier for you to move in response to job demands.

Fewer Responsibilities. Renters have fewer responsibilities than homeowners because they usually do not have to be concerned with housing maintenance and repairs. However, they are expected to do regular household cleaning. Renters also have fewer financial concerns. Their main housing costs are rent and utilities, while homeowners incur expenses related to property taxes and upkeep.

Lower Initial Costs. It is less expensive to take possession of a rental unit than to buy a home. While new tenants may have to pay a relatively small security deposit, a new homebuyer usually has to make a high down payment—several thousand dollars at the least. Also, renters are often able to avail themselves of recreational facilities such as swimming pools and tennis courts, amenities that would be far more costly for homeowners.

Disadvantages of Renting

The disadvantages of renting are that it offers few financial benefits, imposes a restricted lifestyle, and entails legal concerns.

Few Financial Benefits. Renters do not have the financial advantages that homeowners have. They get no tax deductions for mortgage interest and property taxes. They do not benefit from the increased value of real estate. They are subject to rent increases over which they have little control.

Restricted Lifestyle. When you rent, the types of activities that you can pursue in your place of residence are generally limited. Noise from a stereo system or parties is usually monitored closely. Restrictions regarding pets and decoration are often imposed.

Legal Concerns. Most tenants sign a **lease**, the legal document that defines the conditions of a rental agreement. This document describes the rented property and states the monthly rent and the time period of the agreement. It also includes information on cleaning fees, responsibilities for repairs and maintenance, and penalties for late payments. Many leases contain restrictions and regulations regarding such matters as family size, pets, remodeling, parking, trash disposal, and water beds.

Some leases give you the right to *sublet* the rental unit. Subletting may be necessary if you must vacate the premises before the lease expires. The privilege of subletting allows you to have another person take over rent payments and live in the rental unit.

Most leases are in writing, but oral leases are also valid. With such a lease, one party to the lease must give a 30-day notice to the other party before terminating the lease or imposing a rent increase.

A lease provides protection to both the landlord and the tenant. The tenant is protected from rent increases during the term of the lease unless the lease has a provision allowing a rent increase to cover the landlord's higher operating costs. In most states, too, the tenant of a leased dwelling unit cannot be locked out or evicted without a court hearing. The lease gives the landlord the right to take legal action against a tenant for nonpayment of rent or destruction of property.

Costs of Renting

You may incur renting expenses even before you sign a lease. For example, you may be charged a fee by a rental agent or an apartment hunting service. Unless absolutely necessary, however, you should avoid paying someone for finding your rental unit. Frequently, this service is paid for by the landlord.

A security deposit is usually required when you sign a lease. This is an amount of money held by the landlord to cover the cost of any damages that may be done to the rental unit during the lease period. The security deposit is usually one month's rent.

Several state and local governments require that the landlord pay you interest on your security deposit. After you vacate a rental unit, your security deposit should be refunded within a reasonable time. Many states require that it be returned within 30 days of the end of the lease. If money is deducted from your security deposit, you have the right to see the receipts for any repairs or maintenance.

As a renter, besides paying the monthly rent, you will incur other living expenses. For most apartments, water is covered by the rent, but other utilities are not. If you rent a house, you will probably pay for heat, electricity, water, and telephone. When you rent, you should obtain insurance coverage for your personal property. Renter's insurance is discussed in detail in Chapter 12.

HOME OWNERSHIP

Owning a home is a financial goal for many people. This goal may be achieved with one of several types of housing alternatives. When planning to buy your residence, consider the advantages and drawbacks that accompany home ownership.

Housing Units You Can Buy

● Types of Housing Units People Can Buy

Several options are available to the person who wants to buy a home. Single-family dwellings are the most popular type of housing. These residences include previously owned houses, new houses, and custom-built houses. Older houses are preferred by people who want a certain style and quality of housing. However, such houses may need major repairs and renovation.

When buying a newly built house, you should carefully inspect the construction and investigate potential problems. The reputation of the construction company and real estate developer are an indication of the long-term quality of the house.

The styles of single-family houses range from one-story dwellings and ranch houses to two-story and split-level residences. Ease of access to bedrooms and other living areas will influence the style of house you choose. The amount of living space you require will also influence your choice.

Multiunit dwellings—dwellings that comprise more than one living unit— include duplexes and town houses. A duplex is a building that contains two separate homes. A town house is a building that contains two, four, or six single-family living units. While multifamily housing appeals to some people, others want more privacy than it affords.

A **condominium** is an individually owned housing unit in a building with a number of such units. Individual ownership does not include the common areas, such as hallways, outside grounds, and recreational facilities. These areas are owned by the condominium association, which consists of the people who own the housing units. The condominium association oversees the management and operation of the housing complex. The condominium owners are charged a monthly fee to cover the maintenance, repairs, and improvements of the building and the common areas. A condominium is not a type of building structure; it is a legal form of home ownership. Many housing units previously rented as apartments have been converted to condominiums, with individuals purchasing their living units.

Cooperative housing is a form of housing in which a building containing a number of units is owned by a nonprofit organization. A member of the cooperative has the right to live in one of the units by paying rent. The living units of a co-op, unlike condominiums, are not owned by the residents but by the co-op. Rents in a co-op can increase quickly if living units become vacant, since the maintenance costs of the building must be covered by the remaining residents.

Finally, a **manufactured home** is a housing unit that is fully or partially assembled in a factory before being moved to the living site. There are two basic types of manufactured homes. One type is the prefabricated home, whose components are built in the factory and then assembled at the housing site. Recent estimates are that about one third of new single-family homes are of this type.[4]

The second type of manufactured home was previously called a *mobile home*. However, since very few mobile homes are moved from their original site, the term is no longer accurate. These housing units are usually less than 1,000 square feet in size, but they usually offer the same features as a conventional house—for example, fully equipped kitchens, fireplaces, cathedral ceilings, and whirlpool baths. The site for a mobile home may be either purchased or leased in a development specifically designed for such housing units.

The safety of mobile homes is continually debated. Fires do not occur any more frequently in these housing units than in other types of homes. But due to the size and construction of mobile homes, a fire spreads faster in them than in conventional houses. Manufacturers' standards for the fire safety of mobile homes are higher now than they were in the past. Still, when a fire occurs in a mobile home, the unit is usually completely destroyed.

Advantages of Home Ownership

● Positive and Negative Aspects of Home Ownership

Whether you purchase a house, a condominium, or a manufactured home, you will enjoy the pride of ownership, financial benefits, and lifestyle flexibility.

Pride of Ownership. Having a place to call their own is a primary motive of many homebuyers. Stability of residence and a personalized living location are important to homeowners. Their pride of ownership is reflected in involvement in civic and community activities.

---

[4]"Real Estate," *Consumers Digest*, November 1985, p. 85.

Pepper . . . and Salt

"Sorry, but your tree is going condo."

From *The Wall Street Journal*, with permission of Cartoon Features Syndicate.

Financial Benefits. Home ownership has several financial benefits. One of these benefits is the deductibility of mortgage interest and real estate tax payments for federal income tax purposes. A frequent benefit is an increase in the value of the property. Homeowners establish a good credit rating that can be of financial value in the future. Finally, homeowners may be able to borrow against their equity in their homes. Equity is the value of the home less the amount still owed on the mortgage.

Lifestyle Flexibility. While renting gives you greater mobility than home ownership, home ownership gives you more opportunity to express your individuality. Homeowners have greater freedom than renters in decorating and redesigning their dwelling units and in entertaining friends. The flexible lifestyle afforded by home ownership is also seen in the varied activities in which homeowners participate in or near their homes.

Disadvantages of Home Ownership

The American Dream of buying your own home does not guarantee a totally glamorous existence. This investment has the disadvantages of financial risks, limited mobility, and higher living costs.

Financial Risks. Among the financial risks commonly associated with buying a home are difficulty in obtaining the money needed for a down payment. Obtaining mortgage financing may also be a problem, due to your personal situation or current economic conditions. Finally, changing property values in a living area can affect your financial investment.

Limited Mobility. As mentioned, home ownership does not provide the ease in changing living location that renters have. If changes in your situation make it necessary for you to sell your home, the process of doing so may be difficult. High interest rates combined with a low demand for housing can create poor market conditions for selling a home.

Higher Living Costs. As most homeowners will verify, owning your place of residence can be expensive. The homeowner is financially responsible for maintenance and must bear the costs of repainting and repairs for plumbing, roofing, and appliances. The homeowner must also fund home improvements.

Real estate taxes are another expense related to home ownership. As property values and tax rates increase, so too does the amount paid for local government services. When the federal government stopped providing certain services in the early 1980s, the pressure on state and local governments to maintain these services resulted in increases in the property taxes paid by homeowners.

THE HOME BUYING PROCESS

If you decide to buy a home, you should follow a logical procedure. The steps of the home buying process are presented in Figure 9–2.

● Process of Buying a Home

Determining Housing Needs

As you start the process of buying a home, you should determine how much you can spend for a house and how much house you want.

Price. The amount you can afford to spend for a house will be affected by the cash you have available for a down payment, by your regular income, and by your current living expenses and financial obligations. Other factors that you should consider are the current mortgage rates, the potential future value of the property you want to buy, and your ability to make monthly mortgage payments and to cover other living costs, maintenance, repairs, and home improvements. The relationship between your financial situation and the home you plan to buy will be discussed later in this chapter.

FIGURE 9-2   The Home-Buying Process

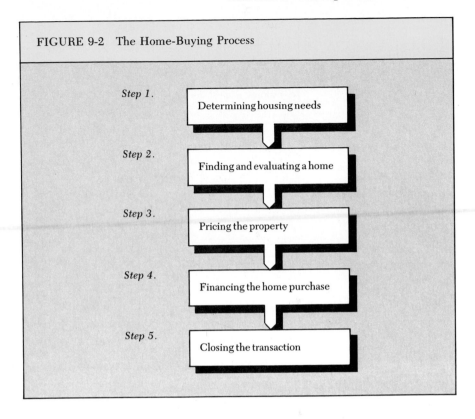

Step 1.   Determining housing needs

Step 2.   Finding and evaluating a home

Step 3.   Pricing the property

Step 4.   Financing the home purchase

Step 5.   Closing the transaction

Quantity and Quality. When buying your first home, be realistic. While many of us would like to live in a mansion, most people have to start at a less extravagant level. You may not get all the features you want in your first home, but financial advisers suggest that you should get into the housing market by purchasing what you can afford. Studies show that the most desired features in a home are a basement, a large garage, abundant closet and storage space, and a large, modern kitchen. As you move up in the housing market, your second or third home can include more of the features that you want. A recent survey reported the amenities that people would like their dream home to have (see Table 9–2).

Ideally, the home you buy will be in good condition. In certain circumstances, however, you may be willing to buy a *handyman's special*—a home that needs work but that you are able to get at a lower price because of its poor condition. Then you will need to either put more money into the house for repairs and improvements, or to invest some *sweat equity* by doing some of the work yourself. Home improvement information and assistance are available from hardware stores and other home product retailers. Also, home improvement shows are frequently held at convention centers featuring speakers, exhibitors, and demonstration sessions.

TABLE 9-2   What's in Your Dream House?

Readers of *Sylvia Porter's Personal Finance* magazine ranked the following home features as most desirable:

1. Swimming pool	11. Art collection
2. Modern kitchen	12. Wine cellar
3. New home interior	13. Sports court
4. Home spa	14. Tennis court
5. Computer center	15. Stress relief system
6. Greenhouse	16. Mini golf course
7. Home gym	17. Playroom
8. Minitheater	18. Bowling alley
9. Rare collectibles	19. Arcade room
10. Robotic house helper	20. Gaming room

Source: "Dream Home Survey," *Sylvia Porter's Personal Finance*, February 1984, p. 86.

Finding and Evaluating a Home

Next, you should select a location, consider using the services of a real estate agent, and conduct a home inspection.

Selecting a Location. While visiting friends, traveling, or reading newspapers and magazines, you will see housing types and home features that will influence what you want. But an old adage of real estate people says, "The three most important factors to consider when buying a home are location, location, and location!"

Do you prefer an urban, a suburban, or a rural setting? Or perhaps you want to live in a small town or in a resort area near a lake or skiing facilities. In selecting a neighborhood, consider the character of the community. Is there a strong community spirit and high neighbor involvement? Compare your values and lifestyle with those of current residents.

If you have or plan to have a family, the school system should be assessed. Educators recommend that schools be evaluated on the basis of variety of programs, the achievement level of students, the percentage of students who go on to college, the dedication of faculty members, the available facilities, and the involvement of parents. Homeowners without children also benefit from strong schools since the educational advantages of a community affect property values.

Accessibility to churches, shopping, public transportation, and other activities will also affect your choice of a location. Public services such as water supply, police protection, and recreational facilities are other location factors. Finally, **zoning laws** are restrictions on how the property in an area can be used. The location of businesses and the anticipated construction of industrial buildings may influence your decision to settle in a particular area.

Utilizing the Services of Real Estate Agents. To minimize the time and effort involved in buying a home, the use of a real estate agent should be considered. A real estate agent works to bring together homebuyers and home sellers.

A real estate agent can help you assess your housing needs and determine the amount you can afford to spend on a home. Real estate agents are usually willing to share information on the communities in which you are interested. The Multiple Listing Service used by real estate agents is a directory of the homes that are available for purchase in a geographic area. This system provides a fast method of searching the market for homes that meet your personal and financial needs.

Finally, a real estate agent can be helpful in presenting your offer to the seller, negotiating a settlement price, assisting you in obtaining financing, and representing you at the closing. Your real estate agent can recommend lawyers, insurance agents, inspectors, and mortgage companies that will serve your needs. The real estate agent's commission is paid by the seller in a housing sale. The role of the real estate agent in selling a house is considered later in this chapter.

Conducting a Home Inspection. Before reaching your decision about a specific home, conduct a complete evaluation of the property. This evaluation can help minimize future problems. Do not assume that because someone now lives there, everything is in proper working condition. Being cau-

Technology for Today
Video Tours of Homes

With the use of a video-based multiple listing service, in just a few hours you can tour several hundred homes that are for sale. A number of real estate companies have introduced electronic programs that feature several photographs of available properties. Prospective customers can eliminate unacceptable houses without leaving the broker's office. This procedure saves a great deal of time for both the real estate agent and the homebuyer.

The video presentation includes instant access to photographs of the neighborhood, local public areas, and an aerial view of the home. More sophisticated and costly systems include several exterior and interior photos as well as a floor plan and a narrative that describes the property. As the costs of real estate videos decrease and customer and broker acceptance increases, homebuying will be as easy as watching television.

Source: Lew Sichelman, "Video Unit Cuts Home-Tour Costs," *Chicago Tribune,* June 14, 1986, sec. 3, pp. 1–2.

FIGURE 9-3 Conducting a Home Inspection

Exterior facilities
- Appearance of neighborhood
- Condition of streets and sidewalks
- Location of street lights, fire hydrants
- Quality of landscaping, trees, shrubs
- Condition of driveway and garage
- Outdoor lighting
- Condition of patio or porch
- Appropriate drainage system

Exterior construction
- Material quality and condition of building
- Construction and condition of foundation
- Condition of bricks, wood, or other siding
- Condition and quality of windows
- Condition and quality of roof and gutters
- Type and condition of chimney

Interior design
- Size and arrangement of rooms
- Amount of closet and storage space
- Door sizes for moving furniture
- Counter space and layout of kitchen
- Condition of kitchen appliances
- Ventilation for cooking
- Adequate laundry area
- Location of bedrooms compared to other areas
- Accessibility to attic and basement
- Adequate electrical outlets

Interior construction
- Condition of electrical fixtures and wiring
- Condition of plumbing fixtures
- Adequate water pressure; water heater condition
- Type and condition of heating unit
- Quality/condition of walls, floors, and doors
- Cracks or potential ceiling problems
- Ease of operation of windows
- Type and condition of floor covering
- Condition, potential use of basement
- Condition of stairways

tious and aggressive will save you headaches and unplanned expenses. The purpose of a home inspection is to evaluate the neighborhood, the exterior of the house, the roof, the foundation, the plumbing, the wiring, the interior construction, and the condition of appliances. Figure 9–3 presents a more detailed format for inspecting a home.

Pricing the Property

● Determining and Negotiating the Purchase Price

After you select a home you desire, your efforts must turn to determining an initial offer price and negotiating a final buying price.

Determining the Home Price. Making an offer on the property you wish to purchase is an initial concern. What price should you offer for the home? The main factors you should consider are recent sales prices in the area, the current demand for housing, the length of time the house has been on the market, the owner's need to sell, the financing options, and the features and condition of the home. Each of these items can affect your offer price. For example, you will have to offer a higher price in times of low interest rates and high demand for homes. On the other hand, a home that has been on the market for over a year could mean an opportunity to offer a lower price. The services of an appraiser can assist you in assessing the current value of the home you wish to buy.

Your offer will be in the form of a purchase agreement, or contract (see Table 9–3). This document constitutes your legal offer to purchase the home. Usually, your first offer price will not be accepted.

Negotiating the Purchase Price. If your initial offer is accepted, you have a valid contract to buy the home. But if your offer is rejected, you have several options, depending on the actions of the seller. A counteroffer from the owner indicates a willingness to negotiate a price settlement. If the counteroffer is only slightly lower than the asking price, you are probably expected to move closer to that price with your next offer. If the counteroffer is quite a bit off the asking price, you are closer to the point where you can split the difference with the seller to arrive at the purchase price. If no counteroffer is forthcoming, you may wish to make another offer to see whether the seller is willing to do any negotiating on the price.[5] In times of high demand for housing, negotiating is minimized. In mid-1986, a duplex on the North Side of Chicago sold for $149,500; it had a listing price of $120,000. The bidding for the building consisted of seven offers, all higher than the asking price![6]

Once a price has been agreed upon, the purchase contract becomes the basis for the transaction. At this time, the buyer must deposit **earnest money**—a portion of the purchase price that is forfeited if the buyer de-

[5]Susan Bondy, "How to Decide How Much to Bid for a House," *Chicago Sun-Times*, August 1, 1986, p. 50.

[6]"Wanted: Home in My Range," *U.S. News & World Report*, August 11, 1986, p. 45.

TABLE 9-3   The Components of a Home Purchase Agreement

The contract between a buyer and a seller for a real estate transaction consists of the following information:

1. The names and addresses of the buyer and seller.
2. A description of the property.
3. The price of the house.
4. The amount of the mortgage that will be needed.
5. The amount of the earnest money deposit.
6. The date and time of the closing.
7. Where the closing will take place.
8. Provision to extend the closing date.
9. Provision for the disposition of the deposit money if something goes wrong.
10. Adjustment to be made at the closing.
11. Details of what is included in the sale—home appliances, drapes, carpeting, and other items.
12. Special conditions of the sale.
13. Inspections that the buyer can make before the closing.
14. Property easements, such as the use of an area of the property for utility lines or poles.

Source: *Homeownership: Guidelines for Buying and Owning a Home* (Richmond: Federal Reserve Bank of Richmond, 1986).

faults. At the closing of the home purchase, the earnest money is applied toward the price of the property.

Home purchase agreements often contain a *contingency clause*. This contract condition states that the agreement is binding only if a certain event occurs. For example, a real estate contract often stipulates that the contract will be invalid if the buyer does not obtain financing for the purchase within a certain time period.

Financing the Home Purchase

Buying a home is an expensive proposition. During the late 1970s and early 1980s, high interest rates and rising prices made the purchase of a home impossible for most Americans. In 1985, more than half of the homes bought had a value greater than $80,000. This situation resulted in various new financing methods to stimulate home sales.

The financial aspects of buying a home involve obtaining down payment money, qualifying for a mortgage, and evaluating mortgage types.

Down Payment Sources. The main expenses of a home purchase are the down payment, the monthly mortgage payment, and the closing costs. The first of these will be discussed here; the other two will be covered later in this chapter.

How much cash you have available for a down payment will affect the size of the mortgage loan you require. A large down payment, such as 20 percent or more, will make it easier for you to obtain a mortgage.

Personal savings, pension plan funds, sales of investments or other assets, and assistance from relatives are the most common sources of down payment money. Parents can help their children in the purchase of a home by giving them a cash gift or a loan, depositing money with the lender to reduce the interest rate of the loan, cosigning the loan, or acting as comortgagors.[7]

• Actions Necessary to Qualify for a Mortgage

Qualifying for a Mortgage. Do you have the funds you need for a down payment? Do you earn enough to make mortgage payments while also covering other living expenses? Do you have a favorable credit rating? Unless you pay cash for a home, you will be required to respond affirmatively to these questions in order to obtain financing. A **mortgage** is a long-term loan on a specific piece of property, such as a home or other real estate. Payments on a mortgage are made over an extended period, for example, 15 or 30 years. Financial institutions such as banks, savings and loan associations, credit unions, mortgage companies, and insurance companies are the most common home financing sources.

To qualify for a mortgage, you must meet criteria similar to those that must be met for other loans. Your credit history must show that you have consistently paid your financial obligations. Your current and projected income must be high enough to make the monthly mortgage payments. Your available funds must be sufficient to meet the down payment. The home you buy will serve as the security, or collateral, for the mortgage loan. The current level of interest rates will affect the amount and cost of your mortgage.

Financial institutions base the amount they will lend you to purchase a home on three items. First, they consider your monthly gross income less any long-term debts, such as car payments. Most home financing sources estimate that about 30 percent of this amount is the monthly payment you can afford. For example, a person with a monthly gross income of $3,023 and a car payment of $190 would be able to afford a monthly housing payment of $850 ($3,023 − $190 × 0.30).

Second, they subtract estimated taxes ($120) and home insurance ($30) from the monthly housing payment to obtain the appropriate mortgage payment ($700). Finally, they consider current interest rates in determining the loan amount. A person can quality for a larger mortgage loan when interest rates are low than when they are high. For example, a person who can afford a monthly mortgage payment of $700 will qualify for a 30-year loan of

$86,995 at 9 percent
$79,765 at 10 percent
$73,503 at 11 percent
$68,052 at 12 percent
$63,279 at 13 percent
$59,078 at 14 percent
$55,360 at 15 percent

[7]"Home Buying: Six Ways Parents Pitch In," *Changing Times*, December 1985, pp. 75–79.

As interest rates rise, fewer people are able to afford the cost of an average-priced home.

Mortgage interest rates, like interest rates on other loans, vary by lending institution. Compare mortgage costs by checking with several mortgage companies. When you compare costs, the interest rate you are quoted is not the only factor you should consider. The required down payment and the points charged will affect the interest rate. **Points** are prepaid interest charged by the lender. Each point is equal to 1 percent of the loan amount. It may be more costly to borrow from a lender that offers a lower interest rate than another lender but requires more points.

The lending policies of financial institutions also vary. Some limit the amount of the mortgage. Others minimize their risk by restricting the ratio between loan amount and the property value. This reduces their chances of financial loss if the property must be sold due to a failure of the borrower to make the mortgage payments.

Obtaining a mortgage requires the potential borrower to submit an application form containing personal and financial data. Most lenders charge a loan application fee of between $100 and $300, according to a survey conducted by the Consumer Federation of America. Of the lenders surveyed, 31 percent did not charge an application fee.[8]

Once the loan application has been reviewed, an interview is usually

[8]Naphtali Hoffman and Stephen Brobeck, *The Bank Book* (New York: Harcourt Brace Jovanovich, 1986), p. 176.

Pepper . . . and Salt

"If not for anything else, you should try to make your marriage work for the sake of your 7% mortgage."

From *The Wall Street Journal*, with permission of Cartoon Features Syndicate.

scheduled. At this meeting, the lender requests additional information and gives the potential borrower an opportunity to prove employment, level of income, ownership of assets, and amounts owed.

Other common charges associated with the mortgage application process are loan origination fees, property appraisal fees, and a credit report charge. The final decision to grant the loan is based on the creditworthiness of the potential borrower and an evaluation of the home, including its location, condition, and value.

The loan commitment is the financial institution's decision to provide the funds needed to purchase a specific property. The approved mortgage application locks in an interest rate for 30 to 90 days. At this point, the purchase contract for the home becomes legally binding.

● Types of Mortgages Available to Finance a Home Purchase

Types of Mortgages. The main types of mortgages are the conventional mortgage, government-guaranteed financing programs, adjustable rate and flexible payment mortgages, the graduated payment mortgage, the buy down, the growing equity mortgage, the balloon mortgage, and the shared appreciation mortgage (see Table 9–4).

1. The **conventional mortgage** has equal payments over, say, 15 or 30 years based on a fixed interest rate. This mortgage offers homebuyers certainty about future loan payments. The mortgage payments are set at a level that allows **amortization** of the loan. That is, the balance owed is reduced with each payment. Since the amount borrowed is large, the payments made during the early years of the mortgage are applied mainly to interest, with only small reductions in the principle of the loan. As the amount owed declines, the monthly payments have an ever greater impact on the loan balance. Near the end of the mortgage term, nearly all of each payment is applied to the balance.

In the past, many conventional mortgages were *assumable*. This feature allowed the homebuyer to continue with the seller's original agreement. Assumable mortgages were especially attractive when the mortgage rate was lower than market interest rates at the time of the sale. Due to volatile interest rates, very few assumable mortgages are currently offered by lending institutions.

2. Government-guaranteed financing programs include insured loans by the Federal Housing Authority (FHA) and loans guaranteed by the Veterans Administration (VA). These government agencies do not provide the mortgage money, but they do help homebuyers obtain low-interest, low–down payment loans.

To qualify for an FHA-insured loan, an individual must meet a few conditions related to down payment and fees. Most low- and middle-income people in our society can qualify for the FHA loan program. The required down payment is between 3 and 5 percent, depending on the amount of the loan. This lower down payment makes it easier for a person to purchase a home. FHA-insured loans have interest rates lower than market interest rates since the FHA's involvement reduces the risk for the lending institution. The

TABLE 9-4   Mortgage Loans from A to Z

Loan Type	Benefits	Drawbacks
1. Fixed rate, fixed payment		
a. Conventional 30-year mortgage	Fixed monthly payments for 30 years provide absolute certainty on housing costs.	Higher initial rates than adjustables.
b. Conventional 15-year mortgage	Lower rate than 30-year fixed; faster equity buildup and quicker payoff of loan.	Higher monthly payments.
c. FHA/VA fixed rate mortgages (30-year and 15-year)	Low down payment requirements and fully assumable with no prepayment penalties.	May require substantial points; may have application red tape and delays.
d. "Balloon" loans (3–10-year terms)	May carry discount rates and other favorable terms, particularly when the loan is provided by the homeseller.	At the end of the 3–10-year term, the entire remaining balance is due in a lump-sum or "balloon" payment, forcing the borrower to find new financing.
2. Adjustable rate, variable payment		
a. Adjustable rate mortgage (ARM)—payment changes on one-year, three-year, and five-year schedules	Lower initial rates than fixed rate loans, particularly on the one-year adjustables. Generally assumable by new buyers. Offers possibility of future rate and payment decreases. Loans with rate "caps" may protect borrowers against increases in rates. In some cases, may be convertible to fixed rate plans after three years.	Shifts far greater interest rate risk onto borrowers than fixed rate loans. Without "caps," may also sharply push up monthly payments in future years.
b. Graduated payment mortgage (GPM)—payment increases by prearranged increments during first five–seven years, then levels off	Allows buyers with marginal incomes to qualify. Higher incomes over next five–seven years expected to cover gradual payment increases. May be combined with adjustable rate mortgage to lower further initial rate and payment.	May have higher annual percentage rate (APR) than standard fixed rate or adjustable rate loans. May involve negative amortization—increasing debt owed by lender.
c. Growing equity mortgage (GEM)—contributes rising portions of monthly payments to payoff of principal debt. Typically pays off in 15–18 years, rather than 30.	Lower up-front payments, quicker loan payoff than conventional fixed rate or adjustable.	May have higher effective rates and higher down payments than other loans in the marketplace. Tax deductions for interest payments decrease over time.

Source: *Real Estate Today*, March–April 1986, p. 21.

borrower is required to pay a fee for insurance that protects the lender against financial loss due to default. Despite the protection given the lender, the lower-than-market interest rate can result in extra prepaid interest, *points,* as a condition of the loan.

The VA-guaranteed loan program assists eligible veterans of the armed services in purchasing a home. As with the FHA program, the funds from VA loans come from a financial institution or a mortgage company and the risk is reduced by government participation. A VA loan can be obtained without a down payment. The points charged by the lending institution must be paid by the home seller, but the veteran is usually responsible for other charges, such as origination and funding fees.

Both FHA-insured loans and VA-guaranteed loans can be attractive financing alternatives. Each imposes limits on the amount that can be borrowed, however, and a backlog of processing applications and approving loans can occur during periods of high demand for housing.

3. Adjustable rate and flexible payment mortgages give individuals a better opportunity to buy homes in times of high interest rates. The **adjustable rate mortgage (ARM)**, also referred to as a flexible rate mortgage or a variable rate mortgage, has an interest rate that increases or decreases during the life of the loan based on the changing economic market for money. When mortgage rates were at record highs, many people took out variable rate home loans based on the expectation that interest rates would eventually go down.

There are many types of adjustable rate mortgages; in some areas, nearly 50 variations have been offered by financial institutions. The types of variable rate home loans are affected by limits placed on the changes in interest rate and on the changes in the monthly payment. A **rate cap** restricts the amount that the interest rate can increase during the loan term. This limit prevents the borrower from paying an interest rate significantly higher than the one stipulated in the original agreement. A rate cap is usually accompanied by a limit on interest rate decreases, so that the lender is assured a certain return on the investment.

A **payment cap** keeps the payments on an adjustable rate mortgage at a given level, or limits the amount to which those payments can rise. When mortgage payments do not rise but interest rates do, the amount owed can increase in months in which the mortgage payment does not cover the interest owed. This increased loan balance, called *negative amortization,* means that the amount of your home equity is decreasing instead of increasing. As a result of such increases in the amount owed, the borrower usually has to make payments for a period longer than originally planned.

You should consider several factors when you evaluate adjustable rate mortgages. First, consider the frequency of and the restrictions on allowed changes in interest rates. Second, consider the frequency of and the restrictions on changes in the monthly payment. Third, investigate the possibility that the loan will be extended due to negative amortization and find out whether the mortgage agreement limits the amount of negative amortization. Finally, find out what index the lending institution will use to set the mortgage interest rate over the term of the loan. A lending institution will revise the rate for an adjustable rate mortgage based on changes in either U.S. Treasury security rates, the Federal Home Loan Bank Board's mortgage rate index, or its own cost-of-funds index.

4. **A graduated payment mortgage** is a financing agreement in which payments rise to different levels every five or ten years during the term of the loan. During the early years, the payments are relatively low. This mortgage is especially beneficial to individuals who anticipate an increase in income in future years.

5. **A buy down** is an interest rate subsidy from a builder or a real estate developer that reduces the mortgage payments during the first few years of the loan. This assistance is intended to stimulate sales among homebuyers who cannot afford conventional financing. After the buy down period, the mortgage payments increase to the level that would have existed without the financial aid.

6. **A growing equity mortgage** provides for increases in payments that allow the amount owed to be paid off more quickly. With such a mortgage, a person would be able to pay off a 30-year home loan in 15 to 18 years. A growing equity mortgage may be desired by high-income individuals who want to quickly build equity in their homes.

7. The historically high mortgage rates of the late 1970s and early 1980s (Table 9–5) helped stimulate various innovative lending plans for homebuyers. One such plan is the **balloon mortgage,** which has fixed monthly payments and a very large final payment, usually after three or five years. This financing plan is designed for individuals who wish to buy a home during periods of high interest rates but expect to be able to refinance the loan before or when the balloon payment is due.

8. The **shared appreciation mortgage (SAM)** is an arrangement in which the borrower agrees to share the increased value of the home with the lender when the home is sold. This agreement provides the homebuyer with a below-market interest rate and with lower payments than those of a conventional loan. To obtain these conditions, the borrower typically has to agree to give the lending institution 30–50 percent of the home's appreciation when the home is sold.

TABLE 9-5   Mortgage Rates through the Years

The national average of interest rates paid for new home loans in the years listed was as follows:

1965	5.81%	1982	15.14%
1970	8.45	1984	12.38
1975	9.00	1985	11.58
1978	9.56	1986	9.82
1980	12.66%		

Source: *Savings Institution Sourcebook* (United States League of Savings Institutions, 1986).

9. **A second mortgage,** more commonly called a *home equity loan,* allows a homeowner to borrow on the paid-up value of the property. Traditional second mortgages allow a homeowner to borrow a lump sum against the equity and to repay it in monthly installments. More recently, lending institutions have offered a variety of home equity loans, including a line-of-credit program that allows the borrower to obtain loan funds by writing a check. When considering this type of loan, homeowners should beware of uncapped variable rate loans and the possibility of losing their home due to an inability to make required payments on both the first and second mortgages.[9]

During the course of your mortgage, you may want to obtain a **refinance** on your home—that is, a new mortgage on your current home at a lower interest rate. Before taking this action, be sure that the costs of refinancing do not offset the savings of a lower interest rate. Refinancing is most advantageous when you can get a mortgage rate 2 or 3 percent lower than your current rate and when you plan to own your present home for at least two more years. With recent changes in the law, also be sure to consider the tax deductibility of refinancing costs.

The maze of mortgages can overwhelm a prospective homebuyer. Before accepting any home financing agreement, compare the interest rates, points, and other mortgage conditions of different lending institutions. Computerized mortgage services can assist you in finding the best arrangement. For a fee, these information networks will research the mortgage conditions of various financial institutions.

Not all lenders have the same mortgage agreement. For example, your loan contract may have a *prepayment penalty,* which can result in extra costs should you decide to pay off your mortgage early. A prepayment penalty requires that a certain amount of interest must be paid even if the loan is paid off in less than the time stipulated in the original agreement. When in doubt on any aspect of mortgages, seek information and assistance from a real estate agent, a lawyer, a financial adviser, or a lending officer of the mortgage company.

Closing the Transaction

The closing of a home purchase involves a meeting of the buyer, seller, and lender of funds, or representatives of each party, to complete the transaction. Documents are signed, last-minute details are settled, and appropriate amounts are paid.

- Costs Associated with Finalizing a Real Estate Transaction

A number of expenses are incurred at the closing. The **closing costs,** also referred to as settlement costs, are the fees and charges paid when a real estate transaction is completed. At this time, the buyer must pay the lender's points and other charges. A credit report fee, the cost of a property survey, a notary's fee, a termite inspection charge, and document preparation fees may also have to be paid. The fees of a real estate agent, lawyer, or

[9]"Should You Hock Your Home?" *Consumer Reports,* November 1986, pp. 739–43.

appraiser are due at the closing. Most of these are costs of the buyer. The real estate commission, however, is paid by the seller from the proceeds of the sale.

Title insurance is another closing cost. This coverage has two phases. First, the title company defines the boundaries of the property being purchased and conducts a search to determine whether the property is free of claims, such as unpaid real estate taxes. Second, the title company provides insurance that protects the owner and the lender during the mortgage term against financial loss resulting from future defects in the title and from other unforeseen property claims not excluded by the policy.

Also due at closing time is the fee for recording the deed. The **deed** is the document that transfers ownership of property from one party to another. Mortgage insurance is another possible closing cost. If required, mortgage insurance protects the lender from loss as a result of a mortgage default.

The Real Estate Settlement Procedures Act of 1974 was enacted to assist homebuyers in understanding the closing process and closing costs. This legislation requires that loan applicants be given certain information, including an estimate of the closing costs, before the actual closing.

At the time of closing and when you make your monthly payments, you will probably have to deposit money that will be used to pay home-related expenses. An **escrow account** is money deposited with a financial institution for the payment of property taxes and homeowners insurance. This account protects the lender from financial loss due to unpaid real estate taxes or damage from fire or other hazards.

As a new homebuyer, you might also consider purchasing an agreement that affords you protection against the cost of defects in the home. Implied warranties created by state laws may cover some problem areas, but other repair costs can also occur. Home builders and real estate sales companies offer warranties to buyers. Coverage purchased from the Home Owners Warranty Corporation includes protection against structural, wiring, and plumbing defects and defects in the heating system and other mechanical systems. About one fourth of the nation's home builders participate in this program, which offers a 10-year warranty on new homes. Or a new homeowner may wish to purchase a service contract from a real estate company such as Electronic Realty Associates (ERA) which warrants appliances, plumbing, air-conditioning systems, the heating unit, and other items for one year. As with any service contract, you must decide whether the coverage provided and the chances of repair expenses justify the cost.

SELLING A HOME

- Decisions Involved in Selling a Home

Most of the people who buy a home will eventually be on the other side of the transaction. Common reasons for selling your home range from such lifestyle factors as your need for more space or your desire for a modern kitchen to such practical considerations as a job change or poor community services. Selling your home requires preparing it for selling, setting a price, and deciding whether to sell it yourself or to sell it through a real estate agent.

Preparing Your Home for Selling

The effective presentation of your home can result in a fast, financially favorable sale. Real estate salespeople recommend that you make needed home repairs and apply a fresh coat of paint to the exterior and interior areas that need one. Clear the garage and exterior areas of toys, debris, and old vehicles, and keep the lawn cut and the leaves raked. Keep the kitchen and bathroom clean and clear of dirty clothes, wet towels, and toilet articles. Avoid offensive odors by removing garbage and keeping pets and their areas clean. Remove excess furniture and dispose of unneeded items to make the house and its closets and storage areas look larger. When showing your home, open drapes and turn on lights to give it a pleasant atmosphere. This effort will give your property an improved image and enable you to sell it sooner.

Determining the Selling Price

Putting a price on your home can be a difficult decision. You face the risk of not selling it immediately if the price is too high, and you may not get a fair settlement if the price is too low. An **appraisal,** which is an estimate of the current value of the property, can provide a good indication of the price you should set for it. Your asking price will be influenced by the recent selling price of comparable homes in your area, demand in the housing market, and the availability of financing based on current mortgage interest rates.

The home improvements you have made may or may not increase the selling price. A hot tub or exercise room may have no value for potential buyers of your home. But certain home improvements almost always contribute to a higher resales value.

Among the improvements most often wanted by homebuyers are energy-efficient features, a remodeled kitchen, an additional or remodeled bathroom, added rooms and storage space, a converted basement, a fireplace, and an outdoor deck or patio.

The time to think about selling your home is when you buy it and every day you live in it. Daily maintenance, timely repairs, and home improvements will increase the future sales price.

Sale by Owner

Each year, about 10 percent of home sales are made by the owner. If you decide to sell your home without the use of a real estate professional, after pricing the home, plan to advertise it through local newspapers and through fliers describing it in detail. Obtain a listing sheet from a real estate office as an example of the information to include on your flier. Distribute the flier through stores, and other public areas, community activities, and so on.

When selling your own home, obtain information on the availability of financing and on the qualifications required for financing. This information will help you and potential buyers to determine whether a sale is possible. Use the services of a lawyer to assist you with the contract, the closing, and other legal matters.

Require potential buyers to provide their names, addresses, telephone numbers, and other background information, and show your home by appointment only. As a security measure, show the home only when two or more adults are at home. You can save several thousand dollars in commission by selling your own home, but you must invest the time and effort needed to do so.

Listing with a Real Estate Agent

If you decide to sell your home with the assistance of a real estate agent, you have many real estate offices in your area from which to choose. These businesses range from one-person-owned firms to nationally advertised companies. A primary selection factor should be the real estate agent's knowledge of all aspects of your community and a willingness to actively market your home.

Your real estate agent will assist you in various ways. These services include suggestions of a selling price, making potential buyers and other agents aware of your home, providing advice on features to highlight, con-

---

Today's Lifestyles
Do-It-Yourself Homeowners

Americans spend $40 billion a year on home repair and improvement materials. The most popular do-it-yourself efforts are interior painting, weatherstripping and caulking, exterior painting, and repair of bathroom and kitchen faucets.

The Do-It-Yourself Research Institute of the National Retail Hardware Association has divided those involved in home repairs and improvements into five lifestyle categories. The *expedients* are people with more money than time who concentrate on improvement and replacement rather than repair. The *inflation-pressured* are young, shrewd shoppers who recognize value and must do it themselves or do without. The *self-assured* are knowledgeable, prudent shoppers who may spend an above-average amount on home improvements. The *price-constrained* focus on inexpensive repair projects and obtain materials through discount stores. The *contemporary female* category consists of female heads of households who are aggressive shoppers and concentrate on decorative projects.

Approximately 75 percent of all households obtain financial and personal satisfaction from repair and home improvement activities.

Source: Kate Callen, "Do-it-Yourself Repairs on Rise—$40 Billion Worth," *News-Sun* (Waukegan, Illinois), September 27–28, 1986, sec. 4, p. 1.

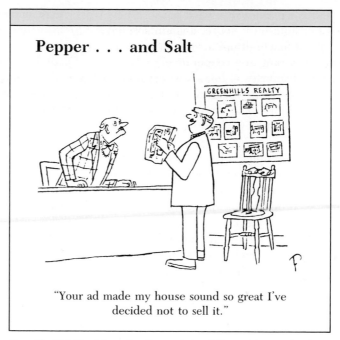

From *The Wall Street Journal*, with permission of Cartoon Features Syndicate.

ducting showings of your home, and handling the financial aspects of the sale. The real estate agent can especially be helpful in screening potential buyers to determine if they will be able to qualify for a mortgage to make the purchase.

You will need to familiarize yourself with many details in addition to those presented in this chapter when you choose, buy, or sell a home. Among other things, you will have to look into changing business policies and tax laws. You can usually obtain the necessary additional information through library research or from a real estate office, financial institution, lawyer, or government agency.

SUMMARY

- Your needs, lifestyle, and financial resources will affect the type of housing you select. Renting, buying, or building your place of residence are the three major housing options.

- The main advantages of renting are mobility, fewer responsibilities, and lower initial costs. The main disadvantages of renting are that it offers few financial benefits, imposes a restricted lifestyle, and entails legal concerns.

- You can buy a previously owned house, a new house, a custom-built house, a manufactured home, a unit in a multiunit dwelling, a condominium, or a unit in a cooperative.
- The main advantages of home ownership are pride of ownership, financial benefits, and lifestyle flexibility. The disadvantages are financial risks, limited mobility, and higher living costs.
- The process of buying a home consists of the following steps: (1) determining housing needs, (2) finding and evaluating a home, (3) pricing the property, (4) financing the home purchase, and (5) closing the transaction.
- The price offered for a home should be based on the prices of other homes in the area, housing market conditions, the situation of the seller, and the availability of financing. The purchase price usually results from a series of offers and counteroffers by the buyer and the seller.
- To qualify for a mortgage, a person must have an established credit record and an income high enough to make the payments on the loan desired. In determining the size of the loan, the lending institution also evaluates the condition and value of the property.
- The main types of mortgages available to homebuyers are the conventional fixed rate mortgage, FHA-insured loans, VA-guaranteed loans, adjustable rate and flexible payment mortgages, the graduated payment mortgage, the buy down, the growing equity mortgage, the balloon, the shared appreciation mortgage, and the second mortgage (also called a home equity loan).
- The costs associated with closing are prepaid interest, fees for processing the mortgage, legal charges, title insurance, a deed fee, and an escrow account deposit.
- When you sell your home, you must decide whether to make certain repairs and improvements, determine the selling price, and decide whether to sell it yourself or to use the services of a real estate agent.

GLOSSARY

Adjustable rate mortgage (ARM). A home loan with an interest rate that can change during the mortgage term due to changes in market interest rates; also called a flexible rate mortgage or a variable rate mortgage.

Amortization. The reduction of a loan balance through payments made over a period of time.

Appraisal. An estimate of the current value of a property.

Balloon mortgage. A home loan with fixed monthly payments and a large final payment, usually after three or five years.

Buy down. An interest rate subsidy from a builder or a real estate developer that reduces a homebuyer's mortgage payments during the first few years of the loan.

Closing costs. Expenses associated with the settlement of a real estate transaction; also called settlement costs.

Condominium. An individually owned housing unit in a building with a number of such units.

Conventional mortgage. A fixed rate, fixed payment home loan.

Cooperative housing. A form of housing in which a nonprofit organization owns a building with a number of housing units that are rented to the organization's members.

Deed. The document that transfers ownership of property from one party to another.

Earnest money. A portion of the price of a home that serves as a deposit for the purchase and is forfeited if the buyer defaults.

Escrow account.   Money deposited with a financial institution for the payment of property taxes and homeowners insurance.

Graduated payment mortgage.   A home financing agreement with payments that rise to different levels during the loan term.

Growing equity mortgage.   A home loan agreement with increases in payments that allow the amount owed to be paid off more quickly.

Lease.   A legal document that defines the conditions of a rental agreement.

Manufactured home.   A housing unit that is fully or partially assembled in a factory before being moved to the living site.

Mortgage.   A long-term loan on a specific piece of property, such as a home or other real estate.

Payment cap.   A limit on the payment increases for an adjustable rate mortgage.

Points.   Prepaid interest charged by a lending institution for a mortgage; each point is equal to 1 percent of the loan amount.

Rate cap.   A limit on the changes in the interest rate charged on an adjustable rate mortgage.

Refinance.   The process of obtaining a new mortgage on a home in order to get a lower interest rate or a more favorable loan agreement.

Second mortgage.   A cash advance based on the paid-up value of a home; also called a home equity loan.

Shared appreciation mortgage (SAM).   A home loan agreement in which the borrower agrees to share the increased value of the home with the lender when the home is sold.

Title insurance.   Insurance that protects the owner or the lender during the mortgage term against financial loss resulting from future defects in the title and from other unforeseen property claims not excluded by the policy.

Zoning laws.   Restrictions on how the property in an area can be used.

REVIEW QUESTIONS

1. What factors determine your housing needs?
2. What actions would you take before and during the building of a home?
3. What are the main advantages and disadvantages of renting?
4. What are the major costs associated with renting a place to live?
5. What types of housing are available to homebuyers?
6. What are the advantages and disadvantages of buying your residence?
7. What are the major steps in the home buying process?
8. How can a real estate agent assist you in buying a home?
9. What factors will affect your offer price on a home you wish to buy?
10. What activities are involved in qualifying for a mortgage?
11. What types of mortgages are available to homebuyers?
12. What are the closing costs of a home purchase transaction?
13. What factors should you consider when you are deciding whether to sell your home yourself or to use the services of a real estate agent?

DISCUSSION QUESTIONS AND ACTIVITIES

1. How can the Starkmans benefit from buying a home that needs improvements?

2. How might Barbara Zeller have found out when mortgage interest rates were at a level that would make refinancing her condominium more affordable?

3. Although the Alcotts had good reasons for deciding to continue renting, what equally good reasons might influence an individual or a family to buy a home?

4. Using newspaper advertisements and information from rental offices, prepare a report comparing the costs, facilities, and features of available apartments in your area.

5. Interview a lawyer to identify the most common legal problems associated with renting.

6. Visit the sales offices of condominiums, new housing developments, and mobile home companies. Obtain information on the costs and features of these housing alternatives. What are the benefits and potential problems of each type of residence?

7. How can the quality of the local school system benefit all of the homeowners in an area, even those who do not have school-age children?

8. Interview a real estate agent about the process involved in selecting and buying a home. Ask about the housing prices in your area and about the services offered by the real estate agent. What does the real estate agent think will happen to housing prices over the next two years?

9. Talk to several people about the type of mortgage they have. Do most people have a fixed rate or a variable rate home loan? Are any of the mortgages insured by the FHA or guaranteed by the VA?

10. Visit four open house showings of homes for sale. What features of these homes would appeal most to potential buyers? What problems might these homes present for their new owners?

ADDITIONAL READINGS

Homeownership: Guidelines for Buying and Owning a Home. Richmond: Federal Reserve Bank of Richmond, 1986.

How to Buy a House, Condo, or Coop. Consumers Union, 256 Washington Street, Mount Vernon, NY 10553.

Money Guide: Your Home. Kansas City, Mo.: Andrews, McMeel, & Parker, 1986.

The Mortgage Money Guide. Washington, D.C.: Federal Trade Commission.

Real Estate Today: Home Guide. Chicago: National Association of Realtors, March–April 1986.

CASE 9–1 Which Residence for Sam and Betty?

Sam and Betty Crawford were recently married and are looking for a permanent residence. Sam, a computer operator, is learning programming as a part-time student. Betty works part-time as a receptionist and is taking courses toward a degree in health care administration. They have $2,000 in a savings account.

Sam and Betty are considering renting an apartment that has a monthly rent of $575 and requires a $600 security deposit. They are also looking into a condominium that they can buy with a $2,300 down payment and monthly mortgage payments of $730.

Questions

1. What factors should Sam and Betty consider before choosing their housing?

2. Besides the housing alternatives mentioned above, what other choices might be available to Sam and Betty?

3. What future events might affect their current choice?

4. What should Sam and Betty do?

CASE 9–2 What Kind of Mortgage for Nelda?

Nelda Vesper is planning to buy a small house instead of continuing to rent. This home will cost $82,000, and she will be able to make a down payment of $22,000. While applying for a mortgage, Nelda was given the choice between a fixed rate mortgage and a variable rate mortgage. The payments on the fixed rate mortgage will be $80 more a month than those on the variable rate mortgage. If interest rates rise, however, the payments on the variable rate mortgage may increase.

Questions

1. What financial factors should Nelda consider before buying a home?

2. Under what circumstances should Nelda take the variable rate mortgage?

3. What factors could cause interest rates to rise and Nelda's monthly payment to increase?

4. What action should Nelda take?

10

Buying Transportation

Few of us live, work, and shop within a small geographic area. Most of us need transportation in order to go to work or school or for other reasons. Transportation, and more specifically the automobile, has become a necessity for most of the people in our society. For about 75 years, the automobile has affected the way we live and the way we do business. The financial demands of transportation make it necessary to carefully plan this expenditure. Your selection and use of transportation alternatives are a fundamental component of your personal financial plan.

After studying this chapter, you will be able to:

- Discuss factors that affect transportation decisions.

- Use automobile information sources.

- Explain the basic decisions that are made in buying an automobile.

- Describe the process involved in buying a used car.

- Identify the strategies involved in buying a new car.

- Discuss the alternatives for financing the purchase of an automobile.

- Explain the process of selling an automobile.

- Describe the financial aspects of owning and operating a car.

- Recognize legal and social concerns associated with automobiles.

Interview with **Holly A. Fryman,** Sales Manager, and **Gene Curelo,** Salesperson, Shamrock Olds, Downers Grove, Illinois

Holly A. Fryman, Sales Manager of Shamrock Olds, Downers Grove, Illinois, has been involved in automobile sales for over 10 years. She recently completed a program of study in dealership management at General Motors University. Gene Curelo, Salesperson at Shamrock Olds, has been involved in automobile sales and sales management since 1971.

Except for buying a home, the purchase of a car is probably the most important financial decision you will make. You have to look for a car that fits your needs and budget. Automobile comparison shopping means learning about a car in terms of fuel efficiency, maintenance costs, and insurance rates.

If you are buying a used car, find the type of car you want and then inspect it thoroughly. Generally, the best buy is a two- or three-year-old car because it has already suffered its heaviest depreciation, but you won't have a lot of costly repairs.

When you buy a used or new car, fuel efficiency will be one of your most important considerations. Fuel economy is affected by such factors as transmission, axle ratio, engine size, tires, and cruise control and by air-conditioning and various other power options.

A manual transmission is generally more fuel efficient than an automatic transmission. The lower axle ratio will slow acceleration, but it will pay off in increased fuel economy during highway driving. The smallest engine that provides adequate performance for your needs will also provide you with the best fuel economy. Radial tires can improve your miles per gallon by 3–7 percent over conventional bias ply tires. The cruise control feature can save fuel because driving at constant speed uses less fuel than changing speeds frequently.

Air-conditioning adds weight to your car, and thus the need for more horsepower. It can cost you one to three miles per gallon in city driving. Power options such as power steering, brakes, seats, windows, and roofs can reduce your miles per gallon by adding weight to your vehicle. Power steering alone can account for a 1 percent drop in fuel economy.

Preventive maintenance and repairs are a significant cost of ownership. Preventive maintenance is the periodic servicing— for example, changing the oil and oil filter—that the manufacturer specifies as necessary to keep your car running properly. These maintenance efforts can help preserve the significant financial investment you make when you buy a car.

Opening Scenario
And Away We Go!

Brad and Barbara Mahoney have never owned a car during their 17 years of marriage. Work is a short commute by train or bus; taxi service takes care of their need to get to shopping, the theater, or friends in town. Several times a year, the Mahoneys rent a car for use on a weekend trip or on an extended visit with friends. Owning a car is not a necessity for everyone in our society. Brad has said a number of times, "Living in the city is

expensive enough. If we had to have a car, it would be impossible to control our finances in a sane manner."

Bob and Karen Hamlin both work, so they both need cars. Both of their teenage sons also have cars, with which they get to school and their part-time jobs. But wait—the Hamlins are still one car short. Their daughter goes to the college across town, so she needs a car or a ride. Coordinating work, school, and other schedules so

as to satisfy the transportation needs of all the Hamlins can be a major task. And the Hamlins also have to satisfy the financial demands of being a four-car family.

In transportation decisions, needs, lifestyles, and financial resources are intertwined. Most individuals and families are required to make some important value judgments and economic choices regarding the transportation component of their financial planning efforts.

TRANSPORTATION ALTERNATIVES

- Factors that Affect Transportation Decisions

Because of our need and desire to go to work or school and to engage in other activities that require us to travel, transportation is an integral use of our time and money. Our lifestyle is a major influence on whether we choose public transportation, a new car, or a used car. Information assists us in the financial decision-making process required to make our transportation choices.

Your Lifestyle and Transportation

Your needs and desires to move from one place to another have a major effect on your finances. Many aspects of your life are affected by the relationship between those needs and desires and your ability to pay for the transportation required to satisfy them.

Your financial situation impels you to make a rational transportation decision. However, emotional factors are also involved. A desire for convenience may be a primary motivator of the travel modes you choose. Such factors as luxury, style, and appearance can also affect your choices, especially if you need to project a certain business or professional image. Table 10–1 presents lifestyle factors that influence the purchase of different automobile models.

If simplicity characterizes your lifestyle, this will be reflected in your use of a bicycle as your primary vehicle. The bicycle is a transportation alternative that provides convenience and low-cost operation and has health and fitness benefits as well. Your selection of transportation, like any other purchase you make, reflects many economic and personality factors.

The Public Transportation Option

Some people do not want the problems associated with owning and operating an automobile. Other people cannot afford an automobile. **Mass transit** refers to systems of public transportation, such as bus or train lines, that allow the fast, efficient movement of many people. Many people select mass transit to fill their transportation needs. As the demand for public transportation has increased, government has made efforts to upgrade and expand it. Modern buses and additional intracity train routes, supported by public funds, have made this travel alternative more attractive.

A person's lifestyle will affect his or her use of public transportation. Some people whose primary work and other activities are within areas served by mass transit systems use these systems because they enjoy the convenience

---

TABLE 10-1 Who Buys What?

Certain types of individuals buy certain types of cars. The profiles of common types of car buyers—and the cars they typically buy—include the following.

Buyer Profile	Typical Car
Young customers (teens to 35), household income under $30,000; or older, affluent, price-conscious consumers who desire a second or third car for the family	Low-priced compact or subcompact such as Toyota Tercel, Ford Escort, Plymouth Horizon, and Renault Encore
Upwardly mobile people between late 20s and late 30s, household income between $35,000 and $50,000; includes blue-collar workers, middle-level managers, and office workers	Compact car with many options such as Chevrolet Cavalier, Ford Tempo, Plymouth Reliant, and Nissan 200 SX; or midsize car such as Buick Century, Chrysler New Yorker, Mercury Cougar, and Toyota Cressida
In late 30s, household income from $40,000 to $65,000	Imports or medium-priced sports car such as Volvo DL, Saab Turbo, Ford Thunderbird, Camaro, and Firebird
Older consumers to mid-60s, household income from $40,000 to $65,000	Large domestic car such as Oldsmobile 98, Chevrolet Caprice, Buick Electra, Dodge Diplomat, and Cadillac DeVille
Professionals, 35 to 60 years old, household income from $45,000 to $100,000	High-priced sports cars such as Porsche, BMW, Jaguar, Mercedes-Benz
Professionals ages 45 to 60, minimum household income of $75,000 but may be $250,000; includes doctors, attorneys, and corporate officers	Ultraluxury vehicles such as Ferrari, Aston Martin, Rolls-Royce

Source: *USA Today,* February 3, 1986, pp. 4E–5E. Copyright 1986 USA TODAY. Excerpted with permission.

and because they want to avoid traffic and parking difficulties. Some people are motivated by the time and money that public transportation saves. Finally, people with environmental concerns may use public transportation so as not to contribute to the pollution caused by automobile emissions.

New or Used: Which Is for You?

Since most people buy an automobile, a primary decision that most people have to make is whether to buy a new automobile or a used one. This decision is based primarily on financial factors. Can you afford the costs associated with buying a new automobile? In general, a used car is less expensive to buy and operate than a new car. But this may hold true only until maintenance and repair costs begin to escalate.

Your decision to buy a new automobile will be influenced by your financial resources and by economic conditions. Your income and your financial situation may allow you to buy a new car regularly. Or increased prices and high interest rates may impair your ability to buy a new car. Such economic factors will frequently modify your decision on whether to buy a new or used car.

Automobile Information Sources

● Automobile
Information Sources

As with other financial decisions, relevant information is a vital component of the decision to buy an automobile. Readily available data sources include industry information, media sources, product testing organizations, and government agencies.

Industry Information. Automobile manufacturers are a primary source of information. Promotional brochures provide data about models, styles, and options on currently available vehicles. Automobile dealers can provide price information.

Media Sources. Television and radio reports can help you in buying an automobile. Even more valuable are newspapers and magazines. Many newspapers have special sections on automobile purchasing and maintenance. Popular magazines offer suggestions on buying a used car, financing your purchase, and leasing an automobile. Specialized periodicals such as *Motor Trend* and *Car and Driver* provide in-depth data about automobile specifications and maintenance procedures.

Testing and Rating Organizations. Each April, *Consumer Reports* gives the results of the automobile testing efforts of Consumers Union. This annual summary provides extensive data about quality, price, safety, and per-

From *The Wall Street Journal*, with permission of Cartoon Features Syndicate.

formance. Other automobile ratings are published by *Changing Times* and *Consumers Digest*.

Government Agencies. Several divisions of the U.S. Department of Transportation provide information and assistance to automobile owners. The Federal Highway Administration monitors automobile operating costs and the safety features of highways. The National Highway Traffic Safety Administration provides test results to inform consumers about the safety and performance features of motor vehicles. Finally, the Urban Mass Transportation Administration assists in the planning and development of public transportation systems.

The Federal Trade Commission regulates automobile sales practices and provides information about used car purchase disclosures, deceptive advertising, and financing. See Appendix D for government agencies and other organizations that may be contacted for information and assistance with regard to automobiles.

AUTOMOBILE PURCHASING PROCEDURES

The mechanical complexity and financial demands of an automobile make it a unique purchase. The decision-making process in buying an automobile involves several basic choices. The strategies used in buying a used car differ from those used in buying a new car. Finally, the financing of the purchase requires some attention. These factors are displayed in Figure 10–1.

Some Fundamental Decisions

• Basic Decisions Made when Buying an Automobile

Buying an automobile involves a number of choices and alternatives. The process should begin with some basic decisions related to finances and to vehicle size, style, and model.

Budget. Your financial situation will be a major influence on your decision to buy a car. If housing, food, clothing, and other living expenses account for most of your income, your spending on transportation will require tight

In the Real World
Automobile Testing at Consumers Union

How would you like to buy 35 new cars a year? That's exactly what Consumers Union, publisher of *Consumer Reports*, does. To provide readers with accurate test results, it inspects, drives, and crashes today's most popular models. It buys these vehicles in the same manner as you would buy a car. That is, Consumers Union has shoppers bargain with dealers for the best price.

The testing process for a car starts with an inspection of the car's features. The car's cargo space and seating comfort and the location and convenience of its gauges, switches, and pedals are evaluated. To determine the ease of starting in cold weather, the car is not kept in a garage. The climate control features of the car are tested under different conditions.

During road testing, engineers take turns driving each car over a 195-mile course and record their comments and impressions on tape and in writing. This test drive examines the car's noise level and its ability to maintain a steady course, the ease of steering and control, fuel economy, and the comfort of the ride with various passenger loads.

The sports car track phase of the investigation includes acceleration timing measurements, measurements of the braking distance at different speeds, tests of the control of the car during quick stops, and avoidance maneuver tests that use swerves similar to those that may be needed to avoid a collision. Finally, low-speed bumper-basher to bumper crashes are conducted to determine the extent of vehicle

damage. After two impacts at five miles per hour and one corner impact at three miles per hour, a professional estimates the cost of repairs.

The data from this extensive research are used to develop an overall rating for each vehicle. Ratings on 76 items are combined with information from readers of *Consumer Reports* on their experiences with various models. The resulting frequency-of-repair charts and tables can provide a valuable indication of your potential satisfaction with a particular automobile.

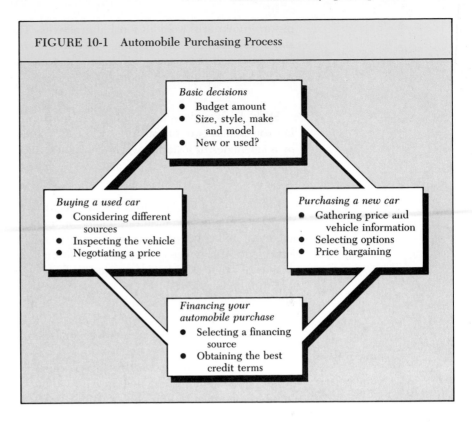

FIGURE 10-1   Automobile Purchasing Process

Basic decisions
- Budget amount
- Size, style, make and model
- New or used?

Buying a used car
- Considering different sources
- Inspecting the vehicle
- Negotiating a price

Purchasing a new car
- Gathering price and vehicle information
- Selecting options
- Price bargaining

Financing your automobile purchase
- Selecting a financing source
- Obtaining the best credit terms

control. But if money is available, you may elect to use a large portion of your available resources for an automobile.

Deciding how much to budget for transportation will be determined by two factors. First, the value of the vehicle you can afford will be based on your savings or your potential for borrowing. Second, you must allocate money for operating costs, such as gas, oil, insurance, and maintenance.

Size. Consumers can choose from over 200 different kinds of automobiles. This maze of choices can be reduced by first deciding what car size you want. Subcompacts have a low price, inexpensive operating costs, and ease of handling in congested areas. But they do not have the power and comfort of a larger car.

Compacts, like subcompacts, offer low-cost operation, but they provide more room than subcompacts. However, compacts have limited power and they usually do not have the options available on larger vehicles. Midsize automobiles, also called intermediates, have a good balance between small and large, providing both economy and comfort for passengers.

Full-size automobiles, despite their higher operating costs, are preferred by individuals who want the best performance, power, and size. Vans and pickup trucks are two additional alternatives. They both come in a full-size and a less-than-full-size version. Once again, your desire for comfort, performance, and cargo space will influence your choice. Table 10–2 can assist you in assessing the vehicle size you prefer.

Style. Body style is most influenced by the number of doors you prefer. Do you want a two- or four-door vehicle? Will your needs be better served by a hatchback or a station wagon? Or does your lifestyle call for a convertible, a minivan, or a pickup truck?

Make and Model. You must choose between a foreign car and a domestic vehicle. Some people base this choice on a desire for efficiency or performance; others base it on a desire for easy servicing. In recent years, several joint ventures between American and foreign car manufacturers have produced cars that include the strengths of knowledge and quality offered by two production systems.

The specific model is your final consideration. Most manufacturers offer twin models with different names. For example, certain Mercury models are also available as Fords. General Motors has similar models of Buicks, Chevrolets, Oldsmobiles, and Pontiacs. For many years, the Chevrolet Camaro and the Pontiac Firebird had twin bodies. Foreign competitors also have duplications among their models. The Chevrolet Nova, assembled in this country, is similar to the Toyota Corolla.[1]

Buying a Used Car

- Process Involved in Buying a Used Car

According to recent estimates, the annual operating cost of a new car was $5,726, compared to $3,318 for a used car.[2] Many people prefer a previously owned vehicle for reasons of cost. A used car may be purchased from a variety of sources. Regardless of the source, you will need to inspect the vehicle and negotiate a price.

Used Car Sources. Americans spend over $90 billion a year to purchase more than 18 million used cars. New car dealers usually have a good supply of used vehicles. These automobiles are late-model vehicles received as trade-ins for new car purchases. New car dealers generally give you a better warranty on a used car than do other sellers, and they have a service department that reconditions the cars they sell. These services mean higher used car prices at new car dealers.

---

[1]"How to Get the Best Deal," *Consumer Reports*, April 1986, p. 212.
[2]"Annual Survey: Overall, Used Is Cheaper," *USA Today*, July 28, 1986, p. 5E.

TABLE 10-2 Which Size Is for You?

The features you desire in a car can help you determine the size car you should buy. Rate each of the statements below from 1 to 5:

1—indicates no agreement with the statement.
2—indicates little agreement with the statement.
3—indicates some agreement with the statement.
4—indicates much agreement with the statement.
5—indicates total agreement with the statement.

_____ 1. I want a car to have the longest list of available options.

_____ 2. I frequently need towing power.

_____ 3. Gasoline prices have no effect on the size car I buy.

_____ 4. I need a car that is very quiet at highway speeds.

_____ 5. In my car, a very smooth ride is very important.

_____ 6. I always use my car to entertain.

_____ 7. I drive many more highway miles than city miles.

_____ 8. My family needs a car with a lot of room.

_____ 9. I always need to carry large packages in my trunk.

_____ 10. The cost of maintenance is not important to my car buying decision.

_____ 11. I want the highest level of luxury in my car.

_____ 12. I don't feel comfortable in a car with a small interior.

_____ 13. I frequently travel with more than four passengers.

_____ 14. I would rather have a car with a large interior than one that has top fuel economy.

_____ 15. Passing power and towing ability are more important to me than fuel economy.

_____ 16. A large rear seat is more important to me than ease of parking.

_____ 17. Six-passenger room is very important to me.

_____ 18. Eight-cylinder performance is more important to me than low driving costs

_____ 19. I want room to stretch out in my car when I drive.

_____ 20. The level of luxury and the amount of room in my car have to make me look successful.

_____ 21. I feel more comfortable in a car that weighs a lot.

_____ 22. My car will be the primary family car, not a second car.

_____ 23. Room and luxury are more important to me than the price of the car.

_____ 24. Having many options is more important to me than paying the lowest price.

_____ 25. Excellent power and performance are very important to me.

_____   Total score

25–40 Subcompact   40–65 Compact   65–85 Midsize   85 + Full size

Source: *Car Buying Made Easier* (Lincoln Park, Mich.: Ford Motor Company), p. 4.

Used car dealers specialize in the sale of previously owned vehicles. They usually offer vehicles that are older than those offered by new car dealers. They are unlikely to have a service department, and if they give you a warranty, its coverage is very limited. In exchange for these shortcomings, however, you will probably be able to obtain a lower price from a used car dealer than from a new car dealer.

Other used car sources are auctions and dealers that sell automobiles previously owned by government agencies, auto rental companies, and other businesses. While these automobiles were probably serviced regularly, most of them had many different drivers or, as with police vehicles, underwent extreme use. Care must be taken to avoid buying a car that seems to be in good shape but has undergone extreme use.

The Federal Trade Commission requires businesses that sell used cars to place a buyers guide sticker in the window of a car that is available for sale. This disclosure assists and protects potential buyers. It must state whether the car comes with a warranty and, if so, what specific warranty protection the dealer will provide. If no warranty is offered, the car is sold "as is" and the dealer assumes no responsibility for any repairs, regardless of any oral claims that might have been made about the car. About one half of all the used cars sold by dealers come without a warranty; this means that once you buy such a car, you must pay for any repairs that are needed to correct problems.

While a used car may not have an express warranty, most states have implied warranties that protect basic rights of the used car buyer. An implied warranty of merchantability means that the product is guaranteed to do what it is supposed to do. Thus, the used car is guaranteed to run—at least for a while!

The buyers guide required by the FTC encourages you to have the used car inspected by a mechanic and to get all promises in writing. You are also provided with a list of the 14 major systems of an automobile and some of the major problems that may occur in these systems. This list can be helpful in comparing the vehicles and warranties offered by different dealers.[3]

FTC used car regulations do not apply to vehicles purchased from private owners. This means that you must take extra care when you buy a used car through a newspaper ad or some other form of local advertising. The many used cars bought from private parties are sold "as is"; to minimize the problems that may arise from the purchase of such a car, you should carefully consider the condition of the car's major systems. Limited information may be available, but ask the seller whether you can see the receipts for maintenance and repairs.

You should follow two general rules when you buy a used car. First, buy your car from a source that gives some assurance of the car's reliability. Second, make a detailed investigation of the car's condition and performance potential.

---

[3]"Buying a Used Car," *Facts for Consumers*, Federal Trade Commission, May 1985.

Inspecting a Used Car. The appearance of a used car can be deceptive. A well-maintained engine may be found inside a body with unsightly rust; a clean, shiny exterior may be concealing some major operational problems. A used car inspection has three major phases.

The first phase is the exterior inspection. Examine the paint for signs of accidents. A magnet will indicate whether body filler has been used to repair damages. Properly fitting doors and windows are also important. Odors in the car from water leakage can indicate accident damage.

Second, a test drive is necessary. Determine whether the car will perform properly without warming up. Does it provide acceptable performance in both highway and stop-and-go city driving? During the road test, have a friend follow you to look for wobbly wheels, white or blue smoke, or other visual problems.

Third, have a mechanic check the car to estimate the costs of currently needed or potential repairs. This service will enable you to avoid surprises when the vehicle becomes yours. Many vehicle defects and much owner dissatisfaction could be avoided through careful inspections before buying. Figure 10–2 details the items that should be considered in a used car inspection.

Although federal law makes odometer tampering illegal, the problem still exists. Mileage may be turned back to give a vehicle a newer appearance. Signs of possible odometer fraud are the failure of digits to line up straight or the presence of broken plastic in the speedometer case.[4] If the brake pedal, tires, or upholstery look very old or very new for the number of miles shown on the odometer, there may have been odometer tampering.

Before making your final decision on a used car, you should find out whether there have been any safety recalls on the car you plan to buy. If so, have the necessary adjustments been made? Between 1966 and 1985, over 150 million automobiles were recalled for safety inspections and corrections. Information about recalls may be obtained from the National Highway Traffic Safety Administration, a division of the U.S. Department of Transportation. This agency has an auto safety hot line for consumers (1-800-424-9393).

Used Car Price Negotiation. The final step in buying a used car is agreeing on a price. You can begin the process of determining a fair price by checking newspaper ads for the prices of comparable vehicles. Other sources of current used car prices are *Edmund's Used Car Prices* and the National Automobile Dealers Association's *Official Used Car Guide*, commonly called the *blue book*. These publications are available at banks, credit unions, libraries, and bookstores. Since the blue book is updated monthly, some automobile sellers and buyers use the *black book*, a weekly report of automobile auction sales published by National Auto Research of Gainesville, Georgia.

The basic price of a used car is also influenced by a number of other

---

[4]"Odometer Tampering," *U.S. News & World Report,* March 10, 1986, p. 69.

FIGURE 10-2   Checking Out a Used Car

Outside the car
- Look for major dents and signs of accidents
- Inspect the trunk and spare tire
- Check tire tread wear
- Observe smoothness of springs and
    shocks when pushing down on car
- Check operation of doors and windows
- Look for leaking fluids under vehicle

Inside the car
- Look for wear on pedals and steering column
- Check for operation of dash lights
    and accessories
- Check instrument panel for operation of gauges
- Start engine and check operation of power
    accessories such as radio, wipers, heater

The engine
- Check for leakage of fluids and overheating
- Check oil level and for signs of leaks
- Check radiator cap, radiator for cracks
    and repairs, and for oil in coolant
- Check battery and cables
- Expect a smooth clean start

The road test
- Let vehicle warm up
- Test drive car on a road with which
    you are familiar
- Listen for smoothness of acceleration
    and transmission
- Check brakes at different speeds

factors. The used car guides provide information on the effect that some of these factors have on price, while the effect of other factors has to be estimated. The number of miles that the car has been driven and the car's special features and options will directly affect its price. A low-mileage car will have a higher price than a comparable car with high mileage. The overall physical condition of the car and the demand for that model will also influence its price.

Used car prices follow the trend of new car sales. If more people buy new cars and trade in or sell their present cars, the increased supply of used cars keeps their prices down. But when the demand for new cars is low and people keep their present cars longer, the prices of used cars increase.

Buying a New Car

● Strategies Involved in Buying a New Car

When you are buying a new car, the time you spend in obtaining information and the time you spend at dealers talking with salespeople and test-driving vehicles will be of value in your decision-making process. Being aware of your personal needs and desires and being able to negotiate price will also help you make a satisfying buying choice.[5]

Gathering information, selecting options for your new car, and bargaining for price are the primary phases of buying a new car.

Gathering Information. As already discussed in this chapter, consumers have a wide variety of automobile information sources. The data provided by these sources range from ratings of current models to details on the factors that should be considered in selecting a car. General Motors has even gone as far as distributing personal computer disks with new car prices and financing information.

An important source of price information is on every new car. The **sticker price** is the suggested retail price of a new car and its optional equipment displayed in printed form on the vehicle. This information label presents the base price of the car along with details about the costs of accessories and other items. The dealer's cost, or *invoice price*, is an amount less than the sticker price. The difference between the sticker price and the dealer's cost is the range available for negotiation. This range is larger for full-size, luxury cars; subcompacts do not usually have a wide negotiation range.

Information about the dealer's cost may be obtained from several sources. *Edmund's New Car Prices*, available in libraries and bookstores, is quite helpful. This publication details the negotiating ranges between the dealer's costs and the suggested selling prices of current models. More sophisticated car cost data are available from computerized services. For a fee, several organizations offer computer printouts comparing the cost and list prices of both the basic vehicle and the optional equipment of specific makes and models. Consumers Union, publisher of *Consumer Reports*, has this service available. For a minimal fee, a prospective buyer can obtain information about standard features, options, and costs. The Consumer Reports Auto Price Service is a worksheet that allows you to select the options you desire

[5]David H. Furse, Girish H. Punj, and David W. Stewart, "A Typology of Individual Search Strategies among Purchasers of New Automobiles," *Journal of Consumer Research*, March 1984, p. 426.

and to compute two totals, one for the suggested list price and the other for the dealer's cost. This information will be used to bargain for the best deal.

Also helpful in planning your purchase of a new car is a knowledge of economic conditions in the automobile industry. A monthly report of car sales is published in *The Wall Street Journal* and in the business section of newspapers. This report provides an indication of how flexible a dealer may be in the prices he charges. When automobile sales are lower than they were in previous months and years, your chances of getting a lower price are improved.

Your prospects for obtaining a favorable deal may also be influenced by the time of day, the month, and the year. You will usually get the best attention during morning or early afternoon visits to the showroom. Shopping near the end of the month may get you a better price, since salespeople may have to make a quota. Sometimes few sales are made at the beginning of the month, which gives you a chance for a bargain. Finally, while some experts recom-

---

In the News
Which Hue for You?

Automobile manufacturers conduct extensive research to determine the appeal and safety effects of vehicle color. The color of the car you select can affect the resale value of the car. Of the 50 colors used in a year, white is the most popular; other driver favorites are charcoal metallic, medium blue metallic, dark blue, silver, dark red, and bright red for sports cars.

Colors project various images. Navy blue, burgundy, and black cherry are luxury tones; yellow is sporty; and black-and-white vehicles have a classic image.

Different parts of the country demand different colors. Black cars will not sell in Florida, but the North and the Midwest demand dark colors; pastels are the favorites in warm areas.

One way to get a car whose color will increase its resale value is to select the color that matches the car color in the company ads. Research has probably been conducted to present the most eye-appealing color. So if you buy a car with that color, when you are ready to sell the car, it should appeal to many in the market.

Viewing cars on backgrounds of concrete, meadows, and snow helps you determine the safest colors. Luminous orange is the most visible color, followed by white, though white is difficult to see in snow and very bright sunshine. Other safe colors are yellow and light shades of orange, gray, and blue. Browns, greens, dark gray, dark blue, and black are difficult to see.

Source: Rich and Jean Taylor-Constantine, "Which Hue for You? Choose Carefully!" *Parade*, October 5, 1986, pp. 18–19.

mend that you buy your new car at the end of the model year (that is, in late summer), winter and early spring, when sales are very slow, have also been suggested.

Selecting Options. Luxury features are desired by most people. These options can easily increase the cost of your new automobile by several thousand dollars. Knowing what you really need, and can afford, is vital to making a wise financial decision.

The most popular optional equipment can be grouped into three categories. The first category comprises mechanical devices that improve performance and ease of operation, such as larger engines, special transmissions, power steering, power brakes, and cruise control. The second category, comfort and convenience options, includes reclining seats, air-conditioning, stereo systems, power locks, rear window defoggers, and tinted glass. The third category consists of aesthetic features that add to the vehicle's visual appeal, such as metallic paint, special trim, and plush upholstery.[6]

Several options may be available for a single price. For example, a convenience package may include power door locks, power windows, power mirror adjustment, and a push-button trunk opener. The package price may save you money, but do you want all of these items? Remember, too, that these power items will increase the operating cost of the vehicle by reducing fuel efficiency.

You may be able to save money on optional equipment by selecting the deluxe edition of a model. Items that cost extra with the basic, low-price edition may be included as standard equipment with the higher-priced limited edition. Again, be sure that you want all of the options and compare the prices of the two editions to make sure that the cost difference is justified by the additional accessories. Your willingness to accept different editions or comparable models of a different make will improve your negotiating position.

An option that you may want to do without is a service contract. This agreement can cover the cost of repairs not included in the warranty provided by the manufacturer. Service contracts range in price from $200 to over $1,000, but they do not always include everything you might expect. Most of these contracts have long lists of parts that are not covered as well as provisions that may negate the coverage of a part if the part's failure is caused by problems with an uncovered part. Failure of the engine cooling system is covered by all service contracts, but some service contracts exclude coverage of such failures if they are caused by overheating.[7]

Because of their costs and exclusions, service contracts may not be a wise financial decision. You can minimize your concern about expensive repairs by setting aside a fund of money to pay for them. Then, if repairs are needed, the money to pay for them will be available. If the automobile performs as expected, you will be able to use the money in other ways. Most

---

[6]"Options: Which to Take, Which to Leave," *Consumer Reports*, April 1986, pp. 224–25.

[7]"Auto Service Contracts," *Consumer Reports*, October 1986, p. 667.

people spend less on repair costs than they would have to spend on a service contract.

Price Bargaining. Nearly all of the consumer purchases in our society are based on set prices associated with a product or service. The buying of an automobile is one of the few situations in which you are expected to bargain for price. Price information and other data discussed earlier in this chapter will assist you in your negotiations.

You should start your price bargaining by comparing the prices of similar automobiles at several dealers. This information will provide you with background on selling prices in relation to the sticker price. Be prepared to be flexible about the kind of car you choose. Your determination to buy a certain make, model, and style will weaken your negotiating position. You must be willing to go to another dealer or to purchase a different kind of car.

Use dealer's cost information in your effort to get a vehicle price that is only a couple of hundred dollars over the dealer's cost. The closer your price is to the dealer's cost, the better the deal you are getting. Don't be fooled by an offer of a price far below the sticker price; the dealer's cost is the number that should concern you.

If a salesperson isn't willing to give you what you consider a fair price, be willing to visit another dealer or to buy a different automobile. Models in high demand may not have a wide bargaining range. In certain situations, you may even have to pay an amount above the sticker price to get the automobile you desire.

Will you receive a better deal by purchasing a car off the lot or by ordering one from the factory? The answer is not clear. Selling a car in stock helps a dealer clear inventory, but you may not get a good price deal on the car if it is in high demand among potential buyers. Moreover, the car on the lot may have options you don't want. Ordering a car means waiting several weeks or months, but it eliminates the dealer's inventory carrying cost. This arrangement could result in a lower price since the dealer is merely serving as a purchasing intermediary for your sale.

When dealing with a car salesperson, be cautious of two potential manipulative techniques. **Lowballing** occurs when a buyer is quoted a very low price that add-on costs increase before the deal is concluded. **Highballing** occurs when a new car buyer is offered a very high price for a trade-in vehicle, with the amount made up by increasing the price of the new car. To prevent confusion in determining the true price of the new car, do not mention a trade-in vehicle until the cost of the new car has been settled. Then ask how much the dealer is willing to pay for your old car. If the offer price is not acceptable, sell the old car on your own.

To avoid the time and effort involved in price bargaining, you may wish to use a **car buying service**, a business that helps a person obtain a specific vehicle at a reasonable price with little effort. Also referred to as auto brokers, these businesses offer desired models with options for a price ranging between $50 and a couple of hundred dollars over the dealer's cost. The buying process starts with the auto broker charging the customer a small fee for price information on desired models. Then, if you decide to buy a car, the auto broker arranges the purchase with a dealer near your home. An auto broker can save you time and money. Car buying services are frequently available through credit unions, churches, community organizations, and motor clubs.

Manufacturers and dealers may offer financing to assist you in your automobile purchase. Until the new car price has been set, however, you should not indicate that you intend to use the dealer's credit plan. Studies have revealed that low-cost loans are frequently offset by increased vehicle prices.

Before the sale is complete, you must sign a **sales agreement,** the legal document that contains the specific details of an automobile purchase. As with any contract, make sure that you understand the sales agreement before signing it. Also, be sure that everything you expect from the deal is presented in the sales agreement. If an item isn't in writing, you have no assurance that it will be included. Your copy of the sales agreement will be your proof, for example, if some option isn't included, or if you are charged for an option you didn't request, or if an option is inferior in quality.

The sales agreement or another receipt will serve as proof of any deposit you pay. Obtain in writing the conditions that would allow you to get back your deposit. Make your deposit as small as possible to cut your losses in case you cancel the deal and are unable to get a refund.

Financing an Automobile Purchase

- Alternatives for Financing an Automobile Purchase

Ideally, to minimize the total costs associated with purchasing and owning an automobile, you will pay cash for your car. Since automobiles are very expensive, many people buy them on credit. The efforts involved in borrowing the money needed to buy an automobile are selecting a financing source and obtaining the best deal.

Financing Sources. As discussed in Chapter 6, car loans are available from banks, credit unions, consumer finance companies, and other financial institutions. Dealer financing is another option. In an effort to make automobile buying more attractive, General Motors Acceptance Corporation, Ford Motor Credit Company, and Chrysler Financial Corporation have created new types of credit plans, such as balloon payment loans, variable rate loans, and special loans to meet the needs of recent college graduates. With a balloon payment loan, which is illegal in some states, for 48 months you make payments that are smaller than the payments on a regular loan. After 48 months, you have the option of continuing to make payments until the balance has been paid; returning the car to the dealer for a fee; or selling the car, paying off the loan, and keeping any leftover funds.[8]

Obtaining the Best Financing. The lowest interest rate or the lowest payment does not necessarily mean the best credit plan. As discussed earlier in

[8]Betsy Bauer, "Tax Change: Driving Up Car Costs," *U.S. News & World Report,* September 29, 1986, p. 62.

"Just take a look at this onboard computer. It
can figure square roots, percentages and the
interest rate of your monthly installment."

From *The Wall Street Journal*, with permission of Cartoon Features Syndicate.

this book, the annual percentage rate (APR) is the best indicator of the true
cost of credit. The federal Truth-in-Lending law requires that the APR be
clearly stated in advertising and other communications to potential borrowers. Low payments may seem like a good deal, but they mean that you will
be paying longer and that your total finance charges will be higher. Consider
both the APR and the total finance charges when you compare the credit
terms of different lenders.

Recently, automobile manufacturers offered several very low loan financing opportunities, including one at 2.9 percent for a three-year loan. They
offered rebates at the same time, giving buyers a choice between a rebate
and a low-interest loan. Although most people were taking the low-interest
financing, the rebate was more advantageous under certain conditions. It
could be used to lower the amount borrowed to buy the automobile with
financing at a bank or a credit union. In several situations, car buyers could
save money by taking the manufacturer's rebate and obtaining their own
financing.[9]

[9]Dale D. Buss, "Rebate of Loan: Car Buyers Need to Do the Math," *The Wall Street Journal*,
October 1, 1986, p. 31.

SELLING YOUR AUTOMOBILE

- Process of Selling an Automobile

At some time, you are likely to be on the selling side of an automobile transaction. Your decision to sell your car on your own may result from a low trade-in offer from a dealer combined with your belief that you can do better by yourself. The selling process starts with an awareness of the documents that must be filed with your state department vehicle registration agency. Contact this agency to obtain the necessary forms as well as information on the regulations that affect the sale of an automobile.

Use current advertisements in local newspapers along with the used car pricing guides discussed earlier in this chapter to assist you in setting a sales price. Maintenance and minor repairs will help improve your car's appearance and increase its price and customer appeal.

Next, you need to make others aware of the car. Put a "For Sale" sign with a telephone number on it. Place it in a location that will allow many people to see it. Information about the car can be distributed through stores, church, or community bulletin boards. Advertisements in local newspapers and weekly shopper newspapers will increase the number of people who are aware that the car is for sale.

Require people who are interested in buying your car to provide you with their addresses and telephone numbers, and have them make appointments to see and test-drive the car. As a precaution, be sure to accompany prospective buyers on the road test. If you have kept a file of maintenance and repair receipts, use this information to document the condition of the car. In negotiating price, consider the condition, mileage, and potential demand.

When completing the transaction, be sure that all of the necessary paperwork has been completed. To avoid getting a bad check or handling large amounts of cash, insist that the car be paid for with a cashier's check or a money order. Provide the buyer with a receipt stating the details of the transaction.

FINANCIAL ASPECTS OF AUTOMOBILE OPERATION

- Financial Aspects of Owning and Operating an Automobile

Buying a car is the beginning of your financial obligations for automobile transportation. Most people spend more of their income on an automobile and related expenses than on any other item except housing and food. For many households, when insurance, license plates, and road taxes are included, the amount spent on an automobile exceeds the amount spent on food. Over a period of 50 years, you can expect to spend nearly $200,000 on automobile costs; this is seven times as much as the average person spends on education.[10] Automobile operating costs, proper maintenance, sources of vehicle servicing, and automobile leasing are the major financial aspects of owning and operating an automobile.

Automobile Operating Costs

Your driving costs will vary based on two main factors—the size of your automobile and the number of miles you drive. The American Automobile

[10]"What Your Car Really Costs: How to Keep a Financially Safe Driving Record," *Economic Education Bulletin*, April 1985, pp. 1–2.

Association recently estimated that, given an annual mileage of 10,000, a subcompact would cost 23.1 cents a mile; a midsize car, 29.6 cents; and a full-size car, 31.2 cents.[11] These cost estimates are reached by considering two categories of expenses:

Fixed Ownership Costs	Variable Operating Costs
Depreciation	Gasoline and oil
Interest on auto loan	Tires
Insurance	Maintenance and repairs
License, registration, taxes, and fees	Parking and tolls

Fixed Ownership Costs. The largest fixed expense associated with a new automobile is **depreciation,** the loss in the vehicle's value due to time and use. Since money is not paid out for depreciation, many people do not consider it an actual expense. But this decreased value of an automobile is a cost that owners incur as they use the automobile and time goes by. Depreciation becomes a monetary cost when the vehicle is sold, traded in, or scrapped and money must be used to purchase a replacement vehicle. Not all automobiles depreciate. Very old vehicles in excellent condition may *appreciate*, or increase in value.

While depreciation is considered a fixed cost of automobile ownership, the actual amount of the decreased value depends on two factors—the amount that the automobile is used and the care that is taken to maintain it. Low-mileage, well-maintained automobiles retain a larger portion of their original value than do other automobiles. Also, certain high-quality, expensive models, such as BMWs or Cadillacs, depreciate at a slower rate than other models. Most automobile models depreciate less quickly today than was the case in earlier years. Such models as the Volvo, the Corvette, and the Camaro are reported to have a value of at least 80 percent of their original cost after five years of use.[12]

Another fixed ownership cost is the interest charge for financing your automobile purchase. This charge is based on the loan amount, the interest rate, and the length of time it will take you to pay off the loan.

Other fixed costs associated with automobile ownership are insurance, license and registration fees, and taxes. Since fixed costs are fairly constant, they are easier to anticipate than variable costs.

Variable Operating Costs. Certain expenses are directly related to the operation of an automobile and vary in relation to the amount of its use and to its age. The cost of such items as gasoline, oil, and tires increase with the

[11]*Your Driving Costs*, rev. ed. (American Automobile Association, 1986), p. 1.

[12]"What Your Car Really Costs: How to Keep a Financially Safe Driving Record," *Economic Education Bulletin*, April 1985, pp. 3, 6.

number of miles that an automobile has been driven. Planning for expenses of this kind is made easier if the number of miles you drive during a given period of time is more or less uniform. Unexpected trips will increase such costs.

As your car gets older, maintenance and repair costs usually increase. You should expect to replace such relatively low-priced components as fan belts, hoses, the battery, or the muffler. More costly repairs—for example, brake, transmission, and electrical system repairs—will also be needed. As discussed in Chapter 3, budgeting a certain amount of savings for such unplanned expenses can help minimize their financial burden. Proper maintenance is discussed later in this chapter.

Increasing outlays for maintenance and repairs can result in the decision to get another car. Despite the ability of some people to carefully maintain a car and to drive it well over 100,000 miles, at some point your car will no longer serve your needs.

Automobile Expense Records. An awareness of the total cost of owning and operating an automobile can be valuable in your overall financial planning. Figure 10–3 presents a summary of the major expenses for three sizes of automobiles.

A simple, yet complete, automobile recordkeeping system can help you control your automobile expenses. Detailed cost information can guide you in deciding when to get rid of your current vehicle and to obtain one with lower operating costs. If you use your automobile for business purposes, your records will provide a basis for calculating tax deductions.

An automobile expense record should include the dates of odometer readings. Recording your mileage each time you guy gas will allow you to compute the fuel efficiency of your car. For tax-deductible travel, the Internal Revenue Service requires specific information on the mileage, location, date, and purpose of trips. You can use a notebook to keep records of your regular operating expenses, such as gas, oil, parking, and tolls. You should also keep files on your maintenance, repair, and replacement part costs. Finally, you should record such infrequent expenditures as insurance payments and license and registration fees.

Proper Maintenance

People who sell, repair, or drive automobiles for a living say that regular vehicle care is one of the best investments you can make. While owner's manuals and articles suggest mileage or time intervals for certain servicing, more frequent oil changes or tune-ups can minimize major repair expenses and maximize the life of the car.

The systems of your car that should be monitored and maintained on a regular basis are the engine, cooling system, transmission, brakes, steering mechanism, exhaust components, and suspension. Figure 10–4 presents additional details on automobile maintenance. It is not intended to be a

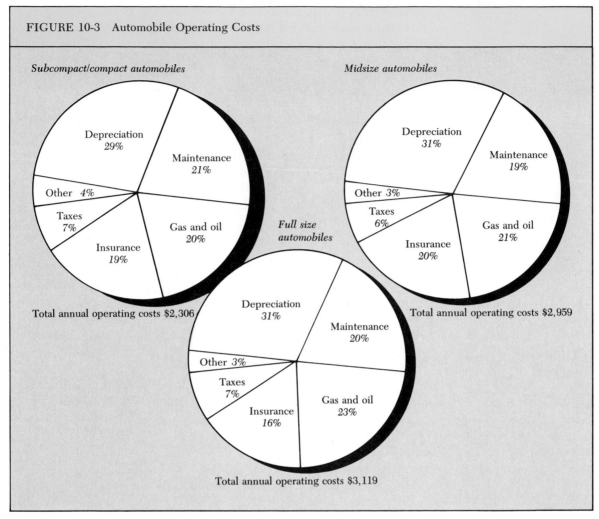

FIGURE 10-3   Automobile Operating Costs

Subcompact/compact automobiles

Depreciation
29%

Maintenance
21%

Other 4%

Taxes
7%

Gas and oil
20%

Insurance
19%

Total annual operating costs $2,306

Midsize automobiles

Depreciation
31%

Maintenance
19%

Other 3%

Taxes
6%

Gas and oil
21%

Insurance
20%

Total annual operating costs $2,959

*Full size
automobiles*

Depreciation
31%

Maintenance
20%

Other 3%

Taxes
7%

Gas and oil
23%

Insurance
16%

Total annual operating costs $3,119

Sources: *Cost of Owning and Operating Automobiles and Vans* (Washington, D.C.: Department of Transportation); and *Your Driving Costs* (American Automobile Association, 1986).

complete guide, but it should serve as a reminder of areas that could result in expensive problems.

Automobile Servicing Sources

Automobile maintenance and repair service is offered by many types of businesses, including car dealers, service stations, repair shops, department and discount stores, and specialty shops. Several precautions can be taken to get reliable, cost-efficient automobile servicing.

Car Dealers. The service department of a car dealer engages in a wide range of car care efforts. Since car dealers are required to perform routine

FIGURE 10-4   Extended Vehicle Life through Proper Maintenance

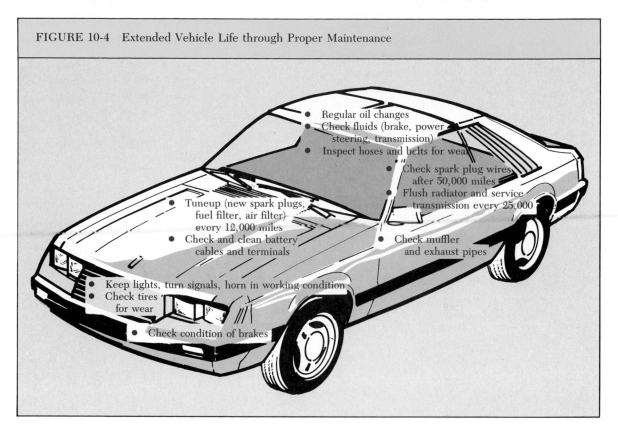

- Regular oil changes
- Check fluids (brake, power steering, transmission)
- Inspect hoses and belts for wear
- Check spark plug wires after 50,000 miles
- Flush radiator and service transmission every 25,000
- Tuneup (new spark plugs, fuel filter, air filter) every 12,000 miles
- Check and clean battery cables and terminals
- Check muffler and exhaust pipes
- Keep lights, turn signals, horn in working condition
- Check tires for wear
- Check condition of brakes

maintenance, major repairs, and body work, they have a complete inventory of parts for most vehicles. The service charges of car dealers are generally higher than those of other types of servicing facilities.

Service Stations. Local gas stations often provide convenience and reasonable prices for routine maintenance and most repair needs. The number of full-service gas stations has declined in recent years due to lower profits and competition from other types of automobile servicing businesses. Today, most people buy gas at a combination gas station and convenience food store. For automobile servicing, drivers must consider other alternatives.

Automobile Repair Shops. Independent repair shops serve a wide variety of automobile servicing needs at fairly competitive prices. As with any service, the quality of these repair shops varies. You should find out whether previous customers were satisfied before doing business with an automobile repair shop.

Department and Discount Stores. Mass merchandise retailers such as Sears, K mart, and Zayre offer convenient, low-cost automobile service. These retailers usually emphasize the sale of tires, batteries, mufflers, and other replacement parts. As required, they will also replace brakes and do oil changes or tune-ups. They offer moderate prices, but they may hire less experienced mechanics to keep their costs down.

Specialty Shops. These limited-service businesses offer a single product or maintenance effort at a reasonable price with fast, quality results. Mufflers, tires, automatic transmissions, and oil changes are among the replacement parts or services that these specialized facilities provide.

In comparing and selecting servicing sources for your automobile, consider the following:

Does the servicing source have a favorable reputation in the community?

Is it approved by the American Automobile Association (AAA), or are its mechanics certified by the National Institute for Automotive Service Excellence (NIASE)?

Will it give you a price estimate over the phone and an estimate of the time needed to complete the work?

Is it operated in an organized manner?

Does it provide written estimates and call you to approve additional repairs?

Does it offer to show you or give you the parts that it replaced?

When a major repair is involved, does it encourage you to get a second opinion?

Since automobile maintenance and repairs can be expensive, be sure to seek out competent service for the money you spend on them. To avoid unnecessary expense, be aware of the common repair frauds presented in Table 10–3.

Many individuals avoid problems and minimize costs by working on their own vehicles. This can be especially worthwhile for routine maintenance and minor repairs, such as oil changes, tune-ups, and replacement of belts, hoses, and batteries. Many books on automobile servicing are available at libraries and bookstores. Also, local high schools and colleges frequently offer courses on the basics of automobile maintenance.

Leasing instead of Buying

It may be possible to have the use of a new car without making a down payment. **Leasing** is a contractual agreement under which you make monthly payments for the use of an automobile over a set period of time—three, four, or five years. At the end of the lease term, you return the automobile to the leasing company.

Some leases require a down payment, and all leases have requirements similar to those that must be met to qualify for credit. For example, you must have a certain income and a good record of making bill payments on

TABLE 10-3   Common Automobile Repair Frauds

The vast majority of automobile servicing sources are fair and honest. But sometimes dollars are wasted when consumers fall prey to the following tricks:

When checking the oil, the attendant may put the dipstick only partway down and then use it to show you that you need oil.

An attendant can cut a fan belt or puncture a hose. Carefully watch when someone checks under your hood.

A garage employee may put some liquid on your battery and then try to convince you that it is leaking and you need a new battery.

Removing air from a tire instead of adding air to it can make an unwary driver open to buying a new tire or to paying for a patch on a tire that is in perfect condition.

The attendant may put grease by a shock absorber or on the ground and then tell you that your present shocks are dangerous and you need new ones.

You may be charged for two gallons of antifreeze with a radiator flush, when only one gallon is put in.

Dealing with reputable businesses and having a basic knowledge of your automobile are the best methods of preventing deceptive repair practices.

time. After signing a lease agreement, you are committed to making monthly payments for the term of the contract.

Lease payments are usually lower than payments on an automobile loan since at the end of the lease you return the vehicle to the leasing company. With a *closed-end* lease, the leasing agent agrees to take back the car at the end of the contract; this is the most popular arrangement. With an *open-end* lease, you may have higher-than-expected costs since you may be required to pay the difference between the value of the car in the contract and the amount for which the leasing agent sells it. Another factor that you should take into account when you are considering leasing is that the lease agreement may limit the number of miles you may drive the leased car during the lease period; more miles would result in an additional charge.

Since the lease agreement provides detailed costs for tax purposes, leasing an automobile can be beneficial to individuals who use their automobiles extensively in their work. Another advantage of leasing is that the leasing company pays for major repairs since the leased vehicle legally belongs to it. Although leasing may sound like a favorable alternative, be sure to investigate all of its costs and benefits in relation to your driving and financial situation.

AUTOMOBILE LEGAL AND SOCIAL CONCERNS

Each day, our transportation habits affect many aspects of our lives. The legal, energy, environmental, and safety concerns associated with owning and operating an automobile can influence our financial decisions with regard to transportation.

Consumer Protection

● Legal and Social
Concerns Associated
with Automobiles

New car warranties provide buyers with some assurance of quality. These warranties vary in the time and mileage of the protection and in the parts they cover. The main conditions of a warranty are the coverage of basic parts against manufacturer's defects; the power train coverage for the engine, transmission, and drivetrain; and the corrosion warranty, which usually applies only to holes due to rust, not to surface rust. Other important conditions of a warranty are a statement regarding whether the warranty is transferable to other owners of the car and details on the charges, if any, that will be made for major repairs in the form of a *deductible*.[13]

Some automobile manufacturers make free repairs or adjustments on certain parts even after the warranty period. This free service, sometimes called a *secret warranty*, is usually the result of the manufacturer's decision to correct design faults that owner complaints have brought to its attention. Ford and General Motors have established toll-free telephone numbers to communicate such information to car owners. Information on secret warranties may also be obtained from the National Highway Traffic Safety Administration.[14]

In the past, when major functional problems occurred with a new car and warranty service didn't solve the difficulty, many consumers lacked a course of action. As a result, 40 states and the District of Columbia enacted *lemon laws* that required a refund for the vehicle after the purchaser had made repeated attempts to obtain servicing. In general, these laws apply to situations in which a person has attempted four times to get the same problem corrected and to situations in which the vehicle has been out of service for more than 30 days within 12 months of purchase or the first 12,000 miles. The terms of the state laws vary, contact your state consumer protection office for details.

The lemon laws triggered the various arbitration programs of automobile manufacturers. These programs were discussed in Chapter 8. Although the manufacturers' intention was to resolve the complaints of auto buyers by means of arbitration, some critics say that these arbitration programs have not been effective for consumers since the automobile manufacturers fund and control them.[15]

Energy

Few people remember that in the early 1970s gas prices were about 32 cents a gallon. Ten years later, fuel costs stabilized at around the $1.20 to $1.30 range. There have been some moderate and drastic price drops since then, but the cost of gasoline has never returned to the price level that existed before the 1974 Middle East oil embargo.

[13]Jack Gillis, *The Car Book* (New York: Harper & Row, 1986), p. 76.

[14]Ibid., p. 75.

[15]Bridgett Davis, "Car Buyers Discover 'Lemon Laws' Often Fail to Prevent Court Trip," *The Wall Street Journal*, October 21, 1986, p. 35.

Technology for Today
A Cushion of Safety

F or more than a decade, various organizations and government agencies have been testing the air bag as a safety option for automobiles. This device, consisting of an air pillow mounted in the dashboard or on the steering wheel, is activated and inflated by nitrogen in a frontal collision (see Figure 10–5). The U.S. Department of Transportation estimates that air bags could save 7,000 lives a year.

The use of air bags has saved several lives in limited road tests and in vehicles equipped with air bags that consumers and organizations have purchased. Research has shown that air bags will not accidentally inflate when a bump is hit or when a low-speed collision occurs. Tests have been conducted in which the air bag inflated while the car was being driven. Since it inflates and starts to deflate in about ¹⁄₂₅ of a second, the test drivers were all able to keep control of the car.

All automobile manufacturers are required to offer air bags as an option on some models. In 1986, the U.S. government purchased 10,300 Ford Tempos equipped with air bags. During the same year, consumers could purchase this option on the Tempo for $815 but also had to buy an automatic transmission for $440, air-conditioning for $740, and power steering for $220. These requirements were imposed because in filling the government order, Ford had set up production facilities to build cars with these items.

The road for air bags has been slow, but they should be more readily available in the near future.

Sources: *About Air Bags* (Insurance Institute for Highway Safety, 1985); Albert R. Karr and Laurie McGinley, "Auto Shoppers Encounter Stiff Resistance when Seeking Air Bags at Ford Dealers," *The Wall Street Journal*, July 31, 1986, p. 23; and Jim Mateja, "Air Bag Tempo," *Chicago Tribune*, July 27, 1986, sec. 17, p. 1.

FIGURE 10-5   Air Bags

When a gas tank could be filled for a couple of dollars, fuel efficiency, the number of miles per gallon, was not a major consumer concern. But as gas prices rose, demand increased for automobiles that provided more miles per gallon. Since imported cars had already improved their fuel efficiency, the demand for such cars increased while consumers waited for more efficient domestic models. Today, a wide range of choices is available for those who wish to maximize gas mileage.

Each year, the Environmental Protection Agency (EPA) conducts tests to determine the fuel efficiency of automobiles sold in the United States. In 1987, the results ranged from over 50 miles a gallon for the Chevrolet Sprint ER and the Honda Civic to about 10 miles a gallon for the Rolls-Royce. EPA mileage information can guide you in selecting an automobile that will give you the fuel efficiency you desire. Since the EPA tests are conducted under laboratory conditions, the mileage you get from your car will probably differ from the EPA figure; still, the EPA data are a reliable indication of automobile fuel efficiency.

Ecology

Social concern over the impact of the automobile on the environment has resulted in mechanical changes in automobiles. An emission control device is a mechanism in an automobile that reduces air pollution from the vehicle's exhaust system. When such devices were originally mandated, they were criticized as costly and as reducing fuel efficiency. Today, there is general acceptance of emission control devices since technology has helped reduce their cost and minimize their effect on fuel efficiency. The environmental efforts of the federal government have been supplemented by the efforts of heavily populated areas such as Chicago and its suburbs, which conduct emission control tests to assure that vehicles meet required pollution control standards.

Automobile Safety

With the publication of *Unsafe at Any Speed* in the mid-1960s, Ralph Nader ushered in a new era of awareness about automobile safety. Since then, a number of efforts made by government, industry, and individual consumers have resulted in safer vehicles and fewer highway deaths and injuries.

Among these efforts were the required installation of seat belts, windshields that safely shatter into small pieces upon impact, crash-resistant fuel tanks, and warning signals to encourage seat belt use. Since less than 20 percent of automobile passengers use seat belts, the U.S. Department of Transportation proposed the installation of automatic crash protection devices, such as an inflatable air bag, to protect those involved in a frontal collision. As a compromise, state legislatures started to pass laws making seat belt use mandatory.

Another safety effort was the passage of child seat belt laws by all 50 states.

Although these laws vary by state, in general young children are required to ride in a safety seat specifically designed for transporting them in automobiles. Older children (usually over three or five years old, depending on the state) may use regular seat belts.

SUMMARY

- Your lifestyle, financial situation, and personality are the main influences on your transportation decisions.
- The main automobile information sources are industry materials, media sources, testing and rating organizations, and government agencies.
- The fundamental decisions that need to be made when you buy a car are how much to spend; what size, style, make, and model to buy; and whether to buy a used or new car.
- Buying a used car involves considering different sources of used cars, inspecting the car, and negotiating a price.
- When you are buying a new car, you should obtain vehicle and dealer cost information, select the options you desire, compare price and services at different dealers, and attempt to negotiate the best price.

- Your automobile purchase may be financed through a bank, a credit union, a consumer finance company, and other financial institutions or through dealer financing.
- Selling an automobile involves pricing the vehicle, advertising, negotiating a price, and completing the necessary legal documents.
- The fixed ownership costs of an automobile are depreciation, interest on financing, insurance, license, registration, taxes, and fees.
- The variable operating costs of an automobile are gasoline, oil, tires, maintenance, repairs, parking, and tolls.
- Warranty conditions, the arbitration process, fuel efficiency, emission control devices, and automobile safety are among the legal and social concerns of automobile owners.

GLOSSARY

Car buying service. A business that helps a person obtain a specific new car with minimal effort or at a reasonable price; also called an auto broker.

Depreciation. The loss in value of an automobile—or other asset—due to time and use.

Emission control device. A mechanism in an automobile that reduces air pollution from the vehicle's exhaust system.

Fuel efficiency. The number of miles per gallon obtained by an automobile.

Highballing. A sales technique in which a high price is offered for a trade-in vehicle, with the amount made up by increasing the price of the new automobile.

Leasing. A contractual agreement under which a person makes monthly payments for the use of an automobile over a set period of time.

Lowballing. A sales technique in which a buyer is quoted a very low price that add-on costs increase before the deal is concluded.

Mass transit.   Systems of public transportation such as bus or train lines, that allow the fast, efficient movement of many people.

Sales agreement.   The legal document that contains the specific details of an automobile purchase.

Sticker price.   The suggested retail price of a new automobile and its optional equipment displayed in printed form on the vehicle.

REVIEW QUESTIONS

1. How does a person's lifestyle affect his or her transportation needs?

2. What factors influence a person's decision to use public transportation?

3. What basic decisions must you make when you decide to buy a car?

4. What are the advantages of each of the sources of used cars?

5. What process for inspecting a used car is recommended?

6. What factors influence the value of a used car?

7. How is the sticker price of an automobile used in negotiating the price you will pay?

8. What actions should you take when selling a car?

9. How does the size of a car affect its operating costs?

10. What are the main costs associated with owning and operating an automobile?

11. What are the benefits of the various types of automotive service businesses?

12. Who could benefit from leasing an automobile instead of buying one?

13. What purpose do *lemon laws* serve?

14. What actions have been taken to improve the safety of automobiles?

DISCUSSION QUESTIONS AND ACTIVITIES

1. What personal or financial changes could occur in Brad and Barbara Mahoney's lives that might create a need to purchase an automobile?

2. Is having four cars in the Hamlin family based on needs, lifestyle, or financial factors? Do you see any alternatives for the Hamlins?

3. Should federal or local governments take actions to limit the use of automobiles in highly populated areas? Explain your answer.

4. Talk to people who regularly use public transportation. Find out why they use it. How does their transportation budget compare with that of people who use an automobile as their primary means of transportation?

5. Compare the prices of used cars at several businesses. What factors account for any differences in the prices these businesses charge for similar cars?

6. Ask some friends or relatives to share with you their experiences in buying new cars. What did they do to get the best deal?

7. Since no money is paid for depreciation, should it be considered an operating cost of a car? Explain your answer.

8. What types of preventive maintenance are likely to extend the life of an automobile?

9. Compare the cost of buying and installing a new battery, a muffler, shock absorbers, or tires at different automotive service businesses.

10. What types of automobile safety features might be considered as options to offer car buyers?

ADDITIONAL READINGS

"Annual Auto Issue." *Consumer Reports*. April of each year.

Gillis, Jack. *The Car Book*. New York: Harper & Row, 1986.

What Your Car Really Costs. Great Barrington, Mass.: American Institute for Economic Research, 1985.

Your Automobile Dollar. Prospect Heights, Ill.: Money Management Institute, Household Financial Services.

CASE 10–1 Should Shelly Drive?

Shelly Carlton uses a two-year-old car to travel to her office management job, a trip of about four miles each way. About twice a month, Shelly drives to another city for regional staff meetings. In addition to gas and other operating costs, Shelly pays a daily parking fee of $4.50. In contrast, monthly public transportation tickets are $42 and allow unlimited travel for 30 days on the city transit system. Even though public transportation offers obvious cost savings for Shelly, she prefers to drive to work.

Questions

1. What factors may have influenced Shelly's decision to drive to work?

2. How much could Shelly save each month if she used public transportation?

3. If Shelly decided to sell her car, how would her living expenses change? How could not having a car affect her job situation?

CASE 10–2 The Garrisons Pick a Car

Kathy and Bill Garrison needed a new car. Their current automobile was seven years old, had been driven 93,000 miles, and needed major repairs. They had $2,700 for a down payment. After talking with several friends and visiting three new car dealers, the Garrisons couldn't decide what type of car to buy and how much they should spend. A few days later, however, Kathy and Bill decided to buy a full-size car that cost $15,000.

Questions

1. What additional actions could the Garrisons have taken before deciding to buy a new car?

2. What car buying alternatives were not used by Kathy and Bill?

3. What financial factors did the Garrisons forget to consider?

4. For future car buying, what suggestions would you make to the Garrisons?

Comprehensive Case for Part Three
Buy the Way!

After 16 years of school, during which he depended on his parents, Jerry Nelson was starting his own household. He rented a one-bedroom apartment that was eight miles away from the company he worked for as an assistant product manager. Some furniture, dishes, towels, and linens that he was able to obtain from his parents and friends helped reduce his move-in costs. He planned to use some of the $1,100 he had in savings to buy additional furniture, decorations for his apartment, and new speakers for his stereo.

Jerry realized that before making these planned household purchases, he had to budget for transportation costs. Currently, he was driving a seven-year-old car that needed major repairs. He was thinking about using his savings for a down payment on a car that was in better condition. In the process of examining purchasing alternatives, he found the following ads for cars that seemed to meet his needs:

If he selected the vehicle in the first ad, the financing could be handled through the dealer's financing plan. Otherwise, he would use a bank or a credit union to finance the automobile purchase.

Beside budgeting transportation costs, Jerry had to budget money for food and to take the time and effort needed to go grocery shopping. While eating at various types of restaurants was convenient, even the fast-food restaurants were more costly than eating at home. Jerry usually went to the grocery store whenever he needed something. He didn't shop consistently at any one store but would shop at the store nearest to the location of the activity in which he happened to be engaged. When selecting brands, he chose the items with which he was most familiar.

Besides budgeting various household, automobile, and food costs, Jerry had to budget other expenses,

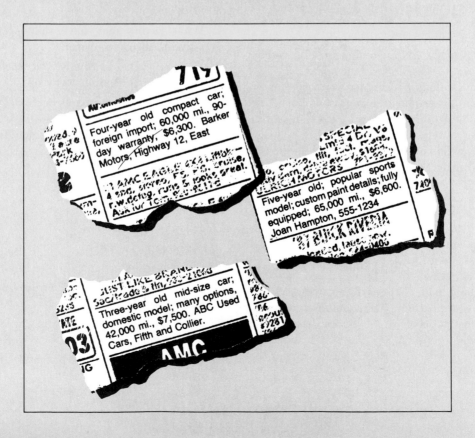

such as electricity and telephone bills. He also had to buy clothing appropriate for his job.

Financial independence can be very pleasant and enjoyable, but it is expensive. Just when you think you've got all your expenses covered, it's time to make your automobile payment, to meet your apartment insurance premium, or to buy your mother a birthday gift.

Questions

1. What will influence Jerry's priorities in spending his available funds?

2. Other than personal experience, how can a person anticipate the types and amounts of expenses for housing, transportation, food, clothing, and other necessities that he or she will encounter?

3. Prepare a list of items and costs that are necessary to start living on your own.

4. What actions should Jerry take before deciding on which car to buy? Should he keep the car he now has, or should he buy a different one?

5. What food-buying habits should Jerry develop?

6. How will Jerry's spending affect his overall financial existence and his future financial security?

PART FOUR

Protecting Your Resources

Part Four of *Personal Finance* is meant to help you protect your resources. We begin with an overview of insurance and its importance in our daily lives. We suggest how you can plan your personal insurance program and what steps you should take to purchase your insurance coverage. Then we discuss home and automobile insurance. Next we examine health care and medical insurance—the types of health insurance coverages, their benefits and limitations. Finally, we cover the important topic of life insurance—its mean-ing, history, purpose, and principle. We conclude by discussing the different types of life insurance policies, their important provisions, and the steps you should take in buying life insurance. Included in this part are:

11

The Nature of Insurance

Insurance deals with property and people. The beneficial impact of insurance on people and businesses in America is so great that we can hardly imagine how our society would function without it. By providing protection against the many risks of financial uncertainty and unexpected losses, insurance makes it possible for people to plan confidently for the future.

After studying this chapter, you will be able to:

- Explain the meaning of insurance.

- Outline the history of insurance.

- Interpret the nature of insurance.

- Define risk management and explain the methods of managing risk.

- Assess the bases of insurance.

- Plan your personal insurance program.

- Purchase your insurance coverage intelligently.

Interview with **Joseph G. Bonnice,**
Assistant Professor of Marketing, Manhattan College

Joseph G. Bonnice is currently an Assistant Professor of Marketing at Manhattan College and also teaches at the College of Insurance. Dr. Bonnice previously served as the Director of Education for the Insurance Information Institute. He is the author of several publications on insurance and risk management.

Insurance is just one part of an overall risk management program involving three steps: (1) identify risks; (2) analyze risks; and (3) control risks. These three steps are the same for a multimillion-dollar company as for an individual or a family.

In the first step of risk management, you should attempt to identify *all* of the potential risks that you face in your situation. Some people will recognize a risk only after they experience a financial loss; this can be a very expensive way of identifying risks. Instead, conduct an investigation that will help you anticipate all of the risks presented by your personal situation.

In the analysis step of risk management, Dr. Bonnice suggests looking at the frequency and severity of a risk or potential loss. It would be rather impractical to insure high-frequency, low-severity events, such as employee theft of paper clips. But your potential losses from low-frequency, high-severity risks, such as being named in a liability lawsuit, require careful analysis.

Finally, you have several options for controlling risks. You can *reduce risks* by actions, such as using a home security system or practicing careful health habits; you can *retain risks* by not taking any special action with regard to them; you can *accept part of risks* by buying insurance with a deductible or by choosing the upper limit of an insurance policy; or you can *transfer risks* to an insurance company.

The process of risk management and insurance planning is vital to financial success. Yet many individuals seem to proceed on the mistaken assumption that "it can never happen to me—it only happens to someone else."

Connie Schnoebelen bristled when she recalled the ad in her church bulletin. It promised up to $25,000 in low-interest student loans for college without a lot of hassle. "It sounded too good to be true," she said.

And she was right. Ms. Schnoebelen, who with her husband ran a small printing company in Des Moines, Iowa, soon discovered that the ad really sold life insurance to parishioners. The Schnoebelens found a loan for their daughter's education elsewhere.

Once in the door, insurance agents frequently link insurance policies with student loans. Witness the case of Ava Measels, a secretary in Carlisle, Arkansas. She purchased $30,000 in life insurance only because an agent told her that she required the insurance in order to get a loan for her daughter's education. But the college later rejected the loan because the Measels' income was too high, although the agent had insisted that the family would qualify. Ms. Measels demanded her $397 premium from the insurance company and eventually got it back.

David Hatton, 20, who also bought insurance to get a loan, complained of high-pressure sales tactics by an agent. Mr. Hatton, who wanted to study computer science at Indiana University, later discovered

INSURANCE: AN INTRODUCTION

- Meaning of Insurance

Your decisions about insurance will be easier if you keep a few fundamentals in mind. First, you should know what insurance is supposed to do. Basically, its purpose is to help protect you and your family against financial hardship due to hazard, accident, death, and the like. Rebuilding your home after a fire, paying a large court judgment, or providing for your family in the event of your early death may require more money than you have. Dealing with damage to your car or theft of your property, however, may be within your means.

To select the right insurance, then, you must know your risks. Start by looking at your property and your family responsibilities. Think about the chances of mishaps or events that could cause major trouble or expense. It is wise to insure against them. Do not insure against little losses that will not hurt. Unless yours is one of the few families that can afford all the protection they need, you should insure the greater risks first.

A little study before you see an insurance agent will help you make your money go as far as it can in fitting you with proper insurance. An agent will answer questions and advise you on details, but the final decision is yours. You can choose from many kinds of insurance. Figuring out how much insurance you need and how much you can spend for it will help you decide which kind to buy. If your financial resources are extremely limited, for example, you might consider temporary (term) insurance on your life.

that he didn't need the $300 policy for the loan, so he stopped payment on the check. Within days, the agent and an insurance executive visited him. "They tried to rush me [to reconsider] because they said there were all kinds of other people who want the money." Mr. Hatton, a data processing clerk for the Indiana state police, later complained to the Indiana insurance department.

Such selling ploys gall some insurance industry officials. Misusing the loan program is "an example of life insurance sales practices at their worst," said Robert MacDonald, president of ITT Life Insurance Company, who turned down three proposals by independent brokers to offer student loans. "Our incentive was to be millions in new insurance premiums," Mr. MacDonald recalled. "We rejected the scheme on the basis that, at best, it was confusing and deceptive and, at worst, immoral and illegal."

In this chapter, you will learn, among other things, what insurance is and how to choose an insurance agent and an insurance company.

*Adapted from Richard Gibson, "Insurers Forcing People to Buy Policy to Qualify for Student Loan," *The Wall Street Journal*, September 10, 1985, p. 33.

How much insurance you buy depends largely on what you can afford. Young families can seldom buy all the insurance they need. However, you should aim at an amount that will give you the money you need to live on and pay sickness, funeral, or other expenses—keeping in mind other sources of income that you will be able to fall back on, such as savings and social security benefits. Then you should buy what you can.

Choosing the amounts and kinds of insurance that fit your needs will take continued study. Insurance problems will always be with you as your situation and responsibilities change. That usually makes it desirable to choose an agent in whom you have full confidence and with whom you can work out a sensible insurance program. The agents recommended by your parents, friends, relatives, neighbors, or bankers are likely to be the best for you.

What Insurance Is

Insurance is protection. Although there are many types of insurance, they all have one thing in common—they give you the peace of mind that comes from knowing that money will be available to meet the needs of your survivors, to pay medical expenses, to protect your home and belongings, and to cover personal or property damage caused by your car. Thus, the principle of all insurance is the same: it protects people against possible financial loss.

Life insurance replaces income that would be lost if the policyholder should die. Health insurance helps meet medical expenses when the policyholder gets sick or helps replace income lost when illness makes it impossible for the policyholder to work. Automobile insurance helps cover property and personal damage caused by the policyholder's car.

What an Insurance Company Is

An **insurance company,** or **insurer,** is a risk-sharing firm that agrees to assume financial responsibility for losses that may result from an insured risk. A person joins the risk-sharing group (the insurance company) by purchasing a contract (a **policy**). Under the policy, the insurance company agrees to assume the risk for a fee (the **premium**) paid periodically by the person (the **insured** or the **policyholder**).

Generally, an insurance policy is written for a period of one year. Then, if both parties are willing, it is renewed for a year. It specifies the risks that are covered by the policy, the dollar amounts that the insurer will pay in case of a loss, and the amount of the premium.

EARLY INSURANCE DEVELOPMENTS[1]

- History of Insurance

The insurance policy is a relatively recent development. The concept of insurance, however, is not new. The idea of transferring the risk of loss from the individual to a group originated thousands of years ago. When a family's hut burned down, for instance, the entire tribe would rebuild it. Traces of rudimentary insurance practices may be seen among the few primitive tribes that still exist.

The first American insurance company, the Friendly Society for the Mutual Insuring of Houses against Fire, was formed in 1735. A fire in 1740 put it out of business.

In 1752, Benjamin Franklin was instrumental in founding a fire insurance company, the Philadelphia Contributorship for the Insurance of Houses from Loss by Fire. Also known as Hand in Hand, it is America's oldest continuously operated fire insurance company. The Insurance Company of North America, founded in 1792, was the first U.S. insurance company to underwrite large risks. By the close of the 18th century, 14 insurance companies had been formed in the United States.

NATURE OF INSURANCE

You face risks every day. You can't cross the street without some danger that you'll be hit by a car. You can't own property without taking the chance that it may be lost, stolen, damaged, or destroyed. Insurance companies offer financial protection against such dangers and losses by promising to

[1]This section is adapted from *Insurance Handbook for Reporters,* 2nd ed. (Allstate Insurance Group, 1985), p. 20. © Allstate Insurance Group, 1985. Authorization is granted to use information in this book with attribution, when appropriate, to Allstate Insurance Company, Northbrook, Il. 60062.

Nature of Insurance

compensate the insured for a relatively large loss in return for the payment of a much smaller, but certain, expense, called the premium.

Risk, *peril*, and *hazard* are important terms in insurance. While in popular use these terms tend to be interchangeable, each of them has a distinct, technical meaning in insurance.

Risk refers to the uncertainty as to loss that faces a person or property covered by insurance. Uncertainty of loss exists for the insured. Insurance companies frequently refer to the person or property insured as the risk.

Peril is the cause of a possible loss. It is the contingency that causes someone to take out insurance. People buy policies for financial protection against such perils as fire, windstorm, explosion, robbery, and accident.

Hazard increases the likelihood of loss through some peril. For example, defective house wiring is a hazard that increases the likelihood of the peril of fire.

Types of Risks

The most common risks are classified as personal risks, property risks, and liability risks.

Personal risks are the uncertainties surrounding loss of income or life due to premature death, illness, disability, old age, and unemployment.

Property risks are the uncertainties of direct or indirect losses to personal or real property due to fire, wind, accident, theft, and other hazards.

Liability risks are possible losses due to negligence resulting in bodily harm or property damage to others. Such harm or damage could be caused by an automobile, professional misconduct, injury on one's property, and so on.

Personal risks, property risks, and liability risks are types of **pure risk** (see Figure 11–1), or insurable risk, since there would always be a chance of loss if the specified events occurred. Pure risks are accidental and unintentional. The nature and financial cost of the loss can be predicted. These risks are insurable.

A **speculative risk** is one in which there is a chance of either loss or gain. Starting a small business that may or may not succeed is an example of speculative risk. So is gambling. Speculative risks are legally defined as uninsurable.

RISK MANAGEMENT

Risk management is an organized strategy for protecting and conserving assets and people. It helps reduce financial losses caused by destructive or damaging events. Risk management is a long-range planning process. The risk management needs of people change at various points in the life cycle. If you understand risks and how to manage them, you can provide better protection for yourself and your family against the effects of personal risks, property risks, and liability risks. In this way, you can reduce your financial losses and thereby improve your chances for economic, social, physical and emotional well-being throughout life. Since most families cannot afford to cover all risks, they need to understand how to obtain the best protection

Methods of Risk Management

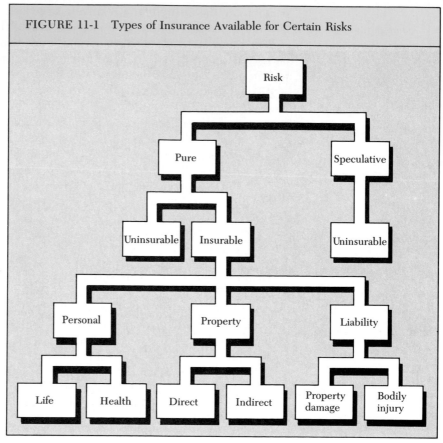

FIGURE 11-1   Types of Insurance Available for Certain Risks

Source: David L. Bickelhaupt, *General Insurance*, 11th ed. (Homewood, Ill.: Richard D. Irwin, 1979), p. 11. Copyright 1983, Richard D. Irwin, Inc.

that they can afford. A combination of strategic alternatives to cover major risks is usually advisable. Figure 11–1 shows what types of insurance are available to cover certain risks.

Methods of Managing Risk[2]

Most people think of risk management as buying insurance. But insurance is not the only method of dealing with risk, and in certain situations other methods may be less costly. In this section, we will discuss the five general risk management techniques.

Risk Avoidance. You can avoid the risk of an automobile accident by not riding in a car. General Motors can avoid the risk of product failure by not introducing new models. Risk avoidance would be practiced in both in-

[2]Adapted from Robert J. Hughes and Jack R. Kapoor, *Business* (Boston: Houghton Mifflin, 1985), pp. 479–81. © 1985 Houghton Mifflin Company.

stances, but at a very high cost. You might have to give up your job, and General Motors might lose out to competitors that introduce new models.

There are, however, situations in which risk avoidance is a practical technique. At the personal level, individuals avoid risks by not smoking or by not walking through high-crime neighborhoods. At the business level, jewelry stores avoid losses through robbery by locking their merchandise in vaults before closing. Obviously, no person or business can avoid all risks. By the same token, however, no one should assume that all risks are unavoidable.

Risk Reduction. It may be possible to reduce risks that cannot be avoided. You can reduce the risk of injury in an auto accident by wearing a seat belt. You can install smoke alarms and fire extinguishers to protect life and reduce potential damage in case of fire.

Risk Assumption. Risk assumption is the act of taking on responsibility for the loss or injury that may result from a risk. Generally, it makes sense to assume a risk when the potential loss is too small to worry about, when effective risk management has reduced the risk, when insurance coverage is too expensive, and when there is no other way of obtaining protection against a loss. For instance, you might decide not to purchase collision insurance on an older car. Then, if an accident occurs, you would bear the costs of fixing the car.

Risk Pooling. Pooling is cooperative participation to spread expenses from losses among a group of people (the pool). This reduces the cost of risk coverage to individuals. Group life insurance and health insurance plans are examples of pooling.

Risk Shifting. The most common method of dealing with risk is to shift, or transfer, it to an insurance company or some other organization.

Figure 11–2 summarizes various risks and appropriate strategies for managing them.

INSURANCE IN OPERATION[3]

- Bases of Insurance

Insurance is not a gamble. It provides protection because it is based on proven principles—on truths or rules of science that explain how things act. These principles are supported by extensive records that insurance companies have kept for many decades. The principles, or laws, include human mortality, probability, and the law of large numbers.

Human Mortality

As you will see in Chapter 14, life insurance companies compile their own mortality tables, based on their own experiences with their policyholders, and these tables are revised regularly. It is from these tables that such companies secure the basic data they need in order to establish the cost of life insurance.

[3]Condensed from Robert I. Mehr, *Fundamentals of Insurance* (Homewood, Ill.: Richard D. Irwin, 1986), pp. 38–39. Copyright 1986, Richard D. Irwin, Inc.

FIGURE 11-2   Examples of Risks and Risk Management Strategies

| Risks | | Strategies for Reducing Financial Impact | | |
Personal Events	Financial Impact	Personal Resources	Private Sector	Public Sector
Disability	Loss of one income Loss of services Increased expenses Other losses	Savings, investments Family observing safety precautions Other resources	Disability insurance Other strategies	Disability insurance

Illness	Loss of one income
	Catastrophic hospital
	    expenses
	Other losses
		Health-enhancing
		    behavior
			Health insurance
			Health maintenance
			    organizations
			Other strategies
				Military health
				Medicare, Medicaid

Death	Loss of one income
	Loss of services
	Final expenses
	Other expenses
		Estate planning
		Risk reduction
		Other resources
			Life insurance
			Other strategies
				Veteran's life
				    insurance
				Social security
				    survivor's benefit

Retirement	Decreased income
	Other expenses
		Savings
		Investments
		Hobbies, skills
		Other resources
			Retirement and/or
			    pensions
			Other strategies
				Social security
				Pension plan for
				    government
				    employees

Property loss	Catastrophic storm
	    damage to property
	Repair or replace-
	    ment cost of theft
		Property repair and
		    upkeep
		Security plans
		Other resources
			Automobile insurance
			Homeowners insurance
			Flood insurance
			    (joint program
			    with government)
				Flood insurance
				    (joint program
				    with business)

Liability	Claims and settle-
	    ment costs
	Lawsuits and legal
	    expenses
	Loss of personal
	    assets and income
	Other expenses
		Observing safety
		    precautions
		Maintaining property
		Other resources
			Homeowners insurance
			Automobile insurance
			Malpractice insurance
			Other strategies	

Source: *Personal and Family Financial Planning: A Staff Development Workshop for Secondary School Trainers and Teachers* (Washington, D.C.: American Council of Life Insurance, 1983), p. vi/13d.

Probability and the Law of Large Numbers

At first glance, it may seem strange that a combination of individual risks would result in the reduction of total risk. The principle that explains this phenomenon is called the **law of large numbers**, sometimes loosely termed the law of averages or the law of probability. However, the law of large numbers is only a part of the subject of probability, which is not a law but a field of mathematics.

Probability is the mathematics of chance. The word *chance* is one we use very frequently. Like many words, it is used in a variety of ways. We may say that we took a chance crossing the street or that we took a chance on a raffle. We discuss the chances that a football team will win their next game or that our next missile will reach the moon. We may say "I haven't a chance of getting an A" or "I'm sure the professor wouldn't give us a test today." However, the notion of chance is given a definite mathematical meaning when we define probability.

In order to set premiums, an insurance company must know how to measure the risks against which people are buying insurance. A fire insurance company must have some way of knowing how many fires will occur. An automobile insurance company must be able to predict the number of accidents involving injury, loss of life, and property damage. A life insurance company must know what the expected number of deaths will be in a given group of policyholders.

How will these companies make their estimates? How will they estimate the probability that (1) an 18-year-old male driver will be involved in an automobile accident this year? (2) a new all-brick house in your community will burn? (3) a 70-year-old man will be hospitalized this year? (4) a 16-year-old person will die before reaching age 17?

In order to arrive at such estimates, data must be collected. The automobile insurance company has to gather data on 18-year-old male drivers in order to find out how many accidents this group of drivers has. The fire insurance company must compile statistics on fires among all-brick houses in communities with good fire departments. The life insurance company must have statistics that show how many 16-year-olds die.

Data for the above probabilities must be based on large numbers of events. The law of large numbers assumes that seemingly chance incidents actually have a predictable pattern if enough such incidents are observed. This means that the longer the number insured for a particular risk are observed, the more accurately the expected losses can be predicted.

Consider the experiment of tossing a coin. There are two possible outcomes: heads or tails. It seems reasonable to assume that each of these two events is equally likely to happen. Based on this assumption, we state that the probability of heads is one half and that the probability of tails is also one half. But if we toss a coin only six times, we may not get three heads and three tails. However, if we toss the same coin 1,000 times, the probability of getting approximately 500 heads and 500 tails becomes a reality. The mathematical law of large number prevails only if there are a large number of coin tosses. Coin tossing is a very old human activity, and most of us tossed coins long before we ever reached the stage of talking about probability.

The **actuary** makes all of the probability calculations used by insurance companies. Actuaries are highly specialized insurance company mathematicians who have been professionally trained in the risk aspects of insurance. Their functions include determining proper insurance rates and conducting various aspects of insurance research. Interested in being an actuary? Read the accompanying boxed feature.

Principle of Indemnity

Indemnity is a legal doctrine that limits recovery under an insurance policy to the lesser of the actual cash value of a loss or the amount that will

Careers in Personal Finance
The Actuarial Profession

To choose a career intelligently, you must know and understand yourself and your interests, abilities, and ambitions. And then you must select a type of work that will provide a satisfying outlet for your talents and energy. If you are skilled in math and are looking for a career in which you can make a worthwhile contribution to society, consider becoming an actuary. Actuaries work with facts, figures, and people, and they must possess the curiosity and drive needed to find answers to complex questions.

An actuary is a business professional who uses mathematical skills to define, analyze, and solve business and social problems. Actuaries are disciplined problem solvers who create and manage insurance and pension programs to reduce the financial impact of the expected and unexpected things that happen to people, such as illnesses, accidents, unemployment, and premature death. That's why people buy insurance and participate in pension plans—to protect themselves financially.

College training is not specifically required to become an actuary, but such training is almost essential to pass the actuarial examinations you'll have to take for professional qualification. Good all-around preparation for an actuarial career is a mathematics or statistics major, a business administration major with a math or statistics minor, or an economics major with a math or statistics minor. Your math courses should include calculus, probability, and statistics. Some colleges and universities have specific undergraduate or graduate programs in actuarial science.

Actuarial salaries compare favorably with salaries in other professions that require similar skills and training. In the actuarial profession, as in any profession, certain factors will help determine your salary. These are:

- Your own ability, imagination, creativity, and integrity.
- Your education and experience, and how well you apply them.
- Your employer—whether you work in private industry, government, consulting, education, or for yourself.
- The law of supply and demand.

Actuarial salaries vary geographically, but broadly estimated salary ranges in 1985 indicated the following earning potential at various experience levels:

No exams	$18,000–$21,000
One exam	$20,000–$23,000
Two exams	$22,000–$25,000
Three exams	$24,000–$28,000
SOA new associates (five exams)	$30,000–$35,000
CAS new associates (seven exams)	$31,500–$42,000
SOA associates (six or more exams, five years' experience)	$35,000–$40,000
CAS and SOA new fellows (10 exams)	$40,000–$50,000
Fellows (several years' experience)	$55,000 and up

Source: *The Actuarial Profession* (Itasca, Ill.: Casualty Actuarial Society and Society of Actuaries, 1985), pp. 4–10.

restore the insured to his or her financial position prior to the loss. To indemnify is to restore lost value or to compensate for damage or loss sustained. Property and liability insurance contracts, for example, are contracts of indemnity; they provide for the compensation of the amount of loss or damage. Thus, if you have insured your house with a market value of $90,000 for $120,000 and the house burns down, the most that an insurance company will reimburse you is $90,000, not $120,000. Consequently, there is no point in insuring any item for more than its value.

An important principle stems from the doctrine of indemnity; this principle is known as insurable interest.

Insurable Interest

The principle of *insurable interest* is basic to the structure of insurance. In property insurance, an exposure to a financial loss must exist to create an insurable interest. The law requires an insurable interest so that insurance policies are neither gambling devices nor tools for those who would profit deliberately from destroying the property of others. In life insurance, an insurable interest is any reasonable expectation of financial loss caused by the death of the person whose life is insured. Thus, husband and wife, partners in a hardware store, the lender of a home mortgage, and parents and their children have an insurable interest in a life insurance policy. But college roommates and an employer and most employees do not have an insurable interest in a life insurance policy because the death of a roommate or an employee does not cause a financial loss to the other roommate or the employer. Related to the principle of insurable interest is the concept of insurable risk.

Insurable Risk

As discussed earlier, only pure risks (not speculative risks) are insurable. Insurable risks have the following characteristics: they are common, definite, accidental, not catastrophic, not trivial, calculable, and economically affordable.

Insurable Risks Are Common to a Large Number of People. For example, a fire insurance company cannot write insurance covering only 100 or 150 homeowners for loss of their homes. Remember, the law of large numbers plays a vital role in insurance. In life insurance, many persons are needed in each age, health, and occupational classification.

Insurable Risks Are Definite. The loss should be difficult to counterfeit. Death comes closest to perfection in meeting this criterion. An insured can collect disability insurance more easily from an automobile accident than from illness, because auto accident disability is more definite.

Insurable Risks Are Accidental or Fortuitous. The loss should be beyond the control of the insured. An insured will not collect insurance by deliberately setting his or her house on fire. The beneficiary of a life insurance will not collect if the insured commits suicide, because the death was not accidental or fortuitous.

Insurable Risks Frequently Do Not Cause Catastrophic Loss. Losses must be individually random; that is, no loss can be connected with any other loss. No insurer can afford to write insurance for a type of loss that is likely to happen to a large percentage of insureds. A life insurer would go bankrupt if all its policyholders died prematurely, as would a fire insurer whose policyholders all lost their homes by fire. That's why catastrophic losses, such as mass destruction of property and life in a war, are not insurable. Life insurers insert war clauses in new policies when war seems imminent.

Insurable Risks Are Not Trivial. The peril covered by insurance should be capable of producing a loss so large that the insured could not bear it without financial hardship. For example, you would not buy a life insurance policy on your pet parakeet or insurance against breakage of a shoestring. The loss involved is too small to warrant the time, effort, and expense necessary to insure against the occurrence.

Insurable Risks Are Calculable. Some probabilities can be determined by logic alone—for example, the probabilities in the flip of a coin, discussed earlier. Others must be determined by tabulating experience and projecting that experience into the future. Mortality tables, for example, are tabulations of past experiences that are used to calculate the number of deaths for a group of people of the same age, sex, and so forth.

Some chances of loss, however, are incalculable—that is, they cannot be determined either by logic or from experience. Unemployment is an example of an incalculable cost, because it occurs with such irregularity that no one has yet succeeded in determining its future incidence. In such cases, insurers rely heavily on subjective rather than objective probabilities in estimating the chance of loss.

Insurable Risks Are Economically Affordable. Theoretically, an insurance company could issue a life insurance policy to a 99-year-old male. But the premium (the cost) would be so prohibitive that the policy would be neither feasible for the insured nor practical for the insurer—because the law of large numbers is inoperative at that age level.

PLANNING A PERSONAL INSURANCE PROGRAM

Because each individual and each family has its own needs and goals—many of which change over the years—a financial security insurance program should be tailored to those needs and goals and to the changes they undergo.

If you buy a pair of shoes, for example, you know it will fit because the size is right. But the feet of people who wear the same size of shoes differ somewhat. So if your shoes were custom made, you would give more attention to making sure that each part of the shoes fitted you exactly. The same is true of a well-planned insurance program.

● Planning Your
Personal Insurance
Program

In the early years of marriage, when the children are young and the family is growing, most families need certain kinds of insurance protection. This protection may include fire insurance on an apartment or a house, life and disability insurance for the breadwinner, and adequate health insurance (with maternity benefits for the wife) for the whole family.

Later, when the family has a higher income and different financial requirements, its protection needs will change. There will be long-range provision for the children's education, more life insurance to match higher income and living standards, and revised health insurance protection. Still later, when the children have grown and are on their own, there will be consideration of retirement benefits, further changing the family's personal insurance program.

In the accompanying boxed feature, we suggest several guidelines to follow in planning your insurance program.

Set Your Goals[4]

In managing risks, your goals are to minimize personal, property, and liability risks. Your insurance goals should define what you expect to do about covering the basic risks present in your life situations. Covering the

[4]*Life and Health Insurance: A Teaching Manual* (Washington, D.C.: American Council of Life Insurance, Health Insurance Association of America, 1986), p. 11/16. Copyright 1986, ACLI.

In the Real World
How Can You Plan an Insurance Program?

 Seek advice from a competent and reliable insurance adviser.

Determine what insurance is required to provide the family with sufficient protection if the breadwinner dies.

Consider what portion of the needed family protection is met by social security and by group insurance, if any.

Decide what other needs must be met by insurance (funeral expenses, savings, retirement annuities, etc.).

Decide what types of insurance best meet your needs.

Plan on an insurance program and stick to it except for periodic reviews of changing needs and changing conditions.

Don't buy more insurance than you need or can afford.

Don't drop one policy for another.

basic risks means providing a financial resource to cover costs resulting from a loss.

Suppose your goal is to buy a new car. You must plan to make the purchase and to protect yourself. Auto insurance on the car lets you enjoy the car without worrying that an auto accident might leave you worse off, financially and physically, than before.

Each individual has unique goals. Social attitudes, income, age, family size, experience, and responsibilities enter into the goals you set—and the insurance you buy must reflect those goals. In general, financial advisers say that a basic risk management plan must set goals to reduce:

1.   Potential loss of income due to the premature death, illness, accident, unemployment, or old age of a wage earner.
2.   Potential loss of income and extra expense resulting from illness, disability, or the death of a spouse.
3.   Additional expenses due to the injury, illness, or death of other family members.
4.   Potential loss of real or personal property due to fire, theft, and other hazards.
5.   Potential loss of income, savings, and property due to personal liability.

Plan to Reach Your Goals

Planning is a sign of maturity, a way of taking control of life instead of letting life happen to you. What risks do you face? Which of them can you afford to take without having to back away from your goals? What resources—public programs, personal strengths, or private risk-sharing plans—are available to you?

To understand and use the resources at your command, you need good information. In insurance, this means a clear picture of the available insurance, the strength and reliability of different insurers, and the comparative costs of the coverage you need.

Put Your Plan into Action

As you carry out your plan, you obtain financial and personal resources, budget them, and use them to reach your risk management goals. If, for example, you find that the insurance protection you have is not enough to cover your basic risks, you may act to purchase additional coverage, to change the kind of insurance coverage you have, to restructure your personal or family budget to cover additional insurance costs, and to strengthen your savings or investment programs to reduce the long-term risk of economic hardship.

The best risk management plans have an element of flexibility. Savings accounts, for example, are available as emergency funds for any number of sudden financial problems. The best insurance plan is also flexible enough to respond to changing life situations. Your goal should be an insurance program that expands (or contracts) with the changing size of your protection needs.

Check Your Results

Evaluate your insurance plan periodically. Among the questions you should ask yourself are: Does it work? Does it adequately protect my plans and goals? An effective risk manager consistently checks the outcomes of decisions and is alert to changes that may reduce the effectiveness of the current risk management plan.

A young working couple may be entirely happy with their life and health insurance coverage. But when they add an infant to the family, it's time to review the protection plans. Suddenly, the risk of financial catastrophe to the family (should one or both parents die or be disabled) is much greater. Yesterday's decisions about insurance coverage are in need of revision.

The needs of a single person differ from those of a family, a single parent, a couple, or a group of unrelated adults living in the same household. All of these people face similar risks, but their financial responsibility to others differs greatly. In each case, the vital question is: Have I provided the financial resources and risk management strategy needed to take care of my basic responsibilities for my own well-being and the well-being of others?

PURCHASING YOUR INSURANCE COVERAGE[5]

To put your risk management plan to work, you must answer four basic questions: what should be insured, and for how much, what kind of insurance should be bought, and from whom?

● Intelligent Insurance
  Purchases

What Should Be Insured?

As stated earlier, insurance decisions should be planned to cover clearly defined risks. The questions center on goals again. What do you want your insurance protection to do? Protect a big-ticket purchase (car, home)? Provide income for your family if you should die or become totally disabled? Cover the risk of theft or fire at your home? Before purchasing insurance, you should work to develop a clear sense of the purposes you want insurance to serve.

How Much Insurance?

A proper insurance plan covers all unaffordable losses. Properly used, insurance pays for major losses that would cause real economic hardship if left uncovered. A rule of thumb is that you absorb minor loss and insure major loss. No sensible person will pay the cost of buying an insurance policy against the loss of trivial possessions: pens, hats, costume jewelry, and so

[5]Ibid., pp. 11/17–18.

forth. Such losses can be absorbed into the personal budget without creating financial problems. But what if the economic loss were $50,000—the fee for a surgical technique required by a member of the family? Such a loss could not be absorbed by most people; therefore, it should be insured against.

Answering the question how much requires a hard analysis of what you need to protect your economic well-being and what you can afford to pay for protection.

Need Analysis. Taking an inventory of your personal finances is a good way to start thinking about the protection you need. The inventory should list your assets, such as real estate, savings and investments, and personal property; your liabilities, such as outstanding loans, charge accounts, and mortgages; and your estimated income and expenses. If you are dealing with life and health insurance, estimate what your income and expenses would be if the wage earner dies or is disabled; in other insurance situations, an estimate will indicate how much leeway your income and expenses give you in meeting smaller losses. In short, the expected loss minus the assets available to cover it roughly equals the amount of insurance needed.

Affordability. When major economic losses are possible, few of us can afford to be without adequate protection. A sudden illness in the family, for instance, could cause a six-figure medical bill. The question, then, isn't just "What can I afford?" but "How can I afford to buy the insurance I need?"

Affording protection may require a shift in the way you manage resources: extending a saving program or cutting down on nonessential spending. Above all, look for ways to get the best protection for the least money.

What Kind of Insurance?

Consumers should be aware of the variety of available insurance products. In the next three chapters, we will discuss the range of life, health, and property insurance products that are available to consumers. Variety makes it possible for you to find flexible insurance plans tailored to your special needs. Young families, for instance, can protect their income with low-cost term life insurance that fits their budgets. Before making a commitment to one insurance plan, look over the variety of available products. If the first policy you review isn't a good fit, you can assume that there is another plan better suited to your insurance needs.

From Whom to Buy?

Look for insurance coverage from financially strong companies with professionally qualified representatives. It is not unusual for a relationship with an insurance company to extend over a period of 20, 30, even 50 years. For that reason alone, consumers should choose carefully when they decide on an insurance company or an insurance agent. Fortunately, you do have a choice of sources.

Sources. Protection is available from a wide range of private and public sources, among which are insurance companies and their representatives; private groups, such as employers, labor unions, and professional or fraternal organizations; government programs, such as Medicare and social security; and other sources, such as financial institutions and manufacturers offering credit insurance.

Rating Insurance Companies. Some of the strongest, most reputable insurance companies in the nation provide excellent insurance coverage at reasonable costs. In fact, the financial strength of an insurance company may be a major factor in holding down premium costs for consumers.

Locate an insurance company by checking the reputations of local agencies. Ask members of your family, friends, or colleagues about the insurers they prefer. For a more official review, look for a copy of *Best's Agents Guide* or *Best's Insurance Reports* in the public library. The Best's ratings are an authoritative guide to the financial stability of the nation's insurers. Best's has five rating classifications: A+ or A (excellent), B+ (very good), B (good), C+ (fairly good), and C (fair).

Choosing Your Insurance Agent. An insurance agent handles the technical side of insurance. But that's only the beginning. The really important part of the agent's job is to apply his or her knowledge of insurance to help you select the proper kind of protection within your financial boundaries.

Choosing a good agent is among the most important steps in the process of

---

Personal Financial Planning and You
Guidelines for Choosing an Insurance Agent

1. The agent must be available when he or she is needed. Clients sometimes have problems that need immediate answers. These problems can occur on weekends and evenings.

2. The agent wants the client to have a balanced financial plan. Each part of the plan should be necessary to the client's overall financial protection.

3. The agent does not pressure the client. The client should be free to make a rational decision about insurance coverage.

4. The agent keeps up with changes in his or her field through education. Agents often attend special classes or study on their own so that they can serve their clients better.

5. As a professional, the agent is happy to answer questions. He or she wants the client to know exactly what is being paid for in an insurance policy.

Source: American Council of Life Insurance.

building your insurance program. How do you find an agent? One of the best ways to begin is by asking your parents, friends, neighbors, and others for their recommendations. You may also want to know something about an agent's membership in professional groups. Agents who belong to a local Life Underwriters Association are often among the more experienced agents in their communities. A **Chartered Life Underwriter (CLU)** is a life insurance agent who has passed a series of college-level examinations on insurance and related subjects. Such agents are entitled to use the designation CLU after their names.

Once you have learned of an agent who sounds promising, you must decide which policy is right for you. The best way to do this is to talk to your agent. Remember, this does not obligate you to buy insurance.

You can size up an agent by asking yourself a few questions about the advice he or she offers. How does the agent explain that a particular type of policy is right for you? Does the agent describe in detail the benefits that you can receive? Does the policy fit in with the rest of your financial picture—social security, company pension, group life insurance, health insurance, and your savings plan?

Understanding Your Insurance Policy

According to the Insurance Information Institute, a common consumer complaint is that people do not know enough about the insurance they are paying for and do not know whether or not they are paying too much for it.[6] The informed consumer questions the agent or company representative and reads insurance contracts for complete understanding of their terms and clauses. In the past, people felt intimidated by the legal terminology of most insurance policies. The simplified writing of auto and homeowner's contracts has eased the burden of reading and understanding these documents.

Understanding the various parts of an insurance policy is vital to knowing whether the proper coverage has been purchased. A general policy has the following components.

The Declaration. The declaration is a separate sheet that is fastened to the policy. It is a statement about the property to be insured, and it takes up such matters as deductibles and the amount of coverage.

The Insuring Agreement. This section explains who and what various coverages of the policy protect.

The Conditions. This section explains the duties and obligations of both the insurer and the policyholder.

---

[6]"A Report to Educators on Property and Casualty Insurance," *Insurance Insights*, Insurance Information Institute, November 1985, pp. 2–3.

The Exclusions. This section describes the properties, losses, and perils that are not covered.

Endorsements. An **endorsement** is a written document that modifies the policy in some way, perhaps adding or deleting coverage.

To be properly informed about buying insurance, there is no substitute for sitting down and talking with an agent or a company representative. Communication is the key to better learning.

How to File an Insurance Claim

Sustaining a loss is frustrating, but the problem can be compounded if care is not taken to secure proper information about the loss prior to filing a claim.

The Insurance Information Institute advises all policyholders to review their policies (both auto and homeowner) *before* a loss to ensure proper coverage and clarify any uncertainties.

The institute offers the following general tips:[7]

1. Maintain receipts on all purchases. Providing receipts will help the insurance company reimburse the policyholder fairly for a loss. Receipts leave no doubts as to the value of a piece of property.

2. Contact the police after a loss, and obtain a written police report, if possible.

3. Take notes about what happened, and include the names of the persons to contact.

4. In the case of an auto accident, get the names of all the parties involved, including witnesses, along with addresses, telephone numbers, driver's license numbers, and license plate numbers.

5. In the case of a homeowner's claim, list all damaged or stolen property. Locate original receipts whenever possible, including repair receipts. Gather repair estimates or estimates of the value of property.

6. Contact the insurance company or the agent as soon as possible.

SUMMARY

- Insurance is protection. The principle of all insurance is the same: people buy insurance policies to protect themselves against possible financial loss.

- Although the insurance policy is a recent development, the concept of insurance is not new. The first American insurance company was formed in 1735. In 1752, Benjamin

[7]Ibid.

Franklin cofounded a fire insurance company that still operates today.

- Risk, peril, and hazard are important terms in insurance. Risk refers to a chance of loss with respect to person, liability, or the property of the insured. Peril is the cause of a possible loss, such as fire, windstorm, theft, explosion or riot. Hazard is the presence of a condition that increases the likelihood of loss through some peril. Risks can be personal risks, property risks, or liability risks.

- Risk management, a long-range planning process, is an organized strategy for protecting and conserving assets and persons. The five general risk management techniques are risk avoidance, risk reduction, risk assumption, risk pooling, and risk shifting.

- All insurance is based on the principles of human mortality, probability, and the law of large numbers. The three most basic principles in insurance are indemnity, insurable interest, and insurable risk. Insurable risks are common to a large number of people. These risks are common, definite, accidental, not catastrophic, not trivial, calculable, and economically affordable.

- The steps in planning your personal insurance program are: setting your goals, making plans to reach your goals, putting your plans into action, and checking your results.

- Four basic questions that you should ask in purchasing your insurance coverage are: What should be insured? How much insurance is needed and affordable? What kind of insurance should be bought? From whom should it be bought? Once you have purchased the insurance, understand the various parts of the policy and learn how to file an insurance claim.

GLOSSARY

Actuary. A highly specialized insurance company mathematician who has been professionally trained in the risk aspects of insurance.

Chartered Life Underwriter (CLU). A life insurance agent who has met certain standards of education and proficiency.

Endorsement. A written document that modifies an insurance policy.

Hazard. Increases the likelihood of loss through some peril.

Indemnity. A legal doctrine limiting recovery under an insurance policy.

Insurance. Protection against possible financial loss.

Insurance company. A risk-sharing firm that assumes financial responsibility for losses that may result from an insured risk.

Insured. A person who is covered by an insurance policy.

Insurer. An insurance company.

Law of large numbers. The longer the number insured for a particular risk are observed, the more accurately the expected losses can be predicted; also called the law of averages and the law of probability.

Peril. The cause of a possible loss.

Policy. A written contract of insurance.

Policyholder. A person who owns an insurance policy.

Premium. The amount of money that a policyholder is charged for an insurance policy.

Probability. The mathematics of chance.

Pure risk. Risk in which there is only a chance of loss; only pure risks are insurable; also called insurable risk.

Risk. Chance or uncertainty of loss; also used to mean "the insured."

Speculative risk. A risk in which there is a chance of either loss or gain.

REVIEW QUESTIONS

1. What is insurance? What fundamentals must be kept in mind when buying insurance?

2. Trace the historical development of the insurance concept.

3. Define risk, peril, and hazard. Why are these concepts important in insurance?

4. Describe the various types of risks. How can they be classified? What is the difference between pure and speculative risks?

5. Define risk management. What are the five methods of managing risk?

6. Define the concept of probability, the principle of indemnity, the law of large numbers, insurable interest, and insurable risks.

7. What are the seven characteristics of insurable risk?

8. What steps must you take in planning your personal insurance program?

9. What four basic questions must you ask before purchasing your insurance coverage?

10. State five guidelines for choosing an insurance agent.

11. Name and describe five components of an insurance policy.

12. What general tips for filing an insurance claim are offered by the Insurance Information Institute?

DISCUSSION QUESTIONS AND ACTIVITIES

1. How could Connie Schnoebelen, Ava Measels, and David Hatton have protected themselves against unethical insurance agents?

2. List the potential risks of not providing for insurance protection in the family budget.

3. Compile a list of the various insurance sources used by your family and your neighbors. Discuss these sources, and classify them as private or public sources.

4. Interview a qualified insurance agent. Ask him or her what a competent insurance agent can and will do to help you purchase various types of protection.

5. List the risks that you or your family will probably face over the next four years. Then list the personal, private, and public resources that you will use to reduce the financial impact of each type of risk.

6. Examine yours or your parents' life insurance and automobile insurance policies. What are the major components of each of these policies?

7. Do you believe that surviving family members have the right to expect protection for their current lifestyle? How important, in your opinion, is the father's (or mother's) obligation to provide that protection?

ADDITIONAL READINGS

Bickelhaupt, David L. *General Insurance.* 11th ed. Homewood, Ill.: Richard D. Irwin, 1983.

Insurance Insights, A Report to Educators on Property and Casualty Insurance, Insurance Information Institute, November 1985, pp. 2–3.

Mehr, Robert I. *Fundamentals of Insurance.* Homewood, Ill.: Richard D. Irwin, 1986.

Mehr, Robert I., Emerson Cammack, and Terry Rose. *Principles of Insurance.* 8th ed. Homewood, Ill.: Richard D. Irwin, 1985.

Policies for Protection. Washington, D.C.: American Council of Life Insurance, 1982.

Sets, Probability, and Statistics. Washington, D.C.: American Council of Life Insurance, 1978.

CASE 11–1 Buying Adequate Insurance Coverage*

Kathy Jones was a junior at Glenbard High School. She had two younger sisters. Her father, the manager of a local supermarket, had take-home pay of $2,000 a month. He had a small group health insurance policy and a $20,000 life insurance policy. He said that he could not afford to buy additional insurance. All of his monthly salary was used to meet current expenses, including car and house payments, food, clothing, transportation, children's allowances, recreation and entertainment, and vacation trips.

One evening, Kathy was talking with her father about insurance, which she was studying in an economics course. She asked what kind of insurance program her father had for their family. This question started Mr. Jones thinking about how well he was planning for his wife and children. Since the family had always been in good health, Mr. Jones felt that additional health and life insurance was not essential. Maybe after he received a raise in his salary and after his daughter

was out of high school, he could afford to buy more insurance.

Questions

1. Do you think Kathy's father was planning wisely for the welfare of his family? Can you suggest ways in which this family could have cut monthly expenses and thus set aside some money for more insurance?

2. Although Mr. Jones's salary was not big enough to buy insurance for all possible risks, what protection do you think he should have had at this time?

3. Suppose Mr. Jones had been seriously injured and unable to work for at least a year. What would the family have done? How might this situation have affected his children?

*Source: Adapted from *Policies for Protection* (Washington, D.C.: American Council of Life Insurance, 1982), p. 16.

CASE 11–2 The Importance of Planning Ahead†

Michael Beale worked in a gift shop in the city. His take-home pay was about $1,600 a month. He had a four-year-old son, and he and his wife were expecting another child. Last year, he told his insurance agent that he felt his family was suffi-

ciently protected with a $40,000 life insurance policy and a hospital expense health insurance policy.

†Source: Adapted from *Policies for Protection* (Washington, D.C.: American Council of Life Insurance, 1982), p. 16.

His shop was successful, and he felt that additional protection was not necessary. Besides, he felt that he would have plenty of time to save for his children's education. Then, several months ago, he was injured when he fell from a ladder. The accident left him disabled and unable to work.

Questions

1. Did Mr. Beale have the right kind of insurance protection for his family? How will his disability affect the welfare of his growing children?

2. If Mr. Beale didn't think he had any financial worries, why should he have considered loss of income insurance?

3. What are some ways in which Mr. Beale's insurance program could have been improved?

12

Home and Automobile Insurance

Each year, there are more than 3 million burglaries and 500,000 fires and 200,000 more homes are damaged by other hazards, causing billions of dollars of financial losses for homeowners and renters. The cost of injuries and property damage caused by automobiles is also very large. Most people use insurance to reduce the chances of economic loss from these risks. Giving your attention to the types and costs of the property and liability coverages available to individuals is a vital component of personal financial planning.

After studying this chapter, you will be able to:

- Recognize the importance of property and liability insurance.

- Describe the coverages included in homeowners and renters insurance.

- Name the types of home insurance policies.

- Discuss the factors that determine the amount of home insurance coverage.

- Explain the factors that affect the cost of home insurance.

- Recognize the importance of automobile insurance.

- Describe the types of automobile insurance coverages.

- Explain the factors that affect the cost of automobile insurance.

Interview with **Rod Iwema,** Agent, State Farm Insurance Companies

Rod Iwema has been an Agent for State Farm Insurance for the past five years. Before that, he served as a School Administrator. In that capacity, he was involved in the purchase of property and liability insurance.

The basic purpose of property and liability insurance is to protect your financial assets against potential loss. While most people have adequate protection against loss due to fire or theft, many people lack adequate liability coverage. These people could lose their savings or investments as a result of a liability judgment against them. In today's legal environment, the more you own, the greater the amount for which you are likely to be sued.

Many insurance companies now offer *guaranteed replacement* coverage for the home. Under this type of policy, your home will be replaced even if the insurance company did not anticipate the total cost. For example, if an insurance company calculates that it would

cost $100,000 to replace your home and insures it for that amount, with guaranteed replacement coverage, your home would be rebuilt even if it were completely destroyed and replacing it costs $120,000. Mr. Iwema also stresses the need of renters for property and liability insurance since they have belongings of value and can be held legally responsible for certain actions.

The cost of home insurance is mainly influenced by the *protection class* of your property. This is determined by such factors as the type of fire fighting equipment used in your area, the local water pressure, and access to fire hydrants.

Although the most important aspect of automobile insurance is liability coverage, you also need to protect your vehicle. Many people believe that when a car ages, dropping collision coverage can save money. This may be true, but you should also consider that a seven- or eight-year-old car may be worth $1,500 while the cost of

collision insurance may be less than $100 a year.

A feature of every automobile liability package is uninsured motorists coverage. If the other driver is at fault in an accident and has no auto insurance or is a hit-and-run driver, this coverage will pay for your bodily injury losses. Underinsured motorists coverage protects you if the other driver is at fault and has liability coverage less than the amount of your bodily injury losses. These coverages are very important to your financial well-being.

You should consider agent availability and company reliability in your planning for property and liability insurance. A company whose rates are low may provide poorer service than you expect when settling a claim. Moreover, a number of cut-rate, poorly managed companies have gone bankrupt in recent years, leaving homeowners and drivers without insurance coverage.

Nathan and Lola Lemton are a typical couple, with two children, Alison, 22, and Andy, 17. They have fire insurance on their home and they are considering the purchase of a burglary policy since they collect antiques and have four rare items as well as a number of other pieces.

The Lemtons' dog, Barky, is one of the most popular pets in the neighborhood. Barky can be seen playing with children almost every day.

Alison Lemton shares an apartment with a friend, Ruth Bowman. Since Alison and Ruth don't have much furniture or other belongings, they have decided not to get insurance. Although they are assuming some risks, they are also saving the cost of insurance.

Andy Lemton drives to school each morning, then to his part-time job. He also uses his car for social trips on evenings and weekends. He has the minimum amount of automobile liability insurance required by the state.

As you can see, the Lemtons have some financial risks that they could reduce with insurance. Damage to their home and property, harm done by their pet, injuries to people in their dwelling, and automobile accidents causing property damage and injuries are a few of the areas in which the Lemtons might consider purchasing additional insurance. Striking the proper balance between too much insurance and not enough insurance is a difficult financial decision. Knowing the risks and the available coverages related to your home and your automobile can help you make your property and liability insurance choices.

PROPERTY AND LIABILITY INSURANCE

- Importance of Property and Liability Insurance

Recently, an automobile insurance company paid $3,600 for damages to a car in an accident caused by a mouse. The critter apparently got into the car while it was parked and then crawled up the driver's pants leg when the car was on an interstate highway. The driver lost control of the vehicle and crashed into a roadside barrier.

Another claim resulted when a barbecued steak fell off a 17th-floor balcony and dented a car.

A weather report recommended that homeowners "crack" their windows to minimize damage from an approaching hurricane. Instead of opening the windows slightly, one individual used a hammer to crack them. The damage was covered by a home insurance policy.[1]

While these incidents have a humorous side, most accidents—and the property losses and legal actions connected with them—do not. Your home

[1] Frank E. James, "Say It Isn't So: Insurance Has a Funny Side," *The Wall Street Journal*, July 9, 1986, p. 23.

and automobile are probably the two most expensive purchases you will make. The main types of risks related to these purchases are property damage or loss, and your responsibility for injuries to others or damage to the property of others.

Potential Property Losses

Houses, automobiles, furniture, clothing, and other personal belongings represent a substantial financial commitment. In connection with that commitment, property owners face two basic types of risks. The first type is physical damage that may be caused by such hazards as fire, wind, water, and smoke. These hazards can cause destruction of your property or temporary loss of its use. For example, if a windstorm causes a large tree branch to break your automobile windshield, you lose the use of the vehicle while it is being repaired.

The second type of risk faced by property owners is the threat of robbery, burglary, vandalism, or arson. Home and automobile insurance coverages minimize the potential financial loss due to these events.

Liability Protection

In a wide variety of circumstances, a person can be judged legally responsible for injuries or damages to others. For example, if a child walks across your property, falls, and sustains severe injuries, the child's family can sue you. Or if you accidentally damage a rare painting while assisting a friend with home repairs, the friend can take legal action against you to recover the cost of the painting.

Liability is legal responsibility for the financial cost of another person's losses or injuries. In many situations, your legal responsibility can be caused by **negligence**—failure to take ordinary or reasonable care. Doing something in a careless manner, such as improperly supervising children at a swimming pool or not removing items from a frequently used staircase, may be ruled as negligence in a liability lawsuit.

Another type of legal responsibility is **vicarious liability,** a situation in which a person is held responsible for the actions of another person. If financial or physical harm to others is caused by the behavior of a child, the parent may be held responsible; if it is caused by the activities of an employee, the employer may be held responsible.

Liability lawsuits can affect society as well as individuals. The settlements for such cases result in higher insurance premiums and higher prices for goods and services. For example, the cost of liability insurance for the Texas World Music Festival increased from $9,800 in 1985 to $88,000 in 1986, resulting in higher concert ticket prices. Most rock concerts have experienced increases in their liability insurance costs.[2]

[2]Christina Wiser, "Rock Insurance: A Ticket to Rise," *USA Today,* June 17, 1986, p. 5D.

In an effort to keep liability insurance costs down, in 1986 32 states took action to limit damage awards. The purpose of these legislative measures was to keep insurance premiums reasonable for businesses and consumers. Florida's liability award limit was imposed on the condition that premiums be reduced for insurance customers.[3]

INSURANCE FOR YOUR HOME AND PROPERTY

Your home and your personal belongings are the major portion of your assets. Loss of some or all of these possessions could cause financial disaster. Whether you rent your dwelling or own a house, condominium, or manufactured home, property insurance is vital to you. **Homeowners insurance** is coverage for your place of residence and its associated financial risks, such as damage to personal property and injuries to others. Types of home insurance that protect renters and condominium owners are also available. In addition, there are home insurance policies that cover particular financial risks.

[3]Leslie Wayne, "Putting Limits on Liability," *New York Times*, August 5, 1986, p. 30.

Careers in Personal Finance
The Insurance Industry

The insurance industry offers a variety of careers ranging from sales positions to positions in statistical analysis. In these careers, you help individuals and businesses reduce the risk of financial loss through the use of insurance.

Insurance agents and brokers have the main responsibility of representing the insurance company in selling financial protection to customers. They also assist people in assessing their insurance needs. In this role, insurance agents can make an important contribution to the financial security of individuals and families. While some college education is desirable for insurance agents, most of their training comes from the company and on-the-job experience.

An actuary computes insurance risks and premium rates. These tasks require an ability to work with statistics and to interpret data on accidents, illness, fires, and other risks that insurance companies cover. Underwriters review risk data and insurance applications to determine whether the applications should be accepted and what rates should be charged for insurance.

The insurance industry also affords career opportunities for safety engineers, risk managers, and claim adjusters. For further information on insurance careers, contact the Insurance Information Institute, 110 William Street, New York, NY 10038, or the American Council of Life Insurance, 1001 Pennsylvania Ave., NW, Washington, DC 20004-2599.

Sources: *Careers in Insurance* (New York: Insurance Information Institute); *Occupational Outlook Handbook*, 1986–87, pp. 72–74, 255–57.

Homeowners Insurance Coverages

● Coverages Included in
   Homeowners and
   Renters Insurance

A homeowners policy provides coverages against financial loss from a variety of risks. These coverages are for the building and other structures, additional living expenses, personal property, personal liability and related coverages, and specialized coverages.

Building and Other Structures. The main component of homeowners insurance is protection against financial loss due to damage or destruction to a house or other structure. Your dwelling and attached structures are covered for fire and other damages. Detached structures on the property, such as a garage, toolshed, or bathhouse, are also protected. Finally, trees, shrubs, and plants are included in the coverage.

Additional Living Expenses. If a fire or other damage prevents the use of your home, additional living expense coverage pays for the cost of living elsewhere. While your home is being repaired, this loss of use coverage reimburses you for the cost of living in a temporary location. Additional living expense coverage is limited to 10–20 percent of the home's coverage and is paid for a maximum of 6–9 months.

Personal Property. Your household belongings, such as furniture, appliances, and clothing, are called *personal property*. These articles are covered for damage or loss up to a portion of the insured value of the home, usually 50 percent. For example, a home insured for $80,000 would have $40,000 of coverage for household belongings. Personal property coverage has limits for certain items, such as $1,000 for jewelry, $2,000 for firearms, and $2,500 for silverware. Items whose value exceeds these limits can be protected with a **personal property floater,** which covers the damage or loss of a specific item of high value. A floater requires a detailed description of the item and periodic appraisals to verify its current value. This coverage protects the item regardless of its location, which insures the item while you are traveling with it or transporting it.

Floaters to protect home computers and related equipment are recommended. This additional coverage can prevent financial loss due to damage or loss of your computer. Contact your insurance agent to determine whether the equipment is covered against damage from spilled drinks, mischievous pets, dropping, or power surges.[4]

Personal property coverage usually provides protection against the loss or damage of an article that you take with you when you leave home. For example, possessions that you take with you when you go on vacation or use while you are living at school are usually covered up to a limit of 10 percent of your policy value. Property that you rent, such as a video recorder or a rug shampoo machine, is insured while it is in your possession.

[4]*Insurance Insights,* Insurance Information Institute, August 1986, p. 4.

In case of damage or loss of property, you must be able to prove both ownership and value. A **household inventory** is a list or other documentation of personal belongings, with purchase dates and cost information. You can get a form for such an inventory from an insurance agent or an office supplies store. Figure 12–1 provides a reminder of the items that should be included in the inventory. For items of special value, you should have receipts, serial numbers, brand names, model names, and written appraisals of value.

Your household inventory can include photographs or a video recording of your home and its contents. Make sure that the closet and storage area doors are open. On the backs of the photographs indicate the date and the value of the object. Regularly update your inventory, photos, and appraisal documents; also keep a copy of each document in a secure location such as a safe-deposit box.

Personal Liability and Related Coverages. Each day, we face the risk of financial loss due to injuries to others or damage to property for which we are responsible. Some examples of this risk are:

- A neighbor or guest falls on your property, resulting in permanent disability.
- A spark from burning leaves starts a fire that damages a neighbor's roof.
- A member of your family accidentally breaks an expensive glass statue while at another person's house.

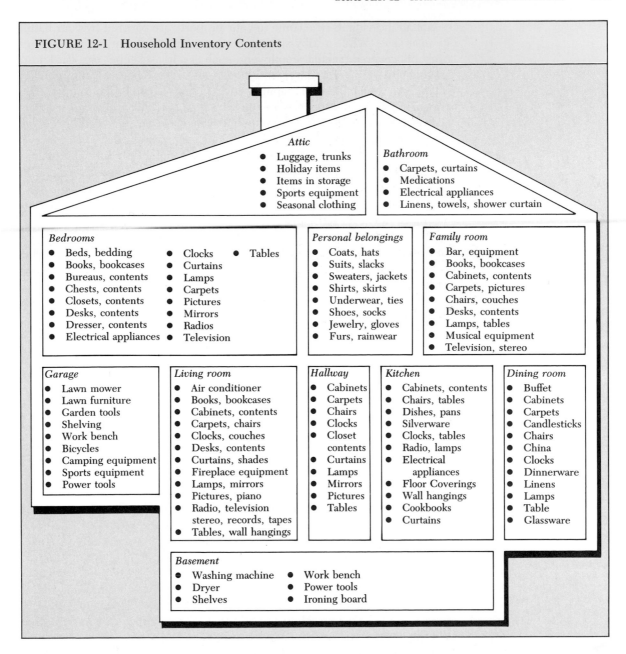

FIGURE 12-1   Household Inventory Contents

Attic
- Luggage, trunks
- Holiday items
- Items in storage
- Sports equipment
- Seasonal clothing

Bathroom
- Carpets, curtains
- Medications
- Electrical appliances
- Linens, towels, shower curtain

Bedrooms
- Beds, bedding
- Books, bookcases
- Bureaus, contents
- Chests, contents
- Closets, contents
- Desks, contents
- Dresser, contents
- Electrical appliances
- Clocks
- Curtains
- Lamps
- Carpets
- Pictures
- Mirrors
- Radios
- Television
- Tables

Personal belongings
- Coats, hats
- Suits, slacks
- Sweaters, jackets
- Shirts, skirts
- Underwear, ties
- Shoes, socks
- Jewelry, gloves
- Furs, rainwear

Family room
- Bar, equipment
- Books, bookcases
- Cabinets, contents
- Carpets, pictures
- Chairs, couches
- Desks, contents
- Lamps, tables
- Musical equipment
- Television, stereo

Garage
- Lawn mower
- Lawn furniture
- Garden tools
- Shelving
- Work bench
- Bicycles
- Camping equipment
- Sports equipment
- Power tools

Living room
- Air conditioner
- Books, bookcases
- Cabinets, contents
- Carpets, chairs
- Clocks, couches
- Desks, contents
- Curtains, shades
- Fireplace equipment
- Lamps, mirrors
- Pictures, piano
- Radio, television stereo, records, tapes
- Tables, wall hangings

Hallway
- Cabinets
- Carpets
- Chairs
- Clocks
- Closet contents
- Curtains
- Lamps
- Mirrors
- Pictures
- Tables

Kitchen
- Cabinets, contents
- Chairs, tables
- Dishes, pans
- Silverware
- Clocks, tables
- Radio, lamps
- Electrical appliances
- Floor Coverings
- Wall hangings
- Cookbooks
- Curtains

Dining room
- Buffet
- Cabinets
- Carpets
- Candlesticks
- Chairs
- China
- Clocks
- Dinnerware
- Linens
- Lamps
- Table
- Glassware

Basement
- Washing machine
- Dryer
- Shelves
- Work bench
- Power tools
- Ironing board

In each of these situations, you could be held responsible for the costs incurred. The personal liability component of a homeowners policy protects you from financial losses resulting from legal action or claims against you or family members due to damages to the property of others. Included in this coverage is the cost of your legal defense.

Not all individuals who come to your property are covered by your liability insurance. While a baby-sitter and others who assist you occasionally are probably covered, regular employees, such as a housekeeper or a gardener, may require worker's compensation coverage. Most homeowners policies provide a basic personal liability coverage of $100,000, but additional amounts are frequently recommended. An **umbrella policy,** also called a personal catastrophe policy, supplements your basic personal liability coverage. This added protection covers you for such personal injury claims as libel, slander, defamation of character, and invasion of property. Extended liability policies are sold in amounts of $1 million or more and are especially useful to individuals involved in business activities. If you are a business owner, you may also need other types of liability coverages. Contact an insurance agent for assistance.

Medical payments coverage pays the cost of minor accidental injuries on your property and minor injuries caused by you, family members, or pets away from home. Settlements under medical payments coverage are made without determining fault. This protection allows fast processing of small claims, generally up to $1,000. Suits for more severe personal injuries are covered by the personal liability portion of the homeowners policy.

Should you or a family member accidentally damage the property of others, the *supplementary coverage* of homeowners insurance is designed to pay for these minor mishaps. This protection is usually limited to items costing $250 or less. Again, payments are made regardless of fault. Any property damage claims for greater amounts would require action under the personal liability coverage.

Specialized Coverages. Homeowners insurance does not cover losses from floods and earthquakes. Therefore, people living in areas with these two risks need to obtain special coverage. In various communities, the National Flood Insurance Program makes flood insurance available. This protection is a coverage separate from your homeowners policy. An insurance agent or the Federal Emergency Management Agency of the Federal Insurance Administration can give you additional information about this coverage.

Earthquake insurance can be obtained as an **endorsement,** or addition of coverage, to your homeowners policy. Since the most severe earthquakes occur in the Pacific Coast area, most of the insurance against this risk is bought by people in that region. You should remember, however, that every state is vulnerable to earthquakes and that this insurance coverage is available in all areas for an additional charge. Both flood and earthquake insurance are frequently required by lenders for a mortgage to buy a home in an area that faces these risks.

Renters Insurance

For people who rent, home insurance coverages include personal property protection, additional living expenses, and personal liability and related coverages. Protection against financial loss due to damage or loss of personal property is the main component of renters insurance. While 9 out of 10 homeowners have insurance, only 3 out of 10 renters are covered.[5] Quite often, renters believe that they are covered under the insurance policy of the building owner. In fact, the building owner's property insurance does not cover the personal property of tenants unless the building owner can be proven negligent. If needed repairs for wiring caused a fire and damaged a tenant's furniture, the renter may be able to collect for damages from the building owner. Renters insurance is relatively inexpensive and provides protection from financial loss due to many of the same risks covered in home-owners policies.

Home Insurance Policy Forms

● Types of Home Insurance Policies

Until the mid-1950s, a person had to buy separate insurance coverage for fire, theft, and other risks. Since then, the insurance industry has created a series of homeowners and renters policies that provide package protection. The primary types of home insurance policies are the basic, broad, special, tenants, condominium owners, and modified coverage forms.

Basic Form. As presented in Figure 12–2, the *basic form* of homeowners insurance protects your home and property against 11 risks. Although this policy is adequate for many situations, damage from falling objects, weight of ice, or freezing are not covered.

Broad Form. The *broad form* expands the basic coverage by including protection against several additional risks (see Figure 12–2). The broad form also increases the coverage for such risks as theft and vehicle damage.

Special Form. The *special form* of homeowners policy provides risk coverage for all causes of loss or damage except those specifically excluded by the policy. Common exclusions are flood, earthquake, war, and nuclear accidents (see Table 12–1).

Tenants Form. The *tenants form* protects the personal property of renters against all risks except those excluded by the policy. As mentioned, renters insurance does not include coverage on the building or other structures.

Other Policy Forms. *Condominium owners* insurance protects your personal property and any additions or improvements you make to the living unit, such as bookshelves, electrical fixtures, and wall or floor coverings.

[5]"Homeowners Insurance," *Consumer Reports*, August 1985, p. 476.

FIGURE 12-2   Types of Home Insurance Policies

Basic form
- Fire, lightning
- Windstorm, hail
- Explosion
- Riot or civil commotion
- Aircraft
- Vehicles
- Smoke
- Vandalism or malicious mischief
- Theft
- Glass breakage
- Volcanic eruption

Broad form
All basic form risks plus:
- Falling objects
- Weight of ice, snow or sleet
- Discharge of water or steam
- Tearing apart of heating system or appliance
- Freezing
- Accidental damage from electrical current

Special form
Covers all basic and broad forms risks plus any other risks except those specifically excluded from the policy such as:
- Flood
- Earthquake
- War
- Nuclear accidents

Tenants form
Provides coverage on personal belongings against the risks covered by the basic and broad forms of the homeowners policies.

The other major coverages of each policy are:
- Personal liability
- Medical payments
- Additional living expenses

Insurance on the building and other structures is purchased by the condominium association.

Finally, the *modified coverage form,* or older home policy, covers residences with a low market value but a high replacement cost due to age or special design. This homeowners policy provides the same coverages as the basic form at a more reasonable cost because the homes are older and more difficult to replace.

Manufactured housing units and mobile homes usually qualify for insurance coverage with conventional policies. But certain mobile homes may require a special arrangement and higher rates since their construction makes them more prone to fire and wind damage.

In addition to the property and liability risks previously discussed, home insurance policies include coverage for:

- Credit card fraud, check forgery, and counterfeit money.
- The cost of removing damaged property.
- Emergency removal of property to protect it from damage.
- Temporary repairs after a loss to prevent further damage.
- Fire department charges in areas with such fees.

TABLE 12-1   Not Everything's Covered

Certain personal property is specifically excluded from the coverage provided by homeowners insurance:

Articles separately described and specifically insured, such as jewelry, furs, boats, or expensive electronic equipment.

Animals, birds, or fishes.

Motorized land vehicles, except those used to service an insured's residence that are not licensed for road use.

Any device or instrument for the transmission and recording of sound, including any accessories or antennas, while in or upon motor vehicles. This includes stereotape players, stereotapes, and citizens band radios.

Aircraft and parts.

Property of roomers, boarders, and other tenants who are not related to any insured.

Property contained in an apartment regularly rented or held for rental to others by any insured.

Property rented or held for rental to others away from the residence premises.

Business property in storage, or held as a sample, or for sale, or for delivery after sale.

Business property pertaining to business actually conducted on the residence premises.

Business property away from the residence premises.

Source: George E. Rajda, *Principles of Insurance* (Glenview, Ill.: Scott, Foresman, 1982). Copyright 1982 by Scott, Foresman and Company. Reprinted by permission.

HOME INSURANCE COST FACTORS

Financial losses caused by fire, theft, wind, and other risks amount to billions of dollars each year. Each property owner must decide whether to choose insurance or accept the potential financial risks. If you choose insurance, you can get the best value for each premium dollar by selecting the appropriate amount of coverage and by being aware of the factors that affect insurance costs.

How Much Coverage Do You Need?

- Factors that Determine the Amount of Home Insurance Coverage

Several factors determine how much insurance coverage you need for your home and property. Your insurance protection should be based on the amount of money you need to rebuild or repair your house, not on the amount you paid for it. As construction costs increase, you should increase the amount of coverage. Most homeowners policies do not automatically increase coverages to account for higher prices.

Some insurance companies offer an inflation increase feature in homeowners policies. This coverage adjustment may be based on the Consumer Price Index, which may not accurately reflect the changing value of your property. A more appropriate alternative is to adjust your policy to changes in the value of your home and changes in construction and building costs in your geographic area.

Most homeowners insurance policies contain a provision requiring that the building be insured for at least 80 percent of the replacement value. Under this **coinsurance clause,** the homeowner must pay for part of the losses if the property is not insured for the specified percentage of the replacement value. Only 80 percent is required because even if your property is completely destroyed, the land and the building foundation will probably still be usable.

When you insure for less than the 80 percent minimum, the insurance company will base its payment of claims on the portion of coverage carried. The following formula is used:

$$\frac{\text{Amount of insurance coverage}}{0.80 \times \text{Replacement cost of building}} \times \begin{array}{l}\text{Amount of property}\\ \text{damage or loss}\end{array} = \begin{array}{l}\text{Insurance}\\ \text{company}\\ \text{payment}\end{array}$$

For example, a $100,000 home with $60,000 of insurance would be below the 80 percent limit. Wind damage of $8,000 to the roof of the house in this situation would mean a settlement of $6,000 ($60,000/$80,000 × $8,000 = $6,000). On the other hand, any coverage over the amount needed to meet the 80 percent coinsurance clause—that is, over $80,000—is wasted spending for insurance since it would not increase the maximum amount that the insurance company would pay you for your loss. The coinsurance requirement is an important reason to monitor the value of your home and adjust the policy amount accordingly.

If you are financing a home, the lending institution will require you to have property insurance in an amount that covers its financial investment. Remember, too, that the amount of insurance on your home will determine the coverage on the contents. Personal belongings are generally covered up to an amount equal to 50 percent of the insurance on the dwelling.

Insurance companies base claim settlements on one of two methods. Under the **actual cash value (ACV)** method, the payment you receive is based on the current replacement cost of a damaged or lost item, less depreciation. This means that you would get $180 for a five-year-old television set that cost you $400 and had an estimated life of eight years if the same set now costs $480. Your settlement amount is determined by taking the current cost of $480 and subtracting five years of depreciation from it—$300 for five years at $60 a year.

Under the **replacement value** method for settling claims, you receive the full cost of repairing or replacing a damaged or lost item; depreciation is not considered. However, many companies limit the replacement cost to 400 percent of the item's actual cash value. The replacement value method does not apply to antiques and collectibles.[6] Such personal belongings require a

---

[6] Peter D. Lawrence, "All about Home Insurance," *New York,* October 24, 1983, p. 84.

personal property floater. Replacement value coverage is about 10 to 20 percent more expensive than ACV coverage.

What Factors Affect Home Insurance Costs?

- Factors that Affect the Costs of Home Insurance

Several factors affect the premium paid for home and property insurance. The main influences are the location of the home, the coverage amount and policy type, discounts, and company differences.

Location of Home. The type of home and the construction materials are important influences on the costs of insurance coverage. A brick house, for example, would cost less to insure than a similar house made of wood. Also, the age and style of the house can cause more potential risks and thus increase insurance costs.

The location of your residence also affects insurance rates. The efficiency of the fire department and the frequency of the thefts in an area will influence your property insurance premium. If more claims have been filed in an area, the rates for those living there will be higher.

Coverage Amount and Policy Type. The policy you select and the financial limits of coverage will also determine the premium you pay. It costs more to insure a $90,000 home than a $70,000 home. The special form of homeowners policy costs more than either the basic policy or the broad form policy.

The amount of the deductible on your policy will also affect the cost of your insurance. If you increase the amount of your deductible, your premium will be lower since the company will pay out less in claims. The most common deductible amount is $250. Increasing the deductible from $250 to $500 can reduce the premium 15 to 20 percent.

Home Insurance Discounts. Most companies offer incentives that reduce home insurance costs. Your premium may be lower if you have smoke detectors or a fire extinguisher. Deterrents to burglars, such as dead bolt locks or an alarm system, may save you money. You can also reduce your premium by buying a long-term policy. A three- or five-year policy is less expensive per year than an annual policy.

Company Differences. Reports have shown that you can save up to 25 percent on homeowners insurance by comparing companies. Contact both insurance agents who work for one company and independent agents who represent several. The information you obtain in this way will enable you to compare rates.

Don't select a company on the basis of price alone. Also consider service and coverage. Not all companies settle claims in the same way. In Maryland, for example, a number of homeowners had two sides of their houses dented by hail. Since the same type of siding was no longer available, all of the siding had to be replaced. Some insurance companies paid for the complete replacement of the siding, while others only paid for the replacement of the damaged areas.[7] State insurance commissions, other government agencies, and consumer organizations can provide information about the reputation of insurance companies.

AUTOMOBILE INSURANCE COVERAGES

- Importance of Automobile Insurance

A major reason for having automobile insurance is that minor damages to your car are no longer possible. Due to escalating labor costs, even repairing a dent can cost hundreds of dollars. Steep rises in medical care costs and the costs of legal settlements have resulted in even more rapid increases in the costs of injuries.

A **financial responsibility law** is state legislation that requires drivers to prove their ability to cover the cost of damage or injury caused by an automobile accident. All of the states have such ordinances to protect the public

---

TABLE 12-2   Automobile Financial Responsibility/Compulsory Insurance Limits (as of October 1986)

State	Liability Limits	State	Liability Limits
Alabama	20/40/10	Montana*	25/50/5
Alaska*	50/100/25	Nebraska	25/50/25
Arizona*	15/30/10	Nevada*	15/30/10
Arkansas	25/50/15	New Hampshire	25/50/25
California*	15/30/5	New Jersey*	15/30/5
Colorado*	25/50/15	New Mexico*	25/50/10
Connecticut*	20/40/10	New York*	10/20/5
Delaware*	15/30/10	North Carolina*	25/50/10
District of Columbia*	10/20/5	North Dakota*	25/50/25
Florida	10/20/5	Ohio*	12.5/25/7.5
Georgia*	15/30/10	Oklahoma*	10/20/10
Hawaii*	35/unlimited/10	Oregon*	25/50/10
Idaho*	25/50/15	Pennsylvania*	15/30/5
Illinois	15/30/10	Rhode Island	25/50/10
Indiana*	25/50/10	South Carolina*	15/30/5
Iowa	20/40/15	South Dakota*	25/50/25
Kansas*	25/50/10	Tennessee	20/40/10
Kentucky*	25/50/10	Texas*	20/40/15
Louisiana*	10/20/10	Utah*	20/40/10
Maine	20/40/10	Vermont*	20/40/10
Maryland*	20/40/10	Virginia	25/50/10
Massachusetts*	10/20/5	Washington	25/50/10
Michigan*	20/40/10	West Virginia*	20/40/10
Minnesota*	30/60/10	Wisconsin	25/50/10
Mississippi	10/20/5	Wyoming*	10/20/5
Missouri*	25/50/10		

*State with compulsory automobile liability insurance.

Sources: Insurance Information Institute and American Insurance Association.

---

[7]"Homeowners Insurance," *Consumer Reports*, August 1985, p. 473.

from physical harm and property damage losses caused by drivers. When there are injuries or significant property damage in an accident, the drivers involved are required to file a report with the state and to show financial responsibility. As of mid-1986, 36 states had compulsory automobile insurance laws. In other states, most people meet the financial responsibility requirement by buying insurance, since very few people have the financial resources needed to meet this legal requirement on their own. Table 12–2 presents each state's minimum limits for financial responsibility and compulsory insurance liability.

The main coverages of automobile insurance can be grouped into two categories, bodily injury and property damage coverages (see Figure 12–3). Other coverages include wage loss insurance and towing service.

Bodily Injury Coverages

● Types of Automobile Insurance Coverages

Most of the money paid in claims by automobile insurance companies is for the legal expenses of injury lawsuits, medical expenses, and related expenses. The main bodily injury coverages are bodily injury liability, medical

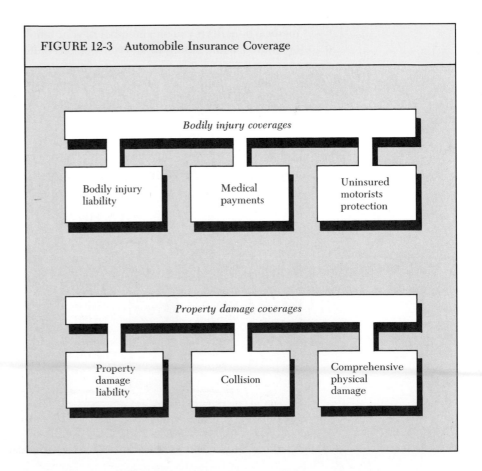

FIGURE 12-3   Automobile Insurance Coverage

Bodily injury coverages

| Bodily injury liability | Medical payments | Uninsured motorists protection |

Property damage coverages

| Property damage liability | Collision | Comprehensive physical damage |

payments, and uninsured motorists protection. The development of no-fault systems in a number of states has influenced the process of settling bodily injury claims.

Bodily Injury Liability. **Bodily injury liability** provides coverage for the risk of financial loss due to legal expenses, medical expenses, lost wages, and other expenses associated with injuries caused by an automobile accident for which you were responsible. This insurance is your most crucial automobile coverage as it protects you against extensive financial losses.

Bodily injury liability is usually expressed as a split limit, such as 10/20 or 100/300 (see Figure 12–4). These amounts represent thousands of dollars of coverage. The first number is the limit for claims that can be paid to one person; the second number is the limit for each accident; the third number is discussed below in the "Property Damage Coverages" section.

Medical Payments. While bodily injury liability pays for the costs of injuries to persons who were not in your automobile, **medical payments** covers the costs of health care for people who were injured in your automobile, including yourself. This protection covers friends, car pool members, and others who ride in your vehicle. Medical payments insurance also provides medical benefits if you or a member of your family is struck by an automobile or injured while riding in another person's automobile.

Uninsured Motorists Protection. If you are in an accident caused by a person without insurance, **uninsured motorists protection** covers the cost of injuries to you and your family, but not property damage. This insurance

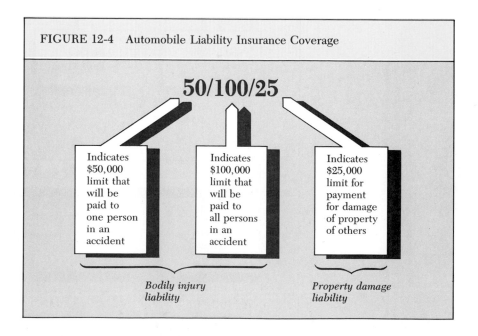

FIGURE 12-4   Automobile Liability Insurance Coverage

also provides protection against financial losses due to injuries caused by a hit-and-run driver or by a driver who has less coverage than the cost of your injuries.

No-Fault Insurance. Difficulties in settling claims for medical expenses and personal injuries resulted in the creation of the **no-fault system,** under which drivers involved in an accident collect medical expenses, lost wages, and related injury costs from their own insurance company. The system is intended to provide fast and smooth methods of paying for damages without taking the legal action frequently necessary to determine fault.

In 1971, Massachusetts was the first state to implement no-fault insurance. As of mid-1986, 26 states had some variation of the system. While no-fault automobile insurance was intended to reduce the time and cost associated with the settlement of automobile injury cases, it has not always achieved this result. One reason for continued difficulties is that no-fault systems vary from state to state. Some no-fault states set limits on medical expenses, lost wages, and other claim settlements, whereas other states allow lawsuits under certain conditions, such as permanent paralysis or death. And some states include property damage in no-fault insurance. Drivers should investigate the coverages and implications of no-fault insurance in their state.

Property Damage Coverages

The three coverages that protect you from financial loss due to the damage of the property of others and damage to your vehicle are property damage liability, collision, and comprehensive physical damage.

Property Damage Liability. **Property damage liability** protects you against financial loss when your car damages the property of others. This coverage applies mainly to other vehicles, but it also includes damage to street signs, lampposts, buildings, and other property. Property damage liability protects you and others covered by your policy when you are driving another person's automobile with his or her permission. The policy limit for property damage liability is frequently given with your bodily injury coverages. The last number in the groups 50/100/25 and 100/300/50 is for property damage liability ($25,000 and $50,000, respectively).

Collision. **Collision** insurance pays for damage to your automobile when it is involved in an accident, regardless of who is at fault. But if another driver caused the accident, your insurance company would try to recover the repair costs for your vehicle from the other driver's property damage liability coverage.

The amount you can collect with collision insurance is limited to the retail value of the automobile at the time of the accident. This amount is usually based on the figures provided by some appraisal service, such as the *Official Used Car Guide* of the National Association of Automobile Dealers. If you have an automobile with many add-on features or one that is several years old and has been restored, you should obtain a documented statement of its condition and value before an accident occurs.

Comprehensive Physical Damage. Another protection for your automobile involves financial losses from damage to it caused by a risk other than a collision. **Comprehensive physical damage** covers you for such risks as fire, theft, glass breakage, falling objects, vandalism, wind, or hail, or damage caused by hitting an animal. This insurance may not cover all of the articles in your vehicle; frequently excluded are some types of radios and stereo equipment. These items may be protected by the personal property coverage of your home insurance. As with collision, comprehensive coverage applies only to your car and claims are paid without considering fault.

Both collision and comprehensive coverage are commonly sold with a

---

In the Real World
Are You Covered?

Quite often, we believe that our insurance will cover various financial losses. For each of the following situations, name the type of home or automobile insurance that would protect you.

1. While you are on vacation, clothing and other personal belongings are stolen. _____

2. Your home is damaged by fire, and you have to live in a hotel for several weeks. _____

3. You and members of your family suffer injuries in an automobile accident caused by a hit-and-run driver. _____

4. A delivery person is injured on your property and takes legal action against you. _____

5. Your automobile is accidentally damaged by some people who are playing baseball. _____

6. A person takes legal action against you for injuries you caused in an automobile accident. _____

7. Water from a local lake rises and damages your furniture and carpeting. _____

8. Your automobile needs repairs because you hit a tree. _____

9. You damaged a valuable tree when your automobile hit it, and you want to pay for the damage. _____

10. While riding with you, in your automobile, your nephew is injured in an accident. He incurs various medical expenses. _____

Answers: (1) Personal property coverage of home insurance; (2) additional living expenses of home insurance; (3) uninsured motorists protection; (4) personal liability coverage of home insurance; (5) comprehensive physical damage; (6) bodily injury liability; (7) flood insurance—requires coverage separate from home insurance; (8) collision; (9) property damage liability of automobile insurance; (10) medical payments.

deductible to help reduce insurance costs. If a broken windshield costs $250 to replace and you have a $100 deductible on your comprehensive coverage, the insurance company would pay $150 of the damage. Deductibles keep insurance premiums lower by reducing the number of small claims that the company pays.

Other Automobile Coverages

In addition to the basic bodily injury and property damage coverages of automobile insurance, other protection is available. Wage loss insurance will reimburse you for any salary or income lost due to injury in an automobile accident. Wage loss insurance is required in states with a no-fault insurance system; it is available on an optional basis in other states.

Towing and emergency road service pays for the cost of breakdowns and mechanical assistance. This coverage can be especially beneficial on long trips or during inclement weather. Towing and road service pays for the cost of getting the vehicle to a service station or starting it when it breaks down on the highway, but not for the cost of repairs. If you belong to an automobile club, towing coverage may be included in your membership. Purchasing duplicate coverage as part of your automobile insurance could be a waste of money.

AUTOMOBILE INSURANCE COSTS

Like other insurance premiums, automobile insurance premiums reflect the amount that the insurance company pays for injury and property damage claims. Your automobile insurance is directly related to the coverage amounts and to such other factors as the vehicle, your place of residence, and your driving record. You can reduce the amount you pay for automobile insurance by taking various actions.

● Factors that Affect the Costs of Automobile Insurance

The Amount of Coverage

"How much coverage do I need?" This fundamental question will affect the amount you pay for insurance. Our legal environment and constantly increasing property values influence your decision on coverage amounts.

Legal Concerns. As discussed, every state has laws that either require or encourage automobile liability insurance coverage. Since very few people can afford to pay an expensive court settlement with their personal assets, most drivers buy automobile liability insurance.

Until about 15 years ago, bodily injury liability coverage of 10/20 was considered adequate. In fact, a few states still have these amounts as their minimum limits for financial responsibility. But legal and insurance advisers now recommend 100/300, and in recent injury cases some people have been awarded millions of dollars. Additional liability coverage that provides protection of up to $1 million is available with an umbrella policy. This coverage was discussed in the section "Insurance for Your Home and Property."

Pepper . . . and Salt

"I'd sure like to get my hands on the robot
that put this car together."

From *The Wall Street Journal*, with permission of Cartoon Features Syndicate.

Property Values. Just as medical expenses and legal settlements have increased, so too has the cost of automobiles. Therefore, a policy limit of more than $5,000 or $10,000 for property damage liability is appropriate; $50,000 or $100,000 is suggested.

The higher cost of automobile replacement parts also contributes to the need for increased property damage coverage. The list price for a 1985 Chevrolet Camaro was $10,682. The Alliance of American Insurers determined that purchasing its parts individually would cost $37,014, not including labor![8]

Automobile Insurance Premium Factors

The premium you pay for automobile insurance is influenced by several factors. The main factors are automobile type, rating territory, and driver classification.

Automobile Type. The year, make, and model of your automobile have a strong impact on your automobile insurance costs. Expensive replacement parts and complicated repairs due to body style cause higher rates. Also, certain makes and models are stolen more often than others. According to the Highway Loss Data Institute, the Oldsmobile Firenza, Mercury Lynx,

[8]Jack Gillis, *The Car Book* (New York: Harper & Row, 1986), p. 92.

and Plymouth Reliant have low theft records, whereas the BMW, Cadillac, Buick Riviera, and Mercedes have the highest theft records.[9]

Rating Territory   Your rating territory is your place of residence to determine your automobile insurance premium. Geographic locations have different costs due to differences in the number of claims made. For example, fewer accidents and less vandalism occur in rural areas than in large cities. During the first half of 1986, 39,712 vehicles were stolen in New York City, 25,088 in Los Angeles, and 23,071 in Chicago. These cities had the highest incidence of automobile theft.[10]

Driver Classification. As an individual, you are compared with other drivers when your automobile insurance premium is set. **Driver classification** is a category based on the driver's age, sex, marital status, driving record, and driving habits; the driver's category is used to determine his or her automobile insurance rates. In general, young, unmarried male drivers have more accidents and can expect to pay higher premiums, (see Figure 12–5). In recent years, some states have barred the use of sex as a factor in setting insurance premiums. As a result, young female drivers have had premium increases of from $200 to over $1,000. Insurance companies argue that young

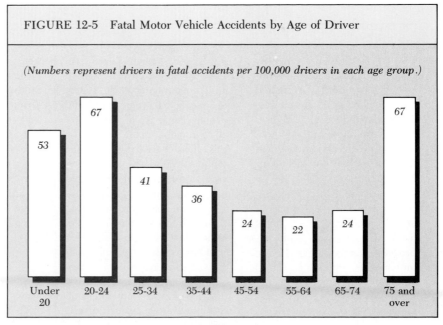

FIGURE 12-5   Fatal Motor Vehicle Accidents by Age of Driver

(Numbers represent drivers in fatal accidents per 100,000 drivers in each age group.)

Under 20	20-24	25-34	35-44	45-54	55-64	65-74	75 and over
53	67	41	36	24	22	24	67

Source: *Accident Facts* (Chicago: National Safety Council, 1985), p. 54.

[9] Ibid., pp. 88–89.

[10] "Where Cars Are Hot," *USA Today*, October 28, 1986, p. 1A.

male drivers should pay more than young female drivers since they have more moving violations, license suspensions, and revocations.[11]

Your driver classification is also influenced by the number of accidents and traffic violations that you have received within the past three years. A poor driving record will increase your insurance costs. Finally, you will pay less for insurance if you do not drive to work than if you use your automobile for business purposes. Belonging to a car pool instead of driving to work alone can reduce your insurance costs.

The number of claims you have filed with your insurance company also affects your insurance premiums. Expensive liability settlements or extensive property damage will increase your rates. If you have many expensive claims or a poor driving record, your company may cancel your policy. Then it is usually difficult to obtain coverage from another company. To deal with

[11]"Unisex Auto Insurance Rating," *Home and Away*, Chicago Motor Club, July–August 1986, pp. 3–4.

In the News
Stronger Regulation of Drunk Drivers

The National Highway Traffic Safety Administration has estimated that 65 percent of automobile accidents involve alcohol use. Drunk driving results in thousands of deaths and injuries and in $24 billion in accident-related costs.

Two major efforts have attempted to reduce the impact of this problem. First, states have strengthened and improved enforcement of driving under the influence (DUI) laws. In many states, a person who violates such a law automatically has driving privileges suspended for a period of three to six months.

Second, the minimum drink-ing age has been raised. In 1984, President Reagan signed a bill encouraging all the states to make 21 the minimum drinking age. As of late 1986, all but eight states had done this. This legislation is an attempt to reduce the number of young Americans who die each year in alcohol-related automobile accidents; most recently, the death toll was 9,500 people under the age of 25.

While a reduction in alcohol-related accidents will lower the insurance premiums of all drivers, the primary motivation of the movement against drunk driving has been to reduce the human suffering associated with such accidents. Organiza-tions such as Mothers Against Drunk Driving (MADD) and Students Against Driving Drunk (SADD) spearheaded that movement, and their efforts continue. They advocate a ban on alcohol sales at gas stations, sponsor nonalcoholic events for young people, and discourage the use of illegal drugs.

Sources: *Accident Facts* (Chicago: National Safety Council, 1985), p. 52; "Drunk Driving Is Costly," *Insurance Insights*, Insurance Information Institute, August 1986, p. 3; and Stewart Powell and Mary Galligan, "State Drinking Laws Come of Age," *U.S. News & World Report*, June 9, 1986, p. 21.

this problem, every state has an **assigned risk pool** consisting of people who are unable to get automobile insurance. Some of these people are assigned to each of the insurance companies operating in the state. These drivers pay several times the normal rates, but they do get coverage. Once they establish a good driving record, they can reapply for insurance at the regular rates. Critics of the assigned risk system contend that good drivers help cover the costs of poor drivers. However, if assigned risk drivers were in accidents without insurance, the potential financial burden on society might be even greater.

Reducing Automobile Insurance Premiums

Several methods to help lower your automobile insurance costs are available. These methods include comparing companies and taking advantage of discounts.

Comparing Companies. Rates and service vary among automobile insurance companies. Among companies in the same area, premiums can vary as much as 100 percent. The Center for the Study of Services found a difference of $668 for comparable coverage from companies in the Washington, DC, area; in San Francisco, the difference was $999.[12] If you relocate, don't assume that the company offering the best rates in your former area also offers the best rates in your present area.

Also consider the service provided by the local insurance agent. Will this company representative be available to answer questions, change coverages, and handle claims as needed? A company's reputation for handling claims and other matters can be checked with such sources as *Consumer Reports* magazine, the Better Business Bureau, and your state insurance department.

Premium Discounts. Most insurance companies offer premium discounts for various reasons. Drivers under 25 can qualify for reduced rates by completing a driver training program and by maintaining good grades in school. If a young driver is away at school without a car, the family is likely to get a reduction in its automobile premium since he or she will not be using the vehicle on a regular basis.

Installing security devices such as a fuel shutoff switch, a second ignition switch, or an alarm system will decrease your chances of theft and thus lower your comprehensive insurance costs. Equipping your automobile with air bags may qualify you for a discount. Establishing a safe driving record and becoming a nonsmoker can qualify you for lower automobile insurance premiums. Discounts are also offered for participating in a car pool and insuring two or more vehicles with the same company. Ask your insurance agent about other methods for lowering your automobile insurance rates.

As discussed, increasing the amount of deductibles will result in a lower

[12] "The Right Way to Cut Insurance Costs," *U.S. News & World Report*, September 1, 1986, p. 53.

premium. Also, some people believe that an old car is not worth the amount paid for the collision and comprehensive coverages and therefore dispense with them.

If you change your driving habits, get married, or alter your driving status in other ways, be sure to notify the insurance company. Premium savings can result. Also consider making your insurance payments once a year rather than on a more costly semiannual, quarterly, or monthly basis. Some employers make group automobile insurance available to workers. As with other types of group insurance plans, the cost of such insurance is usually less than the cost of an individual policy.

Before you buy a car, find out which makes and models have the lowest insurance costs. This information can result in a purchasing decision that is beneficial to your overall financial existence.

SUMMARY

- Home and automobile owners face the risks of property damage or loss and the risks of legal actions by others for the costs of injuries or property damage.
- Homeowners insurance includes protection for the building and other structures, additional living expenses, personal property, and personal liability. Renters insurance includes the same coverages except protection for the building and other structures, which is the concern of the building owner, not the tenant.
- The main types of home insurance policies are the basic, broad, special, and tenants forms. These policies differ in the risks and property they cover.
- The amount of home insurance coverage is determined by the replacement cost of your dwelling and your personal belongings.

- The cost of home insurance is influenced by the location of the home, the coverage amount, the policy type, discounts, and company differences.
- Automobile insurance is used to meet the financial responsibility laws of the state and to protect drivers against financial losses associated with bodily injury and property damage.
- The major types of automobile insurance coverages are bodily injury liability, medical payments, uninsured motorists, property damage liability, collision, and comprehensive physical damage.
- The cost of automobile insurance is affected by the amount of coverage, the automobile type, the rating territory, the driver classification, company differences, and premium discounts.

GLOSSARY

Actual cash value (ACV). A claim settlement method in which the insured receives payment based on the current replacement value of a damaged or lost item, less depreciation.

Assigned risk pool.   Consists of people who are unable to obtain automobile insurance due to poor driving or accident records and who obtain coverage at high rates through a state program that requires insurance companies to accept some of them.

Bodily injury liability.   Coverage for the risk of financial loss due to legal expenses, medical costs, lost wages, and other expenses associated with injuries caused by an automobile accident for which you were responsible.

Coinsurance clause.   A policy provision that requires a homeowner to pay for part of the losses if the property is not insured for the specified percentage of the replacement value.

Collision.   Automobile insurance that pays for damage to the insured's car when it is involved in an accident.

Comprehensive physical damage.   Automobile insurance that covers financial loss from damage to your vehicle caused by a risk other than a collision, such as fire, theft, glass breakage, hail, or vandalism.

Driver classification.   A category based on the driver's age, sex, marital status, driving record, and driving habits; used to determine automobile insurance rates.

Endorsement.   An addition of coverage to a standard insurance policy.

Financial responsibility laws.   State legislation that requires drivers to prove their ability to cover the cost of damage or injury caused by an automobile accident.

Homeowners insurance.   Coverage for your place of residence and its associated financial risks.

Household inventory.   A list or other documentation of personal belongings, with purchase date and cost information.

Liability.   Legal responsibility for the financial cost of another person's losses or injuries.

Medical payments.   Home insurance that pays for the cost of minor injuries on your property; also automobile insurance that covers the cost of the medical care of people injured in your car.

Negligence.   Failure to take ordinary or reasonable care in a situation.

No-fault system.   An automobile insurance program in which drivers involved in an accident collect medical expenses, lost wages, and related expenses from their own insurance company.

Personal property floater.   Additional property insurance to cover the damage or loss of a specific item of high value.

Property damage liability.   Automobile insurance coverage that protects you against financial loss when your car damages the property of others.

Rating territory.   Your place of residence that is used to determine your automobile insurance premium.

Replacement value.   A claim settlement method in which the insured receives the full cost of repairing or replacing a damaged or lost item.

Umbrella policy.   Supplementary personal liability coverage; also called a personal catastrophe policy.

Uninsured motorists protection.   Automobile insurance coverage for the cost of injuries to you and members of your family caused by a driver without insurance or by a hit-and-run driver.

Vicarious liability.   A situation in which a person is held legally responsible for the actions of another person.

REVIEW QUESTIONS

1. What types of financial losses do property and liability insurance cover?

2. What are the main coverages in a homeowners insurance policy?

3. What is covered by the personal liability portion of home insurance?

4. How does renters insurance differ from other home insurance policies?

5. What factors influence the amount of home insurance coverage a person buys?

6. What factors affect the cost of home insurance?

7. How does bodily injury liability protect a driver against potential financial losses?

8. What costs are covered by medical payments and uninsured motorists protection?

9. What protection is provided by property damage liability?

10. How does collision coverage differ from comprehensive physical damage coverage?

11. What factors influence how much a person pays for automobile insurance?

12. What actions can a driver take to reduce the cost of automobile insurance?

DISCUSSION QUESTIONS AND ACTIVITIES

1. What additional insurance coverages might the Lemtons consider obtaining?

2. What factors should the Lemtons consider when deciding whether they have enough insurance or require additional coverages?

3. Talk to several friends and relatives about their household inventory records. In case of damage or loss, would they be able to prove the value of their personal belongings?

4. Interview an insurance agent about the cost differences for various types of home insurance policies. Which form is most commonly used? What type of coverage does the agent recommend?

5. Examine a homeowners or renters insurance policy. What coverages does the policy include? Does the policy contain any unclear features or wording?

6. What factors should a person consider when selecting an insurance company for home or automobile coverage?

7. Should all states require automobile liability insurance before a person is issued license plates for a vehicle? Give reasons for your answer.

8. What actions should government agencies take to reduce automobile accidents and injuries?

9. Compare the costs of automobile insurance with three agents representing different companies. What might be the reasons for any difference in rates among the companies?

10. Should female drivers be charged less than male drivers for comparable automobile insurance coverage? Should unmarried drivers be charged more than married drivers? Give reasons for your answers.

ADDITIONAL READINGS

"Auto Insurance." *Consumer Reports*, September 1984, pp. 501–13.

Berman, Eleanor. "How Good Is Your Homeowners Policy?" *Sylvia Porter's Personal Finance*, May 1986, pp. 62, 64, 66–67.

How to Protect What's Yours. New York: Insurance Information Institute, 1985.

Mehr, Robert I. *Fundamentals of Insurance*. 2nd ed. Homewood, Ill.: Richard D. Irwin, 1986.

"Renters Need Insurance, Too." *Changing Times*, November 1985, p. 98.

Your Insurance Dollar. Prospect Heights, Ill.: Money Management Institute, Household Financial Services, 1986.

CASE 12–1 Insuring a Home

John Collier recently bought a home for $83,000 in an area with many older homes that are being remodeled and improved with new roofs and room additions. John has about $6,000 worth of personal belongings other than his automobile. He has a busy work schedule, and he travels to other cities several times each month. He is not sure what type or amount of home insurance he should have.

Questions

1. As a homeowner, what financial risks does John face?

2. How should John determine how much insurance he needs on his home?

3. What types of home insurance are available to John?

4. What type of policy and amount of coverage would you recommend?

CASE 12–2 Insuring a Car

Fran Bowen owns a four-year-old automobile that she drives to work each day. She also uses it for visits to friends and for vacations. She drives about 14,000 miles a year. Currently, Fran has full coverage for all phases of bodily injury and property damage insurance. The amount she pays each year for this coverage increases as the value of her car decreases. She would like to reduce her living expenses for automobile insurance while assuming some of the risk of financial loss associated with driving her car.

Questions

1. What automobile insurance coverage could Fran eliminate?

2. What other actions could Fran take to reduce the cost of her automobile insurance?

3. How would changes in Fran's automobile insurance coverages affect her financial risks?

4. What actions should Fran take?

13

Health Care and Medical Insurance

Health insurance is one way people protect themselves against economic losses due to illness, accident, or disability. The coverage is available through private insurance companies, service plans, health maintenance organizations, and government programs. Employers often offer health insurance as part of an employee benefit package, called group health insurance, and health care providers sell it to individuals.

After studying this chapter, you will be able to:

- Define health insurance.

- Explain why people buy health insurance.

- Differentiate between group and individual health insurance.

- Analyze the benefits and limitations of the various types of health insurance coverages.

- Discuss private sources of health insurance and health care.

- Describe sources of government health programs.

- Explain why the costs of health insurance and health care are increasing.

Interview with **Thomas Drews,** Director,
Corporate Affairs, Blue Cross/Blue Shield of Illinois

Thomas J. Drews currently serves as Director and Consultant to Blue Cross/Blue Shield of Illinois on issues involving public relations, government relations, and media relations. He also serves as the organization's Coordinator of Educational Programs, including its Annual Symposium, which features comprehensive discussions on health care issues and trends by prominent personalities inside and outside the health care field.

Because of the astronomical increases in the costs of providing health care, the purchasers of health insurance, such as large corporations and unions, have been demanding accountability. Blue Cross/Blue Shield is attempting to contain the costs of providing medical care. This can be done in various ways.

For example, thanks to the many advances in medical science, dozens of surgical procedures can now be successfully performed in the outpatient department of a hospital or in a freestanding ambulatory surgical care facility. If you need a procedure of this type, Blue Cross/Blue Shield urges you to take advantage of the time-saving, dollar-saving benefits of having outpatient surgery. Eliminating even one night in the hospital saves *big* dollars— dollars that can make an important difference in the premiums you or your company must pay for health care benefits.

Another way of reducing medical and health care costs is the coordinated home care program. This enables you to leave the hospital earlier by providing skilled care at home. It's the convenient, relaxed way to recover from an illness, operation, or injury.

Under the coordinated home care program, a licensed nurse visits and cares for the discharged patient at home. Such services as changes of dressings, injection of antibiotics, and physical therapy are provided on a regular basis. "Receiving care at home, surrounded by family and friends, does wonders for the patient's morale," states Mr. Drews. And shortening the hospital stay trims dollars from the cost of health care. At current prices, charges for at-home services range from $50 to $100 a day. Compare this with the average charge of $300 a day for just one day's room and board in a hospital, and you can readily see that the savings effected by coordinated home care can be enormous.

By using such services as coordinated home care and ambulatory surgery, you and your family can contribute toward reducing the high cost of health care. Hospitalization is vital when you need it—and a wasteful expense when you don't.

HEALTH INSURANCE: AN OVERVIEW

- What is Health Insurance?

The purpose of health insurance, like that of other forms of insurance, is to reduce the financial burden of risk by dividing losses among many individuals. Health insurance works in the same ways as life insurance, homeowners insurance, or automobile insurance. You pay the insurance company a specified premium, and the company guarantees you some degree of protection. As with other types of insurance, health insurance premiums and benefits are figured on the basis of average experience. To establish rates and benefits, insurance company actuaries rely on general statistics that tell them how many people in a certain population group will become ill and how much their illnesses will cost.

Unlike life insurance or homeowners insurance, however, health insurance is not measured by the actual amount promised as a benefit, as in a $25,000, $50,000, or $100,000 life or homeowners policy. And unlike automobile liability insurance, which fixes a limit on the amount that the company will pay, health insurance is open-ended. That is, no one can determine the maximum benefit return on any given policy. Health insurance limits are often measured by time (90 days, six months, one year, etc.) rather than by dollar amounts, and the value of health insurance is measured by the extent to which it reduces your potential risk (which is unknown) in the

than for comprehensive plans. David Glueck, vice president of a consulting firm, says that 30–40 percent of hospital plan premiums go to nonclaim expenses and insurance firm profits, compared with only 3–7 percent of the premiums for major policies. "Hospital plans are highly profitable for insurers," Glueck says. "They aren't good buys for consumers."

Charles J. Sherfey, a principal with A. S. Hansen, Inc., a Chicago consulting firm says that the alternatives to hospital indemnity insurance are better deals. As one example, he cites interest payments on home equity loans used to cover medical expenses, which are tax deductible under the new tax law. Sherfey also recommends that employees find out whether their company allows workers to make pretax contributions to an account that can be used for medical expenses. Sherfey says that the new tax law continues to allow these plans, which about 1,000 major businesses now have.

If a person has good basic health insurance coverage, the best way to meet uncovered health expenses is with savings, says Stephen Huth, managing editor at the Chicago-based Charles D. Spencer & Associates, publisher of employee benefits information "Most major employer insurance plans," he notes, "are adequate for people who have moderate savings."

*Condensed from the *Your Money Matters* Column of Elliot D. Lee, "Hospital Care: Is Extra Insurance Worth the Cost?" *The Wall Street Journal*, December 10, 1986, p. 33.

event of illness. In short, how much money would you still owe after your group or individual and other supplemental insurance benefits were exhausted? The unpredictability of illness and its costs is the major reason why people buy health insurance.

HEALTH INSURANCE AND FINANCIAL PLANNING

- Why People Buy Health Insurance

From the individual consumer's perspective, illness must be regarded as totally unpredictable. Nearly everyone has friends or loved ones who have been unexpectedly afflicted with serious illness. The reaction often is: "I never would have believed it could happen to so-and-so." Conversely, we all know of people who thought they were desperately ill, yet lived to a ripe old age. In short, both sickness and good health often come as a surprise. This kind of thinking, though very natural, must be excluded from your approach to health insurance. As a health insurance buyer, you must be concerned with potential risks that seldom occur but that everyone faces.

A trip to the dentist for a regular checkup or to the doctor for a routine physical examination can be paid for out of your family's budget. When you are confronted by a major illness or disability, however, health insurance protection is essential. In 1986, daily hospital room rates averaged over $400 and average costs for a routine delivery of a baby were about $3,200, according to the Health Insurance Institute of America (the costs of a Caesarean delivery exceeded $5,000).[1] Even after the insurance payments, families paid about 20 percent of those charges.[2] It is impossible to predict the kind and amount of health services one will need during a lifetime. The way millions of Americans help pay for these services is through private health insurance. This kind of coverage helps protect people from unexpected medical emergencies that may cause their financial devastation.

There are many ways in which individuals, or groups of individuals, can obtain health insurance protection. Planning a health insurance program takes careful study because the protection should be shaped to the needs of the individual or family. For many families, however, the task is simplified because a foundation for their coverage is already provided by the group health insurance they obtain at work.

GROUP AND INDIVIDUAL HEALTH INSURANCE

At year-end 1983, more than 800 private U.S. insurance companies provided group or individual health insurance covering nearly 111 million persons.[3] Most health insurance policies are sold to employers, who in turn offer the benefits of these policies to employees and their dependents.

Group Health Insurance

● Differences between Group and Individual Health Insurance

Group plans comprise more than 85 percent of all the health insurance issued by life insurance companies. As shown in Figure 13–1, most of these plans are employer sponsored and the employer often pays part or all of their cost. Group insurance will cover you and your immediate family.

The protection provided by group insurance varies from plan to plan. If you have group coverage, check with your personnel department or your union office to see exactly what benefits your plan provides. Those benefits may not cover all of your health insurance needs, or they may be lost if you lose your job. In such cases, you will have to start thinking about replacing your insurance or supplementing it with individual health insurance.

Individual Health Insurance

Individual health insurance covers either one person or a family. If the kind of health insurance you need is not available through a group or if you need coverage in addition to the coverage that a group provides, then you should obtain an individual policy—a policy tailored to your particular needs—from the company of your choice. This requires careful shopping because coverage and cost vary from company to company.

[1] *The Wall Street Journal*, April 16, 1986, sec. 2, p. 29.

[2] Ibid.

[3] *Source Book of Health Insurance Data, 1984–1985* (Washington, D.C.: Health Insurance Association of America, 1986), p. 5.

FIGURE 13-1   Most Employers Pay Health Insurance Premiums for Their Employees, Many Require Employee Contributions

Medical coverage

These percentages of surveyed companies require employee contributions to obtain medical coverage for:

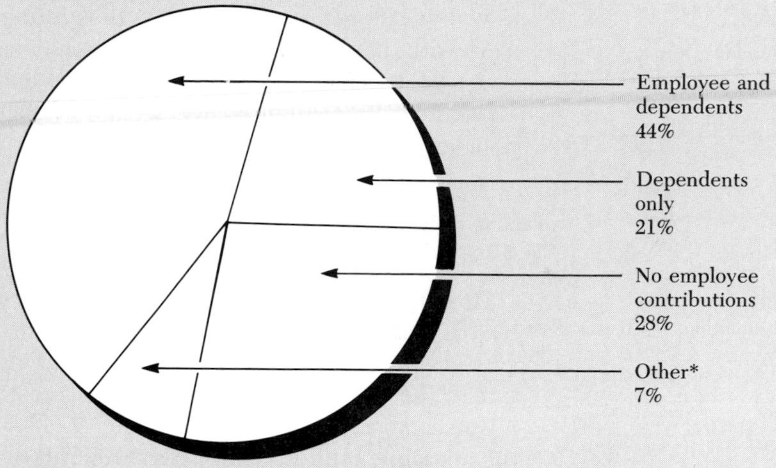

Employee and dependents
44%

Dependents only
21%

No employee contributions
28%

Other*
7%

*Depends on option selected by employee

Source: *The Wall Street Journal,* June 18, 1986, p. 23.

So find out what your group insurance will pay for and what it won't. Make sure you have enough insurance, but don't try to overinsure, because that costs money.

Supplementing Your Group Insurance

A sign that your group coverage needs supplementing would be its failure to provide benefits for the major portion of your medical care bills, mainly hospital, doctor, and surgical charges.

If, for example, your group policy will pay only $150 per day toward a hospital room and the cost in your area is $300, you should look for an individual policy that covers most of the other amount. Similarly, if your group policy will pay for only about half of the going rate for surgical procedures in your area, you need individual coverage for the other half. And if your major medical group policy maximum for all cases is only $50,000, you should be looking for an individual policy that will increase your coverage to at least $250,000.

If you have any questions about your group plan, you should be able to get answers from your employer, your union, or your association. But if you have questions about an individual policy, talk with your insurance company representative.

You should understand the various types of coverages that are available to you or your family.

TYPES OF HEALTH INSURANCE COVERAGES

With today's high cost of health care, it makes sense to be as well insured as you can afford to be. Combining the group plan that is available where you work with the individual policies offered by insurance companies will enable you to put together enough coverage to give you peace of mind. Several types of health insurance coverage are available under group and individual policies.

Hospital Expense Insurance

- Benefits and Limitations of Health Insurance Coverages

Hospital expense insurance pays part or all of hospital bills for room, board, and other charges. Frequently, a maximum amount is allowed for each day in the hospital, up to a maximum number of days. At most other times, the benefit equals the semiprivate room and board charge of the hospital. An additional stated payment is allowed toward such items as use of the operating room and in-hospital laboratory tests, X-rays, and drugs. More people have hospital insurance than any other kind of health insurance.

Surgical Expense Insurance

Surgical expense insurance pays part or all of the surgeon's fee for an operation. A policy of this kind usually lists a number of specific operations and the maximum fee allowed for each. The higher the maximum fee allowed in the policy, the higher the premium charged. Sometimes the benefit is stated in the form of reimbursement up to the usual and customary surgical charges in the geographic area where the operation is performed. Surgical expense insurance is often bought in combination with hospital expense insurance.

Physician's Expense Insurance

Physician's expense insurance helps pay for physician's care that does not involve surgery. Like surgical expense insurance, it lists maximum benefits for specified services. Its coverage may include visits to the doctor's office and the doctor's calls on the patient at home or in the hospital. This type of insurance is usually bought in combination with hospital and surgical insurance. The three types of insurance are called **basic health insurance coverage.**

Major Medical Expense Insurance

Major medical expense insurance protects against the large expenses of a serious injury or a long illness. It adds to the protection offered by basic health insurance coverage. The costs of a serious illness can easily exceed the benefits under hospital, surgical, and physician's expense policies. Major medical pays the bulk of the additional costs. The maximum benefits payable under major medical insurance are high—$50,000, $100,000, or even more.

Major medical helps pay most kinds of hospital and nonhospital expenses for treatment prescribed by the physician. Such expenses may include doctor bills, nursing care, X-ray and laboratory charges, medicines, ambulance service, a wheelchair, crutches, and so on. Because major medical insurance offers such a wide range of benefits and provides high maximums, it contains two features to help keep the premium within the policyholder's means.

One of these features is a **deductible** provision that requires the policyholder to pay a basic amount before the policy benefits begin—for example, the first $500 under an individual plan and a lesser amount under a group plan. (Sometimes part or all of the deductible amount is covered by the benefits of a basic hospital and surgical plan.)

The other feature is a **coinsurance** provision that requires the policyholder to share the expenses beyond the deductible amount. Many policies pay 75 or 80 percent of expenses above the deductible amount. The policyholder pays the rest.

Some major medical policies contain a **stop-loss** provision. This requires the policyholder to pay up to a certain amount, after which the insurance company pays 100 percent of all remaining covered expenses. Typically, the out-of-pocket payment is $2,000.

Comprehensive Major Medical Insurance

Comprehensive major medical insurance is a type of major medical insurance that has a very low deductible amount, often $100 or $200, and is offered without any separate basic plan. This all-inclusive health insurance helps pay hospital, surgical, medical, and other bills.

Many major medical policies have specific maximum benefits for certain expenses, such as hospital room and board and the cost of surgery. Some of these policies pay 75 or 80 percent of the semiprivate room rate and the usual and customary charges of the area.

Disability Income Insurance

Disability income insurance benefits provide for the partial replacement of income lost by employees as the result of an accident, illness, or pregnancy. Generally, disability income policies are divided into two types: (1) those that provide benefits for up to two years (short-term) and (2) those that provide benefits for a longer period, usually for at least five years but often to age 65 or for life (long-term).

The amount of the benefits may vary, depending on whether the disability is total or partial. The duration of the benefits may vary, depending on whether the disability results from an accident or from an illness. Some policies include a provision whereby monthly income benefits are increased each year according to a predetermined formula, which may be related to the cost of living.

When disability income policies are provided on a group basis, the benefits are usually integrated with benefits from social security and other public programs. The total benefits from these sources are generally set at a level that does not exceed 60 percent of salary.

Individual disability income policies usually provide a fixed dollar amount of coverage. This amount may be greater for persons who are turned down by social security. Individual disability income policies have many forms, designed to fit the special needs of the policyholder.

Most disability income policies provide for a waiting period before payments begin, such as a week, a month, two months, or 90 days. The longer the waiting period, the lower the premium cost of the policy. Which choice a salaried employee makes will depend in part on how long the employer will continue to pay the salary during a period of disability. Another consideration is the family's savings or other resources. By meeting the expenses of a short illness out of savings and using insurance to protect against longer disability, a family can buy disability protection at a lower cost.

An important feature of individual health insurance policies is the **incontestable clause,** which specifies that the company must continue the policy unless the policyholder stops paying the premiums. This clause takes effect once the policy has been in effect for a period of time, usually two or three years, depending on state law and the type of policy.

Keep in mind the following rules when you shop for disability income insurance. Ask for noncancelable and guaranteed renewable coverage. Either coverage will protect you against having your insurance company drop you if your health turns bad. Second, consider long-term coverage, to age 65 or beyond, if you are still gainfully employed. The possibility of being disabled permanently makes such coverage worth considering. Third, buy both accident and sickness coverage. Some policies will pay only for accidents. You want to be insured for illness, too.

Always remember that you may already have some form of disability insurance. Your employer may have some form of wage continuation policy that lasts a few months, or an employee group disability plan may provide long-term protection. There is also state worker's compensation for job-connected disability, and there is social security. You are eligible for benefits in the sixth month of disability, so long as the disability has lasted or is expected to last at least 12 months and you are under age 65.

It is a good idea to know exactly how much coverage you have. This will keep you from buying more insurance than you need. What's wrong with overinsuring? First, it is almost always unwise to buy more of anything than you really need. Second, many overinsured people take far more time than they need to return to work.

Hospital Indemnity Policies

A **hospital indemnity policy** pays benefits only when you are hospitalized, but these benefits are paid to you in cash and you can use the money for medical, nonmedical, or supplementary expenses. While such policies have limited coverage, their benefits can have wide usage. The hospital indemnity policy is not a substitute for basic or major medical protection but a supplement to it.

Hospital indemnity policies of many kinds are available from insurance companies by mail, as described in the Opening Scenario, or through insurance agents. Usually, these policies promise to pay between $50 and $100 a day. This represents only a small fraction of daily hospital charges, which now average over $400. A hospital indemnity policy provides no financial security once Medicare contributions have been reduced or expire. Moreover, many of these policies begin to pay benefits only after you have been hospitalized for a specified number of days. The average benefit return does not justify the premium cost.

Many people buy hospital indemnity policies in the hope that they will make money if they get sick. A hospital indemnity policy in this way is like buying a lottery ticket. If your potential risk does not justify buying the policy, because that risk is either too high or too low, doing so would be throwing your money away. You should not sacrifice supplemental health insurance coverage in order to pay the premiums of a hospital indemnity policy.

Interim or Short-Term Medical Insurance

When you lose your job, you are almost certain to lose any group health insurance you may have had. But there are steps you can take to protect yourself and your family until you find another job.

First, find out whether your insurance will continue after your last day at work and if so, exactly how long. It may continue for 30 days or longer, depending on your employer's policy. Next, find out whether you can convert your group coverage to an individual policy. Remember that your benefits under an individual policy will probably not be as good as they were before and that the policy will be more expensive.

If your spouse is employed, find out whether you can receive coverage through his or her employer.

However, if you are healthy and not more than 60 years old and you want more complete protection, you might consider an interim or short-term medical policy.

An interim policy will frequently insure you from two to six months and make payments toward hospitalization, intensive care treatment, doctor in-hospital visits, surgical expenses, miscellaneous hospital expenses, and nursing home care. Such a policy also includes outpatient diagnostic X-ray or laboratory procedures and ambulance coverage.

Most interim policies are effective immediately or within 30 days of purchase. Many interim policies may be reissued once during a 12-month period.

As with other types of health insurance, you should take an interim policy in which you absorb the small medical bills while your insurance handles the big ones. An example of such a policy is one that requires you to pay the first $100 or $500, after which the insurance company pays 80 percent of the next $5,000 and 100 percent of all additional expenses up to your maximum benefit of $25,000 or more.

Dental Expense Insurance

Dental expense insurance provides reimbursement for the expenses of dental services and supplies and encourages preventive dental care. The coverage normally provides for oral examinations (including X rays and cleanings), fillings, extractions, inlays, bridgework, and dentures as well as oral surgery, root canal therapy, and orthodontics.

Dental coverage is generally available through insurance company group plans, prepayment plans, and dental service corporations.

Vision Care Insurance

In the past few years, an interesting development in health insurance coverage has been vision insurance, which has been offered, usually to groups, by an increasing number of insurance companies and prepayment plans.

Pepper . . . and Salt

"He used to sing protest songs about racism and injustice. <u>Now</u> he sings protest songs about meat loaf and orthodontist bills."

From *The Wall Street Journal*, with permission of Cartoon Features Syndicate.

Vision care coverages include eye examinations, prescription lenses, frames, and contact lenses. Not covered are certain services and materials, such as vision training, multifocal plastic lenses, coated or oversized lenses, nonprescription lenses, and tinted lenses.

Accident Insurance

Accident insurance is not really health insurance. Accident insurance policies pay hospital and medical costs only if you have been injured as a result of an accident. The policies frequently impose limits on benefits that are far below the real costs of rehabilitation.

Accident indemnity policies promise to pay a specified amount for the loss of one or both eyes, arms, or legs in an accident. The policies are so narrowly written, however, that they apply in only a very small set of circumstances. Amputees who have had their limbs removed for clinical reasons are not protected by such policies. This kind of insurance can be a waste of money.

Dread Disease and Cancer Insurance Policies

Dread disease and cancer policies, which are usually solicited through the mail, in newspapers and magazines, or by door-to-door salespeople working on commission, are notoriously poor values. Their appeal is based on unrealistic fears, and a number of states have prohibited their sale. Such policies provide coverage only for very specific conditions and are no substitute for comprehensive insurance.

Even if you do contract a disease insured by such a policy, the chances are that you will not be in the hospital long enough to see a benefit return that justifies the premiums. Moreover, these policies normally do not provide protection against many types of costs incurred as a result of the disease, such as home care, transportation, and rehabilitation.

National Insurance Consumer Oganization (NICO), based in Alexandria, Virginia, advises that cancer or dread disease insurance is simply a bad buy, citing its narrow coverage. "If you have a heart attack, cancer insurance doesn't do any good," says Robert Hunter, president of NICO.

Companies that sell cancer insurance policies, including Mutual of Omaha, defend the policies on the ground of their use as a supplement to other plans. Mutual of Omaha, which pays $2,500 immediately upon diagnosis of cancer and then up to $150,000 for subsequent treatment, says that its $2,500 immediate payment can be used even for incidental items such as telephone and transportation.

Contact Lens Insurance

A policy covering the loss of contact lenses typically costs $25 for one year and $48 for two. The insured, however, generally pays a deductible of about $8 to $12.

Unless the policyholder tends to lose contact lenses frequently or has unusually expensive lenses, such insurance is rarely desirable. Two major optical retailers in the New York City area currently sell some contact lenses for $25 to $30 each.

Nursing Home Insurance

Nursing home insurance policies are relatively new products whose nature is changing quickly. In Illinois, for example, most nursing home insurance products provide benefits for skilled care only. A few companies offer additional benefits for intermediate or custodial care.

Skilled care is care given by the nursing home staff to provide supervision and/or total assistance to meet all of the resident's medical and physical needs on a 24-hour basis. Generally, skilled care includes medical or therapeutic services that can only be performed under the direct supervision of nurses, physical therapists, or other medically trained professionals.

Intermediate care is care given in an institutional setting for those who are chronically ill and incapable of independent living. These services are less intensive than skilled care.

Custodial care is care given to assist with everyday activities such as bathing and dressing. This care is for individuals who do not need health-related services.

Home health care is care received at home for such services as cleaning wounds, changing bandages, and giving injections. In some cases, this care replaces institutional care.

Most nursing home policies require a certain amount of skilled care before intermediate or custodial benefits are provided. Some policies also require the nursing home facility to meet certain standards. For example, you may have to be admitted to a certified, skilled facility to receive benefits.

An insurance company usually allows you a minimum of 10 days to review the nursing home policy. If you find that you are not completely satisfied, you may return it for a refund of premium within the time allowed.

In this section, we have discussed 14 types of health insurance coverages. A natural question is: How should you choose among these many types of coverages?

Which Coverage Should You Choose?[4]

Now that you are familiar with the available types of health insurance, let's look at the reality of it all. The most important thing to understand is that the more money you are ready to pay for insurance, the more coverage you can get.

When it comes to medical insurance, you have three choices. You can buy (1) basic, (2) major medical, or (3) both of them.

[4]*What You Should Know about Health Insurance*, Consumer Series (Washington, D.C.: Health Insurance Association of America, 1986), pp. 10–11.

If your pocketbook is very limited, then it is a toss-up between choosing a basic plan and choosing a major medical plan. In many cases, either plan will handle the lion's portion of your hospital and doctor bills. In the event of an illness involving catastrophic costs, however, you will need the protection given by a major medical policy. Ideally, you should get a basic plan and a major medical supplementary plan. Or you should get a comprehensive major medical policy that combines the values of both these plans in a single policy.

Let's look at the hypothetical cases of the Jones family, which has basic and major medical coverage, and the Brown family, which has only the basic coverage.

Let's suppose that the breadwinner in each of these families requires a coronary bypass operation. Both breadwinners recover—after heart surgery and a hospital stay lasting 15 days.

The Jones family has a major medical policy that pays 80 percent of the total bills up to a maximum of $250,000 after the family pays a $5,000 deductible. To offset this deductible, the family also has a basic hospital-surgical expense policy paying $150 a day toward hospital room and board for 180 days ($300 a day for time in an intensive care unit), with an additional in-hospital allowance of $1,000 and a $1,500 maximum benefit for surgery.

On the other hand, the Browns have an identical basic policy but no major medical policy.

Table 13–1 shows about what the bills would amount to for the two fami-

---

TABLE 13-1   Hospital Cost for Two Families

Services	Charges
Hospital daily room and board, 5 days at $400 a day (intensive care) plus 10 days at $200 a day, semiprivate accommodation	$ 4,000
Additional in-hospital services such as operating room, operation of heart-lung machine, and X-ray and laboratory tests	1,400
Private duty nursing (2 days)	400
Surgeon's fee, including in-hospital postoperative consultation and care	3,300
Cardiologist's fee	1,300
Out-of-hospital physician services only	700
Total expenses	$11,100
Paid by basic insurance	$ 5,500
Paid by major medical	4,880
Total paid by Jones's insurance	10,380
Total paid by Brown's insurance	5,500
Total paid by Jones*	720
Total paid by Brown	5,600

*Deductible, coinsurance, and certain miscellaneous expenses.

Source: *What You Should Know about Health Insurance*, Consumer Series (Washington, D.C.: Health Insurance Association of America), p. 11.

lies. It illustrates the importance of major medical coverage in handling catastrophic bills—bills that are not likely to hit the average family but that most definitely can.

PRIVATE SOURCES OF HEALTH INSURANCE AND HEALTH CARE

Health insurance is available from more than 800 private insurance companies, from service plans such as Blue Cross/Blue Shield, from health maintenance organizations, from government programs such as Medicare, and from fraternal organizations and trade unions.

Private Insurance Companies

As discussed earlier, at year-end 1983, more than 800 private U.S. insurance companies were writing individual group health insurance covering nearly 111 million persons.[5] Policies issued by insurance companies provide for payment either directly to the insured for reimbursement of expenses incurred or, if assigned by the insured, to the provider of services.

Most private insurance companies sell health insurance policies to employers, which in turn offer the benefits to employees and their dependents, as fringe benefits. The premiums may be wholly or partially paid by employers.

Hospital and Medical Service Plans

Blue Cross and Blue Shield are statewide organizations similar to commercial health insurance companies. Each state has its own Blue Cross and Blue Shield.

Blue Cross plans provide *hospital care benefits* on essentially a "service type" basis. Through a separate contract with each member hospital, the organization reimburses the hospital for covered services provided to the insured.

Blue Shield plans provide benefits for *surgical and medical services* performed by physicians. The typical Blue Shield plan provides benefits similar to those provided under the benefit provisions of hospital-surgical policies issued by insurance companies.

The rates and coverages of Blue Cross and Blue Shield are administered locally. Both organizations have contracts with participating hospitals and doctors that set the amounts they will pay for the covered services. These amounts are often less than the amounts charged to cash patients and insurance companies. The "Blues" always pay the hospital or doctor directly. In 1984, there were 90 Blue Cross and Blue Shield plans.[6]

- Private Sources of Health Insurance and Health Care

---

[5] *Source Book of Health Insurance Data, 1984–1985*, p. 5.
[6] Ibid.

Health Maintenance Organizations (HMOs)

Health maintenance organizations represent one of the most revolutionary changes that have been taking place in health care. A **health maintenance organization** is a health insurance plan that directly employs or contracts with selected physicians to provide you with health care services in exchange for a fixed, prepaid monthly premium. HMOs operate on the premise that maintaining your health through preventive care will minimize future medical problems.

The preventive care provided by HMOs includes periodic checkups, screening programs, diagnostic testing, and immunizations. HMOs also provide a comprehensive range of other health care services. These services are divided into two categories—basic and supplemental. *Basic health services*

In the Real World
Tips on How to Use and Choose an HMO

How to Use an HMO When you first enroll in an HMO, you must choose a plan physician (family practitioner, internist, pediatrician, or obstetrician-gynecologist) who provides or arranges for all of your health care services. It is extremely important that you receive your care through the plan physician. If you don't, you are responsible for the cost of the service rendered.

The only exceptions to the requirement that care be received through the plan physician are medical emergencies. A medical emergency is a sudden onset of illness or a sudden injury that would jeopardize your life or health if it were not treated immediately. In such instances, you may use the facilities of the nearest hospital emergency room. All other care must be provided by hospitals and doctors under contract with the HMO.

How to Choose an HMO

If you decide to enroll in an HMO, there are a number of additional factors that you should consider:

1. *Accessibility.* Since you must use plan providers, it is extremely important that they be easily accessible from your home or office.
2. *Convenient Office Hours.* Your plan physician should have convenient office hours.
3. *Alternative Physicians.* Should you become dissatisfied with your first choice of a physician, the HMO should allow you the option of changing physicians.
4. *Second Opinions.* You should be able to obtain second opinions.
5. *Type of Coverage.* You should compare the health care services offered by various HMOs, paying particular attention to whether you will incur out-of-pocket expenses or copayments.
6. *Appeal Procedures.* The HMO should have a convenient and prompt method of resolving problems and disputes.
7. *Price.* You should compare the prices charged by various HMOs to see that you are getting the most services for your health care dollar.

include inpatient, outpatient, maternity, mental health, substance abuse, and emergency care. *Supplemental services* include vision, hearing, and pharmaceutical care, which are usually available for an additional fee.

Types of HMOs. Health maintenance organizations vary widely in the types of health care delivery systems that they use. In a *staff model HMO*, the physicians, nurses, and other support personnel are all salaried employees of the HMO. *Group model HMOs* provide professional treatment through a multispecialty medical group practice that is under contract with the HMO. *Independent practice association (IPA) model HMOs* provide care through independent physicians who are under contract with the HMO. However, regardless of the delivery system used, the HMO will provide or arrange for your health care through hospitals, physicians, and specialists.

Whether or not an HMO is right for you depends largely on your willingness and ability to use its network of health care providers. If, for example, you take extended vacations or spend a lot of time out-of-state, an HMO may not be an acceptable option. The accompanying boxed feature on page 407 offers tips on how to use and choose an HMO.

Growth of HMOs. During the past 10 years, the HMO movement has become a viable, dynamic industry. Beginning as a handful of prepaid plans scattered across the country, HMOs are now a well-established health care system. From 1980 to 1985, as Figure 13–2 shows, the number of HMOs almost doubled (from 244 to 480) and the membership of HMOs more than doubled (from less than 10 million to over 20 million).[7]

Future of HMOs. The future of HMOs seems very promising. Across the nation, they have already changed the course of health care. By 1990, they are expected to enroll as many as 30 million members and to generate $25 billion in revenues.[8] That expectation is based on recent trends reflecting the ever-growing acceptance of the HMOs among consumers, employers, and health professionals.

The future will also bring changes in the HMOs. With the support of business, labor, medical, and local government leaders, new HMO plans will be introduced. National profit and nonprofit HMO firms are certain to develop and expand, providing the HMO industry with the advantages of capital resources and management expertise. Excellent profits on investments will be a by-product of well-run HMOs. Read the accompanying boxed feature to learn how some life insurance companies plan to market their health care systems in the future.

[7] Jennifer Bingham Hull, "Physicians Organize to Stop HMOs from Altering Practice of Medicine," *The Wall Street Journal*, June 23, 1986, p. 23.

[8] *A History of Achievement, a Future with Promise*" (Washington, D.C. National Industry Council for HMO Development, 1984), p. 28. This work updates *The Health Maintenance Organization Industry: Ten-Year Report, 1973–1983*.

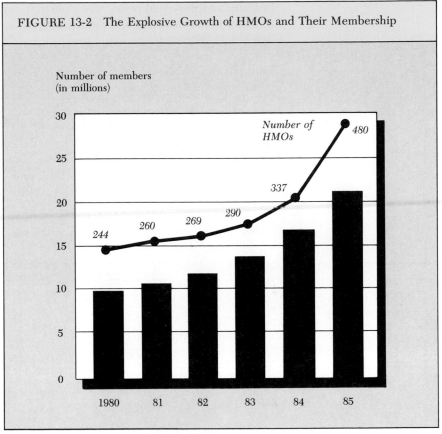

FIGURE 13-2   The Explosive Growth of HMOs and Their Membership

Source: Jennifer Bingham Hull, "Physicians Organize to Stop HMOs from Altering Practice of Medicine," *The Wall Street Journal*, June 23, 1986, p. 23.

Health Associations

Health associations (not to be confused with HMOs) are usually local organizations designed to provide routine and emergency health care more conveniently in relatively isolated areas. These organizations usually operate one or more clinics and employ a small number of physicians, dentists, and supporting staff.

For a nominal fee of $15 to $30 per year, anyone can join a health association. Membership entitles you to participate in the association's programs and allows you to make appointments with doctors and dentists at the association's clinics. Health associations provide no health insurance, however. You are responsible for any charges. You must have your own insurance. Aside from the convenience offered by health association membership, there is another advantage. Health associations participating in Medicare must agree to accept Medicare payment as payment in full. Thus, if you have a

Medicare supplemental policy that does not cover the difference between Medicare's reasonable fee and the actual cost, membership in a health association may be wise.

Home Health Agencies[9]

Home health care providers furnish and are responsible for supervision and management of preventive medical care in a home setting in accordance with a medical order. Rising hospital care costs, new medical technology, and the increasing number of the elderly and infirm have helped make home care one of the fastest-growing areas of the health care industry. Other factors that have contributed to the growth of home health care are government support through Medicare and Medicaid program payments, the inclusion of

[9]"Health Services," in *U.S. Industrial Outlook, 1986* (Washington, D.C.: U.S. Government Printing Office, 1986), p. 54–4.

In the News
New Options in Health Insurance: COBRA

H ealth insurance—it's something you probably take for granted if you or your spouse work, since many employers offer it as part of an employee benefit package. But what if you lost your job or became divorced from a spouse under whose plan you were covered? Until now, termination of employment or divorce probably meant that you also lost your health benefits.

But there is some good news for people in these situations. A law passed by the U.S. Congress in 1986 provides new health insurance options to people facing the termination of their employer-sponsored coverage. These options apply to such situations as the loss of a job, divorce, death of a spouse, or a number of other events.

Under the Consolidated Omnibus Budget Reconciliation Act of 1986 (COBRA) many employers are required to offer employees and dependents who would otherwise lose group health insurance the option of continuing their group coverage for a set period of time, at their own expense.

COBRA, which became effective between July 1, 1986 and June 30, 1987, requires most employers of more than 20 people to offer an option which would continue group health insurance for periods ranging from 18 months to three years. Eligible former employees and dependents have the right to the same coverage as active members of the group. For example, if your employer offers such features as vision or dental care, you would be entitled to those same features if you become a participant in the continued group health insurance plan.

Employees of private companies and state and local governments are covered by this new law. Employees of the federal government and churches are not.

Source: *Consumer Notes*, American Council of Life Insurance, Washington, D.C., April, 1987.

TABLE 13-2   Medicare-Certified Home Health Agencies (HHAs)

Year	Number of Non-Hospital-Based HHAs	Medicare Expenditures ($ millions)
1966	1,713	$ 5
1977	2,296	339
1980	2,509	645
1984	4,343	1,631

Source: *U.S. Industrial Outlook*, 1986, p. 54–4.

home health care in an increasing number of health insurance policies, and the tendency of hospitals to discharge patients before they have fully recovered.

Home health care costs can range from $30 per visit by a paramedic to help a patient with dressing changes to $70,000 per year for certain types of difficult health care cases. A patient requiring three weeks of antibiotic therapy in the Washington, D.C., metropolitan area could save $5,640 by being treated at home rather than in a hospital.

The number of non-hospital-based home health agencies (HHAs) certified by Medicare rose from 1,713 in 1966 to 4,343 in 1984. As shown in Table 13–2, the number of HHAs almost doubled from 1980 to 1984. Table 13–2 also shows that Medicare expenditures for certified home health care grew from $5 million in 1966 to over $1.6 billion in 1984.

Home health care is an entry point for posthospitalization treatment, which hospital administrators see as a profitable opportunity. Hence, hospitals are rapidly moving into the home health care business, posing a threat to independent home care agencies. Discharging patients promptly and then sending them to home health care centers enables hospitals to reduce their overhead costs in fulfilling the Medicare program requirements and also to profit from their home health care activities.

The major national home care chains are Upjohn Healthcare Services, with about 300 offices in 44 states, Canada, and the United Kingdom; H&R Block's Medical Personnel Pool, with about 200 offices in 41 states and Canada; Quality Care, with 163 offices in 43 states; and Staff Builders, with 100 offices in 27 states.

Employer Self-Funded Health Plans

Certain types of health insurance coverage are made available by plans administered by employers, labor unions, fraternal societies, or communities. Usually, these groups provide the amount of protection that a specific group of people desires and can afford.

It is estimated that about 39 percent of the total 1983 insurance company group coverage was represented by administrative service only (ASO) arrangements and minimum premium plans (MPPs). Under these systems, corporations and other organizations establish self-funded health plans. Under ASO arrangements, insurance carriers or private organizations are paid a fee by the self-funded group to process the claims and benefits paperwork. Under MPPs, many employers also insure against a certain level of large, unpredictable claims. These two types of arrangements represented about 5 percent of total insurance company group coverage prior to 1975.[10]

It is important to note that self-funded groups must assume the financial burden if the medical bills are greater than the amount covered by premium income. While private insurance companies have the assets to fall back upon should the need arise, self-funded plans often do not. The results can be disastrous.

In addition to the private sources of health insurance and health care discussed in this section, there are government health programs covering over 31 million people.

GOVERNMENT HEALTH CARE PROGRAMS

Federal and state governments offer health coverage in accordance with laws that define the premiums and benefits they can offer. Specific requirements as to age, occupation, length of service, and family income may be used to determine eligibility for coverage. Two sources of government health insurance are Medicare and Medicaid.

Medicare

● Government Sources of Health Insurance

Medicare is a federal health insurance program for people 65 or older, people of any age with permanent kidney failure, and certain disabled people. The program is administered by the Health Care Financing Administration. Local Social Security Administration offices take applications for Medicare, assist beneficiaries in filing claims, and provide information about the program.

Medicare has two parts—hospital insurance (Part A) and medical insurance (Part B). Hospital insurance helps pay for inpatient hospital care and certain follow-up care. Medical insurance helps pay for your doctor's services and many other medical services and items.

Hospital insurance is financed from part of the social security tax. Voluntary medical insurance is financed from the monthly premiums paid by people who have enrolled for it and from general federal revenues.

Hospital Insurance. Some people have to apply for hospital insurance protection before it can start. But if you are receiving social security checks, your hospital insurance protection automatically begins at 65. If you are not eligible for hospital insurance at 65, you can buy it. The basic premium in

[10] *Source Book of Health Insurance Data, 1984–1985*, p. 6.

1986 was $214 a month. To buy hospital insurance, you also have to enroll for medical insurance and pay a $15.50 monthly premium.

Hospital Insurance Benefits. Medicare hospital insurance can help pay for inpatient hospital care, inpatient care in a skilled nursing facility, home health care, and hospice care.

If you need inpatient care, hospital insurance helps pay for up to 90 days in any participating hospital for each spell of illness. In 1986, hospital insurance paid for all but the first $492 of covered services for the first 60 days. For the 61st through the 90th day, hospital insurance paid for all covered services over $123 a day.

Medical Insurance. Almost anyone who is 65 or older or who is eligible for hospital insurance can enroll for Medicare medical insurance. You don't need any social security or federal work credits to get medical insurance. The basic premium was $15.50 a month in 1986.

Medical Insurance Benefits. Medicare medical insurance helps pay for your doctor's services and for a variety of other medical services and supplies that are not covered by hospital insurance. Each year, as soon as you meet the annual medical insurance deductible, medical insurance will pay 80 percent of the approved charges for the covered services that you receive during the rest of the year. In 1986, the annual deductible was $75.

Table 13–3 presents a summary of benefits that were available through Part A and Part B of Medicare in 1986.

Medicaid

Title XIX of the Social Security Act provides for a program of medical assistance to certain low-income individuals and families. In 1965, the program, known as Medicaid, became federal law.

Medicaid is administered by each state within certain broad federal requirements and guidelines. Financed by both state and federal funds, it is designed to provide medical assistance to those groups or categories of persons who are eligible to receive payments under one of the cash assistance programs, such as Aid to Families with Dependent Children and Supplemental Security Income. States may also provide Medicaid to the medically needy, that is, to persons who fit into one of the categories eligible for public assistance.

Many members of the Medicaid population are also covered by Medicare. Where such dual coverage exists, most state Medicaid programs pay for the Medicare premiums, deductibles, and copayments and for services not covered by Medicare.

To qualify for federal matching funds, state programs must include: inpatient hospital services; outpatient hospital services; laboratory and X-ray services; skilled nursing and home health services for individuals aged 21 and older; family planning services; early and periodic screening, diagnosis, and

TABLE 13-3   Summary of Medicare Benefits

Medicare Service	Benefit	Medicare Pays (1986)	You Pay (1986)
Medicare Part A: Hospital-insurance-covered services per benefit period			
Hospitalization: Semiprivate room and board, general nursing and hospital services, supplies	First 60 days	All but $492	$492
	61st–90th day	All but $123 a day	$123 a day
	91st–150th day	All but $246 a day	$246 a day
	Beyond 150 days (60 reserve days)	Nothing (All but $246 a day)	All costs ($246 a day)
Posthospital skilled nursing facility care in facility approved by Medicare— after you've been in hospital at least 3 days and enter facility within 30 days after hospital discharge	First 20 days	100% of approved amount	Nothing
	Additional 80 days	All but $61.50 a day	$61.50 a day
	Beyond 100 days	Nothing	All costs
Home health care	Unlimited visits as medically necessary	Full cost	Nothing
Hospice care	Two 90-day periods and one 30-day period	All but limited costs for outpatient drugs and inpatient respite care	Limited cost sharing for outpatient drugs and inpatient respite care
Blood	Blood	All but first 3 pints	For first 3 pints

Note: The 60 reserve hospital days may be used only once. All payment figures may change each year. The "benefit period" starts on the first day you receive service as an inpatient in a hospital and ends after you have been out of the hospital or skilled nursing facility for 60 days in a row.

Medicare Service	Benefit	Medicare Pays (1986)	You Pay (1986)
Medicare Part B: Medical-insurance-covered services per calendar year			
Medical expense: Physicians' and surgeons' services, inpatient and outpatient medical services and supplies (X rays, wheelchairs, etc.), physical and speech therapy, ambulance . . .	Medicare pays for medical services in or out of the hospital	80% of approved amount, after $75 deductible	$75 deductible plus 20% of balance of approved amount plus any charge above approved amount
Home health care visits	Unlimited, as medically necessary	Full cost	Nothing
Outpatient hospital treatment	Unlimited, as medically necessary	80% of approved amount, after the deductible	The deductible plus 20% of balance of approved amount
Blood	Blood	80% of approved amount, after first 3 pints	For first 3 pints plus 20% of balance of approved amount

Source: *Citicorp Consumer Views*, March 1986. Copyright by Citicorp, 399 Park Avenue, New York, NY 10043.

treatment for individuals under 21; and physicians' services in the home, office, hospital, or nursing home or elsewhere.

HEALTH CARE COSTS

• Why the Costs of Health Insurance and Health Care Are Increasing

Many people think that the monster of health care inflation has been licked or at least driven back into its cave. In 1986, it was stated that "spending on health care in 1985 rose at the lowest level in two decades." Unfortunately, reports about the defeat of the "health care monster" may be vastly exaggerated.[11]

In 1986, we spent almost $470,000,000,000 on health care, 10.6 percent of the gross national product (see Figure 13–3). It amounts to $1,773 per person! Hospital costs accounted for 40.8 percent of all health expenditures.[12]

The nation's health care bill is estimated at a little over $1.25 billion a day. An average length of 6.6 days in the hospital cost $3,811 in 1986, and the

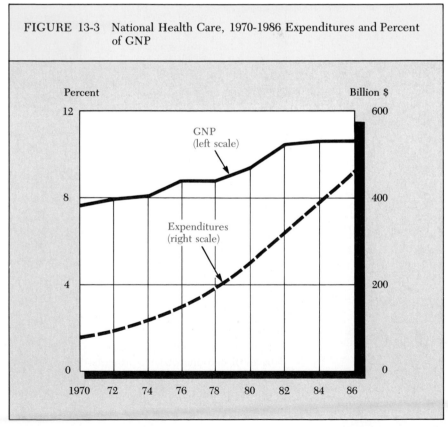

FIGURE 13-3   National Health Care, 1970-1986 Expenditures and Percent of GNP

Source: *U.S. Industrial Outlook*, 1986, p. 54–1.

[11] Uwe E. Reinhardt, "Battle Over Medical Costs Isn't Over," *The Wall Street Journal*, October 22, 1986, p. 28.

[12] *U.S. Industrial Outlook, 1986*, p. 54–1; and *USA Today*, January 30, 1986, sec. D, p. 1.

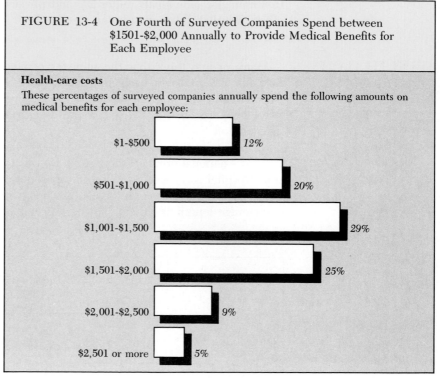

FIGURE 13-4   One Fourth of Surveyed Companies Spend between
$1501-$2,000 Annually to Provide Medical Benefits for
Each Employee

Health-care costs

These percentages of surveyed companies annually spend the following amounts on
medical benefits for each employee:

$1-$500	12%
$501-$1,000	20%
$1,001-$1,500	29%
$1,501-$2,000	25%
$2,001-$2,500	9%
$2,501 or more	5%

Source: *The Wall Street Journal,* November 28, 1986, p. 11.

prices of prescription drugs have been increasing twice as fast as the Consumer Price Index.[13]

In 1983, executives at Norton Company were stunned when they studied
the firm's skyrocketing medical bills. The cost of health care for employees
was threatening to wipe out the company's $45 million annual profit.[14]

According to the Commerce Department, U.S. companies spent about
$91 billion in 1986 to provide health insurance for more than 130 million
employees and members of their families. They spent $25.5 billion little
more than a decade earlier.[15] Employer premiums for group health insurance have been increasing 20–40 percent annually in recent years, depending on employer size and location. A recent study found that in many companies health care costs comprised almost 25 percent of the payroll. The
Bureau of National Affairs projects that companies and workers will be paying $850 billion for health care by 1990.[16] Figure 13–4 shows that one fourth
of the companies spend between $1501–$2000 annually to provide medical
benefits for each employee.

[13] *Changing Times,* January 1986, p. 40.

[14] *Time,* June 30, 1986, p. 64.

[15] Ibid.

[16] *Fair Payment,* Health Insurance Communications Program Fact Sheet (Washington, D.C.:
Health Insurance Association of America, 1984).

What Can You Do to Reduce Health Care Costs?

The best way to avoid the high cost of sickness is to stay well. The prescription is the same as it has always been:

1. Eat a balanced diet, and keep your weight under control.
2. Avoid smoking, and don't drink to excess.
3. Get sufficient rest and relaxation.
4. Drive carefully, and watch out for accident and fire hazards in the home.

Personal Financial Planning and You
Some Final Consumer Tips on Health and Disability Insurance

1. If you pay your own premiums directly, try to arrange for paying them on an annual or quarterly basis rather than a monthly basis. It is cheaper.
2. Policies should be delivered to you within 30 days. If not, contact your insurer and find out, in writing, why. If a policy is not delivered in 60 days, contact the state department of insurance.
3. When you receive a policy, take advantage of the free look provision. You have 10 days to look it over and to obtain a refund if you decide that it is not for you.
4. Unless you have a policy with no inside limits, read your contract over every year to see whether its benefits are still in line with medical costs.
5. Don't replace a policy because you think it is out-of-date. Switching may subject you to new waiting periods and new exclusions. Rather, add to what you have if necessary.

But . . .

6. Don't keep a policy because you've had it a long time. You don't get any special credit from the company for being an old customer.
7. Don't try to make a profit on your insurance by carrying overlapping coverages. Duplicate coverage is expensive. Besides, most group policies now contain a coordination of benefits clause limiting benefits to 100 percent.
8. Use your health emergency fund to cover small expenses.
9. If you're considering the purchase of a dread disease policy such as cancer insurance, understand that it is supplementary and that it will pay for only one disease. You should have full coverage before you consider it. Otherwise, it's a gamble.
10. Don't lie on your insurance application. If you fail to mention a preexisting condition, you may not get paid. You can usually get paid, even for that condition, after one or two years have elapsed if during that period you have had no treatment for the condition.
11. Keep your insurance up-to-date. Some policies adjust to inflation better than others. Some make sure that their benefits have not been outdistanced by inflation. Review your policies annually.
12. Never sign a health insurance application—such applications are lengthy and detailed for individually written policies—until you have recorded full and complete answers to every question.

Source: Health Insurance Association of America.

Learn to minimize, through intelligent self-care, the need for medical attention.

It is also essential, however, to find a personal physician and to follow his or her orders. Have a periodic physical checkup, especially for blood pressure, signs of diabetes, or cancer symptoms.

Finally, take part in community health activities and support programs to clean up the environment or to further medical research.

SUMMARY

- Health insurance is protection that provides payment of benefits for covered sickness or injury.
- Health insurance is one way in which individuals protect themselves against economic losses due to illness, accident, or disability.
- Health insurance is available in either group or individual contracts. More than 85 percent of all the health insurance issued by insurance companies is in the form of group plans. If the kind of health insurance your family needs is not available through a group, you can purchase an individual policy from the company of your choice.
- Five basic types of health insurance are available under group and individual policies: hospital expense insurance, surgical expense insurance, physician's expense insurance, major medical expense insurance, and comprehensive major medical insurance. Other types of

health insurance are dental expense insurance, vision care insurance, accident insurance, accident indemnity insurance, dread disease insurance, contact lens insurance, and nursing home insurance.
- Health insurance and health care are available from private insurance companies, from service plans such as Blue Cross/Blue Shield, and from health maintenance organizations (HMOs).
- Federal and state governments offer health coverage in accordance with laws that define the premiums and benefits. Two well-known government plans are Medicare and Medicaid.
- Americans spend over $1.25 billion a day on health care, and the nation's health care bill is increasing faster than the Consumer Price Index.

GLOSSARY

Basic health insurance coverage.   Hospital expense insurance, surgical expense insurance, and physician's expense insurance.

Blue Cross.   An independent, nonprofit membership corporation that provides protection against the cost of hospital care.

Blue Shield.   An independent, nonprofit membership corporation that provides protection against the cost of surgical and medical care.

Coinsurance.   A provision under which both the insured person and the insurer share the covered losses.

Comprehensive major medical insurance.   A type of major medical insurance that has a very low deductible amount.

Deductible.   An amount that the insured must pay before benefits by the insurance company become payable.

Disability income insurance.   Provides payments to replace income when an insured is unable to work.

Health maintenance organization.   Provides a wide range of comprehensive health care services at a fixed periodic payment.

Hospital expense insurance.   Pays part or all of hospital bills for room, board, and other charges.

Hospital indemnity policy.   Provides a stipulated daily, weekly, or monthly indemnity during hospital confinement.

Incontestable clause.   A stipulation that the insurer may not contest the validity of the contract, usually after two or three years.

Major medical expense insurance.   Pays most of the costs exceeding those covered by the hospital, surgical, and physician's expense policies.

Physician's expense insurance.   Provides benefits for doctor's fees for nonsurgical care, X rays, and lab tests.

Stop-loss.   A provision under which an insured pays a certain amount, after which the insurance company pays 100 percent of the remaining expenses.

Surgical expense insurance.   Pays part or all of the surgeon's fees for an operation.

REVIEW QUESTIONS

1. Define health insurance. What is its purpose? Why do people buy health insurance?

2. What is the difference between group and individual health insurance? Which is more prevalent, and why?

3. Define and distinguish among hospital expense insurance, surgical expense insurance, and physician's expense insurance. Why are the three grouped together called basic health insurance coverage?

4. What is comprehensive major medical insurance? How does it differ from basic health insurance coverage?

5. What is disability income insurance? Who needs it, and why? Describe the waiting period and incontestable clause provisions in a disability income insurance policy.

6. What are the major sources of health insurance and health care?

7. How do hospital and medical service plans such as Blue Cross and Blue Shield operate? What specific coverages are provided by each of these organizations?

8. What is a health maintenance organization? How does it operate? What are three types of HMOs?

9. Describe the growth experienced by HMOs from 1980 to 1985 and evaluate the prospects of HMOs.

10. How do health associations and home health care agencies operate? What is their cost structure?

11. What are employer self-funded health plans, and how do they operate?

12. Describe the benefits provided by Medicare and Medicaid.

DISCUSSION QUESTIONS AND ACTIVITIES

1. Will you buy supplementary health insurance from a hospital indemnity insurance company? Why or why not?

2. List health services that you and your family members have used during the past year. Assign an approximate dollar cost to each of these services, and identify the financial resources (savings, health insurance, government sources, etc.) that were used to pay for the services.

3. Contact health insurance companies in your area, and collect information on the coverages that these companies provide (group, individual, disability, supplemental, etc.). Also collect information on the services provided by the HMOs in your area. Compare the provisions and benefits of the various plans. List advantages and disadvantages of each plan.

4. Discuss the need for private health insurance coverage and government health insurance coverage. Discuss the populations comprised by these two types of coverage and the costs of providing the coverage.

5. Make a list of the benefits included in your employee benefit package, such as health insurance, disability insurance, and life insurance. Discuss the importance of such a benefit package to the consumer.

6. Review several disability income insurance plans. Look for the following terms, and develop a definition for each: maximum benefit, benefit period, waiting period, and cancellation clause.

7. Develop a list of hazardous occupations and a list of hazardous hobbies or recreational activities. How do these occupations, hobbies, and activities affect your health and disability insurance?

ADDITIONAL READINGS

Castro, Janice. "Pinned Down by Medical Bills." *Time*, June 30, 1986, p. 64.

Davidson, Joe. "Research Mystery: Use of Surgery, Hospitals Vary Greatly by Region." *The Wall Street Journal*, March 5, 1986, p. 34.

Grady, Denise. "The Health Care Crisis." *Discover*, May 1986, p. 24.

"Guide to Health Insurance for People with Medicare." Washington, D.C.: U.S. Department of Health and Human Services, 1986.

Hull, Jennifer. "Physicians Organize to Stop HMOs from Altering the Practice of Medicine." *The Wall Street Journal*, June 23, 1986, p. 23.

Montana, Constanza. "Confusing, Error-Riddled Bills Frustrate Consumers." *The Wall Street Journal*, February 23, 1986, p. 23.

"Paying for Medical Care after You're 65." *Citicorp Consumer Views*, March 1986, pp. 1–4.

Reinhardt, Uwe. "Battle over Medical Costs Isn't Over." *The Wall Street Journal*, October 22, 1986, p. 28.

Steptoe, Sonja. "Insurers' Audits: Hospitals Seek Second Opinions." *The Wall Street Journal*, June 16, 1986, p. 33.

What You Should Know about Health Insurance. a Consumer Series. Washington, D.C.: Health Insurance Association of America, n.d.

CASE 13–1 Disastrous Disability*

Gene and Dixie are parents of a two-year-old girl. They live in an apartment in a small city in Illinois, where Gene, 24, earns $18,000 a year as a computer salesman. His monthly take-home pay is $1,180. Dixie has given up her job as a secretary to care for their daughter. Gene has no prior military or civil service that might qualify him for government disability programs. Since Gene and Dixie live in a rented apartment, they have no mortgage disability insurance to cover basic housing costs in case of a disability. Unexpectedly, Gene suffers increasingly serious emotional and mental crises. He is unable to function at his job, and a psychiatrist declares him totally disabled.

Gene's employer provides a long-term disability benefit that pays 50 percent of the average earnings of the prior three years. Since Gene did not work long enough to qualify for full coverage, his benefit is based on an assumed average salary of only $10,000—rather than the $18,000 he actually earned. He is ineligible for social security disability benefits because he hadn't been working in covered employment long enough. He is also ineligible for worker's compensation because the disability is not job-related.

The long-term disability policy provided by his employer will pay Gene $417 a month. But Gene and Dixie now have to pay monthly premiums of $100 to continue their group life and medical insurance. While Gene was working, these premiums were paid by the employer. Therefore, Gene, Dixie, and their daughter must now live on a monthly replacement income of only $317.

If Gene and Dixie had realized the inadequacies in Gene's disability income coverage, due partly to the fact that he was relatively new in his job, they could have purchased an individual policy for a nominal fee. A consultation with their agent could have helped them build the income coverage they needed to protect them against the financial disaster they now face.

Questions

1. What, if anything, can Gene and Dixie do to alleviate their present problems?
2. Why do you think Gene did not take advantage of the additional disability insurance that he could have purchased at work?
3. What advice would you offer to someone in Gene's situation? Why?

*Adapted from *What You Should Know about Disability Insurance*, Consumer Series (Washington, D.C.: Health Insurance Association of America, November 1982), pp. 10–11.

CASE 13–2 Paulette's Pile of Problems*

Paulette, a widow in her mid-30s, lives with her two young children, for whom she receives social security based on her deceased husband's account. She does not have a regular job. To earn a little extra income, she works occasionally, staying under the social security earnings limitation. Paulette currently has no marketable job skills for regular full time work.

Due to the illness of one of her children, Paulette has large medical and hospital bills. Medicaid stepped in and picked up most of the bills because hers is considered a low-income family. Paulette's husband left her with no life insurance, no health insurance, no savings, and a pile of debts.

Questions

1. Look at Paulette's situation, and analyze the need for life and health insurance for her family.

2. Is major medical insurance needed? Can Paulette afford the premiums?

3. What other options might be available to Paulette?

*Adapted from *Personal and Family Financial Planning* (Washington, D.C.: American Council of Life Insurance, 1983), p. VI/33d.

14

Life Insurance

You probably own some life insurance—through a group plan where you work, as a veteran, or through a policy you bought yourself. Perhaps you are considering the purchase of additional life insurance to keep pace with inflation or to cover your growing family. If so, you should prepare for that purchase by learning as much as possible about life insurance and how it can apply to your needs.

This chapter will help you make decisions about life insurance. It describes what life insurance is and how it works, the major types of life insurance coverages, and how you can use life insurance to protect your family.

After studying this chapter, you will be able to:

- Define life insurance, outline its history, and describe its purpose.

- Interpret the life insurance principle.

- Determine your life insurance needs.

- Distinguish between the two types of life insurance companies.

- Categorize various types of life insurance policies.

- Explain important provisions in life insurance contracts.

- Develop a plan to buy your life insurance.

- Indicate how annuities provide security.

Interview with **Jerome Houghton,** General Manager, Personal Financial Security Division, Aetna Life and Casualty Insurance Company

Jerome Houghton joined Aetna Life and Casualty Insurance's downtown Chicago Life Agency in 1958 as an Assistant Supervisor. He became General Agent in Skokie, Illinois, in 1971 and in Oak Brook, Illinois, in 1975. In 1982, he was named General Manager of Aetna's new Personal Financial Security Division in Chicago, with responsibilities for most of the state of Illinois.

There is no simple answer to the question "How much life insurance is enough?" Mr. Houghton states, "You will have to consider the other sources of income your family will have if you die—savings, employee benefits, social security, investments, and real estate." Some experts figure that a surviving spouse with children will need about 60 to 75 percent of the family's present after-tax income. If there are no children or the children are grown, a spouse might be able to get by on as little as 40 percent of the present combined income of husband and wife.

If you don't have an agent, be very careful when you select one. Ask your friends and relatives for advice. Find an agent who is well trained and knows the business thoroughly—one in whom you can have confidence.

In all states, the agent must be licensed to sell life insurance. The good agent has had extensive education and training in life insurance, financial planning, and other subjects related to serving the needs of clients. Agents often continue their education on their own initiative, frequently under company auspices or through a professional organization such as the National Association of Life Underwriters. An agent may be a graduate of the two-year course offered by the Life Underwriter Training Council and may have also received the designation of Chartered Life Underwriter (CLU), awarded by the American College of Life Underwriters following an intensive college-level course of study.

How do you compare the costs of life insurance policies? You can do this only if the policies being compared are for the same amount and have about the same features. Ask your agent to give you all the details about the premiums, benefits, cash values, and—for participating policies—dividend payments. Just inspecting these figures will often help tell you which policy is the best buy. The agent can give you interest-adjusted index numbers. Although subject to some limitations, these have been adjudged the most practical method now available for comparing policy costs.

"This plan is believed to be the best group life insurance plan available today," boasted the brochure of the University of Kansas alumni association. "We endorse this plan and encourage our members to participate in it."

But one recipient of the unsolicited mailed offer was skeptical enough to show it to her husband, J. Robert Hunter, president of the National Insurance Consumer Organization, a consumer advocacy group in Alexandria, Virginia. After studying this 1983 offer, Hunter concluded that the premiums for some participants were at least three times as high as they should be. The insurance was "a very bad deal," he told the university.

As a benefit of membership, many nonprofit groups, associations, and professional organizations promote group insurance—at rates they say are low. But insurance experts contend that these policies often offer limited coverage or are priced higher than equal or better coverage available to individuals.

"Just because it's group life insurance, that doesn't make it cheaper," Hunter says. Concedes Robert Waldron, a spokesman for the American Council of Life Insurance, a trade group: "Many of the offers that come in the mail can be beaten in the open marketplace."

Moreover, the members of nonprofit groups that endorse policies may not realize that the groups often receive money from the insurers. (The University of Kansas alumni group wouldn't comment on what compensation, if any, it received.)

Consumers have a right to know about all such arrangements, argues James H. Hunt,

LIFE INSURANCE: AN INTRODUCTION

- Meaning, History, and Purpose of Life Insurance

Consumer awareness of life insurance has changed very little over the years. Life insurance is still more often sold than bought. In other words, while most people actively seek to buy insurance for their property and health, many people avoid a life insurance purchase until they are approached by an agent. Let us see what life insurance is.

Meaning of Life Insurance

Life insurance is neither mysterious nor difficult to understand. It works in the following manner. A person joins a risk-sharing group (an insurance company) by purchasing a contract (a policy). Under the policy, the insurance company promises to pay a sum of money at the time of the policyholder's death to the person or persons selected by him or her (the beneficiaries). In the case of an endowment policy, the money is paid to the policyholder (the insured) if he or she is alive on the future date (maturity date) named in the policy. The insurance company makes this promise in return for the insured's agreement to pay it a sum of money (the premium) periodically.

an insurance consultant and consumer advocate in Massachusetts. But many nonprofit groups make no general disclosure.

Whether or not nonprofit groups disclose pacts with insurers, some of these groups draw fire by endorsing types of coverage that have dubious value. Cancer insurance, for example, is "an unnecessary product," because comprehensive health insurance policies typically cover cancer, says Kevin Foley, a spokesman for the insurance department of New York State.

Such reasoning doesn't deter the John Wayne Foundation in Beverly Hills, California. "For just $5.00 you can help . . . find a cure for cancer," it tells people. It asks them to become members by mailing the money to the foundation's "administrative center" in Omaha, Nebraska. In actuality, the "center" is Mutual of Omaha Insurance Company; foundation members are eligible to buy the company's cancer insurance.

Besides cost, there may be other reasons to turn down a group coverage policy obtained through nonprofit groups. "Association group life coverage isn't as flexible or reliable as a good one-year renewable term policy issued on an individual basis," says Joseph M. Belth, a professor of insurance at Indiana University. This type of group insurance, he notes, can be terminated by either the group or the insurer.

*Condensed from "Your Money Matters," Walt Bogdanich, "Nonprofit Groups Offer Insurance, but Often the Prices Are Beatable," *The Wall Street Journal*, March 13, 1986, sec. 2, p. 31.

Brief History of Life Insurance

Almost every civilization is known to have had some type of life insurance. Around 1800 B.C., the Babylonians specified in the Code of Hammurabi that "if a life [has been lost] the city or district governor shall pay one mina of silver to the deceased's relatives."[1] Burial insurance was available to residents of ancient Greece. The Romans developed an annuity table that the government of Tuscany used well into the 19th century.

In modern times, there is a record of a life insurance policy issued in 1583. In that year, "William Gybbons, citizen and salter of London," paid 32 pounds for one year of protection. He died within the year, and his heirs collected 400 pounds.

A form of life insurance was used by the synod of the Presbyterian Church of Philadelphia in 1759, when it set up a relief and pension fund for widows

[1]All historical facts are taken from *Insurance Handbook for Reporters*, 2nd ed. (Allstate Insurance Group, 1985), p. 102. Copyright 1985 by Allstate Insurance Company, Northbrook, Ill.

and children of deceased ministers. The first general life company in the United States was set up in 1794. It sold six policies in five years and then went out of the life insurance business.

In 1986, the life insurance industry consisted of about 2,260 companies employing over 554,000 workers.[2] Over 90 percent of the companies in the industry are stock companies owned by public shareholders. The remainder, termed mutual life insurance companies, are owned by their policyholders. During the past few years, a growing number of mutual companies have converted to stock ownership. The reasons generally given were that such conversion would give greater access to capital to enhance corporate growth and would provide potential tax savings.

New life insurance purchased in 1985, the latest year for which industry data are available, reached over $1.2 trillion. Consumers purchased $910.9 billion of term or whole ordinary life insurance. The balance was group and industrial insurance purchased by individuals.

Today, life insurance is an essential part of overall financial planning for most people. In the United States, about 9 out of 10 families and 2 out of 3 individuals have some form of life insurance coverage.

The Purpose of Life Insurance

Life insurance is purchased primarily to provide an immediate estate that did not previously exist. Most people buy life insurance to protect someone who depends on them from financial losses caused by their death. That "someone" could be the nonworking spouse and children of a single-income family. It could be the wife or husband of a two-income family. It could be an aging parent. It could be a business partner or a corporation.

Individuals and families purchase life insurance to fill financial needs created by the loss of the breadwinner. Those needs are: money to meet final expenses, money to live on while the family readjusts itself to the new conditions, an income for the family while the children are growing up, and an income for the surviving parent after the children have left home.

The money from a life insurance death benefit payable to the specified beneficiary is immediately and automatically available to the beneficiary. Unlike a savings account or stocks, that money cannot be impounded or tied up in probate.

Here are typical examples of uses that are made of life insurance proceeds:[3]

Paying off a home mortgage or other debts at the time of death by way of a decreasing term policy.

---

[2]All 1985 and 1986 data are taken from *U.S. Industrial Outlook, 1987* (Washington, D.C.: U.S. Government Printing Office), pp. 51–1, 2.

[3]*Insurance Handbook for Reporters*, p. 105. Copyright 1985 by Allstate Insurance Company.

Providing lump-sum payments through an endowment to children when they reach a specified age.

Providing an education or income for children.

Making charitable bequests after death.

Providing a retirement income.

Accumulating savings.

Establishing a regular income for survivors.

Setting up an estate plan.

Making estate and death tax payments.

Life insurance is one of the few ways to provide liquidity at the time of death.

THE BASIS OF LIFE INSURANCE

- The Life Insurance Principle

The Principle of Life Insurance

The principle of home insurance discussed in Chapter 12 can be applied to the lives of persons. From records covering many years and including millions of lives, mortality tables have been prepared that show the number of deaths for various age groups during any year. In the 1950s, the life insurance industry developed and the National Association of Insurance Commissioners (NAIC) approved a mortality table known as the Commissioners 1958 Standard Ordinary (CSO) Mortality Table (shown in Table 14–1). In 1980, the NAIC approved a new Standard Ordinary Mortality Table based on experience during 1970–75 (Table 14–2). Unlike the 1958 CSO Table, which combined the mortality experience of males and females, the 1980 CSO Table separates the experience by sex.

The data in the table can be used to illustrate the insurance principle for lives of human beings. Let us assume that a group of 100,000 males, aged 29, wish to contribute a sufficient amount to a common fund each year so that $1,000 can be paid to the dependents of each group member who dies during the year. A glance at Table 14–2 shows that the death rate for males at age 29 is 1.71 per thousand; therefore, 171 members of the group can be expected to die during the year.

Thus, each of the 100,000 members must contribute $1.71 at the beginning of the year in order to provide $1,000 for the dependents of each of the 171 who will die before the end of the year. If the survivors desire to continue the arrangements the following year, each of the remaining 99,829 members alive at the beginning of the next year, when they will be 30 years old, must contribute $1.73 in order to protect the dependents of the 173 individuals in the group who will die during that year.

If the group of 100,000 were females, aged 29, the per member cost for providing $1,000 of benefits to those who died during the year would be $1.30 since the female mortality rate per 1,000 is 1.30 at 29 years of age. This example may make it easier for you to see why life insurance premiums are usually less for females than for males.

TABLE 14-1   Table of Mortality: Commissioners 1958 Standard Ordinary

Age	Number Living	Deaths Each Year	Deaths Per 1,000	Age	Number Living	Deaths Each Year	Deaths Per 1,000	Age	Number Living	Deaths Each Year	Deaths Per 1,000
0	10,000,000	70,800	7.08	35	9,373,807	23,528	2.51	70	5,592,012	278,426	49.79
1	9,929,200	17,475	1.76	36	9,350,279	24,685	2.64	71	5,313,586	287,731	54.15
2	9,911,725	15,066	1.52	37	9,325,594	26,112	2.80	72	5,025,855	294,766	58.65
3	9,896,659	14,449	1.46	38	9,299,482	27,991	3.01	73	4,731,089	299,289	63.26
4	9,882,210	13,835	1.40	39	9,271,491	30,132	3.25	74	4,431,800	301,894	68.12
5	9,868,375	13,322	1.35	40	9,241,359	32,622	3.53	75	4,129,906	303,011	73.37
6	9,855,053	12,812	1.30	41	9,208,737	35,362	3.84	76	3,826,895	303,014	79.18
7	9,842,241	12,401	1.26	42	9,173,375	38,253	4.17	77	3,523,881	301,997	85.70
8	9,829,840	12,091	1.23	43	9,135,122	41,382	4.53	78	3,221,884	299,829	93.06
9	9,817,749	11,879	1.21	44	9,093,740	44,741	4.92	79	2,922,055	295,683	101.19
10	9,805,870	11,865	1.21	45	9,048,999	48,412	5.35	80	2,626,372	288,848	109.98
11	9,794,005	12,047	1.23	46	9,000,587	52,473	5.83	81	2,337,524	278,983	119.35
12	9,781,958	12,325	1.26	47	8,948,114	56,910	6.36	82	2,058,541	265,902	129.17
13	9,769,633	12,896	1.32	48	8,891,204	61,794	6.95	83	1,792,639	249,858	139.38
14	9,756,737	13,562	1.39	49	8,829,410	67,104	7.60	84	1,542,781	231,433	150.01
15	9,743,175	14,225	1.46	50	8,762,306	72,902	8.32	85	1,311,348	211,311	161.14
16	9,728,950	14,983	1.54	51	8,689,404	79,160	9.11	86	1,100,037	190,108	172.82
17	9,713,967	15,737	1.62	52	8,610,244	85,758	9.96	87	909,929	168,455	185.13
18	9,698,230	16,390	1.69	53	8,524,486	92,832	10.89	88	741,474	146,997	198.25
19	9,681,840	16,846	1.74	54	8,431,654	100,337	11.90	89	594,477	126,303	212.46
20	9,664,994	17,300	1.79	55	8,331,317	108,307	13.00	90	468,174	106,809	228.14
21	9,647,694	17,655	1.83	56	8,223,010	116,849	14.21	91	361,365	88,813	245.77
22	9,630,039	17,912	1.86	57	8,106,161	125,970	15.54	92	272,552	72,480	265.93
23	9,612,127	18,167	1.89	58	7,980,191	135,663	17.00	93	200,072	57,881	289.30
24	9,593,960	18,324	1.91	59	7,844,528	145,830	18.59	94	142,191	45,026	316.66
25	9,575,636	18,481	1.93	60	7,698,698	156,592	20.34	95	97,165	34,128	351.24
26	9,557,155	18,732	1.96	61	7,542,106	167,736	22.24	96	63,037	25,250	400.56
27	9,538,423	18,981	1.99	62	7,374,370	179,271	24.31	97	37,787	18,456	488.42
28	9,519,442	19,324	2.03	63	7,195,099	191,174	26.57	98	19,331	12,916	668.15
29	9,500,118	19,760	2.08	64	7,003,925	203,394	29.04	99	6,415	6,415	1000.00
30	9,480,358	20,193	2.13	65	6,800,531	215,917	31.75				
31	9,460,165	20,718	2.19	66	6,584,614	228,749	34.74				
32	9,439,447	21,239	2.25	67	6,355,865	241,777	38.04				
33	9,418,208	21,850	2.32	68	6,114,088	254,835	41.68				
34	9,396,358	22,551	2.40	69	5,859,253	267,241	45.61				

Source: American Council of Life Insurance.

How Long Will You Live?

Life expectancy, shown in Table 14–2, does not indicate the age at which a person has the highest probability of dying. For example, the table shows that the life expectancy of a male at the age of 30 is 43.24 years. This does not mean that males 30 years old will probably die at the age of 73.24 years. It means that the average number of years all males who are alive at 30 years of age, will still live is 43.24.

But all of them will die sometime, and all could die soon. Covering the financial need arising from the risk of untimely death is the function of life insurance. Modern life insurance policies are designed to meet almost every circumstance in which there is loss of earning power.

TABLE 14-2   1980 Commissioners Standard Ordinary Mortality Table

Age	Male Mortality Rate Per 1,000	Male Expectancy, Years	Female Mortality Rate Per 1,000	Female Expectancy, Years	Age	Male Mortality Rate Per 1,000	Male Expectancy, Years	Female Mortality Rate Per 1,000	Female Expectancy, Years
0	4.18	70.83	2.89	75.83	50	6.71	25.36	4.96	29.53
1	1.07	70.13	.87	75.04	51	7.30	24.52	5.31	28.67
2	.99	69.20	.81	74.11	52	7.96	23.70	5.70	27.82
3	.98	68.27	.79	73.17	53	8.71	22.89	6.15	26.98
4	.95	67.34	.77	72.23	54	9.56	22.08	6.61	26.14
5	.90	66.40	.76	71.28	55	10.47	21.29	7.09	25.31
6	.85	65.46	.73	70.34	56	11.46	20.51	7.57	24.49
7	.80	64.52	.72	69.39	57	12.49	19.74	8.03	23.67
8	.76	63.57	.70	68.44	58	13.59	18.99	8.47	22.86
9	.74	62.62	.69	67.48	59	14.77	18.24	8.94	22.05
10	.73	61.66	.68	66.53	60	16.08	17.51	9.47	21.25
11	.77	60.71	.69	65.58	61	17.54	16.79	10.13	20.44
12	.85	59.75	.72	64.62	62	19.19	16.08	10.96	19.65
13	.99	58.80	.75	63.67	63	21.06	15.38	12.02	18.86
14	1.15	57.86	.80	62.71	64	23.14	14.70	13.25	18.08
15	1.33	56.93	.85	61.76	65	25.42	14.04	14.59	17.32
16	1.51	56.00	.90	60.82	66	27.85	13.39	16.00	16.57
17	1.67	55.09	.95	59.87	67	30.44	12.76	17.43	15.83
18	1.78	54.18	.98	58.93	68	33.19	12.14	18.84	15.10
19	1.86	53.27	1.02	57.98	69	36.17	11.54	20.36	14.38
20	1.90	52.37	1.05	57.04	70	39.51	10.96	22.11	13.67
21	1.91	51.47	1.07	56.10	71	43.30	10.39	24.23	12.97
22	1.89	50.57	1.09	55.16	72	47.65	9.84	26.87	12.28
23	1.86	49.66	1.11	54.22	73	52.64	9.30	30.11	11.60
24	1.82	48.75	1.14	53.28	74	58.19	8.79	33.93	10.95
25	1.77	47.84	1.16	52.34	75	64.19	8.31	38.24	10.32
26	1.73	46.93	1.19	51.40	76	70.53	7.84	42.96	9.71
27	1.71	46.01	1.22	50.46	77	77.12	7.40	48.04	9.12
28	1.70	45.09	1.26	49.52	78	83.90	6.97	53.45	8.55
29	1.71	44.16	1.30	48.59	79	91.05	6.57	59.35	8.01
30	1.73	43.24	1.35	47.65	80	98.84	6.18	65.99	7.48
31	1.78	42.31	1.40	46.71	81	107.48	5.80	73.60	6.98
32	1.83	41.38	1.45	45.78	82	117.25	5.44	82.40	6.49
33	1.91	40.46	1.50	44.84	83	128.26	5.09	92.53	6.03
34	2.00	39.54	1.58	43.91	84	140.25	4.77	103.81	5.59
35	2.11	38.61	1.65	42.98	85	152.95	4.46	116.10	5.18
36	2.24	37.69	1.76	42.05	86	166.09	4.18	129.29	4.80
37	2.40	36.78	1.89	41.12	87	179.55	3.91	143.32	4.43
38	2.58	35.87	2.04	40.20	88	193.27	3.66	158.18	4.09
39	2.79	34.96	2.22	39.28	89	207.29	3.41	173.94	3.77
40	3.02	34.05	2.42	38.36	90	221.77	3.18	190.75	3.45
41	3.29	33.16	2.64	37.46	91	236.98	2.94	208.87	3.15
42	3.56	32.26	2.87	36.55	92	253.45	2.70	228.81	2.85
43	3.87	31.38	3.09	35.66	93	272.11	2.44	251.51	2.55
44	4.19	30.50	3.32	34.77	94	295.90	2.17	279.31	2.24
45	4.55	29.62	3.56	33.88	95	329.96	1.87	317.32	1.91
46	4.92	28.76	3.80	33.00	96	384.55	1.54	375.74	1.56
47	5.32	27.90	4.05	32.12	97	480.20	1.20	474.97	1.21
48	5.74	27.04	4.33	31.25	98	657.98	.84	655.85	.84
49	6.21	26.20	4.63	30.39	99	1,000.00	.50	1,000.00	.50

Source: American Council of Life Insurance.

DETERMINING
YOUR LIFE
INSURANCE
NEEDS[4]

- Determining Life Insurance Needs

You should consider a number of factors before you buy insurance. These factors include your present and future sources of income, other savings and income protection, group life insurance, group annuities (or other pension benefits), and social security. But first you should determine your life insurance objectives.

[4]Much of this discussion is adapted from *Understanding Your Life Insurance* (Washington, D.C.: American Council of Life Insurance, 1982), pp. 34–41.

Determining Your Life Insurance Objectives

Before you consider types of life insurance policies, you must decide what you want your life insurance to do for you and your dependents.

First, how much money do you want to leave to your dependents if you should die today? Will you require more or less insurance protection to meet their needs as time goes on?

Second, when would you like to be able to retire? What amount of income do you feel you and your spouse would need then?

Third, how much will you be able to pay for your insurance program? When you are older, are you most likely to earn more than, the same as, or less than you do now? Are the demands on your family budget for other expenses of living likely to be greater or less as time goes on?

When you have considered these questions and developed some approximate answers, you are ready to select the types and amounts of life insurance policies that will help you accomplish your objectives.

Once you have decided on what you want your life insurance to accomplish, the next difficult question is to decide how much to buy.

Estimating Your Life Insurance Requirements

How much life insurance should you carry? This question is important for every person who owns or intends to buy life insurance. Because of the various factors involved, the question cannot be answered by mathematics alone. Nevertheless, an insurance policy does put a price on the life of the person insured; therefore, methods are needed to estimate what that price should be.

The money worth of an individual is reflected, at least in part, by his or her current earnings and probable future earning power. One method, then, for determining how much life insurance you should carry is to compute the present value of the estimated income that you will earn during the remainder of your probable lifetime.

There is a rule of thumb that a good target is life insurance totaling four to five times your annual income. As shown in Figure 14–1, in 1985, the average coverage of insured U.S. families was about $75,000. A person with several dependents and other major obligations, such as a mortgage, will usually need more than that amount. A person with relatively few obligations may need less.

Another way of figuring how much life insurance a wage earner should carry is to simply estimate the needs of surviving family members during certain predictable stages after the wage earner's death. In a traditional family setting, these stages are:[5]

1. The survivors adjust their financial affairs. They need perhaps one to three years after the wage earner's death to do this. For example, a

[5]*What You Should Know about Life Insurance* (Washington, D.C.: American Council of Life Insurance, n.d.).

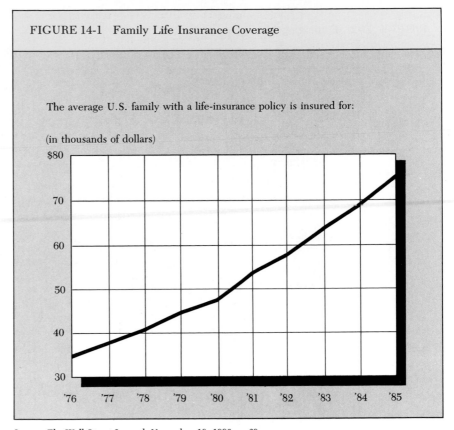

FIGURE 14-1   Family Life Insurance Coverage

The average U.S. family with a life-insurance policy is insured for:

(in thousands of dollars)

Source: *The Wall Street Journal*, November 18, 1986, p. 39.

spouse who had been at home or employed part-time may now need to find a full-time job to become self-supporting.

2.   The children are growing up and in school. During this stage, life insurance proceeds, used together with social security payments, can maintain the living standards of the family.

3.   The children have grown and are out on their own and social security payments to the surviving spouse stop until age 60. Life insurance benefits can then supplement the income of the surviving spouse or provide a nest egg for emergencies.

4.   The surviving spouse has reached retirement age and is likely to qualify for social security retirement payments.

Filling out Figure 14–2 will provide you with an excellent start toward analyzing your life insurance needs. Invite your spouse or another family member to join you, and carefully consider each item in the figure.

You should now have a better idea of your income, assets, expenses, and liabilities. This information should help you determine what financial resources are available to your family and how much income would need to be

FIGURE 14-2   Estimating Life Insurance Needs

This figure will help you determine how much income your family will have after your death and how much income will be needed by your family to continue in the same or a similar lifestyle.

Personal financial statement— current net worth

Assets

Real estate
Home (full market value) $_____
Business   _____
Other   _____

Life insurance
Cash value of your life insurance   _____
Cash value of family members'
  life insurance   _____

Cash or equivalent funds
Cash in bank   _____
Emergency fund   _____
Permanent savings   _____
Checking account   _____
Money market fund/certificates   _____
Pension plan   _____

Investments
Bonds   _____
Stocks   _____
Mutual funds   _____

Personal property
Home furnishings   _____
Car   _____
Jewelry, clothes, silver, china,
  furs, art, etc.   _____
Miscellaneous   _____

Total $_____

Liabilities

Mortgates $_____
Installment loans   _____
Education loans   _____
Other loans   _____
Charge accounts   _____
Other debts   _____

Total $_____

Total assets $_____
Total liabilities $_____
Net worth $_____

Estimate of family resources after policyholder's death

Income	*Annual*
Survivor's salary	$_____
Interest	_____
Dividends on savings	_____
Real estate rent received	_____
Annuity income	_____
Benefits	
Social security	_____
Veterans'	_____
Life insurance	_____
Pension	_____
Trust income	_____
Other income	_____
Total	$_____

Estimated Expenses

	Annual
Housing	$_____
Rent	_____
Mortgage	_____
Utilities	_____
Other	_____
Food	
Home	_____
Away	_____
Clothing/upkeep	_____
Transportation	_____
Education	_____
Entertainment and recreation	_____
Medical and dental expenses	_____
Insurance premiums	
Life	_____
Health	_____
Disability	_____
Auto	_____
Other	_____
Payments	
Loan	_____
Installment	_____
Taxes	
Local	_____
State	_____
Property	_____
Income	_____
Other	
Total	$_____
Total income	$_____
Total expenses	$_____

Source: *A Consumer's Guide to Life Insurance* (Washington, D.C.: American Council of Life Insurance), n.p., n.d.

replaced if the insured dies. These amounts will need to be adjusted periodically to reflect new living arrangements, inflation, and other variables.

The information collected in Figure 14–2 can be summarized to determine the dollar amount of extra life insurance needed.

You can purchase the new or extra life insurance you need from two types of companies. Mutual life insurance companies sell participating policies, while stock life insurance companies sell nonparticipating policies.

TYPES OF LIFE INSURANCE COMPANIES

- Types of Life Insurance Companies

Companies sell life insurance to provide guaranteed protection over long periods of time. Even with mortality tables and past experience, a life insurance company cannot predict what its exact costs will be. There are two approaches to this problem. Under one approach, the life insurance company sells participating (or par) policies. A **participating policy** has somewhat higher premiums than nonparticipating policy, thus providing a built-in cushion to allow for fluctuations in company earnings and expenses. At the end of the year, the company figures its actual costs and profit and refunds any portion of the premium that it does not need. The refund is called the *policy dividend.* If you purchase a participating policy, you should expect the net cost to be lower due to the refund. There is no guarantee, however, that dividends will be paid each year that the insurance contract is in force. Most participating policies are sold by mutual life insurance companies.

Mutual Insurance Companies

A mutual insurance company has no stockholders. Its management is directed by a board elected by the policyholders for whose benefit the company is operated. Nearly all mutual companies issue only participating policies; a few issue nonparticipating policies, but the owners of such policies have no voice in the management.

Stock Insurance Companies

Under the second approach, a stock insurance company sells **nonparticipating (or nonpar)** policies. If the premiums charged bring in more money than the company pays out, it keeps the profit; if the company's outlays exceed the revenues it obtains from premiums, it suffers a loss. The policyholder does not participate in either the profit or loss of the company. Thus, no dividends are declared on *nonpar* policies.

A stock insurance company is owned by stockholders who finance its operations and assume the risks and responsibilities of ownership and management. Most stock companies issue only nonparticipating policies; a few issue both nonparticipating and participating policies; a very few issue participating policies only.[6]

---

[6]*Understanding Your Life Insurance,* p. 8.

Which One Should You Buy?

If you wish to pay exactly the same premium each year, you would choose a nonparticipating policy, with its guaranteed premiums. However, you may prefer life insurance whose annual price reflects the company's experience with its investments, the health of its policyholders, and its general operating costs—that is, a participating policy.

Both mutual insurance companies and stock insurance companies sell three basic types of life insurance—term, whole life, and endowment insurance. In the next section, you will learn about the various types of insurance coverages.

TYPES OF LIFE INSURANCE

- Types of Life Insurance Policies

Figure 14–3 shows the common types of policies issued by life insurance companies. We will discuss not only these common types but also more fashionable new types, and we will examine the purposes for which each type is best suited.

Term Life Insurance

Term insurance is protection for a specified period of time, usually 1, 5, 10, or 20 years or up to age 65. A term insurance policy pays a benefit only if you die during the period that the policy covers. If you stop paying the premiums, the insurance stops. Term insurance is therefore sometimes called temporary life insurance.

Renewability Option. The coverage of term insurance ends at the end of the term, but it can be continued for another term if you have a renewable option. For example, the term insurance of Teachers Insurance and Annuity Association is renewable at your option for successive five-year periods to age 70 without medical reexamination. Level premiums are paid during each five-year period. The premiums increase every five years.

A 30-year-old man who buys $30,000 of coverage might pay a premium of $95 for one-year renewable term insurance the first year and these premiums in later years:

Age 40 $108/one-year renewable term
Age 50 $240/one-year renewable term
Age 60 $525/one-year renewable term

Conversion Option. If you have convertible term insurance, you can exchange it for a whole life policy without a medical examination and at a higher premium. The premium for the whole life policy stays the same for the rest of your life.

Decreasing Term Insurance. Term insurance is also available in a form that pays less to the beneficiary as time passes. The insurance period you select might depend on your age or on how long you decide the coverage will

FIGURE 14-3   Major Types and Subtypes of Life Insurance

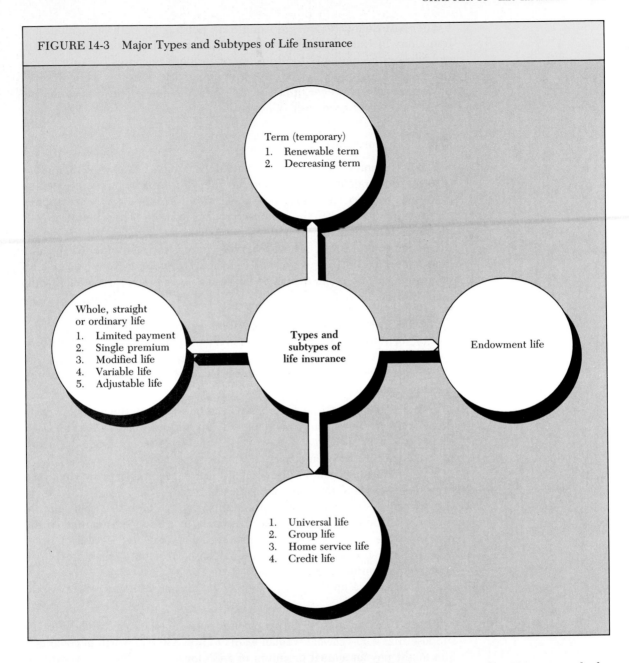

Term (temporary)
1. Renewable term
2. Decreasing term

Whole, straight
or ordinary life
1. Limited payment
2. Single premium
3. Modified life
4. Variable life
5. Adjustable life

Types and
subtypes of
life insurance

Endowment life

1. Universal life
2. Group life
3. Home service life
4. Credit life

be needed. For example, a decreasing term contract for 25 years might be appropriate as coverage of a mortgage loan balance on a house because the coverage would decrease as the balance on the mortgage decreases. You could get the same result by purchasing annual renewable term policies of diminishing amounts during the period of the mortgage loan. An annual renewable policy would offer more flexibility to change coverage if you were to sell the house or remortgage it.

There are sound reasons for using term policies for both permanent and temporary life insurance requirements. *Consumer Reports* and many financial advisers recommend term insurance for both purposes because it provides maximum protection for each premium dollar. Since term life provides protection only, however, it has no cash value. Whole life insurance, on the other hand, does have cash value.

Whole Life Insurance

The most common type of permanent life insurance is the **whole life policy** (also called a straight life or ordinary life policy), in which you pay a specified premium each year for as long as you live. In return, the insurance company pays a stipulated sum to the beneficiary when you die. The amount of your premium depends primarily on the age at which you purchase the insurance.

One important feature of whole life insurance is its cash value. **Cash value** is an amount that increases over the years and that you receive if you give up the insurance. A table in the whole life policy enables you to tell exactly how much cash value it has (see Table 14–3).

Nonforfeiture Clause. Another notable feature of the whole life policy is the **nonforfeiture clause.** This provision allows you not to forfeit all accrued benefits. For example, if you decide not to continue paying premiums, you can exercise certain options with your cash value. The nonforfeiture clause and cash values can be used in various ways, including the following:

1. With your policy as collateral, you can borrow from the company up to the amount of the current cash value. (If you die and the loan has not been repaid, the amount owed plus interest will be deducted from the death proceeds paid to the beneficiary.)

2. If you miss a premium, the company can, if so authorized by you, draw from the cash value to keep your policy in force.

3. If you wish to stop paying premiums, the accrued cash value can be used to continue some whole life insurance in a reduced amount or the policy can be continued as term insurance for a specific period of time.

4. You can use the cash value to purchase an annuity that provides a guaranteed monthly income for life.

5. You can give up the policy completely, and the company will pay you the cash value.

To see the workings of the whole life policy and its cash value, let us suppose that a 30-year-old woman wants to buy $30,000 worth of coverage. She might pay an annual premium of $435 for a whole life policy with no policy dividends. Here's how the cash would grow:

Age 35	$1,830
Age 40	$4,260
Age 45	$6,990
Age 50	$9,960

A substantial reserve is accumulated by the insurance company during the

TABLE 14-3 An Example of Guaranteed Cash Values

Plan and Additional Benefits	Amount	Premium	Years Payable
Whole Life (Premiums payable to age 90)	$10,000	$229.50	55
Waiver of Premium (To age 65)		4.30	30
Accidental Death (To age 70)	10,000	7.80	35

A premium is payable on the policy date and every 12 policy months thereafter. The first premium is $241.60.

TABLE OF GUARANTEED VALUES

END OF POLICY YEAR	CASH OR LOAN VALUE	PAID-UP INSURANCE	EXTENDED TERM INSURANCE YEARS	DAYS
1	$ 14	$ 30	0	152
2	174	450	4	182
3	338	860	8	65
4	506	1,250	10	344
5	676	1,640	12	360
6	879	2,070	14	335
7	1,084	2,500	16	147
8	1,293	2,910	17	207
9	1,504	3,300	18	177
10	1,719	3,690	19	78
11	1,908	4,000	19	209
12	2,099	4,300	19	306
13	2,294	4,590	20	8
14	2,490	4,870	20	47
15	2,690	5,140	20	65
16	2,891	5,410	20	66
17	3,095	5,660	20	52
18	3,301	5,910	20	27
19	3,508	6,150	19	358
20	3,718	6,390	19	317
AGE 60	4,620	7,200	18	111
AGE 65	5,504	7,860	16	147

Paid-up additions and dividend accumulations increase the cash values; indebtedness decreases them.

Direct Beneficiary Helen M. Benson, wife of the insured
Owner Thomas A. Benson, the insured
Insured Thomas A. Benson   **Age and Sex** 37 Male
Policy Date November 1, 1988   **Policy Number** 000/00
Date of Issue November 1, 1988

Source: *Sample Life Insurance Policy* (Washington, D.C.: American Council of Life Insurance), p. 2. n.d.

early years of the whole life policy in order to pay the benefits in the later years when your chances of dying are greater. At first, the basic premium for whole life is higher than that for term insurance; however, the premium for a whole life policy remains constant throughout your lifetime, whereas the premium for a term policy increases with each renewal.

Several types of whole life insurance have been developed to meet different objectives. A few of the popular types are discussed next.

Limited Payment Policy. One type of whole life policy is called the limited payment policy. Under the limited payment plan of insurance, you pay premiums for a stipulated period, usually 20 or 30 years, or until you reach a specified age, such as 60 or 65 (unless your death occurs earlier). However, you remain insured for life under the terms of the contract and the company will pay the face amount of the policy at your death. Because the premium payment period for a limited payment policy is shorter than that for a whole life policy, the annual premium is larger.

The reserve of a limited payment policy accumulates rapidly during the period in which the premiums are being paid, so that the reserve, together with the interest earned on it, is sufficient to pay death claims after the policy has been paid up—that is, requires no more premium payments.

A special form of the limited payment plan is the single-premium policy. Under this type of contract, you make only one premium payment.

An advantage of the limited payment policy is that you make all your insurance payments during your maximum earning period. However, the premium for this form of insurance is considerably higher than that for whole life. This means that the amount of death benefit you get for the same premium is smaller for the limited payment policy than for the whole life policy. Because few people have sufficient income to afford all of the insurance they need, limited payment policies are a luxury that most people cannot afford.

Under the Tax Reform Act of 1986, annuities (to be discussed later in this chapter) and single-premium whole life insurance have retained their tax-deferred benefits. You pay no federal, state, or local income tax on the interest, dividends, or capital gains that your money earns while the policy remains in force. Increases in cash value are taxed only if and when they are distributed to you. Furthermore, beneficiaries pay no income tax on policy proceeds.

Modified Life Insurance Policy. Modified life is another variation of whole life insurance. Its premium is relatively low in the first several years but increases in the later years. It is intended for those who want whole life insurance but wish to pay lower premiums in their younger years.

Variable Life Insurance Policy. The cash values of a variable life insurance policy fluctuate according to the yields earned by a separate fund, which can be a stock fund, a money market fund, or a long-term bond fund. A minimum death benefit is guaranteed, but the death benefit can go higher than that minimum, to a level that depends on the earnings of the dollars invested in the separate fund. The premium payments for a variable life policy are fixed.

Adjustable Life Insurance Policy. The adjustable life insurance policy is another relatively new type of whole life insurance. You can change such a policy as your needs change. For example, if you want to increase or decrease your coverage, you can change either the premium payments or the period of coverage.

Endowment Policy

An **endowment policy** enables you to accumulate a sum of money that is paid to you on a date named in the policy (the maturity date). If you die before the maturity date, the money is paid to the beneficiary. The premium of an endowment policy is higher than that of a limited payment policy or a whole life policy, but the endowment policy builds higher cash values.

You select the date on which you are to receive the money. This date may fall at the expiration of a definite number of years (such as 20 or 30 years) or when you reach a certain age (such as age 65).

The endowment policy is for persons who need not only life insurance protection for dependents but a definite sum of money or income for themselves at some future date.

An Example. Jim Monez is a buyer in a department store. He is 38 years old, and he has a wife and a four-year-old daughter. He now has $70,000 of life insurance, including $25,000 of group insurance, which, together with social security, would provide a modest income until his daughter is out of high school and then still leave something for his wife.

Mr. Monez has just received an increase in salary, and he wants to save a good part of it. He buys a $10,000 endowment policy that matures when he reaches age 65. The policy will enable him to accumulate money for retirement. With this endowment, plus his company pension and his social security payments, he will have a fairly comfortable retirement income. However, if Mr. Monez does not live to be 65, the endowment, added to his present insurance and social security, will provide a more adequate income for his wife.

The accompanying boxed feature compares term, whole life, and endowment policies. It also explains how these three types of insurance policies fit various lifestyles.

Figure 14–4 shows approximate annual premium rates for $1,000 of whole life, limited payment (20 payments), endowment at age 65, and five-year term policies. Notice that the premiums for term insurance are the lowest.

Over the years, variations on term, whole life, and endowment insurance have been developed. The details of these policies may differ from company to company. So check with individual companies to determine the best policy for your needs.

Other Types of Life Insurance Policies

Universal Life. Subject to certain minimums, **universal life** insurance is designed to let you pay premiums at any time in virtually any amount. The

FIGURE 14-4   Approximate Annual Premium Rates for $1,000 of Each of Four Types of Life Insurance Policies.*

Bought at Age	Whole Life	Limited Payment (20-payment)	Endowment (at age 65)	Term (5-year renewable— convertible)
15	$ 7.65	$17.57	$12.55	$ 4.95
20	8.87	19.64	14.87	4.95
25	10.50	21.81	17.79	4.95
30	12.82	24.43	21.68	5.11
40	19.35	31.65	34.69	7.03
50	30.30	42.32	65.40	12.85

*The rates shown are approximate premium rates for nonparticipating life insurance policies for men. The rates for women are somewhat lower because of women's somewhat lower mortality. The rates of participating policies would be slightly higher, but the cost would be lowered by annual dividends. The premium rates shown here are per $1,000 of protection if the policies are purchased in units of $10,000.

Source: *Policies for Protection* (Washington, D.C.; American Council of Life Insurance, 1982), p. 7.

amount of insurance can be changed more easily in a universal life policy than in a traditional policy. The increase in the cash value of a universal life policy reflects the interest earned on short-term investments. Thus, the universal life policy clearly combines term insurance and investment elements.

Universal life has become the hot insurance product of our time, even as it has stirred considerable controversy within the insurance industry. As with other types of policies, the details of universal life policies vary from company to company. The key distinguishing features of universal life policies are explicit, separate accounting to the policyholders of (1) the charges for the insurance element, (2) the charges for company expenses (commissions, policy fees, etc.), and (3) the rate of return on the investment (cash value) of the policy. The rate of return is flexible; it is guaranteed to be not less than a certain amount (usually 4 percent), but it may be more, depending on the insurance company's decision.

The three features mentioned above are a part of all permanent-type insurance policies, but these features are usually buried from the policyholder's view. In effect, universal life represents the insurance industry's answer to the "buy term and invest the difference" recommendation of many independent financial advisers. The industry had little choice, because insurance buyers were doing just that in larger and larger numbers. Now the insurance companies offering universal life policies are trying to capture the investment portion of your savings in open competition with other financial institutions: brokerage houses, money market mutual funds, savings institutions, banks, pension funds, investment trusts, and so on.

Since your primary reason for buying a life insurance policy is the insurance component, the cost of that component should be your primary consideration. Universal life policies that offer a high rate of return on the cash value but charge a high price for the insurance element should generally be avoided.

Group Life Insurance Policy. During recent decades, group life insurance has become widely popular. A group insurance plan insures a large number of persons under the terms of a single policy without medical examination. In general, the same principles that apply to other forms of insurance also apply to group insurance.

Fundamentally, group insurance is term insurance, which was described earlier. Usually, the cost of group insurance is split between an employer and the employees in such a way that the cost of insurance per $1,000 is the same for each employee, regardless of age. The employer pays a larger portion of the costs of the group policy for older employees. Group insurance is therefore a rare bargain for older employees, but even younger employees usually find it inexpensive.

Group insurance is advantageous because it provides some protection for the dependents of individuals who cannot afford to carry the amount of insurance they need or whose physical condition does not permit them to buy individual insurance at a reasonable cost. Moreover, an employee can usually convert a group policy to a permanent plan of individual insurance without a medical examination within 31 days after his or her employment has been terminated. This feature alone might justify group insurance for individuals who are in poor health.

The payments required for group insurance are relatively small for several reasons. First, usually no part of the premium is employed to accumulate a cash value for the individual policyholder. Second, the acquisition expenses are less than those for other types of insurance because medical examinations are eliminated and because commissions for group policies are much lower per person than commissions for individual policies. Third, the premiums are usually collected or paid by the employer, so that collection costs are minimized. Finally, because the employer pays part or all of the premium, the cost to the employee is reduced further.

Recently, various plans of group permanent life insurance have been developed. The cost of these plans is higher than that of group term insurance. However, the employee who leaves the job retains some part of the group protection as fully paid permanent insurance. The employee also has the right to buy an individual policy without evidence of insurability.

Originally, when an employee retired, his or her group life insurance stopped. But now it is generally continued by the employer, though the amount of coverage is usually reduced. For some, the reduction is immediate and to a nominal amount of $3,000 to $8,000; for others, the reduction is made in steps over a five-year period, to about 50 percent of the benefit prior to retirement.

Home Service Life Insurance. Home service life insurance is a relatively new name for industrial life insurance and monthly debit ordinary insurance. A home service life insurance policy is an individual insurance policy serviced by agents who call at the insured's home to collect the premiums. The policy is for an amount less than $3,000. This form of insurance is normally issued without medical examination, although the company may request an examination. Since the cost of collection is high, it is one of the most expensive forms of life insurance.

Credit Life Insurance. Credit life insurance is used to repay a personal

Today's Lifestyles
Types of Life Insurance

Lifestyle	Term Insurance	Whole Life Insurance	Endowment
	Low initial premium Coverage for a specific period of time May be renewable and/or convertible Premium rises with each new term Provides pure life insurance coverage for specific risks	Coverage for life Fixed premium Growing cash value Higher initial premium than term Available as universal, variable, and adjustable life Cash value can be used by you or your dependents	Insurance plus rapid cash accumulation Higher premium than term or whole life You can arrange the policy to coincide with future events
Single	Useful in protecting against temporary debts Available as decreasing term to cover a long-term decreasing debt, such as a mortgage	Useful in protecting dependents, such as elderly parents Useful in providing legacies to charities, schools Useful in building an emergency fund Useful for possible future responsibilities	Useful in circumstances where policyholder has a specific dollar savings goal
Young married— no children	Useful in protecting spouse against temporary debt Available as decreasing term to cover a long-term debt, such as a mortgage Useful in providing spouse with temporary financial protection in event of insured's death	*See Single* Useful in protecting spouse Useful as a source of retirement income	*See Single*

debt should the borrower die before doing so. It is based on the belief that "no person's debts should live after him or her." It was introduced in the United States in 1917, when installment financing and purchasing became popular. Originally, and for many years, credit life coverage was provided by policies that individuals purchased for themselves. Now the vast majority of such coverage is group insurance provided under a master contract issued to a bank or other type of lending agency or to a retail store selling goods on the installment plan. Credit life insurance accounts for about 5 percent of all life insurance in the United States.

Modern life insurance policies contain numerous provisions and clauses.

Lifestyle	Term Insurance	Whole Life Insurance	Endowment
Married with children	Useful in providing spouse and children with high amount of financial protection for low cost during specific time Useful as a decreasing term to cover long-term decreasing debt, such as a mortgage Useful in providing financial protection for high-cost, short-term obligations, such as education	Can guarantee coverage for life regardless of future problems related to insurability Useful in providing college funds Useful in providing protection for postretirement needs Useful in providing estate taxes Useful in building an emergency fund Favorable investment performance can result in increased life insurance coverage	*See Single* Useful in providing college funds
Married— middle-aged	Useful in covering substantial temporary debts such as acquisition of property	*See Single* Useful in protecting spouse Useful in providing protection for postretirement needs	*See Single* Useful in providing retirement dollars
Retired		Accumulated cash values can be used to purchase an annuity Useful in providing estate taxes	

Source: *Life Insurance Teacher's Guide* (Washington, D.C.: American Council of Life Insurance, 1982), p. 14.

The terminology of these policies can be confusing, but understanding their special provisions is very important for the insurance buyer.

IMPORTANT PROVISIONS IN A LIFE INSURANCE CONTRACT

Your life insurance policy is valuable only if it meets your objectives. When your objectives change, however, it may not be necessary to give up the policy. Instead, study the policy carefully and discuss its provisions with your agent. Here are some of the most common provisions.

● Life Insurance
   Contract Provisions

Naming Your Beneficiary

An important provision in every life insurance policy is the right to name your beneficiary. A beneficiary is a person who is designated to receive something, such as life insurance proceeds, from someone.

Under group insurance, you can name one or more persons as contingent beneficiaries who will receive your policy proceeds if the primary beneficiary dies before you do.

The Grace Period

When you buy a life insurance policy, the insurance company agrees to pay a certain sum of money under specified circumstances and you agree to pay a certain premium regularly. The grace period allows 28 to 31 days to elapse, during which time the premium may be paid without penalty. After that time, the policy lapses if the premium has not been paid.

Policy Reinstatement

A lapsed policy can be put back in force—reinstated—if it has not been turned in for cash. To reinstate the policy, you must again qualify as an acceptable risk and you must pay overdue premiums with interest. There is a time limit on reinstatement.

Incontestability Clause

The incontestability clause stipulates that after the policy has been in force for a specified period (usually two years), the insurance company cannot dispute its validity during the lifetime of the insured for any reason, including fraud. One reason for this provision is that the beneficiaries should not be forced to suffer because of the acts of the insured who cannot defend the company's contesting of the claim.

Suicide Clause

The suicide clause provides that if the insured dies by suicide during the first two years that the policy is in force, the death benefit will equal the amount of the paid premium. After the two-year period, the suicide becomes a risk covered by the policy and the beneficiaries of a suicide receive the same benefit that is payable for death from any other cause. Many years ago, policies were issued in which no benefit was ever payable in the event of suicide.

Automatic Premium Loans

Under this option, which the insured may elect, if the insured does not pay the premium within the grace period, the insurance company automatically pays it out of the policy's cash value if that cash value is sufficient. This prevents the insured from inadvertently allowing the policy to lapse.

Misstatement of Age Provision

This provision says that if the company finds out that the insured's age was incorrectly stated, the company will pay the benefits that the insured's premiums would have bought if his or her age had been correctly stated. The provision sets forth a simple procedure to resolve what could otherwise be a complicated legal matter.

Policy Loan Provision

A loan from the insurance company is available on a whole life or endowment policy after the policy has been in force for one, two, or three years, as stated in the policy. This feature, known as the policy loan provision, permits the owner of the policy to borrow any amount up to the cash value of the policy.

Riders to Life Insurance Policies

An insurance company can make changes in the provisions of a policy by attaching a rider to the policy. A rider is any document attached to the policy that modifies its coverage by adding or excluding specified conditions or altering its benefits.[7] A whole life insurance policy may include a waiver of premium disability benefit or an accidental death benefit, or both.

Waiver of Premium Disability Benefit. Under this benefit, the company waives any premiums that are due after the beginning of total and permanent disability. In effect, the company pays them. The disability must occur before you reach a certain age, usually 60, and before the policy matures if it is an endowment.

Accidental Death Benefit. Under this provision, the insurance company promises to pay twice the face amount of the policy if the death of the insured occurs by accidental means. The accidental death benefit is often

[7]Robert William Richards, *The Dow Jones-Irwin Dictionary of Financial Planning* (Homewood, Ill.: Dow Jones-Irwin, 1986), p. 288.

called **double indemnity**. Accidental death must occur within a certain time after the injury, usually 90 days, and before the insured reaches a certain age, usually 60 or 65.

Guaranteed Insurability Option. This option allows you to buy specified additional amounts of life insurance at stated intervals without proof of insurability. Thus, even if you do not remain in good health, you can increase the amount of your insurance as your income rises.

Now that you know the various types of life insurance policies and the major provisions of and riders to such policies, you are ready to make your buying decisions.

BUYING YOUR LIFE INSURANCE

- A Plan to Buy Life Insurance

You should consider a number of factors before buying life insurance. As discussed earlier in this chapter, these factors include your present and future sources of income, other savings and income protection, group life insurance, group annuities (or other pension benefits), and social security.

In Chapter 11, you learned how to select an insurance company and what guidelines to follow in choosing an insurance agent. But comparing life insurance costs may not be as easy as pricing a certain appliance make and model. In this section, you will learn how insurance companies price their products.

Comparing Policy Costs

Each life insurance company designs the policies it sells to make them attractive and useful to many policyholders. One policy may have features that another policy doesn't have; one company may be more selective than another company; one company may get a better return on its investments than another company. These and other factors affect the price of life insurance policies.

In brief, the price that a company charges for a life insurance policy is affected by five factors: the company's cost of doing business; the return on its investments; the mortality rate that it expects among its policyholders; the features contained in its policy; and competition among companies with comparable policies.

The price of life insurance policies can therefore vary considerably among life insurance companies. Moreover, a particular company will not be equally competitive for all policies. Thus, one company might have a competitively priced policy for 24-year-olds but not for 35-year-olds.

Ask your agent to give you interest-adjusted indexes. An **interest-adjusted index** is a method of evaluating the cost of life insurance by taking into account the time value of money. Combining premium payments, dividends, cash value buildup, and present value analysis into an index number makes possible a fairly accurate cost comparison among insurance companies. The lower the index number, the lower is the cost of the policy.

Obtaining a Policy

A life insurance policy is issued after you submit an application for insurance and the application is accepted by the insurance company. Figure 14–5 shows a typical life insurance application.

Examining a Policy: Before the Purchase

When you buy a life insurance policy, read every word of the contract and, if necessary, ask your agent for a point by point explanation of the language. Many insurance companies have rewritten their contracts to make them more understandable. Remember that these are legal documents and that you should be familiar with what they promise, even though technical terms are used.

The National Association of Insurance Commissioners and many state insurance departments have prepared buyers guides to help you understand life insurance terms, benefits, and relative costs. These guides are distributed through your agent and your insurance company. Be sure to ask for one. If you have more questions about life insurance companies or policies, you can check with the office of your state insurance commissioner.

Examining a Policy: After the Purchase

After you buy new life insurance, you have a 10-day "free look" period, during which you can change your mind. If you do so, the company will return your premium without penalty.

It's a good idea to give your beneficiaries and your lawyer a photocopy of your policy. Your beneficiaries should know where the policy is kept, because in order to obtain the insurance proceeds, they will have to send it to the company upon your death, along with a copy of the death certificate. It is not necessary to keep a life insurance policy in a safe-deposit box, but copy down the name of the company and the policy number so that you can have the policy replaced if you mislay or lose it.

Your beneficiaries need not take your insurance proceeds in one lump sum. Many people select other options, such as monthly income and a specific sum set aside for other purposes, perhaps education. Ask your agent about the settlement options that are available.

Choosing Settlement Options

A well-planned life insurance program should cover the immediate expenses resulting from the death of the insured, but that is only one of its purposes. In most instances, the primary purpose of life insurance is to protect dependents against a loss of income resulting from the premature death of the primary breadwinner. Thus, selecting the appropriate settlement option is an important part of designing a life insurance program. Perhaps the most common settlement options are lump-sum payment, lim-

FIGURE 14-5 Life Insurance Application

PART I   Life Insurance Application To *The COUNCIL Life Insurance Company*

IMPORTANT NOTICE—This application is subject to approval by the Company's Home Office. Be sure all questions in all parts of the application are answered completely and accurately, since the application is the basis of the insurance contract and will become part of any policy issued.

1. Insured's Full Name (Please Print-Give title as Mr., Dr., Rev., etc.)

MR. DENNIS SMITH

Mo., Day, Yr. of Birth	Ins. Age	Sex	Place of Birth	Social Security No.
8/25/63	29	M	TULSA, OKLA.	001-30-0000

Single ☑ Married ☐ Widowed ☐ Divorced ☐ Separated ☐

2. Addresses last 5 yrs.

	Number Street	City	State	Zip Code	County	Yrs.
Mail to ☑ Home: Present	711 SUNSET DRIVE	WASH.	D.C.	20000	U.S.A	3
Former						
☐ Business: Present						
Former						

3. Occupation

	Title	Describe Exact Duties	Yrs.
Present	COMPUTER SPECIALIST	DEVELOP PROGRAMS FOR CLIENTS	3
Former	COMPUTER ANALYST	DEVELOP SOFTWARE PACKAGES	6

4. a) Employer ABC COMPUTER CONSULTANTS
   b) Any change contemplated? Yes ☐ (Explain in Remarks) No ☑

5. Have you ever   Yes No
   a) been rejected, deferred or discharged by the Armed Forces for medical reasons or applied for a government disability rating?   ☐ ☑
   b) applied for insurance or for reinstatement which was declined, postponed, modified or rated?   ☐ ☑
   c) used LSD, heroin, cocaine or methadone?   ☐ ☑

6. a) In the past 3 years have you
   (i) had your driver's license suspended or revoked or been convicted of more than one speeding violation?   ☐ ☑
   (ii) operated, been a crew member of, or had any duties aboard any kind of aircraft?   ☐ ☑
   (iii) engaged in underwater diving below 40 feet, parachuting, or motor vehicle racing?   ☐ ☑
   b) In the future, do you intend to engage in any activities mentioned in (ii) and (iii) of a) above? (If "Yes" to 5a or any of 6, complete Supplemental Form 3375)   ☐ ☑

7. Have you smoked one or more cigarettes within the past 12 months?   ☑ ☐

8. Are other insurance applications pending or contemplated?   ☐ ☑

9. Do you intend to go to any foreign country?   ☐ ☑

10. Will coverage applied for replace or change any life insurance or annuities? (If "Yes", submit Replacement Form)   ☐ ☑

11. Total Life Insurance in force $_____   None ☑

12. Face Amount $ 40,000   Plan TERM
    Accidental Death ☐ Waiver of Premium ☐
    Purchase Option–Regular ☐ Preferred ☐ PEP ☐ GOR ☐
    _____ units of Wife's Term–name: _____
    $_____ initial amount Decreasing Term, _____ Years
    (Joint ☐) (Mot. Pro. ☐) (Straight Line ☐)
    Children's Term ☐ Other: _____

13. Auto. Prem. Loan provision operative if available? Yes ☑ No ☐

14. Dividend Option
    Additions (other than Term policies) ☐ Deposits ☐
    Reduce premium, if applicable, otherwise cash ☐
    Supplemental Protection (Keyman only) ☐
    1 Year Term–any balance to
    Deposits ☐ Additions ☐ Reduce prem. (cash if mo.) ☐

15. Beneficiary—for children's, wife's or joint insurance as provided in contract; for other insurance as follows, subject to policy's beneficiary provisions:

    (Name) (Relationship to Insured)
    1st KARYN SMITH   MOTHER   if living,
    2nd RONALD R. SMITH FATHER   if living, if not
    3rd JEAN SMITH   SISTER   if living, if not
    the executors or administrators of: Insured ☐ Other (use Remarks) ☐
    (Joint beneficiaries will receive equally or survivor, unless otherwise specified.)

16. Flexible Plan settlement (personal beneficiary only)   ☑

17. Rights—During Insured's lifetime all rights belong to
    Insured ☑ Other: _____
    Trustee _____ (attach Trust)
    (After Insured's death as provided in contract on wife's insurance.)

18. Premium—Frequency MO. Amt. Paid $ 109.80 None ☐
    Have you received a Conditional Receipt? Yes ☑ No ☐

REMARKS [Include details (company, date, amt., etc.) for all "Yes" answers to questions 4b, 5b, 5c, 8, 9 and 10.]

SMOKES ONE PACK A DAY

I agree that: (1) No one but the Company's President, a Vice-President or Secretary has authority to accept information not contained in the application, to modify or enlarge any contract, or to waive any requirement. (2) Except as otherwise provided in any conditional receipt issued, any policy issued shall take effect upon its delivery and payment of the first premium during the lifetime of each person to be insured. Due dates of later premiums shall be as specified in the policy.

Dated at WASH, D.C. on Jan 15, 1989 Signature of Insured Dennis Smith

Signature of Applicant (if other than Insured) who agrees to be bound by the representations and agreements in this and any other part of this application N/A
(Name) (Relationship) (Complete address of Applicant)

Countersigned by Michael C. Baker
Field Underwriter (Licensed Resident Agent)

Source: American Council of Life Insurance.

FIGURE 14-5   Life Insurance Application (*concluded*)

PART 1A	Statements Forming Part Of Application To *The COUNCIL Life Insurance Company* [Complete this Part if any Non-Medical or Family Insurance is Applied For]

1. Name of Insured DENNIS SMITH   Ins. Age **29**   Height **5** ft. **10** in.   Weight **165** lbs.

2. If Family, Children's, Wife's or Joint Insurance desired, other family members proposed for insurance:

Wife (include maiden name)	Ins. Age	Mo., Day, Yr. of Birth	Height ft. in.	Weight lbs.	Life in Force $	Place of Birth

Children	Sex	Ins. Age	Mo., Day, Yr. of Birth	Children	Sex	Ins. Age	Mo., Day, Yr. of Birth

3. Has any eligible dependent (a) been omitted from 2? Yes ☐ No ☑ (b) applied for insurance or for reinstatement which was declined, postponed, modified or rated or had a policy cancelled or renewal refused? Yes ☐ No ☑ (Give name, date, company in 8)

4. Have you or anyone else proposed for insurance, so far as you know, ever been treated for or had indication of (underline applicable item)

	Yes	No
a) high blood pressure? (If "Yes", list drugs prescribed and dates taken.)	☐	☑
b) chest pain, heart attack, rheumatic fever, heart murmur, irregular pulse or other disorder of the heart or blood vessels?	☐	☑
c) cancer, tumor, cyst, or any disorder of the thyroid, skin, or lymph glands?	☐	☑
d) diabetes or anemia or other blood disorder?	☐	☑
e) sugar, albumin, blood or pus in the urine, or venereal disease?	☐	☑
f) any disorder of the kidney, bladder, prostate, breast or reproductive organs?	☐	☑
g) ulcer, intestinal bleeding, hepatitis, colitis, or other disorder of the stomach, intestine, spleen, pancreas, liver or gall bladder?	☐	☑
h) asthma, tuberculosis, bronchitis, emphysema or other disorder of the lungs?	☑	☐
i) fainting, convulsions, migraine headache, paralysis, epilepsy or any mental or nervous disorder?	☐	☑
j) arthritis, gout, amputation, sciatica, back pain or other disorder of the muscles, bones or joints?	☐	☑
k) disorder of the eyes, ears, nose, throat or sinuses?	☑	☐
l) varicose veins, hemorrhoids, hernia or rectal disorder?	☐	☑
m) alcoholism or drug habit?	☐	☑

5. Have you or anyone else proposed for insurance, so far as you know, (underline applicable item)

	Yes	No
a) consulted or been examined or treated by any physician or practitioner in the past 5 years?	☑	☐
b) had, or been advised to have, an x-ray, cardiogram, blood or other diagnostic test in the past 5 years?	☐	☑
c) been a patient in a hospital, clinic, or other medical facility in the past 5 years?	☐	☑
d) ever had a surgical operation performed or advised?	☐	☑
e) ever made claim for disability or applied for compensation or retirement based on accident or sickness?	☐	☑

6. Are you or any other person proposed for insurance, so far as you know, in impaired physical or mental health, or under any kind of medication? ☐ Yes ☑ No

7. Weight change in last 6 months of adults proposed for insurance:

Name	Gain	Loss	Cause
N/A			

8. Details of all "Yes" answers. For any checkup or routine examination, indicate what symptoms, if any, prompted it and include results of the examination and any special tests. Include clinic number if applicable.

Question No.	Name of Person	Illness & Treatment	No. of Attacks	Dates: Onset-Recovery	Doctor, Clinic or Hospital and Complete Address
4H	DENNIS SMITH	BRONCHITIS	6	1960-1967	DR. WILLIAM BILLS 29 CURRK ST, TULSA, OKLA.
4K	DENNIS SMITH	CONJUNCTIVITIS	1	1981	DR. J.L. MARSHALL
5B	DENNIS SMITH	CHEST X-RAY JOB	1		99 ELM ST, WASH, D.C.
5D	DENNIS SMITH	BROKEN KNEECAP	1	1972-1973	DR. WILLIAM BILLS

So far as may be lawful, I waive for myself and all persons claiming an interest in any insurance issued on this application, all provisions of law forbidding any physician or other person who has attended or examined, or who may attend or examine, me or any other person covered by such insurance, from disclosing any knowledge or information which he thereby acquired.

I represent the statements and answers in this and in any other part of this application to be true and complete to the best of my knowledge and belief, and offer them to the Company for the purpose of inducing it to issue the policy or policies and to accept the payment of premiums thereunder. I also agree that payment of the first premium (if after this date) shall be a representation by me that such statements and answers would be the same if made at the time of such payment.

Dated at ___WASH., D.C.___ on ___Jan 15, 19 89___   Signature of Insured ___Dennis Smith___

Witnessed by ___Michael C. Baker___   Signature of Wife (if insured) ___N/A___
Field Underwriter (Licensed Resident Agent)

AUTHORIZATION

For purposes of determining my eligibility for insurance, I hereby authorize any physician, practitioner, hospital, clinic, institution, insurance company, Medical Information Bureau, or other organization or person that has records or knowledge of me or my health to give any such information to the Council Life Insurance Company.

If application is made to The Council Life Insurance Company for insurance on any member of my family, this authorization also applies to such member. A photostatic copy of this authorization shall be as valid as the original.

Signed on _____ , 19 __   ___Dennis Smith___
Signature of Insured

ited installment payment, life income option, and proceeds left with company.

Lump-Sum Payment. In the lump-sum payment option, the company pays the face amount of the policy in one installment to the beneficiary or to the estate of the insured. This form of settlement is the most widely used option.

Limited Installment Payment. This option provides for payment of the life-insurance proceeds in equal periodic installments for a specified number of years after your death.

Life Income Option. Under the life income option, payments are made to the beneficiary for as long as the beneficiary may live. The amount of each payment is based primarily on the sex and attained age of the beneficiary at the time of the insured's death.

Proceeds Left with the Company. Under this option, the life insurance proceeds are left with the insurance company at a specified rate of interest. The company acts as trustee and pays the interest to the beneficiary. The guaranteed minimum interest rate paid on the proceeds varies among companies.

Read your policy diligently, and know its benefits and limitations. The accompanying boxed feature provides a comprehensive insurance policy checklist.

Switching Policies

If you already own whole life insurance, think twice if someone suggests that you replace it. Before you give up this protection, make sure you are still insurable (check medical and any other qualification requirements). Also remember that you are now older than you were when you purchased your policy and that a new policy will cost more because of your age. Moreover, the older policy may have provisions that are not duplicated in some of the new policies. We are not saying that you should reject the idea of replacing your present policy, but rather that you should proceed with caution. We recommend that you ask your agent or company for an opinion about the new proposal, so as to get both sides of the argument.

As you have seen so far, life insurance provides a set sum at your death. But what if you want to enjoy benefits while you are still alive. Then you might consider annuities. An annuity protects you against the risk of outliving your assets.

Personal Financial Planning and You
Do You Know What Is in Your Life Insurance Policy?

Read your policy, and know its benefits and restrictions. The following questions will help you know what is in your present policy and those you may buy in the future.

1. Which insurance company issued the policy? _____

2. What type of policy is it? _____

3. What is the face value of the policy? _____

4. What is the *annual* premium if paid annually? _____

   What is the *annual* premium if paid quarterly? _____

   What is the *annual* premium if paid semiannually? _____

   What is the *annual* premium if paid monthly? _____

5. Who is the beneficiary? Who is the contingent beneficiary (the person who receives the policy proceeds at the death of the insured if the first beneficiary is deceased)? _____

6. How long is the grace period? _____

7. If the premium is unpaid at the end of the grace period, does this policy automatically lapse? __

8. May the insured reinstate the policy if it has lapsed? _____

9. When does the policy become incontestable (during the time the policy is contestable, the company can seek release from the policy if it is discovered that false statements of a material nature were made in the application for insurance)? _____

10. Is there an annual dividend on the policy? If so, what will be the anticipated annual dividend this year? At the end of the 10th policy year? At the end of the 20th policy year? _____

11. If the policy pays dividends, what choices do you have as to how they will be used? _____

12. How soon after issue may a policy loan be made? _____

13. What rate of interest is charged on money borrowed from the policy? _____

14. What is the cash value or loan value of this policy in its 5th year? In its 10th year? In its 15th year? In its 20th year? _____

15. What nonforfeiture provisions are available if the policy is allowed to lapse? _____

16. May this policy be converted to any other type of policy? _____

17. What settlement options does this policy have? _____

18. Does this policy include a provision for waiver of premium in event of disability? If so, what is the additional premium charge for this provision? _____

19. If this is a term policy, is it guaranteed renewable? _____

20. Other pertinent information about the policy _____

Source: *Life Insurance Teacher's Guide* (Washington, D.C.: American Council of Life Insurance, 1982), p. 32.

FINANCIAL
PLANNING
WITH
ANNUITIES

● How Annuities
Provide Security

An **annuity** is a financial contract written by an insurance company to provide you with a regular income. Generally, you receive the income monthly, with payments often arranged to continue as long as you live. The payments may begin at once or at some future date. The annuity is often described as being the opposite of life insurance. It pays while you live; life insurance pays when you die.

Why Buy Annuities?

A prime reason for buying an annuity is to give you retirement income for the rest of your life. We will discuss retirement income in Chapter 19, "Retirement Planning."

Although people have been buying annuities for many years, the appeal of fixed annuities has increased recently because of rising interest rates and the relative safety of annuities as compared to securities. A *fixed annuity* is a contract stating that the annuitant (the person who is to receive the annuity) will receive a fixed amount of income over a certain period or for life. A *variable annuity,* on the other hand, is a plan under which the monthly payments will vary because payments are based on the income received from stocks or other investments.

Some of the recent growth in annuities can also be attributed to the passage of the Employee Retirement Income Security Act (ERISA) of 1974. Annuities are often purchased for individual retirement accounts (IRAs), which were made possible by the act. They may also be used in Keogh-type plans for the self-employed. As you will see in Chapter 19, contributions to both IRA and Keogh plans are tax deductible up to specified limits.

What about Taxes?

When you buy an annuity, the interest on the principal, as well as the interest compounded on that interest, builds up free of current income tax. The Tax Reform Act of 1986 preserves the tax advantages of annuities (and insurance), while curtailing deductions for IRAs. With an annuity, there is no maximum annual contribution. And if you die during the accumulation period, the beneficiary is guaranteed no less than the amount invested.

"I fully expect annuities (and variable life) to become one of the hottest products in the financial services industry over the next few years," says Arthur H. Goldberg, president of a New York securities and real estate firm.[8]

As with any other hot product, however, the advantages of annuities are tempered by drawbacks. In the case of variable annuities, these drawbacks include reduced flexibility and fees that lower investment return.

Figure 14–6 gives examples of the annual retirement income beginning at age 65 that can result from placing various amounts in a deferred annuity for different periods of time.

[8]Karen Slater, "Variable Annuities, Life Insurance: Tax-Favored Investing—At a Price," *The Wall Street Journal,* September 8, 1986, p. 21.

FIGURE 14-6   Examples of Annual Retirement Income Beginning at
Age 65

The examples in this table are based on contributions of $2,000 a year and representative rates for men in early 1982. The accounts are assumed to accumulate at 8 percent per year. Taxes are not considered, either before or after retirement.

	Total Accumulated	Annual Payout Starting at Age 65
Invested over 30 years:		
$60,000	$244,692	$27,750
Invested over 20 years:		
$40,000	$ 98,846	$11,200
Invested over 10 years:		
$20,000	$ 31,291	$ 3,550

Source: *What You Should Know about Annuities* (Washington, D.C.: American Council of Life Insurance, December 1982), p. 10.

SUMMARY

- Life insurance is a contract between an insurance company and a policyholder, under which the company agrees to pay a specified sum to a beneficiary upon the death of the insured. The first U.S. life insurance company was set up in 1794. Today, in the United States, about 9 out of 10 families and 2 out of 3 individuals have some form of life insurance. People buy life insurance to protect someone who depends on them from financial losses caused by their death.

- Insurance provides protection because it is based on proven principles of human mortality, probability, and the law of large numbers.

- In determining your life insurance needs, you must first determine your insurance objectives and then estimate your insurance requirements. One rule of thumb is that a good target is life insurance totaling four to five times your annual income.

- The two types of life insurance companies are

  stock companies, which are owned by stockholders, and mutual companies, which are owned by policyholders. In general, stock companies sell nonparticipating policies and mutual companies sell participating policies.

- The three basic types of life insurance are term, whole life (also called straight life or ordinary life), and endowment policies. There are many variations and combinations of the three basic types.

- The naming of the beneficiary, the grace period, policy reinstatement, the incontestability and suicide clauses, automatic premium loans, the misstatement of age provision, and the policy loan provision are important provisions in most life insurance policies. Common riders in life insurance policies are the waiver of premium disability benefit, accidental death benefit, and guaranteed insurability options.

- Before buying life insurance consider your

present and future sources of income, group life insurance, and social security. Then compare policy costs. Examine your policy before and after the purchase, and choose appropriate settlement options.

● An annuity is the opposite of life insurance. It pays while you live; life insurance pays when you die. An annuity provides you with a regular income during your retirement years. Annuities are given a favorable income tax treatment under the Tax Reform Act of 1986.

GLOSSARY

Annuity. A contract that provides an income for a specified period of time.

Beneficiary. A person who receives insurance proceeds at the death of an insured.

Cash value. The cash surrender value of a life insurance policy.

Double indemnity. An additional benefit equal to twice the face value of the policy if death occurs due to an accident.

Endowment policy. Provides payment after a specified number of years to the insured (if living) or the beneficiary.

Incontestability clause. A provision stating that the insurer cannot dispute the validity of a policy after a specified period.

Interest-adjusted index. A method of evaluating the cost of life insurance by taking into account the time value of money.

Modified life. A variation of the whole life policy in which low premiums are paid during the initial years.

Nonforfeiture clause. A provision that allows the insured not to forfeit all accrued benefits.

Nonparticipating policy. Life insurance that does not provide policy dividends; also called a nonpar policy.

Participating policy. Life insurance that provides policy dividends; also called a par policy.

Rider. An amendment to a policy.

Suicide clause. A provision stating that if the insured dies by suicide, the benefit will be limited to the amount of premium paid.

Term insurance. Protection for a stated period.

Universal life. A policy that combines term insurance and investment elements.

Whole life policy. A plan of insurance for the whole of life, with premiums payable for life; also called a straight life policy or an ordinary life policy.

REVIEW QUESTIONS

1. What are the components involved in life insurance coverage?

2. Describe the purpose of life insurance, and list some typical examples of personal uses of life insurance proceeds.

3. What is the principle of life insurance? Who developed the Standard Ordinary Mortality Table. Why?

4. Define the following types of insurance policies, and list their advantages and disadvantages:

   a. Term life insurance.
   b. Whole life insurance.
   c. Limited payment policy and single-premium policy.
   d. Endowment policy.

e. Modified life insurance policy.

f. Universal life insurance policy.

g. Variable life insurance policy.

h. Flexible premium variable life insurance policy.

i. Group life insurance policy.

5. Define the eight provisions found in most life insurance policies. What are their advantages, if any?

6. What is a rider? List the three riders to life insurance policies and their benefits.

7. Describe each of the steps that you should take in buying life insurance.

8. How do you compare insurance policy costs? What five factors affect the price of a life insurance policy?

9. What is an annuity? Why do people buy annuities?

DISCUSSION QUESTIONS AND ACTIVITIES

1. Do you believe that nonprofit groups should endorse the types of coverage mentioned in the Opening Scenario? Why or why not?

2. Examine your life insurance policies and the life insurance policies of other members of your family. Note the contractual provisions of each policy. What does the company promise to do in return for premiums?

3. Discuss the importance of giving accurate information on an insurance application form.

4. Obtain life insurance premium rates for $25,000 whole life and term life policies from local insurance firms. Compare the costs and services rendered by each company.

5. Why should you buy additional insurance if you already have group insurance? Discuss.

6. Review the settlement options on your family's life insurance policies and discuss with your family which would be the best choice for them at this time.

7. Contact your state insurance department to get information about whether your state requires interest-adjusted cost disclosure.

8. Visit your library or an insurance company to review *Best's Insurance Reports*, which provides statistical data and comments on insurance companies and ratings of these companies.

9. Discuss why you or your parents bought life insurance from a specific company or agent.

10. Ask an insurance company for its annual report, and see how that report can help you in planning to buy your life insurance.

ADDITIONAL READINGS

Bogdanich, Walt. "Nonprofit Groups Offer Insurance, but Often the Prices Are Beatable." *The Wall Street Journal*, March 13, 1986, p. 31.

"Insurance, U.S." In *U.S. Industrial Outlook, 1986*, Washington, D.C.: U.S. Government Printing Office, p. 51–1.

"Life Insurance." *Consumer Reports*, June 1986, p. 371.

On the Way Up. Hartford, Conn.: Corporate Communications, Aetna Life and Casualty Company, n.d.

Penn, Stanley. "Playing Dead." *The Wall Street Journal*, July 1, 1986, p. 1.

"Risk and How It Affects the Price of Insurance." Washington, D.C.: American Council of Life Insurance, Spring 1986.

Slater, Karen. "Return on Universal Life Insurance Can Be a Lot Less than Expected." *The Wall Street Journal*, February 11, 1986, p. 35.

_____. "Variable Annuity, Life Insurance Tax-Favored Investing—at a Price." *The Wall Street Journal*, September 8, 1986, p. 21.

Topolnicki, Denise M. "Life Insurance." *Money*, June 1986, p. 183.

Welker, Ernest P. "Life Insurance: From the Buyer's Point of View." *Economic Education Bulletin*, July 1982.

CASE 14–1 Identifying the Need for and Amount of Insurance

Jeff and Ann are both 28 years old. They have been married for three years, and they have a son who is almost two. They expect their second child in a few months.

Jeff is a head teller in a local bank. He has just received a $30 a week raise. His income is $480 a week, which, after taxes, leaves him with $1,648 a month. His company provides $20,000 of life insurance, a medical hospital surgical plan, and a major medical plan. All of these group plans protect him as long as he stays with the bank.

When Jeff received his raise, he decided that part of it should be used to add to his family's protection. Jeff and Ann talked to their insurance agent, who reviewed their insurance through Jeff's job. Under social security, they also had some basic protection against the loss of Jeff's income if he became totally disabled or if he died before the children were 18.

But most of this protection was only basic, a kind of floor for Jeff and Ann to build on. For example, monthly social security payments to Ann would be approximately $1,250 if Jeff died leaving two children under age 18. Yet the family's total expenses are higher now than they were before the birth of the second baby. Although the family's expenses would be lowered if Jeff died, they would be at least $250 a month more than social security would provide.

Questions

1. What type of policy would you suggest for Jeff and Ann? Why?

2. In your opinion, do Jeff and Ann need additional insurance? Why or why not?

CASE 14–2 Pam's Stage One

Pam is single, age 21, and a college senior in excellent health. She has no dependents and no plans for marriage. She wants to get established in her career before settling down. She is working part-time to supplement her college grant and meet school and living expenses. She does not receive any support from her widowed mother, who works and just meets her own living expenses.

Pam plans to go to graduate college for her Master of Business Administration degree before looking for a full-time job.

Questions

1. Analyze Pam's need for life insurance. How much life insurance, if any, does she need at this time?

2. What kind of insurance should Pam choose? What options should she select?

Comprehensive Case for Part Four
Highway Hazards

The scene is familiar to all too many of us. Emotion-torn students, a memorial service, an empty classroom seat previously occupied by a student who was a lively participant in school activities one day and a statistic the next day—another life snuffed out by an automobile accident. Yet cars and highways are now safer and drivers more skillful than they have ever been. So why does this senseless carnage continue?

The fact is that, all too often, a major factor in traffic fatalities is the drunk driver—who is often a teenager. The statistics on teenage drinking and driving are shocking:

1. Each year, nearly 5,000 teenagers are killed and 130,000 more are injured in auto accidents in which alcohol is a factor.
2. Of all fatal nighttime alcohol-related crashes, 44 percent are caused by persons 16–24 years old, who make up only 22 percent of the licensed population.
3. Teenage drunk driving costs close to $6 billion a year in damages, hospital costs, and lost work.
4. Almost half—49 percent—of all teenagers drink in cars, and 23 percent of these teenagers drive after drinking.

Reducing the carnage will take the combined efforts of state legislatures, law enforcement agencies, the judicial branch, the media, the educational community, and the insurance industry.

One project—the International Symposium on Alcohol and Driving—was jointly conducted by the Insurance Information Institute and the American Insurance Association. The symposium was held in Washington, D.C., in November 1982. It brought together nearly 600 persons from all parts of the world, among whom were representatives of government, the insurance industry, educators, citizens' groups, and the media. All of those present were determined to join forces to bring about an end to the terrible waste in lives, injuries, and money that drunk driving causes.

Consider the work of one dedicated educator, Robert Anastas, who formed a student organization, Students Against Drunk Driving (SADD), in 1981 at Wayland (Massachusetts) High School after the school introduced a mandatory health education program that included material on the effects of alcohol. The stated purpose of SADD is to:

1. Help save the lives of students and others.
2. Educate students concerning the problem of drinking and driving.
3. Develop peer counseling among students about alcohol use.
4. Increase public awareness and knowledge among all age groups of ways to confront the problem of drunk driving.

Less than two years after its founding, SADD chapters involving 2.5 million teenagers had been established in 5,000 schools. Anastas observes that many young people drink because of peer pressure and that educators can use peer pressure to help students avoid, or at least limit, their drinking.

Questions

1. What solutions can you suggest to reduce the number of automobile accident fatalities among teenagers?
2. Do you think that the mandatory drinking age should be increased to 21 in all the states? Why or why not?
3. Why is the insurance industry so concerned about automobile accidents?
4. In your opinion, are such groups as Students Against Drunk Driving (SADD) effective in reducing the number of deaths that result from drunk driving?
5. What effect does drunk driving have on health care and medical insurance costs?
6. How do auto accidents influence the cost of life insurance for young people?

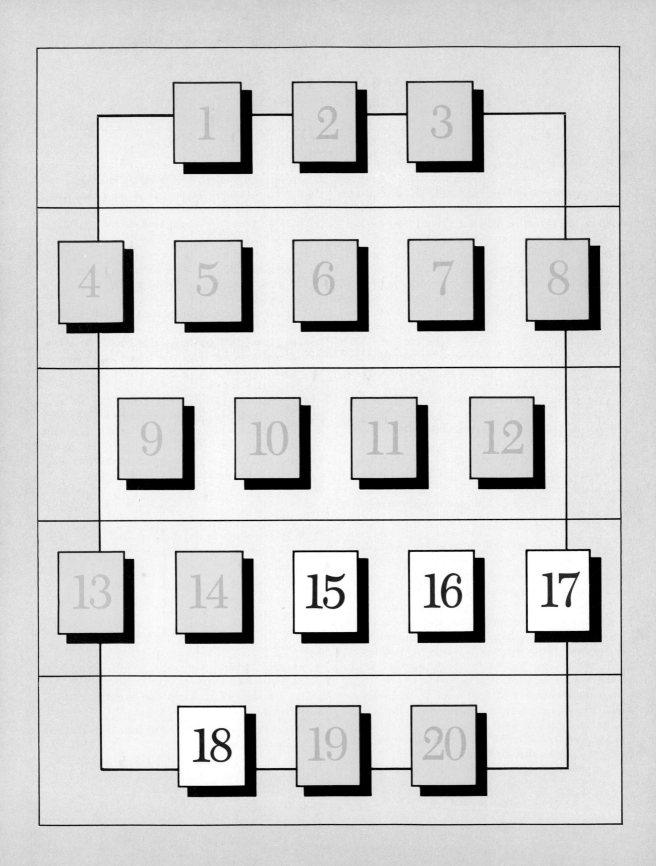

PART FIVE

Investing Your Money

In this part, we are concerned with another personal resource—money. Nobody likes being poor, least of all investors. As a result, investors work, save, and invest to provide financial security and to meet their retirement needs. We begin by discussing the fundamentals required to establish a personal investment program. Then we examine different investments in stocks, bonds, mutual funds, and real estate. Finally, we look at more speculative investments, which include buying stock on margin, selling short, trading commodities and options, and collecting metals, gemstones, and other collectibles. Included in this part are:

15

Fundamentals of Investing

There are people who get rich quick by buying and selling a hot stock issue at just the right time. These people often seem to hit it lucky without formulating a plan or using additional investment information. And yet, sooner or later, their luck plays out and they eventually lose money. Over a long period of time, there is no substitute for systematically evaluating potential investments. If you expect your investment program to earn money for you, you must be willing to invest some time and effort in gathering and analyzing the information you need to make quality decisions. In developing your personal investment plan, there are many different types of investment opportunities from which you can choose. One very safe method of accumulating money is the traditional savings account. You can also purchase common stock, preferred stock, bonds, mutual funds, or commodities. Each of these investment alternatives has advantages and disadvantages, which we will examine in detail. We will also look at financial information and investment services that help you evaluate your possible choices.

After studying this chapter, you will be able to:

- Explain why it is to your advantage to establish an investment program.

- Discuss the importance of preparing for an investment program.

- Identify the major types of investment alternatives available to investors.

- Describe how the factors of safety, income, growth, liquidity, and risk affect your investment options.

- Recognize the role of the professional financial planner in your investment program.

- List the various sources of financial information that can reduce investment risks.

Anthony J. Mooney
Robert W. Petrie
Gene R. Huxhold
Jack Rasmussen

Anthony J. Mooney is Tax Advantaged Investment Coordinator, Assistant Branch Manager, and Associate Vice President at Dean Witter Reynolds, Inc. Robert W. Petrie is Account Executive and Equity Coordinator at Dean Witter Reynolds, Inc. Gene R. Huxhold is Advanced Sales Representative at Kemper Financial Services, Inc. Jack Rasmussen is Real Estate Manager and Broker at Merrill Lynch.

The type of equity security with which most people are familiar is stock. When an investor buys stock, he or she becomes an owner of some share of a company's assets. The most common form of corporate debt is the bond, which is a certificate promising to repay, no later than a specified date, a sum of money that the investor, or bondholder, has loaned to the company. Bonds issued by states, cities, or certain agencies of local governments, such as school districts, are called municipal bonds.

All experts suggest that if you are thinking about investing your money, it is important to get reliable information about your potential investment. If you are unsure about how to proceed, you may want to seek advice from a qualified person whom you trust. But always remember that the final decision is yours. After all, it's your money!

In investing, one of the most basic relationships is that between risk and reward. Very often, investments that offer potentially high returns are accompanied by some relatively higher risk factors. Therefore, it is up to you to decide how much risk you can assume. Always remember that your overall financial situation includes both your current needs and your future needs. In general, prospective investors should avoid risky investments unless they have a steady income, adequate insurance, and an emergency fund of accessible cash. If you need help to make the most suitable choices for your needs, you should consult books on investing, a registered investment adviser, a broker/dealer, or, in certain cases, an attorney, accountant, financial counselor, or bank.

You should be as careful about buying securities as you would be about any costly purchase. The majority of securities professionals are honest, but be aware that misrepresentation and fraud do take place. The experts suggest the following basic safeguards when shopping for investments.

Don't buy securities offered by telephone or through similar cold call procedures; ask for written information. Don't buy because of tips or rumors. Not only is it safer to get the facts first, but it is also illegal to buy or sell securities based on inside information that is not available to other investors. Beware of salespeople who try to pressure you into acting immediately. Get advice if you don't understand something in a prospectus or a piece of sales literature. Be skeptical of quick profits. Check on the credentials of anyone you don't know who tries to sell you securities. Remember that in an investment arrangement past success is no guarantee of future success.

For the beginning investor, making money by investing is not as easy as it might seem. In fact, "Teaching yourself to become an investor is a little like trying to build a house in your spare time. If you persist you'll probably master carpentry, but you'll live with a lot of swollen thumbs."* Although there are hundreds of investment strategies, three basic factors may help eliminate some of those swollen thumbs.

First, good investors do their homework. Many conscientious amateur investors spend at least 10 hours a week evaluating investment alternatives. Their activities include studying corporate reports, talking to a financial planner, evaluating real estate opportunities, and reading business periodi-

cals, newspapers, and financial information available from investment services. This type of homework does pay off. Peggy Schmeltz, an Ohio housewife, was 54 years old in 1972, when her father died and left her $50,000. She knew nothing about the stock market. Ten years later, she had a portfolio of 88 stocks that was worth almost $250,000. Her secret is simple: she spent 10 to 15 hours a week evaluating stocks and maintaining comprehensive records on several hundred companies.†

Second, in addition to doing their homework, good investors follow the 10 basic rules listed below:‡

1. Think before buying.

2. Deal only with investment firms you know.

3. Beware of investment opportunities offered on the telephone by any firm or salesperson you do not know.

4. Guard against all high-pressure sales talks.

5. Beware of promises of quick, spectacular price rises.

6. Be sure you understand the risk of loss as well as the prospect of gain.

7. Get the facts—do not buy on tips or rumors.

8. Ask the person offering investment opportunities over the telephone to mail you written information about the investments. Save all such information for future reference.

9. If you do not understand the written information, consult a person who does.

PREPARING FOR AN INVESTMENT PROGRAM

- Establishing An Investment Program

Personal investment is the use of one's personal funds to earn a financial return. The overall objective of investing is to earn money with money. But that objective is completely useless for the individual because it is so vague.

Establishing Investment Goals

To be useful, investment objectives must be specific and measurable. They must be tailored to the particular financial needs of the individual. Some financial planners suggest that investment goals be stated in terms of money: By December 31, 1999, I will have total assets of $120,000. Other financial planners believe that investors are more motivated to work toward goals that are stated in terms of the particular things they desire: By January 1, 1998, I will have accumulated enough money to purchase a second home

10. Give at least as much thought to making an investment as you would to acquiring any valuable property.

Third, once investments have been made, good investors continually evaluate them. They never sit back and let their money manage itself. All investments need constant care by active and well-exercised financial minds. In addition to monitoring the value of individual investments, you should also monitor the composition of your investments. An investor's objectives change as he or she passes through different stages in life. Stocks suitable for a young, married couple with three small children may be totally inappropriate for a middle-aged couple with grown children. All investors benefit from a thorough investment checkup on a regular basis. A little self-analysis with the help of a financial planner can often be helpful.§ Close surveillance will keep you informed if your investment increases in value, remains the same, or falls in value.

Over the long run, people who invest on the basis of hunches or tips generally lose. An investment, even a small one, is a business venture. Moreover, like other business ventures, investing requires knowledge, skill, and experience. The problem of deciding how to invest is complicated by the many factors you should consider. Where do you begin? The three factors described above are a beginning, but there are other factors that you must consider before you can establish any kind of investment program. In fact, the purpose of this chapter is to help you establish a sound investment program and learn how to evaluate potential investments.

*Robert H. Runde. "What to Do when It's Time to Invest," *Money*, October 1982, p. 84.
†Ibid.
‡*The NASD: What It Does to Protect the Public* (National Association of Securities Dealers Executive Office 1735 K Street, Washington, DC 20006).
§Ann C. Brown, "Out-of-Shape Portfolios," *Forbes*, May 9, 1983, p. 338.

in the mountains. Like the objectives themselves, how they are stated depends on the individual to whom they apply. Some questions that may help establish valid investment objectives are:

1. What will the money be used for, and what are the consequences if it is not obtained?
2. How much money is needed to satisfy the investor's goals?
3. How will the money be obtained?
4. How long will it take to obtain this amount?
5. What possible economic or personal conditions could alter the investment goals?
6. Considering the individual's economic circumstances, is the dollar amount reasonable?

7.   Is the individual willing to make the necessary sacrifices to ensure that the investment goals are met?

Investment objectives must always be oriented toward the future. In Chapter 3, objectives were classified according to the amount of time required to accomplish each type of objective. A *short-term objective* was defined as an objective that would be accomplished within a two-year period. An *intermediate objective* was defined as an objective that would be accomplished within a period of two to five years. Finally, a *long-term objective* was defined as an objective that would take more than five years to accomplish. These classifications and time periods are also useful when planning an investment program. For example, an investor may establish a short-term objective of accumulating $3,000 in a savings account over the next 18 months. The $3,000 may then be used to finance intermediate or long-term investment objectives.

Performing a Financial Checkup

● Preparing for an Investment Program

For the past 10 years, Jon and Mary Santanna have been talking about beginning an investment program. And yet they never seem to have any money left over after all the monthly bills are paid. In fact, their savings account balance is actually smaller today than it was 10 years ago. Unfortunately, the Santannas are not alone. Today, many people are in the same financial boat. Before beginning an investment program, you must make sure your personal financial affairs are in order. Then, and only then, can you proceed with an investment program. In this section, we will examine different factors that you must consider before making the first investment.

Learn to Live within Your Means. Many potential investors must learn to live within their means before an investment program can become a reality. Many individuals spend more than they make on a regular basis. They purchase items on credit and then must make monthly installment payments. Finance charges for credit purchases range between 14 and 24 percent. Obviously, it makes no sense to purchase items on credit with the idea that you are going to invest your excess cash in an investment that returns considerably less than the finance charges you incur on credit purchases. In this situation, it makes more sense to use your money to pay off credit obligations. To remedy this situation, credit purchases should be limited to only the necessities or to purchases required to meet emergency situations. A good rule of thumb is to limit installment payments to 10 to 20 percent of your net monthly pay after taxes. Eventually, the amount of cash remaining after the bills are paid will increase and can be used to start a savings program or finance other investment projects. A word of caution: corrective measures take time, and it is impossible to improve a bad situation overnight. But reducing credit purchases and the resulting installment payments is the foundation of any investment program.

Provide Adequate Insurance Protection. The topic of insurance was discussed in detail in Part Four, and it is not our intention to cover the material again. However, it is essential for individuals to consider their insurance

From *The Wall Street Journal*, with permission of Cartoon Features Syndicate.

needs before beginning an investment program. The types of insurance and the amount of coverage will vary from one person to the next. For example, a married couple with three small children needs more life insurance coverage than a single individual who is retired. Remember, the purpose of life insurance is to replace lost income if the insured should die. In addition to examining your life insurance before you start investing, you should examine the amount of your insurance coverage for hospitalization, the family home and other real estate holdings, automobiles, and any other assets that may need coverage.

Personal Financial Planning and You
An Obvious Need for Financial Planning

Mike Denton, 36, was a chemical engineer employed by Exxon Corporation. During 1986, he earned $55,000 a year. Julie, his wife, was employed as a medical technician for a local hospital and earned $30,000 a year. Since they were married three years ago, they had purchased a new home in an exclusive Houston suburb and two new BMWs. They both had their own American Express and VISA credit cards, which they used to purchase almost anything they wanted. They both enjoyed their present lifestyle and were looking forward to the future. According to Mike, everything seemed to be right on track.

One year later, everything was off track. It all started when Mike lost his job—he simply got the boot. He had always taken his job for granted. As a result, he and Julie had never thought much about money because there seemed to be plenty of it. Now that he was unemployed, they were suffering because of their lack of financial planning. Not only was he trying to find another job, but he also had to try to pay the monthly bills on a lot less money.

When Mike lost his job, the Dentons had $2,100 in the bank. They had monthly expenses that totaled more than $4,500. Until Mike found a new job, they had to find a way to live on Julie's $30,000 salary. First, they decided to sell one of the BMWs. Next, they took out a bank loan to pay off their credit card debts. Finally, they put their home up for sale, but because of the depressed Houston economy, their house didn't sell. Eventually, the mortgage company foreclosed on their home, and they lost it. As a result, they began living in a one-bedroom apartment.

Hopefully, what happened to the Dentons won't happen to you. The Dentons thought they had plenty of time to get their finances in shape. And yet when Mike lost his job, everything fell apart. Like most Americans they made two mistakes. First, Mike had a job, and they never thought he would lose that job. Second, they postponed establishing a financial plan assuming they could do it later. The suggestions that follow will help you avoid the problems that the Dentons experienced.

Start an Emergency Fund. Most financial planners suggest that an investment program should begin with the accumulation of an emergency fund. An *emergency fund* is a certain amount of money that can be obtained quickly in case of immediate need. This money should be deposited in a savings account at the highest available interest rate. (Although savings accounts are actually time deposits, the money in them can almost always be withdrawn immediately.) You may want to review the discussion on savings in Chapter 4 before deciding where to place the money in your emergency fund.

Plan Your Financial Future. Determine short-term and long-term financial objectives that are important to you. Each individual goal and objective should be translated into a written statement because putting your ideas in writing gives you something concrete to work toward.

Learn to Budget. Most people just spend money without thinking. A better approach is to determine which expenditures are important and which ones are unnecessary. Money devoted to unnecessary expenditures can be diverted to finance your investment program.

Keep Accurate Records. Most experts believe this is one of the most important steps in financial planning. A good recordkeeping system lets you see where your money is going.

Establish Your Emergency Fund. The amount of the emergency fund should be determined by the amount of your monthly income and the amount of your monthly expenses. It should be at least three times your monthly salary.

Take Advantage of Windfalls. Unexpected inheritances, tax refunds, bonuses, and other windfalls should be used to obtain the long-term investment goals in your financial plan.

Reevaluate Your Investment Plan. An individual's goals and objectives may change over time. You should be able to change your investment plan in order to meet revised goals and objectives. Reevaluation can be a source of encouragement when you begin to obtain your goals and objectives.

Fifteen months after Mike Denton lost his job, he got another engineering job, and he and Julie began to rebuild their lives. This time, they both vowed to develop a financial plan. They had learned their lesson well, and they didn't want to make the same mistakes again.

For more information, see "Where Does All the Money Go?," *Consumer Reports*, September 1986, p. 581; "Taking Charge of Your Finances," *Parade Magazine*, February 1, 1987, p. 12b; Diane Harris, "How Are You Doing?," *Money*, December 1986, p. 55+; Denise M. Topolnicki, "Six Steps to Financial Freedom," *Money*, November 1986, p. 70+; and "The 1987 Investor's Guide, *Fortune* Magazine, Fall 1986, p. 2+.

The amount of money that should be salted away in the emergency fund varies from person to person. However, most financial planners agree that an amount equal to three months' salary (after taxes) is reasonable.[1] For example, Debbie Martin earns $24,000 a year. Her monthly take-home pay after deductions is $1,600. Before Debbie can begin investing, she must save $4,800 ($1,600 × 3 months) in a savings account or other near cash investment to meet any unexpected emergencies. A few financial planners suggest that the amount in an emergency fund should be based on the amount of expenses the individual must pay each month. If you adopt this guideline, an amount equal to three months' expenses is reasonable.

Establish a Line of Credit. In addition to starting an emergency fund, most financial planners also recommend establishing a line of credit at a commercial bank, savings and loan association, or credit union. A **line of credit** is a short-term loan that is approved before the money is actually needed. Because all the necessary paperwork has already been completed and the loan has been preapproved, the individual can later obtain the money as soon as it is required. This type of financing provides an alternative source of funds if an emergency situation that requires immediate attention does develop.

Getting the Money Needed to Start an Investment Program

Once you have established your investment goals and completed your personal financial checkup, it's time to start investing—assuming that you have enough money to finance your investments. Unfortunately, that is a wrong assumption in many cases because the needed financing doesn't automatically appear. In today's world, you must work to accumulate the money you need to start any type of investment program.

Priority of Investment Goals. How badly do you want to achieve your investment goals? Are you willing to sacrifice some short-term purchases in order to provide financing for your investments? The answers to both questions are extremely important. As pointed out when the material on budgeting was discussed in Chapter 3, no one can make you save money to finance your investment program. You have to want to do it, and the *you* may be the most important factor. Some suggestions that may help you obtain the money needed for a successful investment program are presented below.

You must pay yourself first. Too often, individuals save or invest what is left over after everything else has been paid. As you might guess, there is nothing left over in many cases, and your investment program is put on hold for another month. A second and much better approach is to (1) pay your monthly bills, (2) save a reasonable amount of money, and (3) use whatever money is left over for personal expenses such as entertainment. This ap-

---

[1]Robert H. Runde, "What to Do when It's Time to Invest," *Money*, October 1982, p. 83.

proach allows you to make savings for an investment program a top budget priority.

You should participate in an elective savings program. Many employees can elect to have a specific amount of money withheld from their paychecks each payday. The money withheld by the employer is then deposited in an account for the employee at a bank, savings and loan association, or credit union. Generally, this type of program works because employees learn to live on less take-home pay. It should be pointed out that employees can always withdraw their money from the savings account, but they must make a special trip to the bank, savings and loan association, or credit union to do so. When this type of program is used, it is much easier to put money into an account than it is to get money out of the account.

You can also make a special savings effort one month per year. In order to obtain additional money for investment purposes, some financial planners recommend that investors really cut back to the basics for one month per year. Every expenditure during this month is examined, and only the most essential ones are allowed. Expenditures that are not necessities are eliminated.

You should take advantage of gifts, inheritances, and windfalls. During your lifetime, there will be times when you will receive unexpected sums of money. Unexpected sums of money may result from gifts, inheritances, a salary increase, an end-of-the-year bonus, or a federal income tax refund. Most individuals will opt to spend this money on something that they could not afford under normal circumstances. An alternative approach is to use this extra money to fund your investment program.

The Value of Long-Term Investment Programs

Many individuals never start an investment program because they only have a small sum of money. But even small sums of money grow over a long period of time. For example, if you invest $10,000 for 20 years at a 10 percent annual interest rate, your investment will grow to $67,270 during the 20-year period. This means that if you invest $10,000 on your 30th birthday, your investment will have increased to over $67,000 by the time you are 50. Most long-term investors appreciate the value of letting a bank account or investment compound on a regular basis. The rate of return for an investment does make a difference. Examine Figure 15–1 and notice that an increase in the interest rate results in a larger return to the investor at the end of 1 year, 5 years, and 10 years.

Figure 15–1 illustrates the concept of future value presented in Chapter 3. Notice that the amount of money returned to the investor increases for each year that the initial investment is left on deposit. For example, the original $5,000 deposited at 8 percent will return $7,345 at the end of five years. This represents an increase of $2,345 over and above the original investment. You may want to review the material presented in Chapter 3 before you begin to invest.

FIGURE 15-1   Growth Rate for $5,000 Invested at Current Interest Rates (compounded annually)

Fixed Savings: Starting balance = $5,000

Rate	Balance at the End of Year		
	1	*5*	*10*
6%	$5,300	$6,690	$ 8,955
7	5,350	7,015	9,835
8	5,400	7,345	10,795
9	5,450	7,695	11,835
10	5,500	8,053	12,969
11	5,550	8,425	14,197

A Personal Plan of Action for Investing

Where do you begin? Planning for an individual investment is quite similar to planning for a business. To be a successful investor, you must develop a plan and then implement it. Investment planning begins with establishing realistic goals. The next step is for the individual to perform a personal financial checkup to make sure he or she is ready to invest. If your goals are realistic and you are ready to invest, investment opportunities will be available. Each opportunity must be evaluated, including the potential return and the risk involved. At the very least, this requires some expert advice and careful study. Then, generally through a process of comparison and elimination, particular alternatives are chosen and combined into an investment plan.

The steps required for an effective personal plan of action are presented in Figure 15–2. The first step is to determine the amount of money that will be obtained by a specific date. The total amount of money specified in Step 1 should be based on the objectives that each individual has established. In Step 2, different investment alternatives are listed. Step 3 and Step 4 examine the factors of potential return and potential risk. The choice of investments is reduced to the top three investment alternatives in Step 5. A final decision to choose the top two alternatives is made in Step 6. Step 7 provides for periodic evaluation of the investments at least twice a year.

To illustrate, let's fill in the blanks in Figure 15–2, using the case of Sally Morton, who got a promising job in advertising after college graduation. After three years, Sally is earning $30,000 a year. Her take-home pay after deductions is $2,000 a month. Her living expenses come to about $1,600 a month, which leaves a surplus of $400. Sally has no family responsibilities, so she must decide what to do with the extra money. If Sally applies the model for personal financial planning presented in Figure 15–2 to her specific situation, she will develop a plan that establishes the goals she thinks are important. Sally's plan is illustrated in Figure 15–3.

Your own plan may be quite different from Sally's, but the principle is the same. Each individual has different ideas and goals. Establish your personal financial priorities first, and then follow through.

Reevaluation of Investment Goals

An investor's circumstances may change as he or she goes through life. As a result, investors are often forced to change or adapt their planning to meet new situations. An investor may take a new job at a substantially higher salary. As a result, his or her investment goals may change and the present plan may become obsolete.

Also, possible investment alternatives may change because of changes in economic and financial conditions. During 1980 and 1981, many investors sold their common stock holdings and invested the money in certificates of deposits (CDs) that paid high guaranteed interest. A short time later, many of the same investors began to cash in their CDs, which were now paying lower interest rates, and purchased common stocks because of the potential

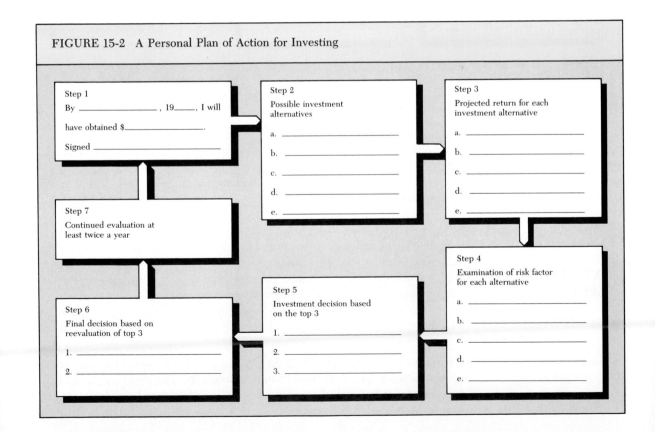

FIGURE 15-2   A Personal Plan of Action for Investing

FIGURE 15-3   A Personal Plan of Action for Sally Morton

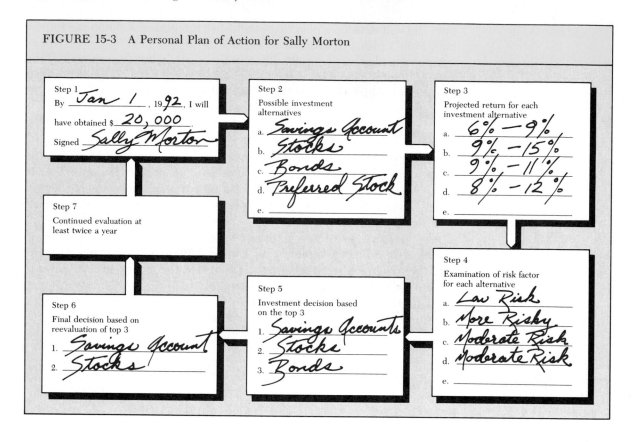

gain that could be made as stocks rebounded from low values. If, after careful evaluation, you feel that your investment objectives or your financial plan needs changing, for any reason, then change them. As noted in the Opening Scenario, periodic evaluation and modification are essential ingredients in every investment plan.

AN OVERVIEW OF INVESTMENT ALTERNATIVES

In the Opening Scenario, we noted that successful investors must do their homework, follow the rules, and continually evaluate their investments. When establishing an investment program, the first step is to gather as much information about investment alternatives as possible. Then investors are in a position to decide whether purchasing stocks, bonds, mutual funds, or some other investment alternative is a better use of their money than putting it in the bank.

- Major Investment Alternatives

As pointed out in Chapter 4, the majority of Americans have a passbook savings account at some time. Savings accounts, also referred to as time deposits, provide a safe place to store money. The usual passbook savings account earns about 5.5 percent in commercial banks and savings and loan associations and slightly more in credit unions. A second option for individuals is a certificate of deposit (CD). A *certificate of deposit* is a document stating that the bank will pay the depositor a guaranteed interest rate for leaving money on deposit for a specified period of time. The chief advantage of a CD when compared to a passbook savings account is that the CD pays a higher rate of interest. A third option is a NOW (negotiable order of withdrawal) account. *A NOW account* is an interest-bearing checking account. Normally, banks pay 5.25 percent interest on money deposited in this type of checking account. In addition to NOW accounts, some financial institutions offer Super NOW accounts. Super NOWs pay a little higher interest rate than the regular NOW accounts and generally have unlimited checking.

Once you have established your emergency fund in a savings account or an interest-bearing checking account, it is time to consider other investment alternatives. In this section, we will provide an overview of the different investment alternatives that you may use to fulfill your investment program. More detailed information on each investment alternative is provided in the remaining chapters of Part Five.

Stock or Equity Financing

Equity capital is money obtained from the owners of the business. If a business is a sole proprietorship or a partnership, equity capital is acquired when the owners invest their own money in the business. In the case of corporations, equity capital is provided by stockholders who buy shares of stock in the company. Since all stockholders are owners, they share in the success of the corporation. This can make buying stock an attractive investment opportunity.

However, you should consider at least two factors before investing in stock. First, a corporation is not obligated to repay the money obtained from the sale of stock or to repurchase the shares at a later date. If a purchaser decides to sell his or her stock, it is sold to another investor. Second, a corporation is under no legal obligation to pay dividends to stockholders for their shares. Dividends are paid out of earnings, but if a company should have a bad year, its board of directors can vote to omit dividend payments and retain the funds for business operations.

There are two types of stock—common stock and preferred stock. Both types have advantages and disadvantages that you should consider before deciding on which to use for an investment program.

Common Stock. A share of common stock represents the most basic form of corporate ownership. Most large corporations sell common stock to satisfy a large part of their financing needs. In return for the financing provided by selling common stock, management must make specific concessions to stockholders that may restrict or change corporate policies. For example, corporations are required by law to have an annual meeting where stockholders have a right to vote. Other factors that you should consider before purchasing common stock will be discussed in Chapter 16.

Preferred Stock. A corporation generally issues only one type of common stock, but it can issue many types of preferred stocks, with different features and different dividends or dividend rates. The most important priority an investor in preferred stock enjoys is receiving cash dividends before common stockholders are paid any cash dividends. This factor is especially important when a corporation is experiencing financial problems and cannot pay cash dividends to both preferred and common stockholders. Also, preferred stockholders, when compared to common stockholders, have a preferred claim to corporate assets should the corporation dissolve or enter bankruptcy. Corporations sometimes issue preferred stock with one or more additional features that may make the preferred stock a more attractive investment. Each of these features will be discussed in detail in the next chapter.

Corporate and Government Bonds

Debt capital is money that corporations or governments obtain by borrowing from outside sources. In many cases, the outside sources are investors like you. There are two types of bonds that an investor should consider. A **corporate bond** is a corporation's written pledge that it will repay a specified amount of money, with interest. A **government bond** is the written pledge of a government or a municipality that it will repay a specified sum of money, with interest. Regardless of who issues the bond, you need to consider two major questions before investing in bonds. First, will the bond be repaid at maturity? The maturity dates for most bonds range between 15 and 40 years. An investor who purchases a bond has two options: keep the bond until maturity and then redeem it, or sell the bond to another investor. In either case, the value of the bond is closely tied to the ability of the corporation or the government agency to repay the bond indebtedness. Second, will the corporation or government agency be able to maintain interest payments to bondholders? Bondholders normally receive interest payments every six months. Again, if a corporation or a government agency cannot pay the interest on its bonds, the value of those bonds will decrease.

Holding bonds until maturity is one way of making money on this type of investment. Investors also use two other methods that can provide more liberal returns on bond investments. Each of these methods will be discussed in Chapter 17.

Mutual Funds

A **mutual fund** is an investment alternative available to individuals who pool their money to buy stocks, bonds, certificates of deposit, and other securities based on the selections of professional managers who work for an investment company. Professional management is an especially important factor for small investors with little or no previous experience in financial matters. Another reason why investors choose this type of investment is *diversification*. Since mutual funds invest in various types of securities, an occasional loss in one security is often offset by gains in other securities.

The goals of one investor may differ from those of another investor. The managers of mutual funds realize this and tailor programs to meet individual needs and objectives. While most investors consider mutual funds a long-term, conservative investment, some mutual funds are more speculative than others. In fact, mutual funds range from very conservative to extremely speculative investments. Although investing money in a mutual fund provides professional management, even the best managers can make errors in judgment. The responsibility for choosing the right mutual fund is still the individual investor's. More information on the different types and costs of mutual funds is presented in Chapter 17.

Real Estate

Real estate ownership represents one of the best hedges against inflation. But not all property will increase in value. Poor location, for example, can cause a piece of property to decrease in value. A number of people who bought land in the Florida Everglades were taken by unscrupulous promoters. There are many factors that you should consider before investing in real estate. The real estate checklist presented in Figure 15–4 cites some of these factors.

Any investment has its disadvantages, and real estate is no exception. To sell your property, you must find an interested buyer who is able to obtain enough money to complete the transaction. Finding a buyer can be difficult if loan money is scarce, if the real estate market is in a decline, or if you overpaid for a piece of property. If you are forced to hold your investment longer than you originally planned, taxes and installment payments must

---

FIGURE 15-4   Real Estate Checklist

1. *Carefully evaluate all potential property.*
   a.   Is the property priced competitively with similar property?
   b.   What type of financing, if any, is available?
   c.   How much are the taxes?

2. *Inspect the surrounding neighborhood.*
   a.   What are the present zoning requirements?
   b.   Is the neighborhood's population increasing or decreasing?
   c.   What is the average income of people in the area?
   d.   Evaluate the state of the surrounding property. Do most of the buildings and houses need repair?

3. *Before making a final decision, answer the following questions.*
   a.   Why are the present owners selling the property?
   b.   How long will you have to hold the property before selling it to someone else?
   c.   How much profit can you reasonably expect to obtain?
   d.   What are the risks involved?
   e.   Is there a chance that the property will decrease in value?

also be considered. As a rule, real estate increases in value and eventually sells at a profit, but there are no guarantees. Success in real estate investment depends on how well you evaluate alternatives. Information on how to evaluate a real estate investment is presented in Chapter 18.

Other Investment Alternatives

A **speculative investment** is an investment that is made in the hope of earning a relatively large profit in a short time. Any investment may be speculative by its very nature—that is, it may be quite risky. However, a true speculative investment is speculative because of the methods that investors use to earn a quick profit. This section provides a brief overview of speculative investments in commodities, options, and precious metals, gemstones, and collectibles.

Commodities. The ownership of certain commodities—cattle, hogs, pork bellies, wheat, corn, soybeans, rice, oats, sugar, coffee, cocoa, cotton, and many others—is traded on a regular basis. The principal commodity exchanges include the Chicago Mercantile Exchange, the Kansas City Board of Trade, and the New York Futures Exchange. A commodity exchange provides a place for investors and speculators to buy and sell commodity contracts. While it is possible to buy commodities for immediate delivery (this is sometimes called *spot trading*), most transactions involve a future delivery date. A **futures contract** is an agreement to buy or sell a commodity at a guaranteed price on some specified future date. Commodities are not something to fool around with unless the investor understands all of the procedures and risks that are explained in Chapter 18.

Options. An **option** is the right to buy or sell a specified amount of stock at a specified price within a certain period of time. Investors who think that a stock's market value or price will increase during a short period of time may decide to purchase a call option. A **call option** gives the purchaser the right to buy the stock at a specified price before a definite expiration date. On the other hand, some investors may feel that a stock's price will go down during the option period. To safeguard their investment, these investors may purchase a put option. A **put option** gives the purchaser the right to sell the stock at a specified price before a definite expiration date.

Whether the investor purchases a call option or a put option, the expiration date must be considered. If either type of option cannot be exercised before the expiration date, the investor loses the cost of the option. Needless to say, options are risky business and not something for the inexperienced investor. The practical details needed for investing in options are presented in Chapter 18.

Precious Metals, Gemstones, and Collectibles. Investments included in this category include gold, silver, and other strategic metals; gemstones; and such collectibles as coins, stamps, antiques, and paintings. Without exception, investments of this kind are normally referred to as high-risk investments for one reason or another. For example, the gold market is ridden with unscrupulous dealers who sell worthless gold-plated lead coins to unsuspecting, uninformed investors. With each of the investments in this category, it is extremely important that you deal with reputable dealers and recognized investment firms. It pays to be careful. While investments in this category can lead to large dollar gains, they should not be used by anyone who does not fully understand the risks involved. Information on precious metals, gemstones, and collectibles is presented in Chapter 18.

FACTORS AFFECTING THE CHOICE OF INVESTMENTS

Millions of Americans have a savings account, buy stocks or bonds, purchase gold and silver, or make similar investments. And they all have reasons for investing their money. Some individuals want to supplement their retirement income when they reach age 65, while others want to become millionaires before they are 50. Although each investor may have specific, individual reasons for investing, there are a number of factors that all investors must consider.

The Safety Factor

● Factors that Affect Your Investment Options

Safety in an investment means minimal risk of loss. When considering the safety factor, investors must decide how much risk they are willing to assume. One basic rule may help answer this question:

The potential return of any investment should be directly related to the risk that is assumed.

Investments range from very safe to very risky. At one end of the spectrum are very safe investments that attract conservative investors. As stated in Chapter 4, when money is deposited at a bank, a savings and loan association, or a credit union, it is virtually risk free because it is usually guaranteed by a government agency. For a conservative investor, securities in the safe category may include corporate or municipal bonds, preferred stock, or certain common stock. Stocks and bonds in this safe category are often called blue-chip investments. A **blue-chip investment** is usually defined as one in which virtually no risk is involved. Corporate characteristics to watch for in evaluating more conservative stocks and bonds include (1) leadership in an industrial group, (2) a history of stable earnings over a number of years, and (3) consistency in paying dividends or bond interest through the years. Examples of blue-chip corporations include Du Pont, Exxon, Xerox, IBM, and General Motors. It is also possible to purchase mutual funds and real estate that are very safe investments.

As pointed out in the last section, there are a number of risky, and potentially profitable, investments. Speculative stocks, certain bonds, commodities, options, strategic metals, gemstones, and collectibles are risk-oriented investments. While each of these risk-oriented investments is discussed in detail in later chapters, such investments are often considered too risky for the smaller, beginning investor.

The Risk Factor

The factor of risk associated with a specific investment does change from time to time. For example, the stock of Computer-Tabulating-Recording Company was considered a risky investment. Today, the company is known as International Business Machines (IBM) and its stock is part of most conservative investment portfolios. When choosing an investment, you must carefully evaluate changes in the risk factor. In fact, the overall risk factor can be broken down into the following four component parts.

Inflation Risk. During inflationary times, there is a risk that the financial return on an investment will not keep pace with the rate of inflation. To see how inflation reduces the buying power of savings, let's say that you have deposited $1,000 in the bank at 7 percent interest. At the end of one year, your money would have earned $70 in interest ($1,000 × 7% = $70). Assuming an inflation rate of 9 percent, it would cost you $1,090 to purchase the same amount of goods that you could have purchased for $1,000 a year earlier. Thus, even though your bank account earned $70, you have lost $20 in actual purchasing power.

Interest Rate Risk. The interest rate risk associated with investments in preferred stock and bonds is the result of changes in the interest rates in the economy. The value of these fixed return investments decreases when overall interest rates increase and increases when overall interest rates decrease. Increases or decreases in interest rates are a result of fluctuation in the supply of or the demand for money. For example, suppose that you purchase a $1,000 corporate bond that matures in 15 years and pays 9 percent interest until maturity. This means that the corporation will pay you $90 ($1,000 × 9% = $90) each year for the next 15 years. If bond interest rates increase to 11 percent, the market value of your 9 percent bond will decrease. No one is willing to purchase your bond at the price you paid for it since at that price a comparable bond that pays 11 percent can be purchased. As a result, you would have to sell your bond for less than $1,000 or hold the bond until maturity. If you decide to sell the bond, the approximate dollar price that you could sell it for would be $818 ($90 ÷ 11% = $818). This price would provide the purchaser with an 11 percent return, and you would lose $182 ($1,000 − $818 = $182) because you owned a bond with a fixed interest rate during a period when overall interest rates in the economy increased.

Business Failure Risk. The risk of business failure is associated with investments in common stock, preferred stock, and bonds. With each of these investments, you face the possibility that bad management, unsuccessful products, or a host of other reasons may cause a business to be less profitable than was originally anticipated. Lower profits usually mean lower dividends or no dividends at all. If the business continues to operate at a loss, even interest payments and repayment of bond indebtedness may be questionable. The business may even fail and be forced to file for bankruptcy, in which case your investment may become totally worthless. Of course, the best way to protect yourself against such losses is to evaluate carefully the companies in which you invest.

Market Risk. The price of stocks, bonds, and other investments may fluctuate because of the behavior of investors in the marketplace. As a result, economic growth is not as systematic and predictable as most investors would like to believe. Generally, a period of rapid expansion is followed by a period of recession. During periods of recession, it may be quite difficult to sell such investments as real estate. Fluctuations in the market price for stocks and bonds may have nothing to do with the fundamental changes in the financial health of corporations. Such fluctuations may be caused by political or even social conditions. For example, the price of petroleum stocks may increase or decrease as a result of political activity in the Middle East.

The Income Factor

How much income should be expected from an investment? To a certain extent, the answer to this question depends on how much risk the investor is willing to assume. The safest investments, passbook savings accounts and CDs, are also the most predictable source of income for an investor. With either of these investments, the investor knows exactly what the interest rate is and how much income will be paid on a specific future date.

If dividend or interest income is a primary objective, most investors choose corporate bonds, preferred stock, or conservative common stock issues. When purchasing stocks or bonds for potential income, most investors are concerned about a corporation's overall profits, future earnings picture, and dividend policies. For example, some corporations are very proud of their long record of consecutive dividend payments and will maintain that policy if at all possible (see Figure 15–5). For some corporations, consistent dividend policies are a matter of pride. For other corporations, maintaining dividend payments is an obvious reward to stockholders who purchase their stock and an incentive to purchase more.

Some investors purchase specific stocks because these stocks pay dividends in certain months of each year. By using this method, an investor is assured of a predictable income each month throughout the year. For example, an individual can choose the companies in the top group of stocks listed in Figure 15–6 for dividend checks in January, April, July, and October. Of course, many different combinations of stocks and bonds will provide the same type of uniform payout.

Other investments that provide income potential are mutual funds and real estate rental property. Although the income from mutual funds is not guaranteed, investors can choose funds whose primary objective is income.

FIGURE 15-5   Corporations with Consecutive Dividend Payments for at Least 80 Years

Corporation	Dividends Since	Type of Business
Allied Corporation	1887	Chemical and petroleum products
American Telephone & Telegraph	1881	Telephone utility
Borden, Inc.	1899	Foods
Burroughs Corporation	1895	Computers
Citicorp	1903	Banking
Commonwealth Edison Company	1890	Electric utility
Continental Corporation	1854	Insurance
Du Pont (E. I.) de Nemours & Co.	1904	Chemicals
Eastman Kodak Company	1902	Photography
Exxon Corporation	1882	Chemical and petroleum products
General Electric Company	1899	Electrical equipment
Kroger Company	1902	Foods
Norfolk & Western Railway	1901	Railroad
PPG Industries, Inc.	1899	Glass
Procter & Gamble Company	1891	Soap products
Standard Oil Company (Indiana)	1894	Chemical and petroleum products
Sterling Drug, Inc.	1902	Drugs
Union Pacific Corporation	1900	Railroad

Income from real estate rental property is not guaranteed because there is always the possibility of either vacancies or unexpected repair bills. Yet one of the objectives in investing in rental property is to generate income. The more speculative investments, such as commodities, options, precious metals, gemstones, and collectibles, offer little, if any, potential for regular income.

The Growth Factor

To investors, growth means that their investment will increase in value. To some extent, all investments may grow. The chief difference among investments is how fast that growth occurs. Often, the greatest opportunity for growth is an investment in common stock. During the first part of the 1980s, investors found that stocks issued by corporations in the electronics, energy, health care, and financial services industries provided the greatest growth potential. In fact, goods and services provided by companies in these industries will be in even greater demand in the next 5 to 10 years.

When growth stocks are purchased, investors must often sacrifice immediate cash dividends in return for greater dollar value in the future. For most growth companies, dividends that would normally be paid to common stockholders are reinvested in the corporation in the form of *retained earnings*. While most companies pay stockholders between 30 and 70 percent of what

FIGURE 15-6   Corporate Stock Issues that Provide Predictable Monthly Income.

Company	Recent Price	Annual Dividend	Percent Yield	Estimated 1985 Earnings/Share	P/E Ratio
Buy for dividend checks in January, April, July, and October:					
Chemical New York Corporation	40	$2.48	6.2	$7.40	5.0
Dow Chemical*	29	1.80	6.2	3.50	10.0
GTE Corporation	41	3.08	7.5	5.75	7.1
Manufacturers Hanover*	36	3.20	8.9	7.75	4.6
Pacific Gas & Electric*	17	1.72	10.1	2.70	6.3
SCANA Corporation	24	2.16	9.0	2.90	8.3
Southern California Edison*	24	2.04	8.5	3.35	7.2
Buy for dividend checks in February, May, August, and November:					
Ameritech	83	$6.60	8.0	$11.00	7.5
BankAmerica Corporation*	19	1.52	8.0	2.25	8.4
Commonwealth Edison Company	30	3.00	10.0	4.50	6.7
Illinois Power Company	25	2.64	10.6	3.92	6.4
Iowa Resources	31	3.08	9.9	4.25	7.3
New York State Electric & Gas*	24	2.44	9.8	3.55	6.8
PacifiCorp*	28	2.32	8.2	3.80	8.0
Buy for dividend checks in March, June, September, and December:					
Central Illinois Public Service	19	$1.60	8.4	$2.33	8.2
Florida Progress Corporation*	25	2.16	8.6	2.80	8.9
Houston Industries	23	2.48	10.8	4.10	5.6
Potomac Electric Power*	28	2.16	7.7	3.31	8.5
Southern Company	20	1.92	9.6	3.10	6.5
United Telecommunications	22	1.92	8.7	2.80	7.9

*Dividend payable after first of month.

Source: *Market Letter,* Wayne Hummer & Co., May 1985 p. 2. Courtesy of Wayne Hummer & Co., 175 West Jackson Boulevard, Chicago, Ill 60604.

they earn, growth companies often pay stockholders a much smaller portion of corporate profits or nothing at all. The money kept by the corporations can provide at least part of the capital needed for future growth and expansion. As a result, the company grows at an even faster pace. Growth financed by retained earnings normally increases the dollar value of stock for the investor.

Assuming that an investor carefully chooses investments, both mutual funds and real estate may offer substantial growth possibilities. More speculative investments, such as strategic metals, gemstones, and collectibles, offer less predictable growth possibilities, while investments in commodities and options usually stress immediate returns as opposed to continued growth. Generally, corporate and government bonds are not purchased for growth.

The Liquidity Factor

Liquidity is the ease with which an asset can be converted to cash. Investments range from cash or near cash to a frozen investment where it is impossible to get your money. Cash is the most liquid asset because no conversion is necessary. Checking and savings accounts are also very liquid investments because they can be quickly converted to cash. There are no withdrawal penalties with a savings account, but there may be a waiting period before you get your money. Although most banks don't make you wait for your money, they may, at their option, require that you wait three or more days. Another type of bank account, a certificate of deposit, is not quite as liquid as a checking or savings account. With a certificate of deposit, there are penalties for withdrawing money before the maturity date.

With other investments, you may be able to sell quickly, but because of market conditions, economic conditions, or many other reasons, you may not be able to regain the amount of money you originally invested. For example, the owner of real estate may have to lower the asking price in order to find a buyer. It may even be difficult to find a buyer for investments in such collectibles as antiques and paintings.

The factors that were discussed in this section are summarized in Figure 15–7. All of the investments included in the figure are ranked high, average, or low for each of the factors discussed in this section.

FIGURE 15-7   The Risks Involved with Typical Investment Alternatives

Type of Investment	Factor to Be Evaluated				
	Safety	*Risk*	*Income*	*Growth*	*Liquidity*
Bank accounts	High	Low	Average	Low	High
Common stock	Average	Average	Average	High	Average
Preferred stock	Average	Average	High	Average	Average
Corporate bonds	Average	Average	High	Low	Average
Government bonds	High	Low	High	Low	High
Mutual funds	Average	Average	Average	Average	Average
Real estate	Average	Average	Average	Average	Low
Commodities	Low	High	N/A	Low	Average
Options	Low	High	N/A	Low	Average
Strategic metals, gemstones, and collectibles	Low	High	N/A	Low	Low

N/A = Not applicable.

FINANCIAL PLANNERS AND OTHER FACTORS THAT REDUCE INVESTMENT RISK

- Using a Financial Planner in Your Investment Program

More information is available to investors today than ever before. Sources of investment information include financial planners, newspapers, corporate reports, and investors' services. Even your own financial records should help you fine-tune your investment program. In the last section of this chapter, we will examine the factors that can spell the difference between success and failure for an investor.

The Role of a Financial Planner

Personal financial planning was defined in Chapter 1 as the art and science of putting your money to work for you and living within your means. In an attempt to achieve these objectives, most individuals seek professional help. In many cases, they turn to lawyers, accountants, bankers, or insurance agents. However, these professionals are specialists in one specific field and may not be qualified to provide the type of advice required to develop a thorough financial plan. The problem of finding qualified help in personal financial planning is compounded by the fact that many people who call themselves financial planners are in reality nothing more than salespersons for various financial investments, tax shelters, or insurance plans.

A true financial planner has had at least two years of training in securities, insurance, taxes, real estate, and estate planning and has passed a rigorous examination. As evidence of training and successful completion of the qualifying examination, the College of Financial Planning in Denver allows individuals who have completed the necessary courses and successfully passed the examination to use the designation Certified Financial Planner (CFP). In a similar manner, the American College in Bryn Mawr, Pennsylvania, allows individuals to use the designation Chartered Financial Consultant (ChFC) if they complete the necessary requirements. Most CFPs and ChFCs don't sell a particular investment product or charge commissions for their investment recommendations. Instead, they charge consultant's fees that range between $75 and $100 an hour.

Before choosing a financial planner, you should ask some questions to determine whether you and the financial planner are on the same wavelength with regard to investment goals and objectives. Typical questions include:

1. How much training and experience does the financial planner have?
2. Can you talk to clients who have used the financial planner's services?
3. What do local bankers, lawyers, and accountants say about the financial planner?
4. How much will consultation with the financial planner cost?
5. After the initial consultation, do you feel you will be able to achieve your investment objectives with the help of the financial planner?

Don't be surprised if your financial planner wants to ask you a few questions, too. In order to provide better service, he or she must know what type of investment program you want to establish. Often this initial conversation will last a couple of hours. It is important that you be honest with the financial planner. Your honesty ensures that both parties understand their responsibilities. If, after a reasonable period of time, you become dissatisfied with your investment program, do not hesitate to discuss this with the financial planner. You may even find it necessary to choose another financial planner if your dissatisfaction continues. This step is not at all uncommon. But when all is said and done, it is your money and you must make the final decisions that help meet your investment goals. Further information on selecting a financial planner is presented in Appendix A.

Your Role in the Investment Process

Good investors continually assess the value of their investments. They never sit back and let their money manage itself. Obviously, different types

---

In the Real World
How to Choose a Financial Adviser

P icking a financial adviser isn't easy. Their professional qualifications and personal virtues vary tremendously. And if you select the wrong adviser, the financial results can be disastrous.

After years of managing their own toy factory, Rudolf and Anastasia Koestner of Norwalk, Connecticut, decided it was time to retire. They sold their factory for $975,000 and invested their money with James L. Condron—an investment adviser in Wilton, Connecticut. The Koestner's chose Condron because he told them that the government checked his books every two weeks. He also told them that his own fa-

ther invested with him. Mr. Condron was so convincing that he was able to raise more than $4 million over a two-year period. Most investors were happy because Condron convinced them that their investments were increasing in value. In reality, however, the value of investments that Condron managed had decreased to less than $1 million. In February 1985, the Securities and Exchange Commission (SEC) charged Mr. Condron and his associates with fraud, lying to investors, and misappropriating assets. Investors have also initiated legal actions against Mr. Condron.*

Actually, the Koestner's were like a lot of investors

today. Investors, on the whole, don't ask enough questions. While the majority of financial advisers are honest, a few are not. When you choose someone to help you manage your investments, you ought to be curious about where the adviser's ideas come from and what factors determine his or her investment strategies. Questions that may help you evaluate both the financial adviser and his or her suggestions include:†

1. What type of newsletters, professional journals, magazines, and other publications does he or she read?
2. What type of courses or seminars has he or she at-

of investments will require different methods of evaluation. Some basic elements of investment evaluations are described below.

Monitor the Value of Your Investment. If you choose to invest in stocks, bonds, mutual funds, commodities, or options, the value of your holdings can be determined by looking at the price quotations reported daily in the financial section of your local newspaper. If you invest your money in a savings account, a checking account, or a certificate of deposit, most financial institutions will provide you with a detailed statement of all activity in the accounts. Your real estate holdings may be compared with similar properties that are currently available for sale in the surrounding area. The value of your strategic metals and gemstones may be determined by checking with reputable dealers and investment firms. Finally, the value of collectibles is usually determined by comparing your investment with the value of similar

tended during the last two years?

3. Has he or she written any scholarly articles that have been published in professional journals?

4. Does he or she have personal contacts with other professionals (accountants, lawyers, tax experts, etc.) that will be needed to help you properly plan your investment program?

The trick to finding the right financial adviser is to take enough time to ask the right questions. Actually, most reliable financial planners encourage questions because it is one way of telling if the investor understands the adviser's suggestions.

In addition to asking questions, try to determine if the prospective financial adviser is making investment suggestions based on what has been successful in the past. Suggestions of this type represent what has happened historically, not what will happen in the future. A good financial adviser should be able to identify good investments and justify those suggestions based on his or her knowledge of the volatile financial world.

One last point. The number of financial advisers registered with the SEC has almost doubled since 1981.‡ As a result, investors have more financial advisers to choose from. If you don't feel comfortable with a

prospective financial adviser, keep looking until you find one that will help you obtain your investment objectives.

*"SEC Files Show How Easily People Take Dubious Investment Advice," *The Wall Street Journal*, November 18, 1986, p. 39.

†Jeff Kosnett, "Is Your Adviser As Sharp as You Think," *Changing Times*, February 1981, p. 37+.

‡"Sec Files, p. 39.

For More Information, see Jill Rachlin, "They've Got Your Money in Their Hands," *U.S. News & World Report*, February 16, 1987, p. 59+; and "Brokerage Firms Scramble to Offer Investment Advice Tied to Tax Bill, *The Wall Street Journal*, October 6, 1986, p. 31.

articles. Regardless of which type of investment you choose, close surveillance will keep you informed of whether your investment increases in value,
remains the same, or falls in value.

Keep Accurate and Current Records. Maintaining accurate records of all
transactions and expenses related to an investment is extremely important.
Accurate recordkeeping is necessary for tax purposes and can help the investor reduce dollar losses.

For stocks and bonds, mutual funds, commodities, and options, all information relating to a particular investment should be kept together so that it
is readily retrievable. For example, you may need to know whether the
company has increased or decreased its dividend to stockholders or what the
current dividend yield is. The dividend yield is a useful means of comparing
investments and is quite easy to calculate. The basic rule is to divide annual
return by the value of the investment. For example, General Motors pays an
annual dividend of $5. Assume that a share of General Motors is selling for
$80. The current dividend yield is 6.25 percent, as calculated below:

$$\frac{0.0625 = 6.25\%}{\$80)\overline{\$5.00}}$$

Although this example involves common stock, the same procedure will
work for bonds, mutual funds, and other investments. Unless you keep up-
to-date records on the value of your investments and follow their progress,
you may not be aware of the best time to sell or to invest additional funds.

Tax Considerations

The dividends, interest, and profits you receive from your investments are
subject to federal income tax. It is therefore every investor's responsibility to
determine how taxes and current tax rulings affect his or her investments.
Areas of concern include dividend and interest income, capital gains, and
capital losses.

Dividend and Interest Income. A dividend is a distribution of money,
stock, or other property that a corporation pays to stockholders. Dividend
income is reported on your federal tax return as ordinary income just like
wages or salaries. Generally, the payer will send you a Form 1099-DIV that
states how much dividend income has been reported to the Internal Revenue Service in your name.

Interest from banks, credit unions, and savings and loan associations is
subject to federal taxation. Interest that you receive from notes, loans,
bonds, and U.S. securities must also be reported as income. Generally, the
payer will send you a Form 1099-INT that states how much interest income
has been reported to the Internal Revenue Service in your name. There is
no exclusion for interest income, and the total amount of such income must
be reported as ordinary income on your income tax return.

Capital Gains and Capital Losses. Under the Tax Reform Act of 1986, profits resulting from the sale of investments are taxed as ordinary income. For example, assume that Joe Coit sold 100 shares of General Motors stock for a profit of $1,000. If Joe is in the 28 percent tax bracket, his tax on the $1,000 profit is $280 ($1,000 × 28% = $280). If he had sold the stock at a loss, he could have used the dollar amount of the loss to offset or reduce ordinary income.

Sources of Investment Information

In the Opening Scenario of this chapter, it was stated that successful investors spend at least 10 hours a week evaluating potential investments. Generally, they use the type of information presented in this section to help evaluate investment opportunities. For most investments, there is more information than an investor can read and comprehend. Therefore, an investor must be selective in the type of information he or she uses for evaluation purposes. With other investments, only a limited amount of information is available. For example, a wealth of information is available on stocks, whereas the amount of information on a strategic metal such as cobalt or manganese may be limited to one source. Regardless of the number or the availability of sources, it is always the investor's job to determine how reliable and accurate the information is. Listed below are sources of information that an investor can use to evaluate present and future investments.

- Investment
  Information Sources

Newspapers. The most available source of information for the average investor is the financial page of a daily metropolitan newspaper or *The Wall Street Journal*. There you will find a summary of the day's trading on the two most widely quoted stock exchanges in the United States, the New York Stock Exchange and the American Stock Exchange. In addition to stock coverage, most newspapers also provide information on stocks traded in the over-the-counter markets, corporate and government bonds, commodities, options, and some strategic metals. Detailed information on how to read price quotations for stocks, bonds, mutual funds, commodities, and options will be presented in the remaining chapters of Part Five.

Business Periodicals. Most business periodicals are published weekly so that the financial information they contain is up-to-date. *Business Week, Fortune, Forbes, Dun's Review*, and similar business periodicals provide not only general economic news about the overall economy but also detailed financial information about individual corporations on a selected basis. There are even business periodicals—for example, *Advertising Age* and *Business Insurance*—that focus on information about firms in a specific industry. In addition to business periodicals, more general magazines such as *U.S. News & World Report, Time*, and *Newsweek* provide investment information as a regular feature. Finally, *Money, Consumer Reports, Changing Times, Sylvia Porter's Personal Finance*, and similar magazines provide information and advice designed to improve the individual's investment skills.

Corporate Reports. The federal government requires corporations selling new issues of securities to disclose information about corporate earnings, assets and liabilities, products or services, and the qualifications of top management in a prospectus that they must give to investors. In addition to the prospectus, all publicly owned corporations send their stockholders an annual report and quarterly reports that contain detailed financial data about the company. Included in both annual and quarterly corporate reports is a statement of financial position, which describes changes in assets, liabilities, and owners' equity. Also included in these reports is a profit and loss statement, which provides dollar amounts for sales, expenses, and profit or loss.

Stock Averages. Investors often gauge the stock market by following one or more widely recognized averages. A stock index is simply an average of current market prices for selected stocks. How much importance should an investor attach to a stock index? Averages show trends and direction, but they do not pinpoint the performance of individual stocks. A similar situation exists when your instructor walks into class and says that the class average on the last major test was 75. This information is useful, but it doesn't tell you how you scored on the test. By tracking averages, an investor can get an overall feel for whether stock prices are increasing or decreasing. The commonly used stock indexes are described below.

Established in 1897, the oldest of the most popular averages used today is the Dow Jones Industrial Average. This index is a weighted average of the prices of the 30 common stocks listed in Figure 15–8. In addition to the Industrial Average, Dow Jones publishes an average composed of 20 leading

---

FIGURE 15-8   The 30 Stocks Included in the Dow Jones Industrial Average

Allied Signal	International Paper
Aluminum Company	McDonald's
American Express	Merck
AT&T	Minnesota M & M
Bethlehem Steel	Navistar International
Boeing	Philip Morris
Chevron	Primerica
CocaCola	Procter & Gamble
Du Pont	Sears Roebuck
Eastman Kodak	Texaco
Exxon	Union Carbide
General Electric	United Technologies
General Motors	USX Corporation
Goodyear	Westinghouse Electric
IBM	Woolworth

Source: *The Wall Street Journal*, Friday, May 15, 1987, p. 46.

transportation stocks, an average composed of 15 leading utility stocks, and a composite average made up of the 65 stocks included in the Dow Jones Industrial, Transportation, and Utility Averages.

The Barron's Stock Index, the Standard & Poor's 500 Stock Average, the New York Stock Exchange Index, and the Value Line Stock Index are composite averages that reflect the prices of more stocks than are included in the Dow Jones averages. *Barron's*, a Dow Jones publication, publishes Barron's 50 Stock Average and an index of low-priced securities that meets the needs of many smaller investors. *Barron's* also publishes Barron's Group Stock Averages, a weekly average covering 32 industry groups. The Standard & Poor's 500 Stock Average is a composite average of 400 industrial companies, 40 utilities, 40 financial stocks, and 20 transportation issues. The New York Stock Exchange Index, an average of approximately 1,500 common stocks listed on the New York Stock Exchange, is weighted to reflect the number and value of the shares outstanding. The Value Line Stock Index consists of 1,700 stocks. Although most of the stocks included in this index are listed on the New York Stock Exchange, the index also includes selected stocks listed on the American Stock Exchange, regional exchanges, and over-the-counter markets.

Investor Services and Newsletters. An individual can also subscribe to services that provide investment information. The fees for investor services generally range from $30 to $300 a year.

There are three widely accepted services for investors who specialize in stocks and bonds:

1. *Standard & Poor's Reports.* These up-to-date reports on corporations listed on the major stock exchanges cover such topics as recommendations, sales and earnings, prospects, recent developments, profit and loss statements, and statements of financial position.
2. *Value Line.* These reports supply detailed information about major corporations—earnings, dividends, sales, liabilities, and the like.
3. *Moody's Investment Service.* Moody's reports help investors evaluate potential investments in corporate securities and provide information similar to that contained in the Standard & Poor's and Value Line reports.

Other investment services and newsletters that may help you evaluate potential investments in stocks include Dun & Bradstreet's *Key Business Ratios,* the *Dow Jones-Irwin Business and Investing Almanac,* and the Wiesenberger Services annual issue on mutual funds. There are even investor services and newsletters for more speculative investments. The *Commodity Yearbook* is a yearly publication that can be supplemented by the *Commodity Yearbook Statistical Abstract* three times per year. The International Monetary Market publishes the *I.M.M. Weekly Report,* which discusses interest rates, foreign exchange markets, and gold. The Chicago Board of Trade publishes the *Interest Rate Futures Newsletter.* Scott Publishing Company publishes the *Stamp Market Update*, which is a quarterly report on current trends and prices of the philatelic market.

The above discussion of investor services and newsletters is not exhaustive, but it does give you some idea of the amount and scope of the information that is available to serious investors. Although most small investors find that Standard & Poor's, Value Line, Moody's, and many of the other services and newsletters described here are too expensive for personal subscriptions, some of these investors obtain copies from stockbrokers or financial planners. This type of information is also available at most public libraries.

SUMMARY

- Personal investment is the use of one's personal funds to earn a financial return. Investment objectives must be specific and measurable and should be classified as short-term objectives (two years or less), intermediate objectives (two to five years), and long-term objectives (longer than five years).
- Before beginning an investment program, you must make sure your personal affairs are in order. Most financial planners suggest that an investment program should begin with an emergency fund that is equal to three months' salary (after taxes).
- Investment alternatives include stock, bonds, mutual funds, and real estate. More speculative investments include commodities, options, precious metals, gemstones, and collectibles.

- Although each investor may have specific individual reasons for investing, the factors of safety, risk, income, growth, and liquidity must be considered by all investors.
- A true financial planner has had at least two years of training in securities, insurance, taxes, real estate, and estate planning and has passed a rigorous examination. Financial planners can help individuals obtain their investment goals.
- Since there is more information on investments than most investors can read and comprehend, investors must be selective in the type of information that they use for evaluation purposes.

GLOSSARY

Blue-chip investment. An investment in which virtually no risk is involved.

Call option. Gives the purchaser the right to buy a specified amount of stock at a specified price before a definite expiration date.

Corporate bond. A corporation's written pledge that it will repay a specified amount of money, with interest.

Debt capital. Money that corporations or governments obtain by borrowing from outside sources.

Dividends.   A distribution of money, stock, or other property that a corporation pays to stockholders.

Equity capital.   Money obtained from the owners of the business.

Futures contract.   An agreement to buy or sell a commodity at a guaranteed price on some specified future date.

Government bond.   The written pledge of a government or a municipality that it will repay a specified sum of money, with interest.

Line of credit.   A short-term loan that is approved before the money is actually needed.

Liquidity.   The ease with which an asset can be converted to cash.

Mutual fund.   An investment alternative available to individuals who pool their money to buy stocks, bonds, certificates of deposit, and other securities based on the selections of professional managers who work for an investment company.

Option.   The right to buy or sell a specified amount of stock at a specified price within a certain period of time.

Personal financial planning.   The art and science of putting your money to work for you and living within your means.

Personal investment.   The use of one's personal funds to earn a financial return.

Put option.   Gives the purchaser the right to sell a specified amount of stock at a specified price before a definite expiration date.

Speculative investment.   An investment that is made in the hope of earning a relatively large profit in a short time.

REVIEW QUESTIONS

1. What is the overall objective of investing?

2. Before beginning an investment program, an individual should perform a financial checkup. What four factors should be evaluated before the first investment is made?

3. What is an emergency fund? Why do investors need to establish an emergency fund before investing money in stocks, bonds, or other investments?

4. What suggestions were offered in this chapter to help individuals get the money they need to start an investment program?

5. From an investor's standpoint, how do corporate and government bonds differ from common and preferred stock?

6. An individual may invest in stocks either directly or through a mutual fund? How do the two investment methods differ?

7. What questions should an investor ask before purchasing a piece of real estate for investment purposes?

8. What factors account for the increased risk that is involved in purchases of commodities, options, precious metals, gemstones, and collectibles?

9. How do the factors of safety, risk, income, growth, and liquidity influence an individual's investment decisions?

10. What factors should you consider when choosing a financial planner?

11. How does the federal government tax dividends, interest, and capital gains?

12. What kinds of information would you like to have before you invest in a particular common stock? Where can you get that information?

DISCUSSION QUESTIONS AND ACTIVITIES

1. What basic factors of investing were described in the Opening Scenario? How can those principles help you become a better investor?

2. What pitfalls will investors avoid if they follow the 10 basic rules listed in the Opening Scenario?

3. Why should investors continually evaluate their investments and the composition of their investment portfolio?

4. What personal factors should an individual consider before establishing an investment program?

5. Develop at least two short-term objectives, two intermediate objectives, and two long-term objectives that you could use to support your investment program.

6. Assume that you are single and have graduated from college. Your job pays you $25,000 a year, your take-home pay is $1,750 a month, and your monthly expenses are $1,500, which leaves you with a monthly surplus of $250. Develop a personal plan of action for investing like the one illustrated in Figure 15–2.

7. What personal circumstances might lead some investors to emphasize income rather than growth in their investment planning? What personal circumstances might lead them to emphasize growth rather than income?

8. Suppose you have just inherited 500 shares of General Motors stock. What would you do with or about it, if anything?

ADDITIONAL READINGS

Barrett, Katherine, and Richard Greene. "The Money-makers (Successful Women Investors)." *Ladies' Home Journal*, October 1986, p. 102.

"The 500: The Fortune Directory of the Largest U.S. Industrial Corporations." *Fortune*, April 28, 1986, p. 182.

Kallen, Barbara. "Have I Got a Money Manager for You." *Forbes*, September 22, 1986, p. 198.

Schurenberg, Eric. "Getting a Lead on a Retirement Plan." *Money*, August 1986, p. 69.

Stechert, Kathryn. "Why You Fight about Money (and How You Can Stop)." *Better Homes and Gardens*, August 1986, p. 34.

"Twelve Worry Free Investments." *Money*, September 1986, p. 62.

"Where Does All the Money Go?" *Consumer Reports*. September 1986, p. 581.

CASE 15–1 From Inheritance to Investment

Joe and Mary Garner were married nine years ago, and they have an eight-year-old child. Four years ago, they purchased a home, on which they owe about $80,000. They also owe $6,000 on their two-year-old automobile. All of their furniture is paid for, and they have no monthly credit card payments.

Joe is employed as an engineer and makes

$35,000 a year. Mary works part-time and earns about $5,000 a year. Their monthly income after deductions is $2,725. Their monthly expenses are listed below:

Fixed expenses:		
Home mortgage payment	$840	
Automobile loan	220	
Insurance	150	
Emergency fund	140	
		$1,350
Total fixed expenses		
Variable expenses:		
Food	310	
Clothing	150	
Gasoline	90	
Automobile repairs	70	
Gifts and donations	100	
Electricity	95	
Gas	65	
Water	25	
Telephone	60	
Medical costs	130	
Recreation	120	
Total variable expenses		1,215
Total expenses		$2,565
Surplus for additional savings ($2,725 − $2,565 − $160)		$ 160

About six months ago, the Garners decided that it was time to get serious about finances.

Based on the above information, they decided to pay themselves first and save $160 a month. After each payday, they deposited $160 in a savings account designated as their emergency fund. Now, after six months, they have $960 in the fund. They also have about $2,000 in a separate savings account.

Last month, Joe and Mary were notified by a lawyer that Mary's uncle had died and left them $75,000. While they were saddened by the death of the uncle, they certainly appreciated their newfound wealth. Now they must decide how to invest their inheritance.

Questions

1. How would you rate the financial status of the Garners before they inherited the $75,000?

2. If you were Joe or Mary Garner, what would you do with the $75,000 inheritance?

3. Which of the investment alternatives described in this chapter would you recommend for the Garners? Why?

4. Where would you go to gather information to support your investment recommendation?

16

Investing in Stocks

As you learned in Chapter 15, there are many investment alternatives that serious investors must consider. Two of these alternatives—common stock and preferred stock—are discussed in this chapter. An investment in either type of stock is based on two simple assumptions. First, a corporation sells stock to raise money. Second, investors purchase the corporation's stock because it represents a "good investment." Today, about one out of every six Americans owns shares of common or preferred stock. In this chapter, we will examine why these investment alternatives are so popular and what factors successful investors use to evaluate potential stock investments.

After studying this chapter, you will be able to:

- Discuss why people invest in common stock and preferred stock.

- Identify the most important features of common stock and preferred stock.

- Explain the factors that can influence the market price for a share of stock.

- Describe how stocks are bought and sold through brokerage firms and securities exchanges.

- Select a brokerage firm and a stockbroker.

- Explain the traditional trading techniques used by long-term investors.

Interview with **Anthony J. Mooney,** Associate Vice President, Dean Witter Reynolds, Inc.

Anthony J. Mooney graduated from Northwestern University with a degree in Business and Marketing. Mr. Mooney currently is an Associate Vice President at Dean Witter, specializing in Basic Financial Planning and Equity Portfolios. In 1985, Dean Witter awarded Mooney the Pacesetter Award for Outstanding Achievement.

The term *securities* encompasses a broad range of investment instruments, which include stocks and bonds, mutual funds, options, and municipal bonds.

Securities are bought and sold in a number of markets. The best-known markets are the New York Stock Exchange and the American Stock Exchange, both located in New York City. There are also regional exchanges, located in cities throughout the country. Also, many securities are not traded on an exchange, but are traded over the counter (OTC), through a large network of securities brokers and dealers.

Investors who buy or sell securities on an exchange or over the counter are usually associated with a broker/dealer firm, where their direct contact

is a registered representative. This professional, often called an account executive, is registered with the National Association of Securities Dealers (NASD), a self-regulatory organization whose operations are overseen by the Securities and Exchange Commission (SEC). The registered representative is the link between the investor and traders and dealers who actually buy and sell securities on the floor of an exchange or elsewhere.

Stocks are designated as common—the most widely known form—or as preferred. The latter is so called because its holders have priority over owners of common stock regarding dividends, and regarding assets if the company is liquidated.

Generally, stocks are traded in blocks or multiples of 100 shares, which are called round lots. An amount of stock consisting of fewer than 100 shares is called an odd lot.

Investors may be concerned about the safety of securities and funds that are held in brokerage accounts. For instance, what would happen if the brokerage firms were to go out of business? To help protect in-

vestors, Congress passed the Securities Investor Protection Act of 1970. This act is administered primarily by the Securities Investor Protection Corporation (SIPC), a nonprofit membership corporation. Most of the securities broker/dealer firms registered with the SEC are members of SIPC.

It's important to remember, states Mr. Mooney, that the law provides financial protection for the securities and cash balances held in customer accounts with broker/dealers, if a firm is forced to liquidate. If the liquidating firm lacks funds or securities to settle all customer claims, the SIPC will satisfy the remaining claims up to a maximum of $500,000 per customer.

Also, brokerage firms may carry insurance on accounts that exceed SIPC coverage. When opening an account, investors should ask about this insurance. However, remember that the insurance pays off only through default of the brokerage firm. It does not cover losses sustained through securities transactions or other investment decisions.

Like many small investors, Martin and Sally Wallace didn't have a lot of money to invest back in 1963. They had just graduated from college, and their main asset was a 1960 Chevrolet that had been driven over 75,000 miles. In addition, the Wallaces were expecting their first child and they had just purchased their first home. Nevertheless, Sally talked Martin into buying 50 shares of Dr Pepper stock at $14.25 per share for a total of $756.49, including the broker's commission.

During the next six months, the Wallaces received a grand total of $21.50 in dividends from their Dr Pepper investment. They were disappointed,

but they decided to hold their investment a little longer. Then, on the 25th of March, 1964, Dr Pepper announced a 2-for-1 stock split. A stock split is the division of each outstanding share of a corporation's stock into a much greater number of shares. The Wallace's original 50 shares were almost magically transformed into 100 shares. Although the 2-for-1 stock split caused the dollar value of a share of Dr Pepper stock to go down, this didn't seem to matter because the Wallaces owned twice as much stock. And besides, the price per share eventually went even higher than their original purchase price of $14.25 per share. Now both Sally and Martin

were tempted to sell their stock because they could more than double their original investment. Again, Sally persuaded Martin to be patient and hold onto their Dr Pepper stock. As a result, they experienced a 3 for 1 stock split in 1970 and 2 for 1 stock splits in 1968 and 1972. Their 50 shares of stock had grown to 1,200 shares.

Twelve years after the last stock split, on February 28, 1984, the Wallaces were forced to sell their stock when a majority of the corporation's stockholders voted to sell the entire company for $22 a share to the New York investment firm of Forstmann, Little, & Co. The Wallaces received $26,400 for their 1,200 shares.

COMMON STOCK

Equity capital, as mentioned in the last chapter, is money obtained from the owners of the business. In the case of a corporation, equity capital is provided by stockholders who buy shares of stock in the corporation. There are two types of stock, common stock and preferred stock. Common stock is discussed in this section, and preferred stock is discussed in the next section. A common stock certificate and a preferred stock certificate are shown in Figure 16–1.

Since common stockholders are the actual owners of the corporation, they share in its success. However, finding a successful corporation is more difficult than just picking a name out of the financial section of the newspaper. Successful stockholders evaluate a number of factors before they invest in any stock. The first factor they evaluate is why a corporation sells common stock.

Why Corporations Issue Common Stock

Corporations sell common stock to finance their business start-up costs and help pay for their ongoing business activities. Today, corporations are

In addition, they had received over $9,000 in dividends since 1963. Although their original investment was only $756.49, their total dollar return was in excess of $35,000. They used almost $15,000 of their profits to purchase a new car and invested the remainder in Xerox and International Business Machines (IBM). They believed that their new investments would do quite well because both Xerox and IBM were heavily engaged in developing new products.

On the surface, it looks as if the Wallaces were just lucky. However, their investment in Dr Pepper was just the beginning. After that first investment in 1963, they continued to invest in stocks whenever they could afford it. As a result, in 1987 their total portfolio consisted of 15 stocks valued at more than $200,000. According to Martin Wallace, the secret of their investment success is that they concentrate on long-range investment goals and don't try to make a big killing overnight.

Of course, a lot of people share this investment philosophy. Why? The answer to that question is quite simple. Stocks, as measured by Standard & Poor's 500 Stock Average, have provided an average annual return of 9.5 percent since 1926, which is as far back as complete stock market returns have been recorded.* In fact, the annual return on stocks has been more than double the annual return on corporate bonds (4.4 percent) and U.S. Treasury bills (3.3 percent) over the same period of time.* Moreover, most financial experts are predicting that the annual return on stocks will be even higher in the future. Therefore, any serious investor must learn as much as possible about corporate stocks and the role they play in establishing a valid investment program.

*John J. Curran, "Finding a Path between Fear and Greed," *Fortune, 1986 Investor's Guide*, p. 10.

classified as either private corporations or public corporations. A *private corporation* is a corporation whose stock is owned by relatively few people and is not traded openly in stock markets. A *public corporation* is a corporation whose stock is traded openly in stock markets and may be purchased by any individual. Public corporations may have thousands, or sometimes even millions, of stockholders. American Telephone & Telegraph, for example, has about 2.8 million stockholders, while General Motors has over 2 million stockholders. Corporate managers prefer selling common stock as a method of financing for several reasons.

● Features of Common Stock

Common Stock: A Form of Equity. Corporations don't have to repay the money a stockholder pays for stock. Generally, a stockholder in a public corporation may sell his or her stock to another stockholder. The selling price is determined by how much a buyer is willing to pay for the stock. Stock transactions between stockholders are a practical example of the supply and demand theories presented earlier in Chapter 1. If the demand for a particular stock increases, the price of the stock will increase. If the demand for a particular stock decreases, the price of the stock will decrease.

FIGURE 16-1 Common and Preferred Stock. Money or Capital Is Provided to the Company by Stockholders When They Purchase Shares of Stock in the Company.

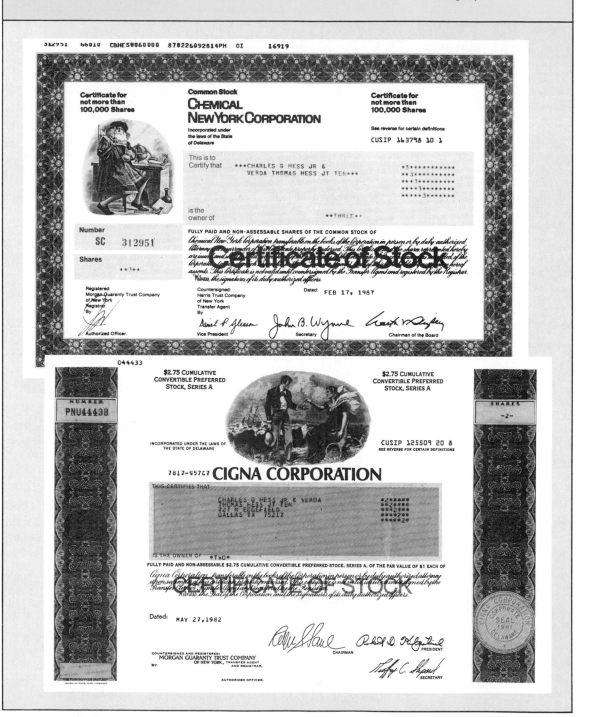

Occasionally, a corporation will buy its own stock, but only because this is in its best interest. For example, IBM, faced with excess profits to invest, recently decided to purchase its own stock. IBM officials believed that this was the best investment they could make at that time.

Common Stock: Dividends Not Mandatory. Dividends are paid out of profits, and dividend payments must be approved by a corporation's board of directors. Dividend policies vary among corporations, which usually distribute from 30 to 70 percent of their earnings to stockholders. However, some corporations follow a policy of smaller dividend distributions to stockholders. In general, these are rapidly growing firms that retain a large share of their earnings for research and development. On the other hand, utility companies and other financially secure enterprises may distribute 80 to 90 percent of their earnings. If a corporation has a bad year, board members may vote to omit dividend payments to stockholders.

Common Stock: Voting Rights and Control of the Company. In return for the financing provided by selling common stock, management must make concessions to stockholders that may restrict or change corporate policies. For example, corporations are required by law to have an annual meeting where stockholders have a right to vote, usually casting one vote per share of stock. Stockholders may vote in person or by proxy. A **proxy** is a legal form that lists the issues to be decided at a stockholders' meeting and requests that stockholders transfer their voting rights to some individual or individuals. The common stockholders elect the board of directors and must approve major changes in corporate policies. Typical changes of this kind include (1) any amendment of the corporate charter or bylaws, (2) the sale of certain assets, (3) possible mergers, (4) the issuance of preferred stock or corporate bonds, and (5) changes in the amount of common stock. A typical proxy form is illustrated in Figure 16–2.

Most states require that a provision for preemptive rights be included in the charter of every corporation. A **preemptive right** is the right of current stockholders to purchase any new stock that the corporation issues before it is offered to the general public. By exercising their preemptive rights, stockholders are able to maintain their current proportion of corporate ownership. This may be important when the corporation is a small one and management control is a matter of concern to stockholders.

Finally, corporations are required by law to distribute annual and quarterly reports to stockholders. These reports contain detailed information about sales, earnings, profits and losses, and other vital financial matters. This information is designed to inform current stockholders about the financial health of the corporation.

Although the money that corporations acquire through the sale of common stock is essentially cost free, few investors will buy common stock if they cannot foresee some return on their investment. We'll examine common stock from the point of view of the investor in the next section.

FIGURE 16-2   A Typical Proxy Form Used by Large Corporations

Receipt of the Notice of said meeting and of the Proxy Statement and Annual Report of UNITED MERCHANTS AND MANUFACTURERS, INC. accompanying the same is hereby acknowledged.

Dated ...., 1986   ....

3347-000000050

CHARLES G HESS JR &
VERDA THOMAS HESS JT ETC
612 TIFFANY TRAIL
RICHARDSON   TX 75081

....
Signature of Stockholder(s)

Please sign this proxy exactly as your name appears hereon. Joint owners should each sign. Trustees, executors, administrators and others signing in a representative capacity should indicate that capacity. An authorized officer may sign on behalf of a corporation and should indicate the name of the corporation and his capacity.

Please date, sign and mail this proxy in the enclosed envelope, which requires no postage if mailed in the U.S.A.

PROXY   Solicited by
                                                                   The Board of Directors

UNITED MERCHANTS AND MANUFACTURERS, INC.
Annual Meeting of Stockholders, November 14, 1986

The undersigned, revoking all prior proxies, hereby appoints M. J. SCHWAB, U. RUSKIN and L. MARX, JR., or any of them, proxies, with full power of substitution, to vote all the shares which the undersigned is entitled to vote at the Annual Meeting of Stockholders of United Merchants and Manufacturers, Inc., to be held at The Sheraton Heights, 650 Terrace Avenue, Hasbrouck Heights, New Jersey, on Friday, November 14, 1986, at 2:00 o'clock in the afternoon; and at any adjournment thereof. **The shares represented by this proxy will be voted as designated below, or if no designation is made, will be voted FOR Items 1, 2, 3 and 4.**

Directors recommend a vote FOR the following:

1. Election of Directors—Nominees are:
   R. M. Andreoli, R. Bassuk, P. A. Cohen, T. Furth, S. A. Hickox, S. O. Margolis, L. Marx, Jr., R. D. Mathews, J. H. Nusbaum, W. M. Rees, U. Ruskin, J. K. Schemmer, M. Schiff and M. J. Schwab.

Mark ⎧   □ FOR ALL Nominees Listed Above
One ⎨   □ FOR ALL Nominees Listed Above EXCEPT the following: ....
Box ⎪
Only ⎩   □ WITHHOLD Authority to Vote For ALL Nominees Listed Above

2. Proposal to amend the Certificate of Incorporation of the Company limiting certain liabilities of the directors.
   □ FOR   □ AGAINST   □ ABSTAIN

3. Selection of KMG Main Hurdman as Auditors.
   □ FOR   □ AGAINST   □ ABSTAIN

4. Shareholder Proposal—Ownership by Each Director of at least 100 Shares of the Company's Common Stock.
   □ FOR   □ AGAINST   □ ABSTAIN

5. Upon any other matter that may properly come before such meeting, or any adjournment thereof, as the proxies in their discretion may determine.

                                                              (To be dated and signed on the other side)

Why Investors Purchase Common Stock

● Reasons for Investing in Common Stock

How do you make money by buying common stock? Basically, there are three ways that an investment in common stock can increase in value. These three ways—income from dividends, dollar appreciation of stock value, and increased value from stock splits—are described below.

Income from Dividends. While the corporation's board members are under no legal obligation to pay dividends, most board members like to keep stockholders happy (and prosperous). It should be noted that few things will unite stockholders into a powerful opposition force more rapidly than omitted or lowered dividends. Therefore, board members usually declare dividends if the corporation's after-tax profits are sufficient for them to do so. Since dividends are a distribution of profits, intelligent investors must be concerned about future after-tax profits. In short, how secure is the dividend?

Corporate dividends for common stock may be in the form of cash, additional stock, or company products. However, the last type of dividend is extremely unusual. If a cash dividend is declared by the board of directors, each stockholder by law receives an equal dollar amount per share. Although dividend policies vary, most coporations pay dividends on a quarterly basis. Some corporations, particularly those having large swings in earnings, declare special year-end or extra dividends in addition to their regular quarterly dividends.

In order to determine who actually owns stock and is entitled to receive dividends on a certain date, this simple rule is followed: dividends remain with the stock until four business days *before* the date of record. The **date of record** is the date when a stockholder must be registered on the corporation's books in order to receive dividends. On the fourth day before the date of record, the stock begins selling ex-dividend. Anyone who purchases an ex-dividend stock is not entitled to receive dividends for this quarter. In this case, dividends are paid to the previous owner of the stock.

For example, General Dynamics declared a quarterly dividend of 25 cents per share to stockholders owning the stock on July 18, 1986 (see Figure 16–3). The stock went ex-dividend on July 14, 1986, four business days before the July 18 date. A stockholder who purchased the stock on July 14 or after was not entitled to this quarterly dividend payment. The actual dividend payment was made by General Dynamics on August 15, 1986, to stockholders who owned the stock on the date of record.

Dollar Appreciation of Stock Value. In most cases, a stockholder purchases stock and then holds onto that stock for a period of time. If the market value of the stock increases, the stockholder must decide whether he or she wants to sell the stock at the higher price or continue to hold it. If the stockholder decides to sell the stock, the dollar amount of difference between the purchase price and the selling price represents profit.

Let's assume that on September 8, 1987, you purchase 100 shares of Eastman Kodak at a cost of $61 a share and that your cost for the stock is $6,100 plus $90 in commission charges, for a total investment of $6,190. Let's also assume that you hold your 100 shares until September 8, 1988, and then sell them for $69 each and that during the 12 months you own Eastman Kodak the company pays quarterly dividends totaling $2.52 a share. Your return on investment is shown in Figure 16–4. In this case, you make money through a dividend paid every three months and through an increase in stock value from $61 per share to $69 per share.

Increased Value from Stock Splits. Investors can also increase earnings and potential profits through a stock split. A **stock split** is a procedure in which the shares of common stock owned by existing stockholders are divided into a larger number of shares. In 1986, for example, the F. W. Woolworth board of directors approved a 2-for-1 stock split. After the stock split, a

FIGURE 16-3   Information on Corporate Dividends Is Presented in *The Wall Street Journal, Barron's Financial Weekly*, and Other Financial Publications.

CORPORATE DIVIDEND NEWS

INTERNATIONAL MULTIFOODS CORP. said directors approved a 3-for-2 stock split, payable on or about July 24 to stock of record June 30. The Minneapolis-based food company had about 9.6 million shares outstanding as of May 5.

* * *

Dividends Reported June 5

Company	Period	Amt.	Payable date	Record date
REGULAR				
Atlntc City El 5⅞%pf	Q	1.46⅞	8- 1-86	7- 3
Brown Group Inc	Q	.36	7- 1-86	6-16
Canadian Imprl Bk Com	Q	b.27	7-28-86	6-28
Citicorp adj pf4	Q	1.673¼	6-30-86	6-16
DST Systems Inc	Q	.05	7-14-86	6-13
Dallas Corp	Q	.16½	7- 3-86	6-19
Duro-Test Corp	S	.20	7-15-86	7- 1
Farah Manufacturing	Q	.22	9- 2-86	8- 4
General Dynamics	Q	.25	8-15-86	7-18
General Host Corp	Q	.05½	7- 3-86	6-16
Homestead Fincl Corp	Q	.10	7- 7-86	6-20
Illinois Power Co	Q	.66	8- 1-86	7-10
Illinois Pwr 4.08%pf	Q	.51	8- 1-86	7-10
Illinois Pwr 4.20%pf	Q	.52½	8- 1-86	7-10
Illinois Pwr 4.26%pf	Q	.53¼	8- 1-86	7-10
Illinois Pwr 4.42%pf	Q	.55¼	8- 1-86	7-10
Illinois Pwr 4.70%pf	Q	.58¾	8- 1-86	7-10
Illinois Pwr 7.56%pf	Q	.94½	8- 1-86	7-10
Illinois Pwr 8%pf	Q	1.00	8- 1-86	7-10
Illinois Pwr 8.24%pf	Q	1.03	8- 1-86	7-10
Illinois Pwr 8.94%pf	Q	1.11¾	8- 1-86	7-10
Illinois Pwr 11.66%pf	Q	1.45¾	8- 1-86	7-10
Illinois Pwr 11.75%pf	Q	1.46⅞	8- 1-86	7-10
Illinois Pwr adjpfA	Q	.75	8- 1-86	7-10
Illinois Pwr adjpfB	Q	.87½	8- 1-86	7-10
Lucky Stores Inc	Q	.29	7- 3-86	6-16
MDC Holdings Inc	Q	.09	6-30-86	6-16
Mercantile Stores	Q	.37½	9-15-86	8-29
Midland Co	Q	.10	7- 7-86	6-20
Natl Convenience Strs	Q	.09	7-11-86	6-27
Planning Research	Q	.05	7-31-86	7-11
Pratt & Lambert Inc	Q	.18	7- 1-86	6-16
Prime Motor Inns	Q	.02	7-31-86	7- 3
Rowe Furniture Corp	Q	.04	7-15-86	6-25
SPS Technologies	Q	.22	6-30-86	6-16
Scherer (RP) Corp	Q	.08	7- 3-86	6-17
Skyline Corp	Q	.12	7- 1-86	6-19
Sperry Corp	Q	.48	9-15-86	7-10
Stanadyne Inc	Q	.27	7- 1-86	6-13
Stokely-Van Camp 5%prf	Q	.25	7- 2-86	6-16
VSE Corp	Q	.05	8-15-86	8- 1
Wal-Mart Stores Inc	Q	.04¼	7- 9-86	6-20
Washington National	Q	.27	7- 1-86	6-16
Washington Natl $2.50pf	Q	.62½	7- 1-86	6-16
Wayne-Gossard Corp	Q	.05	7- 1-86	6-16
Wayne-Gossard $1.60pf	Q	.40	7-10-86	6-16

Source: *The Wall Street Journal*, June 6, 1986, p. 31.

FIGURE 16-4   Sample Stock Transaction for Eastman Kodak

Assumptions: 100 shares of common stock purchased September 8, 1987, sold September 8, 1988; dividends of $2.52 per share

Costs when purchased:		Return when sold:	
100 shares @ $61 =	$6,100	100 shares @ $69 =	$6,900
Plus commission	+$90	Minus commission	−100
Total investment	$6,190	Total return	$6,800

Transaction summary:

Total return	$6,800
Minus total investment	−6,190
Profit from stock sale	$ 610
Plus dividends	+252
Total for the transaction return	$ 862

stockholder who originally owned 100 shares now owned 200 shares. The most common stock splits are 2-for-1, 3-for-1, and 4-for-1.

Why do corporations split their stock? In many cases, a firm's management has a "theoretical" ideal price range for the firm's stock. If the market price of the stock rises above the ideal price range, a stock split brings the market price back in line. In the case of Woolworth, the 2-for-1 stock split reduced the market price to about half of the stock's previous price. The lower market price for each share of stock was the result of dividing the dollar value of the company by a larger number of shares of common stock. Also, a decision to split a company's stock makes the stock issue more attractive to the investing public. Although there are no guarantees that a stock's price will go up after a split, the investing public feels that there is a potential for an increase because the stock is offered at a lower price.

A less common type of stock split occurs when the number of outstanding shares of common stock is reduced. This usually occurs when the market price of a corporation's stock has dropped to the point where the directors consider it too low. In a *reverse split,* stockholders exchange their shares for a proportionately lesser number of shares. As a result, the market price is adjusted upward by a proportionate amount.

PREFERRED STOCK

- Reasons for Investing in Preferred Stock

In addition to purchasing common stock, investors also purchase preferred stock. Certain factors must be considered before purchasing preferred stock. The most important priority that an investor in preferred stock enjoys is receiving cash dividends before common stockholders are paid any cash dividends. This factor is especially important when a corporation is experiencing financial problems and cannot pay cash dividends to both preferred and common stockholders. The dollar amount of the dividend on preferred stock is known before the stock is purchased—unlike the amount of the dividend on common stock. The dividend amount is either a stated amount of money for each share of stock or a certain percentage of the par value of the preferred stock. The **par value** is an assigned (and often arbitrary) dollar value that is printed on a stock certificate. Usually, the dollar amount of the dividend or the specific rate of dividend is set forth in the preferred stock agreement. The dividend is paid from net income after taxes and before any dividend payments are made to common stockholders.

While preferred stock does not represent a legal debt that must be repaid, if the firm is dissolved or declares bankruptcy, preferred stockholders do have first claim to the corporation's assets after creditors (including bond-holders). Generally, a preferred stock certificate contains a clause that allows the corporation to recall the preferred stock issue. **Callable preferred stock** is stock that a corporation may exchange, at its option, for a specified amount of money. A corporation usually calls in a preferred stock issue because management can issue new preferred stock at a lower dividend rate, or perhaps because it can issue common stock with no specified dividend. The price the corporation pays is usually slightly above the going market price for the preferred stock.

Corporations issue preferred stock for two reasons. First, financing through preferred stock is an alternative to financing through corporate bonds or common stock. Second, potential investors often consider preferred stock a less risky investment than common stock because preferred stockholders are paid dividends before common stockholders. In order to make a preferred stock issue even more attractive to investors, some corporations offer the additional features described below.

The Cumulative Feature of Preferred Stock

- **Features of Preferred Stock**

If the corporation's board of directors believes that omitting dividends is justified, it can vote to omit not only the dividends paid to common stockholders but also the dividends paid to preferred stockholders. One way preferred stockholders can help protect against omitted dividends is to purchase cumulative preferred stock. **Cumulative preferred stock** is a stock issue whose unpaid dividends accumulate and must be paid before any cash dividend is paid to the common stockholders. If a corporation does not pay dividends to the cumulative preferred stockholders during one dividend period, the amount of the missed dividends is added to the following period's preferred dividends. For example, assume that the Bartlett Jones Corporation has issued a block of cumulative preferred stock that pays $4 a year. In 1988, Bartlett Jones is faced with a substantial loss and the board of directors votes to omit dividends to both preferred and common stockholders. In 1989, the board of directors decides that profits are high enough to pay the required preferred dividend and also a $2 dividend to all common stockholders. The holders of the cumulative preferred stock will receive $8 per share ($4 for 1988 and $4 for 1989). The holders of common stock will receive only the $2 per share dividend declared for 1989. Without this cumulative feature, the preferred stockholders would lose the omitted dividends.

An investor might expect cumulative preferred stock to be valued at the amount of omitted dividends plus the stock's investment value, but for two reasons this is seldom the case. First, omitted dividends are not a liability of the corporation in the same sense that interest payments are a liability. However, because no dividends may be paid to common stockholders until omitted preferred dividends have been paid, the cumulative preferred stockholder is in a somewhat stronger position than the owner of regular preferred stock. Second, if the corporation wishes to pay dividends to common stockholders, it must either pay the entire amount of omitted dividends or reach an agreement with the preferred stockholders. Typically, the corporation either purchases the preferred stock or satisfies the preferred stockholders' claims with a negotiated payment of something less than the total amount of the omitted dividends.

The Participation Feature of Preferred Stock

One problem that a corporation may face is lack of interest in its preferred stock issue because investors realize that they can earn only a certain cash dividend regardless of how profitable the corporation may be. To make a preferred stock issue more attractive, corporations sometimes add a participation feature. This allows preferred stockholders to share in the earnings of the corporation with the common stockholders. Although participating preferred stock is a rare form of investment, Moody's Financial Service does list approximately 90 issues of this kind.[1]

The participation feature of preferred stock works like this: (1) the required dividend is paid to preferred stockholders; (2) a stated dividend, usually equal to the dividend amount paid to preferred stockholders, is paid to common stockholders; and (3) the remainder of the earnings available for distribution is shared by both preferred and common stockholders. For example, assume that Martin & Martin Manufacturing corporation has issued a block of participating preferred stock that pays a dividend of $3 a year. In 1988, the success of a new product increases Martin & Martin's profits substantially. As a result, the board of directors approves the regular $3 dividend payment to preferred stockholders and also approves a $3 dividend payment to common stockholders. Finally, the board approves an additional $1.50 dividend payment to both preferred and common stockholders. In this situation, the preferred stockholders receive an additional $1.50 a share because of the participation feature of their preferred stock. If the preferred stock did not have the participation feature, the preferred stockholders would receive only the regular dividend and the excess dividends would be paid to the common stockholders. Obviously, participating preferred stock offers a higher potential return than does preferred stock without the participating feature.

[1] Wilbur W. Widicus and Thomas E. Stitzel, *Personal Investing*, 4th ed. (Homewood, Ill.: Richard D. Irwin, 1985), p. 220.

The Conversion Feature of Preferred Stock

Convertible preferred stock is preferred stock that can be exchanged, at the stockholder's option, for a specified number of shares of common stock. Approximately one third of all preferred stock issues are convertible to common stock. The conversion feature provides the investor with the safety of preferred stock and the possibility of greater speculative gain through conversion to common stock.

All of the information relating to the number of shares of common stock that may be obtained through conversion of preferred stock is stated in the corporate records and usually printed on the preferred stock certificate. For example, assume that the Martin & Martin participating preferred stock described above is also convertible. This convertible preferred stock is convertible into two shares of common stock for each share of preferred stock. Assume that the market price of Martin & Martin's convertible preferred stock is $24 and that the stock pays an annual dividend of $2 a share. Also assume that the market price of the company's common stock is $9 and that the common stock currently pays a dividend of $1 a share. Under these circumstances, a preferred stockholder would keep the preferred stock. If the market price of the common stock were to increase to above $12 a share, however, the preferred stockholder would have an incentive to exercise the conversion option.

The decision to convert preferred stock to common stock is complicated by two factors. First, the dividends paid on preferred stock are more secure than the dividends paid on common stock. Second, because of the conversion factor, the price of convertible preferred stock usually increases as the price of common stock increases.

There are also other factors that an investor should evaluate before purchasing either preferred stock or common stock. Additional information that will help you evaluate potential stock investments is discussed in the next section.

EVALUATION OF A STOCK ISSUE

A wealth of information is available to investors in stocks. The sources of this information include newspapers and business periodicals, corporate reports, and investor services. Most local newspapers carry several pages of business news, including reports of securities transactions. *The Wall Street Journal* (which is published on weekdays) and *Barron's* (which is published once a week) are devoted almost entirely to financial and economic news. Obviously, different types of investments require different methods of evaluation, but a logical place to start the evaluation process for common and preferred stock is with the most available source of information—the daily newspaper.

How to Read the Financial Section of the Newspaper

Most daily newspapers contain information about stocks listed on the major stock exchanges and stocks of local interest. Although not all newspa-

FIGURE 16-5 Financial Information about Common and Preferred Stock that Is Available in the Daily Newspaper

52 Weeks High	Low	Stock	Div.	Yld %	P-E Rat.	Sales 100s	High	Low	Close	Net Chg.
68⅞	48	IngerR	2.60	4.0	17	109	65	64¼	64¼	– ½
45½	33	IngRpf	2.35	5.2	...	25	45¼	45¼	45¼	+ ¼
20¾	11⅝	IngrTec	.54	2.8	17	8	19⅜	19⅜	19⅜	...
28⅜	19½	InldStl	.38i	...	...	392	23¼	23	23	...
55½	42⅝	InldStpf	4.75	9.2	...	14	51½	51⅜	51½	+ ¼
24½	16⅝	Insilco	1.00	4.4	17	61	22⅞	22½	22⅞	+ ⅛
6⅝	4¼	InspRs		...	...	987	5⅜	5	5¼	...
40¼	17	IntgRsc		...	18	221	27¼	27	27¼	...
51	31	IntgRpf	4.25	9.9	...	8	43	42¾	43	...
18	6⅜	Intlogn	1.62†	9.5	15	194	17⅛	16¾	17	...
11½	9	Intlogpf	1.50	13.0	...	1	11½	11½	11½	+ ⅛
14⅞	8¾	IntRFn		...	...	266	14¼	13⅝	13⅞	+ ¼
23¼	18⅝	ItcpSe	2.10a	9.5	...	52	22⅛	21⅞	22	...
89	62¾	Interco	3.08	3.4	15	276 u	89½	87⅞	89½	+ 1⅜
189¼	140	Interpf	7.75	4.1	...	1 u	190	190	190	+ ¾
12⅛	6⅛	Intrfst	.10	1.2	12	x 1185	8⅜	8⅛	8⅜	+ ¼
83¼	44½	Intrlk	2.60	3.2	16	58	82¼	80⅞	82	+ ⅞
14⅝	6⅜	Intmed		...	...	88	14⅝	14¼	14⅜	...
24¾	16½	IntAlu	.72	3.5	13	13	20¾	20½	20½	– ⅛

52 Weeks High	Low	Stock	Div.	Yld %	P-E Rat.	Sales 100s	High	Low	Close	Net Chg.
1	2	3	4	5	6	7	8	9	10	11
68⅞	48	IngerR	2.60	4.0	17	109	65	64¼	64¼	– ½
45½	33	IngRpf	2.35	5.2	...	25	45¼	45¼	45¼	+ ¼
20¾	11⅝	IngrTec	.54	2.8	17	8	19⅜	19⅜	19⅜	...
28⅜	19½	InldStl	.38i	...	...	392	23¼	23	23	...
55½	42⅝	InldStpf	4.75	9.2	...	14	51½	51⅜	51½	+ ¼
24½	16⅝	Insilco	1.00	4.4	17	61	22⅞	22½	22⅞	+ ⅛
6⅝	4¼	InspRs		...	...	987	5⅜	5	5¼	...
40¼	17	IntgRsc		...	18	221	27¼	27	27¼	...

1. Highest price paid for one share during the past year.
2. Lowest price paid for one share during the past year.
3. Abbreviated name of the corporation.
4. Total dividends paid per share during the last 12 months; pf denotes a preferred stock.
5. Yield percentage, or the percentage of return based on the current dividend and current price of the stock.
6. Price-to-earnings ratio: the price of a share of the stock divided by the corporation's earnings per share of stock outstanding over the last 12 months.
7. Number of shares traded during the day, expressed in hundreds of shares.
8. Highest price paid for one share during the day; u denotes unchanged.
9. Lowest price paid for one share during the day.
10. Price paid in the last transaction for the day.
11. Difference between the price paid for the last share today and the price paid for the last share on the previous day.

Source: *The Wall Street Journal,* June 9, 1986, p. 38.

pers print exactly the same information, the basic information is usually provided. Stocks are listed alphabetically, so your first task is to move down the table to find the stock you're interested in. Then, to read the stock quotation, you simply read across the table. The market price for the stocks on each line of the table is quoted in dollars and fractional equivalents of one eighth. Thus, ⅛ means $0.125, or 12.5 cents, and ¾ means $0.75, or 75 cents. For Insilco, the sixth stock down from the top in Figure 16–5, you would find the following information. (The numbers in this list refer to the column numbers that have been added to the figure.)

1. The highest price paid for a share of Insilco during the past 52 weeks was $24½, or $24.50.
2. The lowest price paid for a share of Insilco during the past 52 weeks was $16⅝, or $16.625.
3. The name of the corporation (often abbreviated) is listed in the third column.
4. The dividend paid to holders of Insilco common stock over the past year was $1.00 per share.
5. The current annual yield for Insilco is $1.00 ÷ $22.875 = 0.0437, or 4.4 percent.
6. The current price of Insilco common stock is 17 times the firm's per share earnings.
7. On this day, 6,100 shares of Insilco were traded.
8. The highest price paid for a share of Insilco on this day was $22⅞, or $22.875.
9. The lowest price paid for a share of Insilco on this day was $22½, or $22.50.
10. The price of the last share of Insilco traded on this day was $22⅞, or $22.875.
11. The last price paid for a share of Insilco on this day was $0.125 higher than the last price paid on the previous trading day. In Wall Street terms, Insilco "closed up ⅛" on this day.

If a corporation has more than one stock issue, the common stock is always listed first. Note that there are two listings of Ingersoll-Rand Corporation in Figure 16–5. The first is for the company's common stock. The second is for its preferred stock, as indicated by the letters *pf*.

Classification of Stock Investments

When evaluating a stock investment, stockbrokers, financial planners, and investors often classify stocks into different categories. In this section, we will describe five commonly used classifications.

A **blue-chip stock** is a very safe investment that generally attracts conservative investors. Stocks of this kind are issued by the strongest and most respected companies, such as IBM, Hewlett-Packard, and Dow Chemical.

Company characteristics to watch for when evaluating this type of stock include leadership in an industrial group, a history of stable earnings, and consistency in paying dividends.

An **income stock** is a stock that pays higher than average dividends. In order to pay above-average dividends, a corporation must have a steady, predictable source of income. Stocks issued by electric, gas, telephone, and other utility companies, are generally classified as income stocks. Investors purchase these stocks because of their income potential and not necessarily because they will increase in price.

A **growth stock** is a stock issued by a corporation that is earning above-average profits when compared to other firms in the economy. Key factors to evaluate when choosing a growth stock include an expanding product line of quality merchandise and an effective research and development department. In fact, most growth companies retain a large part of their earnings to pay for their research and development efforts. As a result, such companies generally pay out less than 35 percent of their earnings in dividends to their stockholders. Therefore, most investors purchase growth stocks in the hope that the market price of these stocks will "grow" or increase.

A **cyclical stock** is a stock that follows the business cycle of advances and declines in the economy. Typically, the increases and decreases in the price of a cyclical stock are directly related to the advances and declines in the nation's overall economic activity. When the economy expands, the market price of a cyclical stock increases. When the economy declines, the market price of a cyclical stock decreases. Most cyclical stocks are in basic industries such as automobiles, steel, paper, and heavy manufacturing. Investors try to buy cyclical stocks just before the economy expands and try to sell them just before the economy declines.

A **defensive stock** is a stock that remains stable during declines in the economy. For this reason, stocks in this classification are sometimes referred to as countercyclical. Generally, companies that issue such stocks have a history of stable earnings and are able to maintain dividend payments to stockholders during periods of economic decline. Many stocks that are classified as income stocks are also classified as countercyclical stocks because of their stable earnings and consistent dividend policies.

Stock Advisory Services

Another source of information that investors can use to evaluate potential stock investments is a stock advisory service. Although there are hundreds of stock advisory services that charge fees for their information, the investor must be concerned about the quality of the information and not just quantity of information. The information provided by advisory services ranges from a simple alphabetical listing to detailed financial reports. For example, Standard & Poor's stock rankings range from A+ (the highest) to D (in reorganization).

Standard & Poor's Reports, Value Line, and Moody's Investors Service were briefly described in the last chapter. In this section, we will examine a detailed report for Dow Jones & Company that is published in the *Moody's Handbook of Common Stock* (see Figure 16–6).

The basic report illustrated in Figure 16–6 is divided into six main sections. At the top of the report, information about the capitalization, earnings, and dividends of Dow Jones is provided. In the "Background" section, the company's major operations are described in detail. Dow Jones is described as a publisher with interests in national publications and news services, community newspapers, and books. In the next section, "Recent Developments," current information about the company's net income and sales revenues is provided. The net income of Dow Jones rose 7 percent, to $138.6 million, and its sales revenues rose 8 percent, to $1.03 billion. In the "Prospects" section, the company's outlook is described. The sales and earnings of Dow Jones were expected to "continue higher, benefiting from DJ's strong position in publications and services." The "Statistics" section provides important data on the company for the past 10 years. Among the topics included in this section are gross revenues, operating profit margin, return on equity, and net income. The final section of the report states, among other things, when and where the company was incorporated, where the company's principal office is located, who its transfer agent is, and who its main corporate officers are.

Other stock advisory services provide basically the same types of information that are illustrated in Figure 16–6. It is the investor's job to interpret such information and decide whether the company's stock is a good investment.

Factors that Influence the Price of a Stock

● Underlying Reasons for Price Changes

A *bull market* develops when investors are optimistic about the overall economy and purchase stocks. A *bear market* develops when investors are pessimistic about the overall economy and sell stocks. But how do individual investors determine whether it is the right time to buy or sell a particular stock? The price of a stock is affected by many factors. As mentioned, stocks sold on an exchange are practical examples of the supply and demand theories presented earlier, but an investor must also consider other factors when determining whether a stock is priced too high or too low. In this section, we examine numerical measures for a corporation and the fundamental, technical, and efficient market theories that investors use to determine whether a stock is priced right.

Numerical Measures for a Corporation. With a few exceptions, a company's book value has little direct relationship to the market price of its stock.[2] However, book value per share is such a widely reported measure of a stock's value that it deserves mention. The book value for a share of stock is determined by deducting all liabilities from the corporation's assets and dividing the remainder by the number of outstanding shares of common stock.

[2] Ibid. p. 257.

FIGURE 16-6 Sample Moody's Report for Dow Jones & Company

DOW JONES & COMPANY, INC.

LISTED	SYM.	LTPS•	STPS•	IND. DIV.	REC. PRICE	RANGE (52-WKS.)	YLD.
NYSE	DJ	146.9	95.5	$0.82•	43	50 - 37	1.9%

INVESTMENT GRADE. A LEADING FINANCIAL PUBLISHER, WHOSE PRODUCTS ARE NOTED FOR HIGH QUALITY.

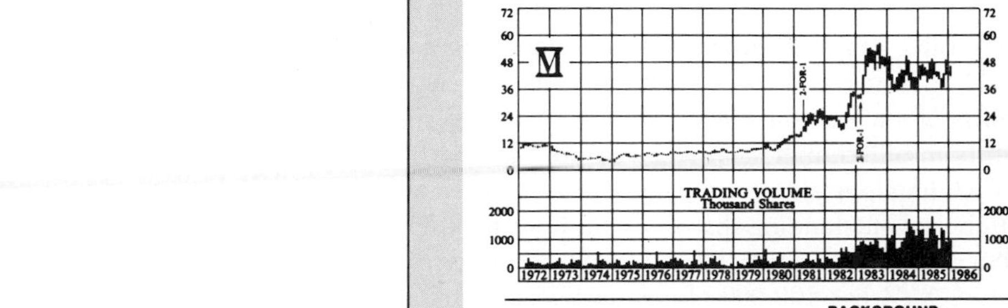

CAPITALIZATION: (12/31/84)

	(000)	(%)
Long-Term Debt	$ 21,020	3.8
Defer. Inc. Taxes	26,554	4.8
Com. & Surp.	505,601	91.4
Total	$553,175	100.0

Shs.($1)-64,303,000

INTERIM EARNINGS:

Qtr.	3/31	6/30	9/30	12/31
1982	0.29	0.38	0.34	0.38
1983	0.37	0.45	0.44	0.32
1984	0.48	0.58	0.41	0.54
1985	0.51	0.59	0.42	0.63

INTERIM DIVIDENDS:

Amt.	Dec.	Ex.	Rec.	Pay.
0.195Q	1/16/85	1/29/85	2/4/85	3/1/85
0.195Q	4/17	4/30	5/6	5/31
0.195Q	6/19	7/30	8/5	8/30
0.195Q	10/16	10/29	11/4	11/29
0.205Q	1/15/86	1/28/86	2/3/86	2/28/86

BACKGROUND:

Dow Jones is a publisher with interests in national publications and news services, community newspapers and books. National publications and services include the Wall Street Journal, Barron's National Business and Financial Weekly and Dow Jones News Services. Community newspapers published by Ottaway Newspapers include 20 dailies. Book publishing is conducted through Richard D. Irwin, Inc. It also has interest in newsprint production, telecommunication equipment manufacturing and rental and business and financial wire services. For 1984, national publications and services accounted for 79% of revenues (89% of operating profit); community newspapers, 16% (13%); and book publishing, 5% (3%); and corporate, 0% (-5%).

RECENT DEVELOPMENTS:

Net income gained 7% to $138.6 million for the year ended 12/31/85. Revenues climbed 8% to $1.03 billion. Advertising linage in the Wall Street Journel declined 5%, while circulation improved slightly to 2,002,800 from 2,001,300. For the Wall Street Journal/Europe, circulation gained 17% to 34,200 and advertising revenues rose 25%. Advertising revenue at the Asian Wall Street Journal was up 17% and circulation increased 5%. Barron's advertising linage was up slightly, while circulations gained 1%. Revenues of the Dow Jones Information Services Group increased 19%. Ottaway Newspapers, Inc. recorded a 19% increase in operating income and an 11% gain in revenues. At year-end the Dow Jones News/Retrieval had a total of 40 databases.

PROSPECTS:

Sales and earnings should continue higher, benefiting from DJ's strong position in publications and services. Continued growth in its major markets will contribute favorably. Future growth will come from increased spending to improve the content of the Wall Street Journal, expand printing capacity, implement production and electronic advances and build the Company's electronic publishing businesses.

STATISTICS:

YEAR	GROSS REVS. ($mill.)	OPER. PROFIT MARGIN %	RET. ON EQUITY %	NET INCOME ($mill.)	WORK CAP. ($mill.)	SENIOR CAPITAL ($mill.)	SHARES (000)	EARN. PER SH.$	DIV. PER SH.$	DIV. PAY. %	PRICE RANGE	P/E RATIO	AVG. YIELD %
76	274.9	22.5	24.0	30.3	35.4	17.4	63,664	0.48	0.26	54	8¾ - 6¾	15.8	3.5
77	317.3	22.7	29.7	39.0	16.6	5.1	61,808	0.63	0.30	48	8⅞ - 7⅜	13.0	3.7
78	363.6	22.7	28.4	44.2	d	8.4	61,952	0.72	0.33	46	9¾ - 7⅜	12.0	3.9
79	440.9	19.5	27.5	51.1	d	15.9	62,108	0.83	0.36	44	10 - 8	10.9	4.0
80	530.7	18.2	26.6	58.9	4.9	8.7	62,306	0.95	0.40	42	15¾ - 8¾	12.9	3.3
81	641.0	21.1	26.5	71.4	d	49.7	60,798	1.14	0.46	40	27⅝ - 14⅞	18.6	2.2
82	730.7	20.5	26.4	88.1	d	35.1	63,813	1.39	0.54	39	35¼ - 17⅞	19.1	2.0
83	866.4	24.3	27.4	114.2	d	16.8	64,087	1.79	0.60	34	56¼ - 32	24.7	1.4
84	965.6	23.8	25.5	129.1	d	21.0	64,303	2.01	0.72	36	51⅜ - 35⅛	21.5	1.7
p85	**1,039.3**			**138.6**				**2.15**	**0.78**	**36**	**50 - 36¾**	**20.2**	**1.8**

•Long-Term Price Score — Short-Term Price Score; see page 4a. Adjusted for 2-for1 split, 4/81 & 2/83.

INCORPORATED:
Nov.22, 1949 – Delaware

PRINCIPAL OFFICE:
22 Cortlandt St.
New York, N.Y. 10007
Tel: (212) 285-5000

ANNUAL MEETING:
Third Wednesday in April

NUMBER OF STOCKHOLDERS:
11,300

TRANSFER AGENT(S):
Morgan Guaranty Trust Co., N.Y., N.Y
Registrar and Transfer Co.,
Cranford, N.J. 07016

REGISTRAR(S):
Morgan Guaranty Trust Co., N.Y., NY

INSTITUTIONAL HOLDINGS:
No. of Institutions: 184
Shares Held: 19,281,948

OFFICERS:
Chmn. & Ch. Exec. Off.
W.H. Phillips
Pres. & Ch. Oper. Off.
R. Shaw.
Sr. V.P.& Ch. Fin. Off.
F.G. Harris
Secretary
R.S. Potter
Treasurer
L.E. Doherty

Source: *Moody's Handbook of Common Stock, Spring 1986* (New York: Moody's Investors Service, Inc., 1986).

For example, assume that XYZ Corporation has assets of $6 million and liabilities of $3 million. Also assume that XYZ has issued 100,000 shares of common stock. In this situation, the book value for a share of XYZ stock is $30 per share, as illustrated below.

$$\frac{\overset{Assets}{\$6,000,000} - \overset{Liabilities}{\$3,000,000}}{100,000 \text{ shares of stock}} = \$30 \text{ per share}$$

Book value may be a useful tool for evaluating a stock issued by a company that has large amounts of capital invested in natural resources. The future profits of such a company are tied directly to the ability to utilize investments in oil, timber, copper, iron ore, and so on.

Earnings per share are a corporation's after-tax earnings divided by the number of outstanding shares of common stock. For example, assume that in 1988 XYZ Corporation has after-tax earnings of $800,000. As mentioned above, XYZ has 100,000 of common stock outstanding shares. This means that XYZ's earnings per share are $8 ($800,000 ÷ 100,000 = $8). Most stockholders consider the amount of earnings per share important because it is a measure of the company's profitability.

The price-earnings ratio is the price of a share of stock divided by the corporation's earnings per share of stock outstanding over the last 12 months. For example, assume that XYZ Corporation's common stock is selling for $112 a share. As determined above, XYZ's earnings per share are $8. XYZ's price–earnings ratio is therefore 14 ($112 ÷ $8 = 14). The price-earnings ratio is a key factor that serious investors use to evaluate stock investments. Generally, the price–earnings ratio for a corporation must be studied over a period of time. For example, if XYZ's price–earnings ratio has ranged from 12 to 30 over the past three years, then its current price–earnings ratio of 14 indicates that it may be a potentially good investment. If XYZ's current price–earnings ratio were 27, toward the high end of the range, then it might be a poor investment at this time. Price–earnings ratios for one firm may be compared with the price–earnings ratios for all firms. For most corporations, price–earnings ratios range between 5 and 20. Again, a low price–earnings ratio indicates that a stock may be a good investment and a high price–earnings ratio indicates that it may be a poor investment.

The beta is an index that compares the risk associated with a specific stock issue with the risk of the stock market in general. The beta for the stock market in general is 1.0. The majority of stocks have betas between 0.5 and 2.0. Generally, conservative stocks have low betas and risky stocks have high betas. For example, assume that XYZ Corporation's stock has a beta of 0.50. This means that its stock is less responsive than the market in general. When the market in general increases by 10 percent, XYZ's stock will go up 5 percent. If, on the other hand, ABC Corporation, has a beta of 2.0, this means that ABC's stock is twice as responsive as the market in general. When the market in general increases by 10 percent, ABC's stock will go up 20 percent.

Investment Theories. Investors use three investment theories to determine a stock's market value. The **fundamental theory** is based on the assumption that a stock's intrinsic or real value is determined by the future earnings of the company. If the expected earnings for a corporation are higher than the present earnings, the corporation's stock should increase in value. If the expected earnings for a corporation are lower than the present earnings, the corporation's stock should decrease in value. In addition to expected earnings, fundamentalists consider (1) the financial strength of the company, (2) the type of industry the firm is in, and (3) the economic growth of the overall economy.

The **technical theory** is based on the assumption that a stock's market value is determined by the forces of supply and demand in the stock market as a whole. It is based, not on the expected earnings or the intrinsic value of an individual stock, but on factors found in the market as a whole. Typical technical factors are the total number of shares traded, the number of buy orders, and the number of sell orders. Technical analysts, sometimes called chartists, construct charts that plot price movements and other market index movements. By means of these charts, they can observe trends and patterns that enable them to predict whether a stock's market price will increase or decrease.

The **efficient market theory**, sometimes called the random walk theory, is based on the assumption that stock price movements are purely random. Advocates of the efficient market theory assume that the stock market is completely efficient and that buyers and sellers have considered all of the available information about an individual stock. Any news on an individual corporation, an oil embargo, or a change in the tax laws that may affect the price of a stock is quickly absorbed by all investors seeking a profit. Thus, a stock's market price reflects its true value. The efficient market theory rejects both the fundamental theory and the technical theory. According to this theory, it is impossible for an investor to outperform the average for the stock market as a whole over a long period of time. Most investors reject the efficient market theory on the assumption that by means of the fundamental theory and the technical theory they can improve their performance in the stock market.

BUYING AND SELLING STOCKS

- Stock Market Transactions

To purchase a pair of jeans, you simply walk into a store that sells jeans, choose a pair, and pay for your purchase. To purchase common or preferred stock, you generally have to work through a financial representative. In turn, your financial representative must buy the stock in either the primary or secondary market. The **primary market** is a market in which an investor purchases financial securities (via an investment bank or other representative) from the issuer of those securities. An **investment bank** is a financial firm that assists organizations in raising funds, usually by helping sell new security issues. An example of stock sold through the primary market is the new common stock issue sold by Chrysler Corporation during the early 1980s. Investors bought this stock through brokerage firms acting as agents for an investment banking firm, and the money they paid for common stock flowed to Chrysler Corporation and not to other investors. The **secondary market** is a market for existing financial securities that are currently traded between investors. Once the Chrysler stock has been sold in the primary market, it can be sold time and again in the secondary market.

Primary Markets for Stocks

How would you sell $100 million worth of common stocks or preferred stocks? For a large corporation, the decision to sell stocks or bonds is often complicated, time consuming, and expensive. There are basically two methods.

First, a large corporation may use an investment bank to sell and distribute the new stock issue. This method is used by most large corporations that

---

In the Real World
How Insider Trading Affects You

The Dennis Levine–Ivan Boesky insider trading case has been described as the largest stock market scandal since the Great Depression of 1929. In terms that a layperson can understand, here is what happened.

Dennis B. Levine was employed as a merger specialist by the investment banking firm of Drexel Burnham Lambert. An investment banking firm is a company that provides assistance to corporations that are in the process of raising money by selling a new stock or bond issue. As a merger specialist, Levine was able to obtain valuable financial information about mergers and acquisitions that were about to take place. He illegally gave this information to Ivan F. Boesky—a professional Wall Street trader. Then Boesky purchased stock in the companies that were merger or acquisition targets on the assumption that the company's stock would increase in value when news about the merger or acquisition became public information. For example, Boesky purchased shares in Carnation based on insider information that Nestlé was about to purchase the Carnation company. When the news became public information and the Carnation stock increased in value, he sold his shares for a $28.3 million profit.* According to the Securities and Exchange Commission (SEC), Boesky did basically the same thing at least eight times before the SEC began to investigate his insider trading activities. Eventually both Levine and Boesky were caught. Levine was found guilty of insider trading and sentenced to two years in prison. Boesky was forced to pay a $100 million fine.

As a result of all the publicity surrounding the Levine-Boesky case and similar incidents, individual investors are becoming concerned about how insider trading affects them. First, remember that insider trading affects only a small percentage of the stocks that are traded on the New York Stock Exchange, the

need a lot of financing. If this method is used, analysts for the investment bank examine the corporation's financial position to determine whether the new issue is financially sound and how difficult it will be to sell the issue.

If the investment bank is satisfied that the new stock is a good risk, it will buy the stock and then resell the stock to its customers—commercial banks, insurance companies, pension funds, mutual funds, and the general public. The investment bank's commission, or spread, ranges from 3.5 to 22 percent of the gross proceeds received by a corporation issuing common stock.[3] Because of the lower risk associated with preferred stock, the commission for selling a new issue of preferred stock is less than the commission for selling a new issue of common stock. In both cases, the size of the commission de-

[3]Eugene F. Brigham, *Fundamentals of Financial Management,* 3rd ed. (New York: CBS College Publishing, 1983), p. 368.

American Stock Exchange, or the over-the-counter market. For example, the New York Stock Exchange uses computers that flag unusual price moves for a particular stock. In 1986, 165 stock issues were flagged. About 60 incidents were referred to the SEC for investigation. In most cases, no action was taken.[†] Second, investors must use common sense when purchasing stocks or bonds. The following suggestions may help you avoid possible losses.

- Invest in quality bonds and high-yield stocks. These investments are less likely to take a nosedive in the event of an averted take-over attempt because they still represent value.
- Don't try to outguess the financial experts. It's hard for a small investor to determine when a merger or acquisition is going to occur.
- Be careful about using information—especially if it is too good to be true. In reality, the SEC will prosecute small investors for using insider information.

If you own stock in a company and the company becomes a takeover target, don't be too greedy. When the price begins to increase, it is time to consider selling the stock. If the merger or acquisition falls through, then your stock's price will rapidly decrease.

[*]Ann Reilly Dowd, David Kirkpatrick, Michael Rogers, Patricia Sellers, H. John Steinbreder, and Daniel P. Wiener, "The Fallout from Wall Street's Greedgate," *Fortune,* March 16, 1987, p. 8.

[†]"Unusual Stock Moves Continue to Raise Questions about Leaks," *The Wall Street Journal,* February 6, 1987, p. 15.

For more information, see George Anders, "Cloudy Cases: Insider-Trading Law Leads to an Array of Interpretations," *The Wall Street Journal,* February 19, 1987, p. 27; "Why Wasn't $1 Million a Year Enough?," *Business Week,* August 25, 1986, p. 72; and Edgerton, "What the Boesky Scandal Means to You and Your Money," *Money,* January 1987, p. 64+.

pends on the quality and financial health of the corporation issuing the new stock. The commission allows the investment bank to make a profit while guaranteeing that the corporation will receive the needed financing.

If the stock issue is too large for one investment bank, a group of investment bankers may form an underwriting syndicate. Then each member of the syndicate is responsible for selling only a part of the new issue. If the investment bank's analysts feel that the new issue will be difficult to sell, the investment bank may agree to take the stock on a best efforts basis, without guaranteeing that the stock will be sold. Because the investment bank does not guarantee the sale of the issue, most large corporations are unwilling to accept this arrangement.

The second method used by a corporation that is trying to obtain financing through the primary market is to sell directly to current stockholders. Usually, promotional materials describing the new stock issue are mailed to current stockholders. These stockholders may then purchase the stock directly from the corporation. As mentioned earlier in this chapter, most states require that a provision for preemptive rights be included in the charter of every corporation. This provision gives current stockholders the right to purchase any new stock that the corporation issues before it is offered to the general public.

You may ask, "Why would a corporation try to sell its own stock?" The most obvious reason for doing so is to avoid the investment bank's commission. Of course, a corporation's ability to sell a new stock issue without the aid of an investment bank is tied directly to the public's perception of the corporation's financial health.

Secondary Markets for Stocks

How does an individual buy or sell common or preferred stock? To purchase common or preferred stock, you have to work through a financial representative—your stockbroker. Then your broker must buy or sell for you in a securities marketplace, which is either a securities exchange or the over-the-counter market.

Securities Exchanges. A securities exchange is a marketplace where member brokers who are representing investors meet to buy and sell securities. The securities sold at a particular exchange must first be listed, or accepted for trading, at that exchange. Generally, the securities issued by nationwide corporations are traded at either the New York Stock Exchange or the American Stock Exchange. The securities of regional corporations are traded at smaller, regional exchanges. These are located in Chicago, San Francisco, Philadelphia, Boston, and several other cities. The securities of very large corporations may be traded at more than one exchange. American firms that do business abroad may also be listed on foreign securities exchanges—in Tokyo, London, or Paris, for example.

The New York Stock Exchange (NYSE) is the largest securities exchange in the United States and accounts for approximately 80 percent of all U.S.

stock transactions. This exchange lists over 2,200 securities issued by approximately 1,500 corporations with a market value of about $1 trillion.[4] The New York Stock Exchange has 1,366 members, or "seats," as they are often called. Most of these members represent brokerage firms that charge commissions on security trades made by their representatives for their customers. The cost of a seat is determined largely by sales volume and stock prices on the exchange. The record membership price of $625,000 was set in 1929.[5] The lowest price in this century was $17,000, paid in 1942. In the early 1980s a seat sold for approximately $350,000.[6]

Before a corporation's stock is approved for listing on the New York Stock Exchange, the firm must meet five criteria:[7]

1. Its annual earnings before federal income taxes must be at least $2.5 million.
2. It must own net tangible assets valued at $16 million or more.

[4] *NYSE's Annual Report and Fact Book* for 1983. The New York Stock Exchange, 11 Wall Street, New York, N.Y. 10005.
[5] Ibid.
[6] Ibid.
[7] Ibid.

From *The Wall Street Journal*, with permission of Cartoon Features Syndicate.

3. The market value of its publicly held stock must equal or exceed $18 million.
4. A total of at least 1.1 million shares of its common stock must be publicly owned.
5. At least 2,000 stockholders must each own 100 or more shares of the firm's stock.

The American Stock Exchange and various regional exchanges also have listing requirements, but typically these are less stringent than the NYSE requirements. The stock of corporations that cannot meet the NYSE requirements, find it too expensive to be listed, or choose not to be listed on the NYSE is often traded on the American Stock Exchange or one of the regional exchanges or through the over-the-counter market.

The Over-the-Counter Market. The **over-the-counter (OTC) market** is a network of stockbrokers who buy and sell the securities of corporations that are not listed on a securities exchange. Usually, the brokers in this network specialize, or make a market, in the securities of one or more specific firms.

Personal Financial Planning and You
Choosing an Account Executive

A good investment program should start before you choose an account executive. First of all, you must establish financial goals and objectives to meet your individual needs. Then you must accumulate enough money to get started. Most authorities suggest maintaining a cash reserve equal to at least three months' salary. Once you have accumulated funds in excess of the cash reserve amount, it's time to choose an account executive.

How Do You Find an Ac- count Executive? All account executives can buy or sell stock for you, but most investors expect more from their account executives. Ideally, an account executive should provide information and advice that can be used in evaluating potential investments. Many investors begin their search for an account executive by asking friends or business associates for recommendations. This is a logical starting point, but remember that some account executives are conservative, while others are risk oriented.

It is quite common for investors to test an account executive's advice over a period of time. Then, if the account executive's track record is acceptable, his or her investment suggestions can be taken more seriously. At this point, most investors begin to rely more heavily on the account executive's advice and less on their own intuition.

Why You Need an Account Executive. Basically, an account executive sees that your order to buy or sell stocks or bonds is correctly executed ac-

The securities of each firm are traded through its specialist, who is generally aware of their prices and of investors who are willing to buy or sell them. Most OTC trading is conducted by telephone. Since 1971, the brokers and dealers operating in the OTC markets have used an electronic quotation system called NASDAQ—the letters stand for the National Association of Securities Dealers Automated Quotation System. NASDAQ is a computerized system that displays current price quotations on a terminal in the subscriber's office.

Brokerage Firms and Account Executives

Most securities transactions are made through an account executive or stockbroker who works for a brokerage firm. An **account executive**, or stockbroker, is an individual who buys or sells securities for his or her clients. (Actually, account executive is the more descriptive title because such individuals handle all types of securities—not just stocks. Most account executives also provide securities information and advise their clients regarding investments.) Account executives are employed by such stock brokerage firms as Merrill Lynch, Prudential-Bache, and A. G. Edwards.

cording to exchange rules. In addition to buying or selling stock for you, your account executive should be able to help you in evaluating your personal financial plan and in establishing goals that are challenging and yet achievable. Your account executive should also be able to provide you with current financial information about the stocks or bonds in which you are interested. There are no guarantees that the securities you buy on the basis of your account executive's recommendation will increase in value, but he or she should help in the evaluation process.

A Final Word of Caution. Before choosing an account executive, you should ask a few questions to determine whether you and the account executive are on the same wavelength with regard to investment goals and objectives. Don't be surprised if your account executive wants to ask you a few questions, too. In order to provide better service, he or she must know what type of investment program you want to establish. If, after a reasonable period of time, you become dissatisfied with your investment program, do not hesitate to discuss your dissatisfaction with the account executive. You may even find it necessary to choose another account executive if your dissatisfaction continues. This is not at all uncommon. But when all is said and done, it is your money and you must make the final decisions that help you meet your investment goals.

The Typical Transaction. Once an investor and his or her account executive have decided on a particular transaction, the investor gives the account executive an order for that transaction. A market order is a request that a stock be purchased or sold at the current market price. Since the stock exchange is an auction market, the account executive's representative will try to get the best price possible and the transaction will be completed as soon as possible. A limit order is a request that a stock be bought or sold at a specified price. A limit order assures you that you will pay no more than the limit price when you buy stock or that you will receive no less than the limit price when you sell stock. For example, if you place a limit order to sell Kellogg common stock for $57 a share, the stock will not be sold for less than that amount. Likewise, if your limit order is to buy Kellogg for $57 a share, the stock will not be purchased until the price drops to $57 a share or lower. Limit orders are used by stockholders to buy stocks at prices thought to be at the low end of a price range and to sell stocks thought to be at the high end of the price range.

Many stockholders are certain that they want to buy or sell their stock if a specified price is reached. A limit order does not guarantee that this will be done. Orders by other investors may be placed ahead of your order. If you want to guarantee that your order is executed, you place a stop order. A stop order is a request that an order be executed at the next available opportunity after the market price of the stock reaches a specified price. For example, assume that you purchased Texaco common stock at $40 per share. Two weeks after your Texaco investment, Texaco is sued for unfair business actions by Pennzoil. Fearing that the market value for your Texaco stock will decrease, you enter a stop order to sell your Texaco stock at $32. This means that if the Texaco stock decreases to $32 or lower, the broker will sell it at the best price he or she can get for you. Both limit orders and stop orders can be day orders that expire at the end of the day if not executed, or they can be good until canceled.

Figure 16–7 illustrates how a market order to sell stock is actually executed. Two things should be noted. First, every stock is traded at a particular trading post, which is a desk on the trading floor. Generally, around 10 or 12 issues are traded at each trading post. Second, each transaction is recorded, and the pertinent information (stock name, number of shares, and price) is transmitted to interested parties through a communications network called a ticker tape. Payment for stocks is generally required within five business days of the transaction.

Commission Charges. Most brokerage firms have a minimum commission charge for buying or selling stock, usually between $20 and $35. Additional commission charges are based on the number of shares and the value of stock bought and sold. On the trading floor of a stock exchange, stocks are traded in round lots or odd lots. A round lot is 100 shares or multiples of 100 shares of a particular stock. Figure 16–8 shows typical commission charges for some round lot transactions. An odd lot is fewer than 100 shares of a particular stock. Brokerage firms generally charge higher per share fees for trading in

FIGURE 16-7   The Steps Involved for a Typical Stock Transaction for Stock Traded on the New York Stock Exchange

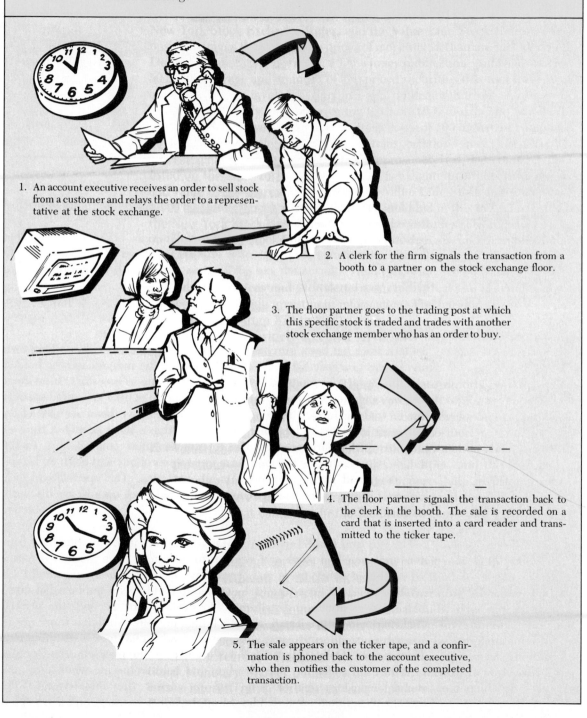

1. An account executive receives an order to sell stock from a customer and relays the order to a representative at the stock exchange.

2. A clerk for the firm signals the transaction from a booth to a partner on the stock exchange floor.

3. The floor partner goes to the trading post at which this specific stock is traded and trades with another stock exchange member who has an order to buy.

4. The floor partner signals the transaction back to the clerk in the booth. The sale is recorded on a card that is inserted into a card reader and transmitted to the ticker tape.

5. The sale appears on the ticker tape, and a confirmation is phoned back to the account executive, who then notifies the customer of the completed transaction.

FIGURE 16-8 Typical Commission Charges for Round Lot Transactions through a Full-Service Broker and a Discount Broker

		Commission	
	Stock Dollar Cost	Full-Service Broker	Discount Broker
100 shares @ $40 per share	$ 4,000	$ 82	$ 35
100 shares @ $60 per share	6,000	90	35
200 shares @ $35 per share	7,000	136	70
400 shares @ $40 per share	16,000	268	140

odd lots, primarily because odd lots must be combined into round lots before they can actually be traded.

Notice that the commission charged by full-service brokers is higher than the commission charged by discount brokers. A full-service broker generally provides more information and advice than a discount broker. Both types of brokers can buy and sell stock for their clients.

Long-Term Techniques for Stockholders

• Stock Trading Techniques

Once stock has been purchased, it may be classified as either a long-term investment or a speculative investment. Generally, individuals who hold an investment for a long period of time are referred to as investors. Individuals who buy and then sell stocks within a short period of time are called speculators or traders. In fact, some account executives have been accused of encouraging investors to buy and sell stocks within a short period of time—a practice called churning—in order to generate more commissions. In this section, we will discuss the long-term techniques of buy and hold, dollar cost averaging, and dividend reinvestment programs. The speculative techniques of selling short, margin transactions, and stock options are discussed in Chapter 18.

The Buy and Hold Technique. Many long-term investors purchase common and preferred stock and hold on to that stock for a number of years. When this is done, there are three ways in which their investment can increase in value. First, they are entitled to dividends if the board of directors approves dividend distributions to stockholders. Second, the price of the stock may go up. Third, the stock may be split. Although there are no guarantees, stock splits usually increase the value of a stock investment over a long period of time. Martin and Sally Wallace—the people in the Opening Scenario of this chapter—used a buy and hold technique when they purchased their Dr Pepper stock in 1963. As a result, they made over $35,000 through a combination of dividends, appreciation in value, and stock splits.

Dollar Cost Averaging. Dollar cost averaging is a long-term technique used by investors who purchase an equal dollar amount of the same stock at equal intervals in time. Assume that you invest $2,000 in XYZ Corporation's common stock each year for a period of three years. The results of your investment program are illustrated in Figure 16–9. Notice that when the price increased in 1989, you purchased fewer shares of stock. When the price of the stock decreased in 1990, you purchased more shares of stock. The average cost for a share of stock, determined by dividing the total investment ($6,000) by the total number of shares (104.1), is $57.64.

Investors use dollar cost averaging to avoid the common practice of buying high and selling low. In the situation shown in Figure 16–9, you would lose money only if you sold your stock at less than the average cost of $57.64. Thus, with dollar cost averaging an investor can make money if the stock is sold at a price higher than the average purchase price.

Dividend Reinvestment Plans. Today, a large number of corporations offer dividend reinvestment plans. **A dividend reinvestment plan** allows current stockholders the option of reinvesting their cash dividends in the corporation's common stock. For stockholders, the chief advantage of this type of plan is that it enables them to purchase stock without paying the typical commission charge to a brokerage firm. For corporations, its chief advantage is that it provides an additional source of capital. As an added incentive, some corporations even offer their stock at a small discount to encourage stockholders to use their dividend reinvestment plan.

Securities Regulation

Government regulation of securities trading began as a response to abusive and fraudulent practices in the sale of stocks. Individual states were the first to react, early in this century. Later, federal legislation was passed to regulate the interstate sale of securities.

State Regulation. In 1911, the first state law regulating securities transactions was enacted in Kansas. Within a few years, a number of states had

---

FIGURE 16-9   Dollar Cost Averaging

Year	Investment	Stock Price	Shares Purchased
1988	$2,000	$50	40.0
1989	2,000	65	30.8
1990	2,000	60	33.3
	$6,000		104.1

passed similar laws. Most of the state laws provide for (1) registration of securities, (2) licensing of brokers and securities salespeople, and (3) prosecution of any individual who sells fraudulent stocks and bonds. These laws are often called blue-sky laws because they were designed to stop the sale of securities that had nothing to back them up except the sky.

Federal Regulation. The Securities Act of 1933, sometimes referred to as the Truth in Securities Act, provides for full disclosure of important facts about corporations issuing new securities. Such corporations are required to file a registration statement containing specific information about the corporation's earnings, assets, and liabilities; its products or services; and the qualifications of its top management. Publication of the prospectus, which is a summary of information contained in the registration statement, is also required by this act.

The Securities Exchange Act of 1934 created the Securities and Exchange Commission (SEC), the agency that enforces federal securities regulations. The operations of the SEC are directed by five commissioners who are appointed by the president of the United States and approved by a two-thirds vote of the Senate. The 1934 act gave the SEC the power to regulate trading on the New York Stock Exchange and the American Stock Exchange. It empowered the SEC to make brokers and securities dealers pass an examination before being allowed to sell securities, and it required that registration statements be brought up-to-date periodically.

Four other federal acts were passed primarily to protect investors:

- The Maloney Act of 1938 made the National Association of Securities Dealers (NASD) responsible for the self-regulation of the over-the-counter securities market.
- The Investment Company Act of 1940 placed investment companies that sell mutual funds under the jurisdiction of the SEC.
- The Federal Securities Act of 1964 extended the SEC's jurisdiction to companies whose stock is sold over the counter if they have total assets of at least $1 million or more than 500 stockholders of any one class of stock.
- The Securities Investor Protection Act of 1970 created the Securities Investor Protection Corporation (SIPC). This organization provides insurance of up to $500,000 for securities left on deposit with a brokerage firm that later fails.

SUMMARY

- People invest in common and preferred stock because of dividend income, appreciation of value, and the possibility of stock splits.

- Dividend payments to both common and preferred stockholders must be approved by a corporation's board of directors. The most important priority that an investor in preferred stock enjoys is receiving cash dividends before common stockholders are paid any cash dividends. In order to make preferred stock more attractive, corporations may add a cumulative feature, a participating feature, and/or a conversion feature to a preferred stock issue.

- A number of factors can make a share of stock increase or decrease in value. Typically, individuals use the fundamental, technical, or efficient market theory to gauge price movements.

- A corporation may sell a new stock issue through an investment bank or directly to current stockholders. Once the stock has been sold in the primary market, it can be sold time and again in the secondary market.

In the secondary market, investors purchase stock listed on a securities exchange or in the over-the-counter market.

- Most securities transactions are made through an account executive or stockbroker who works for a brokerage firm. Most brokerage firms have a minimum commission charge for buying or selling stock. Additional commission charges are based on the number and value of the stock shares that are bought and sold.

- Once stock has been purchased, it may be classified as either a long-term investment or a speculative investment. Traditional trading techniques used by long-term investors include the buy and hold technique, dollar cost averaging, and dividend reinvestment plans.

GLOSSARY

Account executive. An individual who buys or sells securities for his or her clients; also called a stockbroker.

Beta. An index that compares the risk associated with a specific stock issue with the stock market in general.

Blue-chip stock. A very safe investment that generally attracts conservative investors.

Book value. Determined by deducting all liabilities from the corporation's assets and dividing the remainder by the number of outstanding shares of common stock.

Callable preferred stock. Stock that a corporation may exchange, at its option, for a specified amount of money.

Cumulative preferred stock. A stock issue whose unpaid dividends accumulate and must be paid before any cash dividend is paid to the common stockholders.

Cyclical stock. A stock that follows the business cycle of advances and declines in the economy.

Date of record. The date when a stockholder must be registered on the corporation's books in order to receive dividends.

Defensive stock. A stock that remains stable during declines in the economy.

Dividend reinvestment plan. A plan that allows current stockholders the option of reinvesting their cash dividends in the company's common stock.

Dollar cost averaging. A long-term technique used by investors who purchase an equal dollar amount of the same stock at equal intervals in time.

Earnings per share. A corporation's after-tax earnings divided by the number of outstanding shares of common stock.

Efficient market theory. An investment theory that is based on the assumption that stock price movements are purely random; also called random walk theory.

Fundamental theory. An investment theory that is based on the assumption that a stock's intrinsic or real value is determined by the future earnings of the company.

Growth stock.   A stock issued by a corporation that is earning above-average profits when compared to other firms in the economy.

Income stock.   A stock that pays higher than average dividends.

Investment bank.   A financial firm that assists organizations in raising funds, usually by helping sell new security issues.

Limit order.   A request that a stock be bought or sold at a specified price.

Market order.   A request that a stock be purchased or sold at the current market value.

Odd lot.   Fewer than 100 shares of a particular stock.

Over-the-counter (OTC) market.   A network of stockbrokers who buy and sell the securities of corporations that are not listed on a securities exchange.

Par value.   An assigned (and often arbitrary) dollar value that is printed on a stock certificate.

Preemptive right.   The right of current stockholders to purchase any new stock that the corporation issues before it is sold to the general public.

Price-earnings ratio.   The price of a share of stock divided by the corporation's earnings per share of stock outstanding over the last 12 months.

Primary market.   A market in which an investor purchases financial securities (via an investment bank or other representative) from the issuer of those securities.

Proxy.   A legal form that lists issues to be decided at a stockholders' meeting and requests that stockholders transfer their voting rights to some individual or individuals.

Round lot.   One hundred shares or multiples of 100 shares of a particular stock.

Secondary market.   A market for existing financial securities that are currently traded between investors.

Securities exchange.   A marketplace where member brokers who are representing investors meet to buy and sell securities.

Stock split.   A procedure in which the shares of common stock owned by existing stockholders are divided into a larger number of shares.

Stop order.   A request that an order be executed at the next available opportunity after the market price of the stock reaches a specified price.

Technical theory.   An investment theory that is based on the assumption that a stock's market value is determined by the forces of supply and demand in the stock market as a whole.

REVIEW QUESTIONS

1. Why do corporations issue common stock? Why do investors purchase that common stock?

2. What major changes in corporate policies may be decided at the stockholders' meeting of a corporation?

3. Why do corporations split their stock?

4. What priorities do preferred stockholders enjoy when compared to common stockholders?

5. Preferred stock certificates may include a cumulative feature, a participation feature, and/or a conversion feature. What do these features mean to preferred stockholders?

6. How can the information contained in newspaper stock quotations help investors evaluate a specific stock issue?

7. Describe the five classifications of stock that were discussed in this chapter.

8. What type of detailed financial information is provided by stock advisory services?

9. Fundamental theory, technical theory, and

the efficient market theory were described in this chapter. How does each of these theories explain price movements for a stock traded on the NYSE?

10. What is the difference between the primary and secondary markets for stocks?

11. What steps are involved in the purchase of a stock listed on the NYSE?

12. Describe the long-term techniques of buy and hold, dollar cost averaging, and dividend reinvestment plans.

DISCUSSION QUESTIONS AND ACTIVITIES

1. In 1963, Martin and Sally Wallace invested $756.49 in Dr Pepper stock. By 1984, when they sold the stock, their total return on it was over $35,000. Explain how the Wallaces made money on their Dr Pepper stock investment.

2. In 1987, the Wallaces' stock portfolio consisted of 15 stocks valued at more than $200,000. According to Martin Wallace, what is the secret of their investment success? Do you agree with his investment philosophy?

3. What is the difference between common stock and preferred stock. Which type of stock investment do you prefer? Why?

4. What kinds of information would you like to have before you invest in a particular stock issue? Where can you get that information?

5. What factors should you consider when selecting an account executive or stockbroker?

ADDITIONAL READINGS

Baldwin, William. "Cheap-Cheap (Low Price Investing)." *Forbes*, October 6, 1986, p. 200.

Dreman, David. "A Strategy for All Seasons." *Forbes*, July 14, 1986, p. 118.

Fisher, Kenneth L. "Sell? or Hold?" *Forbes*, August 25, 1986, p. 156.

———. "A Time to Buy, a Time to Sell." *Forbes*, July 28, 1986, p. 226.

McFadden, Michael. "Taking a Tip from Tycoons." *Fortune*, October 13, 1986, p. 145.

Ozanian, Michael. "Grapes of Math." *Forbes*, October 6, 1986, p. 195.

Weiner, Leonard. "What to Do when Nothing Looks Good." *U.S. News & World Report*, September 22, 1986, p. 67.

CASE 16–1 One Stockholder's Dilemma

Betty Franklin, 46, is a successful engineer employed by a large electronics manufacturer. Her current salary is $52,000 a year. She owns her own town house, and she has over $30,000 in a certificate of deposit at a local savings and loan association. Her only debt obligation is a $350 monthly car payment.

Betty Franklin also owns common stock in

American Telephone & Telegraph (AT&T), International Business Machines (IBM), General Mills, and USX (formerly U.S. Steel). She admits that she has no idea of what her stock investments are currently worth, because she quit monitoring them back in 1986. She used to keep monthly charts on which she recorded relevant information for each of the stocks she owned, but she stopped doing so because the information didn't seem to change very much. Now she admits that she just got lazy. The chart for October 1986—the last chart she completed—is shown below. All of the information for this chart was taken from *The Wall Street Journal* on Wednesday, October 8, 1986.

Stock	Original Purchase Price	Number of Shares	Current Price per Share	Current Total Value	Current Dividend	Current Yield
AT&T	$ 26	50	$ 22	$1,100	$1.20	5.4%
General Mills	60	40	77	3,080	2.56	3.3
IBM	160	25	133	3,325	4.40	3.3
USX	32	75	27	2,025	1.20	4.4

Questions

1. Assume that you have been asked by Betty Franklin to evaluate her stock investments. Complete the following chart, using *current* information.

2. Based on your findings and on the information provided for 1986, what changes, if any, would you recommend to Betty Franklin?

3. What other information would you need to evaluate these corporations? Where would you get this information?

Stock	Original Purchase Price	Number of Shares	Current Price per Share	Current Total Value	Current Dividend	Current Yield
AT&T	$ 26	50				
General Mills	60	40				
IBM	160	25				
USX	32	75				

Source for the above information: _____ Date _____

17

Investing in Bonds and Mutual Funds

In Chapter 16, we discussed common stock and preferred stock. Here we examine two other investment alternatives—bonds and mutual funds. To invest successfully, an investor must carefully evaluate each of the above investment alternatives. In this chapter, we discuss corporate bonds first. Then we look at bonds issued by federal, state, and local governments. Finally, we examine why an investor would invest in mutual funds. After studying this chapter, you will be able to:

- Discuss why bonds are issued by corporations and by federal, state, and local governments.

- Explain why individuals purchase bonds for investment purposes.

- Evaluate bonds when making an investment.

- Recognize the factors that can influence the market price of a bond.

- Explain why individuals invest in mutual funds.

- Classify mutual funds by investment objective.

- Describe how bonds and mutual funds are bought and sold.

Interviews with **Robert W. Petrie,** Vice President, Thompson McKinnon Securities, Inc., and **Gene R. Huxhold,** Advanced Sales Representative, Kemper Financial Services, Inc.

Gene Huxhold is a specialist in estate, retirement, and financial planning. Mr. Huxhold is the Eastern Regional Director for Retirement Plan Marketing at Kemper Financial Services, Inc., which is located in Chicago. Prior to joining Kemper, Mr. Huxhold was manager of the competition unit at CNA Financial Corporation.

Mr. Huxhold received an undergraduate degree in investment finance and a Masters in Business Economics from DePaul University. He is a Certified Financial Planner and a member of the International Association of Financial Planners and the Institute of Certified Financial Planners.

Robert W. Petrie is currently the Vice President at Thompson McKinnon Securities, Inc. Prior to this position, Mr. Petrie was an account executive and Equity Coordinator for Dean Witter Reynolds, Inc.

The most common form of corporate debt security is the bond, which is a certificate promising to repay, no later than a specified date, a sum of money that the investor, or bondholder, has loaned to the company. In return for the use of money, the company also agrees to pay bondholders a certain amount of interest, which is a percentage of the amount loaned. Since bondholders are not owners of the company, they do not share in dividends or vote on company matters. Usually, the return of their investment is not dependent on how successful the company is in business. Bondholders are entitled to receive the amount of interest originally agreed upon, as well as a return of the principal amount of the bond if they hold it for the time period specified. Most of the bonds issued by corporations are registered with the SEC.

Bonds issued by states, cities, or certain agencies of local governments, such as school districts, are called municipal bonds. An important feature of these bonds is that the Internal Revenue Service does not tax the interest received by the bondholder. Also, the interest is usually exempt from state and local income tax if the bondholder lives in the jurisdiction of the issuing authority. Because of these advantages, however, the interest paid on municipal bonds is generally lower than that paid on corporate bonds. Municipal bonds are not registered with the SEC.

An open-end investment company, usually called a mutual fund, is a company with a managed portfolio of securities that will buy back shares from an investor whenever the investor wishes to sell. The selling price depends on the value of the company's portfolio at that time (the net asset value). There is no secondary trading market for the shares of such investment companies.

If the selling price of the shares of an open-end company includes a sales charge, the company is known as a load fund. The shares of such companies may be purchased directly from the investment company or from its underwriter. Broker/dealers that sell the shares of such a company may charge only a nominal fee for their services.

The investor considering an open-end company should compare the various features, costs, and services of funds— and complexes of funds. Some companies that belong to a fund complex allow shareholders to switch readily from one fund in the complex to another, for example from a fund invested in short-term financial instruments (a money market fund) to a fund specializing in equity investments.

If you are considering an investment in a mutual fund, you should obtain and read a current prospectus before looking at other sales literature.

Bonds and mutual funds used to be considered conservative investments for cautious investors. Traditionally, corporate and government bonds offered a steady source of income, but little prospect of an increase in value. Mutual funds were not much better. In the old days, most mutual funds specialized in risk-free investments that provided steady income rather than growth or appreciation in value. Today, the rules of the game have changed, and bonds and mutual funds have a new dimension that investors must consider.

Take the case of Susan and Bob Thompson. Back in 1978, the Thompsons inherited $53,000. They used $30,000 to pay off all of their debts except for their home. Then they invested the rest of their inheritance in corporate bonds and a mutual fund. They made these investment choices because they wanted security with a minimum of risk. According to Susan, they were both afraid of more speculative investments, such as the stock market.

Based on their own research, the Thompsons decided to purchase 10 Exxon bonds that paid 6 percent interest each year until maturity in 1997. Each bond cost $720, for a total investment of $7,200, plus a commission of $80 paid to their account executive. The Thompsons also invested $15,720 in a mutual fund. Again, based on their own research, they chose the American Capital Enterprise fund. They purchased 2,858 shares of the American Capital Enterprise Fund at $5.50 per share.

On October 8, 1986, eight years later, when their original investment of $23,000 was valued at over $50,000, the Thompsons decided to sell their Exxon bonds because the price had increased to $860 per bond. That decision was based on Bob's belief that the Exxon bonds would decrease in value over the next year. After the account executive's commis-

CORPORATE BONDS

When evaluating a corporate bond for investment purposes, you must answer two major questions. First, will the bond be repaid at maturity? Second, will the corporation be able to maintain interest payments to bondholders until maturity? The information presented in this section will help you answer these two questions.

Bond Characteristics

- The Purpose of Corporate Bonds

A **corporate bond** is a corporation's written pledge that it will repay a specified amount of money, with interest. Figure 17–1 illustrates a typical corporate bond. Note that it includes a box for the dollar amount of the bond, the interest rate, and the maturity date. The usual face value of a corporate bond is $1,000, although the face value of some corporate bonds may be as high as $50,000. The total face value of all the bonds in an issue

sion was paid the Thompsons received $8,500. Thus, they made a $1,200 profit ($8,500 − $7,280 = $1,220). In addition, they received $4,800 in interest during the eight years in which they owned their Exxon bonds. Their total profit on their bond investment was approximately $6,000.

On October 8, 1986, the American Capital Enterprise mutual fund was valued at $14.75 per share. (Remember, the Thompsons' original purchase price was $5.50.) The Thompsons calculated that their investment in the mutual fund was now worth $42,155.50 ($14.75 × 2,858 = $42,155.50).

Although tempted to "cash in" and take a profit of over $26,000, the Thompsons decided to hold on to their mutual fund investment because they thought it would go even higher than the current price. Only time will tell whether their decision was a good one.

In eight years, the Thompsons more than doubled their original investment, and they did it by making what most people would consider conservative investments. Generally, investors choose bonds and mutual funds because these investment alternatives are more attractive than depositing their money in a savings

account or investing in stocks. The Thompsons chose the Exxon bonds and the American Capital Enterprise mutual fund because they were afraid of more speculative investments. As with all investments, you must carefully evaluate a particular bond or mutual fund before making an investment decision. Unfortunately, there are no easy answers, but the success of your investments is tied to your ability to evaluate them. In this chapter, we examine the factors that will help you evaluate a specific investment in corporate bonds, government bonds, or mutual funds.

usually runs into the millions of dollars (see Figure 17–2). Generally, an individual or a firm buys a corporate bond through an account executive that represents a brokerage firm. Between the time of purchase and the maturity date, the corporation pays interest to the bondholder—usually every six months—at the stated interest rate. For example, assume that you purchase a $1,000 bond issued by American Telephone & Telegraph (AT&T). The interest rate for this bond is 8.8 percent. In this situation, you receive interest of $88 ($1,000 × 8.8% = $88) a year from the corporation. The interest is paid in installments of $44 at the end of each six-month period.

The maturity date of a corporate bond is the date on which the corporation is to repay the borrowed money. At the maturity date, the bondholder returns the bond to the corporation and receives cash equaling its face value. Maturity dates for bonds generally range from 15 to 40 years after the date of issue.

FIGURE 17-1   A Typical Corporate Bond. A Corporate Bond Is a Corporation's Written Pledge That It Will Repay a Specified Amount of Money at Maturity.

Because of the long-term maturity dates associated with bonds, the actual legal conditions for a corporate bond are described in a bond indenture. A **bond indenture** is a legal document that details all of the conditions relating to a bond issue. The bond indenture remains in effect until the bonds reach maturity or are repaid by the corporation.

Since corporate bond indentures are very difficult for the average person to read and understand, a corporation issuing bonds appoints a trustee. The **trustee** is an independent firm or individual that acts as the bondholders' representative. Usually, the trustee is a commercial bank or some other financial institution. The corporation must report to the trustee periodically regarding its ability to make interest payments and eventually redeem the bonds. In turn, the trustee transmits this information to the bondholders along with its own evaluation of the corporation's ability to pay. If the corporation fails to live up to the indenture agreement, the trustee may bring legal action to protect the bondholders' interests.

FIGURE 17-2   An Advertisement for 9¼ Percent Bonds Issued by the Burlington Northern Railroad Company

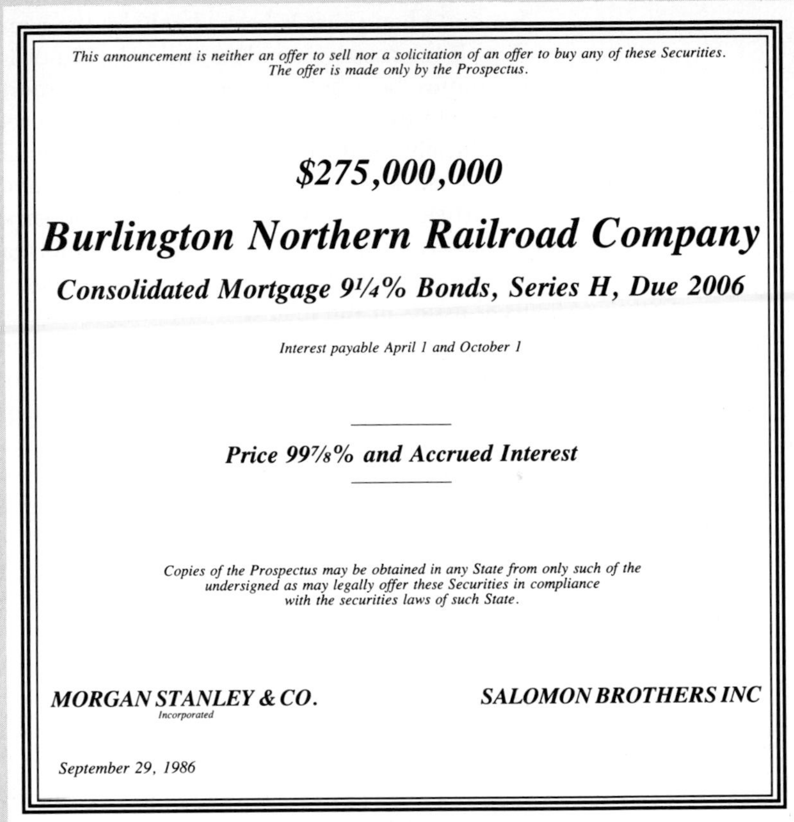

This announcement is neither an offer to sell nor a solicitation of an offer to buy any of these Securities. The offer is made only by the Prospectus.

$275,000,000

Burlington Northern Railroad Company

Consolidated Mortgage 9¼% Bonds, Series H, Due 2006

Interest payable April 1 and October 1

Price 99⅞% and Accrued Interest

Copies of the Prospectus may be obtained in any State from only such of the undersigned as may legally offer these Securities in compliance with the securities laws of such State.

MORGAN STANLEY & CO.
Incorporated

SALOMON BROTHERS INC

September 29, 1986

Source: *The Wall Street Journal,* September 29, 1986, p. 20.

Why Corporations Sell Corporate Bonds

Corporations sell corporate bonds to help finance their ongoing business activities. They usually sell bonds when it is difficult or impossible to sell common stock or preferred stock. While a corporation may use both bonds and stocks to finance its activities, there are important distinctions between the two. Corporate bonds are a form of debt financing, whereas stock is a form of equity financing. Bonds must be repaid at a future date; common stock and preferred stock do not have to be repaid. Interest payments on bonds are mandatory; dividends paid to stockholders are at the discretion of the board of directors. Furthermore, bond interest payments are a tax-deductible business expense, and therefore reduce the amount of income taxes that the corporation pays to the federal government. Finally, in case of bankruptcy, bondholders have a claim to the assets of the corporation prior to that of stockholders. Before issuing bonds, a corporation must decide what type of bond to issue and how the bond issue will be repaid.

Types of Bonds. Most corporate bonds are debenture bonds. A **debenture bond** is a bond that is backed only by the reputation of the issuing corporation. If the corporation does not make either interest or principal payments, debenture bondholders become general creditors, much like the firm's suppliers. In case of bankruptcy, the general creditors can claim any asset not specifically used as collateral for another financial obligation.

To make a bond issue more appealing to investors, a corporation may issue a mortgage bond. A **mortgage bond** is a corporate bond that is secured by various assets of the issuing firm. A first mortgage bond may be backed up by a lien on a specific asset. A general mortgage bond is secured by all of the fixed assets of the firm that are not pledged as collateral for other financial obligations. A mortgage bond is considered more secure than a debenture bond because corporate assets may be sold to repay the bondholders if the corporation defaults on interest or principal payments.

A third type of bond that a corporation may issue is called a subordinated debenture. A **subordinated debenture** is a bond that gives bondholders a claim secondary to that of other debenture bondholders with respect to both income and assets. Investors who purchase subordinated debentures usually enjoy higher interest rates than other bondholders because of the increased risk associated with this type of bond.

A fourth type of bond that a corporation may issue is called a convertible bond. A **convertible bond** is a bond that can be exchanged, at the owner's option, for a specified number of shares of the corporation's common stock. The corporation gains three advantages by issuing convertible bonds. First, the interest rate of such bonds if often lower than that of traditional bonds. Second, the conversion feature attracts investors who are interested in the speculative gain that may be provided by conversion to common stock. And third, if the bondholder converts to common stock, the corporation no longer has to redeem the bond. We will examine convertible bonds from the investor's standpoint later in this chapter.

Provisions for Repayment. Today, most corporate bonds are callable. A **call feature** allows the corporation to buy outstanding bonds from current bondholders before the maturity date. In most cases, corporations issuing callable bonds agree not to call them for the first 5 to 10 years after the bonds have been issued. When a call feature is used, the corporation generally must pay the bondholders a *premium*—an additional amount above the face value of the bond. The amount of the premium is specified in the bond indenture.

A corporation may use one of two methods to ensure that it has sufficient funds available to redeem a bond issue. First, the corporation may establish a sinking fund. A **sinking fund** is a fund to which deposits are made each year for the purpose of redeeming a bond issue. A sinking fund provision is included in the bond indenture, and is generally advantageous to bondholders because it forces the corporation to make arrangements for bond repayment before the bond maturity date. If the terms of the sinking fund provision are not met, then the trustee or bondholders may take legal action against the company. Second, a corporation may issue serial bonds. Serial bonds are bonds of a single issue that mature on different dates. For example, Seaside Productions used a 20-year, $100 million bond issue to finance its expansion. None of the bonds matures during the first 10 years. Thereafter, 10 percent of the bonds mature each year until all the bonds are retired at the end of the 20-year period.

Why Investors Purchase Corporate Bonds

Investors purchase corporate bonds for three reasons: (1) interest income, (2) possible increase in value, and (3) repayment at maturity. First, as mentioned earlier in this chapter, bondholders normally receive interest payments every six months. The dollar amount of interest is determined by multiplying the interest rate by the face value of the bond. For example, if General Electric issues a 7½ percent bond with a face value of $1,000, the investor will receive $75 ($1,000 × 7.5% = $75) a year, paid in installments of $37.50 at the end of each six-month period.

Second, corporate bonds may increase in value. Most beginning investors think that a $1,000 bond is always worth $1,000. In reality, the price of a corporate bond may fluctuate until the maturity date. Changes in overall interest rates in the economy are the primary cause of most bond price fluctuations. When General Electric issued the bond mentioned above, the 7½ percent interest rate was competitive with the interest rate offered by other corporations issuing bonds at that time. The bond's interest rate was slightly higher than the financial return on the traditional savings account or certificate of deposit. If overall interest rates fall, then the General Electric bond will go up in value because of the bond's higher interest rate. On the other hand, if overall interest rates rise, the market value of the General Electric bond will fall. The financial condition of the corporation and the probability of its repaying the bond also affect the bond's value. As a result of these factors, an investor may be able to purchase bonds at less than their face value and, if the value of the bonds increases, sell them at a higher price.

Third, corporate bonds are repaid at maturity. When you purchase a bond, you have two options: you may keep the bond until maturity and then redeem it, or you may sell the bond at any time to another investor. In either case, the value of your bond is closely tied to the corporation's ability to repay its bond indebtedness. In 1986, for example, the LTV Corporation filed for reorganization under the provisions of the U.S. Bankruptcy Act. As a result, the bonds issued by the LTV Corporation immediately dropped in value because of questions concerning the prospects for repayment of the bonds at maturity.

A Typical Bond Transaction. A bond can be a conservative investment alternative because you earn interest for each day you own the bond. Also,

FIGURE 17-3   Sample Corporate Bond Transaction for American Airlines

Assumptions: Interest, 4¼ percent; maturity date, 1992; purchased October 8, 1981; sold October 8, 1986

Costs when purchased:			Return when sold:		
1 bond @ $460	=	$460	1 bond @ $780	=	$780
Plus commission		+10	Minus commission		−10
Total investment		$470	Total return		$770

Transaction summary:

Total return	$770.00
Minus total investment	470.00
Profit from bond sale	$300.00
Plus interest (5 years)	+212.50
Total return for the transaction	$512.50

the corporation will redeem the bond for its face value at maturity. Besides interest and repayment at maturity, you may be able to sell the bond for a profit if you purchased it at a low price and sell it at a higher price. Assume that on October 8, 1981, you purchased a 4¼ percent corporate bond issued by American Airlines. Your cost for the bond is $460 plus a $10 commission charge, for a total investment of $470. Also assume that you held the American Airlines bond until October 8, 1986, before deciding to sell. Finally, assume that on October 8, 1986, you sold the bond at the current market value of $780. The return on your investment is shown in Figure 17–3.

In the above example, you made a total return of $512.50, which came from two sources. After paying commissions for buying *and* selling your bond, you made $300 because the market value of the bond increased from $460 to $780. The increase in the value of the American Airlines bond resulted from two factors. First, overall interest rates in the economy declined during the five-year period in which you owned the bond. Thus, your bond with a fixed interest rate of 4¼ percent became more attractive. Second, American Airlines established a reputation for efficiency and productivity during this five-year period—which enhanced the ability of American Airlines to repay its bonds at maturity in 1992. You also made money on the American Airlines bond because of interest payments. During the five-year period that you owned the bond, American Airlines paid interest payments totaling $212.50. Of course, you should remember that the price of a corporate bond can decrease in value and that interest payments and eventual repayment may be a problem for a corporation that encounters financial difficulties or enters bankruptcy.

Convertible Bonds. Corporations sometimes choose to issue bonds that are convertible into a specified number of shares of common stock. This conversion feature allows investors to enjoy the low risk of a corporate bond but also to take advantage of the speculative nature of common stock by exercising their right of conversion. For example, assume that you purchase a $1,000 corporate bond that is convertible to 50 shares of the company's common stock. This means that you can convert the bond to common stock whenever the price of the company's common stock is $20 ($1,000 ÷ 50 shares = $20) or higher. Assume that at the time of your bond purchase, the company's stock is selling for $12. In this situation, there is no reason to convert because the common stock you receive would be worth only $600 ($12 × 50 shares = $600).

In reality, there is no guarantee that bondholders will convert to common stock even if the market value of the common stock does increase to $20 or higher. The reason for not exercising the conversion feature in the above example is quite simple. As the market value of the common stock increases, the price of the convertible bond also increases. By not converting to common stock, bondholders enjoy the interest income from the bond in addition to the increased bond value caused by the price movement of the stock.

Convertible bonds, like all potential investments, must be carefully evaluated. Remember, not all convertible bonds are quality investments. In fact, the interest rates paid on convertible bonds are often 1 to 2 percent lower than the interest rates paid on corporate bonds without the conversion feature.

GOVERNMENT BONDS AND DEBT SECURITIES

In addition to corporations, the U.S. government and state and local governments also issue bonds to obtain financing. In this section, we discuss bonds issued by the federal government and by state and local governments.

- Bonds Issued by Federal, State, and Local Governments

Treasury Bills, Notes, and Bonds

The federal government sells bonds and securities to finance both the national debt and the government's ongoing activities. The main reason why investors choose U.S. government securities is that most investors consider them risk free. These securities are backed by the full faith and credit of the U.S. government. Because of the decreased risk of default, they offer lower interest returns than corporate bonds. Four principal types of bonds and securities are issued by the U.S. Treasury Department: Treasury bills, Treasury notes, Treasury bonds, and savings bonds. Treasury bills, notes, and bonds can be purchased directly from the 12 Federal Reserve banks or one of their 25 branches. They can also be purchased through banks or brokers. Savings bonds can be purchased through the Federal Reserve banks and branches, commercial banks, savings and loan associations, or other financial institutions. All four types of U.S. government securities can be sold through an account executive, and current price information on them can be found in *The Wall Street Journal* and other financial publications.

Treasury Bills. Treasury bills, sometimes called T-bills, are issued in minimum units of $10,000 with maturities that range from three months to one year. T-bills are discounted securities, which means that they are sold for less than their face value. For example, a six-month $10,000 T-bill with a stated interest rate of 8 percent will initially sell for $9,600. In reality, the interest rate for T-bills is slightly higher than the stated interest rate. In the above example, the investor is receiving $400 ($10,000 × 8% ÷ 2 = $400) interest on a $9,600 investment, which represents an 8.3 percent return on an annual basis. At maturity, the government will repay the face value of the T-bill.

Treasury Notes. Treasury notes are issued in $1,000 or $5,000 units with maturities that range from 2 to 10 years. Interest rates for Treasury notes are slightly higher than interest rates for Treasury bills. Interest for Treasury notes is paid every six months.

Treasury Bonds. Treasury bonds are issued in minimum units of $1,000 with maturities that range from 10 to 30 years. Interest rates for Treasury bonds are higher than interest rates for either Treasury bills or Treasury notes. Like interest on Treasury notes, interest on Treasury bonds is paid every six months.

Savings Bonds. Since 1979, the U.S. government has issued two types of savings bonds. Series EE bonds are issued with maturity values that range from $50 to $10,000. The purchase price for Series EE bonds is one half of their maturity value. Thus, a $50 bond costs $25 when purchased. A Series EE bond purchased after November 1, 1982, and held for at least five years returns a guaranteed minimum of 6 percent or 85 percent of the average yield of five-year Treasury notes during the life of the bond, whichever is higher. Therefore, if Treasury notes earn 9 percent, a Series EE savings bond will earn 7.65 percent, which is 85 percent of the Treasury bond rate. Series EE bonds held for less than five years receive interest ranging from 4.1 percent to 6 percent, depending on the holding period. Series EE bonds must be held a minimum of six months before redemption. These bonds do not pay out interest because all interest is automatically reinvested.

Series HH bonds are sold in denominations of $500 to $10,000. Unlike Series EE bonds, Series HH bonds pay out interest semiannually to investors who hold them for more than six months. The interest payments are made by check.

Federal Agency Debt Issues

In addition to the bonds and securities issued by the Treasury Department, there are also debt securities issued by federal agencies. New agency issues have been running at the rate of $20 billion to $30 billion per year.[1]

[1]Geoffrey A. Hirt, and Stanley B. Block, *Fundamentals of Investment Management*, 2nd ed. (Homewood, Ill.: Richard D. Irwin, 1986), p. 274.

Federal agencies that issue debt securities include the Federal Home Loan Bank, the Federal National Mortgage Association (FNMA), the Federal Housing Administration (FHA), and the Government National Mortgage Association (GNMA).

Although agency issues are, for practical purposes, risk free, they offer a slightly higher yield than government securities issued by the Treasury Department. Securities issued by federal agencies have maturities that range from 1 year to 40 years, with an average life of about 15 years.

State and Local Government Securities

A municipal bond, sometimes called a muni, is a debt security issued by a state or local government. Such securities are used to finance the ongoing activities of state and local governments and major projects such as airports, schools, toll roads, and toll bridges. State and local securities are classified as either general obligation bonds or revenue bonds. A general obligation bond is a bond backed by the full faith, credit, and unlimited taxing power of the government that issued it. A revenue bond is a bond that is repaid from the income generated by the project it is designed to finance. Both types of bonds are relatively safe. Over the years, the default rate on municipal securities has amounted to less than 1 percent of the face value of all municipal bonds.[2] Still, an investor must evaluate each investment in municipals before making the investment. In 1983, for example, the Washington Public Power Supply could not pay off its debt on municipal bonds worth more than $2 billion and thousands of investors lost money. Several years ago, New York City was on the verge of defaulting on a bond issue that was about to mature. Strong financial measures and new loans saved the city and the bondholders, but the experience affected the market value of all New York City bonds. In addition, the city had to pay higher than usual interest rates to attract investors to new bond issues. If the risk of default worries you, you can purchase insured municipal bonds. A number of states offer to guarantee payments on selected securities. There are also two large private insurers—the Municipal Bond Insurance Association and the American Municipal Bond Assurance Corporation. Usually, guaranteed municipal securities carry a slightly lower interest rate than uninsured bonds because of the reduced risk of default.

One of the most important features of municipal securities is that they are exempt from federal taxes. In addition, they are generally exempt from state and local taxes in the state where they are issued. As a result, municipal securities are very popular among wealthy investors. Because of their tax-exempt status, municipal bonds offer less interest than taxable bonds. By using the following formula, you can calculate the *taxable equivalent yield* for a municipal security.

---

[2]Edward Boyer, "Buying Bonds for Income, Not Safety," *Fortune: The 1986 Investor's Guide*, p. 52.

$$\frac{\text{Taxable equivalent}}{\text{yield}} = \frac{\text{Tax-exempt yield}}{1.0 \text{ minus your tax rate}}$$

For example, the taxable equivalent yield on a 7 percent municipal bond for a person in the 28 percent tax bracket is 9.7 percent, as illustrated below.

$$\frac{\text{Taxable equivalent}}{\text{yield}} = \frac{.07}{1.0 - .28} = .097$$

Once the taxable equivalent yield has been calculated, it is possible to compare the return on tax-exempt securities with the return on taxable securities.

THE INVESTOR'S DECISION TO BUY OR SELL BONDS

One of the basic principles that we have stressed throughout this text is the need to evaluate any potential investment. Certainly, corporate and government bonds are no exception. Only after you have completed your evaluation should you purchase bonds. Of course, a decision to sell bonds also requires evaluation. In this section, we examine methods that you can use to evaluate an investment in bonds and we look at the mechanics of buying and selling bonds.

Evaluation of Bonds

● How Individuals Evaluate Bonds

Good investors continually assess the value of their investments. They never sit back and let their money manage itself. Obviously, different types of investments require different methods of evaluation. Some of the basic means for evaluating bond investments are described below.

How to Read the Bond Section of the Newspaper. Not all local newspapers contain bond quotations, but *The Wall Street Journal* and *Barron's* publish complete and thorough information on this subject. Purchases and sales of bonds are reported in tables like that shown at the top of Figure 17–4. In bond quotations, prices are given as a percentage of the face value, which is usually $1,000. Thus, to find the actual price paid, you must multiply the quoted price by 10. For example, a price that is quoted as 84 means a selling price of $84 × 10 = $840. The first row of Figure 17–4 gives the following information for the Chevron corporate bond. (The numbers in this list refer to the column numbers that have been added to the figure.)

1. The abbreviated name of the issuing firm is Chvrn, which stands for Chevron. The bond pays annual interest at the rate of 8¾ percent of its face value, or $1,000 × 8.75% = $87.50 per year. It matures in the year 2005.
2. The annual yield, or return, based on today's market price, is $87.50 ÷ $953.75, or 9.2 percent.

Figure 17-4 Financial Information about Corporate Bonds that is Available in *The Wall Street Journal*

Bonds	Cur Yld	Vol	High	Low	Close	Net Chg.
Chvrn 8¾05	9.2	10	95½	95	95⅜	+ ⅜
ChCft 13s99	12.4	7	104¾	103½	104¾	+ ¾
Chryslr 8s98	9.0	10	89⅛	89	89⅛	+ ⅛
Chryslr 13s97	10.9	7	119	119	119	...
ChryF 9⅜87	9.3	9	101	101	101	+ ½
ChryF 9¾90D	9.4	126	104¼	104¼	104¼	− ⅜
CirclK 8¼05t	cv	20	133	132½	132½	− ½
Citicp 7.2s89t	7.2	10	99⅞	99⅞	99⅞	...
Citicp 8.45s07	9.2	10	91¾	90⅛	91¾	+ 1½
Citicp 8⅛07	9.2	12	89	88⅛	88⅛	− ⅝
Citicp 7.40s04t	7.5	4	98⅛	98⅛	98⅛	− ⅞
Citicp 12½93	11.4	3	109⅜	109⅜	109⅜	− ⅜
Citicp 8s99	8.2	24	00¼	00	98	− 1¾
Citicp 11⅞95	10.7	70	111⅜	110⅞	111⅜	+ ⅜
CitSv 13⅞11	12.5	10	111	110⅞	111	+ ⅛
CitSvc zr86	...	2	96⁹⁄₁₆	96⁹⁄₁₆	96⁹⁄₁₆	...
CitSvc zr87	...	38	89	89	89	...
CitSvc zr88	...	20	81⅜	80⅞	80⅞	...
CitSvc zr89	...	61	74½	74	74⅛	+ ⅛
ClevEl 7⅛90	7.6	15	94	93⅞	93⅞	+ ⅛

Bonds	Cur Yld	Vol	High	Low	Close	Net Chg.
1	2	3	4	5	6	7
Chvrn 8¾05	9.2	10	95½	95	95⅜	+ ⅜
ChCft 13s99	12.4	7	104¾	103½	104¾	+ ¾
Chryslr 8s98	9.0	10	89⅛	89	89⅛	+ ⅛
Chryslr 13s97	10.9	7	119	119	119	...
ChryF 9⅜87	9.3	9	101	101	101	+ ½
ChryF 9¾90D	9.4	126	104¼	104¼	104¼	− ⅜
CirclK 8¼05	cv	20	133	132½	132½	− ½
Citicp 7.2s89t	7.2	10	99⅞	99⅞	99⅞	...
Citicp 8.45s07	9.2	10	91¾	90⅛	91¾	+ 1½
Citicp 8⅛07	9.2	12	89	88⅛	88⅛	− ⅝

1. Abbreviated name of the corporation, the bond's interest rate, and the year of maturity.
2. Current yield, determined by dividing the annual interest in dollars by the current price of the bond. A "cv" in this column indicates that this bond is convertible into a specified number of shares of common stock.
3. Number of bonds traded during the day.
4. Highest price paid for one bond during the day.
5. Lowest price paid for one bond during the day.
6. Price paid in the last transaction for the day.
7. Difference between the price paid for the last bond today and the price paid for the last bond on the previous day.

Source: *The Wall Street Journal*, June 30, 1986, p. 36

3. Ten $1,000 bonds were traded on this day.
4. The highest price paid for a Chevron bond during the day was $95.5 × 10, or $955.
5. The lowest price paid for a Chevron bond during the day was $95 × 10, or $950.

6. The last price paid for a Chevron bond during the day was $95.375 × 10, or $953.75.
7. The last price paid on this day was +$0.375 × 10, or $3.75 higher than the last price paid on the previous trading day. In Wall Street terms, the Chevron bond "closed up ⅜" on this day.

For government bonds, two price quotations are included in most financial publications. The first price quotation, or the *bid price,* is the highest price that has been offered to purchase a particular government security. The bid price represents the amount that a seller could receive for that security. The second price quotation, or the *asked price,* represents the lowest price at which the government security has been offered for sale. The asked price represents the amount at which a buyer could purchase the security. In addition to price quotations, financial publications provide information about the interest rates, maturity dates, and yields of government securities.

FIGURE 17-5   Description of Bond Ratings Provided by Moody's Investors Service and Standard & Poor's

Quality	Moody's	Standard & Poor's	Description
High-grade	Aaa	AAA	Bonds that are judged to be of the best quality. They carry the smallest degree of investment risk and are generally referred to as "gilt edge." Interest payments are protected by a large or exceptionally stable margin, and principal is secure.
	Aa	AA	Bonds that are judged to be of high quality by all standards. Together with the first group, they comprise what are generally known as high-grade bonds. They are rated lower than the best bonds because their margins of protection may not be as large.
Medium-grade	A	A	Bonds that possess many favorable investment attributes and are to be considered upper medium-grade obligations. The factors giving security to principal and interest are considered adequate.
	Baa	BBB	Bonds that are considered medium-grade obligations; i.e., they are neither highly protected nor poorly secured.

Source: Geoffrey A. Hirt and Stanley B. Block, *Fundamentals of Investment Management,* 2nd ed. (Homewood, Ill.: Richard D. Irwin, 1986), p. 285; based on information from *Moody's Bond Record* (published by Moody's Investors Service, Inc.) and *Bond Guide* (Standard & Poor's Corporation).

Bond Ratings. To determine the quality and risk associated with bond issues, investors rely on the bond ratings provided by Moody's Investors Service, Inc. and Standard & Poor's Corporation. Both companies rank thousands of corporate and municipal bonds. Generally, U.S. government securities issued by the Treasury Department and various federal agencies are not graded because they are risk free for practical purposes.

As illustrated in Figure 17–5, bond ratings generally range from AAA (the highest) to D (the lowest). For both Moody's and Standard & Poor's, the first four categories represent investment-grade securities. Bonds in the next two categories are considered speculative in nature. Finally, the C and D categories are used to rank bonds that are in default because of poor prospects of repayment or even continued payment of interest. Although bond ratings may be flawed or inaccurate, most investors regard the work of both Moody's and Standard & Poor's as highly reliable.

FIGURE 17-5 *(concluded)*

Quality	Moody's	Standard & Poor's	Description
Speculative	Ba	BB	Bonds that are judged to have speculative elements; their future cannot be considered well assured. Often, their protection of interest and principal payments may be very moderate.
	B	B	Bonds that generally lack characteristics of the desirable investment. Assurance of interest and principal payments or of maintenance of other terms of the contract over any long period of time may be small.
Default	Caa	CCC	Bonds that are of poor standing. Such issues may be in default, or elements of danger may be present with respect to principal or interest.
	Ca	CC	Bonds that represent obligations that are speculative to a high degree. Such issues are often in default or have other marked shortcomings.
	C		The lowest-rated class in Moody's designation. These bonds can be regarded as having extremely poor prospects of attaining any real investment standing.
		C	Rating given to income bonds on which interest is not currently being paid.
		D	Issues in default with arrears in interest and/or principal payments.

Bond Yield Calculations. For a bond investment, the **yield** is the rate of return earned by an investor that holds a bond for a stated period of time. Two methods are used to measure the yield on a bond investment.

The **current yield** is determined by dividing the annual interest dollar amount of a bond by its current market price. Generally, the current yield for a bond is included in most financial publications, but there are occasions when you must calculate it. The following formula may help you complete this calculation.

$$\text{Current yield} = \frac{\text{Interest amount}}{\text{Market value}}$$

For example, assume that you own a Mobil corporate bond that pays 8½ percent interest on an annual basis. This means that you will receive $85 a year. Also assume that the current market price of the Mobil bond is $930.

In the Real World
The Pros and Cons of Junk Bonds

R ecently, junk bonds paid 13 percent on the average—well above the yield on high-grade corporate bonds or U.S. Treasury bonds. As a result, a large number of investors are buying these bonds in record numbers. And there are more bonds to choose from than ever before. Almost two thirds of all outstanding junk bonds were issued in the last three years, and roughly half were issued in the last two years.* Before deciding on junk bonds, there are a number of factors to consider.

A junk bond is a high-yield bond issued by a corporation rated BB or lower by Standard & Poor's. The Standard & Poor's BB rating stands for "Speculative." According to Wall Street bond analysts, the reason for the high return on junk bonds is the amount of risk. The high return on junk bonds is like insurance against a possible loss.

The risks associated with junk bonds are the result of two factors. First, the ultimate fear for any junk bond investor is the risk of default. Corporate bonds are supposed to be conservative, income-producing investments that are *repaid* at maturity. With a junk bond, there is a higher likelihood that the company will not be able to repay the bond at maturity. For example, LTV, the giant steelmaker, filed for Chapter 11 bankruptcy and stopped payment on bonds with a face value of $2.1 billion. In addition to LTV, 30 other corporations defaulted on bonds in 1986. In fact, the default rate for publicly traded junk bonds averaged 3.4 percent on all bond debt issued between 1980 and 1986.† During the late 1970s, the default rate was less than 1 percent. A second risk associated with junk bonds is the possibility that the corpora-

The current yield is 9.1, percent as illustrated below.

$$\text{Current yield} = \frac{\$85}{\$930}$$
$$= 9.1\%$$

The **yield to maturity** is a yield calculation that takes into account the relationship among a bond's maturity value, the time to maturity, the current price, and the dollar amount of interest. The formula for calculating the yield to maturity is presented below.

$$\text{Yield to maturity} = \frac{\dfrac{\text{Interest}}{\text{amount}} + \dfrac{\text{Face value} - \text{Market value}}{\text{Number of periods}}}{\dfrac{\text{Market value} + \text{Face value}}{2}}$$

tion will be unable to make interest payments to bondholders. Generally, bondholders will receive interest payments every six months until maturity.

Today, Wall Street experts warn that there is more reason than ever to exercise caution. According to Ben Weberman, a senior editor for *Forbes,* "the distinguishing feature about junk bond investing is that there is no such thing as average and that each issue has its own personality."‡ Therefore, each junk bond issue must be evaluated on its own merits. For investors unwilling or un-

able to do their homework, some experts suggest investing in a mutual fund that specializes in junk bonds. Junk bond mutual funds offer greater safety because of increased diversification. Regardless of whether you purchase junk bonds based on your own research and evaluation or through a mutual fund, remember one basic rule of investing: *the potential return should be directly related to the risk assumed.*

*Lorraine Carson, Christopher Knowlton, Terence Pare, and Andrew Evan Serwer, "The Coming

Defaults in Junk Bonds," *Fortune,* March 16, 1987, p. 26+.

†"Underwriters Find Junk Bond Pitfalls," *The Wall Street Journal,* September 29, 1986, p. 15.

‡Ben Weberman, "The Real and the Junk," *Forbes,* July 28, 1986, p. 224.

For more information, see "Junk Bond Jitters," *Dun's Business Monthly,* January 1987, p. 23; Gary Weiss, "Bonds Have More Fun, But They're Not for the Fainthearted," *Business Week,* December 29, 1986, p. 108; and "Junk Bonds: Why the Yields Are Still Fat," *Fortune,* July 7, 1986, p. 107.

For example, assume that you purchase a $1,000 corporate bond issued by Dayton Power on December 31, 1986. The bond pays 8⅛ percent annual interest, and its maturity date is 2001. The current market price is $850. The yield to maturity is 9.9 percent, as illustrated below.

$$\text{Yield to maturity} = \frac{\$81.25 + \dfrac{\$1,000 - \$850}{15}}{\dfrac{\$850 + \$1,000}{2}}$$

$$= \frac{\$91.25}{\$925}$$

$$= 9.9\%$$

In this situation, the yield to maturity takes into account two types of return on the bond. First, the bondholder will receive interest income from the purchase date until the maturity date. Second, the bondholder will receive a payment for the face value of the bond at maturity. If the bond is purchased at a price below the face value, the yield to maturity is greater than the stated interest rate. If the bond is purchased at a price above the face value, the yield to maturity is less than the stated interest rate.

The Mechanics of a Bond Transaction

Bonds are purchased in much the same manner as stocks. Corporate bonds may be purchased in the primary market or the secondary market. (Remember, the *primary* market is a market in which an investor purchases financial securities, via an investment bank or other representative, from the issuer of those securities. The *secondary* market is a market for existing financial securities that are currently traded between investors.) In the secondary market, most corporate bonds are traded on either the New York Bond Exchange or the American Bond Exchange. As mentioned earlier, U.S. government bonds and securities may be purchased through the Federal Reserve System, commercial banks, savings and loan associations, and account executives representing brokerage firms. Municipal bonds are sold through account executives.

Generally, the commissions that brokerage firms charge on bond transactions are smaller than the commissions they charge on stock transactions. In fact, most brokerage firms charge $10 to buy or sell a $1,000 corporate bond.

● Factors that Affect Bond Prices

Bond Prices. All bonds are issued with a stated face value. This is the amount the bondholder will receive if the bond is held until it matures. But once the bond has been issued, its price may be higher or lower than its face value. When a bond is selling for less than its face value, it is said to be selling at a *discount*. When a bond is selling for more than its face value, it is said to be selling at a *premium*. Overall interest rates in the economy, the financial condition of the company or government unit issuing the bond, and the factors of supply and demand are the three primary reasons for an increase or decrease in a specific bond's market price. For example, assume that you purchase a 5 percent $1,000 Eastern Airlines bond whose current market price is $640. Obviously, 5 percent interest is below the rate of return available on other potential investments. Also, the financial condition of the company and the overall unstable conditions in the airlines industry may depress the price of this bond. As a result, an investor is not willing to pay $1,000 for a bond that pays only 5 percent. Therefore, the bond is selling at a discount, or less than its face value.

Registered Bonds or Coupon Bonds. The method used to pay bondholders their interest depends on whether they own registered bonds or coupon bonds. A registered bond is a bond that is registered in the owner's name by the issuing company. Interest checks for registered bonds are mailed directly to the bondholder of record. When a registered bond is sold, it must be endorsed by the seller before ownership can be transferred on the company's books. A coupon bond is a bond whose ownership is not registered by the issuing company. To collect interest on a coupon bond, bondholders must clip a coupon and then redeem it by following the procedures outlined by the issuer. Coupon bonds, sometimes called bearer bonds, are more dangerous than registered bonds. If a coupon bond is lost or stolen, interest on the bond may be collected and the bond may be redeemed by anyone who finds it. For this reason, most corporate bonds are registered.

MUTUAL FUNDS

A mutual fund is an investment alternative available to individuals who pool their money to buy stocks, bonds, certificates of deposit, and other securities selected by professional managers who work for an investment company. Before deciding whether mutual funds are the right investment for you, you should consider certain factors.

Why Investors Purchase Mutual Funds

- Investing in Mutual Funds

The major reasons why investors purchase mutual funds are professional management and *diversification*, or investment in a wide variety of securities. Most investment companies do everything possible to convince individual investors that they can do a better job of picking securities than individual investors can. Sometimes these claims are true, and sometimes they are just so much hot air. Still, investment companies do have professional portfolio managers with years of experience who devote large amounts of time to picking just the "right" securities for mutual funds. In addition, numerous investment companies have developed elaborate systems and procedures to help their portfolio managers make the right selections. But even the best portfolio managers make mistakes. As an investor, you have to evaluate an investment in mutual funds just as you would evaluate any other potential investment.

The diversification of mutual funds spells safety, because an occasional loss incurred with one investment is usually offset by gains from other investments. For example, consider the number of securities included in the portfolio for American Capital Enterprise Fund, illustrated in Figure 17–6.

In addition to professional management and diversification, yet another reason why investors purchase mutual funds is that these funds represent a

FIGURE 17-6   Composition of Securities in the American Capital Enterprise Fund

Investment Portfolio
December 31, 1985

Principal Amount	Short-term investments—5.59%	Market Value
	Corporate notes—1.40%	
$ 9,225,000	Allied Bancshares, Inc., 10%, 1/2/86 (cost $9,219,875)	$ 9,219,875
	U.S. government obligations—4.19%	
28,000,000	U.S. Treasury bills, 7.02% to 7.07%, 3/20/86 to 4/26/86 (cost $27,512,793)	$ 27,518,540
	Total short-term Investments (cost $36,732,668)	$ 36,738,415

Number of Shares	Common stocks—95.36%	
	Aerospace and aircraft manufacturing—2.43%	
100,000	Boeing Co.	$ 5,225,000
200,000	Raytheon Co.	10,725,000
		$ 15,950,000
	Airfreight—1.85%	
*200,000	Federal Express Corp.	$ 12,125,000
	Air Transport—3.00%	
*200,000	AMR Corp.	$ 8,300,000
200,000	Southwest Airlines Co.	5,375,000
*400,000	Texas Air Corp.	6,000,000
		$ 19,675,000
	Auto parts—1.95%	
200,000	Eaton Corp.	$ 12,825,000
	Automotive—5.33%	
500,000	Chrysler Corp.	$ 23,250,000
100,000	General Motors Corp.	7,037,500
5,000	General Motors Corp., Class H	191,250
300,000	Magna International, Inc., Class A	4,537,500
		$ 35,016,250
	Banks—1.50%	
200,000	Citicorp	$ 9,875,000
	Brewers and Distillers—1.16%	
200,000	Seagram Co., Ltd.	$ 9,600,000

*Non-income producing

FIGURE 17-6   *(continued)*

Number of Shares		Market Value
	Building Materials—1.14%	
200,000	Owens Corning Fiberglas Corp.	$ 7,500,000
	Chemicals—1.25%	
200,000	Dow Chemical Corp.	$ 8,200,000
	Computer services—0.76%	
*200,000	Lotus Development Corp.	$ 5,000,000
	Conglomerates—2.92%	
200,000	Allied-Signal, Inc.	$ 9,350,000
200,000	Textron, Inc.	9,800,000
		$ 19,150,000
	Drugs and health care products—4.89%	
*300,000	Cetus Corp.	$ 7,950,000
* 50,000	Genentech, Inc.	3,487,500
300,000	Pharmacia AB, ADR	5,550,000
100,000	Schering-Plough Corp.	5,762,500
200,000	Syntex Corp.	9,325,000
		$ 32,075,000
	Electrical equipment—1.55%	
100,000	General Electric Co.	$ 7,275,000
*100,000	Optical Radiation Corp.	2,925,000
		$ 10,200,000
	Electronics and isntrumentation—5.20%	
500,000	Amdahl Corp.	$ 7,312,500
200,000	Gould, Inc.	6,075,000
200,000	Loral Corp.	7,300,000
200,000	Motorola, Inc.	7,775,000
*400,000	Symbolics, Inc.	5,700,000
		$ 34,162,500
	Financial and leasing—1.97%	
500,000	Federal National Mortgage Assn.	$ 12,937,500
	Forest products—.94%	
200,000	Weyerhaeuser Co.	$ 6,150,000
	Household furnishings and appliances—1.29%	
200,000	Singer Co.	$ 8,500,000
	Insurance—property and casualty—1.86%	
16,500	Fireman's Fund Corp.	$ 509,437
300,000	USF&G Corp.	11,700,000
		$ 12,209,437

†Affiliate as defined in the Investment Company Act of 1940 by reason of ownership of 5 percent or more of its outstanding voting securities.
Source: American Capital Enterprise Fund, Inc., *Annual Report,* December 31, 1985, pp. 2–5.

FIGURE 17-6   *(continued)*

Principal Amount		Market Value
	Leisure time and entertainment—3.16%	
*†200,000	Republic Pictures Corp., Class A	$ 1,675,000
*†15,000	Republic Pictures Corp., Class B	127,500
*300,000	Vestron, Inc.	3,937,500
100,000	Walt Disney Productions	11,287,500
*100,000	Warner Communications, Inc.	3,737,500
		$ 20,765,000
	Medical and hospital supplies—0.76%	
318,900	Baxter Travenol Laboratories, Inc.	$ 4,982,813
	Office and business equipment—3.04%	
*200,000	Data General Corp.	$ 9,075,000
200,000	NCR Corp.	8,050,000
*1,500,000	Storage Technology Corp.	2,812,500
		$ 19,937,500
	Oil—domestic—4.97%	
3,000	Enserch Exploration Partners, Ltd., Units	$ 51,375
300,000	Imperial Oil, Ltd., Class A	10,950,000
*500,000	Mesa Ltd. Partnership, Units	6,250,000
500,000	Mesa Petroleum Co.	1,375,000
300,000	Occidental Petroleum Corp.	9,225,000
75,000	Pennzoil Co.	4,800,000
		$ 32,651,375
	Oil—international—3.01%	
200,000	Shell Transport & Trading	$ 7,750,000
400,000	Texaco, Inc.	12,000,000
		$ 19,750,000
	Oil services and equipment—0.67%	
*800,000	Tom Brown, Inc.	$ 750,400
100,000	Schlumberger, Ltd.	3,662,500
		$ 4,412,900
	Radio and television broadcasting—15.21%	
*†2,500,000	Tele-Communications, Inc., Class A	$ 9,562,500
*†230,00	Tele-Communications, Inc., Class B	8,280,000
		$ 99,842,500
	Retail stores—4.20%	
100,000	Dayton-Hudson Corp.	$ 4,587,500
200,000	Sears Roebuck & Co.	7,800,000
200,000	Southland Corp.	8,800,000
200,000	Wal Mart Stores, Inc.	6,375,000
		$ 27,562,500
	Savings and loan—11.16%	
500,000	H.F. Ahmanson & Co.	$ 24,500,000
1,000,000	Great Western Financial Corp.	34,625,000
1,400,000	Philadelphia Savings Fund Society	14,175,000
		$ 73,300,000

FIGURE 17-6 *(concluded)*

Principal Amount		
	Security and commodity brokers, dealers, and services—1.33%	
200,000	Phibro-Salomon Corp.	$ 8,700,000
	Services—financial information—1.30%	
500,000	Telerate, Inc.	$ 8,500,000
	Services—hospital and medical care—1.12%	
400,000	HBO & Co.	$ 7,350,000
	Telecommunications—1.37%	
*800,000	MCI Communications Corp.	$ 9,000,000
	Telephone and telegraph apparatus—0.14%	
*100,000	DSC Communications Corp.	$ 900,000
	Tire and rubber goods—0.73%	
200,000	Firestone Tire and Rubber Co.	$ 4,825,000
	Tobacco—0.96%	
200,000	R.J. Reynolds Industries, Inc.	$ 6,275,000
	Utilities—telephone and telegraph—0.94%	
*500,000	Western Union Corp.	$ 6,187,500
	Total common stocks (cost $529,012,362)	$626,092,775
	Total investments (cost $565,745,030)—100.95%	$662,831,190
	Excess of liabilities over cash and receivables—(0.95%)	(6,247,523)
	Net assets—100%	$656,583,667

convenient way to invest money. Most transactions can be completed by mail or over the phone. Judging from the number of mutual funds available today, a large number of people believe that these advantages are important. According to Lipper Analytical Services, a firm that tracks the performance of mutual funds, the funds that specialize only in stocks number approximately 500 and have assets of almost $90 billion.[3]

Characteristics of Mutual Fund Investments

Two major types of mutual funds are offered by investment companies. Approximately 10 to 15 percent of all mutual funds are classified as closed-end funds. A **closed-end fund** is a mutual fund in which shares are issued only when the fund is organized. As a result, only a certain number of shares are available to investors. After all the shares originally issued have been

[3]Edward Boyer, "Putting Stock Funds to Work," *Fortune: The 1986 Investor's Guide*, p. 45.

sold, an investor can purchase shares only from another investor who is willing to sell them. Approximately 85 to 90 percent of all mutual funds are classified as open-end funds. An **open-end fund** is a mutual fund in which new shares are issued and redeemed by the investment company at the request of investors. In an open-end fund, there is no limitation on the number of shares that the investment company can issue. Investors are free to buy and sell shares at the net asset value plus a small commission. The **net asset value** (**NAV**) per share is equal to the current market value of the mutual fund's portfolio minus the mutual fund's liabilities divided by the number of shares outstanding. For most mutual funds, the net asset value is calculated at least once a day. In addition to buying and selling shares on request, most open-end funds provide their investors with a wide variety of services that are not provided by the closed-end funds.

The mutual fund investor should compare the cost of investing in a fund with the cost of other investment alternatives, such as purchasing stocks or bonds. With regard to cost, mutual funds are classified as either load funds or no-load funds. A **load fund** is a mutual fund in which investors pay a commission every time they purchase shares. The typical commission charge ranges from 7 to 8½ percent. Commissions are charged only when you buy shares; no commission is charged when you sell your shares of a load fund. A **no-load fund** is a mutual fund in which no sales charge is paid by the individual investor. No-load funds don't charge commissions when you buy shares because there are no salespeople. If you want to buy shares of a no-load fund, you must deal directly with the investment company. The usual means of contact is telephone or mail. While no-load funds do not charge commission to buy shares, some of these do charge a 1 to 2 percent commission for redeeming shares.

Since no-load funds offer the same type of investment opportunities that load funds offer, you may want to investigate them further before making the final decision on which type of mutual fund is best for you. Although the sales commission should not be the deciding factor, saving 8½ percent commission is a factor that you should consider.

Most mutual funds charge a management fee, which is calculated on a yearly basis. The management fee usually ranges from 0.50 to 1 percent of the total dollar amount invested. Typically, management fees are higher for no-load funds than for load funds since no-load funds do not charge sales commissions at the time of purchase.

Classifications of Mutual Funds

● Types of Mutual
  Funds

The managers of mutual funds tailor their investment portfolios to the investment objectives of their customers. The major categories of mutual funds, in terms of the types of securities they invest in, are as follows:

- *Balanced funds,* which apportion their investments among common stocks, preferred stocks, and bonds.

- *Growth funds,* which invest in the common stocks of well-managed, rapidly growing corporations.
- *Growth-income funds,* which invest in common and preferred stocks that pay good dividends and are expected to increase in market value.
- *Index funds,* which invest in common stocks that react in the same way as the stock market as a whole does.
- *Industry funds,* sometimes called specialty funds, which invest in the common stocks of companies in the same industry.
- *Income funds,* which invest in stocks and bonds that pay high dividends and interest.
- *Money market funds,* which invest in short-term corporate obligations and government securities that offer high interest.
- *Municipal bond funds,* which invest in municipal bonds that provide investors with tax-free interest income.

A number of mutual funds are part of a fund complex, sometimes referred to as a fund family. A shareholder may readily switch among the mutual funds in a fund complex. For example, assume that you own shares in the Mutual of Omaha growth fund. At your option, you may switch to the Mutual of Omaha income fund.

If you get the feeling that there are mutual funds designed to meet just about any conceivable investment objective, you are probably right. Hundreds of mutual funds trade daily under the headings "capital appreciation," "small-company growth," and "equity-income." It is your job to determine which fund is right for you. The material in the next section will help you make that decision.

THE INVESTOR'S DECISION TO BUY OR SELL A MUTUAL FUND

Often, the decision to buy or sell shares in mutual funds is "too easy" because most investors assume that there is no need for them to evaluate their investments. Why question what the professional portfolio managers decide to do? Yet the professionals do make mistakes—even if these are few and far between. The responsibility for choosing the right mutual fund rests with the individual investor. After all, you are the only one who knows how a particular mutual fund can help you achieve your financial objectives.

Evaluation of Mutual Funds

Although investing money in a mutual fund provides professional management, individual investors should continually evaluate their mutual fund investments. Some of the basic means for evaluating mutual funds are described below.

How to Read the Mutual Funds Section in the Newspaper. Most local newspapers, *The Wall Street Journal,* and *Barron's* provide information about mutual funds. The net asset value, offer price, and change in net asset value are reported in tables like that shown in Figure 17–7. The third row of

FIGURE 17-7   Financial Information about Mutual Funds that is
Available in *The Wall Street Journal*

```
                        Offer   NAV
                  NAV   Price   Chg.
John Hancock Funds:
  Bond  Fd  16.16 17.66    ...
  Global Tr  14.75 16.12  − .02
  Growth     17.63 19.27  + .03
  Spcl  Eqt   7.16  7.83  + .02
  US  GvSc    9.57 10.46  − .01
  Tax    Ex  10.64 11.63  + .01
  USGG       10.65 11.64    ...
  Kauf Fund   1.13 N.L.   + .02
Kemper Funds:
  Cal   Tax  13.83 14.48  − .01
```

| John Hancock Funds: | Offer | NAV |
NAV	Price	Chg.
1	2	3	4
Bond Fd	16.16	17.66	...
Global Tr	14.75	16.12	− .02
Growth	17.63	19.27	+ .03
Spcl Eqt	7.16	7.83	+ .02
US GvSc	9.57	10.46	− .01
Tax Ex	10.64	11.63	+ .01
USGG	10.65	11.64	...

1. The name of the investment company and the mutual fund is included in column 1.
2. The net asset value (NAV) for one share during the day. (Col. 2)
3. The offer price for one share during the day. (Col. 3)
4. Difference between the price paid for the last share today and the price paid for the last share on the previous day. (Col. 4)

Source: *The Wall Street Journal*, June 27, 1986, p. 28.

Figure 17–7 gives the following information for the John Hancock Growth Fund. (The numbers in this list refer to the column numbers that have been added to the figure.)

1.   The name of this fund is the John Hancock Growth Fund.
2.   The net asset value for the John Hancock Growth Fund during the day was $17.63.
3.   The offer price for the John Hancock Growth Fund during the day was $19.27. (The offer price is determined by adding the sales commission to the net asset value.) Therefore, you could purchase one share of John Hancock Growth Fund for $19.27.
4.   The last price paid for a share of the John Hancock Growth Fund on this day was $0.03 higher than the last price paid on the previous trading day.

If a mutual fund is a no-load fund, it is indicated by the "N.L." in the offer column. For example, the Kaufman Fund is a no-load fund. (Remember, no-load funds don't charge commissions when shares are purchased.)

Other Factors to Consider. Obviously, a mutual fund should help you meet your investment objectives. In Chapter 15, we talked about establishing investment goals. The statement was made that investment objectives must be tailored to the particular financial needs of the individual. This statement applies to mutual funds. You must evaluate such factors as age, income, and future earning power before investing in mutual funds. It is then possible to establish short-term, intermediate, and long-term objectives. After you have performed a personal financial checkup and established an emergency fund, it is time to get serious about evaluating mutual funds along with any other potential investments in which you are interested.

There are numerous sources of information that an investor can use to evaluate mutual fund investments. A good place to start is with investment-oriented magazines. *Forbes, Changing Times, Money,* and other finance or consumer-oriented magazines provide information that may be useful for mutual fund investors. For example, *Forbes* publishes an annual mutual funds survey. A portion of the 1986 survey is illustrated in Figure 17–8. In addition to providing statistical information, the *Forbes* survey ranks funds from A + (the highest) to D (the lowest) on their ability to perform in an up market and a down market.

An investor can also subscribe to services that provide detailed information to mutual fund investors. Moody's Investors Service, Lipper Analytical Services, and the Wiesenberger Investment Companies are three widely used sources of mutual fund information. In addition, various mutual newsletters provide financial information to subscribers for a fee. All of these sources are fairly expensive, but their reports may be available from brokerage firms or libraries.

An investment company sponsoring a mutual fund must provide investors with a prospectus. The prospectus provides valuable information about the fund's investment portfolio. Take a second look at the investment portfolio for the American Capital Enterprise Fund illustrated in Figure 17–6. This fund is typical of most mutual funds because its portfolio comprises a large number of securities that provide a high degree of diversification. Before deciding to invest in any mutual fund, ask yourself these two questions: Do the securities in the fund's investment portfolio match your investment objectives? Is there sufficient diversification in the selection of securities?

One final note on evaluation of mutual funds. Most long-term mutual fund investors will tell you that when evaluating a mutual fund, the most important consideration is long-term performance. The ability to make money in an up market and preserve capital in a down market is what determines a fund's long-term performance. Information on a fund's long-term performance record is available in the prospectus and from other sources of financial information.

FIGURE 17-8   A Portion of the 1986 Annual Mutual Funds Survey Published by *Forbes* Magazine

Performance in UP markets	in DOWN markets	Fund/distributor	Average annual total return 1976-86	Latest 12 months total return	return from income dividends	Total assets 6/30/86 (millions)	% change '86 vs '85	Maximum sales charge	Annual expenses per $100
		Standard & Poor's 500 stock average	14.7%	35.8%	3.2%				
		Forbes stock fund composite	16.7%	32.4%	2.2%				
D	B	AMA Fund¹/AMA	14.3%	32.0%	1.8%	$34	18%	none	$1.60‡
B	A	Amcap Fund/American Funds	22.3	29.7	1.8	1,506	25	8.50%	0.54
C	A+	American Capital Comstock Fund/American Cap	22.0	20.4	2.4	1,001	22	8.50	0.58
A	D	American Capital Enterprise Fund/American Cap	19.4	33.9	1.7	718	13	8.50	0.61
		American Capital Exchange Fund/‡‡	—*	27.7	2.6	51	3	none	0.69
		American Capital OTC Secs/American Cap	—*	21.8	0.3	129	42	8.50	1.19
B	A+	American Capital Pace Fund/American Cap	27.1	23.7	3.2	2,229	47	8.50	0.60
B	A	American Capital Venture Fund/American Cap	24.2	17.8	0.9	415	–5	8.50	0.68
D	A	American Growth Fund/American Growth	17.0	15.1	4.2	71	3	8.50	1.32
B	D	American Investors Fund/American Invest	7.6	22.6	2.3	82	–3	none	1.32
D	B	American Leaders Fund/Federated	12.7	23.3	4.0	116	44	none	1.09‡
D	A	American Mutual Fund/American Funds	18.6	31.7	3.7	1,962	47	8.50	0.46
B	B	American National Growth/Securities Mgmt	18.4	34.6	1.6	102	9	8.50	0.95
D	A	American National Income/Securities Mgmt	14.1	23.4	3.5	62	27	8.50	0.90
		American Pension Investors Trust²/Amer Pension	—*	35.6	5.1	6	NM	5.00b	1.43‡
		American Telecommunications-Growth/‡‡	—*	38.9	2.4	45	23	3.00b	1.32
		American Telecommunications-Income/‡‡	—*	37.5	5.2	104	21	3.00b	1.07
A	C	AMEV Capital Fund/AMEV Investors	20.9	47.6	1.4	106	42	8.50	0.90
		AMEV Fiduciary Fund/AMEV Investors	—*	56.2	0.8	16	103	4.00	1.50‡
A+	C	AMEV Growth Fund/AMEV Investors	25.4	50.2	0.8	163	59	8.50	0.86
•F	•B	Analytic Optioned Equity Fund/Analytic Option	—*	15.6	3.7	84	–25	none	1.23
B	D	Armstrong Associates/Armstrong	14.6	17.8	2.7	12	7	none	1.60
A	C	ASA Limited/closed end	20.2	1.0	4.9	437	–4	NA	0.30
		Associated Planners Stock Fund/AIM	—*	40.7	0.5	5	178	8.50	2.39
B	F	Axe-Houghton Stock Fund/Axe-Houghton	13.5	35.1	0.4	108	8	none	0.95‡
		Babson Enterprise Fund/Jones & Babson	—*	23.7	1.7	62	208	none	1.58
D	D	Babson Growth Fund/Jones & Babson	11.5	35.0	4.0	254	18	none	0.76
		Babson Value Fund/Jones & Babson	—*	29.5	2.0	5	286	none	0.93
•B	•C	Bailard, Biehl & Kaiser International/Bailard	—*	110.6	1.7	131	111	none	0.98
B	B	Baker, Fentress & Co/closed end	19.0	44.0	2.1	456	38	NA	0.54
		Bartlett Capital Trust-Basic Value³/Bartlett	—*	32.2	6.0	65	142	none	1.56‡
		Bascom Hill Investors/Madison	—*	29.2	3.7	7	46	none	1.06
D	B	Beacon Hill Mutual Fund/Beacon Hill	13.3	35.1	none	4	34	none	3.40
D	A	BLC Capital Accumulation Fund⁴/Princor	16.9	37.0	3.5	56	80	8.50	0.80
B	D	BLC Growth Fund/Princor	15.6	42.7	1.7	26	40	8.50	1.00
C	C	Boston Co Capital Appreciation/Boston Co	15.0	38.6	1.3	474	50	none	0.96‡
		Boston Co Special Growth Fund/Boston Co	—*	39.0	1.3	67	49	none	1.35‡
D	C	Boston Mutual Fund/Boston Mutual	11.3	21.6	1.5	7	.19	none	1.36
		Brandywine Fund/Brandywine	—*	—*	—*	41	—	none	1.60

Total return is for 9/30/76 to 6/30/86. For all categories other than money markets, funds are added to this section when they exceed $5 million in net assets and deleted when they drop below $2 million.   Stock and balanced funds are rated only if in operation since 11/30/80.   •Fund rated for two periods only: maximum allowable grade A.   *Fund not in operation for full period.   ‡Fund has 12b-1 plan (hidden load) pending or in force.   ‡‡Exchange fund, not currently selling new shares.   ¹Formerly PRO Fund.   ²Fund pays a 5% premium on share purchases and charges a 5% redemption fee.   ³Formerly Midwest Group-Bartlett Basic Value.   ⁴Formerly BLC Income Fund. b: Includes redemption fee that reverts to distributor.   NA: Not applicable or not available.   NM: Not meaningful.

Table of distributors, showing addresses and phone numbers, begins on page 186.

Source: Excerpted by permission of *Forbes* magazine, September 8, 1986. © Forbes Inc., 1986.

The Mechanics of a Mutual Fund Transaction

- Buying and Selling Mutual Funds

A mutual fund may be purchased through an account executive who is authorized to sell the fund or directly from the investment company that sponsors the fund. Because of the unique nature of mutual fund transactions, we examine how investors buy and sell shares in a mutual fund.

Purchase Options. To purchase mutual funds, you may use these three options: regular accounts, voluntary savings plans, and contractual savings plans. The most popular and least complicated method of purchasing shares in a mutual fund is through a regular account transaction. When a regular account is used, investors decide how much money they want to invest and simply buy as many shares as possible. Commissions, if any, are deducted from the amount of the investment, and the remainder is used to purchase shares.

Voluntary savings plans allow investors to open an account with an investment company for as little as $25. For most investment companies, the minimum amount for opening this type of account ranges between $25 and $1,000. At the time of the initial purchase, the investor declares an intent to make regular minimum purchases of the fund's shares. The chief advantage of the voluntary savings plan is that it allows investors to make smaller purchases than the minimum purchases required by the regular account method described above. For most voluntary savings plans, the minimum purchase ranges from $25 to $100 for each transaction. Although there is no penalty for not making regular purchases, most investors feel an "obligation" to make purchases on a regular basis. Thus, the number of shares they own and their total investment increase.

Contractual savings plans require that investors make regular purchases over a specified period of time—usually 10 to 15 years. These plans are sometimes referred to as front-end load funds because almost all of the commissions are paid in the first few years of the contract period. There are penalties if the investor does not fulfill the purchase requirements. For example, if an investor drops out of a contractual savings plan before completing the purchase requirements, he or she sacrifices the prepaid commissions. Many investors and government regulatory agencies are critical of contractual savings plans. As a result, the Securities and Exchange Commission and many states have imposed new rules on investment companies offering contractual savings plans.

All three purchase options allow investors to buy mutual fund shares over a long period of time. As a result, they can use the principle of dollar cost averaging, which was explained in the last chapter. Dollar cost averaging allows the investor to average many individual purchase prices over a long period of time. Thus, the investor avoids the problem of buying high and selling low. Investors who use dollar cost averaging can make money if they sell their mutual fund shares at a price higher than their average purchase price.

Withdrawal Options. Most mutual funds have a provision that allows investors with a minimum net asset value of at least $5,000 to systematically withdraw money. There are four options that may be used to systematically withdraw money from a mutual fund. First, the investor may withdraw a specified, fixed dollar amount each investment period until the investor's fund is exhausted. Normally, an investment period is three months. Most mutual funds require that an investor withdraw a minimum amount—ranging from $25 to $50—each investment period.

A second option allows the investor to liquidate or "sell off" a certain number of shares each investment period. Since the net asset value of shares in a mutual fund varies from one period to the next, the amount of money that the investor receives will also vary. Once the specified number of shares has been sold, a check is mailed directly to the investor.

A third option allows investors to withdraw a fixed percentage of asset growth. For example, assume that you arrange to receive 60 percent of the asset growth of your investment and that the asset growth of your investment amounts to $800 in a particular investment period. For that period, you

Personal Financial Planning and You
Are Mutual Funds for You?

I n 1986, Americans invested over $190 billion in mutual funds, or about $700 million a day.* In fact, there are over 40 million people who own shares in a mutual fund. Today, there are more mutual funds than ever before—all developed to meet the needs of investors like you. Whether you want your money in conservative, long-term government bonds or in speculative foreign stocks, there is a mutual fund for you. And while putting your money in a mutual fund may seem like a carefree method of investing, you must still develop an overall strategy to obtain your financial objectives. Then, you must choose one or more mutual funds to match that strategy. To be successful, an investor must still evaluate different mutual fund alternatives.

When evaluating a mutual

fund, the first factor to consider is the fund's investment objective. At one end of a broad spectrum are aggressive growth funds whose aim is maximum appreciation of your investment dollar. They invest in speculative stocks and other risk-oriented investments. At the other extreme are conservative funds that invest in U.S. government securities and stress conservation of capital while providing a steady flow of income. Between these two extremes, mutual funds are classified as balanced funds, growth-income funds, index funds, industry funds, income funds, money market funds, or municipal bond funds.

The second factor to consider is a fund's past performance. It is relatively easy to obtain a comparative performance ranking for periods ranging from the last 10 years to the last

quarter. Sources for this type of information include: *Donoghue's Mutual Funds Almanac, The Handbook for No-Load Mutual Funds, The Investor's Guide to No-Load Mutual Funds,* and *Forbes* Magazine. The most comprehensive reference sources for mutual funds are the *Wisenberger Investment Companies Service* and reports published by the Lipper Analytical Services. All of the above publications are available at many libraries.

When looking at past performance, you must remember that top performers can turn into poor performers, and vice versa. For example, the 44 Wall Street Fund had the best five-year performance record in the mutual fund industry in the late 1970s—a 1,019 percent gain—according to Lipper Analytical Services. By 1986, the same fund was the worst

would receive a check for $480 ($800 × 60% = $480). If there is no asset growth, no payment is made to the investor. Under this option, the investor's principal remains untouched.

A final option allows the investor to withdraw all income that results from interest, dividends, and capital gains earned by the mutual fund during an investment period. Under this option, the investor's principal also remains untouched.

performer over the previous five years—a 69 percent decline.[†] A good investor must consider *both* long-term and short-term performance.

Investors may also use mutual fund newsletters to aid in the evaluation process. Thanks to the increased interest in mutual funds, there are now about 45 mutual fund newsletters, almost four times as many as in 1982.[‡] Many of the older newsletters have survived the test of time and provide investors with reliable advice for fees ranging from $85 to $300 a year. But be warned, some newsletters can be misleading. One way that they mislead investors is by backdating the performance of their suggested investment portfolios—a practice somewhat akin to betting on a horse race after it's over. For instance, one newsletter, Rating the Stock Selectors,

tells investors that if they had followed its advice for the last 50 months, they would now have a 380 percent profit. But the newsletter admits that it devised this strategy a little over 14 months ago.[§]

A third factor to consider is the amount of commission you must pay when you invest in a mutual fund. Basically, there are two types of mutual funds. Load funds are sold by brokers and charge 8.5 percent commission of the amount you invest. No-load funds charge no commission because their shares are sold directly by the company and there is no broker involved. Many financial advisors suggest no-load funds. And yet, many investors feel that a broker's advice is well worth the commission charge. Two directories list mutual funds by investment goals and give details on commission charges. A

guide to funds with small or no sales commissions is available for $5 from the No-Load Mutual Fund Association, P.O. Box 2004, JAF Building, New York, NY 10116. A similar guide is available for $1 from the Investment Company Institute, 1600 M Street, N.W., Washington, DC 20036, Attention Guide.[§]

[*]"Mutual Fund Daze," *U.S. News & World Report*, February 16, 1987, p. 52+.
[†]Leonard Wiener, "Choosing a Fund: A Survival Guide for Small Investors," *U.S. News & World Report*, February 16, 1987, p. 56+.
[‡]Jan Wong, "Mutual Fund Newsletters Multiply, but What Do They Offer Readers?," *The Wall Street Journal*, June 30, 1986, p. 23.
[§]Ibid.
[§]Leonard Wiener, "Choosing a Fund," p. 56+.

SUMMARY

- Corporations, the U.S. government, and state and local governments issue bonds and other securities to finance their ongoing activities.
- Investors purchase corporate and government bonds for three reasons: (1) interest income, (2) possible increase in value, and (3) repayment at maturity.
- Four basic means that investors can use to evaluate bonds are bond information in newspapers, bond ratings, the current yield of bonds, and the yield to maturity of bonds.
- The market price of a bond can be influenced by changes in the overall interest rates of the economy, in the financial condition of the company or the government unit issuing the bond, and in the prospects for repayment at maturity.
- The major advantages of a mutual fund invest-

ment are professional management and diversification. A mutual fund investment also represents a convenient way to invest money.
- The major categories of mutual funds, in terms of the types of securities they invest in, are balanced funds, growth funds, growth-income funds, index funds, industry funds, income funds, money market funds, and municipal bond funds.
- Bonds and mutual funds can be purchased through account executives who represent brokerage firms. Government bonds can also be purchased through the Federal Reserve banks and branches, commercial banks, savings and loan associations, and other financial institutions. Mutual funds also can be purchased through the investment companies that sponsor the funds.

GLOSSARY

Bond indenture.   A legal document that details all of the conditions relating to a bond issue.

Call feature.   A feature that allows the corporation to buy outstanding bonds from current bondholders before the maturity date.

Closed-end fund.   A mutual fund in which new shares are issued only when the fund is organized.

Convertible bond.   A bond that can be exchanged, at the owner's option, for a specified number of shares of the corporation's common stock.

Corporate bond.   A corporation's written pledge that it will repay a specified amount of money, with interest.

Coupon bond.   A bond whose ownership is not registered by the issuing company.

Current yield.   Determined by dividing the annual

interest dollar amount by the current market price of the bond.

Debenture bond.   A bond that is backed only by the reputation of the issuing corporation.

General obligation bond.   A bond backed by the full faith, credit, and unlimited taxing power of the government that issued it.

Load fund.   A mutual fund in which investors pay a commission every time they purchase shares.

Maturity date.   For a corporate bond, this is the date on which the corporation is to repay the borrowed money.

Mortgage bond.   A corporate bond that is secured by various assets of the issuing firm.

Municipal bond.   A debt security issued by a state or local government.

Net asset value (NAV).   The current market value of the mutual fund's portfolio minus the liabilities of the mutual fund divided by the number of shares outstanding.

No-load fund.   A mutual fund in which no sales charge is paid by the individual investor.

Open-end fund.   A mutual fund in which new shares are issued and redeemed by the investment company at the request of investors.

Registered bond.   A bond that is registered in the owner's name by the issuing company.

Revenue bond.   A bond that is repaid from the income generated by the project it is designed to finance.

Serial bonds.   Bonds of a single issue that mature on different dates.

Sinking fund.   A fund to which deposits are made each year for the purpose of redeeming a bond issue.

Subordinated debenture.   A bond that gives bondholders a claim secondary to that of other debenture bondholders with respect to both income and assets.

Trustee.   An independent firm or individual that acts as the bondholders' representative.

Yield.   The rate of return earned by an investor that holds a bond for a stated period of time.

Yield to maturity.   A yield calculation that takes into account the relationship among the security's maturity value, the time to maturity, the current price, and the dollar amount of interest.

REVIEW QUESTIONS

1. Why do corporations sell bonds? Why do investors purchase those bonds?

2. What is a debenture bond? How does a debenture bond differ from a mortgage bond?

3. A corporation may use one of two methods to ensure that it has sufficient funds available to redeem a bond issue. Explain the two methods.

4. Why do corporations issue convertible bonds? What are the advantages of purchasing a convertible bond?

5. What is the difference between a Treasury bill, a Treasury note, and a Treasury bond?

6. State and local bonds are classified as either general obligation bonds or revenue bonds. How do these classifications affect repayment of the bonds?

7. Describe the bond rating system used by Standard & Poor's and Moody's.

8. What is the difference between a registered bond and a coupon bond?

9. What are the major advantages of investing through a mutual fund?

10. How is the net asset value for a mutual fund determined?

11. There are closed-end funds, open-end funds, load funds, and no-load funds. How do these classifications affect your investment decisions?

12. What are the three options that investors can use to purchase mutual funds? What are the four options that investors can use to withdraw money from a mutual fund?

DISCUSSION QUESTIONS AND ACTIVITIES

1. In 1978, Susan and Bob Thompson invested $23,000 in Exxon corporate bonds and the American Capital Enterprise Fund. In 1986, their investment portfolio was valued at over $50,000. Explain how the Thompsons made money on their investments.

2. In 1986, the Thompsons decided to sell their Exxon bonds and to keep their shares in the American Capital Enterprise Fund. Would you have made the same decision? Why?

3. How would you evaluate a corporate bond? How would you evaluate a municipal bond?

4. All bonds are issued with a stated face value. But once a bond has been issued, its price may fluctuate. Why?

5. Assume that you are an investor with an extra $1,000 to invest. Would you choose bonds, mutual funds, or some other investment alternative? Why?

6. The managers of mutual funds tailor their investment portfolios to the objectives of their customers. Of the eight types of mutual funds described in this chapter, which seems most appropriate for your investment portfolio?

7. Today, there are all kinds of mutual funds for all kinds of investors. How would you evaluate a specific mutual fund for investment purposes?

ADDITIONAL READINGS

"Best and Worst of the Mutual Funds." *Changing Times*, October 1986, p. 30.

"Find a Fund to Match Your Goals." *Changing Times*, September 1986, p. 63.

"A Guide to Mutual Funds," *Consumer Reports*, June 1987, p. 352

"The Man Who Made Magellan Biggest and Best." *Fortune*, September 1, 1986, p. 58.

"1986 Annual Mutual Funds Survey." *Forbes*, September 8, 1986, Special Section, p. 100.

Steyer, Robert, "Going for High Yields with a Bit More Risk." *Fortune: The 1987 Investor's Guide*, p. 43.

Weinstein, George. "15 Mutual Funds That Let You Start Small." *Better Homes and Gardens*, June 1986, p. 32.

Wiener, Leonard. "The New Glitter in Savings Bonds." *U.S. News & World Report*, July 28, 1986, p. 44.

CASE 17–1 The ABC's of Bond Ratings

Are bonds safer than common or preferred stock? The answer to that question depends on a number of factors, such as who issued the bond, the likelihood of repayment at maturity, the conditions contained in the bond agreement, and the future outlook for the firm or government agency that issued the bond. Most investors rely on two financial services, Standard & Poor's and

Moody's, to provide ratings for bonds. Standard & Poor's bond ratings range from AAA (the highest) to D (the lowest). Moody's bond ratings range from Aaa (the highest) to C (the lowest). For most investors, a bond rated A or better is probably as safe as a blue-chip stock, while a C-rated bond could be as risky as the most speculative stock.

Recently, a number of corporate bond issues that lack an A rating or better from Standard & Poor's have been sold in the bond market. The reasons for the lower bond ratings vary. The corporation may have too much long-term debt. Its earnings may be too low. Changing economic conditions may make payment of interest or repayment of the bond principal doubtful. Whatever the reason, the corporations issuing these bonds had to increase the interest rate to attract purchasers. As a result, the bonds offer extremely attractive current yields to investors that are willing to take a chance. For example, a $1,000 corporate bond issued by Pan American Airlines is paying 13½ percent interest until maturity in the year 2003. The current market price is $960, which means that the yield is 14.1 percent. According to Standard & Poor's, the Pan American bond is rated CCC.

Questions

1. How important are the ratings issued by Standard & Poor's and Moody's? What does the Standard & Poor's CCC rating actually mean?

2. A 14.1 percent yield is at least 3 to 4 percent higher than the interest paid on more conservative corporate bond issues. Is an additional 3 to 4 percent in interest worth the added risks involved in purchasing a bond with lower ratings similar to the Pan American bond described above?

3. What other information would you need to evaluate the Pan American bond described above? Where would you get this information?

CASE 17–2 Fidelity's Magellan Mutual Fund

In 1963, the Magellan mutual fund was organized by Fidelity Distributors Corporation. The success of this fund over the past 23 years has been nothing less than phenomenal. For example, a $10,000 investment in the Magellan fund made back in 1976 was estimated to be worth over $185,000 in 1986. In 1986, the Magellan fund experienced a total return of 52 percent and, the fund had over $7 billion in assets. It is ranked number one in both 10-year and 5-year performance by Lipper Analytical Services. According to fund manager Peter Lynch, one third of the current Magellan portfolio is made up of growth stocks; one third, conservative stocks; and one third, special situation stocks.

Questions

1. Why would Fidelity's Magellan fund outperform all other mutual funds?

2. The minimum dollar amount required to open a Magellan account is $1,000. If you had $1,000, would you invest it in the Magellan fund?

3. The Magellan fund has been extremely successful over the past 10 years. Why is past performance an important factor in the evaluation of a mutual fund?

4. What other information would you need to evaluate the Magellan fund? Where would you get this information?

18

Real Estate and Other Investment Alternatives

In this chapter, we will discuss tangible investments, such as real estate, gold, silver, diamonds and other precious stones, works of art, rare coins, stamps, and antiques. We will also discuss intangible investments, such as commodities and futures, and speculative investments, such as short selling, margin transactions, and stock options and warrants. The advantages and disadvantages of real estate and other investment alternatives will be presented.

Traditionally, Americans have invested in real estate. It is an asset that we can see, touch, and smell, and it is generally a good hedge against inflation. But, as you will see, the choices in real estate investment are bewildering for the new investor. Furthermore, the Tax Reform Act of 1986 has lessened the appeal of investing in real estate.

After studying this chapter, you will be able to:

- Identify types of real estate investments.

- List the advantages of real estate investments.

- Discuss the disadvantages of real estate investments.

- Explain speculative investment techniques.

- Analyze the risks and rewards of investing in precious metals, gems, and other collectibles.

Interview with **Dan Bergman,** President and Owner,
ERA (Electronic Realty Associates) Country Cousin

Dan Bergman is the President and Owner of ERA (Electronic Realty Associates) Country Cousin. He conducts real estate training sessions for his employees and is actively involved in real estate sales.

A second home, a vacation residence, an apartment building, vacant land, and commercial property such as stores or office space are the most common alternatives for the real estate investor. Despite recent tax law changes, purchasing real estate for investment purposes still has definite advantages. If you own rental property, you can take tax deductions for all rental expenses, including depreciation, mortgage interest, property taxes, maintenance, repairs, insurance, and utilities. However, the new tax law does limit the use of losses to offset other income if you are not an active owner or manager of rental property.

Mr. Bergman cautions potential investors in real estate regarding the risks associated with such ventures. Economic conditions and interest rates will affect the demand for your property and your cost of borrowing. An oversupply of buildings in an area will influence your ability to rent space. In 1981, the average vacancy rate for commercial property in the downtown areas of 15 major cities was about 4 percent; in early 1987, the vacancy rate was nearly 16 percent.

Your investment success will also be affected by the condition of the property you buy. For apartment buildings, the best choices are usually buildings that are situated in stable neighborhoods and have low maintenance costs.

Despite the many legal, financial, and economic concerns associated with income-producing property, such property has good long-term investment potential. Current rental income should cover your operating expenses and even give you a positive cash flow; and the capital gain resulting from the appreciated value of the property can contribute to your future financial security.

In 1984, Murray Edwards was offered an unusual real estate deal by a customer who walked into his livestock feed business in rural Winters, Texas. "How'd you like to buy the Buffalo Gap post office?" the customer asked.

In purchasing that post office and three others, Edwards joined the growing number of small investors who buy post offices and then lease them back to the Postal Service. Although individual investors can buy other kinds of government buildings, none of these buildings have become as accessible or as popular as the post office.

In 1986, 28,000 of the approximately 35,000 U.S. post offices were privately owned.

Post offices have attracted investors because they offer both the economic advantage of a tax shelter and the prestige of owning a local landmark. Moreover, there is a wide range of locations and prices. The 106,000-square-foot post office in Wilkes-Barre, Pennsylvania, sold for $2,995,000; the 2,000-square-foot post office in Silverado, California, for $39,000.

With Congress tightening the laws governing tax shelters, many real estate experts be-

lieved that post offices would afford more room for investors who were looking for a profit rather than a shelter. These experts thought that the prices of post offices would drop and that post office leases would probably be structured more liberally for those who owned the buildings. As a result, "more mom and pop investors are going to be getting into post offices," predicted John Dounian, vice president of Chancellor Investments, a Los Angeles real estate firm specializing in the brokerage of post offices.

Investing in a post office, especially an older one, is not a

INVESTING IN REAL ESTATE

- Types of Real Estate Investments

Real estate investments are classified as direct or indirect. In **direct investment**, the investor holds legal title to the property. Direct real estate investments include single-family dwellings, duplexes, apartments, land, and nonresidential real estate.

In **indirect investment**, the investors appoint a trustee to hold legal title on behalf of all the investors in the group. Limited partnerships and syndicates, real estate investment trusts, mortgages, and mortgage pools are examples of indirect real estate investments. Figure 18–1 summarizes the advantages and disadvantages of the two types of investments.

Direct Real Estate Investments

Your Home as an Investment.[1] Until recent years, few people regarded their homes as investments. During a long period, from 1880 to 1945, the prices of single-family houses rose less than the Consumer Price Index

---

[1] This section is based on Wilbur W. Widicus and Thomas E. Stitzel, *Personal Investing*, 4th ed. (Homewood, Ill.: Richard D. Irwin, 1985), pp. 338–40. © 1985 Richard D. Irwin, Inc.

sure bet. Many older post offices have long-term leases that can leave the investor vulnerable to rising costs from inflation or taxes.

King James Weyant, Jr., a retiree from Lauderhill, Florida, said in 1986 that he had already lost more than $7,000 on a post office in Fort Montgomery, New York. Weyant, who built the post office in 1971, said that his 30-year lease hadn't kept pace with inflation. Also, a planned municipal sewer system, unanticipated in 1971, was going to cost Weyant an extra $1,000 a year. "It's been a very, very sad experi-ence for me," said Weyant. "I expect to lose money on this until the lease expires in 2001."

Some investors suggest that people who buy new post offices should insist on short-term leases and should choose post offices on desirable sites so that if the lease is not renewed, the property will be easy to rent or sell. Albert Y. Chow, a medical technologist in Montebello, California, who owned eight California post offices in 1986, insisted on having 10-year leases with no options to renew; he also insisted that the Postal Service pay maintenance expenses. Moreover, he in-vested only in centrally located post offices that had about 10 years remaining on a lease. "I want to be in the driver's seat," he said, "not the Postal Service."

"I think it's a reasonably secure investment," said James T. Coe, director of the Postal Service's Office of Real Estate. "It is very secure in terms of the credit stability of your tenant."

*Adapted from Brett Skakun, "Investors Find Profits, Pitfalls in Post Offices," *The Wall Street Journal*, August 19, 1986, p. 31.

(CPI). Since that time, however, housing prices have risen more rapidly than the Consumer Price Index. Therefore, the family home has become identified as an asset that can maintain its purchasing power.

Figure 18–2 shows percentage increases in the CPI, the Standard and Poor's 500 Stock Average, and an index of the average price of existing homes. In this figure, the base year is 1970. Index numbers for later years are compared with the 1970 index levels. For example, CPI level rose from 116.3 in 1970 to 121.3 in 1971. The percentage change was

$$\frac{121.3 - 116.3}{116.3} = 0.0430, \text{ or } 4.3\%$$

It is obvious from Figure 18–2 that from 1970 to 1983 the value of existing homes increased, on average, more rapidly than did the CPI. Therefore, home ownership was protected against inflation. During the same period, the stock market averages performed poorly relative to either the housing price index or the CPI. (The average stock prices shown in Figure 18–2 do

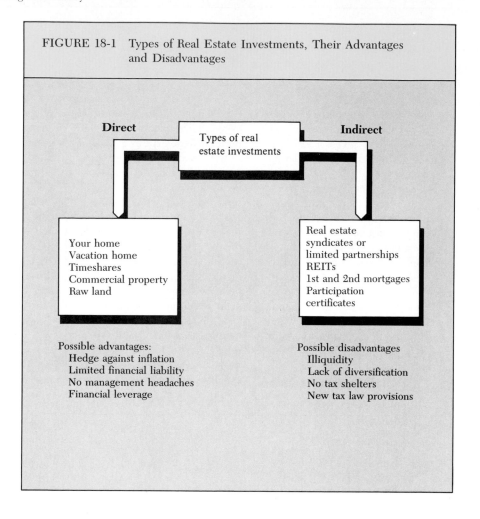

FIGURE 18-1   Types of Real Estate Investments, Their Advantages and Disadvantages

not include dividends received. These increased stock profits somewhat, but not greatly.)

Despite the Tax Reform Act of 1986, your home probably remains the best investment you will ever make.[2] The new act preserves the mortgage interest deduction for your primary residence and for a second house, and you are able to continue writing off your property taxes. However, the deductions for mortgage interest and property taxes are probably worth less to you under the new act because you are likely to be in a lower tax bracket after 1986. Thus, the after-tax cost of owning your home is higher.

The new tax act still allows you to defer taxes on the profits from the sale of your home if you reinvest the money within two years in a dwelling that costs as much as or more than your previous one. If you are 55 or older, you

[2]This discussion is adapted from *Money*, October 1986, p. 166; and *The Wall Street Journal*, December 1, 1986, p. 24D, and October 29, 1986, p. 27.

FIGURE 18-2   Every Year since 1977, the Prices of Existing Homes Increased Faster than the CPI and S&P 500 Index

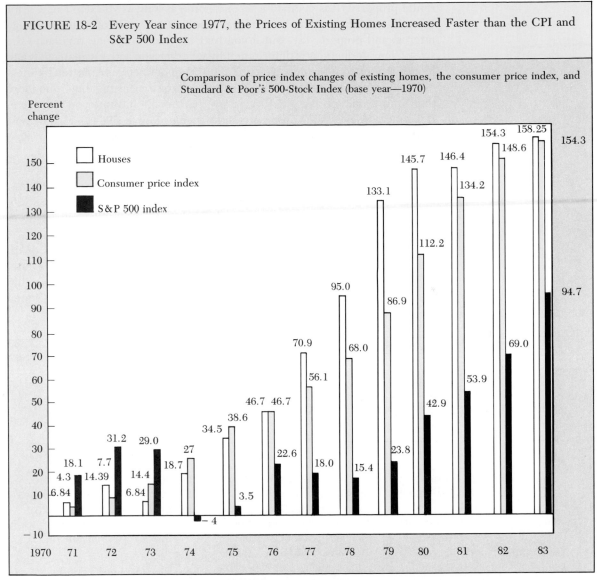

Comparison of price index changes of existing homes, the consumer price index, and Standard & Poor's 500-Stock Index (base year—1970)

Sources: *Federal Home Loan Bank Board Bulletin;* Standard & Poor's, Inc.; and U.S. Bureau of Labor Statistics.

can also take advantage of the onetime $125,000 capital gains exclusion on your profit.

Your Vacation Home.[3] If you have a vacation home, the after-tax cost of owning it rises in 1987. Just how much it rises depends largely on whether the Internal Revenue Service views the place as your second home or as a

[3] Ibid.

rental property. It is deemed a second home as long as you don't rent it for more than 14 days a year, and in that case you can write off your mortgage interest and property tax. But if you rent the vacation home regularly, the size of your deductions is determined by whether you actively manage it and by the size of your income. You are allowed to deduct your mortgage interest, property taxes, and expenses for the house as long as the total is no more than your rental income plus any passive partnership income you may have. If your expenses on the house exceed the income you derive from it, the new rules let you deduct up to $25,000 of your annual losses on the house against your salary and your investment income.

Timesharing or Interval Ownership. Timesharing, or interval ownership, is the use of a vacation home for a limited, preplanned time. According to the Federal Trade Commission, since 1975 timeshare sales have nearly doubled every year.

There are two types of timesharing plans: *deeded* and *nondeeded*. With the deeded plan, you buy an ownership interest in a piece of real estate. With the nondeeded plan, you buy a lease, a license, or a club membership that lets you use the property a specific amount of time each year for a stated

---

Personal Financial Planning and You
What You Should Know about Timesharing

To enable consumers make informed vacation purchases, the National TimeSharing Council (NTC) of the American Land Development Association publishes both a consumer's guide to timesharing and a directory of NTC member resorts.

Timesharing is a relatively new vacation concept that allows consumers to purchase vacation time—generally in one-week increments—at resorts all over the country. In early 1985, approximately 950 timeshare resorts could be found in the United States, primarily in the Sunbelt states but also in other traditional vacation states from the Rocky Mountains to New England.

The *NTC Consumer's Guide to Resort and Urban Timesharing* explains how the timeshare concept works, the various forms of timeshare ownership, how to select a timesharing resort, and what questions to ask the resort developer. The *Directory of NTC Timesharing Resorts* provides a state-by-state list of available properties and the recreational facilities provided at each. It is designed to assist consumers in making informed choices by enabling them to see—and visit—the wide range of available timeshare resorts.

The NTC directory of member resorts and the consumer's guide may be purchased for a combined price of $6. Separately, the directory is $5 and the guide is $2. *Helpful Hints*, a pamphlet, is available for $1. Orders should be sent to the National TimeSharing Council, Suite 510, 1220 L Street, NW, Washington, D.C. 20005.

number of years. With both plans, your cost is proportional to the length of time per year you buy.

Before you sign any papers, evaluate any investment claims made by the seller. The future value of a timeshare depends on many factors. Resale of the timeshare may be difficult. You may meet with competition from the firm that sold you the timeshare, or local real estate brokers may not want to include the timeshare in their listings. Closing costs, broker commissions, and financing charges should also be considered. What you should know about timesharing, including its major advantages and disadvantages, is summarized in the accompanying boxed feature.

Besides investing in your home, your vacation home, and your timeshare, you may consider investing in commercial property.

Commercial Property.[4] The term **commercial property** refers to land and buildings that produce lease or rental income. Such property includes duplexes, apartments, hotels, office buildings, stores, and all sorts of other types of commercial establishments. Aside from a home, the real property

[4]This section is adapted from Widicus and Stitzel, *Personal Investing*, pp. 349–50. © 1985 Richard D. Irwin, Inc.

The major advantages of timeshare ownership are:

1.   Guaranteed availability of space.
2.   Tax deductibility of interest and taxes.
3.   Potential capital gain as an inflation hedge.
4.   Proprietor's interest and pride of ownership.
5.   Flexibility of exchanging time periods.
6.   Possibility of worldwide exchange program.
7.   Some costs are fixed (e.g., mortgage costs).

The major weaknesses of timeshare ownership appear to be:

1.   The price is usually higher than other comparable properties.
2.   The management costs are higher than for condominiums or townhouses.
3.   The investor may have to go to the same place every year at the same time.
4.   It is not like owning your own apartment or a townhouse.
5.   Your anticipated gain might not occur, and with

enough planning you might be able to rent an apartment elsewhere at no greater cost to you and without making a $6,000 to $12,000 investment. In fact, some timeshare ownership units can be sold only to the managers and at the original price, with no gain going to the investor.

Sources: *Midwest Investor*, Wheaton, Illinois, Summer 1985, p. 4; and Frederick Amling and William G. Droms, *Personal Financial Management*, 2nd ed. (Homewood, Ill.: Richard D. Irwin, 1986), p. 490. © 1986 Richard D. Irwin, Inc.

investment most widely favored by the small investor is the duplex, four-plex, or small apartment building. Many investors have been able to acquire sizable commercial properties by first investing in a duplex and then "trading up" to larger units as equity in the original property increased.

The investment potential of commercial property, unlike that of raw land or a personal residence, can be accurately measured. There are several methods for doing this, all of which compare the expected future income from a property with the cost of the property. Figure 18–3 shows one method that may be used to calculate the expected profitability of commercial properties. More sophisticated analytic methods are being used, but this one covers most of the areas of investigation. Its greatest weaknesses are that the analysis covers a maximum of three years and that the expected market or sales price of the property plays no role in the analysis.

Figure 18–3 contains information about a six-year-old 10-unit apartment that is assumed to be for sale. When such a property is placed on the market, the real estate broker listing it prepares information of the type contained in this figure. If the property is not listed, the seller prepares this information. Typically, only current-year information is supplied.

You must examine such information as carefully as possible, paying particular attention to the expense and income items. The information describing Outflow Apartments was created by using expense, income, and other ratios obtained from the National Institute of Real Estate Brokers. This trade group collects cost, revenue, and other information on real property investments on a nationwide basis. The ratios, which are classified by the size, type, and location of property, give a rough guide to what the costs and revenues of different types of commercial properties should be. Some companies and other trade groups compile similar information.

The upper section of the form in Figure 18–3 identifies the property, tells what type of property it is, and furnishes information on its assessed value. The accuracy of the assessed value can usually be checked by examining city or county property tax records.

In this form, the term *land* refers to the real estate on which the commercial property has been built. "Improvements" are the structures and other real property that are considered attached to the land. "Personal property" includes refrigerators, freestanding stoves, furniture, drapes, and other appliances that are not considered real property.

Income and Expenses. "Gross scheduled income" is the total amount of income that would be obtained if the apartments were completely rented and all rents were paid. But commercial properties are seldom fully rented, and rents sometimes cannot be collected. "Gross operating income" is what remains after these losses.

"Operating expenses" are the nonfinancial expenses of operating the apartments. Traditionally, each expense category of this income statement is divided by gross scheduled income to provide a relative measure of each cost. Estimates of income and expenses must be made for new properties. Owners of existing properties typically provide the most recent year's income statement to prospective buyers. Taxes and utility expenses can usu-

FIGURE 18-3 Current Year Income Analysis for Outflow Apartments

Property name _Outflow Apartments_ Type _Ten Plex_

Location _____ List price _$ 200,000_

Assessed value: _$151,500_ _100_ % Less loans _$ 140,000_

    Land _30,000_ _20_ % = List price equity _$60,000_

    Improvements _120,000_ _79_ %

    Personal property _1,500_ _1_ %

	Year 1	%	Year 2	%	Year 3	%
Gross scheduled income	30,000	100				
Less vacancy and credit losses	1,500	5				
= Gross operating income	28,500	95				
Less operating expenses						
Taxes	5,700	19				
Utilities	1,200	4				
Insurance	300	1				
Management	2,400	8				
Services	200	1				
Supplies						
Maintenance	1,500	5				
Other	200	1				
Total expense	11,500	39				
= Net operating income	17,000	56				
Less loan payments	16,022					
= Gross spendable income	978					
Plus principal repayment	2868					
= Gross equity income	3846					
Less depreciation	7272					
= Taxable income	(3426)					

Source: Widicus and Stitzel, _Personal Investing_, p. 350. © 1985 Richard D. Irwin, Inc.

ally be verified by examining receipts. It is much more difficult to check the accuracy of most other expense and income items.

    "Net operating income" represents the income from the investment before financing payments and depreciation. A widely used measure of the gross profitability of such an investment is the ratio of net operating income (NOI) to the cost of the property. In this example, the ratio of operating income earned to the list price is

$$\frac{\text{NOI}}{\text{List price}} = \text{Rate of return}$$

$$\frac{\$17,000}{\$200,000} = 0.085, \text{ or } 8.5\%$$

A similar ratio of gross operating income to market price is also calculated. Both ratios are often used by appraisers and lenders.

   Financing and Depreciation Charges. Financing and depreciation are so important that even after the Tax Reform Act of 1986, they are handled separately from operating expenses. Beginning in 1987, the depreciation stretches to 27½ years for residential buildings and 31½ years for other commercial property. The Tax Reform Act of 1986 dictates straight-line depreciation: an equal percentage of the cost must be deducted each year. In Figure 18–3, the allowed depreciation is $200,000 divided by 27½ years, that is, $7,272 per year.

   Figure 18–4 shows a three-year loan schedule. This schedule assumes that the purchaser can assume the balance of a 25-year, 7.5 percent loan ($89,675) and can obtain an additional loan at 13 percent, for total financing of $140,000. The original loan has 19 more years to run before it is paid off; the second loan will also have a 19-year maturity.

   Returning to Figure 18–3, you can see how financing costs are deducted from net operating income to produce gross spendable income. Adding the yearly principal repayment on loans to gross spendable income produces gross equity income. Subtracting yearly depreciation costs from this figure gives a loss of $3,426 for the first year that this investment is held. Gross

---

FIGURE 18-4   Financing Schedule for Outflow Apartments

Existing financing:

	Principal Amount	Term	Annual Payment	Interest Rate
1st loan	$100,000	25 years	$8,868	7½%

Proposed financing:

	Principal Amount	Term	Annual Payment	Interest Rate
1st loan	$ 89,675	19 years	$ 8,868	7½%
2nd loan	50,325	19 years	7,156	13

Repayment schedule, all loans:

Year	Interest Paid	Principal Paid	Total Payment	Principal Remaining
1	$13,154	$2,868	$16,022	$137,132
2	12,892	3,130	16,022	134,002
3	12,604	3,418	16,022	130,584

Source: Widicus and Stitzel, *Personal Investing*, p. 352. © 1985 Richard D. Irwin, Inc.

spendable income and gross equity income are often divided by the amount of the investor's equity to compare returns with the equity investment.

Outflow Apartments' gross spendable income is only $978, but depreciation reduces the owner's taxable income by $3,426. If the owner were in the new marginal 28 percent income tax bracket, his or her taxes would be lowered by

$$0.28 \times \$3,426 = \$959$$

This amount is often called a *tax saving*. Deducting this amount from the book loss shown on the income analysis form results in an after-tax cost of only $2,467.

$$\$3,426 - \$959 = \$2,467$$

The investment still produces a loss, but that loss is lowered by the investment's income tax effects.

Many real property investors are interested primarily in the yearly after-tax cash returns (or losses) from their investments. Traditionally, these returns are calculated by using the following format, in which amounts from Figure 18–3 have been rearranged to show the after-tax cash cost of holding Outflow Apartments.

Net operating income	$17,000
Less: Financing payments	16,022
= Gross spendable income	978
Less: Income tax	959
Net spendable cash	$ 19

So far, Outflow Apartments appears to be a poorer investment than almost anything you could imagine. However, we have not considered market price appreciation. Practically all real property prices have risen dramatically in recent years. Many people expect these price rises to continue and look to them for profits. They are quite willing to hold real property that breaks even on a cash basis, or even runs a cash loss, hoping to take their profits in a lump sum when they sell the property.

The Outflow Apartments investment would be highly profitable if its value were to increase by 6 percent per year. The investment would then be worth $212,000 in one year, $224,720 in two, $238,203 in three, and $267,645 in five. Because the investor has never had more than $60,000 of equity in the apartments, large profits on invested equity would be created if prices rose at this rate. Continued market price increases will cause real property to be sold at what seem to be unjustifiably high prices.

Under the new tax act, such deductions as the mortgage interest, depreciation, property taxes, and other expenses of rental property are limited to the amount of rental income you receive. Any excess deductions are considered a passive loss and—with some exceptions—can be used only to offset income from a similar activity, such as another rental property. A passive activity is a business or trade in which you do not materially participate or rental activity. Passive loss is the total amount of losses from a passive activity minus the total income from the passive activity.

Raw Land. With the passage of the new tax act, popular real estate investments—the typical suburban garden apartments—were no longer tempting real estate investors. Instead, these investors were favoring more exotic property, such as raw land ripe for development. "Land is a very sexy investment right now," said Lawrence Krause, a San Francisco financial adviser.[5]

There was good reason for the interest. In recent years, land costs had been the fastest-rising component in the cost of housing, increasing 20 percent in 1986 in most eastern, midwestern, and California markets. In addition, syndicators described land investments as unaffected by the new tax act. Moreover, the new act enabled investors to improve raw land without suffering a tax penalty.[6]

If land investments promised tremendous gains, they also posed enormous risks, as investors with land in the oil patch could attest. With their money riding on a single parcel, investors could end up owning overpriced cropland in the event of a building slowdown or an economic downturn.

Many investors buy land with the intention of subdividing it. Purchases of this kind are speculative because of the many risks involved.[7] You must be certain that water, sewers, and other utilities will be available. The most common and least expensive way of obtaining water and sewage service is by hooking onto existing facilities of an adjoining city or town.

Many towns and cities now refuse to annex property or provide water and sewage service without an affirmative vote of the citizens. This adds another element of uncertainty to what is usually an already risky proposition. Wells and septic tanks might serve the same purposes, but they are typically more expensive. In many parts of the country, well water is not easily found. County land zoning ordinances may rule against septic tanks or may allow them only on lots that are at least one-half acre in size. Unless the area is remote, telephone and electric service is seldom a problem because of the ease with which electric lines can be installed.

Thus far, we have focused on direct real estate investments, in which the investor holds legal title to the property. In the next section, you will learn how you can invest in real estate without the hassles of direct ownership.

Indirect Real Estate Investments

Bernice R. Hecker, a Seattle, Washington, anesthesiologist, made her first real estate investment in 1985. She joined a partnership that bought an office building in Midland, Texas. "Why real estate? Probably superstition,"

[5] Robert Guenther, "Future Growth Draws Investors to Land," *The Wall Street Journal*, October 1, 1986, p. 31.

[6] Ibid.

[7] This section is adapted from Widicus and Stitzel, *Personal Investing*, pp. 347–48. © 1985 Richard D. Irwin, Inc.

she said. "I wanted a tangible asset. I felt I could evaluate a piece of property much more readily" than stocks, bonds, or "a cattle ranch."[8]

Dr. Hecker used one of the three basic methods of investing in real estate. The three methods, each of which offers progressively more risk and higher potential rewards, are real estate syndicates, which are partnerships that buy properties; real estate investment trusts (REITs), which are stockholder-owned real estate companies; and direct investments, which were explained in the preceding section.

Real Estate Syndicates or Limited Partnerships. A **syndicate** is a temporary association of individuals or firms, organized to perform a specific task that requires a large amount of capital.[9] The syndicate may be organized as a corporation, as a trust, or, more commonly, as a limited partnership.

The limited partnership works as follows. It is formed by a general partner, who has unlimited liability for its liabilities. The general partner then sells participation units to the limited partners, whose liability is generally limited to the extent of their initial investment, say $5,000 or $10,000. Limited liability is particularly important in real estate syndicates because their mortgage debt obligations may exceed the net worth of the participants.

In addition to limited liability, a real estate syndicate provides professional management for its members. A syndicate that owns several properties may also provide diversification.

Traditionally, real estate syndicates have been tax shelters for the investors, but the Tax Reform Act of 1986 is limiting the creativity of real estate syndicators. It hits real estate syndicates particularly hard by preventing losses from "passive" investments in partnerships from offsetting income from other sources. It also limits deductions of interest and depreciation and increases the tax on capital gains.[10]

Under the new tax act, all real estate investors will have their depreciation deductions for all commercial property spread out, from 19½ to 31½ years. And interest expense and other losses that tax-oriented partnerships generate—passive losses—can offset passive income only—that is, income from other limited partnerships. So if you have dividends, interest income, wages, and so on from other sources, you can't shelter it any more.[11] Whether you can shelter your income or not, Bradford Mead, vice president for finance at Baron Resources Corporation, a firm that sells real estate limited partnerships, stated, "We don't expect the tax overhaul law to affect the investments much, because our properties generate cash—a 12 percent return to investors." Read the accompanying boxed feature to learn how Baron brings business savvy to innkeeping.

[8]Joanne Lipman, "Land and Opportunity," *The Wall Street Journal*, December 2, 1985, p. 22D.

[9]Robert J. Hughes and Jack R. Kapoor, BUSINESS, (Boston, Mass.: Houghton Mifflin Company), p. 82. © Houghton Mifflin Company.

[10]Laurie P. Cohen, "Real Estate Syndicators Changing Tactics in Advance of Tax Overhaul," *The Wall Street Journal*, July 31, 1986, p. 23.

[11]*Financial World*, October 28, 1986, p. 15.

Real Estate Investment Trusts (REITs). Another way for the small investor to invest in big-time real estate deals is the real estate investment trust (REIT). A **REIT** is similar to a mutual fund or an investment company, and it trades on stock exchanges or over the counter. Like mutual funds, REITs pool investor funds, along with borrowed funds, and invest them directly in real estate or use them to make construction or mortgage loans.

There are three types of REITs. Equity REITs—which invest directly in properties—comprise 57 percent of all REITs. Mortgage REITs—which pool money to finance construction loans and mortgages on developed properties—comprise 24 percent. Hybrid REITs—combinations of mortgage and equity REITs—comprise 19 percent.[12]

Federal law requires REITs to:

- Distribute at least 95 percent of their net annual earnings to shareholders.

[12] Jim Henderson, "Real Estate: Beckoning Bargain Buyers," *USA Today*, January 13, 1986, p. 10E.

In the News
Rare Marriage: Investor Brings Business Savvy to Innkeeping

After more than seven years of owning and operating the 39-room New England Inn in North Conway, New Hampshire, Joe and Linda Johnston were unwilling to invest an additional $500,000 to upgrade the place. "We decided we were tired of working and being broke all the time," said Joe Johnston. "That's really what it came down to. It was time for another operator to take over." So in 1986 the Johnstons sold the inn for $1.6 million and moved to their new home on Cape Cod, Massachusetts.

The Johnstons' experience is typical of the cycle that country inn owners go through. Purchasers charmed by what they think is the lifestyle of the innkeeper later discover the realities of the hospitality industry. The major difference in the Johnstons' case is that their buyer wasn't another couple experimenting with innkeeping but a corporation that sells investors shares in real estate limited partnerships.

The buyer, Baron Resources Corporation, has carved a niche for itself with investments in historic New England inns. Since 1984, the small Avon, Connecticut, company has bought and packaged six country inns for investors. It has found that the romance of owning an inn without the day-to-day management headaches appeals to many people, especially when ownership entitles them to a 50 percent discount on their inn bills.

So far, Baron has had little difficulty in finding good properties for sale. Gene Bellows, a former inn owner and now vice president of Baron, says that many inn purchasers expect the lifestyle of the innkeeper in

- Not engage in speculative, short-term holding of real estate in order to sell for quick profits.
- Hire independent real estate professionals to carry out certain management activities.
- Have at least 100 shareholders. No more than half the shares may be owned by five or fewer people.

The new law is expected to increase the attractiveness of organizing and investing in REITs. In fact, the new tax law could be the greatest boon to REITs since the tax code was changed in 1960 to allow REITs to avoid corporate taxes, according to James B. Hoover, a specialist in REITs.[13]

Because the new tax act decreases the marginal tax rates of individuals, income-oriented investments such as REITs are expected to be in greater demand. For example, the price of National Medical's Health Care Property Investors stock (a REIT specializing in the health care industry) rose from

[13] Rhonda L. Rundle, "REITs Find a Home in Health Care Industry," *The Wall Street Journal*, August 27, 1986, p. 6.

"The Bob Newhart Show" only to learn that it's more like the frenetic life that is depicted in "Fawlty Towers," a British TV comedy series. As a result, many owners sell their property within a few years.

It's one thing for a property to look good in a sales brochure but quite another for the property to look attractive to investors. In 1986, Bradford Mead, Baron's vice president for finance, said that the four inns in Baron partnerships in the preceding year averaged a 31 percent return for an investor in the 50 percent tax bracket. And

Mead didn't "expect the tax overhaul bill to affect the investments much, because our properties generate cash—a 12 percent return to investors."

Baron's financial data suggest that from 1971 to 1986 historic inns appreciated at about 15 percent annually. Baron assumes that this robust appreciation will continue and that room rates will increase by an average 5 percent a year, while operating expenses will grow by an average 4 percent a year. Eventually, Baron expects to sell its inns at 10 times net operating income.

But Baron isn't simply counting on inflation to increase the value of its inns. Better marketing, experienced management, and tighter cost controls all play roles in enhancing the returns. As an incentive to star innkeepers, Baron offers an ownership position in the parent corporation.

Source: Robert Guenther, "Rare Marriage: Investor Brings Business Savvy to Innkeeping," *The Wall Street Journal*, September 24, 1986, p. 33.

$20 a share in May 1985, when it went public, to $29.75 a share in October 1986.[14]

The investor may choose among more than 200 REITs. Further information on REITs can be obtained from the National Association of Real Estate Investment Trusts, 1101 17th Street, NW, Washington, DC 20036.

Investing in First and Second Mortgages. Mortgages and other debt contracts are commonly purchased by the more well-to-do members of most communities. Often, the purchaser of a mortgage takes on some sort of risk that the financial institutions that ordinarily provide mortgage financing refuse to accept. Perhaps the mortgage is on a property for which there is no ready market. Perhaps the title to the property is not legally clear. Perhaps the title is not insurable. At any rate, many people purchase such mortgages.

[14] Ibid.

In the Real World
Uncle Sam and His Family

The government securities named Maes and Macs can offer safety and relatively high yields for the right investor.

1. *Ginnie Mae*—Government National Mortgage Association (GNMA)

Introduced the first mortgage-backed securities in 1970 and still dominates this market.

The residential mortgage-backed securities are packaged in pools and then resold to investors as certificates ($25,000), or as shares by mutual funds.

Regular payments to investors are guaranteed by the GNMA—an agency of the Department of Housing and Urban Development.

Ginnie Maes are backed by the full faith and credit of the federal government.

The average life of mortgages is 12 years.

2. *Freddie Mac*—Federal Home Loan Mortgage Corporation (FHLMC)

Issues mortgage-backed securities similar to Ginnie Maes.

The pools of fixed rate home mortgages are made up of conventional home loans rather than mortgages insured by the FHA or the VA.

The timely payment of interest and the *ultimate* payment of principal are guaranteed.

3. *Fannie Mae*—Federal National Mortgage Association (FNMA)

Issues mortgage-backed securities similar to Ginnie Maes and Freddie Macs.

The pools of fixed rate home mortgages are similar to Freddie Macs, not Ginnie Maes.

Like Ginnie Maes, Fannie Maes guarantee a fair share of interest and principal *every month* even if homeowners do not meet their obligations.

As with Ginnie Maes and Freddie Macs, newly issued Fannie Mae certificates require a minimum investment of $25,000; the older certificates

Investments of this kind may provide relatively high rates of return because of their special risk characteristics.

Most financial institutions will not make loans on second or third mortgages; these loans are left mainly to individuals. Such debt contracts are riskier than first mortgages because of their junior legal status, but they pay higher interest yields.

Participation Certificates. If you want risk-proof real estate investment, participation certificates (PCs) are for you. Participation certificates are sold by such federal agencies as the Government National Mortgage Association (Ginnie Mae), the Federal Home Loan Mortgage Corporation (Freddie Mac), the Federal National Mortgage Association (Fannie Mae), and the Student Loan Marketing Association (Sallie Mae). A few states issue little siblings, such as the State of New York Mortgage Agency (Sonny Mae) and the New England Education Loan Marketing Corporation (Nellie Mae).

(whose principal has been partially paid off) require an investment of as little as $10,000.

4. *Sallie Mae*—Student Loan Marketing Association

Created by Congress in 1972 to provide a national secondary market for government-guaranteed student loans.

Issues bonds, each of which is backed by Sallie Mae as a whole, rather than specific pools of loans.

Sallie Mae bonds are considered virtually as safe as government Treasuries.

Brokers sell bonds having minimum denominations of $10,000.

Investors can also buy shares of Sallie Mae *stock:* the corporation is government chartered but publicly owned, and its shares are traded on the New York Stock Exchange.

5. *Sonny Mae*—State of New York Mortgage Agency

Issues bonds backed by fixed rate single-family home mortgages and uses proceeds to subsidize below-market-rate mortgages for first-time home buyers.

As with ordinary bonds, interest on Sonny Maes is paid only until the bonds mature.

Sonny Maes are exempt from federal income tax, and

New York State residents do not pay state income tax on them.

6. *Nellie Mae*—New England Education Loan Marketing Corporation

A nonprofit corporation created by the Commonwealth of Massachusetts.

Provides a secondary market for federally guaranteed student loans issued in Massachusetts and New Hampshire.

The AAA-rated Nellie Mae bonds mature in three years.

The bonds are sold in minimum denominations of $5,000.

Uncle Sam and His Family: Government Participation Certificates

Illustration by Randall Enos in *Money*, November 1984, p. 97. By permission of the artist.

A **participation certificate** is an equity investment in a pool of mortgages that have been purchased by these government agencies. Maes and Macs are guaranteed by agencies closely tied to the federal government, making them just as secure as Uncle Sam's own bonds and notes. At one time, you needed a minimum of $25,000 to invest in PCs. Thanks to Maes and Macs mutual funds, you now need as little as $1,000 to buy shares in a unit trust or a mutual fund whose portfolio consists entirely of these securities. Either way, you assume the role of a mortgage lender. Each month, as payments are made on the mortgages, you receive interest and principal by check, or if you wish, the mutual fund will reinvest the amount for you.[15]

[15] Anne McGrath, "The Saga of Ginnie Mae Takes a Sorry Turn," *U.S. News & World Report*, July 28, 1986, p. 42; "Ginnie Maes: Even Some Brokers Don't Understand Them," *Personal Investor*, April 1985, pp. 50–54; and *Money*, Diane Harris, "Ginnie Mae and Kin," November 1984, pp. 97–104.

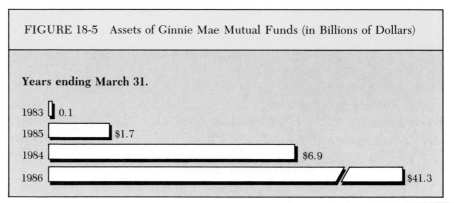

FIGURE 18-5   Assets of Ginnie Mae Mutual Funds (in Billions of Dollars)

Years ending March 31.

1983   0.1
1985 $1.7
1984 $6.9
1986 $41.3

Sources: Lipper Analytical Services; and *U.S. News & World Report*, July 28, 1986, p. 42.

The growth in Ginnie Mae mutual funds has been spectacular. As Figure 18–5 shows, between 1983 (when shares in these funs were first sold) and March 1986, some $41 billion poured in, according to Lipper Analytical Services.[16] Figure 18–6 shows a sample Ginnie Mae certificate. Figure 18–7 shows an advertisement for a Ginnie Mae mutual fund.

Advantages of Real Estate Investments

- Advantages of Real Estate Investments

There are so many kinds of real estate investments that blanket statements about their investment advantages and disadvantages are not possible. However, certain types of real estate investments may possess some of the following advantages.

A Hedge against Inflation. Real property equity investments usually provide protection against purchasing power risk. In some areas, the prices of homes have increased dramatically. For example, in Hawaii, California, and Washington, D.C., they have increased 15 to 20 percent per year or more. It has not been uncommon for real estate investors to buy a house for $100,000 and sell it for $125,000 six months later. One woman sold her house for $160,000. Then, two days after it was put back on the market, she realized that she had sold it too cheaply and bought it back for $165,000. After painting the house inside and out, she sold it for $190,000.

Easy Entry. You can gain entry to a shopping center or a large apartment building by investing as little as $5,000 in a limited partnership. The minimum capital requirements for the total venture may be as high as $1 million or more, which is beyond the limits of a typical real estate investor.

---

[16] Anne McGrath, "The Saga of Ginnie Mae Takes a Sorry Turn," *U.S. News & World Report*, July 28, 1986, p. 42.

FIGURE 18-6   Ginnie Mae Certificates Combine Features of Both Bonds and Mortgages

Source: *The Wall Street Journal,* January 9, 1987, p. 34.

Limited Financial Liability. If you are a limited partner, you are not liable for losses beyond your initial investment. That can be important if the venture is speculative and rewards are not assured. General partners, however, must bear all financial risks.

No Management Headaches. If you have invested in limited partnerships, REITs, mortgages, or participation certificates, you do not need to worry about paperwork and accounting, maintenance chores, and other administrative duties.

Financial Leverage. *Financial leverage* is the use of borrowed funds for investment purposes. It enables you to acquire a more expensive property than you could on your own. This is an advantage when property values and incomes are rising. Assume that you buy a $100,000 property with no loan and then sell it for $120,000. The $20,000 gain represents a 20 percent return on your $100,000 investment. Then assume instead that you invest

FIGURE 18-7   Mutual Fund Firms, such as the Dreyfus GNMA Fund, Have Been Aggressively Promoting Ginnie Maes for Investors.

only $10,000 of your own money and borrow the other $90,000 (90 percent financing). Now you have made $20,000 on your $10,000 investment, or a 200 percent return.

Other traditional advantages of real estate investments, such as deductions for interest, property taxes, depreciation, deferred capital gains, and personal federal income taxes have been restricted or eliminated under the

Tax Reform Act of 1986. Previously, these were tax advantages; now they are disadvantages.

Disadvantages of Real Estate Investments

● Disadvantages of Real
Estate Investments

Real estate investments have several disadvantages. However, these disadvantages do not affect all kinds of real estate investments to the same extent.

Declining Property Values. As discussed earlier, real property investments usually provide a hedge against inflation. But during deflationary and recessionary periods, the value of such investments may decline. For example, hundreds of developers, lenders, and investors have been victims of a deflation in commercial real estate that began sporadically in the early 1980s.[17] In many cities, skyscraper office rentals have dropped 25 to 40 percent. Occupancy rates at certain kinds of hotels, apartments, resort properties, and condominium high-rises have also plummeted, and in most cases so has their value. Cities once thought immune to a real estate recession, such as San Francisco, Salt Lake City, Phoenix, Chicago, and Dallas, have been hammered. In areas already hurt by the energy slump, such as Houston, Denver, and Tulsa, things have grown markedly worse.[18]

Since 1982, banks and thrift institutions have reported real estate–related losses of more than $10 billion, dwarfing the losses in any previous period since the Great Depression. Additional losses of many billions of dollars have hit developers and investors whose equity stakes were wiped out in foreclosures; insurance companies and pension funds that made real estate loans, and the federal insurance agencies that bear the costs of closing banks and thrifts ruined by bad real estate loans.[19]

Illiquidity. Perhaps the largest drawback of direct real estate investments is the absence of large, liquid, and relatively efficient markets for them. Whereas stocks or bonds can generally be sold in a few minutes at the market price, this is not the case for real estate. It may take months to sell your commercial property or your limited partnership shares.

Lack of Diversification. Diversification in direct real estate investments is difficult because of the large size of most real estate projects. REITs, Ginnie Maes, Freddie Macs, and other syndicates, however, do provide various levels of diversification.

To these traditional disadvantages of real estate investments, the Tax Reform Act of 1986 adds the following tax-related problems.

---

[17] Peter Waldman and William Celis III, "Empty Buildings," *The Wall Street Journal*, September 4, 1986, p. 1.

[18] Ibid.

[19] Ibid.

No Tax Shelter. First and foremost, the new act limits the ability of taxpayers to use losses generated by real estate investments to offset income gained from other sources. Thus, investors cannot deduct their real estate losses from income generated by wages, salaries, dividends, and interest. In short, the tax shelter aspect of real estate syndicates is gone.

Elimination of Capital Gains Tax Benefits. Under the new tax act, the long-standing favored treatment afforded long-term capital gains is eliminated entirely. However, the new act reduces all marginal tax rates to a maximum of 15 percent for most taxpayers and to 28 percent for taxpayers with higher incomes. In the past, reduced capital gains taxes have been an important reason for investing in real estate partnerships.

Long Depreciation Period. Before the Tax Reform Act of 1986 went into effect, commercial real estate could be depreciated within 18 years. Under the accelerated cost recovery system (ACRS) adopted in 1980, an investor was allowed to use accelerated depreciation method to recover the costs. Now you are required to use the straight-line depreciation method over 27½ years for residential real estate and over 31½ years for all other types of real estate.

There are other aspects of the tax reform that affect real estate investments, and all of them reduce the value of the tax credits for such investments. Investors are not allowed to take losses in excess of the actual amounts they invest. Furthermore, investment tax credit is eliminated entirely for all types of real estate except low-income housing projects.

Pepper . . . and Salt

"There's a man here who says he's looking for an honest tax shelter."

From *The Wall Street Journal*, with permission of Cartoon Features Syndicate.

ALTERNATIVE INVESTMENTS

- Speculative Investment Techniques

In addition to direct and indirect real estate investment, there are many other ways to invest your money. In this section, we will discuss a few more speculative investment techniques, such as buying stock on margin, selling short, investing in commodity futures, and playing the options market.

An investor who has successfully invested some money in stocks, bonds, or mutual funds might want to consider the following more speculative techniques. Only an investor who fully understands the possible risks as well as the potential returns should use these techniques.

Buying Stock on Margin

When buying stock on **margin,** an investor borrows part of the money necessary to buy a particular stock. The margin requirement is set by the Federal Reserve Board and is subject to periodic change. When the current margin requirement is 50 percent, this means that an investor may borrow up to half of the stock purchase price. Usually, the stock brokerage firm either lends the money or arranges the loan with another financial institution. Investors buy on margin because doing so offers them the potential for greater profits. Figure 18–8 gives an example of buying stock on margin.

As shown in Figure 18–8, it is more profitable to use margin. In effect, the financial leverage of borrowed money allowed the stockholder to purchase a larger number of stock shares. Since the dollar value of each share increased, the stockholder obtained a much greater total profit by buying the stock on margin.

The investor's stock did what it was supposed to do—rise in value. Had the value of the stock gone down, buying on margin would have increased the investor's loss. Because in buying on margin up to 50 percent of the purchase price is borrowed, interest must be paid on the loan. Most broker-age firms charge 1 to 3 percent above the prime interest rate for such loans. Normally, bankers define the *prime rate* as the interest rate they charge their best business customers. The interest charges will absorb the profits if the value of the stock does not increase rapidly enough. Success in buying on margin is tied to how soon the investor can sell the stock at a price higher than the purchase price.

The stock purchased serves as collateral for the loan. If the stock's market value decreases to approximately one half of the original price, the investor will receive a margin call from the brokerage firm. The exact price at which the *margin call* is issued is determined by the amount of money that the investor borrowed when the stock was purchased. Generally, the more money the investor borrows, the sooner he or she will receive a margin call. After the margin call, the investor must pledge additional cash or securities to serve as collateral for the loan. If the investor doesn't have acceptable collateral, the margined stock is sold and the proceeds are used to repay the loan.

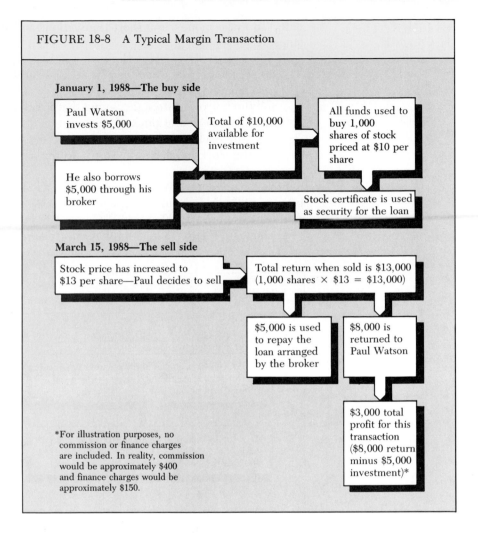

FIGURE 18-8   A Typical Margin Transaction

January 1, 1988—The buy side

Paul Watson invests $5,000

He also borrows $5,000 through his broker

Total of $10,000 available for investment

All funds used to buy 1,000 shares of stock priced at $10 per share

Stock certificate is used as security for the loan

March 15, 1988—The sell side

Stock price has increased to $13 per share—Paul decides to sell

Total return when sold is $13,000 (1,000 shares × $13 = $13,000)

$5,000 is used to repay the loan arranged by the broker

$8,000 is returned to Paul Watson

$3,000 total profit for this transaction ($8,000 return minus $5,000 investment)*

*For illustration purposes, no commission or finance charges are included. In reality, commission would be approximately $400 and finance charges would be approximately $150.

Selling Short

An investor's ability to make money by buying and selling securities is related to how well he or she can predict whether a certain stock or bond is increasing or decreasing in market value. Normally, the investor buys stocks and bonds and assumes that they will increase in value—a procedure referred to as *buying long*. But not all stocks or bonds increase in value. In fact, there are many reasons why the market value of a security may decrease. With this fact in mind, investors oriented to greater risk often use a procedure called selling short to make money when the price of a security is falling. **Selling short** is selling stock that has been borrowed from a stockbroker and must be replaced at a later date. When you sell short, you sell today, knowing that you must buy or cover your short transaction at a later date. To make money in a short transaction, an investor must take these steps:

1. Arrange to borrow a stock certificate for a certain number of shares for a particular stock from a stockbroker.
2. Sell the borrowed stock, assuming that it will drop in price in a reasonably short period of time.
3. Buy the stock at a lower price than the price paid for it in Step 1.
4. Use the stock purchased in Step 3 to replace the stock sold in Step 1.

For example, Paul Watson believes that General Motors is overpriced because of lower demand for cars and numerous other factors. As a result, he decides to sell short 100 shares of General Motors (see Figure 18–9).

As shown in Figure 18–9, Paul Watson's total return for this short transac-

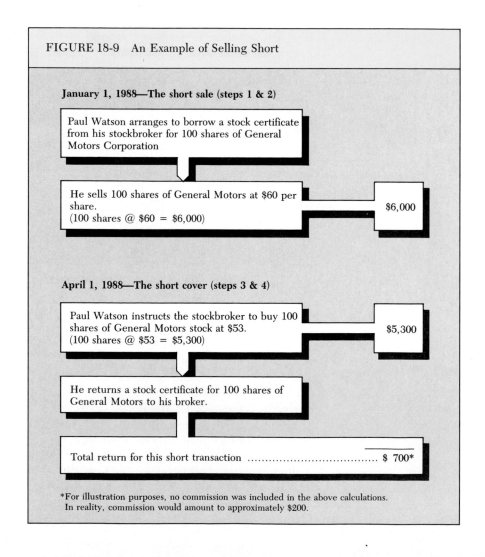

FIGURE 18-9   An Example of Selling Short

January 1, 1988—The short sale (steps 1 & 2)

Paul Watson arranges to borrow a stock certificate from his stockbroker for 100 shares of General Motors Corporation

He sells 100 shares of General Motors at $60 per share.
(100 shares @ $60 = $6,000) $6,000

April 1, 1988—The short cover (steps 3 & 4)

Paul Watson instructs the stockbroker to buy 100 shares of General Motors stock at $53.
(100 shares @ $53 = $5,300) $5,300

He returns a stock certificate for 100 shares of General Motors to his broker.

Total return for this short transaction .... $ 700*

*For illustration purposes, no commission was included in the above calculations. In reality, commission would amount to approximately $200.

tion was $700 because the stock did what it was supposed to do—decrease in value. Such a decrease is especially important to the investor selling short because he or she must replace the stock or bonds that were borrowed from the brokerage firm. If the securities increase in value, the investor will lose money. There is usually no brokerage charge for selling short, since the brokerage firm receives a commission charge when the securities are bought and sold.

The Commodity Markets

The ownership of certain commodities—cattle, hogs, pork bellies, wheat, corn, soybeans, rice, oats, sugar, coffee, cocoa, cotton, gold, silver, copper, and many others—is traded on a regular basis. Among the principal commodity exchanges are the Chicago Board of Trade, the Chicago Mercantile Exchange, the Kansas City Board of Trade, and the New York Futures Exchange. A commodity exchange provides a place for investors and speculators to buy and sell commodity contracts. While it is possible to buy or sell commodities for immediate delivery (this is sometimes called *spot trading*), most commodity transactions involve a future delivery date. A **futures contract** allows the owner to buy or sell a commodity at a guaranteed price at a future date.

Although the procedures in a commodity transaction are similar to those involved in a stock transaction, there are important differences. The margin requirements for commodity transactions are much lower than those for stock transactions. The lower margin requirement encourages speculation because an individual doesn't have to put up as much money to secure a futures contract. The risk factor is normally much greater for commodities than for stocks because of wide price fluctuations, and even relatively small fluctuations can cause great losses—because of the low margins. These fluctuations may result from the pressures of supply and demand, economic conditions, or even something as uncontrollable as the weather. For example, the price of orange juice may go up because of unexpected cold weather in Florida, Texas, or California. Finally, rumors, natural disasters, political events, or just about anything else can send commodity prices up or down in a very short period of time.

Trading in commodities is too risky for a lot of investors. You shouldn't let the lure of quick profits influence your investment decisions. Commodities are not something to fool around with unless you understand all of the procedures and risks.

The Options Market

An **option** gives an investor the right to buy or sell a specific stock at a predetermined price for a specific period of time. An investor who thinks that the market price of a stock will increase during a short period of time may decide to purchase a call option. A **call option** is sold by a stockholder and gives the purchaser the right to *buy* a share of stock at a guaranteed price before a definite expiration date. For instance, Bob Gray invests $150 to purchase 100 call options on Control Data stock at $1.50 per option. His 100 call options enable him to buy 100 shares of Control Data at a guaranteed price of $45 per share before the expiration date. In this case, if the price of Control Data stock does increase, Bob Gray can make money in one of two ways:

1. Before the expiration date, he can sell his options to another investor. Since his options are more valuable as a result of the stock's higher price, he can sell them to another investor at a price higher than he paid for them.
2. He can exercise his options and purchase the stock at the price guaranteed by them. Since the stock price guaranteed by the options is lower than the market price, he can make a profit by turning around and selling the stock at a higher price.

Some stock owners who believe that the price of their stock will go down during the option period will purchase a put option to safeguard their investment. A **put option** is the right to *sell* a share of stock at a guaranteed price before a definite expiration date. For example, Patsy Jones owns 100 shares of Eastman Kodak. She decides to safeguard her investment from a drop in market value by purchasing 100 put options at $3.25 per option, for a total cost of $325. Her 100 put options enable her to sell 100 shares of Eastman Kodak at a guaranteed price of $75 before the expiration date. In this case, if the price of Eastman Kodak stock does go down, Patsy Jones can sell the shares of Eastman Kodak at the higher price guaranteed by the put options.

If you believe that investing in real estate, buying on margin, selling short, investing in commodity futures, and investing in options market are too risky or too complicated, you might want to consider tangible investments. These investments include gold and other precious metals, gems, and other collectibles. But, remember risk and reward go hand in hand.

INVESTING IN PRECIOUS METALS, GEMS, AND OTHER COLLECTIBLES

- Risks and Rewards of Investing in Precious Metals

When the economy picks up, some investors predict higher inflation. Therefore many think the precious metals, such as gold, platinum and silver will regain some of their glitter. In this section, we will discuss several methods for buying precious metals.

Gold

Many factors tend to drive up gold prices: fear of war, political instability, and inflation. On the other hand, the easing of international tensions or disinflation causes a decline in gold prices. High interest rates also depress gold prices because they make it very expensive to carry gold as an investment.

Many people have acquired the metal itself; many others have gone into gold through a number of other kinds of investment that serve a variety of purposes. Some of these investments promise quick profits at high risk; others preserve capital; and yet others provide income from dividends or interest. But none of them are exempt from daily gold price fluctuations. Figure 18–11 shows gold price fluctuations between 1976 and 1987.

Gold Bullion. Gold bullion includes gold bars or wafers. The basic unit of gold bullion is one kilogram (32.15 troy ounces of .995 fine gold). Coin deal-

---

FIGURE 18-10   The Demand for American Eagles Has Been Very Strong

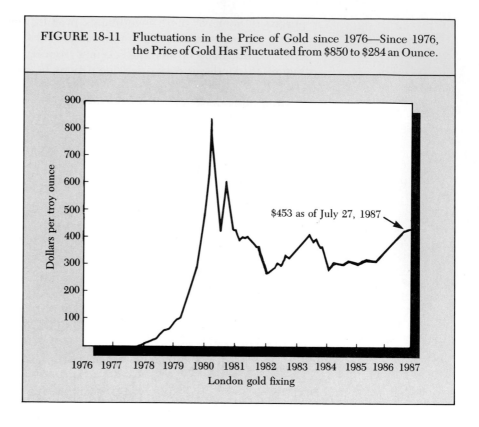

FIGURE 18-11   Fluctuations in the Price of Gold since 1976—Since 1976, the Price of Gold Has Fluctuated from $850 to $284 an Ounce.

ers, precious metals dealers, and some banks sell gold bullion in sizes ranging from five grams (16/100 of a troy ounce) to 500 ounces or more. On small bars, dealers and banks add 5 to 8 percent premium over the pure gold bullion value; on larger bars, the premium is usually 1 to 2 percent. Gold bullion presents storage problems, and unless the gold bar or wafer remains in the custody of the bank or dealer that sells it initially, it must be reassayed before being sold.

Gold Bullion Coins. You can avoid storage and assaying problems by investing in gold bullion coins. In the early 1980s, before the intensification of South Africa's political problems, South African Krugerrands were the most popular gold bullion coins in the United States. Popular gold bullion coins today include the Canadian Gold Maple Leaf, the Mexican 50 Pesos, the Austrian 100 Koronas, and the British Sovereign. The new American Eagle gold coin, the first gold bullion coin ever produced by the U.S. government, was issued in late 1986 (see Figure 18–10). The demand for it was so strong that the initial minting of 558,000 ounces was sold out within a few hours.[20]

[20] Michael Siconolfi, "Eagle's Success Fuels Anger of Coin Dealers," *The Wall Street Journal,* October 22, 1986, p. 31.

Most brokers require a minimum order of 10 coins and charge a commission of at least 2 percent. Later, we will discuss rare gold and silver coins that are purchased for their numismatic value, not the intrinsic value of their gold or silver content.

Gold Stocks. In addition to investing in gold bullion and gold bullion coins, you may invest in gold by purchasing the common stocks of gold mining companies. Among gold mining stocks listed on U.S. stock exchanges are those of Homestake Mining (based in the United States) and Campbell Red Lake and Dome Mines (based in Canada). Because such stocks often move in a direction opposite to that of the stock market as a whole, they may provide excellent portfolio diversification. You may also wish to examine closed-end investment companies with heavy positions in gold mining stocks (such as ARA, Ltd.).

Gold Futures Contracts. Finally, you may wish to consider trading in gold futures contracts. Gold futures are traded on five different U.S. exchanges and on many foreign exchanges.

Silver, Platinum, and Palladium

Investments in silver, platinum, and palladium, like investments in gold, are used as a hedge against inflation and as a safe haven during political or economic upheavals. During the last 55 years, silver prices ranged from a historic low of 24.25 cents per ounce in 1932, to over $50 an ounce in early 1980, and then back to $5.50 an ounce in 1986.

Two less well known precious metals, platinum and palladium, are also popular investments. Both have industrial uses as catalysts, particularly in automobile production. Some investors think that increased car sales could mean higher prices for these metals. Platinum currently sells for about $550 an ounce, palladium for about $125 an ounce.

As discussed earlier, finding storage for your precious metals can be tricky. While $20,000 in gold, for example, occupies only as much space as a thick paperback, $20,000 in silver weighs more than 200 pounds and could require a few safe-deposit boxes. Those boxes, moreover, are not insured against fire and theft.

You should remember, too, that unlike stocks, bonds, and other interest-bearing investments, precious metals sit in vaults earning nothing. And whether you profit on an eventual sale depends entirely on how well you call the market.

Precious Stones

Precious stones include diamonds, sapphires, rubies, and emeralds. Diamonds and other precious stones appeal to investors because of their small size, easy concealment, and great durability and because of their potential as a hedge against inflation. Inflation and the interest in tangible assets helped increase diamond prices 40-fold between 1970 and 1980. A lucky few made fortunes, and brokerage and diamond firms took up the investment diamond business. In 1980, for example, Thomson McKinnon Securities, Inc. offered a diamond trust, a mutual fund sold in $1,000 units with diamonds as its only asset. Thomson McKinnon's timing couldn't have been worse. When the bubble burst in 1980, the value of one benchmark diamond fell 75 percent in just a few months.[21]

Whether you are buying precious stones to store in a safe-deposit box or to wear around your neck, there are a few things to keep in mind about risks. Diamonds and other precious stones are not easily turned into cash. It is hard to know whether you are getting a good stone. Diamond prices can be affected by the whims of De Beers Consolidated Mines of South Africa, Ltd., which controls 85 percent of the world's supply of rough diamonds, and by political instability in diamond-producing countries.[22] Moreover, the average buyer should expect to buy at retail and sell at wholesale, a difference of at least 10–15 percent—and perhaps of as much as 50 percent.

The best way to know exactly what you are getting, especially if you are planning to spend more than $1,000, is to insist that your stone be certified by an independent gemological laboratory, one not connected with a diamond-selling organization. (The acknowledged industry leader in this area is the Gemological Institute of America.) The certificate should list the stone's characteristics, including its weight, color, clarity, and quality of cut. The grading of diamonds, however, is not an exact science, and recent experiments have shown that when the same diamond is submitted twice to the same institute, it can get two different ratings.[23]

Michael Roman, chairman of the Jewelers of America, a trade group representing 12,000 retailers, stated that his group did not recommend diamonds as an investment and scoffed at the notion that local retail jewelers were realizing huge profits on diamond sales to misguided customers. He also did not believe in certification unless the stone in question is a high-grade diamond weighing at least one carat.[24]

Despite the present rosy scenarios for precious metals and gems, the risks in trading them are sizable. Just ask investors who in 1980 bought gold at as much as $850 an ounce, platinum at $1,040 an ounce, silver at $48 an ounce, and a one-carat diamond at $62,000.[25]

Other Collectibles

Collectibles include rare coins, works of art, antiques, stamps, rare books, sports memorabilia, rugs, Chinese ceramics, paintings, and other items that

[21] Doron P. Levin, "A Diamond is Forever; Its Value, However, is Subject to the Vagaries of the Gem Market," *The Wall Street Journal,* August 1, 1983, p. 34.

[22] Ibid.

[23] Ibid.

[24] *U.S. News & World Report,* August 25, 1986, p. 36.

[25] Ibid.

appeal to collectors and investors. Each of these items offers the collector/investor both pleasure and the opportunity for profit. Many collectors have discovered only incidentally that items they bought for their own pleasure had gained greatly in value while they owned them.

Traditionally, antiques, works of art, books, coins, stamps, and rugs have been considered standard collectible investments. Lately, however, the field of collectible objects has expanded to include such items as Mount St. Helens ceramics, posters, badges and buttons (for the freed Iranian hostages), Barbie dolls, "Dynasty" characters Alexis and Krystle, Hummel figurines, *National Geographic* (the March 1984 issue with the laser photo), John Paul II comic books, commemorative plates, and art deco curios from the 1920s.[26]

Collecting for investment purposes is very different from collecting as a hobby. Investing in collectibles can be just as serious as investing in real estate or the stock market and should be approached with equal study and care.

Investment counselors caution that collectibles do not provide interest or dividends, that it may be difficult to sell them at the right price on short notice, and that if they become valuable enough, they must be insured against loss or theft.

[26] *Sylvia Porter's Personal Finance*, October 1986, pp. 59–65; *USA Today*, January 13, 1986, p. 8E; and *Changing Times*, March 1986, pp. 70–76.

Pepper . . . and Salt

"Oh, I don't read them, I buy them as an investment."

From *The Wall Street Journal*, with permission of Cartoon Features Syndicate.

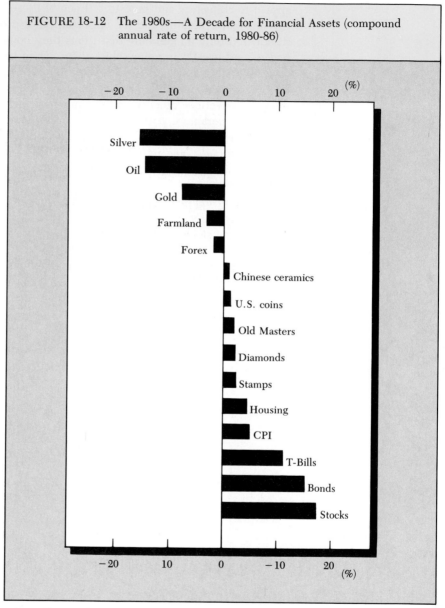

FIGURE 18-12   The 1980s—A Decade for Financial Assets (compound annual rate of return, 1980-86)

Source: Adapted from Sumner N. Levine, ed., *Business and Investment Almanac, 1987* Homewood, Ill.: Dow Jones-Irwin, 1987), p. 268. © Sumner N. Levine, 1987.

Figures 18–12 and 18–13 compare the percentage annual rate of return on various kinds of tangible and intangible assets for the 1980s and the 1970s, respectively. If the 1980s are the decade for financial assets, such as stocks, bonds, and T-bills, then the 1970s were the decade for collectibles and tangibles, such as oil, gold, coins, silver, and stamps.

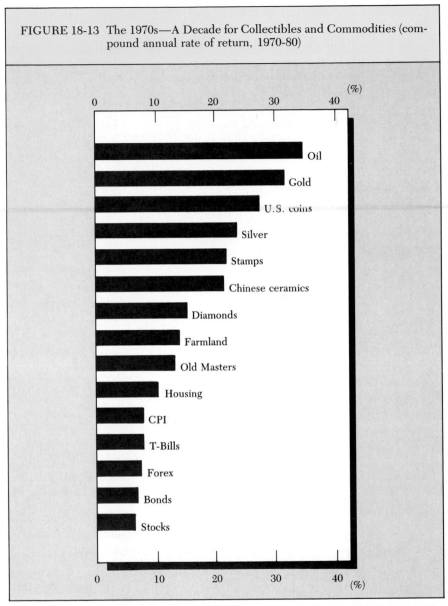

FIGURE 18-13   The 1970s—A Decade for Collectibles and Commodities (compound annual rate of return, 1970-80)

Source: Adapted from Sumner N. Levine, ed., *Business and Investment Almanac, 1987* Homewood, Ill.: Dow-Jones-Irwin, 1987), p. 268. © Sumner N. Levine, 1987.

SUMMARY

- Real estate investments are classified as direct or indirect. Direct real estate investments, in which the investor holds legal title to the property, include a home, a vacation home, a timeshare, commercial property, and raw land. Indirect real estate investments include real estate syndicates, REITs, mortgages, and PCs.

- Real estate investments may have these advantages: a hedge against inflation, easy entry, limited financial liability, no management headaches, and financial leverage.

- Real estate investments may have these disadvantages: declining values, illiquidity, lack of diversification, and the reduction or elimination of tax advantages.

- Some investors may consider more speculative investments, such as buying stock on margin, selling short, owning certain commodities, and playing the options market.

- Other investors prefer to invest in precious metals, such as gold, platinum, and silver; precious stones, such as diamonds; or collectibles, such as stamps, rare coins, works of art, antiques, rare books, and Chinese ceramics. Collectibles do not provide current income, and they may be difficult to sell in a hurry.

GLOSSARY

Call option. The right to buy a share of stock at a guaranteed price before a definite expiration date.

Collectibles. Rare coins, works of art, antiques, stamps, rare books and other items that appeal to collectors and investors.

Commercial property. Land and buildings that produce lease or rental income.

Direct investment. The investor holds legal title to property.

Futures contract. Allows the owner to buy or sell a commodity at a guaranteed price at a future date.

Indirect investment. A trustee holds legal title to property.

Margin. Buying stock with borrowed money.

Option. Gives an investor the right to buy or sell a specific stock at a predetermined price for a specific period of time.

Participation certificate. An equity investment in a pool of mortgages that have been purchased by a federal agency, such as Ginnie Mae.

Passive activity. A business or trade in which the investor does not materially participate.

Passive loss. The total amount of losses from a passive activity minus the total income from the passive activity.

Put option. The right to sell a share of stock at a guaranteed price before a definite expiration date.

REIT. A firm that pools investor funds and invests them directly in real estate.

Selling short. Selling borrowed stock that must be replaced later.

Syndicate. A limited partnership organized to sell real estate.

Timesharing. The use of a vacation home for a limited, preplanned time; also called interval ownership.

REVIEW QUESTIONS

1. Distinguish between direct and indirect real estate investments. Give an example of each.

2. Distinguish among gross scheduled income, gross operating income, operating expenses, net operating income, and rate of return.

3. What is a real estate syndicate or limited partnership? What are the responsibilities of a general partner? a limited partner?

4. Why are real estate investment trusts compared to mutual funds?

5. Describe three types of REITs. What four federal requirements must REITs adhere to in their operations?

6. What are first and second mortgages? What are their usual investment and legal requirements?

7. What is a Ginnie Mae PC? What are the investment characteristics—financial risk, marketability, and purchasing power risk—of this form of investment?

8. Describe the advantages and disadvantages of investing in real estate.

9. Trace the steps required in buying stock on margin and the steps required in selling short.

10. Define the following terms: commodity market, futures contract, options market, call option, and put option.

11. What are the various ways of owning gold, silver, and platinum?

12. Describe some advantages and disadvantages of investing your money in such collectibles as stamps, rare coins, antiques, and sports memorabilia.

DISCUSSION QUESTIONS AND ACTIVITIES

1. Why do such persons as King James Weyant and Albert Y. Chow invest in Postal Service properties?

2. Why might investments in real estate serve as an inflation hedge?

3. In what way does real estate provide a high degree of leverage?

4. "Ownership of a home is one of the best investments you can make." Comment on this statement, paying particular attention to the investment characteristics of the average home.

5. Would you invest your money in a vacation home? in a timeshare? Why or why not?

6. Why will you make direct or indirect real estate investments? Do you have a preference among such investments? If so, why?

7. Who should consider buying stock on margin, selling short, or playing the futures markets? Will you? Why or why not?

8. How have returns on precious metals compared with returns on other investments over the past few years?

ADDITIONAL READINGS

Cox, Meg. "Emotional Investments." *The Wall Street Journal*, December 2, 1985, p. 20D.

Freedman, Alix M. "Comics Attract Investor Interest." *The Wall Street Journal*, July 30, 1986, p. 21.

Guenther, Robert. "All-Cash Deals May Sacrifice Favorable Effects of Leverage." *The Wall Street Journal*, October 29, 1986, p. 27.

_____. "Apartment Vacancies Increase as More Renters Buy Houses." *The Wall Street Journal*, October 15, 1986, p. 31.

_____. "Tax Overhaul Will Encourage Owners to Exchange Property." *The Wall Street Journal*, October 22, 1986, p. 31.

Investment Opportunities in the Hotel/Motel Industry. Kansas City, Mo.: Hotel and Motel Brokers of America, August 1985.

"Investment Scams." *Changing Times*, July 1986, p. 26.

Jordan, Charles J. "What to Collect from the 1980s." *Sylvia Porter's Personal Finance*, October 1986, p. 59.

"Office Building Boom and Bust." *Weekly Letter*, Federal Reserve Bank of San Francisco, October 17, 1986, pp. 1–4.

Topolnicki, Denise M. "Fine Art of Fraud." *Money*, September 1986, p. 73.

CASE 18–1 Cleopatra's Secret*

David Maloney grew fungus on milk because it seemed like a great way to make money. Maloney, a 25-year-old resident of Kansas City, Kansas, wasn't the only one. About 12,000 people across the country may have invested up to $10 million growing these scablike cultures in glasses of warm milk. They called themselves growers or home farmers, and they said their fungal "harvest" was sold as a skin cream ingredient called Cleopatra's Secret.

Law enforcement authorities didn't share Maloney's enthusiasm for the concept. They didn't accuse him of doing anything wrong, but they said that the operation he had invested in was an elaborate Ponzi scheme, an illegal deal in which early investors are paid high returns with money raised from later investors. Such schemes ultimately collapse when the supply of new investors dries up.

By May 1985, more than a half-dozen states had initiated legal action against the promoters of this group, called Kubus Syndicate. Officials of the syndicate denied that they had done anything wrong.

In theory, a Ponzi scheme can work for any kind of investment. Ohio authorities alleged that

a 23-year-old former busboy even ran a Ponzi scheme on scalped tickets. "He went out and sold IOUs, promising to double or triple your money within 15 to 60 days," claimed Roger Marting, head of the Ohio Division of Securities. "The amount owed to the public when we shut him down was $7.3 million."

According to state securities officials, the most common tipoff to a Ponzi scam is the promise of high returns at no risk. "It's the old 'You can have three $5 bills for a 10,'" said Marting. "If it's too good to be true, it is."

Questions

1. Why would any intelligent individual fall prey to Ponzi scams?

2. Why can't federal and state securities authorities put the promoters of such scams behind the bars?

3. How can you protect yourself from such "moneymaking" deals?

*Condensed from Walt Bogdanich, "Ponzi Scams Allegedly Increasing, Fooling Even the Savviest Investors," *The Wall Street Journal*, May 8, 1985, sec. 2, p. 35.

CASE 18–2 Emotional Investments*

When the children approach college age, a lot of parents tighten their belts and head for the bank. But not Donald Hall. He headed for his basement. There Hall, director of the Strasenburgh Planetarium in Rochester, New York, selected choice pieces from his 1930s glassware collection for auction. "I made out like a bandit," he said of the recent sale of the first third of his 6,000-piece hoard. Some plates that cost him as little as a dime years earlier brought as much as $10 each. Altogether, Hall said, the collection could bring more than $30,000 to finance what he called a "Depression-glass scholarship" for his daughter, who was starting high school. Hall spent only about $5,000 acquiring the glass, beginning when his daughter, Elizabeth, was just a year old.

Can other collectors hope to match Hall's performance? Forget it, financial planners say. Nobody can count on outguessing the market for collectibles, they say, and anybody can drop a bundle on them. "Even in times of high inflation, people paid so much of a markup for collectibles like gems that they lost money," says Richard Michi, a Chicago investment adviser. "I tell clients to avoid collectibles. There are so many better investments that are easier to understand, more liquid, and have a higher return."

According to John Gallo, an executive of the Butterfield & Butterfield auction house in San Francisco, a 1920-era Persian rug that sold for about $6,000 in 1980 had dropped to $1,500 by 1982 and would fetch no more than $2,000 in 1985.

On the other hand, in 1985 Christie's International auction house in New York sold for $2,350 a Steiff teddy bear that was probably valued at $300 a decade earlier, said Julie Collier, head of collectibles at Christie's. She said that the value of the toy was greatly enhanced because it had escaped much of the wear and tear normally inflicted by children.

Questions

1. Would you invest in collectibles today, as Donald Hall did years ago, to finance your children's college education? Why or why not?

2. What dangers do you see in such investments?

3. What *should* be the foremost reason for investing in collectibles?

*Adapted from Meg Cox, "Emotional Investments," *The Wall Street Journal*, December 2, 1985, p. 20D.

Comprehensive Case for Part Five
Down, but Hopefully Not Out!

Two years ago, Gene Martin, 43, thought that everything in his life was pretty much on "target." He was happily married with two children, had a good job as a chemical engineer, had $10,000 in the bank, and had even invested $70,000 in conservative stocks and bonds.

Now, two years later, most of that is gone. It all started when the company he worked for was purchased by a larger corporation. Gene, along with a lot of other engineers, was "fired" because he was no longer needed. Of course, the fact that he was unemployed didn't stop the monthly bills, and his unemployment benefits didn't help much. The $10,000 bank account was quickly exhausted. Gene and his wife, Karen, began selling their stocks and bonds to make ends meet.

Then, to make matters worse, Gene and Karen started to argue about finances, career plans, the children, and just about everything else. Karen filed for divorce six months after Gene lost his job. Since Gene and Karen could not agree on a property settlement, they each got a lawyer. Their legal fees totaled $8,500. After another six months, their divorce became final. As part of the property settlement, Karen got the kids, house, and car; one half of their furniture; and one half of the remaining stocks and bonds. She was also required to pay Gene $15,000 for his portion of the equity in their home. Gene got the $15,000 payment from Karen and the other half of the furniture and of the remaining stocks and bonds. Also, Gene was required to pay VISA, MasterCard, and medical bills that totaled $3,700. Finally, he was required to pay $600 a month child support for their two children.

According to Gene, the next nine months were the "low point in his life." He could not find a job, and he was living in a one-room efficiency apartment separated from his two kids. He was existing on the cash settlement he got from Karen and the money he received for his share of the remaining stocks and bonds.

At the end of his second year of unemployment, Gene got a job as a chemical engineer with a large, well-respected company. Because of his past work experience, the company agreed to pay him $56,000 a year. His take-home pay was approximately $2,900 a month, and his problems seemed to be over. But it quickly dawned on him that he was 45 years old—20 years from retirement—and had a grand total of $4,500 in assets. He realized that he had to do some careful financial planning unless he wanted to work forever.

He performed a financial checkup and found that his monthly expenses are $2,450. An itemized list of these expenses is shown below.

Expense	Amount
Apartment	$ 550
Child support	600
Transportation	400
Utilities	200
Food and entertainment	450
Clothing and cleaning	150
Miscellaneous	100
Total monthly expenses	$2,450

After analyzing the results of his financial checkup, Gene realizes that he has about $450 a month, or $5,400 a year, left over after all of his expenses have been paid. Now he must decide what to do with the excess.

Questions

1. How would you rank the Martins' financial condition before Gene lost his job? How could their financial condition have been improved?

2. If the divorce could not be avoided, what could Gene and Karen have done differently? Why do you think they both had to have a lawyer?

3. As a result of the divorce, Gene is a single taxpayer earning $56,000 a year. Because he lives in an apartment and doesn't have any other tax deductions, he is afraid that he will end up paying a large percentage of his income to the federal government. In what ways could Gene minimize the amount of taxes that he pays?

4. Assume that you are a financial planner and Gene is your client. Given the information in this case, develop a thorough financial plan that takes into account Gene's immediate needs and his retirement needs. Be sure to include specific investment goals.

5. What types of investments would you recommend for Gene? Explain.

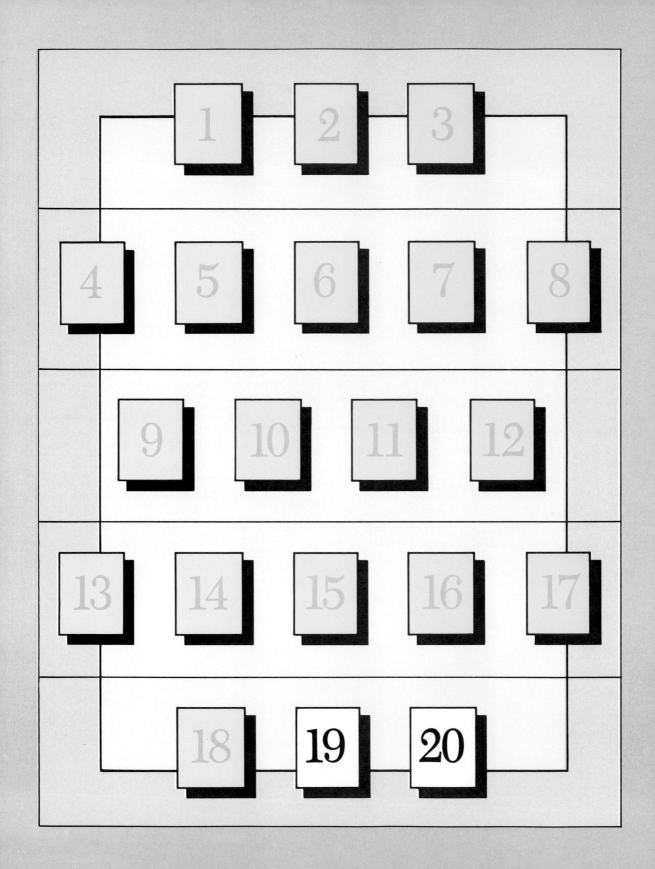

PART SIX

Controlling Your Financial Future

This part of *Personal Finance* emphasizes planning for retirement income and estate management. First, we will discuss the importance of retirement planning and show you how to analyze your retirement assets and liabilities. We will stress why it is vital to estimate your retirement living needs and your retirement expenses. We will examine how you can invest for your retirement years and how you can live on your retirement income. Then we will focus on the steps you should take to protect your family now and in the future. We will discuss wills, trust arrangements, and methods of owning property and the choices that may be the best in your circumstances. We will see what property is included in the valuation of your estate and how your estate is settled. Finally, we will discuss federal and state taxes that can be imposed on your estate, how these taxes are calculated and paid, and what you can do to minimize them. Included in this part are:

19

Retirement Planning

Retirement can be a new and rewarding phase of your life. As with any new venture, however, a successful, happy retirement doesn't just happen—it takes planning and continual evaluation. Thinking about retirement in advance can help you understand the retirement process and gain a sense of control over the future. Anticipating future changes can be useful.

After studying this chapter, you will be able to:

- Recognize the importance of retirement planning.

- Analyze your current assets and liabilities for retirement.

- Estimate your retirement spending needs.

- Identify your retirement housing needs.

- Estimate your retirement expenses.

- Evaluate your planned retirement income.

- Develop a balanced budget based on your retirement income.

Interview with **Howard Shank,** Retirement Planning Author and Retired Advertising Executive

Howard Shank worked in the advertising industry for 37 years. Since retiring in 1980, he has started a new career. He is the author of a recent book entitled *Managing Retirement,* and he has a second book in progress.

Whether you are 18, 38, or 58, it's not too early or too late to plan for a fulfilling retirement. In the simplest terms, retirement planning should involve money and good habits. Since most people have a difficult time saving, forced savings programs such as profit sharing, pension plans, and social security can help "save you from yourself."

Mr. Shank recommends that you take advantage of the *power of accumulation* for both your monetary needs and your psychological needs. From a financial point of view, this power refers to the compounding (future value) of interest. Stock investments are likely to give you the best long-term growth. As you approach retirement, low-risk investments are usually most appropriate.

But retirement planning not only involves putting money in the bank; it also involves developing *intellectual capital* such as skills, abilities, and attitudes. Persuasion, collaboration, and communication skills have ongoing value. The most important skill is learning to learn. This skill assures you that you will always have knowledge that is in demand.

Retirement can be a time to practice the art of *self-reinvention.* In retirement, you will have time to do things that you never had time for in the past. You may also have to redefine the word *important.* The achievements and rewards that seemed important when you were pursuing your career are likely to be replaced by other activities and values.

Most of you will not put these suggestions into practice since retirement may be a long way off. But remember, you will get there sooner than you think. Mr. Shank says that going to get his social security card "seems like yesterday, but it's been 50 years." So start today to create a systematic approach for developing good habits for accumulating money, skills, and attitudes that will serve you a lifetime.

"What's going to happen to all of us?" wondered Margaret Bruno, a 34-year-old saleswoman from Chicago. "We're going to live longer than anyone before us. I don't even have any children, so I can't go knock on someone else's door in 20 years and tell them to take care of me. That's why a person who's as unconcerned with retirement as I am is still concerned with it. I'm not going to have anywhere to go when I'm 65."

Young professionals such as Bruno have a problem. They want to drive sports cars, take expensive vacations, and buy videocassette recorders. But they also want to retire with plenty of money.

In a recent survey, more than half of the young professionals said that they would rather spend money today than save for retirement. Yet 61 percent of them were worried about not having enough money to retire comfortably.

Young professionals are wor-ried about their retirement, but they worry more than they plan. "I can't stand the idea of spending 30, 40 years of my life looking toward the last 10 or 15, when those 10 or 15 years aren't even guaranteed to me," said Robert Seidman, a 36-year-old self-employed sales-man from Edgewater, New Jersey. "It would bother me if I made myself unhappy for 30 years with the hope that some-day in the future that money's going to come in handy."

"I think of retirement all the time, but I don't know where to start," said Sandra Chavez, 35, a maintenance analyst for Chicago's transit system. "I don't even have an IRA. I talk about it, think about it, worry about it, and I spend so much time doing that that I don't get anything done."

These three—Bruno, Seid-man, and Chavez were among 30 young professionals who participated in focus groups conducted in New York and Chicago by Creative Research Associates. All of them had household incomes of at least $30,000. The study revealed that a group of prosperous, educated people want the good life to last forever but aren't sure how to make this happen.

If there is one thing many young professionals count on, it's that the social security sys-tem will die before they do. More than 70 percent of people between the ages of 25 and 39 with household incomes of at least $30,000 said that they had little or no confidence in its fu-ture.

More than 30 percent of the people surveyed said that they would withdraw from the social security system if they could. Many planned to rely on IRAs. In fact, slightly more than half of the interviewed profession-als had put money into IRAs or Keogh plans.

However, saving money didn't come naturally to many in this group. Some of them blamed the inflation of the 70s, which they said made savings

WHY RETIREMENT PLANNING?

- Importance of Retirement Planning

For 40 years, your life, and probably the life of your family, revolves around your job. One day you retire—and practically every aspect of your life is different. There's less money, more time, and no daily structure.

You can expect to spend about 16 to 20 years in retirement—too many years to be bored, lonely, and poor. You want your retirement years to be rewarding, active, and rich in new experiences. But you have to plan—and plan early. It's never too early to begin planning for retirement; some ex-perts even suggest starting while you are in school. Be certain you don't let your 45th birthday roll by without a comprehensive retirement plan. Re-

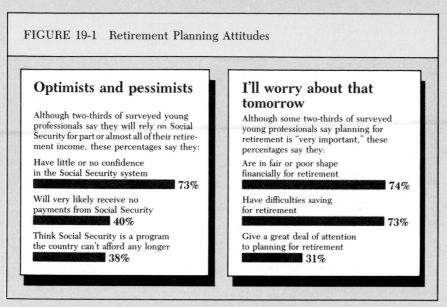

FIGURE 19-1   Retirement Planning Attitudes

Optimists and pessimists

Although two-thirds of surveyed young professionals say they will rely on Social Security for part or almost all of their retirement income, these percentages say they:

Have little or no confidence in the Social Security system
73%

Will very likely receive no payments from Social Security
40%

Think Social Security is a program the country can't afford any longer
38%

I'll worry about that tomorrow

Although some two-thirds of surveyed young professionals say planning for retirement is "very important," these percentages say they:

Are in fair or poor shape financially for retirement
74%

Have difficulties saving for retirement
73%

Give a great deal of attention to planning for retirement
31%

Source: *The Wall Street Journal*, December 10, 1985, p. 33; and *The Wall Street Journal*, December 9, 1985, p. 23.

seem uneconomical. Others blamed their spendthrift ways. "I think our generation is more attached to impulse items," said Jeff Greenberg, 30, an editor at a New York publishing company. "For instance, I have a microwave oven, and I don't really know why I got it. There are lots of things that I have. I have a VCR; do I really need it? The list goes on—it's endless."

Some of the interviewed professionals were fearful that their golden years would be uncomfortable. But others believed that they would be able to live very well in retirement.

Some findings of the study are shown in Figure 19–1.

Source: Adapted from Edwin A. Finn Jr., "Instead of Planning for Retirement, Young Professionals Fret about It," *The Wall Street Journal*, December 9, 1985, p. 23.

member, the longer you wait, the less influence you will have on the shape of your life in retirement.

Retirement planning is both emotional and financial. Emotional planning for retirement involves identifying your personal goals and setting out to meet them. Financial planning for retirement involves assessing your postretirement needs and income and plugging any gaps you find. Financial planning for retirement is vitally important for several reasons:

1.   You can expect to live in retirement for many years. At age 65, the

average life expectancy of a man is 14 years and the average life expectancy of a woman is 19 years.

2.   Social security and a private pension, if you have one, may be insufficient to cover the cost of living.

3.   Inflation may diminish the purchasing power of your retirement savings.

You should anticipate your retirement years by analyzing your long-range goals. What does retirement mean to you? Does it mean an opportunity to stop work and rest, or does it mean time to travel, develop a hobby, or start a second career? Where and how do you want to live during your retirement? Once you have considered your retirement goals, you are ready to evaluate the cost of your plans and whether you can afford them. The accompanying boxed feature suggests where you should be in your retirement planning at various ages.

The Basics of Retirement Planning

Before you decide where you want to be financially, you have to find out where you are. Your first step, therefore, is to analyze your current assets and liabilities. Then you estimate your spending needs and adjust them for inflation. Next you evaluate your planned retirement income. Finally, you increase your income if necessary.

"Retirement plan? I wouldn't worry about that.
You'd be out of your mind to work here
that long."

From *The Wall Street Journal,* with permission of Cartoon Features Syndicate.

CONDUCTING
A FINANCIAL
ANALYSIS

● Analyze Your Current
  Assets and Liabilities

As you learned in Chapter 3, your current assets include everything you own that has value: cash on hand and in checking and savings accounts; the current value of your stocks, bonds, and other investments; the current value of your house, car, jewelry, and furnishings; and the current value of your life insurance and pensions. Your current liabilities are everything you owe: your mortgage, car payments, credit card balances, taxes due, and so forth. The difference between the two totals is your net worth, a figure that you should increase each year as you move toward retirement. Use Figure 19–2 to calculate your net worth now and at retirement.

Personal Financial Planning and You
Retirement Planning: Where You Should Be

A ge 25. Strike a balance between long-term and short-term financial goals. Even if you're saving for a home, don't ignore investments for retirement. Begin saving in a tax-deferred IRA or 401(k) retirement plan.

Age 35. This is the critical age to begin financial planning. If you wait longer, it will just be much harder. When you change jobs, take a close look at the retirement benefits, because they could be based on your longevity with the company. If you plan to buy a home, do it soon, or you may still be paying for it after you retire. If you're going to make some investments that promise big returns but could be risky, now's the time. If you lose money you still have time to make it back before retire-

ment. Try to save about 10 percent of your salary for retirement. Experts say 10 percent is generally enough to get your retirement plans rolling, but not so much that it will derail your day-to-day finances.

Age 45. Invest more, but in low-risk investments. If possible, try to increase the amount you're investing—up to 25 percent of your salary. If you haven't begun saving for retirement, you must start a crash program immediately. It's an ideal time for a complete financial overhaul. See a financial planner to make sure your finances are in order so you'll be able to afford retirement in 20 years. Many parents experience a windfall within the next 10 years. Their children are graduating from college and leaving home, so expenses

drop sharply. Experts say it's a good time to make further investments—it's almost painless because you've got the extra money and you're used to living without it.

Age 55. It's time to start lessening one's dependence on stocks and other investments that are subject to the whims of the market. It may be a good time to sell the family home and to move into something smaller that requires less maintenance. Anytime after age 55, you can take advantage of a tax rule that allows you to sell your house and not be taxed on profits of up to $125,000. If you do opt for a smaller home, stash the cash in safe investments such as certificates of deposit.

Source: *USA Today*, March 3, 1986, p. 11E.

FIGURE 19-2   Review Your Assets, Liabilities, and Net Worth

	Now	At Retirement
Assets		
Savings accounts	$_____	$_____
Checking accounts	_____	_____
Time deposits	_____	_____
U.S. savings bonds	_____	_____
Life insurance (cash value)	_____	_____
Annuities (surrender value)	_____	_____
Pension (vested interest)	_____	_____
Investments (market value)	_____	_____
House (market value)	_____	_____
Other real estate	_____	_____
Business interests	_____	_____
Personal property (auto, jewelry, etc.)	_____	_____
Other assets	_____	_____
Total assets	$_____	$_____
Liabilities		
Mortgage (balance due)	$_____	$_____
Automobile loan	_____	_____
Installment loans	_____	_____
Taxes due	_____	_____
Business debts	_____	_____
Total liabilities	$_____	$_____
Subtract total liabilities from total assets:		
Total assets	$_____	$_____
Total liabilities	_____	_____
Total net worth	$_____	$_____

Review Your Assets

Reviewing your assets to make sure they are suitable for retirement is a sound idea. Make necessary shifts in your investments and holdings to fit your circumstances. In reviewing your assets, consider the following factors.

Housing. If you own your house, it is probably your biggest single asset. The amount tied up in your house may be out of line, however, with your retirement income. If it is, consider selling your house and buying a less expensive one. The selection of a smaller, more easily maintained house can also decrease your maintenance costs. The difference saved can be put into a savings account or certificates or into other income-producing investments.

If your mortgage is largely or completely paid off, you may be able to get an annuity that provides you with extra income during retirement. In this arrangement, a lender uses your house as collateral to buy an annuity for you from a life insurance company. Each month, the lender pays you (the homeowner) from the annuity, after deducting the mortgage interest payment. The mortgage principal, which was used to obtain the annuity, is repaid to the lender by probate after your death. This special annuity is known as a **reverse annuity mortgage.** Such mortgages may not be available in your area. Check with your banker or a savings institution about availability and details.

Life Insurance. You may have set up your life insurance to provide support and education for your children. Now you may want to convert some of this asset into cash or income (an annuity). Another possibility is to reduce premium payments by decreasing the face value of your insurance. Doing this will give you extra money to spend on living expenses or to invest for additional income.

Depending on the terms of your life insurance policy and the interest rate on the loan, you may be able to borrow against the policy and then invest the money at a higher yield. But you should be aware that assets accumulated and passed on as death benefits under a life insurance policy are exempt from federal income taxation, whereas invested assets may be subject to tax. A life insurance loan does not have to be repaid, but any unpaid balance will reduce the death benefit. If you do not pay the annual interest on the loan the unpaid interest is added to the principal of the loan, so that you end up paying interest on interest.

Savings Bonds. You may now want to exchange Series E savings bonds that you bought for investment purposes for Series H bonds that will pay you interest periodically.

Other Investments. Evaluate any other investments you may have. When you chose them, you may have been more interested in making your money grow than in getting an early return. Has the time come to take the income from your investments? You may now want to take dividends rather than reinvest them.

After thoroughly reviewing your assets, estimate your spending needs during your retirement years.

RETIREMENT LIVING EXPENSES

The exact amount of money you will need in retirement is impossible to predict. However, you can estimate your needs by considering changes in spending patterns and where and how you plan to live.

Your spending patterns will probably change. A study conducted by the Bureau of Labor Statistics on how families spend money shows that retired families use a greater share for food, housing, and medical care than

TABLE 19-1   Spending Patterns of Retired and Nonretired Families
(percentage of total family income before taxes)

	Retired	Nonretired
Total family income before taxes	100	100
Consumption expenditures:		
Food	19	14
Housing	29	21
Transportation	11	14
Clothing	4	5
Medical care	9	4
Personal care	2	2
Other	10	11
Taxes	6	16
Gifts and contributions	8	4
Personal insurance	2	7
Miscellaneous	0	2

Source: Department of Labor, Bureau of Labor Statistics.

● Estimate Your
Spending Needs

nonretired families. Although no two families are alike in how they adjust their spending patterns to changes in the life cycle, the Bureau of Labor Statistics tabulation in Table 19–1 can guide you in anticipating your own future spending patterns.

The following expenses may be lowered or eliminated:

Work Expenses. You will no longer have to make payments into your retirement system. You will not be buying gas and oil for the drive back and forth to work or paying train or bus fares. You may be buying fewer lunches away from home.

Clothing Expenses. You probably will not need as many clothes after you retire, and your dress may be more casual.

Housing Expenses. If you have paid off your house mortgage by the time you retire, your cost of housing may be reduced, although increases in property taxes may offset this gain.

Federal Income Taxes. Your federal income taxes will be lower. No federal tax has to be paid on some forms of income, such as social security, railroad retirement benefits, and certain veteran's benefits. A retirement credit is allowed for some sources of income, such as annuities. You will probably be paying taxes at a lower rate because your taxable income will be lower.

Under the U.S. Civil Service Retirement System, your retirement income is not taxed until you have received the amount you have invested in the retirement fund. After that, your retirement income is taxable.

You can also estimate which of the following expenses may increase:

Insurance. The loss of your employer's contribution to health and life insurance will increase your payments. Medicare, however, may offset part of this increased expense.

Medical Expenses. Although medical expenses vary from person to person, they tend to increase with age.

Expenses for Leisure Activities. With more free time, many retirees want to spend more money on leisure activities. You may want to put aside extra money for a retirement trip or other large recreational expenses.

Gifts and Contributions. Many retirees who continue to spend the same amount of money on gifts and contributions find that their spending in this area takes a larger share of their smaller income. Some retirees may want to reevaluate such spending.

PLANNING YOUR RETIREMENT HOUSING

- Estimate Your Retirement Housing Needs

Think about where you will want to live. If you think you will want to live in another city, it's a good idea to plan vacations in areas you might enjoy. When some area begins to appeal to you, visit it during various times of the year to experience the year-round climate. Meet the people. Check into available activities, transportation, taxes. Be honest about what you will have to give up and what you will gain.

Where you live in retirement can influence your financial needs. You must make some important decisions about whether or not to stay in your present community and about whether or not to stay in your present home. Everyone has particular needs and preferences; you are the only one who can determine what location and housing are best for you.

Before moving, consider what this involves. Moving is expensive, and, if you are not satisfied with your new location, returning to your former home may be impossible. Consider the social aspects of moving. Will you want to be near your children, other relatives, and good friends? Are you prepared for new circumstances?

If you decide to stay in the same community, you can estimate your future living costs on the basis of your past expenses. But if you plan to move to a new location, consider renting for a year before you make a final commitment to move. Homes in certain areas of the country cost less than homes in other areas. Figure 19–3 shows cities where homes cost less. Comparing the costs of a certain area or city with the costs of the area or city you live in now will give you an idea of how a change in location will affect your expenses.

Your second big decision with regard to your retirement housing needs is determining the type of housing that is best for you.

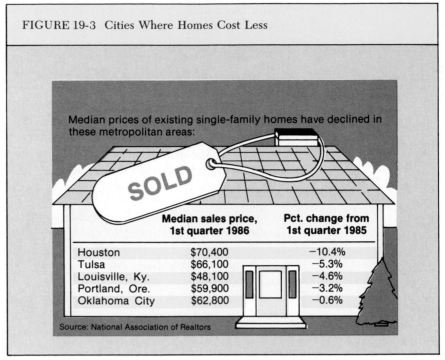

FIGURE 19-3   Cities Where Homes Cost Less

Median prices of existing single-family homes have declined in these metropolitan areas:

	Median sales price, 1st quarter 1986	Pct. change from 1st quarter 1985
Houston	$70,400	−10.4%
Tulsa	$66,100	−5.3%
Louisville, Ky.	$48,100	−4.6%
Portland, Ore.	$59,900	−3.2%
Oklahoma City	$62,800	−0.6%

Source: National Association of Realtors

Source: *USA Today*, May 12, 1986, p. B–1.

Type of Housing

The housing needs of people often change as they grow older. The ease and cost of maintenance and nearness to public transportation, shopping, church, and entertainment often become more important to people when they retire.

There are many housing alternatives, and several of them were discussed in Chapter 9. Here we shall examine how each of the following alternatives would meet a retiree's housing needs.

Present Home. Staying in your present home without renovating it is one alternative. Staying in and renovating your present home is another. However, renovating may be expensive, as shown in Figure 19–4. Loans from the U.S. Department of Housing and Urban Development (HUD) designed to rehabilitate or convert older homes have low interest rates and favorable terms for older adults. For more information on such loans, contact your banker or your county or city government.

Smaller Single-Family House. Yet another alternative is buying a smaller home that is easier and less expensive to care for and is in a more convenient location. The sale of your larger home could provide you with extra cash for retirement. If you are over 55 and have been living in your present home for

FIGURE 19-4 Rooms with a New Look

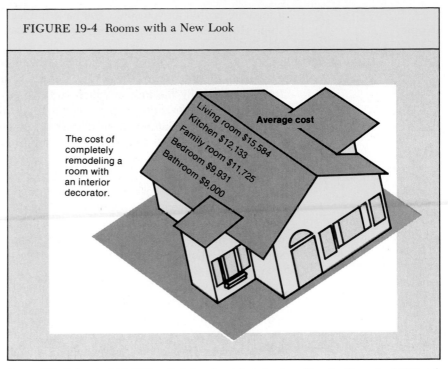

The cost of completely remodeling a room with an interior decorator.

Living room $15,584
Kitchen $12,133
Family room $11,725
Bedroom $9,931
Bathroom $8,000

Average cost

Source: *USA Today,* April 25, 1986, p. D–1; based on information from *Changing Times,* April 1986, and American Society of Interior Designers; 1985 figures.

three of the last five years, you do not have to pay federal income tax on the first $125,000 capital gains profit from its sale. But you may use this exemption only once in a lifetime.

Multifamily Houses. The units in a multifamily house are more like apartments than like single-family homes. Since zoning requirements often limit the areas where multifamily homes can be built, you may find some locations unacceptable for retirement living.

Rented Apartment, Smaller House, or Room in a Hotel. Renting has many advantages for a retiree. It makes moving easier. The monthly costs are usually fixed in the short run. The maintenance and repair costs are minimal. Special services and facilities may be provided at little or no additional charge. If your income is low or moderate, you may be eligible for public or subsidized housing.

Condominium. A condominium is an individually owned home in a multiunit project. In a condominium, you enjoy many of the advantages of apartment living and single-family home ownership. The maintenance of common areas is handled for you. You pay maintenance costs and taxes on common areas through a monthly maintenance fee charged to each unit; you also pay a separate tax bill for your unit. You have the tax advantages of home owner-ship. However, you must not expect the privacy of a house.

Cooperative. A cooperative also combines apartment living with property ownership, although in a way slightly different from that of a condominium. Instead of owning the unit in which you live, you purchase a share in the corporation that owns the cooperative property. Your share of the building's taxes and mortgage interest is tax deductible, as with a house or a condomin-ium. Before you buy a cooperative, be sure to check all of its restrictions.

Mobile Home Park. In warmer climates, mobile home parks are particu-larly popular. Mobile homes cost less, are taxed less, and require less main-tenance than conventional homes of similar size. However, mobile homes depreciate more quickly than conventional homes. The facilities of well-organized mobile home parks are similar to those of retirement villages, and some mobile home parks are designed especially for retired people.

Housing Project for Retirees. Housing projects designed for retired peo-ple are located throughout the country. The housing types, costs, and social surroundings vary with each of these projects. Consider any choice of this kind carefully. You can learn a great deal more about whether you will fit in from a preliminary living arrangement than from a cursory examination.

Retirement Hotel. Many older hotels have been converted to full-time use by retirees. Most of these retirement hotels are located in California, Texas, and Florida. They have many of the advantages and problems of apartment living. The main difference between a retirement hotel and an apartment is that a retirement hotel generally includes meals as part of the rent. Stay in such a hotel for a few days and see whether the accommodations are satisfactory and the neighborhood is acceptable. The local chamber of commerce should be able to help you locate retirement hotels in the areas where you want to live.

Lifetime Housing. Lifetime housing facilities are sponsored by nonprofit fraternal, union, church, and civic organizations. Such facilities are best suited to people who want to ensure having a home as long as they live, without the responsibility of ownership or the insecurity of renting. Facili-ties of this kind usually offer both apartment-style housing and nonhousekeeping living arrangements; in some cases, even nursing home care is provided.

Lifetime housing offers security and, if necessary, an increasing level of care. However, if you choose such housing just after retirement, you may find that you are in close contact with older people who are less active and less healthy than people who live in other kinds of retirement communities.

Whatever your retirement housing alternative is, make sure you know what you are signing and understand what you are buying.

Caveat Emptor. Buying a piece of land for a retirement home is an exciting prospect for many people, but before you sign a contract, be sure you know what you are doing. Land fraud, especially in Florida, Arizona, and New Mexico, is a serious problem. The usually high-pressure sales deal begins with a dinner invitation. You see an attractive film of the area where the parcel is supposed to be located, and then you are encouraged to close a deal with only a few dollars down and a small monthly payment. Although the interstate sale of land is regulated by laws, these laws are sometimes ignored or not adhered to strictly. The HUD Office of Interstate Land Sales Registration (OILSR) regulates interstate land sales and receives nearly 2,500 complaints each year from people who believe they have been treated unfairly in land deals.

While the OILSR has had some success in obtaining refunds or adjustments, it can only act when the developer has clearly violated the law. Developers are required to register with the government, to file a statement describing the land they intend to sell, and to issue accurate property reports, and some developers fail to meet these requirements. One developer in five is suspected of making inaccurate, incomplete, or misleading reports.[1]

Before you buy land, your attorney should review the contract. Write to the state attorney general's office or the state real estate board for information about the developer and the land in question.

Contact OILSR, 451 7th Street, SW, Washington, DC 20410 to determine whether an out-of-state developer is properly registered. Check with your local Better Business Bureau and banker to assess the financial soundness of the developer. Compare prices of land in areas near your site. See the land you are buying, not something similar. Finally, don't take the word of the developer about its quality.

Federal Help. Although your income may be enough to meet most of your housing needs, financing a big project, such as modernizing or rehabilitating your home, may be more than you can afford. Anticipating that problem, the federal government established a group of programs aimed at solving the housing problems of people over 62. Through these programs, federal loan insurance, direct loans, and grants may be available to you. For specific details, people living in metropolitan areas should contact the local HUD office. People who live in rural areas should contact an office of the Farmers Home Administration.

Now that you have considered your probable retirement situation, you are ready to list your estimated expenses. Using the worksheet in Table 19–2, list your present expenses and estimate what these expenses would be if you were retired.

---

[1]*And One Day You Retire* (Hartford, Conn.: Aetna Life and Casualty Company, November 1984), pp. 42–43.

TABLE 19-2   Your Present Expenses and Your Estimated Retirement Expenses

Item	Now		Retirement	
	Per Month	*Per Year*	*Per Month*	*Per Year*
Fixed expenses:				
Rent or mortgage payment	$_____	$_____	$_____	$_____
Taxes	_____	_____	_____	_____
Insurance	_____	_____	_____	_____
Savings	_____	_____	_____	_____
Debt payment	_____	_____	_____	_____
Other	_____	_____	_____	_____
Total fixed expenses	_____	_____	_____	_____
Variable expenses:				
Food and beverages	_____	_____	_____	_____
Household operation and maintenance	_____	_____	_____	_____
Furnishings and equipment	_____	_____	_____	_____
Clothing	_____	_____	_____	_____
Personal	_____	_____	_____	_____
Transportation	_____	_____	_____	_____
Medical care	_____	_____	_____	_____
Recreation and education	_____	_____	_____	_____
Gifts and contributions	_____	_____	_____	_____
Other	_____	_____	_____	_____
Total variable expenses	_____	_____	_____	_____
Total expenses	_____	_____	_____	_____

DAILY LIVING COSTS

● Estimate Your Retirement Expenses

As discussed earlier, your expenses will be less when you retire than they were when you, and your spouse, were working. But how much less? To make a realistic comparison, list your major spending categories, starting with fixed expenses, such as rent or mortgage payments, utilities, insurance premiums, and taxes. Then list less fixed outlays—food, clothing, transportation, and so on. Finally, enter miscellaneous expenditures, such as hospitals, doctors, dentists, prescriptions, entertainment, vacations, gifts, contributions, and unforeseen expenses.

However, be sure you have an emergency fund for unforeseen expenses. Even when you are living a tranquil life, the unexpected can occur.

Also be sure to build a cushion to cope with inflation. Be pessimistic in your estimates of how much the price of goods and services will rise.

Adjust Your Expenses for Inflation

You now have a list of your probable monthly (and annual) expenses if you were to retire today. With inflation, however, those expenses will not be fixed. The possible loss of buying power due to inflation is what makes planning ahead so important. Over the last 20 years, the cost of living rose an

FIGURE 19-5   Rates of Inflation since 1965

Price increases of selected small-ticket consumer goods*

Item	Sep. 1984	Sep. 1986	Percent Change
Ground coffee (1 lb.)	$ 1.79	$ 3.19	78.2%
Liquid detergent (22 oz.)	1.29	1.89	46.5
Toothpaste (5 oz.)	.99	1.39	40.4
Taxi (2-mile ride)	3.10	4.25	37.1
Orange juice (½ gallon)	1.69	2.29	35.5
Pack of gum	.45	.60	33.3
Pizza slice	.95	1.25	31.6
Bananas (1 lb.)	.39	.49	25.6
Ground round beef (1 lb.)	1.99	2.49	25.1
Woman's haircut	20.00	25.00	25.0
Pint of ice cream	1.09	1.35	23.9
Movie	5.00	6.00	20.0
Shoe shine	1.25	1.50	20.0
Peanut butter (18 oz. jar)	1.79	2.09	16.8
Paperback book	3.75	4.35	16.0
Bottle of imported beer	1.30	1.50	15.4
Dry cleaning of a suit	6.00	6.75	12.5
News magazine	1.75	1.95	11.4
Fast food 4-oz. hamburger and milk shake	2.63	2.88	9.5
Full sole and rubber heels	25.00	27.00	8.0
Weighted average increase**	–	–	23.9%

But don't let the 1986 inflation rate fool you, just look at the price increases of selected small-ticket items from 1984 to 1986.

*Prices are at New York City retail levels and are used as examples only.
**Includes items not listed in table.

Source: *Citicorp Consumer Views*, July 1985, pp. 2–3.

average of 6.2 percent a year, though the rate has slowed to 3 or 4 percent between 1983 and mid-1987.[2]

To help you cope with this probable increase in your expenses, plan your retirement income needs accordingly. By using the inflation factor in Table 19–3, you can estimate what your monthly and annual expenses will be when you retire.

First, choose the approximate number of years until your retirement from the left-hand column.

Second, choose an estimated annual rate of inflation. Figure 19–5 shows

[2]"Plan Your Retirement Now, Enjoy It Later," *Citicorp Consumer Views*, July 1985, pp. 2–3.

TABLE 19-3   How Much Inflation in Your Future?

Find the inflation factor below that matches both the number of years until you'll retire and the inflation rate you've picked. To adjust your budget to inflated prices, multiply your annual retirement income by this factor.

Say you're now 55, and will retire in 10 years at age 65 on a budget of $20,000 a year in today's prices. You expect an average inflation rate of 5 percent over the next 10 years, and the table shows an inflation factor of 1.629.

That means living costs would be about 63 percent higher when you retire than they are now. Multiply $20,000 by 1.629. The result shows a retirement tab of $32,580 a year in 1995 prices.

Number of Years until You Retire	Average Annual Rate of Inflation between Now and Retirement					
	3%	4%	5%	6%	7%	8%
4	1.126	1.170	1.216	1.262	1.311	1.360
6	1.194	1.265	1.340	1.419	1.501	1.587
8	1.267	1.369	1.477	1.594	1.718	1.851
10	1.344	1.480	1.629	1.791	1.967	2.159
15	1.558	1.801	2.079	2.397	2.759	3.172
20	1.806	2.191	2.653	3.207	3.870	4.661
25	2.094	2.666	3.386	4.292	5.427	6.848

Source: *Citicorp Consumer Views*, July 1985, pp. 2–3. © Citicorp, 1985.

rates of inflation since 1965, but what the rates will be in the future cannot be predicted accurately.

Third, find the inflation factor corresponding to the number of years until your retirement and the estimated annual inflation rate.

Fourth, multiply the inflation factor by your estimated retirement expenses.

You may wish to refigure your inflated retirement income needs several times during your preretirement years, since unforeseen circumstances may change your estimate of the inflation factor or your retirement expenses. Once you retire, use the inflation factors in Table 19–3 to help you plan ahead.

PLANNING YOUR RETIREMENT INCOME

- Evaluate Your Planned Retirement Income

Social Security

Once you have determined your approximate future expenses, you must evaluate the sources and amounts of your retirement income. Possible sources of income for many retirees are social security, other public pension plans, employer pension plans, personal retirement plans, and annuities.

Social security is the most widely used source of retirement income. It should not be the only source, however. Social security covers almost all kinds of employment and self-employment, employment in federal government being the biggest exception. If you are eligible for social security, you may collect monthly retirement benefits at age 62 or older or disability at any age under 65 if a severe disability prevents you from working for a year or longer. Your eligibility for social security benefits is generally based on your lifetime earnings record (or your spouse's earnings record) and your age.

You must be fully insured under social security to be eligible for retirement and disability benefits on your own earnings record. This means that you must have credit for a certain amount of work covered by social security. The amount needed for both retirement and disability benefits depends on your ages and ranges from 1½ years to 10 years.

A variety of materials are available from the Social Security Administration to assist students and retired, disabled, unemployed, and needy persons who qualify for social security checks. The accompanying boxed feature outlines the social security benefits available to students.

Social security benefits are not paid automatically. You must apply for them. If you have decided when you will retire, phone or visit any social security office about three months before that date to file your application. Bring proof of your age and a record of your most recent earnings (for example, a W-2 statement or a tax return). You may wish to visit the social security office toward the end of the week or month, as it is less crowded then than at other times.

If you are contributing to social security, check your earnings record for accuracy about every three years. At the social security office, request a postcard form to use in requesting a statement of your earnings. If you are age 56 or older, you can also ask for an estimate of what your retirement benefits will be at retirement age.

The amount of your monthly social security check is based on your average

"My ultimate goal? Retirement."

From *The Wall Street Journal*, with permission of Cartoon Features Syndicate.

earnings covered under social security (or those of the insured worker's) and on your age.

Social security benefits are protected against inflation. These benefits automatically increase whenever living costs climbed 3 percent or more in a previous year.

Other Public Pension Plans

Besides social security, the federal government administers several other retirement plans (for federal government and railroad employees). The largest of these plans is the U.S. Civil Service Retirement System. Employees covered under this plan are not covered by social security. The Veteran Administration provides pensions for many survivors of men and women who died while in the Armed Forces and disability pensions for eligible veterans. The Railroad Retirement System is the only retirement system administered by the federal government that covers a single private industry. Many state, county, and city governments operate retirement plans for their employees.

In the Real World
Social Security Is Not Just for the Retired or Disabled

Social Security Checks for Students

Social security checks can be paid to a young unmarried person when a parent insured under social security dies or receives disability or retirement benefits. The son or daughter is eligible if he or she is:

Under 18—whether or not in school.
Under 19—and attending secondary school (high school in most cases) full-time.
Any age—if severely disabled before age 22.

Who Is a "Full-Time Student?"

You are a full-time student if you attend high school, junior high, or elementary school, provided:

The school considers you in full-time attendance.
You are enrolled for at least 20 hours a week in a course of study lasting at least 13 weeks.

When Checks Can Be Paid

Social security checks can be paid for all months you attend high school (or other approved school) up to the month you reach age 19. In some cases,

payment can continue longer—generally until completion of the school year or for two months after the month you are 19, whichever comes first.

You cannot get student checks if you work and your employer asked or required you to attend school and pays you for doing so. Nor can you receive checks if you are imprisoned for conviction of a felony.

If You Will Soon Be 18

If you now get social security checks as a child under 18, you will receive a notice a few

Employer Pension Plans

Another source of retirement income for you may be the pension plan offered by your company. With employer plans, your employer contributes to your retirement benefits—and sometimes you contribute too. Contributions and earnings on those contributions accumulate tax free until you receive them.

Since private pension plans vary, you should go to your firm's personnel office or union office to find out (1) when you become eligible for pension benefits and (2) what benefits you will be entitled to. Most employer plans are defined-benefit or defined-contribution plans.

A **defined-contribution plan** has an individual account for each employee; therefore, these plans are sometimes called individual account plans.[3] The plan document describes the amount that the employer will contribute, but

[3]Burton T. Beam, Jr., and John J. McFadden, *Employee Benefits* (Homewood, Ill.: Richard D. Irwin, 1985), pp. 260–61.

months before your 18th birthday. It will explain what to do to have your benefits continue if you have not yet completed high school.

You must apply for social security if you are a high school student who first becomes eligible for benefits between 18 and 19. This may be when a parent starts receiving retirement or disability checks, or dies. Call any social security office for more information.

How Earnings Can Affect Your Checks

Earnings from a job or self-employment may affect your social security checks if you become entitled. Earnings for the *entire* year have to be counted, including those in months before and after benefits start and in months after benefits end.

Here's how it works. If you earn $5,760 or less in 1986 you get all of your social security payments for the year. If you earn over $5,760, then $1 in benefits is withheld for each $2 you earn above that amount.

There is a special monthly rule that applies in the year benefits start and the year benefits end. If payments start or end in 1986, for example, you can receive a full benefit for any month in 1986 that your earnings do not exceed $480, no matter how high your total earnings are for the year.

The earnings of your parent on whose record you get social security checks may affect your benefits. For example, if your parent does not get a check for one or more months because of excess earnings, then you won't get a check for those months either, even if you did not work.

Source: Social Security Administration, 1986.

it does not promise any particular benefit. When a plan participant retires or otherwise becomes eligible for benefits, the benefit is the total amount in the participant's account, including past investment earnings on amounts put into the account.

Defined-contribution plans include:

1. Money-purchase pension plans, in which your employer promises to set aside a certain amount for you each year, generally a percentage of your earnings.

2. Stock bonus plans, in which your employer's contribution is used to buy stock in your company for you. The stock is usually held in trust until you retire, when you can receive your shares or sell them at their fair market value.

3. Profit sharing plans, in which your employer's contribution depends on the company's profits.

4. Another type of defined-contribution plan is called a salary reduction or 401(k) plan. Under a **401(k) plan**, your employer makes nontaxable contributions to the plan for your benefit and reduces your salary by the same amounts. If your employer is a tax-exempt institution such as a hospital, university, or museum, the salary reduction plan is called a Section 403(b) plan.

The Tax Reform Act of 1986 retains the $30,000 cap on annual contributions for money-purchase pension plans, stock bonus plans, and profit sharing plans. Eventually, the annual limit on such plans will increase in response to inflation. Figure 19–6 is based on a survey of the profit sharing plans of 437 companies.

The new tax act reduces from $30,000 to $7,000 the maximum annual amount that an employee can defer for a 401(k) plan. The maximum amount that you may contribute to a 403(b) plan now ranges from $9,500 annually up to $12,500 if you have worked for the same employer for 15 years or more. The maximum can be higher in plans to which your employer contributes.

Under some circumstances, you are allowed to make withdrawals from a 401(k) plan before age 59½ without penalty. In addition, lump-sum distributions that you receive from your 401(k) are eligible for five-year income averaging if you have been a participant in the plan for at least five years.

What happens to your benefits under an employer pension plan if you change jobs? One of the most important aspects of such plans is vesting. **Vesting** is your right to at least a portion of the benefits you have accrued under an employer pension plan (within certain limits), even though you leave your employer before you retire. The new tax act requires that you be fully vested after five years with the same employer.

In a **defined-benefit plan,**[4] the plan document specifies the benefit promised to the employee at the normal retirement age. The plan itself does not specify how much the employer must contribute annually. The plan's actuary determines the annual employer contribution required so that the plan

[4]Ibid.

FIGURE 19-6 Profit Sharing

A survey of the profit sharing plans of 437 companies showed that:

84 percent used deferred plans, depositing profits in a trust with no optional cash payout.

61 percent required or allowed employee contributions.

41 percent had only one investment fund for employee contributions, and 38 percent had only one fund for employer contributions.

The average contribution of employers in 1985 was 8.7 percent of their total covered payroll.

Source: *The Wall Street Journal*, November 19, 1986, p. 31; based on information from Hewitt Associates.

---

fund will be sufficient to pay the promised benefit as each participant retires. If the fund is inadequate, the employer must make additional contributions. Because of their actuarial aspects, defined-benefit plans tend to be more complicated and more expensive to administer than defined-contribution plans.

See the accompanying boxed feature for an example of how changing jobs affects your pension. Some pension plans allow portability. This enables you to carry earned benefits from one employer's pension plan to another employer's pension plan when you change jobs.

The Employee Retirement Income Security Act of 1974 (ERISA) sets minimum standards for pension plans in private industry and protects more than 50 million workers. The major provisions of the act are summarized in the accompanying boxed feature.

In addition to the retirement plans offered by social security, other public pension plans, and employer pension plans, many individuals have set up personal retirement plans.

Personal Retirement Plans

The two most popular personal retirement plans are individual retirement accounts (IRAs) and Keogh accounts.

Individual Retirement Accounts (IRAs). The **IRA**, which entails the establishment of a trust or a custodial account, is by far the most popular type of personal retirement plan. In 1986, over 40 million people had an IRA.

Before the passage of the Tax Reform Act of 1986, a working person could make a tax-deductible contribution of up to $2,000 a year to an IRA and a nonworking spouse could chip in $250. The IRA's earnings were not taxed until they were withdrawn.

The new tax act makes several important changes in the IRA rules. The rules remain unchanged for those not covered by company pension plans.

But if a pension plan at work covers you or your spouse, the IRA deduction may be reduced or eliminated for both of you. The new act does not affect your IRA deduction if you are covered by a pension plan and have adjusted gross income of less than $25,000 ($40,000 for joint filers). But you are allowed only a partial deduction if you earn between $40,000 and $50,000 on a joint return or between $25,000 and $35,000 on a single return. Beyond those income limits, the IRA deduction is completely eliminated. Table 19–4 summarizes the new IRA limitations.

Today's Lifestyles
Job-Hopping Pares Your Pension Benefits

Thomas Cody seemed to be getting ahead. In the 14 years since graduating from college, the graphic designer had advanced through six jobs and was making twice the salary of his first position.

But in one important respect, Cody, creative coordinator in Standard Oil Company's graphic communications department, was falling further and further behind. At age 36, he had never stayed at one company long enough to become vested in a pension plan or to qualify for long-term benefits. So far, he had built up some retirement savings, but not much of which to speak. As a result, he believed that he might never be able to retire. "I may have to let my talent be my pension," he said.

Cody is typical of many baby boomers. Faced with mergers, layoffs, intense competition from their own ranks—and perhaps their own restlessness—many young professionals change companies every three or four years. Each move is often attractive in the short run. But such individuals usually sacrifice some or all of their long-term benefits, including pensions, stock options, profit sharing, or company contributions to an employee savings plan. The net result: Young job-hoppers will lose financial ground as often as they gain it, many benefit consultants say.

In addition to losing those benefits—which could amount to significant sums when compounded to retirement—the job-hopper loses time. Normally, he must wait through the new employer's vesting period to qualify again for retirement benefit.

Yet even if a job-hopper stays with several companies long enough to become vested, he still gets hit most of the time. The sum of his small pensions won't add up to the one big pension he would have received had he spent his whole career with one company (see accompanying table).

If possible, "you want to get all your job-hopping done by the time you're in your late 30s," said James G. Waters, a vice president of the New York–based management consulting firm Towers, Perrin, Forster & Crosby. Unless an employee is a "top banana," Waters said, his pension will probably be diminished each time he moves. And the older he is at the time of the move, the more he will lose.

Many workers fail to review either their benefits or vesting schedules when considering a move, consultants say. Moreover, such plans can be tricky. An employee might have stayed long enough at a com-

However, whether or not you are covered by a pension plan, you can still make nondeductible IRA contributions and all of the income your IRA earns will compound tax deferred until you withdraw money from the IRA. Remember, the biggest benefit of an IRA lies in its tax-deferred earnings growth, and the longer the money accumulates tax deferred, the bigger the benefit.

Table 19–5 shows the magic of a tax-deferred IRA. If you are 25 years old now, the difference between investing $2,000 a year into a taxable invest-

pany to be eligible for retirement benefits but may have to work through the end of the year to receive them.

"Too often a person makes the decision to move, and then they want to try to save what they can," said P. Thomas Austin tax partner with the Cleveland-based accounting firm, Ernst & Whinney. "By then it's too late."

Source: Adapted from Betsy Morris, "Your Money Matters," *The Wall Street Journal*, July 24, 1986, p. 21.

The High Cost of Job-Hopping

Pension basis: One percentage point per year of service multiplied by final salary.

	Years of Service	Percentage Point Credit		Final Salary		Annual Pensions
Employee A						
1st job	10	10%	×	$ 35,817	=	$ 3,582
2nd job	10	10	×	64,143	=	6,414
3rd job	10	10	×	114,870	=	11,487
4th job	10	10		205,714		20,571
				Total pension: $42,054		
Employee B						
1st job	40	40	×	205,714	=	82,286
				Total pension: $82,286		

Note: Figures assume starting salary of $20,000 and 6 percent annual inflation rate. Pay increases match inflation rate.
Source: Federal Reserve Bank of Boston.

TABLE 19-4   The Quick IRA Contribution Test

The chart below provides an easy way for you to see which type of IRA contribution you are eligible to make under the new tax act.

Income		Covered by a Pension Plan (you or your spouse)?	Type of $2,000 Contribution
Family	Individual		
$40,000 and under	$25,000 and under	Yes	Fully deductible
$40,000 and under	$25,000 and under	No	Fully deductible
$40,001–$50,000	$25,001–$35,000	Yes	Partially deductible
$40,001–$50,000	$25,001–$35,000	No	Fully deductible
Above $50,000	Above $35,000	Yes	Nondeductible
Above $50,000	Above $35,000	No	Fully deductible

If, for example, your income is between $40,000 and $50,000 ($25,000–$35,000 for individuals), you are eligible to make both a deductible *and* a nondeductible IRA contribution—even if you are covered by an employee pension plan.

A simple formula is used to calculate the deductible contribution. Here's how it works:

If your family income is $43,500, that puts you $3,500 above the income limit of $40,000 for a fully deductible $2,000 IRA contribution. You simply divide $3,500 by 10,000 to obtain the percentage of your $2,000 contribution that is nondeductible. Then subtract this amount from $2,000 to obtain the amount of your deductible contribution.

Step 1: $43,500 − $40,000 = $3,500

Step 2: $\dfrac{\$3,500}{10,000} = 35\% \times \$2,000 = \$700$

Step 3: $2,000 − $700 = $1,300

You are able to make a $1,300 fully deductible IRA contribution. And so is your spouse if you are both working. You may also make a $700 nondeductible contribution, for a total allowable IRA contribution of $2,000.

ment versus a tax-deferred IRA can be as much as $211,434 by the time you are 65. That's because in a taxable investment, unlike a tax-deferred IRA, a portion of your interest earnings is taxed away each year.

Simplified Employee Pension Plans–IRA (SEP–IRA). SEP plans are nothing more than individual retirement accounts funded by an employer. Each employee sets up an IRA account at a bank or a brokerage house. Then the employer makes an annual contribution of up to 15 percent of an employee's salary or $30,000, whichever is less.[5]

"A SEP is probably the easiest of any qualified retirement plan to set up, as far as the administrative hassles for an employer go," according to John A. Corsaro, tax manager at Seidman & Seidman/BDO in New York. Because employees manage their own SEP–IRAs, Corsaro noted, an employer doesn't have to pay a lawyer to set up a pension trust fund or an accountant to do an annual audit.[6]

[5]Steven P. Galante, "Simplified Pension Plans Get a Boost From New Tax Law," *The Wall Street Journal*, November 17, 1986, p. 35.

[6]Ibid.

In the Real World
What You Should Know about the Pension Law

More than 50 million workers are protected by the Employee Retirement Income Security Act of 1974 (ERISA). ERISA sets minimum standards for pension plans in private industry. For example, it specifies when you can start building up pension benefits, how long you can be away from your job before you have a break in service, and your spouse's right to part of your pension in the event of your death. ERISA, which was enacted in 1974, was amended in 1984 by the Retirement Equity Act (REA). REA provides additional protections for spouses of participants and liberalizes ERISA rules on participation and vesting.

The law provides that:

Age and service requirements for eligibility for pension plan participation must not be unreasonable.

People who work for a specified minimum period under a pension plan will receive at least some pension at retirement.

The money will be there to pay pension benefits when they are due.

Plan funds must be handled prudently.

Employees and their beneficiaries must be informed of their rights and entitlements under their plans.

Spouses of pensioners are protected (through joint and survivor provisions).

The benefits of workers in some defined-benefit pension plans are protected in the event of a plan termination (through insurance provisions). In a defined-benefit plan, the amount of the pension benefits you will receive when you retire is determined in advance.

You are also entitled to:

Appeal if you are denied benefits.

Exercise your rights under your plan and ERISA without harassment or interference.

Sue in federal court to recover benefits.

Source: *What You Should Know about the Pension Law* (Washington, D.C.: Department of Labor, Office of Pension and Welfare Benefit Programs, December 1985), p. 5.

TABLE 19-5   Value of Deposits at Age 65 Assuming a Constant Rate of 7.5 Percent

Age	Total deposit at Age 65 (@ $2,000/year)	A Taxable Investment	An IRA Investment (tax deferred)	Difference
20	$90,000	$321,662	$664,129	$342,466
25	80,000	243,078	454,513	211,434
30	70,000	181,578	308,503	126,924
35	60,000	133,449	206,798	73,349
40	50,000	95,783	135,955	40,171
45	40,000	66,306	86,609	20,302
50	30,000	43,238	52,236	8,998
55	20,000	25,185	28,294	3,109
60	10,000	11,056	11,616	560

Note: Assumes a 33 percent tax rate.
Source: Insights, Freedom Federal Savings Bank, Fall 1986, p. 3.

Pension planners expect SEPs to get their biggest boost from a provision in the Tax Reform Act of 1986 that allows you to shelter income from taxes by making voluntary contributions to your SEP–IRAs. Starting in 1987, in addition to receiving the employer's contribution, an employee can defer up to $7,000 of his or her annual salary by putting it away in a SEP. That individual contribution, plus the money it earns, is tax exempt until it is withdrawn.[7]

Your investment opportunities for IRA funds are not limited to savings accounts or certificates of deposit; you can put your money in many kinds of investments.

Where to Invest Your IRA Money. You can put your IRA money into almost any kind of investment: certificates of deposit, mutual funds, annuities, stocks, bonds, real estate, and so forth. Only life insurance, precious metals,[8] collectibles, and securities bought on margin are forbidden. Before you make your choice consider how much risk is involved. If you have other secure retirement income, you may elect somewhat risky but potentially profitable IRA investments. But if your IRA is going to provide an important part of your retirement income, it is best to be conservative.

Figure 19–7 shows how 45 million individuals have invested their IRA money. However, the new tax act may change the investment pattern. Without the sugar of a tax deduction, IRAs become considerably less sweet. Some advisers now suggest that their clients buy shares in a tax-exempt bond

[7]Ibid.

[8]The Tax Reform Act of 1986 does permit you to deposit new U.S.–minted gold and silver coins—for example, the American Eagle—in your IRA, but to do this you must name a bank or other institution as custodian and pay a storage fee.

FIGURE 19-7   Investing in Our Retirement

Assets in individual retirement accounts have skyrocketed since 1982, the first year Congress allowed them for all wage earners. Experts predict that low interest rates on bank certificates of deposit and a booming stock market will result in banks and thrifts getting an even smaller share of the market this year.

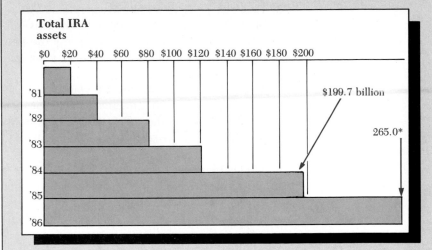

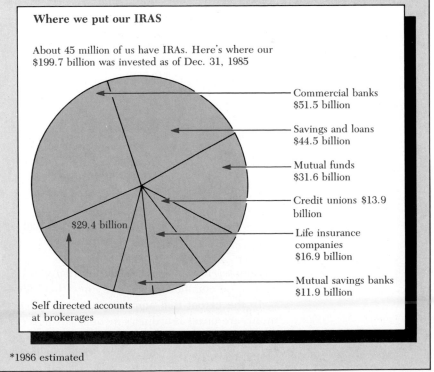

*1986 estimated

Source: *USA Today*, March 31, 1986, p. 4B; 1986 estimate from *USA Today*, January 29, 1986, p. 1B.

fund or purchase a tax-deferred annuity or other investment instead of investing in an IRA.[9]

IRA Withdrawals. When you retire, you will be able to withdraw your IRA in a lump sum, withdraw it in installments over your life expectancy, or place it in an annuity that guarantees payments over your lifetime. If you take the lump sum, the entire amount will be taxable as ordinary income and the only tax break you will have is standard five-year income averaging. IRA withdrawals made before age 59½ are now subject to a 10 percent tax in addition to ordinary income tax, unless the participant dies or is disabled. You can avoid this tax if you roll over your IRA.

The Rollover IRA Strategy. If you change jobs or if you retire before age 59½, one of your most attractive options for managing your retirement plan distribution will be the rollover IRA. This option enables you to avoid the early distribution penalty on pre-59½ distributions.

Keogh Plans. A **Keogh plan,** also known as an H.R.10 plan or as a self-employed retirement plan, is a qualified pension plan that has been developed for self-employed individuals and their employees. Generally, Keogh plans must not discriminate in favor of a self-employed person or any employee. Both defined-contribution and defined-benefit Keogh plans have tax-deductible contribution limits, and other restrictions also apply to Keogh plans. Therefore, you should obtain professional tax advice before using this type of retirement plan. The new tax act did not change the rules for Keogh plans.

The schedule shown in Table 19–6 compares the annual contribution dollar limits under the old and new tax laws for Keogh, 401(k), SEP–IRA, and 403(b) retirement plans.

Annuities

In Chapter 14, you learned what an annuity is and how annuities provide lifelong security. You can outlive the proceeds of your IRA, your Keogh plan, or your investments, but an **annuity** provides guaranteed income for life.

You can buy an annuity as your individual retirement account—with the proceeds of an IRA or a company pension—or as supplemental retirement income. You can buy an annuity with a single payment or with periodic payments. You can buy an annuity that will begin payouts immediately, or, as is more common, you an buy one that will begin payouts at a later date.

To the extent that annuity payments exceed your premiums, these payments are taxed as ordinary income as you receive them, but earned interest on annuities accumulates tax free until the payments begin. Annuities may be fixed, providing a specific income for life, or they may be variable, with

[9]John R. Dorfman, "Many Investors Plan to Drop IRAs, but Some Ought to Think Twice," *The Wall Street Journal,* January 15, 1987, p. 21.

TABLE 19-6   Contribution Limits for Qualified Retirement Plans

The Tax Reform Act of 1986 has changed the contribution dollar limits for some qualified plans. The new contribution limits for retirement plans are shown in the chart below.

Retirement Plan	Annual Contribution Dollar Limit	
	Old Law	New Law
Keogh	$30,000	$30,000
401(k)	30,000	7,000
SEP–IRA	30,000	30,000
403(b)	20,000	9,500

payouts above a guaranteed minimum level dependent on investment return. Either way, the rate of return on annuities is often pegged to market rates.

Types of Annuities. *Immediate annuities* are generally purchased by people of retirement age. Such annuities provide income payments at once. They are usually purchased with a lump-sum payment.

With deferred annuities, income payments start at some future date. Interest builds up on the money you deposit. Such annuities are often used by younger people to save money toward retirement.

A *deferred annuity* purchased with a lump sum is known as a single-premium deferred annuity. In recent years, such annuities have been popular because of the tax-free buildup during the accumulation period.

If you are buying a deferred annuity, you may wish to obtain a contract that permits flexible premiums. With such an annuity, your contributions may vary from year to year. An annuity of this kind can be used to provide funds for an IRA. Most of the deferred annuities sold today are either single-premium or flexible premium annuities.

The cash value of your life insurance policy may be converted to an annuity. If you are over 65 and your children have completed their education and are financially self-sufficient, you may feel that you no longer need all of your life insurance coverage. An option in your life insurance policy lets you convert its cash value to a lifetime income.

Options in Annuities

You can decide on the terms under which your annuity pays off for you and your family. The major options are as follows.

Straight Life Annuity. With a straight life annuity, also called a pure annuity, you receive an income for the rest of your life, but no payments are made to anyone after your death. This type of annuity provides the largest amount of income per dollar of purchase money. It is recommended for a person who needs as much annuity income as possible and either has no dependents or has taken care of them through other means.

Life Annuity with Installments Certain. You receive an income for the rest of your life. If you die within a certain period after you start receiving income, usually 10 or 20 years, your beneficiary receives regular payments for the balance of that period.

Installment Refund Annuity. You receive an income for the rest of your life. However if you die before receiving as much money as you paid in, your beneficiary receives regular income until the total payments equal that amount.

Which Annuity Option Is the Best?

The straight life annuity gives more income per dollar of outlay than any other type. But its payments stop when you die, whether that's a month or many years after the payout begins.

Should you get an annuity with a guaranteed return? There are differences of opinion. Some experts argue that it is a mistake to diminish your monthly income just to make sure that your money is returned to your survivors. Some suggest that if you want to assure that your spouse or someone else continues to receive annuity income after your death, you might choose the joint and survivor annuity. Such an annuity pays its installments until the death of the last designated survivor. There is still another choice that you must make: how your annuity premiums are to be invested.

With a fixed dollar annuity, the money you pay is invested in bonds and mortgages that have a guaranteed return. With such an annuity, you are guaranteed a fixed amount each payout period.

With a variable annuity, the money you pay is generally invested in common stocks or other equities. The income you receive will depend on the investment results.

An annuity guarantees lifetime income, but you have a choice about the form that it will take. Discuss all of the possible options with your insurance agent.

The costs, fees, and other features of annuities differ from policy to policy. Ask about sales and administrative charges, purchase and withdrawal fees, and interest rate guarantees.

Table 19–7 shows how the Tax Reform Act of 1986 affects pension and deferred compensation plans, employee benefits, and employee stock option plans (ESOPs).

TABLE 19-7   Effects of the Tax Reform Act of 1986 on Retirement Planning

Provision	Old Law	New Law
Treatment of tax-favored savings		
Individual retirement accounts (IRAs)	An individual may deduct from gross income up to $2,000 to contribute to an IRA. An IRA also receives tax-deferred accumulation. A nonworking spouse may deduct $250.	Current law deductibility of up to $2,000 retained for taxpayer and taxpayer spouse, regardless of income, if they're not active participants in an employer-sponsored retirement plan, including tax-sheltered annuities, government plans, simplified employee pensions (SEPs) and Keogh plans. Low-income individuals also allowed deductibility, even if taxpayer or spouse is an active plan participant. The $2,000 deduction is phased out at income levels between $40,000 and $50,000 adjusted gross income (AGI) AGI for joint returns ($25,000 and $35,000, single).
		Individuals may make nondeductible contributions to a separate account to the extent that they are ineligible for deductible contributions. Where one spouse has no earned income, the maximum on joint returns is $2,250. The nondeductible contribution is subject to the same dollar limits for deductible contributions of $2,000 of earned income ($2,250 for a spousal account). Income in the account accumulates tax free until distribution. Provision generally effective January 1, 1987. Tax on early withdrawals is 10 percent.
Deferred annuity contracts	Interest credited to the cash surrender value of a deferred annuity is not taxed currently but is taxed when paid to the policyholder. A 5 percent tax is imposed if holder withdraws any amount before age 59½	Investment income earned under a deferred annuity contract is taxable if the contract is owned by a corporation, trust, or other like entity not a natural person.
		Tax on early withdrawals is increased to 10 percent by modifying the circumstances under which early withdrawal is imposed.
Special rules for simplified employee pensions (SEP)	If an IRA qualifies for a SEP, the annual IRA deduction limit is the lesser of 15 percent of pay or $30,000.	Adopts simplifying SEP amendments and permits elective deferrals to employees of small firms up to $7,000. Essentially turns SEP plans into 401(k) plans.

TABLE 19-7 *(continued)*

Provision	Old Law	New Law
Minimum standards for qualified plans		
Coverage requirements for qualified plans	A plan generally satisfies the coverage rules if it meets either the percentage test or the fair cross section test. A plan meets the percentage test if it benefits at least 70 percent of all employees or if it benefits at least 80 percent of all employees eligible to benefit, and at least 70 percent of all employees are eligible. A fair cross section test is one that, as determined by the secretary of the Treasury, covers a classification of employees that does not discriminate in favor of employees who are officers or shareholders or who are highly compensated. No specific rules on line of business or operating unit.	Qualified plans must cover (1) 70 percent of non–highly compensated employees covered, (2) a percentage of non–highly compensated employees equal to at least 70 percent of the percentage of highly compensated employees covered, (3) a reasonable classification test (imposed by Treasury), or (4) an alternative classification test.
Vesting	Employer-provided benefits must be vested upon attainment of normal retirement age, at all times in the benefit derived from employee contributions, and, with respect to employer-provided benefits, at least as rapidly as under the following three alternative schedules: *(a)* upon completion of 10 years of service; *(b)* beginning at 25 percent after completion of 5 years of service, increasing gradually to 100 percent after 15 years; *(c)* 50 percent vesting after 5 years and when the sum of age and years of service is at least 45, and an additional 10 percent vesting for each additional year of service and two-point increases in the sum of age and years of service, until 100 percent vesting has been attained after 15 years of service. Faster vesting is required for top-heavy plans. The requirements apply to multiemployer plans.	Generally, requires full vesting upon completion of five years of service or vesting at 20 percent after three years of service, increased by 20 percent each subsequent year until full vesting at seven years. One hundred percent 10-year vesting required for multiemployer plans. Class year vesting not permitted. Effective generally after December 31, 1988.

TABLE 19-7 *(concluded)*

Provision	Old Law	New Law
Withdrawal of benefits		
Uniform minimum distribution rules	Distribution of a participant's benefits must commence when the participant (1) attains the age of 70½, or (2) with respect to participants who are 5 percent owners, the taxable year in which the participant retires, if later.	For IRAs, qualified plans, and tax-sheltered annuities, distribution must commence no later than April 1 of calendar year following the year in which participant attains age 70½. Sanctions for not abiding by rules amount to a 50 percent excise tax on the minimum amount required to be distributed over the amount actually distributed. Nondeductible tax borne by the recipient. Effective date: January 1, 1989.
Withdrawals before age 59½	An additional 10 percent income tax is imposed on certain early withdrawals.	Generally, conforms to early withdrawal rules for qualified plans and tax-sheltered annuities to the rules for IRAs (requiring a 10 percent tax on early withdrawal). Exceptions include death, disability, distributions as part of a series scheduled by the plan, and retirement at age 55.
Lump sum; other distribution requirements	Certain lump-sum distributions received under a qualified plan may qualify for special 10-year forward averaging treatment. A participant may elect to treat the pre-1974 portion of any qualified plan or tax-sheltered annuity as long-term capital gain.	Retains current law (10-year forward income averaging) for those who reached age 50 by January 1, 1986. Otherwise allows only onetime five-year averaging after age 59½; also phases out capital gains character of the pre-1974 portion of a lump-sum distribution over a six-year period. Extends restrictions to all tax-sheltered annuities. Repeals three-year basis recovery rule and treats each distribution as partly a payment of income and partly a recovery of employee distributions.
Tax deferral under qualified plan		
Asset reversions under qualified plans	Assets may generally not be used except to satisfy employee liabilities, but if they revert to the employer, assets are fully includable in the employer's gross income.	Generally, applies an excise tax of 10 percent of plan funds reverting to employer upon plan termination.

Source: *Taxaction '86* (New York: E. F. Hutton, n.d.), pp. 13–15.

Will You Have Enough Money during Retirement?

Now that you have reviewed all your possible sources of retirement income, use Table 19–8 to estimate what you annual retirement income will be. Don't forget to inflate incomes or investments that increase with the cost

TABLE 19-8   Retirement Income

Source	Amount per Year	
	Income Now	Inflated Income
Social security	$_____	$_____
Other government pension	_____	_____
Private pension	_____	_____
IRA, Keogh	_____	_____
Annuities	_____	_____
Dividends, interest, etc.	_____	_____
Other	_____	_____
	_____	_____
Total income	$_____	$_____

FIGURE 19-8   The Higher Your Salary Is when You Retire, the Lower Is the Percentage of Salary Replaced by Pension Income and Social Security.

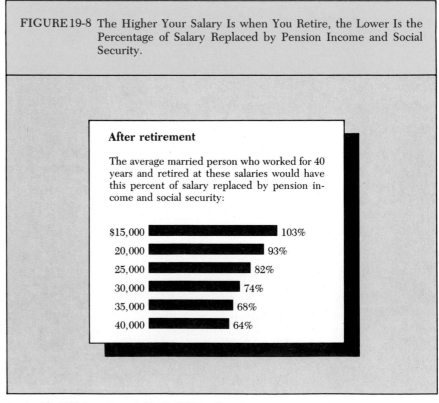

After retirement

The average married person who worked for 40 years and retired at these salaries would have this percent of salary replaced by pension income and social security:

$15,000	103%
20,000	93%
25,000	82%
30,000	74%
35,000	68%
40,000	64%

Source: *The Wall Street Journal*, May 7, 1986, p. 31.

of living (such as social security) to what they will be when you retire. (Use the inflation factors presented in Table 19–3.)

Figure 19–8 shows what an average married person can expect from pension income and social security.

Now compare your total estimated retirement income with your total inflated retirement expenses, as figured earlier. If your estimated income exceeds your estimated expenses and a large portion of your planned income will automatically increase with the cost of living during your retirement, you are in good shape. (You should evaluate your plans every few years between now and retirement to be sure your planned income is still adequate to meet your planned expenses.)

If, however, your planned retirement income is less than your estimated retirement expenses, now is the time to take action to increase your retirement income. Also, if a large portion of your retirement income is fixed and will not increase with inflation, you should make plans for a much larger retirement income to meet your inflating expenses during retirement.

Investing for Retirement

The guaranteed income part of your retirement fund consists of money paid into lower-yield, very safe forms of investment. This part of your fund may already be taken care of through social security or retirement plans discussed earlier. If you would like to add to this part, other low-risk investments, as discussed in previous chapters, are savings accounts and certifi-

---

TABLE 19-9   Determining Investments

If you need this much extra money for retirement,	and it will be _____ years before you retire, you should save _____ each month				
	5	10	15	20	25
	In an investment yielding a 6 percent rate of return				
$ 5,000	$ 74.40	$ 31.57	$ 17.88	$11.32	$ 7.59
10,000	148.81	63.13	35.77	22.64	15.18
15,000	223.21	94.70	53.65	33.97	22.77
20,000	297.62	126.26	71.53	45.29	30.36
25,000	372.02	157.83	89.41	56.61	37.95
30,000	444.05	189.68	107.39	67.95	45.57
	In an investment yielding a 9 percent rate of return				
$ 5,000	$ 69.68	$ 27.43	$14.19	$ 8.14	$ 4.92
10,000	139.35	54.86	28.38	16.29	9.84
15,000	209.03	82.29	42.57	24.43	14.76
20,000	278.71	109.72	56.77	32.58	19.68
25,000	348.38	137.15	70.96	40.72	24.60
30,000	418.06	164.58	85.15	48.86	29.52

cates of deposit, U.S. savings bonds, money market securities, municipal and corporate bonds, and real estate.

Table 19–9 will help you determine how much you should invest monthly in either a low-risk, high-yield investment (guaranteed income) or a high-risk, high-yield investment to reach the goal for additional retirement income that you calculated earlier.

LIVING ON YOUR RETIREMENT INCOME

• Budgeting Retirement Income

As you planned your retirement, you estimated a budget or spending plan. Now you may find that your actual expenses at retirement are higher than you anticipated.

The first step in stretching your retirement income is to make sure you are receiving all the income to which you are entitled. Examine the possible sources of income mentioned earlier to see whether there are more programs or additional benefits that you could qualify for. What assets or valuables could you use as a cash or income source?

To stay within your income, you may also need to make some changes in your spending plans. For example, you could use your skills and time instead of your money. There are probably many things you could do yourself instead of paying someone else to do them. Take advantage of free and low-cost recreation, such as walks, picnics, public parks, lectures, museums, libraries, art galleries, art fairs, gardening, and church and club programs.

"He was a farm boy who made a fortune in the big city so he could buy a farm and become a farm boy again!"

From *The Wall Street Journal*, with permission of Cartoon Features Syndicate.

Tax Advantages

Be sure to take advantage of all the tax savings given to retirees. You may need to file a quarterly estimated income tax return beginning with the first quarter of your first year of retirement. For more information, ask your local IRS for a free copy of *Tax Benefits for Older Americans*. If you have any questions about your taxes, get help from someone at the IRS.

Working during Retirement

You may want to work part-time or start a new part-time career after you retire. Retirement work can provide a greater sense of usefulness, involvement, and self-worth and may be the ideal way to add to your retirement income. You may want to pursue a personal interest or hobby, or you can contact your state or local agency on aging for information on employment opportunities for retirees.

If you decide to work part-time after you retire, you should be aware of how your earnings will affect your social security income. As long as you do not earn more than the annually exempt amount, your social security payments will not be affected. But if you earn more than the annual exempt amount, your social security payments will be reduced. Check with your local social security office for the latest information.

SUMMARY

- Retirement planning is important because you will probably spend many years in retirement; social security and a private pension may be insufficient to cover the cost of living; and inflation may erode the purchasing power of your retirement savings.
- Analyze your current assets (everything you own) and your current liabilities (everything you owe). The difference between your assets and your liabilities is your net worth. Review your assets to make sure they are suitable for retirement.
- The spending patterns of retirees change, so it is impossible to predict the exact amount of money you will need in retirement. However, you can estimate your expenses. Some of those expenses will increase; others will decrease.

- Where you live in retirement can influence your financial needs. You are the only one who can determine the location and housing that are best for you. The types of housing available to retirees include single-family houses, multifamily houses, rentals, condominiums, cooperatives, mobile home parks, and housing projects for retirees. Each of these living arrangements has its advantages and disadvantages.
- Estimate your retirement expenses, and adjust those expenses for inflation, using the appropriate inflation factor.
- Your possible sources of income during retirement include social security, other public pension plans, employer pension plans, personal retirement plans, and annuities.
- Compare your total estimated retirement in-

come with your total inflated retirement expenses. If your income approximates your expenses, you are in good shape; if not, determine additional income needs and sources.

GLOSSARY

Annuity.   A contract that provides an income for life or a certain number of years, or both.

Defined-benefit plan.   A plan in which the participants know in advance what benefits they will receive at retirement.

Defined contribution plan.   A plan—profit sharing, money purchase, Keogh, or 401(k)—in which an individual account is provided for each participant.

401(k) plan.   A plan under which employees can defer current taxation on a portion of their salary.

Individual retirement account (IRA).   A special account in which you set aside a portion of your income; taxes are not paid on the principal or interest until money is withdrawn from the account.

Keogh plan.   A plan intended to fund the retirement of self-employed persons and their employees.

Reverse annuity mortgage.   A mortgage in which the lender uses your house as collateral to buy an annuity for you from an insurance company.

Vesting.   Your right to at least a portion of the benefits you accrue under an employer retirement plan even if you leave the employer before you retire.

REVIEW QUESTIONS

1. Give three reasons why it is important to plan for your retirement.

2. What factors will you consider in reviewing your assets? What determines the suitability of those assets for retirement?

3. What expenses are likely to increase and decrease during retirement? Why?

4. What factors will you consider in estimating your retirement living needs? What types of housing are available to retirees? What are the advantages and disadvantages of these housing types?

5. In estimating your expenses, what two warnings should you remember?

6. List various sources of retirement income. What is a major source of retirement income for most Americans?

7. What are defined-benefit and defined-contribution plans? What are the differences between the two?

8. What are fixed and variable annuities for retirement? How are the payments on these annuities taxed?

9. What steps are taken in determining additional retirement income needs?

10. What are some possible vehicles for investing during retirement? Which of these vehicles are relatively risk free? Which are riskier?

11. Outline the steps you must take in order to live on your retirement income and balance your retirement budget.

DISCUSSION QUESTIONS AND ACTIVITIES

1. If young professionals are worried about their retirement, why don't they do something about it? Where should they start?

2. Discuss: "Probably the most important advice you can get is simply to plan as soon as possible for the future. Don't put it off, and don't wait for things to 'fall in place.'"

3. Why are many of the young professionals who worry about the future reluctant to plan for retirement?

4. Discuss this statement: "Planning for retirement is useless because the future is so uncertain and because present circumstances can change overnight."

5. Although two thirds of surveyed young professionals said that planning for retirement was "very important," 74 percent said that they were in fair or poor shape financially for retirement. How do you explain this?

6. If you were to start retirement planning at age 25, what investment options would you choose? Why?

7. Prepare your balance sheet by listing your assets and liabilities. What assets will you earmark for retirement income?

8. How will your spending patterns change during your retirement years?

9. Which type of housing will best meet your retirement housing needs?

10. Discuss pros and cons of living with one's children during the retirement years.

11. Under what circumstances can students be eligible for social security and disability benefits?

ADDITIONAL READINGS

"Annuities That Pay Off after Retirement." *U.S. News & World Report*, February 24, 1986, p. 60.

"Changing Course." *U.S. News & World Report*, October 6, 1986, p. 46.

Feinstein, Selwyn. "Early Retirement." *The Wall Street Journal*, January 9, 1987, p. 1.

Kehoe, Tom. "Retirement: Sooner than You Think." *USA Today*, March 3, 1986, p. 11E.

Know Your Pension Plan. Washington, D.C.: Department of Labor, Office of Pension and Welfare Benefit Programs, 1986.

Lublin, Joann S. "Costly Retirement Home Market Booms, Raising Concern for Aged." *The Wall Street Journal*, October 22, 1986, p. 31.

Morris, Betsy. "Frequent Job Changes May Hurt Young Workers upon Retirement." *The Wall Street Journal*, July 24, 1986, p. 21.

Often-Asked Questions about Employee Retirement Income Security. Washington, D.C.: Department of Labor, September 1985.

Slocum, Ken. "On the Move." *The Wall Street Journal*, July 16, 1986, p. 1.

Walker, Deborah. "New Retirement Strategies to Beat Tax Reform." *Privileged Information*, February 15, 1987, p. 1.

What You Should Know about the Pension Law. Washington, D.C.: Department of Labor, December 1985.

Wong, Jan. "Despite Their Touted Advantages, IRAs Are Not the Best Investment for Everyone." *The Wall Street Journal*, March 24, 1986, p. 21.

CASE 19–1 Retirement Planning*

Margaret Bruno was 34 years old. In the past 13 years, she had seen her father die and had watched her mother, who now lived with her, grow frail and poor. She was emphatic about how she intended to live her own life.

"My father died at 50, and he had nothing—but he had never done anything either," said this Chicago saleswoman. "If I'm going to go out at 50, I want to make sure I've done as much as I possibly can between now and when I'm 50. If I don't have anything for when I'm 52, I'll handle it. Somehow I'll handle it."

Young adults whose parents were ill prepared to retire and are struggling in retirement would appear to have more incentive to plan for the future. But they don't. They fear that if they deny themselves luxuries now, they still run the risk of not being able to enjoy the good life later.

"My grandfather-in-law hoarded his whole life—every nickel, every penny he could get his hands on he put away in the bank," said Sheryl Gluck, 35, who managed a photography studio. "Then my grandmother-in-law became very sick. The past two years, nursing home and hospitals have taken every penny from him. She is vegetating in a nursing home, dying day by day, and he is now in a retirement home with no money."

But that didn't prompt Gluck to prepare any further for her retirement. On the contrary, she said, "what good was all the hoarding and all the depriving yourself of everything? This man worked an entire lifetime to give all his money away. You can't worry about the future; you don't know what's going to happen."

"There were a lot of family circumstances that happened where one day somebody was fine and the next day they died," said Gluck. "And ever since that started happening, . . . I decided I may not be here tomorrow or I may not be here next week and I'm going to start living for today. That's why I guess I don't see 30 years down the road to retirement."

So had she become more fatalistic? She shook her head. "I see it as realistic," she said.

Questions

1. Is Sheryl Gluck realistic? What fallacies do you detect in her arguments?

2. Are young professionals inclined to shrug off planning for retirement because they live in an economy that encourages spending and discourages saving?

3. Thoughts of providing for themselves, their children, and possibly their parents only seem to make many young adults turn their backs on the future. Why?

*Adapted from Edwin A. Finn Jr., "Instead of Planning for Retirement, Young Professionals Fret about It," *The Wall Street Journal,* December 9, 1985, p. 23.

CASE 19–2 Early Retirement*

Before taking early retirement in 1980, Howard Shank made a list of the things he wanted to do when he was no longer the president at Leo Burnett Company, a Chicago advertising agency. High on his agenda were painting, writing, golf, and traveling. But Shank, who was then 57, wasn't ready to follow his own advice. Instead, he let others tell him how a man of his talent, experience, and vigor should spend his retirement years. So he taught, consulted, and was miserable for 18 months.

When he faced the prospect of early retirement in 1981, Charles Gedge had plenty of misgivings. He was 59 when Sears Roebuck & Co. offered retirement incentives to 2,500 managers, aiming to reduce employment and make room for younger workers eager to move up. The offer was attractive: half pay for three years plus all of his accrued pension benefits in a lump sum. Still, after 30 years with Sears, Gedge wasn't ready to end his career. "I had seen so many people who retired at Sears who were dead in a couple of years," he said.

There was nothing sudden about Frederic Libby's retirement. He had plotted it for more than a decade, and he hadn't had any second thoughts. In 1982, at age 60, he left his job at Eastman Kodak, after 32 years with the company. Eight years earlier, he had bought a lot on North Carolina's Outer Banks. And six years earlier, he had bought a boat suited to the Carolina waters. With a 50 percent Kodak pension and navy benefits, he figured that he could afford to live out his days happily on the beach.

Roger Birk also laid out a retirement schedule when, in 1980, he was asked to become the chairman and chief executive of Merrill Lynch. He said that he would probably retire in five years, when he was only 55. His predecessor, Donald Regan, who became the White House chief of staff, "offered to bet I would change my mind,"

Birk said. But Birk was true to his word, ending his 30 years with the brokerage house in July 1985.

But Arthur Freitas knew he needed supplemental income when, at age 57, he accepted early retirement from Union Carbide Corporation in 1984. His 33 years with Carbide entitled him to one year's pay and a 60 percent pension. But two of his four children were still at home. So he continued to work—first with a nonprofit agency and then as a business broker.

Questions

1. What can be learned from the experiences of Shank, Gedge, Libby, Birk, and Freitas?

2. Do you think it fair for companies to retire older employees early in order to reduce employment and make room for younger workers?

*Condensed from Selwyn Feinstein, "Early Retirement," *The Wall Street Journal*, January 9, 1987, p. 1.

20

Estate Planning

While you work, your objective is to accumulate funds for your future and for your dependants. However, your point of view will change. The emphasis in your financial planning will shift from accumulating assets to distributing them wisely. Your hard-earned wealth should go to those whom you wish to support and not to the various taxing agencies.

Contrary to widely held notions, estate planning, which includes wills and trusts, is not useful only to the rich and the elderly. Trusts can be used for purposes other than tax advantages. Furthermore, most persons can afford the expense of using them.

After studying this chapter, you will be able to:

- Discuss the importance of estate planning.

- Outline the personal aspects of estate planning.

- Identify the legal aspects of estate planning.

- Distinguish among various types and formats of wills.

- Differentiate among various types of trusts.

- Explain the effects of federal and state taxes on estate planning.

Interview with **William Boylan,**
Practicing Attorney, Glen Ellyn, Illinois

William E. Boylan, a doctor of jurisprudence and a certified public accountant, is a partner with the law firm of Kalinich, McCluskey, Sullivan, & Boylan. Licensed to practice law in Illinois and Wisconsin, Mr. Boylan is a member of the Illinois Bar Association and the DuPage Bar Association and served three terms as chairman of the Tax Law Committee of the DuPage Bar Association.

The major objectives of estate planning, states Mr. Boylan, are to minimize taxes while you are alive and after your death and to make sure that your estate is distributed according to your wishes.

The estate tax has changed significantly during the last few years. While the estate tax is imposed by the federal government, inheritance taxes are levied by state or local jurisdictions. Inheritance taxes are imposed on a beneficiary and are geared to the relationship of that beneficiary to the decedent. The tax rates and exemptions vary from state to state.

Estate planning and wills go hand in hand. A will is a directive or a written intent by a person who owns property, as to what's to be done with the property when he or she dies. The purpose of a will is to avoid family squabbles and to effect the orderly transfer of assets to the owner's intended beneficiaries at the owner's death.

Should a person draw his or her own will? Mr. Boylan says yes, if a will is simple; no, if a will incorporates trust arrangements, appoints guardians, or seeks tax advantages. In a complex will, a layperson's omissions and other errors could be costly to the administrator or executor or to the family.

A letter of last instruction can be very helpful. This usually contains instructions regarding burial or cremation plans, and it may contain instructions regarding the donation of bodily organs, such as a heart, a liver, or kidneys. But a letter of last instruction is no substitute for a will since it does not have the legal validity of a will. Most people do not prepare a letter of last instruction, but every adult should prepare a will.

The Spanish artist Casso Aruza originally wanted to be a bullfighter. One Sunday, Casso entered the ring on horseback as a picador, an armored spear carrier who torments the bull. He was unskilled as a pic, and the bull was strong.

Casso was thrown from his horse and was helpless. Before he was rescued by members of the cuadrilla, there was blood on the sand. "That pic has got to be loco," someone muttered, and the name stuck. For the rest of his life, the great artist was known as "Crazy Pic" Casso.

Picasso then emigrated to the United States, became a citizen, married, and raised a family. He was eccentric, unpredictable, colorful, and a genius. He died in 1973 at the age of 92. He left everything to his wife, including about 1,500 paintings worth about $2 million. In his will, Picasso expressed the wish that his wife should sell the paintings only if this were necessary to support herself in the manner to which she had been accustomed. Upon her death, the remainder of the paintings were to go to his many children. There was no estate tax liability, since he left everything to his wife. But when she died, the estate tax problem was serious, primarily because of the paintings. There was a cash shortfall, and the estate had to sell some property to pay the hefty estate tax.*

Consider the plight of the

WHY ESTATE PLANNING? AN INTRODUCTION

- The Importance of Estate Planning

This chapter discusses a subject most people would rather avoid: death—your own or that of your spouse. Many people do not give a single thought to preparing for death. Some people give only cursory attention to setting their personal and financial affairs in order.

As you learned in the previous chapter, most people now live long lives. They have ample time to think about and plan for the future. Yet a large percentage of people do little or nothing to provide for those who will survive them.

It is not always easy to plan for your family's financial security in the event of your death or the death of your spouse. Therefore, the objective of this chapter is to help you initiate discussions about questions that should be asked before that happens. Does my spouse, for instance, know what all of the family's resources and debts are? Does my family have enough insurance protection?

The question whether your family can cope financially without your or your spouse's income and support is a difficult one. This chapter can't provide all of the answers, but it does supply a basis of sound estate planning for you and your family.

Wrigley family† and the heirs of Adolph Coors, Jr. The Coors heirs were forced to sell stock in the Coors Brewery to raise the funds needed to satisfy Uncle Sam's claim against the estate. The Wrigley family had to sell the Chicago Cubs to pay taxes that came due upon the death of two family members.

But estate planning and estate taxes are not just for the Cassos, Coors, and Wrigleys; an estate plan is needed by everyone—rich or poor, single or married, male or female, parent or child. As a result of inflation, many middle-class Americans who own their own homes, have life insurance policies, and are enrolled in company pension plans have a net worth approaching the estate tax threshold.‡

The subject of estate taxes, wills, and trusts is just part of the larger area of estate planning. Estate planning entails analysis of your entire financial picture to determine the best ways to secure your financial well-being and that of your family now and in the future.

*Adapted from *Monthly Tax Report,* December 1985, Laventhol & Horwath, Certified Public Accountants, 1845 Walnut Street, Philadelphia, PA 19103. Copyright by Laventhol & Horwath.

†"Keeping It in the Family," *Changing Times,* January 1986, p. 66.

‡D. Larry Crumbley and Edward E. Milam, *Estate Planning* (Homewood, Ill.: Dow Jones-Irwin, 1986), p. 1.

What Is Estate Planning?

Estate planning is a definite plan for the administration and disposition of one's property during one's lifetime and at one's death. Thus, it involves both handling your property while you are alive and dealing with what happens to that property after your death.

Estate planning is an essential part of retirement planning and an integral part of financial planning. It has two parts. The first consists of building your estate through savings, investments, and insurance. The second consists of transferring your estate, at your death, in the manner you have specified. As this chapter explains, an estate plan is usually implemented by a will and one or more trust agreements.

- **Personal Aspects of Estate Planning**

Nearly every adult is involved with financial decision making and must keep important records. Whatever your status—single or married; male or female; Ph.D. professor or U.S. marine; taxi driver, corporate executive, farmer, rancher, sports champion, or coal miner—you must make financial and personal decisions that are important to you. Those decisions may be even more important to others in your family.

"As a firm believer in reincarnation, I'm leaving
everything to me."

From *The Wall Street Journal*, with permission of Cartoon Features Syndicate.

Knowledge in certain areas and good recordkeeping can simplify those decisions. There are things you should know—and do—to protect your interests and those of your heirs.

At first, planning for financial security and estate planning may seem complicated. Although many money matters require legal and technical advice, if you and your spouse learn the necessary skills, you will find yourself managing your money affairs more efficiently and wisely. Begin by answering the questionnaire in Figure 20–1 to see how much you and your family know about your own money affairs. You and your family should be able to answer some of these questions. Do you find the questions bewildering? They can be if the subjects are unfamiliar to you.

If You Are Married

If you are married, your estate planning involves the interests of at least two people—more if there are children. Legal requirements and responsibilities can create problems for married persons that are entirely different from the problems of single persons. Situations become more complex. Possessions accumulate. The need for orderliness and clarity becomes greater.

FIGURE 20-1   Estate Planning Checklist

	Yes	No
1. Can you locate your copies of last year's income tax returns?	☐	☐
2. Where is your safe-deposit box located? Where is the key to it kept?	☐	☐
3. Do you know what kinds and amounts of life insurance protection you have?	☐	☐
4. Can you locate your insurance policies—life, health, property, casualty, and auto?	☐	☐
5. Do you know the names of the beneficiaries and contingent beneficiaries of your life insurance policies?	☐	☐
6. Do you know what type of health insurance protection you have and what the provisions of your health insurance policy are?	☐	☐
7. Do you and your spouse have current wills? Can you locate those wills, along with the name and address of the attorney who drafted them?	☐	☐
8. Do you have a separate record of the important papers you keep in your safe-deposit box? Where is this record located?	☐	☐
9. Do you have a record of your spouse's social security number?	☐	☐
10. Can you locate your marriage certificate? The birth certificates of all the members of your family?	☐	☐
11. Do you know the name and address of your life insurance agent?	☐	☐
12. Do you have a clear understanding of what the principal financial resources and liabilities of your estate are?	☐	☐
13. Are you knowledgeable about simple, daily, and compound interest rates? About retirement funds and property ownership?	☐	☐
14. Have you given any thought to funerals and burial arrangements?	☐	☐
15. Do you know what papers and records will be important in the event of your death?	☐	☐
16. Can you explain the functions of a bank trust department, the meaning of joint ownership, and so forth?	☐	☐

Source: *Planning with Your Beneficiaries* (Washington, D.C.: American Council of Life Insurance, Education and Community Services, n.d.), p. 2.

Your death will mean a new lifestyle for your spouse. If there are no children or if the children have grown up and lead separate lives, your spouse will once again be single. The surviving spouse must confront problems of grief and adjustment. Daily life must continue. At the same time, the estate must be settled. If not, there may be catastrophic financial consequences.

If children survive you, making sure that your estate can be readily analyzed and distributed may be all the more critical. If relatives or friends are beneficiaries, bequests have to be made known quickly and clearly.

Your wishes and information about your estate have to be accessible, understandable, and legally proper. Otherwise, there may be problems for your beneficiaries and your intentions may not be carried out.

If You Never Married

Never having been married does not eliminate the need to organize your papers. For persons who live alone, as for married persons, it is essential that important documents and personal information be consolidated and accessible.

Remember that in the event of your death difficult questions and situations are going to confront some person at a time of severe emotional strain. That person may not be prepared to face them objectively.

Probably the single most important thing that you can do is take steps to see that your beneficiaries have the information and the knowledge they need to survive emotionally and financially if you die suddenly.

Such action should be taken by everyone. But the need to take it is especially great if you are only 5 or 10 years away from retirement. By then, your possessions will probably be of considerable value. Your savings and checking account balances will probably be substantial. Your investment plans will have materialized. If you stop and take a look at where you are, you may be pleasantly surprised at the worth of your estate.

The Cost of Rationalizing

Daily living gets in the way of thinking about death. You mean to organize things that need to be known in case you die, but you haven't done it yet. One of your rationalizations may be that you are not sure of what information you need to provide.

Think about the outcome of your delay. Your beneficiary will meet people who offer specific types of assistance—morticians, clergy, lawyers, insurance agents, clerks of government federal agencies, and so on. These people will probably be strangers—sympathetic, courteous, helpful, but disinterested. And your bereaved beneficiary may find it difficult to reveal confidences to them.

THE BASICS OF WILLS AND TRUSTS

● Legal Aspects of Estate Planning

In case of death, proof of claims must be produced or the claims will not be processed. If no thought was given to gathering the necessary documents beforehand (with a sufficient number of copies), a period of financial hardship may follow until proof is obtained. If needed documentation cannot be located, there may be irretrievable loss of needed funds. Emotionally painful delays may be experienced until rights have been established.

Some important needed papers are:

1. Birth certificates—yours, your spouse's, your children's.
2. Marriage certificates—always important, but especially important if you or your spouse were married previously.

TABLE 20-1   Important Documents for Which Proof Will Be Needed

Social security documents
Veteran documents
Insurance policies
Transfer records of joint bank accounts
Safe-deposit box records
Registration of automobiles
Title to stock and bond certificates

3. Legal name changes—judgment of court documents pertaining to any legal changes in the names that appear on birth certificates (especially important to protect the adopted children of a previous marriage or children who have been adopted through adoption agencies).

4. Military service records—the standard DD–214 (Armed Forces of the United States Report of Transfer or Discharge) or any other official statement of your military service details, if appropriate.

You can obtain these papers with minimum difficulty. You simply need the determination to follow through on your plan. Table 20–1 lists important documents for which proof is needed.

You should have several copies of certain documents because when you submit a claim, the accompanying proof often becomes a permanent part of the claim file and is not returned. Remember, too, that there are circumstances in which your children may be required to furnish proof of their parents' birth, marriage, or divorce.

One of the most vital records you should have is a will. Every adult should have a written will.

Wills

A will is the legal declaration of a person's mind as to the disposition of his or her property after his or her death. Thus, a will is a way to transfer your property according to your wishes after you die.

Whether you prepare a will before you die or neglect to take that sensible step, you have a will. If you fail to prepare your own will, the state in which you legally reside steps in and controls the distribution of your estate without regard for wishes that you may have had but that you failed to define in legal form. Thus, if you die intestate—without a valid will—the state's law of descent and distribution becomes your will, as shown in Figure 20–2.

Consider the example of a man with a wife and children who died without a will. By default, he has authorized his estate to be disposed of according to the provisions of the fictitious document shown in Figure 20–2. The wording

FIGURE 20-2   What Will the State Do to Your Property if You Die
                Intestate?

My Last Will and Testament

Being of sound mind and memory, I, _____, do hereby publish this as my last Will and Testament.

FIRST

I give my wife only one third of my possessions, and I give my children the remaining two thirds.

A. I appoint my wife as guardian of my children, but as a safeguard I require that she report to the Probate Court each year and render an accounting of how, why, and where she spent the money necessary for the proper care of my children.

B. As a further safeguard, I direct my wife to produce to the Probate Court a Performance Bond to guarantee that she exercise proper judgment in the handling, investing, and spending of the children's money.

C. As a final safeguard, my children shall have the right to demand and receive a complete accounting from their mother of all of her financial actions with their money as soon as they reach legal age.

D. When my children reach age 18, they shall have full rights to withdraw and spend their share of my estate. No one shall have any right to question my children's actions on how they decide to spend their respective shares.

SECOND

Should my wife remarry, her second husband shall be entitled to one third of everything my wife possesses. Should my children need some of this share for their support, the second husband shall not be bound to spend any part of his share on my children's behalf.

A. The second husband shall have the sole right to decide who is to get his share, even to the exclusion of my children.

THIRD

Should my wife predecease me or die while any of my children are minors, I do not wish to exercise my right to nominate the guardian of my children.

A. Rather than nominating a guardian of my preference, I direct my relatives and friends to get together and select a guardian by mutual agreement.

B. In the event that they fail to agree on a guardian, I direct the Probate Court to make the selection. If the court wishes, it may appoint a stranger acceptable to it.

FOURTH

Under existing tax law, certain legitimate avenues are open to me to lower death rates. Since I prefer to have my money used for government purposes rather than for the benefit of my wife and children, I direct that no effort be made to lower taxes.

IN WITNESS WHEREOF, I have set my hand to this, my LAST WILL AND TESTAMENT, this _____ day of _____ 19_____.

in Figure 20–2 represents a pattern of distribution that could occur unless you prepare a valid will specifying otherwise.

This need not happen to a husband only. It could happen to anyone. To avoid such consequences, make a will! Consulting an attorney for this purpose can save your heirs many troubles, especially since the passage of the

Economic Recovery Tax Act of 1981. This act created estate planning opportunities and problems for many people. You may be one of them. The act also created some difficult choices as to type of wills.

Types of Wills

- Types and Formats of Wills

A brief review of the types of wills may be helpful since the tax effects of these wills differ. The four types of wills are the simple will, the traditional marital share will, the exemption trust will, and the stated dollar amount will.

Simple Will. A simple will, sometimes called an "I love you" will, is one in which you leave everything to your spouse. Such a will is sufficient for most smaller estates. But if you have a large or complex estate, especially one involving business interests that you want to pass on to your children, a simple will may not meet your objectives. It might also cause a greater overall amount of taxation because everything would then be taxed in your spouse's subsequent estate.

For example, if your estate is $1,200,000 and you leave it all to your spouse, there would be no tax at your death. However, there would be a tax of $235,000 at your spouse's death (based on 1987 rates and exemptions), assuming that the value of the estate remains constant. To avoid that, you could use a two-part marital will to split your estate into two halves, resulting

". . .to my nephew, Phelps Putney, who always
sneered at my conservative stuffed shirt stance,
I leave him my shirts."

From *The Wall Street Journal*, with permission of Cartoon Features Syndicate.

in no tax at either death. If your spouse had separate property or if the value of your estate increased, the simple will would cause greater taxation.

Traditional Marital Share Will. The traditional marital share will leaves one half of your adjusted gross estate (the gross estate minus debts and costs) to your spouse outright as a marital share. The other half of your adjusted gross estate could go to your children or other heirs or be held in trust for your family. A trust could provide your spouse with a lifelong income and would not be taxed at your spouse's death.

Under this type of will, half of your estate is taxed at your death and half at your spouse's death. This results in the lowest overall amount of federal estate taxes on estates above a certain size (twice the exemption amount). However, there are other considerations. State inheritance taxes might be greater, especially at the first death, due to conflicting federal and state exemption and beneficiary classification. Also, under this type of will, unlike a simple will or an exemption trust, federal estate taxes may have to be paid up front at the first death that involves the loss of use of money. If your spouse has considerable assets in his or her own right, it might not be prudent to increase your spouse's estate by any amount. In such a situation, a will that equalizes estates might be better.

Exemption Trust Will. The exemption trust will has been gaining in popularity due to the increased exemption ($600,000 in 1987). Under this type of will, everything passes to your spouse with the exception of an amount equal to the exemption ($600,000 in 1987), which would pass into trust. The amount passed to your spouse could be by will, trust, or other means. The exemption trust can provide your spouse with a lifelong income.

There would be little or no tax at your death because of the combination of the exemption and the marital deduction. The exemption amount, and any appreciation on it, would not be taxed in your spouse's estate.

This type of will is not practical in small estates because under it not much would pass to the spouse. In 1987, for example, only $200,000 of an $800,000 estate would go to the spouse.

The main advantage of the exemption trust will is that it eliminates future taxation of the exemption amount and any growth on it. This may be an important factor if property values appreciate considerably.

Table 20–2 compares the tax results of the three types of wills discussed above, based on 1987 rates and exemptions. Note that up to $1,200,000 of the marital or exemption will can produce the same result: first an amount equal to the exemption equivalent ($600,000) to your spouse, then the balance up to the same amount to a trust. Other arrangements are certainly possible, with higher or lower amounts to your spouse expressed as percentages or as dollar amounts, but the tax results would fall within the parameters of these three types of wills.

Stated Dollar Amount Will. This type of will allows you to pass to your spouse any amount that satisfies your family objectives. These objectives

TABLE 20-2   Federal Estate Taxes and Type of Will

Adjusted Gross Estate		Simple (All to Spouse) Will	Marital Share (50% to Spouse) Will	Exemption ($600,000) Trust Will
$ 600,000	Your tax	$ 0	$ 0	$ 0
	Spouse's tax	0	0	0
	Total	0	0	0
750,000	Your tax	0	0	0
	Spouse's tax	55,500	0	0
	Total	55,500	0	0
1,000,000	Your tax	0	0	0
	Spouse's tax	153,000	0	0
	Total	153,000	0	0
1,250,000	Your tax	0	9,250	0
	Spouse's tax	255,500	9,250	18,500
	Total	255,500	18,500	18,500
1,500,000	Your tax	0	55,500	0
	Spouse's tax	363,000	55,500	114,000
	Total	363,000	111,000	114,000
2,000,000	Your tax	0	153,000	0
	Spouse's tax	588,000	153,000	320,000
	Total	588,000	306,000	320,000
2,500,000	Your tax	0	255,500	0
	Spouse's tax	833,000	255,500	543,000
	Total	833,000	511,000	543,000
3,000,000	Your tax	0	363,000	0
	Spouse's tax	1,083,000	363,000	784,000
	Total	1,083,000	726,000	784,000
4,000,000	Your tax	$ 0	$ 588,000	$ 0
	Spouse's tax	1,583,000	588,000	1,283,000
	Total	1,583,000	1,176,000	1,283,000
5,000,000	Your tax	0	833,000	0
	Spouse's tax	2,083,000	833,000	1,783,000
	Total	2,083,000	1,666,000	1,783,000
10,000,000	Your tax	0	2,083,000	0
	Spouse's tax	4,583,000	2,083,000	4,283,000
	Total	4,583,000	4,166,000	4,283,000

Source: *ETP: Estate Tax Planning* (Hartford, Conn.: Aetna Life and Casualty Company, January 1982), pp. 12–13.

may or may not include tax considerations. For example, you could pass the stated amount of $600,000 (1987 exemption amount). But the stated amount could be related to anticipated income needs or to the value of personal items.

State law may dictate how much you must leave your spouse. Most states require that your spouse receive a certain amount, usually one half or one third. Some states require that such interests pass outright, and others permit life interests. The stated dollar amount will might satisfy such requirements and pass the balance to others. You might, for example, decide to pass most of your estate to your children, thereby avoiding subsequent taxation in your spouse's estate. It may also make sense to pass interests in a business to children who are involved in the business.

Such plans may increase taxes at your death since all property does not pass to your spouse. However, the taxes at your spouse's subsequent death would be less. Another option is to leave your spouse an outright amount equal to the exemption with a life estate in the balance, or a life estate in trust.

Which Type of Will Is Best for You? The four types of wills discussed above are your basic choices. Which one is best for you?

Prior to the Economic Recovery Tax Act of 1981 many experts would have advocated the traditional marital share will. Today, many attorneys believe that the exemption trust will is best. However, there is no one ideal will. Which will is best for you depends on such factors as the future appreciation of your estate, inflation, the respective ages of the spouses, relative liquidity, and—most important—your objectives.

Formats of Wills

Wills may be holographic or formal. A **holographic will** is a handwritten will that you prepare. It should be written, dated, and signed entirely in your handwriting—no printed or typed information should be on its pages. It should not be witnessed.

A **formal will** is usually prepared with an attorney's assistance. It may be either typed or on a preprinted form. You must sign the will and acknowledge it as your will in the presence of two witnesses, neither of whom is a **beneficiary** (a person you have named to receive property under the will). The witnesses must then sign the will in your presence.

A **statutory will** is one type of formal will. It is a preprinted form that may be obtained from lawyers and stationery stores. There are serious risks in using this or any other preprinted form. One risk is that such a form usually requires you to conform to rigid provisions, some of which may not be in the best interests of your beneficiaries. And if you change the preprinted wording, you may violate the law regarding wills, which may cause the changed sections or the entire will to be declared invalid. There is also a risk that the form is out-of-date and does not reflect current law.

Writing Your Will

The way to transfer your property according to your wishes is to write a will specifying those wishes. Joint ownership is no substitute for a will. Although jointly owned property passes directly to the joint owner and may be appropriate for some assets, such as your home, only with a will can you distribute your property as a whole exactly as you wish. Select a person who will follow your instructions (your executor or executrix). By naming your own executor, you will eliminate the need for a court-appointed administrator, prevent unnecessary delay in the distribution of your property, and minimize estate taxes and settlement costs. See the accompanying boxed feature for important aspects of making a will.

Selecting an Executor. Select an executor who is both willing and able to carry out the complicated tasks associated with the job. These tasks are preparing an inventory of assets, collecting any money due, paying off any debts, preparing and filing all income and estate tax returns, liquidating and reinvesting other assets to pay off debts and provide income for your family

---

Personal Financial Planning and You
The 10 Commandments of Making Your Will

1. Work closely with your spouse as you prepare your will. Seek professional help so that your family objectives can be met regardless of who dies first.

2. Write your will to conform with your current wishes. When your circumstances change (for example, when you retire or when you move to another state), review your will, and if appropriate, write a new one.

3. Do not choose a beneficiary as a witness. If such a person is called upon to validate your will, he or she may not be able to collect an inheritance.

4. If you are remarrying, consider signing a prenuptial agreement to protect your children. If you sign such an agreement before the wedding, you and your intended spouse can legally agree that neither of you will make any claim on the other's estate. The agreement can be revoked later, if you both agree.

5. Consider using percentages rather than dollar amounts when you divide your estate. If you leave $15,000 to a friend and the rest to your spouse, your spouse will suffer if your estate shrinks to $17,000.

6. Both you and your spouse should have a will, and those wills should be separate documents.

7. Be flexible. Don't insist that your heirs keep stock or run a cattle ranch. Should you do so, they may suffer if economic conditions change.

8. Sign the original of your will and keep it in a safe place; keep an unsigned copy at home for reference.

9. Alter your will by preparing a new will or adding a codicil. Don't change beneficiaries by writing on the will itself; this may invalidate the will.

10. Select an executor who is both willing and able to carry out the complicated tasks associated with the job.

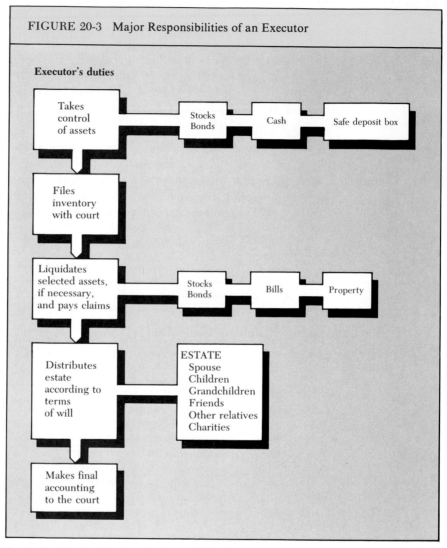

FIGURE 20-3   Major Responsibilities of an Executor

Source: *Trust Services from Your Bank*, rev. ed. (Washington, D.C.: American Bankers Association, 1978), p. 9, ©ABA.

while the estate is being administered, distributing the estate, and making a final accounting to your beneficiaries and to the probate court.

Your executor can be a family member, a friend, an attorney, an account-ant, or the trust department of a bank. Fees for executors, whether profes-sionals or friends, are set by state laws. Figure 20–3 summarizes typical duties of an executor.

Altering or Rewriting Your Will

Sometimes you will need to change the provision of your will. The new 100 percent marital deduction is not automatic. Congress would not alter or rewrite your will. This task was left to you. Therefore, unless you change your will or unless your state passes a law making the new definition applicable, you will have to rewrite your will to make the unlimited marital deduction apply. Because there are many choices of a personal nature, few, if any, states will get involved. For example, some people may not want to leave the entire estate to the spouse, perhaps for valid tax reasons.

You should review your will if any of these things takes place: if you move to a different state; if you have sold property mentioned in the will; if the size and composition of your estate has changed; if you have married, divorced, or remarried; if new potential heirs have died or been born.

Don't make any changes on the face of your will. Additions, deletions, or erasures on a will that has been signed and witnessed can invalidate the will.

If only a few changes are needed in your will, adding a codicil may be the best choice. A codicil is a document that explains, adds, or deletes provisions in your existing will. It identifies the will being amended and confirms the unchanged sections of the will. To be valid, it must conform to the legal requirements for a holographic or formal will.

If you wish to make major changes in your will or if you have already added a codicil, preparing a new will is preferable to adding a new codicil. In the new will, however, include a clause revoking all earlier wills and codicils.

If you are rewriting a will because of a remarriage, consider drafting a prenuptial agreement. This is a documentary agreement between spouses before marriage. In such agreements, one or both parties often waive a right to receive property under the other's will or under state law.

In addition to disposing of your estate, your will should name a guardian and/or trustee to care for minor children if both parents die at the same time, such as in an automobile accident or a plane crash. A guardian is a person who assumes the responsibilities of providing the children with personal care and of managing the estate for them. A trustee, on the other hand, is a person or institution that holds or generally manages property for the benefit of someone else under a trust agreement.

You should take great care in selecting a guardian for your children. You want a guardian whose philosophy on raising children is similar to yours and who is willing to accept the responsibility.

Most states require a guardian to post a bond with the probate court. The bonding company promises to reimburse the minor's estate up to the amount of the bond if the guardian uses the property of the minor for his or her own gain. The bonding fee of several hundred dollars is paid from the estate. However, you can waive the bonding requirement in your will.

Through your will, you may want to provide funds to raise your children. You could, for instance, leave a lump sum for an addition to the guardian's house and establish monthly payments to cover your children's living expenses.

The guardian of the minor's estate manages the property you leave behind for your children. This guardian can be a person or the trust department of a financial institution, such as a bank. Property that you place in trust for your children can be managed by the trustee rather than by the guardian of the minor's estate.

Wills like some of those discussed in this section have existed for thousands of years; the oldest known will was written by the Egyptian pharaoh Uah in 2448 B.C. Recently, a new type of will, called a living will, has emerged.

A Living Will

A living will provides for your wishes being followed if you become so physically or mentally disabled that you are unable to act on your own behalf.

A living will is a document that a person can prepare in anticipation of death, and in that respect it resembles a traditional will. It enables an indi-

---

FIGURE 20-4   A Living Will: Example 1

TO MY FAMILY, MY PHYSICIAN, MY LAWYER, MY CLERGYMAN
TO ANY MEDICAL FACILITY IN WHOSE CARE I HAPPEN TO BE
TO ANY INDIVIDUAL WHO MAY BECOME RESPONSIBLE FOR MY
HEALTH, WELFARE, OR AFFAIRS:

Death is as much a reality as birth, growth, maturity, and old age—it is the one certainty of life. If the time comes when I, _____, can no longer take part in decisions for my own future, let this statement stand as an expression of my wishes, while I am still of sound mind.

If the situation should arise in which there is no reasonable expectation of my recovery from physical or mental disability, I request that I be allowed to die and not be kept alive by artificial means or "heroic measures." I do not fear death itself as much as the indignities of deterioration, dependence, and hopeless pain. I, therefore, ask that medication be mercifully administered to me to alleviate suffering even though this may hasten the moment of death.

This request is made after careful consideration. I hope you who care for me will feel morally bound to follow its mandate. I recognize that this appears to place a heavy responsibility upon you, but it is with the intention of relieving you of such responsibility and of placing it upon myself in accordance with my strong convictions, that this statement is made.

Signed _____

Date _____

Witness _____

Witness _____

Copies of this request have been given to _____
_____
_____
_____

Source: *Don't Wait until Tomorrow* (Hartford, Conn.: Aetna Life and Casualty Company, n.d.), p. 10.

FIGURE 20-5   A Living Will: Example 2

Living Will Declaration

Declaration made this _____ day of _____ (month, year)
I, _____, being of sound mind, willfully and voluntarily make known my desire that my dying shall not be artificially prolonged under the circumstances set forth below, do hereby declare

If at any time I should have an incurable injury, disease, or illness regarded as a terminal condition by my physician and if my physician has determined that the application of life-sustaining procedures would serve only to artificially prolong the dying process and that my death will occur whether or not life-sustaining procedures are utilized. I direct that such procedures be withheld or withdrawn and that I be permitted to die with only the administration of medication or the performance of any medical procedure deemed necessary to provide me with comfort care.

In the absence of my ability to give directions regarding the use of such life-sustaining procedures, it is my intention that this declaration shall be honored by my family and physician as the final expression of my legal right to refuse medical or surgical treatment and accept the consequences from such refusal.

I understand the full import of this declaration, and I am emotionally and mentally competent to make this declaration.

Signed _____

City, County, and State of Residence _____

The declarant has been personally known to me, and I believe him or her to be of sound mind.

Witness _____

Witness _____

Source: *Don't Wait until Tomorrow* (Hartford, Conn.: Aetna Life and Casualty Company, n.d.), p. 11.

vidual, while well, to express the intention that life be allowed to end if he or she becomes terminally ill. Living wills are recognized in many states, and you may consider writing one when you draw a conventional will. Figures 20–4 and 20–5 are examples of typical living wills.

To ensure the effectiveness of a living will, discuss your intention of preparing such a will with the people closest to you. You should also discuss this with your family doctor. Sign and date your document before two witnesses. Witnessing shows that you signed of your own free will.

Give copies of your living will to those closest to you, and have your family doctor place a copy in your medical file. Keep the original document readily accessible, and look it over periodically, preferably once a year, to be sure that your wishes have remained unchanged. To verify your intent, redate and initial each later endorsement.

A living will can become a problem. A once healthy person may have a change of heart and prefer to remain alive even as death seems imminent.

"You can pass living wills around a roomful of young people, and 95 percent will sign them," said a geriatric internist. "But pass them around a nursing home, and you will get a different response." A psychiatrist specializing in the care of elderly people added, "People who are old, enfeebled, slowly dying, are still living existentially. They may enjoy their meals, the sunlight on their skin, sensory pleasures."[1]

FIGURE 20-6   Letter of Last Instruction

In addition to your will, you'll need to prepare a letter of instruction. This document provides your family with the information necessary to locate your assets, carry out funeral arrangements, and collect any survivors' benefits or life insurance proceeds. The letter can't be legally enforced, but it can be the guide your family needs to close your affairs.

Write the letter clearly so that even a stranger could understand it, and check with your attorney to be sure it agrees with the terms of your will. Give copies of the letter to your executor and your closest beneficiaries. Because the letter describes your finances in great detail, the original and copies should be kept in safe places.

When writing your letter of instruction, provide—in detail that includes names, addresses, and telephone numbers—such information as the following.

Notifications

Instruct that these people and institutions be notified of your death: employer, executor, attorney, financial institutions where you have accounts, accountant, broker, insuring agents, and social security office.

List your social security number, and give the location of your card.

Funeral Arrangements

Describe arrangements you've already made or want your family to make.

Include a reminder that the funeral director be asked for at least six copies of the death certificate. These will be needed to collect insurance and other benefits.

Personal Papers

Give the location of your personal documents—will, birth and marriage certificates, military papers, and other documents.

Bank Accounts

List your checking and savings accounts by name of institution, address of the office where the account is located, type of account, and account number.

Give the location of canceled checks and statements.

Safe deposit

Give the location of the box and key and a list of contents.

Credit Cards

List by issuer and card number.

Homeowner Records

Note the location of the deed and mortgage papers.

Provide information on taxes, liens, leases, and so on.

---

[1] *Don't Wait until Tomorrow*, (Hartford, Conn.: Aetna Life and Casualty Company, n.d.), pp. 10–11.

Living wills call for careful thought, but they do provide you with a choice as to the manner of your death. Related to the concept of living will is power of attorney.

Power of Attorney

A **power of attorney** is a legal document authorizing someone to act on your behalf. At some point in your life, you may become ill or incapacitated. You may then wish to have someone attend to your needs and your personal affairs. You can assign a power of attorney to anyone you choose.

FIGURE 20-6   *(concluded)*

Insurance

List all of your life, auto, home, veteran's, medical, and credit insurance policies.
Name the agents, and give the location of all the documents needed to process claims.
Describe any loans you've taken out against your insurance policies that you haven't yet repaid.

Vehicles

Tell where the registration and other papers may be found.

Taxes

Give the location of your income tax returns for at least the past five years.

Investments

List stocks, bonds, and other securities by certificate numbers, issuers, and cost.
Tell where they're located, and identify your stockbrokers.

Trusts

List the type and size of any trust you've established, and give the name and address of the trustee.

Loans

List loans and other accounts you must repay, and give full information on terms, payments, collateral, and so on.

Accounts Receivable

List all debts owed to you, giving the same specifics as for loans.

Survivors' Benefits

List possible sources of benefits not named in your will—for example, social security, veteran's, employee, fraternal association—and how much to expect from each source.

Other

Give the location of receipts, warranties, and other miscellaneous papers.
Explain any unusual provisions of the will, such as disinheritance of a child.

The person you name can be given a limited power or a great deal of power. The power given can be special—to carry out certain acts or transactions; or it can be general—to act completely for you. A conventional power of attorney is automatically revoked in a case of legal incapacity.

Letter of Last Instruction

In addition to your will, you should prepare a letter of last instruction. This document, though not legally enforced, can provide your heirs with important information. It should contain the details of your funeral arrangements. It should also contain the names of the persons who should be notified of your death and the locations of your bank accounts, credit cards, safe-deposit box, and other important items. Figure 20–6 shows what information can be included in a letter of instruction.

Trusts

It is a good idea to discuss with your attorney the possibility of establishing a trust as a means of managing your estate. Basically, a **trust** is a legal arrangement through which your assets are held by a trustee for your benefit or that of your beneficiaries. Read the accompanying boxed feature for information on various types of trusts.

●   Various Types of
      Trusts

Trusts are either revocable or irrevocable. In a **revocable trust,** you retain the right to end the trust or change its terms during your lifetime. You might choose a revocable trust if you think you may need its assets for your own use at a later time or if you want to monitor the performance of the trust and the trustee before the arrangement is made irrevocable by your death. Once you have established an irrevocable trust, however, you cannot change its terms or end it. However, an irrevocable trust offers tax advantages not offered by a revocable trust.

Trustee services are commonly provided by banks and in some instances are provided by life insurance companies. There are three types of trusts: living trusts, testamentary trusts, and insurance trusts. Each has particular advantages and may be the most appropriate for your family situation.

Living Trusts. In a **living trust,** a trustee receives specific instructions as to how your assets are to be managed, how income payments are to be made, and how the principal is to be distributed to specific persons or institutions while you are still alive.

Testamentary Trusts. A **testamentary trust** is a trust established by your will that becomes effective upon your death. Such a trust can be valuable if your beneficiaries are inexperienced in financial matters or if the potential estate tax is substantial. Like a living trust, a testamentary trust provides the benefits of asset management, financial bookkeeping, protection of the beneficiaries, and minimizing of estate taxes.

Insurance Trusts. In many families, the proceeds of life insurance policies are the largest single asset of the estate. A **life insurance trust** is established while you are living. The trust receives your life insurance benefits upon your death and administers them in an agreed upon manner. Such trusts can be canceled if there is a change in your family or financial circumstances or if you wish to make new plans for the future.

In the Real World
In Trusts We Trust

When a person puts assets in a trust, he or she essentially gives them to a third party—the trustee—to manage for the trust's beneficiaries. Testamentary trusts are set up in your will to take effect when you die. Living trusts go to work during your lifetime. Some trusts are designed to bring heirs financial security; others, to minimize estate taxes. Here are a few of the more common varieties.

Minors' Testamentary Trust. Should you and your spouse both die, the assets you bequeath your children will be held for them until they reach a certain age. By leaving instructions about how the income and principal can be spent, you exert some control. If you worry that your children may have unequal needs as they mature, you can include a "sprinkling" clause that allows the funds to be doled out as the trustee sees fit.

Marital Deduction Trust. This is a way to safeguard your estate when your spouse is financially naive. He or she can use the income and some principal of the trust, but a trustee manages it. The trust is free of taxes under the marital deduction, which allows unlimited spouse-to-spouse bequests. A trust with "general power of appointment" gives the surviving spouse the right to choose the eventual beneficiaries.

QTIP Trust. A form of marital deduction trust, a QTIP— qualified terminable interest property—trust guarantees that children from a first marriage will be provided for after your second spouse dies. The trust provides income and perhaps some principal to your spouse, but you dictate who eventually receives the bulk of the property after your spouse dies.

Charitable Trusts. A charitable remainder trust holds your contributions in trust for a charity. You get some income tax deductions as you contribute, and you and your family enjoy the income from the assets until the trust terminates and the charity receives the assets outright. A charitable lead trust provides the charity with a specified payout for a specified period, at the end of which the assets go to the beneficiaries.

Revocable Living Trust. The main advantage of the revocable living trust is that it can circumvent probate, the often cumbersome legal process of sorting through a will's provisions. You transfer title of your assets to the trust but maintain control over them while you live. When you die, the assets go to your beneficiaries. Since you hold the reins, however, the trust is part of your taxable estate.

Source: *U.S. News & World Report*, June 2, 1986, p. 47.

To summarize, a trust is a property arrangement in which a trustee, such as a person or a bank trust department, holds title to, takes care of, and, in most cases, manages property for the benefit of someone else. The creator of the trust is called the **trustor** or grantor. A bank, as trustee, charges a modest fee for its services, generally based on the value of the trust assets. All trust assets added together are known as an estate.

Estates

Your **estate** is everything you own. It includes all of your property—tangible and intangible, however acquired or owned, whether inside or outside the country. It may include jointly owned property, life insurance and employee benefits, and property you no longer own. Thus, an important step in estate planning is taking inventory of everything you own, such as:

1. Cash, checking accounts, savings accounts, CDs, and money market funds.
2. Stocks, bonds (including municipals and U.S. savings bonds), mutual funds, commodity futures, and tax shelters.
3. Life insurance, employee benefits, and annuities.
4. Your home and any other real estate, land and buildings, furniture, and fixtures.
5. Farms, grain, livestock, machinery, and equipment.
6. Proprietorship, partnership, and close corporation interests.
7. Notes, accounts, and claims receivable.
8. Interests in trusts and powers of appointment.
9. Antiques, works of art, collections, cars, boats, planes, personal effects, and everything else.

In the community property states (Arizona, California, Idaho, Louisiana, Nevada, New Mexico, Texas, and Washington), where each spouse owns 50 percent of the property, half of the community assets are included in each spouse's estate. In the other states (the non–community property states), property is included in the estate of the spouse who owns it. The way you own property can make a tax difference.

Joint Ownership. Joint ownership of property between spouses is very common. Joint ownership may also exist between parents and children, other relatives, or any two or more persons. While joint ownership may avoid *probate* (official proof of a will), creditor attachment, and inheritance taxes in some states, it does not avoid federal estate taxes. In fact, it may increase them.

There are three types of joint ownership, and they have different tax and estate planning consequences.

If you and your spouse own property as *joint tenants with the right of survivorship (JT/WROS)*, the property is considered owned 50–50 for estate tax purposes and will automatically pass to your spouse at your death, and vice versa. No gift tax is paid on creating such ownership, nor, due to the unlimited marital deduction, is any estate tax paid at the first death. However, this type of joint ownership may result in more taxes overall at the surviving spouse's later death than would have been the case with a traditional marital share will, discussed earlier.

If you put property in joint ownership with a child (or anyone else other than your spouse), you have made a potentially taxable gift to the child to the extent that the child's share of ownership exceeds his or her own contribution. There are exceptions for U.S. savings bonds and savings accounts. In any event, the property is included in your gross estate except to the extent of the child's contribution.

If you and your spouse or anyone else own property as *tenants in common*, each individual is considered to own a proportionate share for tax purposes, and only your share is included in your estate. That share does not go to the other tenants in common at your death but is included in your probate estate and subject to your decision as to who gets it. While there are no gift or estate tax consequences between spouse joint owners, gifts of joint interests to children or others can cause taxation.

Joint ownership is not a good substitute for a will. It gives you less control over the disposition and taxation of your property. Your state laws govern the types and effects of joint ownership. Some states require that survivorship rights be spelled out in the deed, or at least abbreviated (for example, JT/WROS). Only your attorney can advise you on these matters.

Tenancy by the entirety, the third type of co-ownership, is limited to married couples. Under this type of co-ownership, both spouses own the property; when one spouse dies, the other gets it automatically. Neither spouse may sell the property without the consent of the other.

Life Insurance and Employee Benefits. Life insurance proceeds are free of income tax, excluded from probate, and wholly or partially exempt from most state inheritance taxes.

These proceeds are included in your estate for federal estate tax purposes if the policy contains any incidents of ownership such as the right to change beneficiaries, to surrender the policy for cash, or to make loans on the policy.

Assignment of ownership to your beneficiary or a trust could remove a life insurance policy from your estate. But if your spouse is the intended beneficiary, you do not need to assign ownership, since the proceeds would be free of estate tax due to the marital deduction.

Death benefits from qualified pension, profit sharing, or Keogh plans are excluded from your estate unless they are payable to it or unless your beneficiary elects the special provision for averaging income tax in lump-sum distributions. (Any benefits attributable to your own nondeductible contributions are included.) Benefits from IRA plans are also excluded if they are paid as an annuity or for a period of 36 months or more. Other benefits, such as deferred compensation and stock option plans, are fully included. Such benefits are also subject to income taxation. Careful planning is needed to minimize both income and estate taxes.

Lifetime Gifts and Trusts. Due to the structure of the unified estate and gift tax rates, the value of any taxable gifts made since 1977 are included for estate taxation. Note that this includes the value at the date of the gift, not the value at the date of death.

Gifts or trusts with strings attached, such as retaining the income, use, or control of the property, are fully included at their date of death value, whether your rights are expressed or implied. For example, if you transfer title of your home to a child but continue to live in it, the home is taxed in your estate. Or if you put property in trust and retain certain control over the income or principal, the property is included in your estate even though you cannot obtain it yourself. Also, if you are the beneficiary of a trust established by someone else and you have general rights to the principal during life or the power to appoint it to anyone at death, that amount is included in your estate.

Settling Your Estate

If you have had a will drawn, you are "testate" in the eyes of the law and an executor (named in your will) will carry out your wishes in due time. If you have not named an executor, the probate court (the court that supervises the distribution of estates) will appoint an administrator to carry out the instructions in your will.

If you don't have a will, you would be "intestate" at your death. In this case, what you own is put under the control of a court-appointed administrator for distribution according to laws of the state in which you reside. Your jointly owned property is also untouchable. A surviving owner could make no disposition of the property—sell it, give it away, move it to another location, and so on—without obtaining approval from the probate court, which could be a lengthy, complex process.

TAXATION AND ESTATE PLANNING

● Federal and State Estate Taxes

The tax aspects of estate planning have changed considerably because of recent major changes in the federal tax structure. The maximum tax rate on estates and gifts, for example, is gradually declining.

You can reduce your taxable estate by giving away assets during your lifetime. (But don't give away assets just to reduce your estate tax liability if you may need those assets in your retirement.) No gift tax is due on gifts of up to $10,000 to any one person in any one year. (A married couple, acting together, may give up to $20,000 to one person in one year.) Thus, if at age 82 Picasso had had 20 descendants, he could have given each of them six or seven paintings a year (using his $10,000 annual exclusion from gift tax on each gift). In this way, he would have removed at least 120 paintings a year from his estate tax free (while still keeping them in the family). After 10 years, he would have given away more than 1,000 paintings, two thirds of the total on hand when he died.

Also, if Picasso had died in 1985, he could have made bequests of up to $400,000 to his children or anyone else he wished without paying any tax at all (the exemption was $600,000 in 1987 and thereafter). Then he could have

TABLE 20-3 Unified Transfer Tax Rate Schedules

If the Amount Is:		Tentative Tax Is:		
Over	*But Not Over*	*Tax* +	*Percent*	*On Excess Over*
1984				
$ 0	$ 10,000	$ 0	18	$ 0
10,000	20,000	1,800	20	10,000
20,000	40,000	3,800	22	20,000
40,000	60,000	8,200	24	40,000
60,000	80,000	13,000	26	60,000
80,000	100,000	18,200	28	80,000
100,000	150,000	23,800	30	100,000
150,000	250,000	38,800	32	150,000
250,000	500,000	70,800	34	250,000
500,000	750,000	155,800	37	500,000
750,000	1,000,000	248,300	39	750,000
1,000,000	1,250,000	345,800	41	1,000,000
1,250,000	1,500,000	448,300	43	1,250,000
1,500,000	2,000,000	555,800	45	1,500,000
2,000,000	2,500,000	780,800	49	2,000,000
2,500,000	3,000,000	1,025,800	53	2,500,000
3,000,000	—	1,290,800	55	3,000,000
1988 and thereafter				
0	10,000	0	18	0
10,000	20,000	1,800	20	10,000
20,000	40,000	3,800	22	20,000
40,000	60,000	8,200	24	40,000
60,000	80,000	13,000	26	60,000
80,000	100,000	18,200	28	80,000
100,000	150,000	23,800	30	100,000
150,000	250,000	38,800	32	150,000
250,000	500,000	70,800	34	250,000
500,000	750,000	155,800	37	500,000
750,000	1,000,000	248,300	39	750,000
1,000,000	1,250,000	345,800	41	1,000,000
1,250,000	1,500,000	448,300	43	1,250,000
1,500,000	2,000,000	555,800	45	1,500,000
2,000,000	2,500,000	780,800	49	2,000,000
2,500,000	—	1,025,800	50	2,500,000

left the balance of his estate to his widow. The estate would have been tax free, too, because of the unlimited marital deduction.[2]

Types of Taxes

Federal and state governments levy various types of taxes that must be considered in planning your estate. The four major taxes of this kind are estate taxes, estate income taxes, inheritance taxes, and gift taxes.

Estate Taxes. An estate tax is a federal tax levied on the right of a deceased person to transmit his or her property and life insurance at death. Estate taxes have undergone extensive revision since the mid-1970s. The Economic Recovery Act of 1981 makes important tax concessions—particularly the unlimited marital deduction and the increased exemption equivalent shown in Table 20–3. Figure 20–7 shows Estate Tax Return Form.

Under present law, with intelligent estate planning and properly drawn wills, you may leave all of your property free of federal estate taxes to your surviving spouse. The surviving spouse's estate in excess of $600,000 is faced with estate taxes of from 37 percent to 50 percent.

All limits have been removed from transfers between spouses during lifetime as well as at death. Whatever you give your spouse is exempt from gift and estate taxes. Gift tax returns need not be filed for interspousal gifts. There is still the possibility, however, that such gifts will be included in your estate if they have been given within three years of your death.

Estates and Trusts Federal Income Taxes. Don't confuse the federal estate tax with the federal estates (and trusts) income tax. Under the Tax Reform Act of 1986, trusts and estates must pay quarterly estimated taxes and new trusts must use the calendar year as the tax year.

Table 20–4 shows the effects of the Tax Reform Act of 1986 on federal income taxation of estates and trusts.

Inheritance Taxes. An inheritance tax is levied on the right of an heir to receive all or part of the estate and life insurance proceeds of a deceased person. The tax payable depends on the net value of the property and insurance received. It also depends on the relationship of the heir to the deceased.

Inheritance taxes are imposed only by the state governments. Most of the states levy an inheritance tax, but the state laws differ widely as to exemptions, rates of taxation, and the treatment of property and life insurance. A reasonable average for state inheritance taxes would be 4–10 percent of your estate, with the higher percentages on larger amounts.

In the past few years, many states have been phasing out their inheritance tax provisions—usually over a period of three or four years. This apparently

---

[2]*Monthly Tax Report,* Laventhol & Horwath, December 1985, p. 1.

FIGURE 20-7

Form **706-A**
(Rev. June 1985)

Department of the Treasury
Internal Revenue Service

United States Additional Estate Tax Return

(To report dispositions or cessations of qualified use under
section 2032A of the Internal Revenue Code)

OMB No. 1545-0016

Expires 6/30/88

Name of qualified heir or heiress	Heir's or heiress' social security number
Address of qualified heir or heiress (number and street including apartment number or rural route)	Commencement date (See instructions)
City, town or post office, State and ZIP code	

Decedent's name reported on Form 706	Decedent's social security number	Date of death

Part I   Tax Computation

1 Value at date of death (or alternate valuation date) of all specially valued property which passed from decedent to qualified heir or heiress:
  a Without section 2032A election **1a**
  b With section 2032A election **1b**
  c Balance (subtract line 1b from line 1a) **1c**

2 Value at date of death (or alternate valuation date) of all specially valued property in decedent's estate:
  a Without section 2032A election **2a**
  b With section 2032A election **2b**
  c Balance (subtract line 2b from line 2a) **2c**

3 Decedent's estate tax:
  a Recomputed without section 2032A election (attach computation) . . **3a**
  b Reported on Form 706 with section 2032A election **3b**
  c Balance (subtract line 3b from line 3a) **3c**

4 Divide line 1c by line 2c and enter the result as a percentage . . . . **4**   %
5 Multiply line 3c by percentage on line 4 . . . . **5**
6 Value, without section 2032A election, at date of death (or alternate valuation date) of specially valued property shown on Schedule A **6**
7 Divide line 6 by line 1(a) and enter the result as a percentage . . . . **7**   %
8 Multiply line 5 by percentage on line 7 (see instructions) **8**
9 Enter the total of column (d), Schedule A, page 2 . . . . **9**
10 Enter the total of column (e), Schedule A, page 2 . . . . **10**
11 Balance (subtract line 10 from line 9) **11**
12 Additional estate tax. Enter the lesser of line 8 or line 11 . . . . **12**

Part II   Involuntary Conversions or Exchanges.   Check if for: ☐ Involuntary conversion ☐ Exchange

13 Qualified replacement (or exchange) property

(a) Item	(b) Description	(c) Cost (or FMV)
Total cost (or FMV)		**13**

14 Enter the total of column (d), Schedule A, page 2 . . . . **14**
15 Divide line 13 by line 14 and enter the result as a percentage (Do not enter more than 100%) . . . . **15**   %
16 Multiply line 12 by percentage on line 15 . . . . **16**
17 Additional tax, subtract line 16 from line 12 (Do not enter less than zero) **17**

Under penalties of perjury, I declare that I have examined this return, and to the best of my knowledge and belief, it is true, correct, and complete. Declaration of preparer other than taxpayer is based on all information of which preparer has any knowledge.

Signature of taxpayer .... Date ....

Signature of preparer other than taxpayer .... Date ....

Address (and ZIP code) ....

For Paperwork Reduction Act Notice, see page 1 of the separate instructions.

Form **706-A** (Rev. 6-85)

TABLE 20-4   Estates and Trusts Income Tax Rates

The Tax Reform Act of 1986 reduced 14 income tax rates for estates (and trusts) to 5 rates for 1987 and 4 thereafter.

Taxable Income	Tax	Percent on Excess
1986		
$ 0	$ 0	11
1,135	125	12
2,265	260	14
4,585	585	16
6,800	940	18
9,065	1,347	22
11,440	1,870	25
14,300	2,585	28
17,160	3,386	33
22,875	5,272	38
30,540	8,184	42
44,350	13,985	45
57,195	19,765	49
85,790	33,776	50
1987		
0	0	11
500	55	15
4,700	685	28
7.550	1,483	35
15,150	4,143	38.5
1988		
0	0	15
5,000	750	28
13,000	2,990	33
26,000	7,280	28

reflects a desire to retain older and wealthy citizens as residents and to discourage them from leaving the states where they have lived most of their lives to seek tax havens in such states as Florida and Nevada. The New England states, in particular, are fearful of an exodus of the elderly, with its accompanying loss of sales and income tax revenues. Since the federal estate tax changes have raised exemptions and lowered rates, the state inheritance taxes have become more burdensome for many people. For increasing numbers, state inheritance taxes are the only taxes at death that remain. Increasingly, state legislatures have been questioning the equity of further taxes at death and are opting instead for sales and income taxes to provide state revenues.

Gift Taxes. But the federal government and state governments levy a gift tax on the privilege of making gifts to others. Estate and inheritance taxes can be avoided by giving property during the lifetime of the property owner. For this reason, the federal tax laws provide for taxes on gifts of property. The tax rates on gifts used to be only 75 percent of the tax rates on estates, but since 1976 the gift tax rates have been the same as the estate tax rates. Indeed, the tax rates are now called unified transfer tax rates.

Many states have gift tax laws. The state gift tax laws are similar to the federal gift tax laws, but the exemptions and the dates for filing returns vary widely among the states.

As discussed earlier, the federal gift tax allows you to give up to $10,000 each year to any person without incurring gift tax liability or having to report the gift to the IRS. Gifts from a husband or a wife to a third party are considered as having been made in equal amounts by each spouse. Consequently, a husband and wife may give as much as $20,000 per year to anyone without incurring tax liability.

Property owners sometimes make a formal gift of property to wife or children but actually retain control over the property. In such cases, the courts have often disregarded the gift and have held that the property is still part of the donor's estate. If gifts are made to avoid taxes, they should be make in good faith and the resulting change in ownership should be observed carefully.

Tax Avoidance and Tax Evasion

A poorly arranged estate may be subject to unduly large taxation. Therefore, you should study the tax laws and seek advice to avoid estate taxes larger than those the lawmakers intended you to pay. You should have a clear idea of the distinction between tax avoidance and tax evasion. Tax avoidance is the use of legal methods to reduce or escape taxes; tax evasion is the use of illegal methods to reduce or escape taxes.

Charitable Gifts and Bequests. Gifts made to certain recognized charitable or educational agencies are exempt from gift, estate, and inheritance taxes. Accordingly, such gifts or bequests (gifts through a will) represent one method of reducing or avoiding estate and inheritance taxes.

Table 20–5 highlights the provisions of the Tax Reform Act of 1986 that affect trusts and estates, minor children, and gift and estate taxes.

Calculation of Tax

The estate tax is applied, not to your total gross estate, but to your net taxable estate at death. This estate is your testamentary net worth after your debts, liabilities, probate costs, and administration costs have been subtracted. These items, all of which are taken off your estate before calculating your tax, are cash requirements to be paid by your estate.

Debts and Liabilities. In arriving at your taxable estate, the amount of your debts and other creditor obligations are subtracted. You are liable for the payment of these debts while living; your estate will be liable at your death. Your debts may include mortgages, collateralized loans, margin accounts, bank loans, notes payable, installment and charge accounts, and accrued income and property taxes. They may also include your last illness and funeral expenses.

Probate and Administration Costs. Your estate administration costs will include fees for attorneys, accountants, appraisers, executors or administrators and trustees, court costs, bonding and surety costs, and miscellaneous other expenses. These administration costs may run 5–8 percent of your estate, depending on its size and complexity. While the percentage usually decreases as the size of the estate increases, it may be increased by additional complicating factors, such as handling a business interest.

Next deductions are made for bequests to qualified charities and for prop-

---

TABLE 20-5 Effects of Tax Reform Act of 1986 on Opportunities for Shifting Income among Family Members

Provision	Old Law	New Law
Income taxation of trusts and estates General	In the case of a grantor trust, one where the grantor or other person with the power to revoke the trust has certain powers with respect to the trust, income is taxed directly to the grantor. In the case of a nongrantor trust, each trust is treated as a separate taxable entity.	Nongrantor trusts and estates taxed in the same way as under the old law except that the tax brackets are narrowed. Income of a grantor trust is taxed directly to the grantor under revised definition of grantor trust. Applies to transfers made after March 1, 1986.
Trusts other than grantor trusts	The trust may elect a taxable year other than that of the grantor. Beneficiaries of a trust are taxable on distributions from the trust to the extent of the trust's taxable income for taxable years ending with, or within, the taxable year of the beneficiary. Nongrantor trust separately calculates tax liability at the rate applicable to married taxpayers filing jointly. In calculating tax liability, (a) the personal exemption is limited to $100 or $300, (b) no zero bracket amount is permitted, and (c) an unlimited charitable deduction is available, and a distribution is allowed for distributions to beneficiaries. Trusts will be aggregated if they have substantially the same grantors and beneficiaries and if they are separated to avoid taxes.	All trusts except charitable trusts must use the calendar year as the taxable year. Undistributed income of existing and new nongrantor trusts taxed at: $0–$5,000 15% $5,000+ 28 Benefit of the 15 percent bracket is phased out for income between $13,000 and $25,000. No other changes in calculating the liability or the aggregation of bonds.

TABLE 20-5   *(concluded)*

Provision	Old Law	New Law
Grantor trusts (including "Clifford" trusts)	The grantor is generally taxed directly on trust income. The grantor is generally treated as the owner of all or a portion of the trust if *(a)* the grantor has a reversionary interest that is expected to return to him within 10 years, *(b)* the grantor has the power to control the beneficial enjoyment of the income or corpus, *(c)* the grantor retains certain administrative powers, *(d)* the grantor retains the right to revoke the trust at any time during the first 10 years, and *(e)* the income of the trust may be distributed to the grantor or the grantor's spouse during the first 10 years. A person other than the grantor is treated as the owner of all or a portion of the trust if *(a)* that person has the power to revoke the trust, and *(b)* that person surrendered the power to revoke and that person retained one of the powers listed above.	The 10-year exception of grantor trust taxation ("Clifford" trusts) is eliminated. Powers and interests of the grantor's spouse are not treated as powers and interests of the grantor.
Unearned income of a minor child	If income-producing assets are transferred to a minor child, income earned on those assets is generally taxed at the child's marginal rate.	In general, unearned income of a child under age 14 exceeding $1,000 to be taxed at the marginal rate of the parent if the property was transferred by the parent. Personal exemption not allowed to a child if the child may be claimed as a dependent by parents.

Source: *Taxaction '86* (New York: E. F. Hutton, n.d.), p. 15.

erty passing to your spouse (the marital deduction). That leaves your net taxable estate, to which the rates shown in Table 20–6 are applied to determine your gross estate tax.

Inheritance and estate taxes in your own state are additional costs, and these costs are not deductible in arriving at your taxable estate. In fact, you may have to pay inheritance taxes in two or more states, depending on the location of your property.

Paying the Tax[3]

If after various estate tax reduction techniques have been employed, there is still an estate tax to pay, then consideration must be given as to how best to

[3] This section adapted from *ETP: Estate Tax Planning*, (Hartford, Conn.: Aetna Life and Casualty Company, January 1982), p. 20.

TABLE 20-6   Simplified Tax Table, 1987

Taxable Estate	Estate Tax*	Rate on Excess
$ 600,000	$ 0	37%
750,000	55,500	39
1,000,000	153,000	41
1,250,000	255,500	43
1,500,000	363,000	45
2,000,000	588,000	49
2,500,000	833,000	50

*After deducting the maximum allowable credit.

pay it. The federal estate tax is due and payable in cash nine months after your death. State taxes, probate costs, debts, and expenses usually also fall due within that time. These costs can, and often do, result in a real cash bind, because rarely do wealthy people keep a lot of cash on hand. Their wealth was derived from putting their money to work in businesses, real estate, or other investments. Estate liquidity—having enough cash to pay taxes and costs without forced sales of assets or heavy borrowing—is often a problem.

One way to handle the estate tax is to set aside or accumulate enough cash to pay it when it falls due. The trouble with this suggestion is that you may die before you have accumulated enough cash and that the cash you accumulate may be subject to income tax during your life and to estate tax at your death.

Another way to handle the estate tax would be for your family to sell assets to pay taxes, as did the families of Picasso, Coors, and Wrigley. The first assets that might be sold are stocks, bonds, gold or silver coins, and similar liquid assets. But these assets may be the source of your family's income after your death, and the market for them may be down. Such assets as real estate might also be sold, but prices on forced sales are usually only a fraction of the fair value.

Your family could consider borrowing, but it is unusual to find a commercial lender that will lend money to pay back taxes. And if one were found, personal liability might be required. In any event, borrowing does not solve the problem; it only prolongs it, adding interest costs in the process.

Borrowing from the IRS itself in the form of deferred payments or installments may be possible for reasonable cause. Tax extension and installment payment provisions are helpful, but they still leave a tax debt to be paid by your heirs at your death. Paying that debt, even over an extended period of time, could be a real burden and severely restrict their income and flexibility.

Life insurance may well be the most reasonable, feasible, and economical means to pay your estate tax. Instead of forcing your family to pay off the estate tax and other debts and costs by borrowing or selling, through insurance you can provide your family with tax-free cash at a fraction of the cost of borrowing.

SUMMARY

- Estate planning is an essential part of retirement planning and an integral part of financial planning. The first part of estate planning consists of building your estate; the second part consists of transferring your estate, at your death, in the manner you have specified.
- The personal aspects of estate planning depend on whether you are single or married. If you are married, your estate planning involves the interests of at least two people—more if there are children. Never having been married does not eliminate the need to organize your papers.
- In case of death, proof of claims must be produced, or the claims will not be processed. Among the papers needed are birth certificates, marriage certificates, legal name changes, and military service records.

- The four types of wills are the simple will, the traditional marital share will, the exemption trust will, and the stated dollar amount will. Which type is best for you depends on your personal and financial circumstances.
- Establishing a trust can be an excellent way to manage your estate. Trusts are revocable or irrevocable. Popular forms of trusts include living trusts, testamentary trusts, and insurance trusts. An attorney's help is needed to establish a trust.
- The tax aspects of estate planning have changed considerably because of recent major changes in federal tax structure. The four major federal and state taxes that must be considered in planning your estate are estate taxes, estate income taxes, inheritance taxes, and gift taxes.

GLOSSARY

Adjusted gross estate. The gross estate minus debts and costs.

Beneficiary. A recipient of trust income or of assets.

Codicil. A document that modifies provisions in an existing will.

Estate. Everything you own.

Estate planning. Creating and transferring an estate according to your wishes.

Estate tax. A federal tax on the privilege of transferring property at death.

Exemption trust will. A will in which everything passes to your spouse except the exemption ($600,000 in 1987).

Formal will. A will usually prepared with an attorney's assistance.

Gift tax. Federal and state tax on the privilege of making gifts to others.

Guardian. A person who assumes responsibilities for your children after your death.

Holographic will. A handwritten will.

Inheritance tax.   A tax levied on the right of an heir to receive an estate.

Intestate.   Without a valid will.

Life insurance trust.   A trust in which all or part of a trust's assets are derived from the proceeds of life insurance.

Living trust.   A trust created and providing benefits during the trustor's lifetime.

Living will.   A document prepared in anticipation of death.

Power of attorney.   A legal document authorizing someone to act on your behalf.

Prenuptial agreement.   A documentary agreement between spouses before marriage.

Revocable trust.   A trust whose terms the trustor retains the right to change.

Simple will.   A will that leaves everything to the spouse; also called an "I love you" will.

Statutory will.   A formal will on a preprinted form.

Testamentary trust.   A trust established by your will that becomes effective upon your death.

Traditional marital share will.   A will in which the grantor leaves one half of the estate to the spouse.

Trust.   A legal arrangement through which your assets are held by a trustee.

Trustee.   A person or institution that holds or manages property for the benefit of someone else under a trust agreement.

Trustor.   The creator of the trust; also called the grantor.

Will.   The legal declaration of a person's mind as to the disposition of his or her property after his or her death.

REVIEW QUESTIONS

1. What is estate planning? What special considerations are there in estate planning if your are married? If you are single?

2. What is a will? Describe the four types of wills, and list advantages and disadvantages of each type. What type of will is best for you? Why?

3. What differences are there among a holographic will, a formal will, and a statutory will?

4. Define and explain the following terms: *codicil, prenuptial agreement, guardian, executor, trustor, trustee, living will,* and *power of attorney.*

5. What is a letter of last instruction? Is it a substitute for a will? Why? What information is generally included in a letter of last instruction?

6. What is a trust? Describe a living trust, a testamentary trust, and an insurance trust. What are advantages and disadvantages of each?

7. What is an estate? What property is included in it?

8. Discuss and distinguish among joint tenancy with the right of survivorship, tenancy in common, and tenancy by the entirety. Is one form of ownership better than the others?

9. How is the property of a deceased person assessed for federal estate taxes?

10. Describe estate, inheritance, and gift taxes? Who levies these taxes, and why?

11. How is estate tax calculated? When does it become due?

DISCUSSION QUESTIONS AND ACTIVITIES

1. If Casso Aruza wanted to use the marital deduction and still control who would ultimately receive his paintings, what type of trust could he have established?

2. Where could a person seek assistance if he or she finds estate planning too complicated to handle unaided?

3. Why is it important for each spouse to have a will even though both spouses own all of their property jointly? After all, you don't need a will to get the unlimited marital deduction.

4. Whom would you choose to be an executor of your will? Why did you choose this person?

5. Whom would you want to be the guardian of your children if you and your spouse die in a common accident? Why did you choose this person?

6. Do you think a living will serves any useful function? Would you consider using a living will? Why?

7. If you were to buy a home with your spouse, what type of ownership would you prefer? Why?

8. In your view, is it sound financial planning to name a bank as executor and trustee? Why?

9. What professionals do you currently deal with (lawyer, banker, accountant, life insurance agent) who could help you in developing an estate plan? What other kinds of professionals could provide such assistance?

10. Develop a list of specific long-term estate planning goals with your family. Discuss how those goals could be achieved even if one spouse died unexpectedly?

ADDITIONAL READINGS

Crumbley, Larry D., and Edward D. Milam. *Estate Planning: A Guide for Advisors and Their Clients.* Homewood, Ill.: Richard D. Irwin, 1986.

A Guide to Wills and Trusts. Consumer Information Report 16. San Francisco, Calif.: Bank of America, 1984.

How Much of Your Business Are You Planning to Give to the IRS? Hartford, Conn.: Aetna Life and Casualty Company.

Planning with Your Beneficiaries. Washington, D.C.: American Council of Life Insurance, Education and Community Services. n.d.

Prestopino, Chris J. *Introduction to Estate Planning.* Homewood, Ill.: Richard D. Irwin, 1987.

Slater, Karen. "Been Putting Off a Will? Consider the Consequences of Dying without One." *The Wall Street Journal,* January 9, 1986, p. 19.

Steptoe, Sonja. "Engaged Couples Are Increasingly Going to the Bargaining Table before the Altar." *The Wall Street Journal,* July 23, 1986, p. 23.

"Take Care of Your Heirs." *Changing Times,* September 1986, pp. 33–38.

What Type of Will Is Best for You? Hartford, Conn.: Aetna Life and Casualty Company, 1982.

Zweig, Phillip. "Executors of Estates Discover that Job Can Be Difficult and Sometimes Costly." *The Wall Street Journal,* September 3, 1985, p. 25.

CASE 20–1 Retirement and Estate Planning in a High-Income Family

Rich, 48, and Mariann, 47, have a gross estate of $1,160,000 and a high family income. Last year, their combined gross income was about $175,000, most of which came from a medical clinic, in which Rich and several other physicians are partners. The remaining income came from Mariann's part-time job and from interest and dividends on various stocks, bonds, mutual funds, tax-sheltered investments, and rental property that Rich holds.

Rich and Mariann also own, in joint tenancy with right of survivorship, a home, a summer home, and an undeveloped lot in another state, and Mariann will receive $100,000 from a trust fund next year. Their net worth is about $510,000.

Since their holdings are extensive, Rich and Mariann contacted an estate planner for help in determining the most advantageous way of orga-

nizing their estate. Naturally, they wanted to be sure that the estate was set up in such a way as to minimize tax and probate shrinkage when it was passed on, first to the surviving spouse and ultimately to their four children. They also wanted to accumulate additional assets and to minimize their income taxes.

Questions

1. Should Rich and Mariann retitle some of the assets they currently hold in joint tenancy, so as to take advantage of the unified estate and gift tax credit? Why?

2. Should Rich and Mariann establish a gifting program to reduce their income taxes and build up education funds for their children? Why or why not?

CASE 20–2 Retirement and Estate Planning in a Middle-Income Family

Bob, 42, an account executive for a manufacturing company, makes $45,000 a year. Judy, 42, a teacher, makes $25,000 a year.

With a son and a daughter, aged 15 and 13, respectively, Bob and Judy first want to make sure that they have enough money to pay for their children's education. They also want to make sure that they can retire at about 75 percent of their current monthly income when Bob is 64. Finally, Bob and Judy want to know how these goals and the overall status of their estate would be affected if either of them became disabled or died prematurely.

Questions

1. Assuming a modest rate of growth in their current capital plus monthly additions by each of them, do you think that Bob and Judy will be able to finance their children's education? Would you recommend that they establish an education protection fund?

2. If Judy were to die prematurely, would the family face an income shortage? What if Bob died?

3. What suggestions do you have for Bob and Judy's estate planning? For example, what type of will do you recommend and do you recommend a trust arrangement?

Comprehensive Case for Part Six
*Retirement and Beyond!**

Brett and Robin are a happily married couple in their late 60s who have two children; Neil, aged 36, and Connie, aged 34. Brett retired last year. At present, Brett and Robin have the following property interests. In community property states, assume that all tenancies in common (TIC) held by the spouses are actually held as community property.

$210,000   Home: Joint tenancy; cost, $50,000.

$500,000   Money market fund: spousal TIC.

$21,000   Autos: Brett's property.

$160,000   Face value life insurance policy (L1) on Brett's life: cash value, $31,000. Robin is owner and beneficiary. Premiums are paid with her separate property.

$90,000   Face value life insurance policy (L2) on Robin's life: cash value, $17,000. Brett is owner and beneficiary. Premiums are paid with spousal TIC property.

$130,000   (Replacement value) qualified pension, with income payable to Brett for his life, then to Robin for her life. Brett's contributions (his property) totaled 30 percent of the total contributions made. The employer contributed the rest.

Trust   Revocable trust (Trust A) was set up in 1982, funded with land owned by Brett, then worth $180,000. At present, it is worth $490,000. On Brett's death, the trust terminates and all property passes to Connie.

$960,000   Apartment house: Brett's property.

Brett and Robin are planning to have their first wills—"All to surviving spouse" wills—drafted next month.

In 1982, Brett made the following additional gifts: (a) $26,000 cash outright to Neil, (b) $14,500 cash outright to Connie, and (c) $700,000 in stock into an irrevocable trust (Trust B), with all income accumulated until Neil reaches age 41. At that time, the trust will terminate and all income and principal will be paid to Neil and Connie equally. Brett has never made any other gifts.

Questions

1. How would you evaluate the financial situation Brett and Robin have for their retirement?

2. What are the positive and negative aspects of Brett and Robin's estate planning?

3. Calculate Brett's total taxable gifts for the gift year, assuming gift splitting. This will be a single amount.

4. Assuming that Brett dies in 1988, calculate the amount of Brett's probate estate.

5. Why is retirement and estate planning important for all individuals and families?

* Source: Chris J. Prestopino, *Introduction to Estate Planning* (Homewood, Ill.: Richard D. Irwin, 1987). p. 190. Copyright 1987 Richard D. Irwin, Inc.

Choosing a Financial Planner

Since most people spend most of their time in earning or using income, many people are unable to give their personal financial planning as much attention as it requires. Financial planners are individuals who can help you establish and accomplish financial goals by coordinating your financial decisions. These individuals operate under a variety of titles, such as financial adviser and financial counselor. Legal, competitive, and economic changes in financial services have enabled financial planners to expand their offerings of financial assistance.

Before employing the services of a financial planner, you should consider who the financial planners are, whether you need one, how to select one, how financial planners are certified, and the value of computerized financial plans.

WHO ARE THE FINANCIAL PLANNERS?

Many financial planners represent major insurance companies or investment businesses. Financial planners may also be individuals whose primary profession is tax accounting, real estate, or law. In total, over 200,000 individuals call themselves financial planners.

Financial planners may be placed in one of two categories. The first category consists of the financial planners who charge a fee but have no interest in the financial products they recommend. These individuals are commonly accountants, lawyers, credit counselors, or independent financial advisers.

The second category consists of the financial planners who earn a commission on any insurance, stocks, mutual funds, or other investments that the client buys. These individuals are often employed by financial services companies with a nationwide network of offices. Critics contend that the financial planning assistance provided by such companies is just a marketing ploy to sell other items. These financial supermarkets offer a variety of financial services and use such terms as *money dynamics, financial resources planning,* and *wealth management* to attract customers.[1]

A financial planner's background or the company a financial planner represents is a good gauge of the financial planner's principal area of expertise. An accountant is likely to be most knowledgeable about tax laws, while an insurance company representative will probably emphasize how you can use insurance to achieve your financial goals.[2]

DO YOU NEED A FINANCIAL PLANNER?

The two main factors that determine whether you need financial planning assistance are your income and your willingness to make independent decisions. If you earn less than $40,000 a year, you probably do not need a financial planner. Anything less does not allow for many major financial decisions once you have allocated the funds for the spending, savings, insurance, and tax elements of your personal financial planning. Figure A–1 offers a way to assess your need for a financial planner.

Taking a personal interest in your financial affairs can minimize your need for a financial planner. If you are willing to keep up-to-date on developments related to investments, insurance, taxes, and other personal business topics, you can probably reduce the amount of money you spend on financial advisers. This will require an ongoing investment of time and effort on your finances, but it will enable you to control your own financial direction, which many people consider necessary.

When deciding whether to use a financial planner, also consider the services that financial planners usually provide. First, the financial planner should aid you in assessing your current financial position with regard to spending, savings, insurance, taxes, and potential investments. Second, he or she should offer a clearly written plan with different courses of action for your consideration. Third, he or she should take time to discuss the components of the plan and help you monitor your financial progress. Finally, he or she should guide you to other experts and sources of financial services as needed.

You may not always receive specific advice from a financial planner. A financial planner who charges a flat fee will probably not give you specific investment recommendations. Some consider this approach more objective than that of commission-based planners who push products that increase their earnings.

HOW SHOULD YOU SELECT A FINANCIAL PLANNER?

You can locate financial planners by using a telephone directory, by contacting financial institutions, or by obtaining references from friends, business associates, or professionals with whom you currently deal, such as insurance agents, or real estate brokers.

---

[1]"Financial Planners: How to Pick the Best for You," *Changing Times,* May 1986, p. 35.
[2]Ibid.

FIGURE A-1   Do You Need a Financial Planner?

Compute the following "financial planning need index" to determine if the use of a financial planner would be to your advantage.

Income: For each $5,000 of family income above $20,000, score one point, through $50,000. Over $50,000, score one point for each additional $10,000 up to a 15-point limit. For example, an income of $90,000 would score 10 points. _____

Taxes: For each $1,000 paid in taxes above $5,000 up to $10,000, score one point. Score another point for each $2,000 in taxes over $10,000 up to a maximum of 15 points. For example, $20,000 in federal taxes would score 10 points. _____

Financial assets: In this category, you receive points as follows: one point if you own common stocks or bonds; one point for a margin account or borrowing to finance investments; one point if you own a mutual fund, variable annuity, or more than three life insurance policies; if all of the above apply, take an additional point; double your total of the above if you have more than five investments or use more than one stockbroker, banker, or insurance agent; two additional points for an investment in a venture company or family business or investment real estate; one point for a limited partnership investment, and two more points if this is a private rather than a public offering. The maximum number of points for this category is 10. _____

Financial planning need index (divide total by three): A score of five or higher is usually an indication that you should consider formal assistance for financial planning. _____

Source: Carl E. Andersen, *Andersen on Financial Planning* (Homewood, Ill.: Dow Jones-Irwin, 1986), pp. 20–21.

When evaluating a financial planner, investigate the following:

- Is financial planning the primary activity of the individual, or are other activities primary?
- What is the individual's educational background and formal training?
- What are his or her areas of expertise?
- Are experts in other areas, such as taxes, law, or insurance, available to assist you in your financial planning?
- What professional titles and certification does the individual possess?
- Is the individual licensed as an investment broker or as a seller of life insurance?
- Are you allowed a free initial consultation?
- What method of payment is required? Will you be able to afford the service?
- Does the individual have an independent practice, or is he or she affiliated with a major financial services company?
- What are typical insurance, tax, and investment decisions that the individual makes for current clients?

- Is the individual able to communicate in a manner with which you feel comfortable?

Such an investigation takes time and effort, but remember that you are considering placing your entire financial future in the hands of one person. (Table A–1 presents information on services and fees.)

HOW ARE FINANCIAL PLANNERS CERTIFIED?

The requirements for becoming a financial planner are very loose. Only about 10 percent of those who call themselves financial planners have met specific training requirements for that role. Organizations that provide details on the certification of financial planners are the Institute of Certified Financial Planners, the International Association for Financial Planning, and the National Association of Personal Financial Planners.

Many financial planners use abbreviations for the titles they have earned. Some of these abbreviations are quite familiar—for example, CPA (certified public accountant, JD (doctor of law), and MBA (master of business administration); others are unknown to most people. Less well known abbreviations used by financial planners include CFP (certified financial planner), ChFC (chartered financial consultant in the life insurance industry), and CFA (chartered financial analyst handling stock and bond portfolios).

While these credentials provide some assurance of expertise, not all planners are licensed. The Better Business Bureau estimated that fraudulent planners took consumers for nearly $90 million in bad investments and advice between 1983 and 1985.[3] Such financial planning activities as insurance and investment security sales do come under regulatory control. Some states have proposed or enacted testing and means for monitoring financial planners. Since the financial planning marketplace is likely to remain relatively free of regulation, however, consumers should be wary of and investigate any financial planning operation they are considering.

HOW HELPFUL ARE COMPUTERIZED FINANCIAL PLANS?

Computerized financial plans are an inexpensive alternative to financial planners. The low-priced advice provided by such plans, called *prefab planning* by some, can provide appropriate financial direction. While the cost of a financial planner can range from a couple of hundred dollars to several thousand dollars, computerized assistance ranges in price from nothing at all to a few hundred dollars.

Computerized financial advice has been available for several years from many of the organizations that financial planners represent. Investment brokers, insurance companies, and other financial institutions offer computerized financial evaluations and recommendations. Merrill Lynch offers the "Financial Pathfinder," and the "Money Allocation Program" is a service of E. F. Hutton.

For companies with a financial product to sell, computerized financial

[3]"Financial Planners: What Are They Really Selling?" *Consumer Reports*, January 1986, p. 37.

TABLE A-1   The Price You Pay for Financial Help

Here's a list of some typical financial services and what it costs to hire a professional.

Service	Professional	Average Fee
Basic tax preparation	H&R Block	$45
	Certified public accountant	$100 or more
	Tax lawyer	$82 an hour or more
Tax planning (year-round)	CPA	$75 an hour or more
	Certified financial planner	$50 to $125 an hour
	Tax lawyer	$82 an hour or more
Buying stocks*	Full-service broker	$70 for 100 shares at $30 each
	Discount broker	$35 for 100 shares at $30 each
Buying shares in a mutual fund	Full-service broker	8.5% of initial investment for most funds
	Discount broker	$12 plus 0.8% of initial investment of $3,000 or less worth of shares in no-load fund†
		No charge to buy into no-load (no-fee) fund on your own
Closing a house sale	Lawyer	U.S. average: $316 on $60,000 house ($275 in West Central states to $400 in California)
Retirement planning	Chartered life underwriter or chartered financial consultant	$1,500 to $2,500 plus commissions for middle-aged couple with children, $100,000 income
	Certified financial planner, fee-only‡	$2,000 to $3,000 for middle-aged couple with children, $100,000 income
Financial planning	Chartered life underwriter or chartered financial consultant	$300 to $500 plus commissions for family with two wage earners, $50,000 income
	Certified financial planner, fee-only‡	$1,500 to $2,000 for family with two wage earners, $50,000 income

*Stockbroker fees vary with the price and number of shares traded.
†Figures provided by Charles Schwab & Co.
‡Fee-only financial planners charge an hourly rate or a specific fee for each service. Most financial planners charge a fee plus commissions on certain investments.
Source: *USA Today*, March 3, 1986, p. 4E. Copyright 1986 *USA Today*. Reprinted with permission.

Pepper . . . and Salt

"I feel I owe you an apology,
Mr. McCambridge."

From *The Wall Street Journal*, with permission of Cartoon Features Syndicate.

plans serve to attract new customers. However, when such plans are used, the selling efforts are usually less intensive than the selling efforts made by financial planners. Clients may have the option of meeting with a company representative to interpret results. Again, beware of bias toward insurance or specific types of investments that may have been built into the computerized plan.

Despite their drawbacks, computerized financial plans can have value. Systems users are usually under no obligation to purchase additional products or services. The printed report assesses your current financial position and suggests actions that you can take. You are not likely to get a lot of detail since this type of financial plan is frequently prepackaged to provide general advice and accepted methods for reaching goals. These low-price plans will probably not recommend specific stocks or tax actions.

A computerized financial plan will probably begin with you completing a 15–70 page questionnaire on your current financial and family situation. The information you provide is processed to produce a 20–40 page analysis and recommendations on savings plans, investment strategies, insurance needs, tax estimates, and financial prospects for retirement.[4] This may seem impressive, but you can probably prepare a similar report based on the knowledge you have derived from this book. Still, you may wish to save time and effort by using a computerized financial plan.

[4]"Computerized Financial Plans: How Good?" *Changing Times*, October 1985, p. 48.

B

Buying a Personal Computer and Financial Planning Software

Personal computers make handling personal financial matters easier and faster. Reduced computer costs and increased availability of programs are allowing individuals to budget, plan investments, and prepare their taxes with assistance from an automated information system. Knowing the components of a computer system, the sources of computer buying information, and the types and sources of personal financial software can be of value to you.

PERSONAL COMPUTER SYSTEMS

Before purchasing a personal computer, you should be aware of its main components. The microprocessor is the brains of the system. Its size is expressed in terms of its random-access memory (RAM)—the amount of data that it can store. The unit of measurement of a microprocessor's RAM is the kilobyte, or K, which is 1,024 characters of such data as a digit or a letter. The RAM of early personal computers was 16K or 32K; today, 256K, 512K, and 640K are more common. The size of the microprocessor you select will depend on the types of programs you want to use now and on the future uses you plan to make of your system. A larger memory will allow you to expand your uses to include school research projects and business activities.

The main input device is the keyboard. This allows you to enter and process data. The visual display screen, or monitor, is also used during the input phase of processing. It allows you to see the data or commands that you have entered.

A disk drive is a device that can serve both your input needs and your storage needs. Reading programs and data from diskettes speeds the input phase. After processing data, you can store it on a diskette for future use. As your storage needs increase, you can add a hard disk to your system. A hard disk maintains larger amounts of data than a diskette.

To complement your personal computer, you will probably want a printer that gives you a paper copy of the various reports, documents, and letters produced by the computer. Printers come in a wide variety of styles and prices. Which one you select will depend on the quality and speed you need.

Your personal computer has the potential of being a window on the world. Connecting your telephone to your computer by means of a modem enables you to conduct banking at home, to obtain financial and other news, and to communicate with other personal computers for business or social purposes.

SOURCES OF COMPUTER PURCHASING INFORMATION

Choosing a personal computer will require considering a number of factors and gathering information from various sources. The make, model, and size of the computer you choose will be influenced by the intended uses and your financial constraints. The most popular personal computers are the Apple and the IBM PC and compatibles. A wide range of capabilities and prices exist in the marketplace.

Obtaining product and price information will help you purchase a personal computer that will serve your needs. Personal computer buying guides and magazines are available in bookstores and libraries. Among the publications that can be helpful are *Personal Computing, Family Computing, Compute!, PC Magazine, PC World,* and *A + . Consumer Reports, Changing Times,* and other personal finance periodicals offer computer buying assistance. People who own and work with computers can also offer valuable insights.

The retailers that sell personal computers are another source of information. Stores that specialize in computer equipment and accessories can be found in most areas. These full-service computer stores, which may be locally owned or part of a national chain, will usually demonstrate the computers, printers, software, and other items that they sell.

Most department stores and discount stores sell computers for home and business use. These retailers may not provide the same level of expertise and service as that provided by stores specializing in computers. Advertisements in computer magazines are a helpful source of purchasing information. Mail-order businesses sell all the ingredients of personal computer systems at reasonable prices. But, of course, assistance is not available from out-of-town firms.

Local newspapers advertisements, computer periodicals, and computer stores provide information on used computers. As owners upgrade their systems, trade-ins become available to people who want a low-cost personal computer. As with used cars, be sure to test-drive the used computer by running the software you plan to use.

From *The Wall Street Journal*, with permission of Cartoon Features Syndicate.

SOURCES OF FINANCIAL PLANNING SOFTWARE

Your personal computer will make it easier for you to compose and revise letters and reports. A data base management program provides facilities for storing and retrieving information. Software of this type can be helpful in maintaining the financial records discussed in Chapter 3 or in filing tax information by category.

A spreadsheet program such as Lotus 1-2-3 or the less expensive PC-Calc can be used to establish a budgeting system or to handle other financial planning data. With spreadsheets, numbers can be manipulated, future situations can be projected, and financial statements can be developed.

Also available for personal financial planning are a variety of specialized software packages that are in four categories, home budgeting programs, investment analysis programs, programs for tax recordkeeping and preparation, and financial planning programs. Since over 2,000 microcomputer programs have the words *financial* or *investing* in their titles, the ones mentioned below are only a sampling of those from which you can choose. The prices of such programs range from $15 to $20 to several hundred dollars.

Home Budgeting Programs

These software packages are designed to create spending categories and to help you in planning your budget. Some may also prepare personal financial statements, write checks, and maintain your checkbook balance. Programs available in this category include:

Budget Analysis Pac, Computronics, 50 North Pascack Road, Spring Valley, NY 10977.

Checkbook Management, PC Software Interest Group, 1030 East Duane, Sunnyvale, CA 94086.

Financial Navigator, Money Care, Inc., 253 Martens Ave., Mountain View, CA 94094.

J. K. Lasser's Your Money Manager, Simon and Schuster, 1 Gulf and Western Plaza, New York, NY 10023.

Time and Money, Soft/Plus Research, Box 590, Boonville, CA 95415.

Investment Programs

Microcomputer programs are available to monitor and plan your investments. These software packages can provide you with data on the current value of your portfolio and on individual stock, bond, mutual fund, and commodity investments. Investment software includes:

The Equalizer, Charles Schwab & Co., 101 Montgomery Street, San Francisco, CA 94104.

Compustock, A. S. Gibson and Sons, Inc., Box 130, Bountiful, UT 84010.

Investicalc and *Option Pak*, Software Express, Box 2288, Merrifield, VA 22116.

Market Analyzer Plus, Dow Jones & Company, Inc., Box 300, Princeton, NJ 08540.

Stockpak II, Standard & Poor's, Micro Systems Division, 25 Broadway, New York, NY 10004.

Stock Market Analysis, The Computer Room, Box 1596, Gordonsville, VA 22942.

Your Personal Investment Manager, Timeworks, Inc., 444 Lake Cook Road, Deerfield, IL 60015.

Tax Programs

A wide range of software is available to plan, maintain, and prepare income tax documents. These programs usually require annual updates to provide for tax law changes. You may wish to consider the following:

EZ Tax, EZWare Corporation, Box 620, 29 Bala Avenue, Bala Cynwyd, PA 19004.

J. K. Lasser's Your Income Tax, Simon and Schuster, 1 Gulf and Western Plaza, New York, NY 10023.

Swiftax, Timeworks, Inc., 444 Lake Cook Road, Deerfield, IL 60015.

The Tax Advantage, Arrays, Inc., 6711 Valjean Avenue, Van Nuys, CA 91406.

Tax Preparer, Howard Soft, 1224 Prospect Street, La Jolla, CA 92037.

TurboTax, Chipsoft, Inc., 4901 Morena Boulevard, San Diego, CA 92117.

Financial Planning Programs

Several software packages handle many or all aspects of personal financial planning. Such programs usually include budgeting, personal financial statements, tax records, estimates of tax payments, analysis of investments, and a checkbook feature. Popular programs in this category include:

Andrew Tobias' Managing Your Money, Micro Education Corporation of America, 285 Riverside Avenue, Westport, CT 06880.

Dollars and Sense, Monogram, 8295 South La Cienega Boulevard, Inglewood, CA 90301.

Financial Independence, Broderbund Software, Inc., 17 Paul Drive, San Rafael, CA 94903.

Sylvia Porter's Your Personal Financial Planner, Timeworks, Inc., 444 Lake Cook Road, Deerfield, IL 60015.

Before purchasing any software, you should make sure that it is compatible with your computer system. You should also obtain information regarding its functions, ease of operation, and current cost. Most important, you should make sure that the software serves the needs that it is intended to serve.

ADDITIONAL READINGS

Bruce, David. "Computerizing Your Finances." *Sylvia Porter's Personal Finance*, June 1986, pp. 83–86.

————. "Computerizing Your Taxes." *Sylvia Porter's Personal Finance*, March 1986, pp. 24, 26.

Davidson, Pamela. "Tax Strategies for the Age of Reform." *Personal Computing*, December 1986, pp. 64–69, 71, 73–75.

Meyers, Thomas A. "Rating Investment Software: Portfolio Management." *PC Magazine*, April 15, 1986, pp. 183–221.

Morgenstern, Steve. "A Guide to Personal Finances." *Family Computing*, January 1987, pp. 37–45.

Stern, Matthew. "Your Money and Your Mac." *Family Computing*, April, 1987, p. 16.

"Software That Does the Hard Work." *Changing Times*, June 1986, pp. 71–75.

Wasik, John. "Finally Personal Computers Make Sense." *Consumers Digest*, June 1986, pp. 35–38.

Watkins, Linda M. "Users Find Personal-Accounting Software Doesn't Easily Solve All Financial Woes." *The Wall Street Journal*, March 4, 1986, p. 31.

The Time Value of Money: Future Value and Present Value Computations

The time value of money, more commonly referred to as *interest*, is the price of money that is borrowed or lent. Interest is the cost of using money; it can be compared to rent, the cost of using an apartment or other item. The time value of money is based on the fact that a dollar received today is worth more than a dollar that will be received one year from today, because the dollar received today can be saved or invested and will be worth more than a dollar a year from today. In a similar manner, a dollar that will be received one year from today is worth less than a dollar today.

The time value of money consists of two major aspects: future value and present value. *Future value*, also referred to as compounding, is the amount to which a current sum will increase based on a certain interest rate and period of time. *Present value* is the current value of a future sum based on a certain interest rate and period of time.

In future value problems, you are given an amount to save or invest and you need to calculate the amount that will be available at some future date based on a certain interest rate. With present value problems, you are given the amount that will be available at some future date and you must calculate the current monetary value of that amount based on a certain interest rate. Both future value and present value computations are based on basic interest rate calculations.

**INTEREST
RATE BASICS**

Simple interest is the dollar cost of borrowing or earnings from lending money. The interest is based on three elements:

- The dollar amount, called the *principal*
- The *rate of interest*
- The amount of *time*

The formula for computing interest is:

$$\text{Interest} = \text{Principal} \times \text{Rate of interest} \times \text{Time}$$

The interest rate is stated as a percentage for a year. For example, you must convert 12 percent to either 0.12 or $^{12}/_{100}$ before doing your calculations. The time element must also be converted to a decimal or fraction. For example, three months would be shown as either 0.25 or ¼ of a year. Interest over 2½ years would involve a time period of 2.5.

Example A. Suppose $1,000 is borrowed at 5 percent and repaid in one payment at the end of one year. Using the simple interest calculation, the interest is $50, computed as follows:

$$\$50 = \$1,000 \times 0.05 \times 1 \text{ (year)}$$

Example B. If you deposited $750 in a savings account paying 8 percent, how much interest would you earn in nine months? You would compute this amount as follows:

$$\begin{aligned}\text{Interest} &= \$750 \times 0.08 \times \tfrac{3}{4} \text{ (or 0.75 of a year)}\\ &= \$45\end{aligned}$$

Sample Problem 1. How much interest would you earn if you deposited $300 at 6 percent for 27 months? (*Answers to sample problems are at the end of this appendix.*)

Sample Problem 2. How much interest would you pay to borrow $670 for eight months at 12 percent?

**FUTURE
VALUE OF A
SINGLE
AMOUNT**

The future value of an amount consists of the original amount plus compound interest. This calculation involves the following elements:

$$FV = \text{Future value}$$
$$PV = \text{Present value}$$
$$i = \text{Interest rate}$$
$$n = \text{Number of time periods}$$

The formula for future value is:

$$FV = PV(1 + i)^n$$

Example C. The future value of $1 at 10 percent after three years is $1.33. This amount is calculated as follows:

$$\$1.33 = \$1.00(1 + 0.10)^3$$

Future value tables are available to help you determine compounded interest amounts (see Table C–1): By looking at Table C–1 for 10 percent and three years, you can see that $1 would be worth $1.33 at that time. For other amounts, multiply the table factor by the original amount.

Example D. If your savings of $400 earns 12 percent, compounded monthly, over a year and a half, you would use the table factor for 1 percent for 18 time periods. The future value of this amount is $478.40, calculated as follows:

$$\$478.40 = \$400 \ (1.196)$$

Sample Problem 3. What is the future value of $800 at 8 percent after six years?

Sample Problem 4. How much would you have in savings if you kept $200 on deposit for eight years at 8 percent compounded semiannually?

FUTURE VALUE OF A SERIES OF EQUAL AMOUNTS

Future value may also be calculated for a situation in which regular additions are made to savings. The following formula is used:

$$FV = \frac{(1 + i)^n - 1}{i}$$

This formula assumes that each deposit is for the same amount, that the interest rate is the same for each time period, and that the deposits are made at the end of each time period.

Example E. The future value of three $1 deposits made at the end of the next three years earning 10 percent interest is $3.31. This is calculated as follows:

$$\$3.31 = \$1 \ \frac{(1 + 0.10)^3 - 1}{0.10}$$

With the use of Table C–2, this same amount can be found for 10 percent for three time periods. To use the table for other amounts, multiply the table factors by the annual deposit.

Example F. If you plan to deposit $40 a year for 10 years earning 8 percent compounded annually, you would use the table factor for 8 percent for 10 time periods. The future value of this amount is $579.48, calculated as follows:

$$\$579.48 = \$40(14.487)$$

Sample Problem 5. What is the future value of an annual deposit of $230 earning 6 percent for 15 years?

Sample Problem 6. What amount would a person have in a retirement account if annual deposits of $375 were made for 25 years earning 12 percent compounded annually?

PRESENT VALUE OF A SINGLE AMOUNT

If you want to know how much you need to deposit in the present in order to receive a certain amount in the future, the following formula is used:

$$PV = \frac{1}{(1 + i)^n}$$

Example G. The present value of $1 to be received three years from now based on a 10 percent interest rate is $0.75. This amount is calculated as follows:

$$\$0.75 = \frac{\$1}{(1 + 0.10)^3}$$

Present value tables are available to assist in this process (see Table C–3). Notice that $1 at 10 percent for three years has a present value of $0.75. For amounts other than $1, multiply the table factor by the amount involved.

Example H. If you want to have $300 seven years from now and your savings earns 10 percent compounded semiannually, you would use the table factor for 5 percent for 14 time periods. In this situation, the present value is $151.50, calculated as follows:

$$\$151.50 = \$300(0.505)$$

Sample Problem 7. What is the present value of $2,200 earning 15 percent for eight years?

Sample Problem 8. In order to have $6,000 for a daughter's education in 10 years, what amount should a parent deposit in a savings account that earns 12 percent compounded quarterly?

PRESENT VALUE OF A SERIES OF EQUAL AMOUNTS

The final time value of money situation allows a person to receive an amount at the end of each time period for a certain number of periods. This amount would be calculated as follows:

$$PV = \frac{1 - \dfrac{1}{(1 + i)^n}}{i}$$

Example I. The present value of a $1 withdrawal at the end of the next three years would be $2.49, calculated as follows:

$$\$2.49 = \$1 \left[\frac{1 - \dfrac{1}{(1 + 0.10)^n}}{0.10} \right]$$

This same amount can be found in Table C–4 for 10 percent and three time periods. To use the table for other situations, multiply the table factor by the amount to be withdrawn each year.

Example J. If you would like to withdraw $100 at the end of each year for 10 years from an account that earns 14 percent compounded annually, what amount must you deposit now? Use the table factor for 14 percent for 10 time periods. In this situation, the present value is $521.60, calculated as follows:

$$\$521.60 = \$100(5.216)$$

Sample Problem 9. What is the present value of a withdrawal of $200 at the end of each year for 14 years with an interest rate of 7 percent?

Sample Problem 10. How much would you have to deposit now to be able to withdraw $650 at the end of each year for 20 years from an account that earns 11 percent?

ANSWERS TO SAMPLE PROBLEMS

1. $300 × 0.06 × 2.25 years (27 months) = $40.50.
2. $670 × 0.12 × ⅔ (of a year) = $53.60.
3. $800(1.587) = $1,269.60. (Use Table C–1, 8%, 6 periods.)
4. $200(1.873) = $374.60. (Use Table C–1, 4%, 16 periods.)
5. $230(23.276) = $5,353.48. (Use Table C–2, 6%, 15 periods.)
6. $375(133.33) = $9,998.75. (Use Table C–2, 12%, 25 periods.)

7. $2,200(.327) = $719.40. (Use Table C–3, 15%, 8 periods.)
8. $6,000(.307) = $1,842. (Use Table C–3, 3%, 40 periods.)
9. $200(8.745) = $1,749. (Use Table C–4, 7%, 14 periods.)
10. $650(7.963) = $5,175.95. (Use Table C–4, 11%, 20 periods.)

ADDITIONAL READINGS

ABCs of Figuring Interest. Federal Reserve Bank of Chicago.

The Arithmetic of Interest Rates. Federal Reserve Bank of New York.

Rosen, Lawrence R. *The Dow Jones-Irwin Guide to Interest*. Homewood, Ill.: Dow Jones-Irwin, 1981.

Welsch, Glenn A. and Daniel G. Short. "Future Value and Present Value Concepts." *Fundamentals of Financial Accounting*, 5th ed., pp. 507–17. Homewood, Ill.: Richard D. Irwin, 1987.

TABLE C-1 Future Value (Compounded Sum) of $1 after a Given Number of Time Periods

Period	1%	2%	3%	4%	5%	6%	7%	8%	9%	10%	11%
1	1.010	1.020	1.030	1.040	1.050	1.060	1.070	1.080	1.090	1.100	1.110
2	1.020	1.040	1.061	1.082	1.103	1.124	1.145	1.166	1.188	1.210	1.232
3	1.030	1.061	1.093	1.125	1.158	1.191	1.225	1.260	1.295	1.331	1.368
4	1.041	1.082	1.126	1.170	1.216	1.262	1.311	1.360	1.412	1.464	1.518
5	1.051	1.104	1.159	1.217	1.276	1.338	1.403	1.469	1.539	1.611	1.685
6	1.062	1.126	1.194	1.265	1.340	1.419	1.501	1.587	1.677	1.772	1.870
7	1.072	1.149	1.230	1.316	1.407	1.504	1.606	1.714	1.828	1.949	2.076
8	1.083	1.172	1.267	1.369	1.477	1.594	1.718	1.851	1.993	2.144	2.305
9	1.094	1.195	1.305	1.423	1.551	1.689	1.838	1.999	2.172	2.358	2.558
10	1.105	1.219	1.344	1.480	1.629	1.791	1.967	2.159	2.367	2.594	2.839
11	1.116	1.243	1.384	1.539	1.710	1.898	2.105	2.332	2.580	2.853	3.152
12	1.127	1.268	1.426	1.601	1.796	2.012	2.252	2.518	2.813	3.138	3.498
13	1.138	1.294	1.469	1.665	1.886	2.133	2.410	2.720	3.066	3.452	3.883
14	1.149	1.319	1.513	1.732	1.980	2.261	2.579	2.937	3.342	3.797	4.310
15	1.161	1.346	1.558	1.801	2.079	2.397	2.759	3.172	3.642	4.177	4.785
16	1.173	1.373	1.605	1.873	2.183	2.540	2.952	3.426	3.970	4.595	5.311
17	1.184	1.400	1.653	1.948	2.292	2.693	3.159	3.700	4.328	5.054	5.895
18	1.196	1.428	1.702	2.026	2.407	2.854	3.380	3.996	4.717	5.560	6.544
19	1.208	1.457	1.754	2.107	2.527	3.026	3.617	4.316	5.142	6.116	7.263
20	1.220	1.486	1.806	2.191	2.653	3.207	3.870	4.661	5.604	6.727	8.062
25	1.282	1.641	2.094	2.666	3.386	4.292	5.427	6.848	8.623	10.835	13.585
30	1.348	1.811	2.427	3.243	4.322	5.743	7.612	10.063	13.268	17.449	22.892
40	1.489	2.208	3.262	4.801	7.040	10.286	14.974	21.725	31.409	45.259	65.001
50	1.645	2.692	4.384	7.107	11.467	18.420	29.457	46.902	74.358	117.39	184.57

Percent

TABLE C-1 *(concluded)*

Period	Percent										
	12%	13%	14%	15%	16%	17%	18%	19%	20%	25%	30%
1	1.120	1.130	1.140	1.150	1.160	1.170	1.180	1.190	1.200	1.250	1.300
2	1.254	1.277	1.300	1.323	1.346	1.369	1.392	1.416	1.440	1.563	1.690
3	1.405	1.443	1.482	1.521	1.561	1.602	1.643	1.685	1.728	1.953	2.197
4	1.574	1.630	1.689	1.749	1.811	1.874	1.939	2.005	2.074	2.441	2.856
5	1.762	1.842	1.925	2.011	2.100	2.192	2.288	2.386	2.488	3.052	3.713
6	1.974	2.082	2.195	2.313	2.436	2.565	2.700	2.840	2.986	3.815	4.827
7	2.211	2.353	2.502	2.660	2.826	3.001	3.185	3.379	3.583	4.768	6.276
8	2.476	2.658	2.853	3.059	3.278	3.511	3.759	4.021	4.300	5.960	8.157
9	2.773	3.004	3.252	3.518	3.803	4.108	4.435	4.785	5.160	7.451	10.604
10	3.106	3.395	3.707	4.046	4.411	4.807	5.234	5.696	6.192	9.313	13.786
11	3.479	3.836	4.226	4.652	5.117	5.624	6.176	6.777	7.430	11.642	17.922
12	3.896	4.335	4.818	5.350	5.936	6.580	7.288	8.064	8.916	14.552	23.298
13	4.363	4.898	5.492	6.153	6.886	7.699	8.599	9.596	10.699	18.190	30.288
14	4.887	5.535	6.261	7.076	7.988	9.007	10.147	11.420	12.839	22.737	39.374
15	5.474	6.254	7.138	8.137	9.266	10.539	11.974	13.590	15.407	28.422	51.186
16	6.130	7.067	8.137	9.358	10.748	12.330	14.129	16.172	18.488	35.527	66.542
17	6.866	7.986	9.276	10.761	12.468	14.426	16.672	19.244	22.186	44.409	86.504
18	7.690	9.024	10.575	12.375	14.463	16.879	19.673	22.091	26.623	55.511	112.46
19	8.613	10.197	12.056	14.232	16.777	19.748	23.214	27.252	31.948	69.389	146.19
20	9.646	11.523	13.743	16.367	19.461	23.106	27.393	32.429	38.338	86.736	190.05
25	17.000	21.231	26.462	32.919	40.874	50.658	62.669	77.388	95.396	264.70	705.64
30	29.960	39.116	50.950	66.212	85.850	111.07	143.37	184.68	237.38	807.79	2,620.0
40	93.051	132.78	188.88	267.86	378.72	533.87	750.38	1,051.7	1,469.8	7,523.2	36,119.
50	289.00	450.74	700.23	1,083.7	1,670.7	2,566.2	3,927.4	5,988.9	9,100.4	70,065.	497,929.

Source: Maurice Joy, *Introduction to Financial Management* (Homewood, Ill.: Richard D. Irwin, Inc.)

TABLE C-2 Future Value (Compounded Sum) of $1 Paid in at the End of Each Period for a Given Number of Time Periods

Period						Percent					
	1%	2%	3%	4%	5%	6%	7%	8%	9%	10%	11%
1	1.000	1.000	1.000	1.000	1.000	1.000	1.000	1.000	1.000	1.000	1.000
2	2.010	2.020	2.030	2.040	2.050	2.060	2.070	2.080	2.090	2.100	2.110
3	3.030	3.060	3.091	3.122	3.153	3.184	3.215	3.246	3.278	3.310	3.342
4	4.060	4.122	4.184	4.246	4.310	4.375	4.440	4.506	4.573	4.641	4.710
5	5.101	5.204	5.309	5.416	5.526	5.637	5.751	5.867	5.985	6.105	6.228
6	6.152	6.308	6.468	6.633	6.802	6.975	7.153	7.336	7.523	7.716	7.913
7	7.214	7.434	7.662	7.898	8.142	8.394	8.654	8.923	9.200	9.487	9.783
8	8.286	8.583	8.892	9.214	9.549	9.897	10.260	10.637	11.028	11.436	11.859
9	9.369	9.755	10.159	10.583	11.027	11.491	11.978	12.488	13.021	13.579	14.164
10	10.462	10.950	11.464	12.006	12.578	13.181	13.816	14.487	15.193	15.937	16.722
11	11.567	12.169	12.808	13.486	14.207	14.972	15.784	16.645	17.560	18.531	19.561
12	12.683	13.412	14.192	15.026	15.917	16.870	17.888	18.977	20.141	21.384	22.713
13	13.809	14.680	15.618	16.627	17.713	18.882	20.141	21.495	22.953	24.523	26.212
14	14.947	15.974	17.086	18.292	19.599	21.015	22.550	24.215	26.019	27.975	30.095
15	16.097	17.293	18.599	20.024	21.579	23.276	25.129	27.152	29.361	31.772	34.405
16	17.258	18.639	20.157	21.825	23.657	25.673	27.888	30.324	33.003	35.950	39.190
17	18.430	20.012	21.762	23.698	25.840	28.213	30.840	33.750	36.974	40.545	44.501
18	19.615	21.412	23.414	25.645	28.132	30.906	33.999	37.450	41.301	45.599	50.396
19	20.811	22.841	25.117	27.671	30.539	33.760	37.379	41.446	46.018	51.159	56.939
20	22.019	24.297	26.870	29.778	33.066	36.786	40.995	45.762	51.160	57.275	64.203
25	28.243	32.030	36.459	41.646	47.727	54.865	63.249	73.106	84.701	98.347	114.41
30	34.785	40.588	47.575	56.085	66.439	79.058	94.461	113.28	136.31	164.49	199.02
40	48.886	60.402	75.401	95.026	120.80	154.76	199.64	259.06	337.89	442.59	581.83
50	64.463	84.579	112.80	152.67	209.35	290.34	406.53	573.77	815.08	1,163.9	1,668.8

TABLE C-2 *(concluded)*

Period	12%	13%	14%	15%	16%	17%	18%	19%	20%	25%	30%
1	1.000	1.000	1.000	1.000	1.000	1.000	1.000	1.000	1.000	1.000	1.000
2	2.120	2.130	2.140	2.150	2.160	2.170	2.180	2.190	2.200	2.250	2.300
3	3.374	3.407	3.440	3.473	3.506	3.539	3.572	3.606	3.640	3.813	3.990
4	4.779	4.850	4.921	4.993	5.066	5.141	5.215	5.291	5.368	5.766	6.187
5	6.353	6.480	6.610	6.742	6.877	7.014	7.154	7.297	7.442	8.207	9.043
6	8.115	8.323	8.536	8.754	8.977	9.207	9.442	9.683	9.930	11.259	12.756
7	10.089	10.405	10.730	11.067	11.414	11.772	12.142	12.523	12.916	15.073	17.583
8	12.300	12.757	13.233	13.727	14.240	14.773	15.327	15.902	16.499	19.842	23.858
9	14.776	15.416	16.085	16.786	17.519	18.285	19.086	19.923	20.799	25.802	32.015
10	17.549	18.420	19.337	20.304	21.321	22.393	23.521	24.701	25.959	33.253	42.619
11	20.655	21.814	23.045	24.349	25.733	27.200	28.755	30.404	32.150	42.566	56.405
12	24.133	25.650	27.271	29.002	30.850	32.824	34.931	37.180	39.581	54.208	74.327
13	28.029	29.985	32.089	34.352	36.786	39.404	42.219	45.244	48.497	68.760	97.625
14	32.393	34.883	37.581	40.505	43.672	47.103	50.818	54.841	59.196	86.949	127.91
15	37.280	40.417	43.842	47.580	51.660	56.110	60.965	66.261	72.035	109.69	167.29
16	42.753	46.672	50.980	55.717	60.925	66.649	72.939	79.850	87.442	138.11	218.47
17	48.884	53.739	59.118	65.075	71.673	78.979	87.068	96.022	105.93	173.64	285.01
18	55.750	61.725	68.394	75.836	84.141	93.406	103.74	115.27	128.12	218.05	371.52
19	63.440	70.749	78.969	88.212	98.603	110.29	123.41	138.17	154.74	273.56	483.97
20	72.052	80.947	91.025	102.44	115.38	130.03	146.63	165.42	186.69	342.95	630.17
25	133.33	155.62	181.87	212.79	249.21	292.11	342.60	402.04	471.98	1,054.8	2,348.80
30	241.33	293.20	356.79	434.75	530.31	647.44	790.95	966.7	1,181.9	3,227.2	8,730.0
40	767.09	1,013.7	1,342.0	1,779.1	2,360.8	3,134.5	4,163.21	5,529.8	7,343.9	30,089.	120,393.
50	2,400.0	3,459.5	4,994.5	7,217.7	10,436.	15,090.	21,813.	31,515.	45,497.	280,256.	165,976.

Source: Maurice Joy, *Introduction to Financial Management* (Homewood, Ill.: Richard D. Irwin, Inc.)

TABLE C-3   Present Value of $1 to Be Received at the End of a Given Number of Time Periods

Percent

Period	1%	2%	3%	4%	5%	6%	7%	8%	9%	10%	11%	12%
1	0.990	0.980	0.971	0.962	0.952	0.943	0.935	0.926	0.917	0.909	0.901	0.893
2	0.980	0.961	0.943	0.925	0.907	0.890	0.873	0.857	0.842	0.826	0.812	0.797
3	0.971	0.942	0.915	0.889	0.864	0.840	0.816	0.794	0.772	0.751	0.731	0.712
4	0.961	0.924	0.885	0.855	0.823	0.792	0.763	0.735	0.708	0.683	0.659	0.636
5	0.951	0.906	0.863	0.822	0.784	0.747	0.713	0.681	0.650	0.621	0.593	0.567
6	0.942	0.888	0.837	0.790	0.746	0.705	0.666	0.630	0.596	0.564	0.535	0.507
7	0.933	0.871	0.813	0.760	0.711	0.665	0.623	0.583	0.547	0.513	0.482	0.452
8	0.923	0.853	0.789	0.731	0.677	0.627	0.582	0.540	0.502	0.467	0.434	0.404
9	0.914	0.837	0.766	0.703	0.645	0.592	0.544	0.500	0.460	0.424	0.391	0.361
10	0.905	0.820	0.744	0.676	0.614	0.558	0.508	0.463	0.422	0.386	0.352	0.322
11	0.896	0.804	0.722	0.650	0.585	0.527	0.475	0.429	0.388	0.350	0.317	0.287
12	0.887	0.788	0.701	0.625	0.557	0.497	0.444	0.397	0.356	0.319	0.286	0.257
13	0.879	0.773	0.681	0.601	0.530	0.469	0.415	0.368	0.326	0.290	0.258	0.229
14	0.870	0.758	0.661	0.577	0.505	0.442	0.388	0.340	0.299	0.263	0.232	0.205
15	0.861	0.743	0.642	0.555	0.481	0.417	0.362	0.315	0.275	0.239	0.209	0.183
16	0.853	0.728	0.623	0.534	0.458	0.394	0.339	0.292	0.252	0.218	0.188	0.163
17	0.844	0.714	0.605	0.513	0.436	0.371	0.317	0.270	0.231	0.198	0.170	0.146
18	0.836	0.700	0.587	0.494	0.416	0.350	0.296	0.250	0.212	0.180	0.153	0.130
19	0.828	0.686	0.570	0.475	0.396	0.331	0.277	0.232	0.194	0.164	0.138	0.116
20	0.820	0.673	0.554	0.456	0.377	0.312	0.258	0.215	0.178	0.149	0.124	0.104
25	0.780	0.610	0.478	0.375	0.295	0.233	0.184	0.146	0.116	0.092	0.074	0.059
30	0.742	0.552	0.412	0.308	0.231	0.174	0.131	0.099	0.075	0.057	0.044	0.033
40	0.672	0.453	0.307	0.208	0.142	0.097	0.067	0.046	0.032	0.022	0.015	0.011
50	0.608	0.372	0.228	0.141	0.087	0.054	0.034	0.021	0.013	0.009	0.005	0.003

TABLE C-3 (concluded)

Percent

Period	13%	14%	15%	16%	17%	18%	19%	20%	25%	30%	35%	40%	50%
1	0.885	0.877	0.870	0.862	0.855	0.847	0.840	0.833	0.800	0.769	0.741	0.714	0.667
2	0.783	0.769	0.756	0.743	0.731	0.718	0.706	0.694	0.640	0.592	0.549	0.510	0.444
3	0.693	0.675	0.658	0.641	0.624	0.609	0.593	0.579	0.512	0.455	0.406	0.364	0.296
4	0.613	0.592	0.572	0.552	0.534	0.515	0.499	0.482	0.410	0.350	0.301	0.260	0.198
5	0.543	0.519	0.497	0.476	0.456	0.437	0.419	0.402	0.320	0.269	0.223	0.186	0.132
6	0.480	0.456	0.432	0.410	0.390	0.370	0.352	0.335	0.262	0.207	0.165	0.133	0.088
7	0.425	0.400	0.376	0.354	0.333	0.314	0.296	0.279	0.210	0.159	0.122	0.095	0.059
8	0.376	0.351	0.327	0.305	0.285	0.266	0.249	0.233	0.168	0.123	0.091	0.068	0.039
9	0.333	0.300	0.284	0.263	0.243	0.225	0.209	0.194	0.134	0.094	0.067	0.048	0.026
10	0.295	0.270	0.247	0.227	0.208	0.191	0.176	0.162	0.107	0.073	0.050	0.035	0.017
11	0.261	0.237	0.215	0.195	0.178	0.162	0.148	0.135	0.086	0.056	0.037	0.025	0.012
12	0.231	0.208	0.187	0.168	0.152	0.137	0.124	0.112	0.069	0.043	0.027	0.018	0.008
13	0.204	0.182	0.163	0.145	0.130	0.116	0.104	0.093	0.055	0.033	0.020	0.013	0.005
14	0.181	0.160	0.141	0.125	0.111	0.099	0.088	0.078	0.044	0.025	0.015	0.009	0.003
15	0.160	0.140	0.123	0.108	0.095	0.084	0.074	0.065	0.035	0.020	0.011	0.006	0.002
16	0.141	0.123	0.107	0.093	0.081	0.071	0.062	0.054	0.028	0.015	0.008	0.005	0.002
17	0.125	0.108	0.093	0.080	0.069	0.060	0.052	0.045	0.023	0.012	0.006	0.003	0.001
18	0.111	0.095	0.081	0.069	0.059	0.051	0.044	0.038	0.018	0.009	0.005	0.002	0.001
19	0.098	0.083	0.070	0.060	0.051	0.043	0.037	0.031	0.014	0.007	0.003	0.002	0
20	0.087	0.073	0.061	0.051	0.043	0.037	0.031	0.026	0.012	0.005	0.002	0.001	0
25	0.047	0.038	0.030	0.024	0.020	0.016	0.013	0.010	0.004	0.001	0.001	0	0
30	0.026	0.020	0.015	0.012	0.009	0.007	0.005	0.004	0.001	0	0	0	0
40	0.008	0.005	0.004	0.003	0.002	0.001	0.001	0.001	0	0	0	0	0
50	0.002	0.001	0.001	0.001	0	0	0	0	0	0	0	0	0

Source: Maurice Joy, *Introduction to Financial Management* (Homewood, Ill.: Richard D. Irwin, Inc.)

TABLE C-4 Present Value of $1 Received at the End of Each Period for a Given Number of Time Periods

Period						Percent						
	1%	2%	3%	4%	5%	6%	7%	8%	9%	10%	11%	12%
1	0.990	0.980	0.971	0.962	0.952	0.943	0.935	0.926	0.917	0.909	0.901	0.893
2	1.970	1.942	1.913	1.886	1.859	1.833	1.808	1.783	1.759	1.736	1.713	1.690
3	2.941	2.884	2.829	2.775	2.723	2.673	2.624	2.577	2.531	2.487	2.444	2.402
4	3.902	3.808	3.717	3.630	3.546	3.465	3.387	3.312	3.240	3.170	3.102	3.037
5	4.853	4.713	4.580	4.452	4.329	4.212	4.100	3.993	3.890	3.791	3.696	3.605
6	5.795	5.601	5.417	5.242	5.076	4.917	4.767	4.623	4.486	4.355	4.231	4.111
7	6.728	6.472	6.230	6.002	5.786	5.582	5.389	5.206	5.033	4.868	4.712	4.564
8	7.652	7.325	7.020	6.733	6.463	6.210	5.971	5.747	5.535	5.335	5.146	4.968
9	8.566	8.162	7.786	7.435	7.108	6.802	6.515	6.247	5.995	5.759	5.537	5.328
10	9.471	8.983	8.530	8.111	7.722	7.360	7.024	6.710	6.418	6.145	5.889	5.650
11	10.368	9.787	9.253	8.760	8.306	7.887	7.499	7.139	6.805	6.495	6.207	5.938
12	11.255	10.575	9.954	9.385	8.863	8.384	7.943	7.536	7.161	6.814	6.492	6.194
13	12.134	11.348	10.635	9.986	9.394	8.853	8.358	7.904	7.487	7.103	6.750	6.424
14	13.004	12.106	11.296	10.563	9.899	9.295	8.745	8.244	7.786	7.367	6.982	6.628
15	13.865	12.849	11.939	11.118	10.380	9.712	9.108	8.559	8.061	7.606	7.191	6.811
16	14.718	13.578	12.561	11.652	10.838	10.106	9.447	8.851	8.313	7.824	7.379	6.974
17	15.562	14.292	13.166	12.166	11.274	10.477	9.763	9.122	8.544	8.022	7.549	7.102
18	16.398	14.992	13.754	12.659	11.690	10.828	10.059	9.372	8.756	8.201	7.702	7.250
19	17.226	15.678	14.324	13.134	12.085	11.158	10.336	9.604	8.950	8.365	7.839	7.366
20	18.046	16.351	14.877	13.590	12.462	11.470	10.594	9.818	9.129	8.514	7.963	7.469
25	22.023	19.523	17.413	15.622	14.094	12.783	11.654	10.675	9.823	9.077	8.422	7.843
30	25.808	22.396	19.600	17.292	15.372	13.765	12.409	11.258	10.274	9.427	8.694	8.055
40	32.835	27.355	23.115	19.793	17.159	15.046	13.332	11.925	10.757	9.779	8.951	8.244
50	39.196	31.424	25.730	21.482	18.256	15.762	13.801	12.233	10.962	9.915	9.042	8.304

TABLE C-4 (concluded)

Percent

Period	13%	14%	15%	16%	17%	18%	19%	20%	25%	30%	35%	40%	50%
1	0.885	0.877	0.870	0.862	0.855	0.847	0.840	0.833	0.800	0.769	0.741	0.714	0.667
2	1.668	1.647	1.626	1.605	1.585	1.566	1.547	1.528	1.440	1.361	1.289	1.224	1.111
3	2.361	2.322	2.283	2.246	2.210	2.174	2.140	2.106	1.952	1.816	1.696	1.589	1.407
4	2.974	2.914	2.855	2.798	2.743	2.690	2.639	2.589	2.362	2.166	1.997	1.849	1.605
5	3.517	3.433	3.352	3.274	3.199	3.127	3.058	2.991	2.689	2.436	2.220	2.035	1.737
6	3.998	3.889	3.784	3.685	3.589	3.498	3.410	3.326	2.951	2.643	2.385	2.168	1.824
7	4.423	4.288	4.160	4.039	3.922	3.812	3.706	3.605	3.161	2.802	2.508	2.263	1.883
8	4.799	4.639	4.487	4.344	4.207	4.078	3.954	3.837	3.329	2.925	2.598	2.331	1.922
9	5.132	4.946	4.772	4.607	4.451	4.303	4.163	4.031	3.463	3.019	2.665	2.379	1.948
10	5.426	5.216	5.019	4.833	4.659	4.494	4.339	4.192	3.571	3.092	2.715	2.414	1.965
11	5.687	5.453	5.234	5.029	4.836	4.656	4.486	4.327	3.656	3.147	2.752	2.438	1.977
12	5.918	5.660	5.421	5.197	4.988	4.793	4.611	4.439	3.725	3.190	2.779	2.456	1.985
13	6.122	5.842	5.583	5.342	5.118	4.910	4.715	4.533	3.780	3.223	2.799	2.469	1.990
14	6.302	6.002	5.724	5.468	5.229	5.008	4.802	4.611	3.824	3.249	2.814	2.478	1.993
15	6.462	6.142	5.847	5.575	5.324	5.092	4.876	4.675	3.859	3.268	2.825	2.484	1.995
16	6.604	6.265	5.954	5.668	5.405	5.162	4.938	4.730	3.887	3.283	2.834	2.489	1.997
17	6.729	6.373	6.047	5.749	5.475	5.222	4.988	4.775	3.910	3.295	2.840	2.492	1.998
18	6.840	6.467	6.128	5.818	5.534	5.273	5.033	4.812	3.928	3.304	2.844	2.494	1.999
19	6.938	6.550	6.198	5.877	5.584	5.316	5.070	4.843	3.942	3.311	2.848	2.496	1.999
20	7.025	6.623	6.259	5.929	5.628	5.353	5.101	4.870	3.954	3.316	2.850	2.497	1.999
25	7.330	6.873	6.464	6.097	5.766	5.467	5.195	4.948	3.985	3.329	2.856	2.499	2.000
30	7.496	7.003	6.566	6.177	5.829	5.517	5.235	4.979	3.995	3.332	2.857	2.500	2.000
40	7.634	7.105	6.642	6.233	5.871	5.548	5.258	4.997	3.999	3.333	2.857	2.500	2.000
50	7.675	7.133	6.661	6.246	5.880	5.554	5.262	4.999	4.000	3.333	2.857	2.500	2.000

Source: Maurice Joy, *Introduction to Financial Management* (Homewood, Ill.: Richard D. Irwin, Inc.)

Consumer Agencies and Organizations

The following government agencies and private organizations provide information and assistance on various financial planning and consumer purchasing topics. These groups can serve your needs when you want to:

- Research a financial topic.
- Gather information when planning a purchase.
- Resolve a consumer problem.

Type of Assistance	Federal Agency	State, Local Agency; Other Organizations
Advertising		
False advertising Product labeling Deceptive sales practices Warranties	Federal Trade Commission 6th and Pennsylvania, NW Washington, DC 20580 (202) 523-1670	State Consumer Protection Office c/o State Attorney General or Governor's Office Council of Better Business Bureaus 1515 Wilson Boulevard Arlington, VA 22209 (703) 276-0100
Air travel		
Air safety Airport regulation Airline routes	Federal Aviation Administration 800 Independence Avenue Washington, DC 20591 (202) 426-8058	International Airline Passengers Association Box 660074 Dallas, TX 75266 (800) 527-5888
Product safety appliances		
Potentially dangerous products Complaints against retailers, manufacturers	Consumer Product Safety Commission Washington, DC 20207 (800) 638-CPSC	Major Appliance Consumer Action Panel (MACAP) 20 North Wacker Drive Chicago, IL 60606 (800) 621-0477

Type of Assistance	Federal Agency	State, Local Agency; Other Organizations
Automobiles		
New cars Used cars Automobile repairs Auto safety	Federal Trade Commission (see above) National Highway Traffic Safety Administration 400 Seventh Street, SW Washington, DC 20590 (800) 424-9393	AUTOCAP/National Automobile Dealers Association 8400 Westpark Drive McLean, VA 22102 (703) 821-7144 Center for Auto Safety 2001 S Street, NW Washington, DC 20009 (202) 328-7700
Banking, financial institutions		
Checking accounts Savings accounts Deposit insurance Financial services	Federal Deposit Insurance Corporation 550 17th Street, NW Washington, DC 20429 (800) 424-5488 Federal Savings and Loan Insurance Corporation 1700 G Street, NW Washington, DC 20456 (202) 377-6600 Comproller of the Currency 490 L'Enfnat Plaza, SW Washington, DC 20219 (202) 447-1600 Federal Reserve Board Washington, DC 20551 (202) 452-3946 National Credit Union Administration 1776 G Street, NW Washington, DC 20219 (202) 357-1000	State Banking Authority (in your state capital city) Credit Union National Association Box 431 Madison, WI 53701 (608) 231-4000 American Bankers Association 1120 Connecticut Avenue, NW Washington, DC 20036 (202) 663-5269 United States League of Savings Institutions 111 East Wacker Drive Chicago, IL 60601 (312) 644-3100
Career planning		
Job training Employment information	Bureau of Labor Statistics Department of Labor 441 G Street, NW Washington, DC 20212 (202) 523-1913	State Department of Labor or State Employment Service
Consumer credit		
Credit cards Deceptive credit advertising Truth-in-Lending Act Credit rights of women, minorities	Federal Trade Commission (see above)	Bankcard Holders of America 333 Pennsylvania Avenue, SE Washington, DC 20003 (202) 543-5805
Environment		
Air, water pollution Toxic substances	Environmental Protection Agency 1111 18 Street, NW Washington, DC 20207 (202) 634-7700	Clean Water Action Project 317 Pennsylvania Avenue, SE Washington, DC 20003 (202) 547-1196

Type of Assistance	Federal Agency	State, Local Agency; Other Organizations
Food		
Food grades Food additives Nutritional information	U.S. Department of Agriculture Washington, DC 20250 (202) 447-7025 Food and Drug Administration 5600 Fishers Lane Rockville, MD 20857 (301) 443-2410	Center for Science in the Public Interest Box 14176 Washington, DC 20044 (202) 332-9110
Funerals		
Cost disclosure Deceptive business practices	Federal Trade Commission (see above)	Funeral Service Consumer Action Program 135 West Wells Street Milwaukee, WI 53203 (414) 541-2500
Housing, real estate		
Fair housing practices Mortgages Community development	Department of Housing and Urban Development 451 7 Street, SW Washington, DC 20410 (202) 755-5111 Federal Home Loan Bank Board 1700 G Street, NW Washington, DC 20551 (202) 377-6262	National Association of Realtors 430 North Michigan Avenue Chicago, IL 60611 (312) 329-8200 National Association of Home Builders 15th and M Streets, NW Washington, DC 20005 (202) 822-0200
Insurance		
Policy conditions Premiums Types of coverage Consumer complaints	Federal Trade Commission (see above) National Flood Insurance Program 64 Rockledge Drive Bethesda, MD 20034 (800) 638-6620	State Insurance Commissioners (in your state capital city) American Council of Life Insurance 1850 K Street, NW Washington, DC 20006 (800) 423-8000 Insurance Information Institute 110 William Street New York, NY 10038 (800) 221-4954
Investments		
Stocks, bonds Mutual funds Commodities Investment brokers	Securities and Exchange Commission 500 North Capitol Street Washington, DC 20549 (202) 272-2650 Commodity Futures Trading Commission 2033 K Street, NW Washington, DC 20581 (202) 254-7556	Investment Company Institute 1600 M Street, NW Washington, DC 20036 (202) 293-7700 National Association of Securities Dealers 1735 K Street, NW Washington, DC 20006 (202) 728-8000 Securities Investor Protection Corp. 900 17 Street, NW Washington, DC 20006 (202) 223-8400

Type of Assistance	Federal Agency	State, Local Agency; Other Organizations
Legal matters Consumer complaints Arbitration	U.S. Office of Consumer Affairs 1009 Premier Building Washington, DC 20201 (202) 634-4140 Department of Justice Office of Consumer Litigation Washington, DC 20530 (202) 724-6786	American Arbitration Association 140 West 51 Street New York, NY 10020 (212) 484-4000 American Bar Association 750 North Lake Shore Drive Chicago, IL 60611 (312) 988-5158
Medical concerns Prescription medications Over-the-counter medications Medical devices Health care	Food and Drug Administration (see above) Public Health Service 200 Independence Avenue, SW Washington, DC 20201 (202) 245-7694	American Medical Association 535 North Dearborn Chicago, IL 60610 (312) 645-5000 Pharmaceutical Manufacturers Association 1100 15 Street, NW Washington, DC 20005 (202) 835-3468
Mail order Damaged products Deceptive business practices Illegal use of U.S. mail	U.S. Postal Service Washington, DC 20260-2100 (202) 268-4267	Direct Marketing Association 6 East 43 Street New York, NY 10017 (212) 689-4977
Retirement Old-age benefits Pension information Medicare	Social Security Administration 6401 Security Boulevard Baltimore, MD 21235 (301) 594-7700	American Association of Retired Persons 1909 K Street, NW Washington, DC 20049 (202) 872-4700
Utilities Cable television Utility rates	Federal Communications Commission 1919 M Street, NW Washington, DC 20554 (202) 632-7000	State Utility Commission (in your state capital city) Citizens Utility Board 215 Pennsylvania Ave, SE Washington, DC 20003 (202) 546-9707
Taxes Tax information Audit procedures	Internal Revenue Service 1111 Constitution Avenue, NW Washington, DC 20204 (800) 225-0717	Department of Revenue (in your state capital city) The Tax Foundation One Thomas Circle Washington, DC 20005 (202) 822-9050

Information on additional government agencies and private organizations may be obtained from the following publications:

- *Consumer's Resource Handbook* (Washington, D.C.: U.S. Office of Consumer Affairs).
- *Encyclopedia of Associations* (Detroit, Mich.: Gale Research Company).
- Matthew Lesko, *Information U.S.A.* (New York: Viking Press).

Index

FINANCIAL PLANNING PERIODICALS

The field of personal finance is constantly changing. To keep up with this dynamic field you can read the following periodicals. You can subscribe to these publications or read them at your school or community library.

BARRON'S

BARRON'S
200 Burnett Road
Chicopee, MA 01020

Bottom Line PERSONAL

BOTTOM LINE PERSONAL
Box 1027
Millburn, NJ 07041

BUSINESS WEEK
Box 421
Hightstown, NJ 08520

CHANGING TIMES

CHANGING TIMES
1729 H Street, NW
Washington, DC 20006

Consumers Digest *For People Who Demand Value*

CONSUMERS DIGEST
Box 3074
Harlan, IA 51537

Consumer Reports *

CONSUMER REPORTS
Box 2485
Boulder, CO 80322